AMBITION, PRAGMATISM, AND PARTY

Ambition, Pragmatism, *and* Party

Scott Kaufman

University Press of Kansas

Published by the University Press of Kansas (Lawrence, Kansas 66045), which was organized by the Kansas Board of Regents and is operated and funded by Emporia State University, Fort Hays State University, Kansas State University, Pittsburg State University, the University of Kansas, and Wichita State University

Library of Congress Cataloging-in-Publication Data

Names: Kaufman, Scott, 1969– author.
Title: Ambition, pragmatism, and party : a political biography of Gerald R. Ford / Scott Kaufman.
Description: Lawrence, Kansas : University Press of Kansas, 2017. | Includes bibliographical references and index.
Identifiers: LCCN 2017038277
ISBN 9780700625000 (cloth : alk. paper)
ISBN 9780700625017 (ebook)
Subjects: LCSH: Ford, Gerald R., 1913–2006. | Presidents—United States—Biography. | United States—Politics and government—1945-1989. | United States—Politics and government—1974–1977.
Classification: LCC E866 .K38 2017 | DDC 973.925092[B]—dc23
LC record available at https://lccn.loc.gov/2017038277.

British Library Cataloguing-in-Publication Data is available.

Printed in the United States of America

10 9 8 7 6 5 4 3 2 1

The paper used in this publication is recycled and contains 30 percent postconsumer waste. It is acid free and meets the minimum requirements of the American National Standard for Permanence of Paper for Printed Library Materials Z39.48-1992.

To my colleagues in the Department of History
at Francis Marion University

Contents

Illustrations

Preface

On 9 August 1974, President Richard Nixon, facing impeachment because of his part in the Watergate scandal, resigned, becoming the first and only chief executive in American history to do so. That same day, his vice president, Gerald Ford, became the country's new leader. What made the events of that day even more remarkable was that eight months earlier, Ford was the minority leader of the House of Representatives, where he represented Michigan's Fifth District. He had become vice president only because the incumbent, Spiro Agnew, had also been forced to resign. Now, in August, Ford entered the White House as the country's only unelected president.

Maybe it is because of the unprecedented way in which he became president that the overwhelming majority of the scholarship on Gerald Ford has focused on his tenure in the Oval Office rather than on his whole life. Indeed, only three works have made an attempt at a comprehensive political biography of America's thirty-eighth president. The first was brothers Edward Schapsmeier and Frederick Schapsmeier's *Gerald R. Ford's Date with Destiny*, but its disjointed, jumpy nature and publication nearly twenty years before Ford's death make it wanting. Far more readable is Douglas Brinkley's *Gerald R. Ford*, which covers the entirety of Ford's life. However, it is part of a series designed to offer short histories of each president, thus restricting the depth of coverage. The last, and most recent, is James

Cannon's laudatory *Gerald R. Ford*,[1] but the author passed away before he completed it, and the portions of the book on Ford's presidency read more as his memoir than as a scholarly monograph.

It is possible that the dearth of biographies is due to the fact that, despite a twenty-five-year career in Congress, Ford never sponsored a major piece of legislation, and he failed to achieve his dream of becoming speaker of the House. Perhaps it is because, though he was intelligent, he was not an intellectual on a par with James Madison, John Quincy Adams, Theodore Roosevelt, or Woodrow Wilson. He was not a visionary like Thomas Jefferson or Franklin Roosevelt; indeed, he had a difficult time seeing beyond specific policy proposals and placing them within a broader plan for the country. He did not have the complex personality of Lyndon B. Johnson or Richard Nixon. He was not the center of a major scandal. He was not a member of a famous family. He did not lead the country during a war. Or maybe it originates from the thesis that Ford was a caretaker president,[2] one whose only decision of significance was to pardon Nixon and who otherwise kept the chair in the Oval Office warm pending the outcome of the 1976 presidential election.

If any of these explanations are correct, they are unfair, for they give short shrift to an individual who not only sat in the Oval Office, but whose life experiences and career in and out of Washington covered almost the entire twentieth century. Born in 1913, he was raised by an abused mother who found happiness following a contentious divorce and a stepfather who treated his stepson as his own. His parents suffered through the Depression, which nearly forced his stepfather to close his business. He fought in World War II and joined Congress shortly after the Cold War began. During his tenure in the House of Representatives, he participated in numerous debates both inside and outside of Congress regarding containment policy, the Korean War, the Vietnam War, and the emergence of détente with the Communist world. Likewise, he spoke repeatedly on the extent to which the government should involve itself at home on matters ranging from civil rights to the environment, the economy, and welfare policy. Moreover, he witnessed a Republican Party that increasingly was at war with itself as the GOP's right wing emerged as a force with which to be reckoned.

Though short, Ford's 895-day presidency was marked by more than the Nixon pardon. He oversaw the withdrawal of the remaining U.S. presence in South Vietnam. He had to address crises involving the Cambodian seizure of the American ship *Mayaguez*, Americans' use of energy, and New York City's finances. He sought as well to continue détente with the Soviet Union and tried to figure out how to help the economy emerge from stagflation. Repeatedly, he found himself pulled not only by conservatives in his own party—who challenged him for the Republican nomination for the presidency in 1976—but an increasingly assertive, Democratic-controlled Congress. After leaving the White House, he remained active within Republican politics. But he also began to move more to the political left on social issues, and he developed a close relationship with another former president, Jimmy Carter. Additionally, he used his title of ex-president to make a significant sum of money.

During Ford's ninety-three-year life, three themes emerged. The first was his ambition. Through hard work, he became an Eagle Scout and the captain of his high school football team, endeavored to become an attorney, and clawed his way into Yale Law School. He broke up with his first girlfriend so he could practice law in Michigan. During World War II, he served with the U.S. Navy, used his connections to rise up the chain of command on the aircraft carrier on which he served, and left the service with the rank of lieutenant commander. Not long after joining Congress, he decided he wanted to become speaker of the House and allied himself with a group of younger lawmakers, the "Young Turks," who helped him eventually rise to the position of minority leader. In that post, he sought to convince others to endorse a variety of initiatives he believed would be best for his party and the nation. Instead of becoming speaker, he ended up serving as president of the United States, during which time he cajoled those who opposed him to see the wisdom of the positions he adopted. After losing the 1976 election, he toyed with running again in 1980, but, forgoing that option, he instead became a well-paid member of numerous corporate boards. His desire to assume positions of authority took its toll on Ford's family. He was an absent husband and father, which was difficult for his four children, but it was his wife, Betty, who took Jerry's absenteeism the hardest. She never considered divorcing her husband, but the time he was away made her feel ever more alone. She became addicted to alcohol, which she combined with painkillers she took for a bad back. Yet she refused to permit her suffering to stand in the way of his dreams. Indeed, in many ways she was as determined as he, taking positions as first lady that were out of accord with those of Republican conservatives. She hoped that once she and Jerry left the White House, they would have more time together, but he continued to spend time away. It took a family intervention to help her give up her addictions, and she became a leader in the fight against alcohol and drug abuse.

Second, in addition to seeking authority, Ford was loyal to the Republican Party. He was a moderate conservative, raised in a conservative district of Michigan and in a family that reflected a conservative ethic of achieving success with little government assistance. He was a former isolationist who, as a result of his service in World War II, became an internationalist. Consequently, he developed a hawkish temperament on the issues of containing communism and supporting a free-market economy. On domestic issues, he endorsed welfare programs, civil rights for African Americans, and environmental protections. He preferred, however, to have the states rather than the federal government enforce them. He participated in Wendell Willkie's bid for the presidency in 1940 and, as a congressman, established a voting record that was largely in line with that of the Republican presidents under whom he served. After becoming president, he promoted initiatives that harmonized with his moderate conservatism; as an ex-president, he campaigned for Republicans seeking both state offices and the presidency.

Ford's fealty to the GOP caused him to be inconsistent. As a hawk, he called for heavy spending on the military but stood behind Dwight D. Eisenhower's call for curtailing expenditures on the armed forces in the name of balancing the budget. He resisted policies that in his mind smacked of appeasement to the Soviet Union, such as talks aimed at restricting the testing of nuclear weapons. Yet under President Richard Nixon, he became a champion of the Strategic Arms Limitations Treaty (SALT I) and, as president himself, pursued a SALT II agreement. As a congressman, he railed against China, but he later stood behind Nixon's rapprochement with that Communist country.

His loyalty also led him to overreach at times. He attempted to impeach Supreme Court Justice William Douglas in what appeared to many observers to be revenge for the Senate's refusal to confirm two of President Nixon's nominees to the Court. Ford could also be naive, which, in combination with his friendship with Nixon, convinced him that the former president had had no part in the Watergate scandal, even as evidence to the otherwise became overwhelming.

Ford, however, was a pragmatic partisan, and it is his pragmatism that constitutes the third theme of this biography. Inspired by loving parents who were known for decency and goodwill, Ford developed a reputation for honesty and a strong sense of right and wrong. He was not an ideologue, though. Just as winning a football game required cooperating with other members of the team, so rising up the political ranks and achieving one's goals necessitated a preparedness to compromise and to build coalitions with those whose views might not accord with one's own. Doing so offered a mixed bag for Ford. In Congress, he became known among his fellow Republicans as someone who was approachable and willing to listen to all sides before making a decision. He also exhibited a readiness to work with Democrats, particularly on foreign policy but also to some extent on domestic matters. Yet before and during his tenure as minority leader, that willingness to reach across party lines oftentimes brought Republicans in alliance with conservative Democrats, whose positions, particularly with regard to race, were not necessarily those Ford favored.

As president, Ford wanted to see the country continue down the path of fiscal conservatism and internationalism he had preached as a lawmaker. Building the alliances he had sought to create while on Capitol Hill, though, proved increasingly difficult. By the mid-1970s, conservatives in his party had grown in strength and did not favor many of Ford's decisions, including those related to his pick for vice president, relations with the Soviet Union, or tax policy. A Democratic-controlled and reform-minded Congress determined to rein in presidential power also constrained Ford, who signed legislation that was not fully in accord with what he wanted. That Ford refused to give up his pragmatic partisanship, however, became apparent after he left office. He developed a close friendship with a Democrat, Jimmy Carter, and adopted positions that oftentimes were not in line with a GOP that had continued to move rightward.

Today, polls of laypersons and academics place Gerald Ford among the ranks of mediocre presidents. Fifty-six percent of Americans ranked Ford as "average" in a 2013 Gallup survey, and a Quinnipiac University poll of registered voters taken the following year found that of the twelve chief executives who have served since World War II, Ford ranked eleventh among the best presidents, and eighth among the worst. A C-SPAN poll of U.S. historians in 2009 placed Ford twenty-second among the forty-three presidents.[3] Even if a closer look at Ford's life in politics does not change these impressions, his career will allow readers to experience a period when, despite sometimes vigorous partisan debates, words such as "compromise" and "cooperation" were heard much more often in Washington.

Acknowledgments

This book emerged from a request by Peter Coveney, an editor at Wiley-Blackwell, that I edit a book of historiographical essays on Gerald Ford and Jimmy Carter. Having spent years researching Carter, I was familiar with the literature on his life and presidency, but I knew less about Ford. Desiring to learn more about the country's thirty-eighth president, I began reading books about him and his life. I discovered that while a few biographies about him had been written, there was much about his political career that had been overlooked or given short shrift. I brought up the idea, therefore, of writing a biography of Ford to Fred Woodward, then the director of the University Press of Kansas, and the result is this book.

There are numerous people who made this book possible. First and foremost is the staff at the Gerald R. Ford Library, who went out of their way to assist me: research archivists Donna Lehman, Elizabeth Druga, Tim Holtz, Mark Fischer, and Hannah Brookhart; supervisory archivist Geir Gundersen; grants coordinator Jeremy Schmidt; and the library's director, Elaine Didier. I will forever appreciate their kindness, suggestions for places to see and eat in Ann Arbor, and all the amazing work they are doing to put numerous documents online.

Having conducted research on Jimmy and Rosalynn Carter, I have spent many hours at the Jimmy Carter Presidential Library and Museum in Atlanta, and I want to thank all the archivists there for their help with this project. My appreciation goes out as well to the staffs at the New York Public Library, the Bentley Historical Library in Ann Arbor, the J. Willard Marriott Library at the University of Utah, the John F. Kennedy Presidential Library and Museum in Boston, and the Library of Congress in Washington, D.C. Kathryn Hodson at the University of Iowa Libraries and Monica Blank at the Rockefeller Archive Center were very helpful. Both John Fierst of the Clarke Historical Library at Central Michigan University and Kristen Nyitray at the Frank Melville Jr. Memorial Library at the State University of New York–Stony Brook corresponded with me and provided some very useful materials.

A special note of appreciation goes to Dr. Alissa Warters, professor of political science and associate provost for academic affairs and enrollment management at Francis Marion University, who spent several weeks conducting research at the Ford, Richard Nixon, and Ronald Reagan Libraries. The documents she gave me for this manuscript were invaluable.

I also want to thank Dr. Warters for participating in some of the interviews conducted for this book, as well as those who talked with us about Ford as father, congressman, and president. Ford's youngest son, Steve, was kind enough not only to speak with us for several hours but also to reach out to others who knew his father: Buzz Thomas, the grandson of Willis Ward, who played alongside Ford for the University of Michigan football team, and the former deputy director of the Office of Management and Budget, Paul O'Neill. Several people who served on Capitol Hill—Congresspersons Patricia Schroeder and Lee Hamilton and Senators Bob Dole, Richard Lugar, and Bill Brock—recounted their experiences in government and their memories of Ford. Neal Thigpen, a personal friend who was a member of the South Carolina delegation to both the 1976 and 1980 Republican National Conventions, offered some terrific stories about being part of the process of choosing the party's nominee. I wish to thank as well two history majors at Francis Marion University, Ben Jackson and Troy Tanner, who spent time helping me transcribe these interviews.

The Gerald R. Ford Presidential Foundation offers travel grants to researchers and provided funding to both Dr. Warters and me. Francis Marion University is exceedingly generous in funding faculty research, and I wish to thank the university's president, L. Fred Carter, the History Department, and the Francis Marion University Foundation for their wonderful support.

Prior to submitting the manuscript, my father, Burton Kaufman, himself a former professor of history, reviewed it and made numerous helpful suggestions. Though I was saddened to receive word from Fred Woodward of his decision to retire, the press's editor-in-chief, Joyce Harrison, has been a wonder to work with. I wish to thank as well her editorial assistant, Cole Anneberg, and production editor Larisa Martin. The University Press of Kansas sent the monograph to two readers who offered terrific recommendations. One of them was kind enough to identify himself: John Robert Greene, whose knowledge of Gerald Ford and the Ford administration is second to none.

This is the first book my wife, Julie, has experienced from start to finish. I cannot thank her enough for her love and patience while I spent innumerable days away on research or in my office typing on my computer. That she did not have a heart attack as my office turned into what I call "organized chaos," what with papers and books spread all around, is a testament to her stoicism. My love goes as well to our four-legged "dogter," Lexi; my aunt and uncle, Shirley and Barry Michaelson, with whom I stayed while conducting research in Boston; Kai, Kim, Taro, and Karsten Yamamoto, who opened their doors to me while I was in New York City; my sister, Heather, and her husband, Steve Moore; my stepmother, Jane Bloom, and her family; my brother-in-law, Bill Colman, his wife, Nancy Bason, and their children, Andy and Carolyn; my sister-in-law, Jill Bacchetta, her husband, David, and their son and daughter, Brandon and Taylor; my grandmother, Ruth Kaufman; and my "second parents," Al and Mickey Keithley, and their family.

ONE

A Ford, Not a King

She had had enough. The physical and emotional abuse had become more than she could take. So in July 1913, Dorothy King took her infant son, fled her Nebraska home, and crossed the Missouri River to her parents, who were waiting in neighboring Iowa. It was a first step to a much better life for her and her newborn child, one that set him down a path toward political leadership.

The child's name was Leslie King Jr., but he would become known as Gerald R. Ford Jr. Between his birth and his thirty-fifth birthday, when he entered the U.S. House of Representatives, Ford benefited from a combination of luck, on the one hand, and, on the other, his mother and stepfather, coaches, military officers, girlfriends, and acquaintances from whom he learned the values of patience, determination, honesty, spiritedness, and faith in human nature. He also discovered within himself an overwhelming ambition and a desire to assume positions of leadership. His drive to success was not without its challenges and disappointments. But it was clear to those who knew him that he was one who would not give up on achieving his goals.

A King Becomes a Ford

Ford's mother, Dorothy Gardner, was the granddaughter of Alexander Gardner, who had arrived in America from Scotland, and Sally Miller, whose family traced their lineage back to England. The Millers had moved from New York to Illinois sometime after Sally's birth, and it was in the Prairie State where she met Alexander. Married in 1839, they had six children, the youngest of whom, Levi Addison, was born in 1860. At age twenty-four, Levi exchanged vows with Adele Augusta Ayers in Harvard, Illinois. The couple had two daughters: Tannisse, born in 1887, and, five years later, Dorothy.

Levi developed a successful real estate business and apparently enjoyed politics, serving for a year as Harvard's mayor. Long after he had been president of the United States, Gerald Ford recalled Dorothy's parents as very kind. This kindness passed on to their daughter, who by all accounts was religiously devout, warmhearted, "gregarious," and "a great conversationalist." As events were soon to make clear, she was also an emotionally strong individual who was prepared to stand up to those who tried to intimidate her.[1]

In 1912, Dorothy married Leslie Lynch King, one of five children of a well-off Omaha family. King's father, Charles, was a merchant who in the 1880s had made a fortune establishing stores and banks along the route of what became the Chicago and North Western Transportation Company Railroad. He also helped found several towns, including Chadron, Nebraska, where Leslie was born in 1884. Charles moved the family to Omaha in 1908, constructed a mansion there, and continued to build his fortune, amassing some $20 million.

Dorothy and Leslie met while she was a student at St. Mary's Academy, a woman's college in Knoxville, Illinois; her roommate was one of his sisters. The tall, handsome, and blond twenty-eight-year-old King and the beautiful twenty-year-old Dorothy appeared to be a match made in heaven. After a brief courtship, King asked her father for her hand, assuring him that he was well-off, had a good job in his father's company, and could give her a comfortable life. Levi had no reason to doubt the young courter. A prosperous businessman himself, he knew that Leslie's father was a multimillionaire. Nor did Adele see any cause for concern. With her parents' consent, Dorothy and Leslie married in September 1912 and then boarded a train for the West Coast and their honeymoon.[2]

Dorothy's expectation for a blissful marriage rapidly dissolved when King

Gerald R. Ford around ten months old, circa June 1914. Photo in the Gerald Ford Library, Ann Arbor, Michigan.

hit her repeatedly during that West Coast trip. Not only was he malicious, but he was mendacious: upon returning to Omaha, Dorothy discovered that her husband and father-in-law were on poor terms; the elder King refused to provide his son with financial support; the younger King had been stealing money from the father's business; and despite his thievery, Leslie was deeply in debt. A brief reconciliation gave way to more violence, and to complicate matters, Dorothy in December learned that she was pregnant.[3]

Possibly because she did not want to leave her child without a father figure, Dorothy tried her best to salvage her marriage. She found support from her father-in-law, who agreed to let her use his large home for the baby's delivery and made sure she had a doctor and nurse to provide care, and from her mother, who arrived from Illinois. On 14 July 1913, she bore a son, whom she and Leslie named Leslie Jr. But if she believed that having a child would change her husband and rescue their marriage, she was wrong. King continued to terrorize his wife and even threatened to kill their child. Fearing for both her life and that of her son, Dorothy called a lawyer, who told her to leave Nebraska. Not even taking time to pack clothes, she boarded a carriage and headed across the Missouri River to Council Bluffs, Iowa, where her parents were waiting to take her home to Harvard. Afterward, Dorothy filed for divorce, winning not only custody of her son but an order for Leslie Sr. to pay $3,000 in alimony and $25 a month in child support. Having recently been fired by his father, Leslie claimed impoverishment and inability to pay. Charles stepped in, promising to make good on the court order.[4]

In a way, Dorothy could relax, for she was free of her tormentor and had money coming in from his father. Yet she faced the stigma of being a divorcée. While commonplace in the twenty-first century, divorce was not usual throughout much of America's history. Rather, it was associated with scandal, psychological defect, and societal failure, and it was considered particularly disgraceful where there were children involved. Knowing she could not stay in small-town Harvard, Dorothy moved to Chicago, where she had family, and found a place in Hyde Park. Her parents also left Harvard, not for Chicago but for Grand Rapids, Michigan, where Levi's company had an office. Shortly thereafter, Levi was diagnosed with kidney failure, and Dorothy and her son traveled with increasing frequency to see him. By the time he passed away in 1916, she had left her job in Chicago and moved to Grand Rapids to live with her mother.[5]

Situated on the Grand River, which is also Michigan's longest river, Grand Rapids is about 25 miles east of Lake Michigan and is the seat of Kent County. Native Americans had lived in the region for thousands of years, including the Hopewell and Ottawa tribes. Europeans arrived in the area in the early 1800s and established a trading post. By the mid-1840s, that post had become a town with a population of approximately 1,500; it was over 87,000 at the turn of the twentieth century. While gypsum mining explains some of this growth, the area's forests were key. With 35 million acres of both hard- and softwoods, Michigan appeared to have an unlimited reserve of trees, and the Grand River provided a means of transporting fallen timber to mills at Grand Rapids. As the 1800s neared their end, the city had become a center for furniture manufacturing—earning it the nickname "Furniture City"—supported by a number of attendant industries, among them the manufacture of paint and varnish.[6] After 1900, a small automobile firm, the Austin Automobile Company, also began operations.

Industry meant jobs, and immigrants flooded into Grand Rapids to find work. The largest group was the Dutch, who constituted over 25 percent of the city's population in 1900, but Poles, Germans, Swedes, and Lithuanians had made it home as well. Ethnic neighborhoods and a wide array of churches and temples reflected this diversity, but even more apparent were the class divisions. Downtown lay along the Grand River, and just to the east was a hill. That area became known as the Hill District, where the lumber-mill owners and other wealthy individuals resided. Further east—the East Side—was populated by middle- and upper-middle-class families; the West Side contained predominantly blue-collar families.[7]

Overshadowing the ethnic differences in Grand Rapids was a population that largely adhered to what has been referred to by scholars and by Ford's contemporaries as a midwestern form of conservatism. Like political conservatives, they touted limited government and fiscal frugality. But what set them apart from others of conservative bent was their nonfundamentalist piety and, more importantly, their political moderation and pragmatism and their willingness to engage in compromise. Further drawing the city together was an excellent transportation system, particularly the electric streetcars that made it relatively easy and inexpensive to get from one's home to the city's downtown industries. Though not offering the diversions one could find in nearby Detroit or Chicago, the city provided a symphony, clubs, and theaters. Dorothy and her mother took advantage of what Grand Rapids had to offer, joining various organizations and regularly attending Grace Episcopal Church,[8] located about 5 miles southeast of downtown.

While attending mass, Dorothy caught the attention of Gerald R. Ford. Ford was the son of George Ford, who had been born in Ohio, moved to Michigan, and married Zana Frances Pixley. Making their home in Grand Rapids, they had three children, the youngest of whom, Gerald Rudolph, was born in 1889 on the city's West Side.[9] His father had died in a train accident when Gerald was only seven. To help support his family, he dropped out of school in the eighth grade and never completed his education. He worked selling paint and wallpaper for Heystek and Caulfield, located in the East Side. Ford was by no means as wealthy as the Gardners, but he was financially stable.[10]

Dorothy did not care that her family was better off than Ford's, for she had learned the hard way that money did not buy happiness. And there was much to like about him. He was physically attractive, standing just over six feet tall, with a rectangular face marked by penetrating eyes and an aquiline nose, and a slightly receding line of black hair that he parted down the middle and combed straight back. He was also religiously devout, friendly, emotionally mature, and well respected in the city, in part because of his active community service. He was in many ways the very opposite of the man from whom she had escaped a few years earlier. In 1915, the two began dating regularly. Whether her family approved is not clear, though there is evidence that her mother was less than pleased because of Ford's social status. What was certain was that Dorothy had no intention of rushing into another marriage, waiting until February 1917 to exchange vows.[11]

Ford's stepfather and mother rented a home on Madison Avenue, near the corner with Franklin Street, where there was a firehouse with the city's last horse-drawn steam engine. Ford recalled that when it went out on a call, "the sight was spectacular." The Fords stayed there until 1919, when they moved to a home on Rosewood Avenue. It was an economically well-off part of town, with excellent schools, good health-care facilities, parks, and safe neighborhoods. Those who lived there were, in the words of one author, "thrifty, self-reliant, and active in civic affairs."[12]

The Fords could not have been happier. They loved each other deeply, and Gerald treated his bride with unfettered kindness and respect. The same was true for Dorothy's son, whom she began to call "Junie Ford" as opposed to "Junior," as well as Ford's half-brother, Tom, to whom Dorothy gave birth in 1918. The Fords were strict disciplinarians who made sure Jerry and Tom told the truth, did their chores, and came to dinner on time. But they also had fun. Gerald taught his children how to swim and play sports, including baseball and football. He was part owner of a home on Lake Michigan, and each summer the family went there, where the elder Ford and his stepson fished. It was through his stepfather that Ford learned the importance of independent thinking and doing what he believed was just. While many of the younger Ford's interests and mannerisms began to reflect those of his stepfather, one feature did not: his temper. Like his biological father, he periodically would fly into a rage for no reason, throwing items or pushing or hitting people if he did not get his way. His anger appeared enough in kindergarten that his teacher years later referred to him as "naughty Junior Ford."[13]

Dorothy and Gerald began what became a years-long effort to get Junie to control his temper. If he exhibited anger, Dorothy would have him look at himself in a mirror to see "how silly he looked, or she would laugh at his fits . . . and try to tease him out of them." Gerald was more direct, using "classic motivational talk." As both were devout churchgoers, they also turned to the Bible and had Junie memorize Proverbs 16:32: "He that is slow to anger is better than the mighty; and he that ruleth his spirit than he that taketh a city." Ford also discovered inspiration in Rudyard Kipling, whose poem "If" begins "If you can keep your head when all about you / Are losing theirs and blaming it on you." By high school, the younger Ford had made great strides in controlling his temper—though it did reappear periodically—and credited the love and devotion of his parents as fundamental to his success at doing so.[14]

Junie, who decided to take the name "Jerry" after the man he believed was his biological father, also had to address his stuttering, which began when he was in second grade. It is not clear how long the problem continued, but it certainly affected his self-confidence. Worried about his stammering, he became less and less willing to express himself orally. Another teacher realized that the cause of the problem was that Ford was naturally left-handed, but school custom called for using one's right hand. When he was permitted to use his left hand, the stuttering stopped. Still, the experience had long-term consequences, for throughout elementary and secondary school, Ford became known as someone who was friendly (minus his increasingly infrequent periods of anger) yet taciturn.[15]

About this time, Ford's father ran into financial difficulties. Harry Heystek Jr. had acquired Heystek and Canfield in 1921 after his father passed away, and he began making some poor business decisions that eventually forced the company to close in 1925. One of those decisions was to fire Gerald Sr. He got employment as a salesman for the Grand Rapids Wood Finishing Company, but his salary was not enough to cover the mortgage on the family home. Foreclosure followed. The Fords found a place for rent on Union Avenue, not far from where they had lived after Dorothy and Gerald married. It may have been because of the strain on their finances that Jerry's parents suggested he become a caddy at a golf course in Grand Rapids; additionally, he could learn to play the game. He refused, preferring instead to play football and read, particularly books by Horatio Alger and poems by Edgar Guest. Alger, Ford later commented, wrote "stories about heroes, poor boys who struggled and eventually succeeded." Appearing in the *Detroit Free Press*, Guest's verses offered a sentimental perspective on daily life.[16] Despite his dismissive attitude toward golf, Ford as an adult became known for his love of the game.

Though golf did not interest Ford, the Boy Scouts did. The Cub Scouts did not exist at the time, so a male youth seeking to become a Scout had to wait until his twelfth birthday. With his parents' encouragement, Ford joined Troop 15, sponsored by Trinity M. E. Church, in December 1924. The scoutmaster was Chuck Kindel, the son of the owner of a Grand Rapids furniture company. Jerry excelled in the Boy Scouts, achieving the title of Eagle Scout in only three years. He participated in a summer camp, where he received his first leadership positions, those of assistant counselor and swimming coach. He enjoyed the responsibility and made enough of an impression that in 1929 he was one of twelve Eagle Scouts selected by the state governor to serve as guides at Fort Mackinac, a former military outpost that had played an important role in the War of 1812. The job, which required him to greet visitors and lead talks on the fort, was one he came to adore.[17]

By 1929, Ford had two more siblings, Richard and James. None of the children received any favoritism. All were taught to work hard, be on time, and never lie. Because Gerald Sr. had not finished his education, he insisted his children do so. He made sure all his sons involved themselves in sports, an activity that his stepson recalled taught important lessons of their own: "how to compete but always by the rules, how to be part of a team, how to win, how to lose and come back to try again." Sports also provided insight into human nature. "By the time I entered seventh grade," Ford later wrote, "I was becoming aware of the deep emotions that competition can stir," be it rivalry for the heart of a young woman or a determination to prove oneself better than another during a game. Such competition could breed hate. Ford decided, though, that "everyone . . . had more good qualities than bad. If I understood and tried to accentuate those good qualities in others, I could get along much better."[18]

By the time Ford entered high school, he had largely developed the personality that continued throughout his life. His parents had inculcated in him the values of patience, diligence, and honesty. While Boy Scouts taught him teamwork and playing by the rules, sports firmly rooted those principles in his mind, as well as the idea that one should persevere, even after failure. These were the qualities of leadership. Yet Ford's faith in human nature engendered in him a certain naïveté, which periodically haunted him during his political career.

South High

Where Ford would attend high school was a question for his parents. Their home lay where the districts serving Central High, South High, and Ottawa Hills met. Ottawa Hills was newer and served the wealthier neighborhoods in town, upper-middle-class parents sent their children to Central, and lower-class children predominated at South. South was also the most racially and ethnically diverse. Vacillating, his parents asked Ralph Conger, a teacher and basketball coach at Central, for advice. Though Conger taught at Central, he encouraged the Fords to send Jerry to South. "They have the best teachers," he told them. "And there he will learn more about people, and about living."[19]

It turned out to be a good decision, one that exposed Ford to a more heterogeneous group of peers. "If I had gone to Central," he related years later, "I probably would have been one of those smartass[es]—in the first place I could not afford to do the things that most kids did then." At South, though, "I wasn't any worse off than the rest of the people." He enjoyed the teachers and began to think about what he wanted to do after graduation. His future wife, Betty, later commented that Ford won a trip to Washington, D.C., and while there became interested in politics. Ford himself never confirmed that story—it appears in fact that his desire to become a politician developed later—but he had resolved to go to college and get a law degree. He doubled down on his studies and did well enough to become an honor student.[20]

Also important to Ford's future was football. He loved the game and remained a fan throughout his life. As a freshman he signed up for South High's football team. The varsity coach was Clifford Gettings, a competent leader who was also, in Ford's words, "a stern taskmaster." Seeing the blond, 5-foot-8, 130-pound Ford standing on the practice field, Gettings decided he would play center for the junior varsity (JV) squad. Ford excelled at the position, enough so that when the varsity team's senior center, Orris Burghdorf, suffered an injury before Ford's sophomore year, Gettings called on his JV center to fill the void.[21]

The center was a key position. Football in the 1920s was dissimilar in many ways from today's game. One difference was the size of players. In modern football, it is not uncommon for a center, even in college, to weigh over 300 pounds and to be over 6 feet tall; in the 1920s, a football player who reached 6 feet was considered tall, and he usually weighed less than 200 pounds. For another, modern football is specialized, with each individual having specific responsibilities. For the center, that means snapping the ball to the quarterback—or, in a wildcat formation, to the person who is lined up in the quarterback position—and then immediately blocking an opposing defensive lineman. That was not the case for Ford. In addition to blocking, a center might have to snap the ball to players already in motion. Finally, it is rare in football today for a person who plays on offense to play on defense, and vice versa. Ford, though, was on an eleven-man squad, meaning that everyone played on both sides of the ball.[22]

Ford continued to impress his coach. "Jerry was a hard-working kid and totally dependable," Gettings commented. His center "knew everyone's assignment on every play; having him in the game was like having a coach on the field." For Ford, the game and his coach reinforced lessons he had acquired from earlier experience. "I learned discipline," he recounted. "I learned that you had to consider yourself a part of a team." Gettings taught his players to "give it everything you've got, but [to] always play by the rules." And while the desire was to win, "losing a game . . . was a tragedy, terrible, but you couldn't sit back and let that destroy your whole mental attitude." Not just Gettings but spectators admired Ford's competitive spirit. In 1929, the football team won the city championship, and its center, who had gained 1–2 inches in height and another 10 pounds in weight, received all-city football honors.[23]

Indeed, all the Fords' lives seemed to be on the upswing. Gerald Sr. had begun to do well enough that he was able to buy the home on Union Avenue in 1925. Desiring to continue his climb up the social ladder, he decided, with the support of his boss, to start a company that specialized in interior paint. In October 1929, Ford Paint and Varnish Company opened its doors.[24]

The timing could not have been worse. That same month, the New York stock market crashed, and the nation spiraled into the worst economic depression in its history. Unemployment, which had stood at a mere 3 percent prior to the stock market crash, climbed to 25 percent four years later. Some 4,000 banks went under in the same period. The automobile industry, on which the Michigan economy relied so heavily, was hit especially hard. For instance, Ford Motor Company had in 1932 a workforce more than 60 percent smaller than it had been less than a decade earlier. In Grand Rapids itself, the mayor, George Welsh, found himself having to look after the needs of 20,000 people. With no offers of state or federal relief, Welsh instituted a series of public-works programs, using scrip to pay those in need of employment.[25]

Gerald Sr. managed to hang on. In his own acts of self-reliance, he took a cut in salary, paid himself and his employees five dollars a week, and promised wage increases when the country recovered. The following year, Charles King passed away, putting an end to the child support he had paid to Dorothy for his son. Although Gerald held on to his business, the Fords needed extra income, so they insisted that their son get a job. Jerry found part-time employment with Alex DeMar, a member of the city's Greek community, who ran a local dance hall. Another part-time employer was Bill Skougis, the owner of a Greek diner who loved football and knew it would be good business to have one of the team's stars working for him. In return for two dollars a week and lunch, Ford washed dishes and cooked and served food.[26]

While he was at work the following spring, the younger Ford got one of the greatest shocks of his life. A man came into the diner and, after staring at Jerry for about fifteen or twenty minutes, walked up to him. "I'm Leslie King, your father," he announced. "Can I take you to lunch?" Ford recalled his mother telling him some years earlier that Gerald Sr. was not his biological father, but they had not discussed it further. Now, this stranger had arrived from out of thin air. Skougis gave Ford permission to leave, and the high schooler reluctantly agreed to the offer of lunch. Walking to King's car, Ford met a woman whom King introduced as his wife and their daughter. The conversation between father and son during their meal was, Ford later wrote, "superficial. . . . We didn't mention the divorce or anything else disagreeable." Rather, King explained that he and his family had taken a train from Wyoming to Detroit to purchase a new car, and then, as they were driving back home, he had decided to stop in Grand Rapids to try to locate his son. He then suggested his son join him, but Ford refused. Returning to the diner, King gave Ford twenty-five dollars, told him to buy himself something nice, and left.[27]

That evening, Ford told his parents what had happened. Though his mother was disturbed by the unexpected social call, she gave him details of her first marriage and told him why she had left King. His stepfather "reassured him that he had done nothing wrong." They expressed their love for their son and their trust in him. Yet he was still troubled, unsure what King's intentions were, and was concerned that his mother and stepfather might think he was prepared to consider his biological father's offer. "That night was one of the most difficult of my life," Ford recounted. "When I went to bed that night, I broke down and cried."[28]

Ford, however, had to put the incident behind him and did so. He continued to focus on his classes and sports, though he did find time to date a young woman named Mary Hondorp during his last two years in high school. In his junior year, he suffered an injury to his knee that forced him to sit out several football games, but he still made all-city again. In his senior year, Ford's team chose him as captain, which he called "probably one of [my] most emotional experiences." Adding to that excitement was South's triumph in the state football championship.[29]

Despite the Depression, in 1930 Gerald Sr. believed he had been able to make enough money to purchase a home on Lake Drive, but by the next year he had begun to question whether he could hold on to it. It would have helped the Fords had Leslie King Sr. paid his child support—which a court in 1931 had increased to $100 a month—but he had failed to comply with the judge's order. With their financial situation precarious, it was obvious that the Fords could not afford to send their oldest child to college.[30]

Once asked if he had benefited from luck in his early years, Ford said yes, pointing to his mother's divorce, her decision to move to Grand Rapids, and her second marriage to "one of the truly outstanding people I ever knew in my life." Serendipity now entered his life again, this time in the form of South High principal Arthur Krause. Without telling the Fords, he wrote Harry Kipke, the football coach at the University of Michigan. "We have a boy in this school by the name of Gerald Ford," he informed Kipke. Other universities, including Harvard and Northwestern, had shown an interest in him, yet "I have had my heart set on his entering Michigan and I have done everything possible to steer him that way." He asked Kipke to meet with the young Ford and suggest he become a Wolverine: "All I want you to hold out to the boy is that you will try to get him an honest job to enable him to pay part of his way. He will not need much help if any." Kipke agreed, drove to Grand Rapids, and was impressed with the young man. Michigan did not offer football scholarships, but to pay for his meals—which would be a freshman's largest expense in Ann Arbor—Ford would be able to work at the university's hospital. Knowing that his star center would need $100 to cover his freshman-year tuition, Krause established a scholarship funded by profits from South High's bookstore and made sure Ford was its first recipient.[31]

Ford was one of almost 1,200 students to enter the University of Michigan in 1931. As a freshman, he and his roommate, a basketball player from Grand Rapids, lived in a small room, paying four dollars a week in fees. He pledged the Delta Kappa Epsilon fraternity the next year. He admitted that "the Deke house had a lousy reputation," but it was known for its athletes and its parties. In truth, Ford had little time for diversion. For one thing, he needed money. His stepfather was still suffering from the Depression, and Jerry received no response to a letter he had sent to his biological father asking for financial help. To pay bills, therefore, he washed dishes at the Deke house and took other part-time jobs. He made additional money by donating blood.[32]

Gerald Ford on the football field at the University of Michigan, 1933. Photo in the Gerald Ford Library, Ann Arbor, Michigan.

Ford also had football on his mind and was among twenty-five freshmen to try out for the team. The South High center impressed his new coach. That year, the 6-foot, 198-pounder was the starting center for the freshman team and received a trophy for being "outstanding freshman player in spring practice." He joined the varsity team the following year but largely sat on the bench, as the center was an All-American named Chuck Bernard. Ford believed he was a better offensive player than Bernard, but Bernard was, he admitted, the better overall athlete. He wished he had been a starter throughout his years at Michigan, yet he did not mope. "I learned," he later said, "that there was the potential always that somebody could be better than you." Ford's attitude impressed his coach, who called him "one of the finest boys I have ever met. I'm not talking of football ability, but of character. . . . He has never complained, never crabbed, never felt that he wasn't getting a square deal, always boosting for Bernard, who was keeping him on the bench. . . . Give me eleven boys with the disposition of Jerry Ford."[33]

Ford went into his senior year full of optimism. Bernard had graduated, meaning Ford would be the starting center for the varsity squad. The Wolverines had won college football's national championship the previous two years, and there were high hopes for a three-peat. But injuries to key players hurt. "Our defense struggled mightily, but we just couldn't score," Ford remarked. Michigan lost its first two games, against rivals Michigan State and the University of Chicago, by a combined total of 43–0.[34]

The next game, against Georgia Tech, tested Jerry's character. One of his best friends, and his roommate on away games, was Willis Ward, an African American who was one of the Wolverines' top receivers. Georgia Tech at the time had not integrated and refused to play Michigan if Willis came onto the field. The two schools considered a compromise by which Georgia Tech would have one of its top players sit out if Willis did, a proposal Ford considered "morally wrong." For advice, he called his stepfather, who suggested that his stepson "do whatever the coaching staff decides is right." Still uncertain, Ford spoke to Willis, who urged him to play. "Look," Ford recalled Willis telling him, "the team's having a bad year. We've lost two games and we probably won't win any more. You've got to play Saturday. You owe it to the team." Ford agreed. In its only win that season, the team defeated Georgia Tech 9–2. Yet the Wolverines' center throughout had proven himself a hard player and a team leader. Not only was he named the squad's most valuable player, but also he had earned the respect of players among the Wolverines' opponents. One was Rip Whalen, a guard on Northwestern's squad, who was impressed enough to suggest to his coach that Ford play in college football's All-Star scrimmage, the East-West Shrine Game. Ford's team, East, lost, but he played well enough to receive offers from two professional football teams, the Detroit Lions and the Green Bay Packers.[35]

Looking back, Ford regretted that he had not taken one of the teams up on its offer and played for a year. At the time, though, playing professionally was not what he had in mind. By his senior year in high school, he had decided he wanted to become a lawyer. According to one of his brothers, it was Ford Sr. who convinced his stepson to seek that career path. Whether or not that was the case, his aspirations toward the law offered a third reason why Ford had little time for partying, for he realized that he needed to maintain good grades to get into a high-ranking law school. He did well in the courses for his double major, in history and economics, but he had more difficulty with French and English composition. With the exception of a class on the history of the U.S. South, he scored As and Bs in his history classes and predominantly Bs in his business and economics courses. He never scored higher than a C in composition, got a D in French, and completed his undergraduate career with a B average.[36]

Even if Ford's grades had been good enough for him to get into a prestigious law school, he still had to pay for it. Ford asked to work for Kipke as an assistant, but the Michigan coach did not have the funds. Once again, he got lucky. Kipke called Ford to tell him that Yale University's head football coach, Ducky Pond, would be in Ann Arbor to find an assistant line coach. Ivan Williamson, Yale's end coach, happened to have captained Michigan's football squad when Ford was a sophomore. He recommended his former teammate for the job, as did Kipke, who forwarded his recommendation on to Pond.[37]

Pond interviewed Ford and confirmed what Williamson and Kipke had told him about the Grand Rapids native. The salary Pond offered was also good: $2,400 a year, starting that September. In fact, the pay was yet another reason to forgo professional ball. The Packers and the Lions had offered Ford $2,800, a significant difference at that time. If, however, Ford got injured and proved unable to play after ten days, the team could drop him.[38] Job security was far less a concern if he went to Yale.

Law versus Love

In the intersession between graduation from the University of Michigan in June 1935 and the start of Yale's fall term, Ford worked in his father's paint store. To the delight of his parents, he decided to change his name officially, and in December 1935, a probate court judge granted Ford's request. From that point, he was Gerald Rudolph Ford Jr.[39]

Ford enjoyed his new position at Yale, and the players liked him. Though for the first time he was financially secure and was able to put some money away, he remained wedded to the idea of getting into law school. Pond told him there was no way he could coach, which was itself a full-time job, and take law classes. Yale Law School was also dismissive, arguing not only that he would not have the time, but that it was highly selective, accepting only about 25 percent of applicants.[40] Ford's B average at Michigan was not going to cut it.

For the moment, Ford put off law school. One of his roommates, Ken Loeffler, Yale's basketball coach, told Ford about the exciting time he had had working in national parks out west, and he suggested that Jerry spend the summer of 1936 as a park ranger. "Well, that sounded like a good idea," Ford reminisced, "better than filling paint cans." He wrote one of Michigan's senators, Arthur Vandenberg, who got Jerry hired at Yellowstone National Park. Spending $700 for a car, Ford headed west. He stopped off to see his biological father, who was also in Wyoming, thinking there had "to be some good in the person my mother first married." He stayed one night with the Kings and discovered that King was not impecunious; rather, he had inherited a good sum of money following his father's passing. "There was not much to talk about," Ford recalled, "but while I was there I could see that he had quite a bit of land, and seemed to be doing well." The next day, he left for Yellowstone. Armed with a rifle to protect himself from the park's grizzly bears, his duties included removing trash, providing directions to visitors, and overseeing the campgrounds. Jerry worked until mid-September, earning $1,680 for his service. He performed well enough to receive a recommendation for reappointment, but he turned it down.[41]

It was not that Ford disliked being a park ranger, but he still planned to go to law school. Following another successful year coaching football, including winning the Ivy League title and a $600 pay raise, Ford went back to Ann Arbor to take classes at the University of Michigan Law School. "If I received good grades," he wrote in his memoir, "I could use them as a wedge to try again at Yale."[42]

Ford took two classes in Ann Arbor, receiving Bs in both. Returning to Yale, he again raised with Pond the idea of law school. This time, the Yale coach relented, but only if he took the courses "in the spring term. You can't let it interfere with your coaching responsibilities." Ford's memoir gives the impression that he accepted that deal. In fact, as he confessed later, there was more to the story. "I didn't tell the athletic department I was going to take two courses that fall of '38," he confessed. "And I didn't tell the law school I was going to continue my coaching." He took two classes, "worked my ass off," and got Bs in both. He then formally applied to Yale Law. That he planned on taking classes part-time did not please the faculty, but a well-known professor, Myres McDougal, who had interviewed Ford as part of the application process, was taken enough with the applicant to recommend his admission. With that, Ford formally began his tenure as a Yale law student.[43]

Getting a law degree in a timely manner initially posed a challenge to Ford. On top of working with the football team, he had begun coaching the boxing squad, a job for which he admitted he had no experience and which he did not enjoy. But he eventually saved enough money to quit his coaching positions and attend law school full time. The classes enthralled him. He had to read numerous cases and differences of opinion, mull them over, and determine what the correct answer was. Never one to back away from a challenge, he caught up on his course work, graduating in 1941 in the top third of a class that included Byron White, who served as a Supreme Court justice from 1962 to 1993; Sargent Shriver, the first director of the Peace Corps; and Cyrus Vance, who became President Jimmy Carter's secretary of state.[44]

Throughout, Ford's parents remained on his mind. The Great Depression continued to hold the country captive, taking down businesses and livelihoods. Ford Paint and Varnish, though, was among the companies that survived. A midwestern conservative, the elder Ford adhered to the ideology of the country's interwar Republican presidents, which emphasized self-reliance and rejected government interference in the economy. It was a position that set these individuals apart from President Franklin D. Roosevelt, who insisted that the way to tackle the Depression was through government regulations and government-funded public-works initiatives, all of which were parts of his New Deal domestic program. The younger Ford, having watched his stepfather persevere without federal assistance, came to question whether such oversight and interference in the country's capitalist system was wise or even necessary. As he said during his tenure in the Oval Office, "The Ford Paint and Varnish Company survived the Depression. And I have often wondered if it would have if my father had had to fill out all of today's forms and applications and those thousands and thousands of questionnaires, and at the same time, cope with the patchwork of rules and regulations which face today's businessmen."[45]

The child support Leslie King owed his ex-wife certainly could help. On his way back to New Haven from Yellowstone in the summer of 1936, Ford had stopped off in Ann Arbor and told his mother about King's wealth. Dorothy determined to take King to court, with the help of one of Jerry's fraternity brothers who had recently received his law degree. A federal court in Wyoming ordered King to pay $6,300 and attorney fees. King claimed to be unable to afford that sum and asked Jerry to compromise, but the least Ford would accept was $4,000. It was not until 1939, and only after ending up in jail for not complying with the federal court order, that King agreed to pay. After deductions for attorney fees, Dorothy received a check for nearly $2,400. "I was glad it was over," commented Ford. "I never saw my father again. I never heard from him again."[46]

At about this time, someone new entered Ford's life. When coaching at Yale, he received a letter from a woman he had "dated very casually" in Ann Arbor who suggested he meet Phyllis Brown, a student at the Connecticut

College for Women in nearby New London. "She and I went to prep school together," wrote the friend, "and she is the most beautiful girl I ever knew. She loves athletics, is very active, and I think you would like her." New London was the home of the U.S. Coast Guard Academy, and a short time after receiving this letter, the Yale boxing team went there for a match against the cadets, two of whom were from Grand Rapids and friends of Ford. They seconded the recommendation that he meet Brown, commenting as well on her good looks. Having not found "much in the way of female attraction around New Haven," he gave Brown a call. She agreed to go out with him, and he drove to meet her.[47]

Brown appeared to be a perfect match for the aspiring attorney. She was stunning, standing 5 foot 8, with shoulder-length blonde hair, blue-green eyes, a bright smile, and an hourglass 34-22-34 figure. She considered herself "an Eastern preppy" and thought "anybody who came from west of Pennsylvania was a Westerner. And I thought of [Ford] as being a sort of a hayseed." Yet she found him a "charming hayseed,"[48] one whom she wanted to see again.

Ford later wrote he was "deeply in love for the first time." He was impressed with her beauty, intellect, and energy. She taught him to ski. They danced, "sailed, played tennis . . . [and] went to the theater. . . . He really hadn't done many of these things," she recalled. What moved Brown was his determination. Here was a young man who was simultaneously coaching and taking law classes while courting her. "He was always tired," Brown stated years later. She acknowledged she "was a flirt. . . . I didn't know what I wanted and I had lots of beaus and lots of young men in my life." Yet "Jerry was just hanging in there. . . . He just sort of never gave up."[49]

Their relationship blossomed. "I believed in him," she commented. "Whatever he set out to do, he made a commitment and kept it." He was not an intellectual, but he was intelligent and "cunning." He would listen to what others said, she reminisced, think it over, "and then he would come up with the right answer. He was smart—not clever, not quick, but smart." He "was the first important man in my life, my first love affair, the first man I ever slept with"—an interesting comment that pointed to Ford's preparedness to set aside his midwestern piety. He also enjoyed their time together, even if he did not necessarily express it. His mother's efforts to get him to control his temper had led him to contain all his emotions. Brown knew Ford cared for her, but "he was not very expressive." This is not to say he always kept up his guard. He did not appreciate her flirting, as became clear in New York City, when during a night out, "he put a fist right through [a] door."[50]

Ford and Brown were in New York as a result of a chance encounter Brown had had in 1939 with McClelland Barclay, a famous pinup artist. Taken with the young woman, Barclay suggested she become a model. He sent her to a modeling agency in New York, which immediately hired her. Enjoying her new world, she quit school. Ford traveled to the Big Apple to spend time with her, visiting museums, going to the opera, and enjoying Broadway plays. When *Look* magazine asked her to bring her boyfriend for a ski weekend that would become a story in an upcoming issue, she invited Jerry. The two appeared in the 12 March 1940 edition, with photos depicting a happy couple skiing, snuggling, and being very much in love. Both their families anticipated nuptials in the near future. Ford and Brown too talked about getting married, although he wanted to wait until after he had received his law degree and found a good job.[51]

Their relationship did not last. As Brown's modeling career took off, Ford found himself having to choose between love and law. The aspiring lawyer's refusal to "give up" was indicative of a workaholism that he had developed by the time he graduated from Michigan. That workaholic nature was a double-edged sword. On the one hand, it explained his determination to woo Brown, despite her flirtatiousness and the frustration it caused him. On the other hand, it drove him to get his law degree and even to begin looking into a career in politics. In Ford's case, it meant Brown and his own professional aspirations could not coexist, particularly after he decided to return to Grand Rapids.

What convinced Ford to head back home and think about public office was an incident that took place during the 1940 presidential election, which pitted the Republican nominee, Wendell Willkie, against Franklin Roosevelt, who hoped to win a third term in the White House. World War II had begun the year before, and Roosevelt had taken steps, such as providing fifty old destroyers to Great Britain, to, he declared, protect the world from aggression while keeping the United States out of the conflict. Willkie insisted Roosevelt was being disingenuous, claiming that the New Deal was anathema to private enterprise and warning that the Oval Office's occupant intended to bring the United States into the war. Ford found much in Willkie that appealed to him. That summer, while in Grand Rapids, he told his stepfather that he wanted to serve as a volunteer on Willkie's campaign. Gerald Sr. encouraged him to speak with Frank McKay.[52]

McKay was the local party boss, and his power extended throughout Michigan. Born in 1883 in Grand Rapids, he had begun working in a factory, where he gained the friendship of many of the city's immigrants. Over time, he made a fortune in finance, banking, and real estate. He also became owner of the *Michigan Times* newspaper; invested in the lumber, tire, and food industries; and, consequently, expanded his influence. In the meantime, he received a position as the assignment clerk for the county circuit court, and he used that position to make powerful political connections. Charged with but not convicted of corruption in 1919, he became Michigan's state treasurer in 1925. He held that post until 1930 and used it to expand his influence statewide. By 1940, McKay's power had begun to wane as those loyal to him passed away or became too feeble to help him. Moreover, he started to lose interest in politics. Still, he remained politically formidable and convinced Willkie to let him control all Michigan patronage if the GOP candidate won. Ford disliked the idea of having to turn to such a character as McKay, but he knew that getting a job with the Willkie campaign in Grand Rapids would have to go through him. Accordingly, he made an appointment to meet with the party boss. He waited in McKay's office for "four hours," after which, Ford remembered, "he gave me three minutes. He showed no interest in how I might help the party. He obviously thought I was some young whippersnapper, and ended the discussion."[53]

Ford never forgot the encounter with McKay. Upset by his treatment, he returned to New York City, where he joined the Willkie campaign. He did well enough to attend the GOP National Convention in Philadelphia. Tempering the excitement of that moment was Roosevelt's unprecedented third-term victory in November. Willkie's defeat was another edifying experience for the Yale student. "Not only did I learn a little about politics," he commented, "but more important I learned about myself. I liked politics, everything about it." Ford began to think about seeking public office, "and logic told me the place for that was Grand Rapids."[54]

Further attesting to Ford's determination to return to Michigan was the time he spent in New York improving his speaking. He no longer stuttered, but he knew that whether as lawyer or as a politician, he had to make a case in clear, concise language, oftentimes extemporaneously. During one summer he spent a couple of months in the Big Apple taking lessons from a speech teacher who worked at Carnegie Hall. His advice to Ford, advice that Ford later said he wished he had followed more often, was to "speak as yourself. Don't try to be some outstanding orator. You are most impressive when you speak in your typical Middle Western style."[55]

When he graduated from Yale Law in 1941, therefore, Ford turned down offers to practice on the East Coast, including New York City, and chose to return to Grand Rapids. Going back to Michigan meant a difficult breakup with Phyllis. Ford had never indicated to her that he wanted her to come with him to Michigan. Most likely, she would not have left the Big Apple, since she enjoyed her modeling career and life in the big city. In later years, the two questioned as well whether their relationship would have survived. She admitted she was "a flirt," and Ford acknowledged that a marriage to her "would not have lasted."[56]

Ford Goes to War

Back in Grand Rapids, Ford opened a practice with Philip Buchen, a fellow Deke who had gotten to know Ford when they both took classes at the University of Michigan. Buchen finished at the top of his class and, like Ford, had offers from top law firms. But he shared Ford's vision of opening a practice in Grand Rapids. Both passed the bar exam later that year, and using what little money they had—Ford had some savings from coaching, and Buchen had received a loan from his father—they opened their practice in the middle of that year downtown in the Michigan Trust Building. It was a good choice: the Trust Building was also the location of the Grand Rapids Bar Association, which had an outstanding library that Ford and Buchen could use. Lawyers in the association referred clients to their two colleagues. Ford also rounded up business through his membership in such organizations as the United Way and the Red Cross. The fact that he was well-known in town because of his prowess on the football field and his active service to his church, Grace Episcopal, helped expand his clientele.[57]

The two men made good partners. Buchen had suffered from polio as a child, which limited him physically, and so he spent much of his time in the office while Ford went into the field. Their first client was a friend of Jerry's parents who paid the two attorneys ten dollars to look at some information about a home he wanted to buy. In their first year, they grossed $1,200. Although they took numerous types of cases, Ford preferred trial law and cases involving adoptions. Because of what his mother had gone through, he least enjoyed divorces.[58]

Ford liked law, but Buchen assumed his partner planned on using it as a stepping stone into politics—that is, until 7 December 1941, when Japanese aircraft launched a surprise attack on the U.S. Pacific Fleet at Pearl Harbor, Hawaii. Hearing reports of the attack that evening on his car radio, Ford knew that the United States was going to enter World War II and that he wanted to serve his nation by joining the military.[59]

Quitting his job with the law firm, Ford signed up with the U.S. Navy.

Once again, football helped him. The navy had a pilot-training program in North Carolina, and one of the people in that program, Tom Hamilton, had himself played on the gridiron. Believing good pilots had to be in good physical shape, he made sure the former Michigan center assisted with the pilots' conditioning. "But there was a war going on," Ford commented in his memoir. "I wanted desperately to be part of it, so I wrote letters to everyone I knew, pleading for a billet on a ship." In 1943 he finally received an assignment to the light aircraft carrier *Monterey*.[60]

A newly commissioned vessel, the 622-foot *Monterey* weighed 11,000 tons, had a top speed of about 30 knots, a crew of 1,569, and a complement of forty-five aircraft. Ford's job was to oversee the crews manning the 40-millimeter antiaircraft guns situated on the ship's fantail. The *Monterey* first saw action in November 1943 when the Third Fleet participated in an assault on the enemy-controlled Gilbert Islands. "The Japanese planes came after us with a vengeance," he penned. "We had many general quarters calls and it was as much action as I'd ever hope to see." His desire for a position of leadership, however, overcame any qualms he had about further combat. Once again, chance and football entered the picture. When Ford learned the *Monterey*'s assistant navigation officer had been transferred to another vessel, he requested the post. The carrier's captain, Lester Hundt, "was an avid football fan, and he took a liking to me. And I cozied up to him." Hence, when Ford asked for promotion, Hundt gave it to him. In turn, Ford found himself navigating the ship and, during combat, he was one of the officers who served on the ship's bridge. "Couldn't have had a better place to be," he remembered. "I was right there where everything was going on. . . . It was good duty to be at the center of action." The new post was proof to Ford that "the harder you work, the luckier you are."[61]

Luck seemed to be on the *Monterey*'s side. Between Pearl Harbor and the end of 1944, U.S. and Allied forces had dramatically reduced Japan's Pacific empire, which once had expanded nearly halfway across the ocean. The Solomon, Gilbert, Marshall, and Mariana island chains, as well as virtually all of New Guinea, were in Allied hands. U.S. forces had also begun an offensive against Japanese troops in the Philippines. During this period, the *Monterey* had repeatedly seen action. In addition to the operations in the Gilberts, it had supported amphibious landings on the Marshall Islands of Kwajalein and Eniwetok in January–February 1944 and participated in the Battle of the Philippine Sea that June, during which American pilots destroyed much of Japan's naval air arm. In October, the *Monterey* took part in air attacks on the Japanese-controlled island of Formosa, fighting off relentless enemy attacks against it and other ships in the fleet and barely avoiding a torpedo that damaged the U.S. cruiser *Canberra*.[62] Later that month, it participated in the largest naval battle in world history, the Battle of Leyte Gulf, which witnessed U.S. warships and naval air power destroy most of what remained of Japan's fleet. The *Monterey* thus could claim doing its part in turning the tide against Japan, and doing so unscathed.

That is, until December 1944, when Ford's luck nearly ran out. Still stationed off the Philippines to support U.S. ground forces there, the Third Fleet found itself in the midst of Typhoon Cobra. Although the fleet's commander, Admiral William Halsey, knew of the worsening weather conditions, he had been led to believe the system was located elsewhere and not heading toward his ships. His vessels began refueling operations, only to be battered by huge waves driven by winds topping 100 miles per hour. Some were high enough to flood over the *Monterey*'s flight deck, which sat nearly 60 feet above the water. The clanging bell signaling general quarters rang on the carrier, and Ford smelled smoke. When he went onto the flight deck, the rolling ship nearly threw him overboard; only by catching with his fingers the combing, a two-inch lip that bordered the deck, was he able to avoid falling into the sea. He threw himself onto a catwalk and rushed as fast as safely possible to the bridge, where the ship's captain, Stuart Ingersoll, ordered him below decks to assess the situation. Heading to the hangar, he found that some of the planes, which had been tied down by cables, had broken loose, crashing into one another and starting a fire. Ford recalled that vents designed "to funnel fresh air down to the engine and boiler rooms . . . were funneling smoke. One sailor died of asphyxiation and 33 were injured." Worse, three of the ship's four boilers had failed. If the last one quit, the *Monterey* would lose all water pressure, and the crew would have no ability to fight the flames. Ingersoll sent crewmen "wearing gas masks to the engine and boiler rooms. They brought out the survivors, kept the one boiler functioning and worked to repair the others." Seven hours later, the fire was out, and the ship was on its way to the Caroline Islands and then back to the United States. Every one of the carrier's planes was lost or damaged, three crewmen had died, and another forty had suffered injuries.[63] The typhoon had also damaged over two dozen other vessels, some of them severely, sunk three others, and taken over 700 lives. But the *Monterey* managed to survive the storm and the war.

Ford had hoped for a transfer to another carrier but instead received orders to return to the United States and await further instructions. Ingersoll urged the navy to promote his former navigation officer, calling him "steady, reliable, and resourceful. His unfailing good humor, pleasing personality, and natural ability as a leader made him well liked and respected by the officers and men." Ford spent his time on leave seeing his parents in Grand Rapids. He also visited Phyllis Brown in New York, who had written him while he was in the Pacific and told him she had married and was pregnant. Despite their difficult breakup, Ford may have felt he could reconnect with her. He discovered, however, that his emotional attachment had vanished. "We had cocktails," Ford remarked, "but that was the extent of it."[64]

Time and experience had changed Ford in another way. Prior to World War II, he had been an isolationist. Isolationists, who were particularly numerous in the Midwest, eschewed U.S. involvement in foreign affairs, preferring to focus the nation's affairs on its own security concerns. Participation in the world's second global conflict had transformed him: "I returned understanding we could never be isolated again. We were and are one world. It was clear to me, it was inevitable to me, that this country was obligated to lead in this new world. We had won the war. It was up to us to keep the peace."[65]

Ford had hoped the navy would return him to combat, but instead he received orders to report to the Naval Reserve Training Command in Illinois. In August 1945, Japan surrendered, and in February of the following year, now Lieutenant Commander Ford received his discharge. With his naval career behind him, he decided to go back into law. The office he had opened with Buchen had closed, as Ford had been in combat and his former partner had joined a prestigious Grand Rapids firm, Butterfield, Keeney, and Amberg. Buchen had informed Ford that he too could work there, and now free to do so, Ford sat down with Julius Amberg, one of the senior partners. The naval veteran impressed Amberg, who offered him a job.[66]

Ford enjoyed being back in Grand Rapids. Amberg improved Ford's research skills, taught him the art of writing a good brief, and improved his delivery before a jury and judge. During the Depression, Ford's parents had moved into a house on Santa Cruz Drive, located in the East Side. Once filled by Dorothy, Gerald Sr., and their three younger sons—Ford had been living on campus at the University of Michigan when his folks moved—the house was now an empty nest, as all of the Ford children had become adults with lives of their own. Desiring to spend time with his family, and probably to save money, Ford moved in with his parents.[67]

As driven as ever, Ford worked long hours at Butterfield, Keeney, and Amberg, oftentimes being the first to arrive in the morning and the last to leave at night. Politics, though, continued to attract him. "Without being too subtle about it," wrote one of his biographers, "he began to build a political base," working with the Boy Scouts, the United Way, the Kent County Farm Bureau, the American Legion, the Veterans of Foreign Wars, the National Association for the Advancement of Colored People, and the Urban League. His devotion to his work began to worry his mother. "Jerry," Dorothy asked him, "when are you going to start dating again? Your brothers are all married and raising families. You need to find a nice girl and get married and settle down. You're not getting any younger, you know."[68]

That "nice girl" entered the picture in 1947. In the middle of that year, Ford met Betty Warren at a cocktail party. He later described her as "a good-looking, well-dressed young lady," and at the party he learned that she was in the midst of getting a divorce. He decided to ask her out. He informed a friend, Peg Neuman, of his intentions, and with Ford present, she called Warren, who knew Ford had a reputation as "the town's most eligible bachelor." When Betty hesitated to go out with him, Ford took the phone and urged her to join him on a date. "I'm in the process of getting a divorce, and you're a lawyer, and you ought to know better," she explained. He persisted, and she relented, offering him "twenty minutes" of her time. The two "went to a quiet bar," and what was supposed to have been twenty minutes turned into more than an hour of conversation. He drove her home, leaving the intrigued Warren hoping he would call her again.[69]

It was the beginning of a romance that would turn into a nearly sixty-year marriage. Born in 1918 in Chicago, Elizabeth "Betty" Anne Bloomer was one of three children, and the only daughter, of Hortense Neahr and William Bloomer. Hortense came from a well-off family, and William was a traveling salesman for a rubber company. The family had moved to Grand Rapids when Betty was two years old. As Betty grew up, she began taking dance lessons, hoping eventually to become a professional dancer. When the stock market crashed in 1929, her father's salary dropped precipitously. To earn money for the family, Betty taught various types of dances to children and modeled dresses each Saturday at a local department store called Herpolsheimer's.

There was good reason to foresee Betty making something of herself. Headstrong, Hortense made sure that "her daughter was exposed to the best that Grand Rapids society had to offer." Betty became an active member in service organizations, including the Junior League, and even made the front page of the society section of the *Grand Rapids Press*. She was also more than willing to get into fights or play sports with boys. Betty came to see Eleanor Roosevelt, whom scholars regard as one of the nation's most activist first ladies, as a "role model because [of] her independence. . . . I really liked the idea that a woman was finally speaking out and expressing herself rather than just expressing the views of her husband. That seemed healthy."[70]

Concealed behind what appeared to be an idyllic life were serious family problems that, wrote one of her biographers, "boded ill for Betty's future." One was William's job, which took him away from home for extended periods of time and left her without his presence in her life. His death from carbon monoxide poisoning in 1934—there is some question as to whether it was an accident or suicide—erased that presence altogether. The other was her father's addiction to alcohol, about which Betty did not learn until after his passing. While there are questions about the relationship between genetics and alcoholism, there is conclusive evidence that the disease runs in families.[71] As it turned out, avoiding the bottle proved a challenge for Betty in her later years.

William passed away when Betty was sixteen years old and a student at Central High. She had difficulty coping with her father's loss. She also found it hard to handle her mother, who, following William's death, had to assume the roles of both parents. Her "domineering" personality might have rubbed off on Betty, but it ran headlong into her daughter's own aspirations. There was no better example of that than Betty's dream to dance, which would mean leaving Grand Rapids for New York. Hortense refused to allow it, at least until Betty turned twenty. In the meantime, they arranged a compromise by which her daughter took classes at Bennington College with Martha Graham,[72] who was then and is still today considered one of the greatest figures in the history of modern dance.

Having reached twenty, Betty moved to New York to join Graham's dance troupe as part of the backup group to the first line. Realizing her daughter was serious about living in New York but not prepared to give her complete independence, Hortense convinced her to come back to Grand Rapids for six months to see if anything worked out. If not, she could go back to the Big Apple.

Betty never returned to New York. She founded her own dance studio in Grand Rapids, where she began to date and, in 1942, married Bill Warren, a childhood friend. It proved a terrible mistake. Warren, like Betty's father, was a salesman who had a drinking problem. Worse, he had trouble holding down a job; he and his wife moved from one city to another as he looked for employment, with periodic stays in Grand Rapids. When they were in their hometown, Betty worked at Herpolsheimer's as fashion coordinator. She grew increasingly frustrated with her spouse, who was frequently away from home. Unable to live that way, she filed for divorce. Although Bill did not contest the end of the marriage, the divorce was not granted until 1947.

Ford did not care that Betty's divorce had yet to be finalized. Maybe this was due in part to the fact that his mother had found love following her legal separation from Leslie King. Certainly he found much he liked in the thin, 5-foot-5, brown-haired, square-faced, blue-eyed dancer and model. In addition to being attractive, she was energetic and bright, and she told him what was on her mind. To Betty, Jerry was handsome, driven, and caring. They both were hard workers and enjoyed going out at night to watch football as much as a quiet evening at home. The two began dating regularly and fell in love. In February 1948, Ford finally popped the question, but with a caveat: "I'd like to marry you," he told her, "but we can't get married until next fall and I can't tell you why." Without batting an eye, she accepted his proposal.[73]

What Ford could not reveal to his fiancée was his intention to run for Michigan's Fifth District seat in the U.S. House of Representatives, which included Kent County—the home of Grand Rapids—and the less populous Ottawa County. The district was solidly Republican. In contrast to most of the nation between 1920 and 1948, which had elected a Democrat five times to the presidency, voters in the Fifth had chosen a Democrat to represent their district only once, and that turned out to be for a single two-year term. Even labor unions, some of the Democratic Party's most important constituents, tended to vote Republican in the Fifth because of the GOP's power there. Ford knew, therefore, that if he could win the Republican primary, the seat was his, yet victory was a long shot. He was well-known but lacked political experience. Furthermore, the incumbent, Bartel Jonkman, appeared unbeatable. Jonkman was in his fifth term, a Republican of Dutch background—which mattered a great deal in a district where conservative Dutch voters predominated—and had the backing of the McKay political machine. Ford, however, had reason to challenge Jonkman. He remembered how McKay had treated him in 1940, and he regarded Jonkman's support for isolationism not just out-of-date but dangerous. He also knew that McKay had opposition. Indeed, a few months before Pearl Harbor, Ford had become aware of citizens who had started to organize against McKay. Called the Home Front, the group remained active during and after World War II, raising money and putting up candidates to run against McKay, including Gerald Ford Sr., who, at his son's urging, had challenged the McKay machine in 1944 and won the post of Kent County chairman. His victory represented the beginning of the end of McKay's stranglehold on Grand Rapids politics.[74]

Ford told Buchen of his plans, and he in turn encouraged the prospective candidate to name Jack Stiles, whom both had known at the University of Michigan, as campaign manager. A local businessman and political novice, Stiles agreed to help. Both understood the key contest would be the GOP primary. The first step was to find out if anyone else was prepared to challenge Jonkman. Ford spoke with each of the possible contenders, but no one showed any interest. Next, he needed the support of the Dutch majority. Ford had no Dutch blood in him, but a friend and member of the Home Front, Dr. Willard Ver Meulen, did. Ver Meulen, a local dentist, had turned against McKay after he learned that a doctor at a local sanitarium who worked while drunk had been allowed to continue practicing because he had connections to the political boss. Ford could also rely on some of his classmates from South High, fellow veterans, and people with whom he had served in groups such as the United Way and the Red Cross.[75]

Ford filed to run in June 1948, about three months before the primary, and he and Betty set their wedding date for October, approximately a month after the primary vote. He figured that if he lost, he could return to law. If he won, and knowing the political leanings of his district, getting married prior to Election Day would do him no harm.[76]

Once again, luck was on Ford's side. Jonkman saw no threat from the young newcomer. President Harry Truman, furious with the Republican-controlled Congress's refusal to pass legislation he favored and desiring to win the 1948 presidential election, had called lawmakers back into special session, meaning that Jonkman had to stay in Washington. Furthermore, Ford gained the endorsement of Michigan's well-known Republican senator, Arthur Vandenberg. Like Ford, Vandenberg had been an isolationist prior to World War II, had become an internationalist as a result of the conflict, and had grown disgusted with Jonkman's opposition to a more active U.S. role in world affairs, which included denunciations of Vandenberg himself. Finally, Amberg proved an ally. He told Ford that the latter need come to the office only an hour each day, allowing him to spend the rest of his time on the stump.

A Gerald Ford Republican primary campaign billboard, 1948. Photo in the Gerald Ford Library, Ann Arbor, Michigan.

Ford decided to set up his campaign headquarters in a red, white, and blue Quonset hut (taking advantage of the symbolic significance of a veteran having his campaign's nerve center situated in patriotically painted military housing) in the parking lot in front of Wurzburg's department store, which enabled Amberg to help Ford's campaign another way: McKay's office overlooked the parking lot. Knowing that Wurzburg's was a valued client of Butterfield, Keeney, and Amberg, McKay demanded the store's managers have the hut removed; Wurzberg's, in turn, contacted the law firm. Amberg, a Democrat who knew no member of his party stood a chance of defeating Jonkman and who had no love for the incumbent, called Ford into his office and asked if he was prepared to move his headquarters. Ford refused. "Excellent," replied Amberg. "That's exactly what I hoped you'd say."[77]

Ford campaigned on a message of conservative internationalism. He put up billboards with the slogan "Jerry Ford—to work for you in Congress," and he traveled throughout the district, shaking hands and speaking to anyone who listened. He favored smaller government and lower taxes, positions supported by the many conservatives who lived in his district. Foreign policy was another matter. Even though he knew voters in his part of Michigan tended toward isolationism, he made clear that the United States could no longer limit its involvement in world affairs. Accordingly, he endorsed the creation of the United Nations and the Marshall Plan, the latter of which offered billions of dollars in economic aid to help western Europe recover from the ravages of the war. He called on Jonkman to debate him, but the incumbent, still seeing Ford as no threat, refused.[78]

Jonkman's strategy was shortsighted. For one, he ignored the shift toward internationalism that had taken hold in the country, including in his home state. The best example of this was Senator Vandenberg. While there was no guarantee that voters in the Fifth District shared Ford's and Vandenberg's foreign policy views, the fact that sentiment was growing in favor of America playing a more active role in world affairs should have been a warning. Moreover, even if Ford was a political neophyte, he and his family were well-known in Grand Rapids. That Ford, unlike Jonkman, had veteran credentials was another fact working in his favor.[79]

But Jonkman's biggest errors were yet to come. First, he chastised organized labor, which upset Leonard Woodcock, western Michigan's representative for the United Auto Workers (UAW); Woodcock and the UAW therefore endorsed Ford. The League of Women Voters (LWV) also turned against him. While addressing that group, Jonkman walked out after being criticized. According to Dorothy Judd, a member of the local chapter of the LWV, "this really opened the way for Jerry, I think, people were so angered with Jonkman." Then, in September, just before the primary, Lee Woodruff endorsed Ford. As editor of the largest newspaper in Grand Rapids, the *Grand Rapids Press*, Woodruff was an internationalist who had become upset with Jonkman's denunciations of Vandenberg's foreign-policy views. An infuriated Jonkman began to denounce Woodruff and the *Press*, further cementing sentiment in his district against him.[80]

On 15 September, Ford defeated the five-term incumbent, winning 23,600 votes to Jonkman's 14,300. It was a major victory, one that surprised even Betty and gained him national notice. "Incumbents almost to a man swept the top races in Tuesday's primary elections in seven states," reported the *New York Times*. "One major upset was the defeat of veteran Representative Bartel J. Jonkman in his bid for the Republican nomination in Michigan. He was ousted by Gerald B. [*sic*] Ford Jr., a Grand Rapids attorney."[81]

The primary victory his, Ford turned his attention to two other matters. One was his Democratic opponent, Freddy Barr, who happened to be his and Betty's friend. The other was his wedding. The event offered indications of the type of life he planned and Betty could expect living. During the rehearsal dinner, Jerry departed to give a speech, leaving Betty alone until the couple's minister took the groom's spot. He campaigned on his wedding day, 15 October, and had to change so fast into his formal wear that he forgot to take off his mud-covered shoes. Neither his new wife nor his future mother-in-law were particularly pleased with his appearance. Jerry and Betty then headed to Ann Arbor for their three-day honeymoon, which con-

Gerald R. Ford Jr. and Betty Ford following their marriage, 15 October 1948. Photo in the Gerald Ford Library, Ann Arbor, Michigan.

sisted of celebrating their nuptials with friends, a night at a hotel, and then, the next day, a football game and political rally for New York governor Thomas Dewey, the Republicans' presidential candidate. The seventeenth, a Sunday, was "quiet"; it was followed by a meeting with Ford's political aides on Monday and then a trip back to Grand Rapids. As they entered their hometown, Ford told his wife that he had some meetings that day and asked if she could make him soup and a sandwich. "That was her introduction to married life with a politician," he wrote. She was clearly bothered by what she later called a "complete farce of a honeymoon," and his request made her realize "what it was going to be like from then on."[82]

There was little doubt that Ford would leave law for politics. He was a conservative in a conservative district, meaning it would be difficult for a Democrat to win; even Barr knew he had no chance of victory. Jerry remembered, "Somebody asked [Barr] during the campaign what was his campaign theme, and he said, 'Well, I got nine kids and I need the job.'" Ford realized the seat was his, yet he continued to stump as hard as ever. Betty, who admitted she was not a very politically interested individual, helped out. On 2 November, Ford easily defeated Barr, winning 61 percent of the vote.[83]

The Price of Ambition?

Ford's dictum "The harder you work, the luckier you are" was an accurate reflection of his beliefs. He perceived a clear connection among grit, determination, and achievement. Those traits came from his parents. His mother had escaped an abusive husband who had threatened her life and that of her newborn son. His stepfather had worked hard to provide for his family and taught Ford the values of self-reliance and of tightening one's financial belt.[84] From his parents he also learned the importance of honesty and patience.

Ford's parents, though, were not the only ones to influence him. In the Boy Scouts, he discovered a love for leadership, which carried into sports, particularly football. That sport, which he played in both high school and college, taught him the importance of teamwork and faith in human nature and reinforced the lesson of discipline his parents had inculcated in him. His naïveté regarding what drives people apparently was not shaken. Nor was his own ambition. Phyllis Brown had shown him that life was about more than just work. It was, however, impossible to take the work out of the workaholic whose objective had become a life in politics. Once Ford had settled on that goal, there was virtually nothing to keep him from getting a seat on Capitol Hill.

The question was what this all meant for his new bride. Betty supported his intention to move from the world of law into that of politics. What she did not expect was that he would win or that his new job as a congressman would affect their marriage. "Like every woman," she reflected, "I thought that when you sign that certificate and walk down the aisle, all of a sudden everything changes, and you have all his attention and regular hours. Well, that wasn't to be."[85] Theirs would be a marriage that would last, but her new husband's desire to climb the political ladder, and the time it required him to spend away from her, would offer serious challenges.

TWO

Climbing the Ladder of Power

If Gerald Ford's victory in his district's Republican primary was a surprise, a far greater shock took place at the national level. President Harry S. Truman, who had entered the Oval Office following Franklin D. Roosevelt's death in April 1945, had decided in 1948 to run for the presidency in his own right. It appeared he had no chance of victory, as he faced two other Democratic opponents: J. Strom Thurmond, whose "Dixiecrats" disliked the president's support for African American civil rights, and Henry Wallace, who contended that Truman's determination to contain the threat posed by Soviet communism prevented closer ties with Moscow. With the Democrats nominating three men for the presidency, the single Republican candidate, New York governor Thomas Dewey, seemed to be a shoo-in to win. Every poll had Dewey emerging victorious.[1] Yet in one of the most unexpected outcomes in a presidential election, it was Truman who emerged victorious by leading a well-managed campaign and maintaining behind him the coalition of groups that had stood behind Roosevelt. Moreover, Democrats, who had lost control of both houses of Congress in 1946, retook them.

Ford thus found himself as a freshman among the minority on Capitol Hill. Never one to skirt a challenge, he intended to do all he could to help his party gain and retain majority status in the House. To that end, he pursued a path marked by a moderate, pragmatic conservatism, one that emphasized standing up to communism abroad and at home and a limited federal role when it came to domestic social and economic matters. It was a course that set him apart from his party's liberal and conservative wings. More than that, it was a course that, in combination with his own desire to hold positions of authority, convinced him to seek what for him was the biggest prize of all: becoming speaker of the House. By 1959, luck and grit had taken him several steps closer to that goal.

Settling In

One of the first steps for the Fords was to find a place to live in Washington, D.C. Money was an issue, as it was throughout his congressional career. Because the financial support congressional candidates presently have did not exist in 1948, Ford emerged from his campaign $8,000 in debt, and his $12,500-per-year (later $15,000) legislator's salary would not permit him to pay off his IOUs any time soon. Betty and he rented a two-bedroom apartment at 2500 Q Street, but since Ford's job required him to keep in close contact with voters in his district, they looked for a place in Grand Rapids too. Using what little savings they had, as well as benefits from the GI Bill (a 1944 law that offered benefits to World War II veterans), Ford borrowed about $18,000 at a low interest rate, and in the summer of 1949 he purchased, for $28,000, a two-story apartment home on Sherman Street, located in Grand Rapids' East Side. They rented out the upstairs flat, living downstairs during their visits to their hometown.[2]

Also on Jerry's mind was his new job. He recalled the day he was sworn in as "probably the greatest thrill I had ever had in my life." After taking the oath, he looked up in the gallery and saw Betty sitting with the spouses of the other new freshmen. "She looked as proud as I felt," commented Ford. "From that first day on, I knew I wanted the House to be my career."[3]

Ford found a welcoming reception from several of his new colleagues. One was Richard Nixon, a California Republican serving his second term. Nixon shook Ford's hand and, to the latter's surprise, made mention of the Michigander's upset victory. The two became friends and were among the founders of the Chowder and Marching Society, a Republican social group formed in response to a bill passed through a congressional committee that would give automatic pensions to veterans; the Society's members felt the bill would take too much out of the nation's Treasury. Another new colleague was John F. Kennedy, a Massachusetts Democrat who had come into the House the same year as Nixon and whose office was across the hall from Ford's in the Old House building. Yet almost nobody in the House's Michigan delegation wanted anything to do with a person they regarded as an interloper who had defeated their friend, Bartel Jonkman.[4]

There was, however, an important exception among the Michiganders. Serving in his fifteenth consecutive term in the House, Earl Michener was highly respected by both Democrats and Republicans and was someone from whom Ford could learn the ropes of Capitol Hill. It was Michener who early on offered his young colleague salient advice: "Jerry, you can become one of two kinds of members of the House of Representatives. You can either be a floor man, and learn how to handle debate, the rules of procedure, etc., or you can be a committee expert. It's up to you what you want to become." Ford wanted the latter, but his freshman status meant he lacked the seniority that would permit him access to the juiciest committee assignments. Hence, he ended up on the Public Works Committee, which oversaw matters relating to the nation's infrastructure. Although sitting on that committee gave him exposure to the House's inner workings, he found the post relatively boring, for there "wasn't a hell of a lotta work" involved. Therefore, "I spent a lot of my time on the floor."[5]

Ford had two advantages operating in his favor, however, over other new House members. One was Michener, who introduced Ford to influential lawmakers, including Speaker of the House Sam Rayburn (D-Tex.) and John Taber (R-N.Y.), who sat on the powerful Appropriations Committee and had served as its chair. Ford had found out the benefits of spending time with people in positions of influence, as had been the case of the *Monterey*'s captain, Lester Hundt, and he did the same with Taber. To his pleasure, the New Yorker learned that his policy views coincided with those of Ford's. The second advantage, in Ford's words, was "just horseshit luck." Albert Engel, a Michigan Republican who sat on both the Public Works and Appropriations Committees, decided to resign from Congress and run for Michigan governor. Michener suggested Ford seek Engel's open position on Appropriations. Under House rules, any of the other members of the Michigan delegation, all of whom had seniority to Ford, had first crack at the seat. However, none of them wanted it, for they all held high-ranking positions on other committees and realized that if they took a seat on Appropriations, they would be treated as that body's most junior member. With no one else from his home state willing to jump onto Appropriations, and taking advantage of his friendship with Taber, Ford got the post.[6]

Ford was now on one of the oldest and most powerful committees in Congress. Created in 1865, the Committee on Appropriations controls the power of the purse: it votes on spending bills that are generated in the House as well as on the budget the president sends to Capitol Hill each year. The committee has a number of subcommittees, including defense, foreign aid, and agriculture, to look over the legislation or budget in question and, where necessary, make revisions before submitting the funding request back to the full committee for consideration; the vote of the full committee carries a significant amount of weight when the bill or budget is considered by the full House. Furthermore, because the committee's members are directly tied to the government's wallet, they have a greater chance of drawing federal funding to their districts, which can bring them political points at election time.

The Moderate Conservative

Ford's Republican Party was reeling from not just the defeat of 1948 but also its failure to recapture the White House since Franklin Roosevelt's election in 1932. By 1948, those losses had created a split within the GOP among conservatives, liberals, and moderates. Conservatives favored the Republicans of the 1920s and 1930s who endorsed small government, railed against the New Deal as socialistic, and leaned toward isolationism. Liberals were not unlike the progressive Republicans of the first two decades of the twentieth century: like the Democrats, they endorsed the New Deal, and they were willing to accept government intervention to help America's economic and societal ills; liberals also were prepared to accept Roosevelt's interventionist foreign policy. While not as supportive of big government as liberals, moderates accepted elements of the New Deal, though they shared liberals' belief that the GOP could run that program better than the Democrats.[7] Additionally, they joined liberals in pushing for an internationalist-minded diplomacy.

On the surface, liberals appeared to hold the greatest power in the GOP, as the party's nominees for the presidency in the 1930s and 1940s came from their ranks. However, that power was more superficial than real. A good example was Dewey, who had also run as the Republicans' presidential nominee in 1944 and whose positions had reflected those of conservatives. He chastised Roosevelt for not preparing America to defend itself prior to Pearl Harbor and for conducting "personal secret diplomacy." To him, the New Deal not only had failed to pull the United States out of the Great Depression but had begun to take the country "down the . . . road to regimentation" and had opened the door to Communist control of the nation. Though Dewey at first appeared to have a good chance of winning the election, his assault on Roosevelt and the president's policies turned voters off, and the New York governor lost in a landslide. Unwilling to make the same mistake, Dewey in 1948 had moved more toward the left, adopting a platform that endorsed the Equal Rights Amendment for women, greater protections for African Americans, and internationalism. He too was an anticommunist but refused to link Democrats to that anticapitalist, antidemocratic ideology. Once again, he lost, convincing conservatives that he should have run a campaign more like that of 1944.[8]

Ford sided with Republican moderates. He had already shown himself to be an internationalist, which set him apart from conservatives. Moreover, his position on domestic programs was middle-of-the-road. In promoting the New Deal, Roosevelt had accepted British economist John Maynard Keynes's contention that short-term deficit spending was necessary in times of economic slowdown to jump-start the economy. Although Ford realized Keynesianism might have been needed during the 1930s, he had come from a family that had not relied on the government dole during those years, and he did not favor programs that made individuals reliant on aid from Washington. Moreover, the postwar economy was booming as pent-up consumer demand for products was met by factories that had begun shifting production from military to civilian wares. It was time, believed Ford, for the government to limit (but not fully eliminate) funding for expensive—if not unnecessary—welfare programs, and to save money and raise revenue so as to pay down the country's wartime debt.

This is not to say Ford insisted on a balanced budget. He was a pragmatist who understood that a balanced budget was not always possible and even at times unwise. But to him, it was the job of the government to bring revenue and spending as much in line as possible,[9] as well as to avoid an excessively large debt that took money out of the Treasury, money that could be given back to corporations and individuals in the form of tax breaks.

Ford's moderate conservatism appeared in his response to Truman's first postelection State of the Union address, in which the president outlined a program that became known as the Fair Deal. Largely an extension of Roosevelt's New Deal, the Fair Deal included repeal of the 1947 Taft-Hartley Act—a bill passed over Truman's veto that restricted the power of labor unions, required union leaders to take an oath that they were not Communists, and gave the federal government the power to seek an injunction to prevent strikes that posed a threat to the country's well-being—implementation of a national health-insurance program, federal aid for education, an increase in the minimum wage from forty cents an hour to seventy-five cents, an increase in Social Security benefits, a public-housing program for low-income families, greater financial support for farmers, and a tax primarily on corporations to raise an additional $4 billion in revenue. Furthermore, Truman made clear he planned again to push for legislation designed to protect African American rights and to eliminate poll taxes and Jim Crow laws that denied blacks equal rights.

Ford had mixed feelings about the Fair Deal. He agreed with increasing the minimum wage; however, as a champion of free enterprise, he regarded a call by Representative John Lesinski (D-Mich.), the chair of the Labor Committee, for raising it quickly as detrimental to businesses. Additionally, he liked the idea of expanding Social Security benefits and favored greater protections for African Americans. His position on housing was mixed. He voted for Truman's low-income housing program—which became the 1949 National Housing Act—because it had a provision that helped people in rural areas get a home. With that single exception, he consistently rejected the idea of public housing throughout most of his career in the House, as the program required the use of taxpayer money and gave Americans a disincentive to try to improve their lot without federal assistance. He also opposed a national health-insurance program, favored using block grants instead of federal aid to support education, and called for retaining Taft-Hartley, contending that without it labor unions might become too powerful. Finally, while he did not reject taxes on businesses completely, his free-enterprise sentiment moved him to call for imposing them in a very limited fashion. In short, Ford took a middle position between what he regarded as the liberalism of the Fair Deal and the conservatism of those who rejected everything Truman favored. "We must all recognize that in our present society there must be a certain minimum of well-being for every individual," he commented. "However, the welfare state can go too far and thereby destroy individual initiative. At some point, a balance must be struck and it is the job of the 81st Congress to cooperate in achieving this end."[10]

Ford's past experiences explain his positions on the Fair Deal and civil rights, and they also underscore his desire to have the federal government enforce child support. Early on, he introduced legislation on this subject, telling the House Judiciary Committee in August 1949 that Washington's involvement "will have a salutary effect and will assist materially in bringing about a change in the attitude of the people who will cross State lines with the very definite intention of evading their family responsibility." This would not be the last time Ford attempted to pass such legislation. While he was not the only one who tried to get such a bill through Congress, not until passage of the Child Support Recovery Act in 1992 did the federal government assume responsibility for making sure "deadbeat dads" provided financial support for their children.[11]

Despite the lack of support among his colleagues to help children in need, there is little doubt that conservative-minded individuals on Capitol Hill (and in his district) shared Ford's insistence that the Truman administration do something about a series of union strikes in January 1950 that caused a dramatic cut in coal production. At issue was the workers' desire for a new contract, which the mine owners refused to offer. Ford chastised Truman for not invoking Taft-Hartley, pointing out that "it is 14 degrees below zero in Michigan and the people are getting colder by the hour." The administration succeeded in getting a court injunction to force the miners back to work, but when they failed to comply, the president asked lawmakers for the power to seize the mines. Neither the miners nor the owners favored such a move, prompting the latter to offer their employees a new contract in March.[12]

Ford certainly found even broader favor in his call to tackle the threat posed by Soviet-inspired communism. The Communist takeover of Czechoslovakia in 1948 and of China in 1949 as well as the Berlin Blockade of 1948–1949 were a few of the many events that bred fear of what President Dwight D. Eisenhower would later call the "domino theory": the idea that if not stopped, communism might reach the United States. Indeed, for all Americans knew, there were already Communists in the country seeking to undermine the country's capitalist-democratic system. The result was the Red Scare that extended into the early 1950s. Films such as *Conspirator* and *The Red Menace*, both of which came out in 1949, and George Orwell's novel *1984*, published that same year, depicted the danger communism posed to the nation's welfare. To root out possible subversives, the Taft-Hartley Act included a provision aimed at removing Communists from labor unions, and that same year Truman announced a federal loyalty program. Also in 1947 the House Un-American Activities Committee (HUAC)—which had been established in the 1930s to combat Nazism in the United States but which after World War II turned its attention to communism—subpoenaed dozens of individuals with ties to Hollywood to question them about their Communist affiliations. The next year, HUAC was the scene of hearings into the Communist ties of a former assistant secretary of state, Alger Hiss. Under oath, Hiss denied the charges, but he was later found guilty of perjury and served four years in prison. The Hiss case played into the hands of Senator Joseph McCarthy (R-Wisc.), who became a leader in this anticommunist endeavor. McCarthy accused dozens of persons of serving as Communist sympathizers or agents, though he was never able to prove any of his claims.

Ford was part of the emerging Cold War consensus in the United States that communism was a threat to the country. He praised Nixon, who was a member of HUAC, for combating "the insidious Communist forces that would destroy our Nation" and referred to Owen Lattimore—a university professor who was among those targeted by McCarthy—as a "fellow traveller" because he favored a seat in the United Nations (UN) for Communist China. Ford also endorsed a bill introduced by Representative Karl Mundt (R-S.D.) and Senator Homer Ferguson (R-Mich.) that would require all members of the U.S. Communist Party to register with the federal government; the bill ultimately became a provision of the Internal Security Act of 1950. But in combating communism at home, Ford again was not an ideologue. He rejected the efforts of those in the House who wanted to create another committee, similar to HUAC, that would focus on tax-exempt organizations. Neither Truman nor Ford nor many moderate Republicans liked McCarthy's methods on the grounds that he was dividing the nation. Yet those same GOP moderates worried that denouncing McCarthy publicly risked splitting the party, and therefore they kept their views to themselves. That was certainly the case with Ford, who later wrote, "The fact that I didn't speak out against McCarthy is a real regret."[13]

It was not enough to stand up against communism at home, though. The Soviets, as explained by the influential Sovietologist George Kennan, had no desire to coexist peacefully with the United States. Rather, they would patiently, and through means that offered the least risk of war, spread their power worldwide and weaken that of Washington. A hawk who believed in using America's military power to prevent Kremlin-inspired communism, Ford shared that assessment. He denounced the 1945 Yalta Agreement on the grounds that it permitted Soviet control of Poland and represented a dangerous example of appeasement. "Russia knows no compromise," he told his colleagues in the House. "Why must we surrender to her every wish? . . . Yalta should spur us to a new method in our dealings with this ruthless, atheistic nation. Appeasement has not worked with the Soviet[s]. Appeasement cannot work with bullies and barbarians."[14]

Ford also seconded the judgment of America's leaders that stopping godless communism necessitated a policy of containment. He endorsed U.S. membership in the United Nations because it gave Washington an ability to express its concerns and desires in an international forum. He also liked the Reciprocal Trade Agreements Program (RTAP). During the Great Depression, Roosevelt had signed into law the Reciprocal Trade Agreements Act, giving him the power to adjust tariffs in the hopes that if the United States lowered duties, other nations would do the same, which would in turn promote U.S. commercial sales abroad. While this act proffered clear economic benefit for American business interests, it also had a link to containment. One component of U.S. foreign policy in the Cold War was the export of U.S. culture abroad, as evidenced by the establishment in 1946 of the Office of International Cultural Affairs and the International Press and Publication Division, the latter of which later became the U.S. Information Agency. Selling U.S. products abroad was closely connected to this cultural offensive, for if other peoples (and their leaders) were shown what America's capitalist system could offer, they would have reason to avoid moving toward the Soviet orbit. The Reciprocal Trade Agreements Act set the stage for the RTAP; after 1948 it became part of the larger General Agreement on Tariffs and Trade (GATT), a program Ford consistently supported.[15]

In containing communism, Truman did not ignore military measures. He stood behind the formation in 1949 of the North Atlantic Treaty Organization (NATO). After Communist North Korea attacked the noncommunist South in June of the following year, he asked the UN to provide military help to Seoul. Rather than crying foul for Truman's failure to request a formal U.S. declaration of war against Pyongyang, members of Congress shared the president's desire to react to the North's invasion quickly. The United Nations did as well. At the time, the Soviet Union was boycotting the UN because the United States and its allies refused to permit Communist China to join that organization. As a result, Moscow was unable to veto a resolution passed by the Security Council calling on UN members to help Seoul. Ultimately sixteen nations answered the call. Under the leadership of U.S. General Douglas MacArthur, who had become a hero to Americans by leading their country to victory over Japan during World War II, UN troops succeeded in pushing North Korea's forces out of the South, only to have China enter the war in November. By early 1951, the war had stalemated along a line that largely followed the old North-South boundary.

Throughout, Ford insisted on defending the Korean peninsula. In July 1950, Congress began hearings on the Defense Production Act to mobilize the U.S. economy for the war, permit the president to control wages and prices, and allocate resources. Southern Democrats and conservative Republicans had doubts about the bill, asserting that it gave the central government too much power, but Ford endorsed its passage that September. He worried that an increase in expenditures could cause inflation, but he could not see any justification for restricting military spending at a time when the lives of Americans and their allies were at stake. Following China's intervention, he called for bombing that country's supply bases and blockading its coast. "We are bleeding ourselves to death, which is just what Stalin wants us to do," he declared in the House. "It is utter stupidity to continue with such a policy when we are not fighting with both fists."[16] Such sentiment reflected that of many other Americans, including MacArthur, who found himself relieved of command in April 1951 for openly criticizing the Truman administration's handling of the war.

The 1952 Elections

A stalemated war and a president who had fired a hero and appeared unwilling to take all the measures needed to end the war took their toll on Truman's popularity rating, which fell to 23 percent and stayed there. The opening of negotiations among the belligerents in July 1951 gave some hope for ending the war, yet those too deadlocked. Knowing he had no chance of winning reelection, Truman recruited Illinois governor Adlai Stevenson to run as the Democratic nominee. The question for the Republicans was whom to run against Stevenson. The leading candidate was Senator Robert Taft of Ohio. Known as "Mr. Republican," he was the favorite of the party's conservative wing. But his personality was colorless, and he had been so outspoken against the New Deal that some of his colleagues wondered "whether he can revise his thinking and be positively for something." Most problematic were his isolationist foreign policy views.[17]

For all these reasons, Ford disliked Taft and hoped General Dwight D. Eisenhower would throw his hat in the ring. Eisenhower had commanded Allied forces in Europe during World War II and, like MacArthur, had emerged from that conflict idolized by the American people. Afterward, he served as president of Columbia University and then commanded NATO's military forces. A midwesterner himself—he had been born in Texas but was raised in Kansas—he shared Ford's moderate conservatism on domestic matters and internationalist orientation. Years later Ford stated, "Eisenhower was number one electable, and number two, ideologically I fitted with him." He therefore joined nearly twenty other moderate Republican lawmakers in sending a letter to Eisenhower in February 1952, urging him to announce his candidacy. "There can be no doubt that an overwhelming majority of the people of the United States want you as their leader," they wrote.[18]

Eisenhower appeared to have mixed feelings about running. He regarded becoming president as yet another form of service to the country and as early as 1945 had considered seeking the Oval Office. Nor could he have forgotten a January 1951 meeting he had had with Taft at the Pentagon building in which he offered not to run for the presidency in 1952 if Taft agreed to an internationalist foreign policy. Taft had refused, and now the Ohio senator appeared to be the White House's next occupant. Yet the demands of the war and then of NATO command had been exhausting, and a history of smoking left Eisenhower in less-than-pristine health. His reply to Ford and Ford's colleagues was thus noncommittal. He needed to remain in Europe, he wrote in March, but "I assure you that I shall regularly reexamine my position, bearing in mind your message."[19]

Eisenhower gradually decided in favor of running. In March, he defeated Taft in the New Hampshire primary. Then, following another strong showing in Minnesota, he announced in April that he would give up his post with NATO and campaign full time.[20] He chose as his running mate Nixon, whose conservative, anticommunist credentials and California residency would help Eisenhower gather votes from westerners and from the Republican right wing. Also having behind him many moderates, independents, and even Democrats—in fact, there were many Democrats who had wanted Eisenhower as *their* candidate—the former general secured the GOP's nod at its national convention in July.

It was a tough campaign. Stevenson was a better orator and was more intellectual than Eisenhower, but the latter's smile, self-confidence, effective use of television, and, maybe most important, message resonated: the Democrats, including Truman, were guilty of corruption, as was shown by investigations into the politics of the president's home state of Missouri and by reports of efforts by the government to peddle its influence; it was the Democrats who had mired the United States in Korea; and if elected, promised Eisenhower, he would travel to Korea. Still, it was not easy going for the Republican candidate, whose campaign was embarrassed by news reports that Nixon had a secret fund maintained for him by supporters in California. While there did not exist in 1952 the strict code of ethics that lawmakers are (supposed to be) bound by today, the possibility that Eisenhower's running mate had accepted personal favors raised questions about his trustworthiness. The GOP candidate pondered whether to dump Nixon, but the Californian preempted him by giving an impassioned speech on television in which he used a dog his two daughters had named Checkers as an example of the types of gifts he had accepted. By creating a vision of his children losing their beloved pet, Nixon forced Eisenhower into a corner and suppressed sentiment favoring a different running mate. Stevenson, for his part, did his best to distance himself from Truman,[21] but it was not enough. On Election Day, Eisenhower won 33.9 million votes, or 6.5 million more than Stevenson, and 442 electoral votes to the Democratic candidate's 89. For the first time in twenty years, a Republican had control of the White House.

Throughout, Ford championed the Eisenhower-Nixon ticket. He found the media's focus on Nixon's slush-fund trail confusing, as "other members of Congress—myself included—had maintained reasonably similar funds." Ford put his dollars into a separate bank account and used it for newsletters and travel to Michigan. "Under existing rules, those funds were both legal and appropriate." He wrote the vice-presidential nominee, "Fight it to finish just as you did the smears by the Communists when you were proving charges against Alger Hiss" and simultaneously joined others who urged retention of Nixon on the GOP ticket. In the meantime, he criticized the Stevenson campaign, pointing out that Robert Tufts, who worked for the State Department, had joined the governor's staff. To the Michigander, it was "another piece of tangible proof that Adlai Stevenson is in the political custody of the Truman Administration" and, by extension, of the misbegotten policies and the corruption infecting it.[22]

Eisenhower's victory was only one aspect of what ended up being an exciting year for Ford. The Fifth District's representative realized he had little chance of losing his seat in 1950, but he was by nature very competitive and wanted to retain the position of authority he had won two years earlier. Every time Congress recessed or he had a long weekend, he returned to Grand Rapids to meet constituents, tour farms or local businesses, and give speeches. Furthermore, he began a weekly newsletter and sent audiotapes home to be played on the radio detailing his and Congress's activities, and he polled constituents on issues ranging from the minimum wage to education, labor, and health policy. He made sure to keep up with mail coming to his office, sought to have questions or requests answered as quickly as possible, sent letters to folks back home who had had a major event take place in their lives (such as a birth or wedding), and took pictures with visitors, which he then autographed. He easily won reelection, defeating the Democratic nominee, J. H. McLaughlin, with nearly 67 percent of the vote.[23]

Ford was just as aggressive in 1952. In addition to continuing the newsletter, correspondence, stumping, and meetings, he and Betty joined the

Dwight and Mamie Eisenhower join Gerald and Betty Ford at a Grand Rapids campaign event, 1952. Photo in the Gerald Ford Library, Ann Arbor, Michigan.

president and Mrs. Eisenhower when they made a campaign stop in Grand Rapids. Once again, Ford won by a wide margin, securing another term.[24] Even better, Ford began his third term in Congress as part of a Republican-controlled Capitol Hill, with the GOP holding a two-seat majority in the Senate and eight more than the Democrats in the House. It was the first time in twenty-two years that Republicans had command of both the executive and legislative branches of government.

Ascending New Rungs

Whether Betty Ford shared Jerry's excitement is questionable. Not long after arriving in the capital in 1949, she learned her mother was severely ill. She boarded the first flight out of the capital for Florida, but mechanical problems delayed the aircraft's departure. By the time she arrived at her destination, her mother had passed away from a cerebral hemorrhage. Having lost her only surviving parent was hard enough, but it was compounded

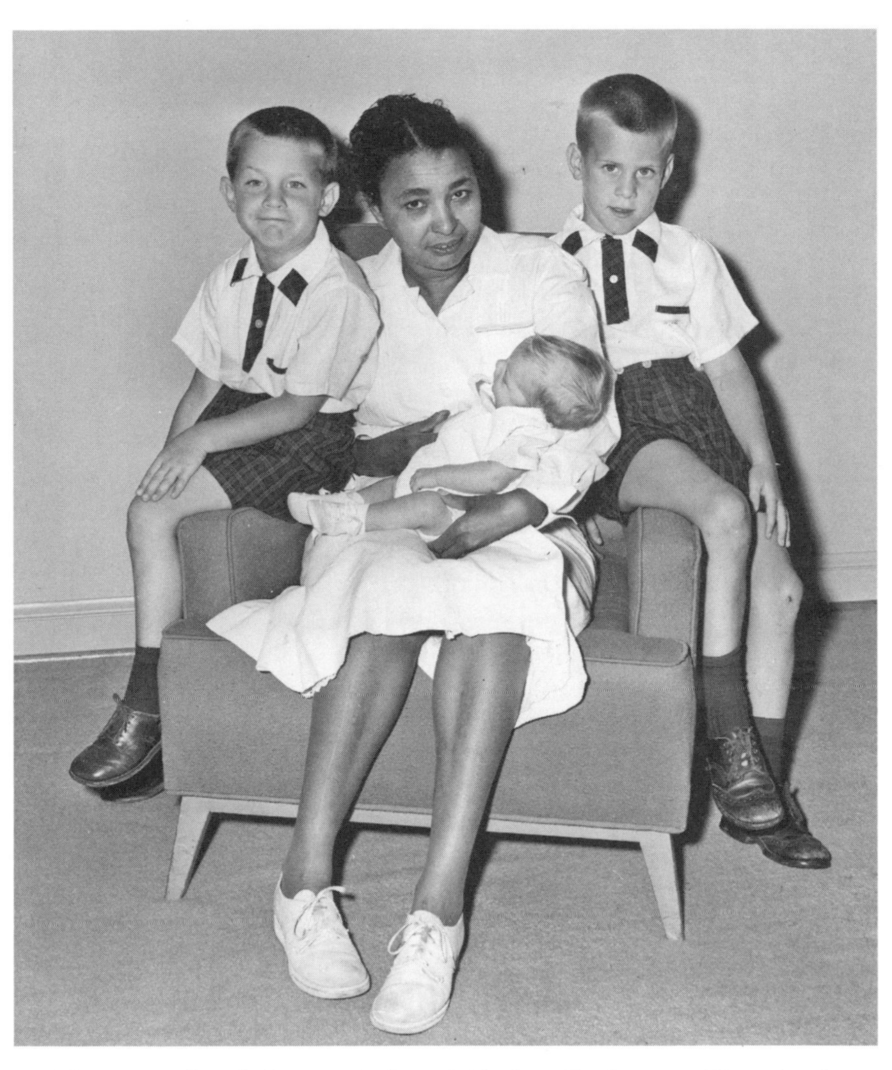

Clara Powell with Steven, Jack, and Michael Ford, 1956. Photo in the Gerald Ford Library, Ann Arbor, Michigan.

by her new lot as a politician's wife. Just before the Fords' wedding, Jerry's sister-in-law Janet—who had wed his half-brother Thomas in 1942—told Betty that "you won't have to worry about other women. Jerry's work will be the other woman."[25]

That work had now entered its third term in office. Mrs. Ford did her best to accept the duties of a congressman's spouse, meeting people from Ford's district who visited the capital, attending social functions, volunteering in his office, and joining the Congressional Club, which was made up of wives of members of Congress, cabinet members, and Supreme Court justices. She read about the responsibilities of a lawmaker to learn more about what her husband's work entailed. She even began to share his aspiration to achieve greater power on Capitol Hill.

Yet throughout, Betty felt insecure. Her growing interest in politics did not come close to matching his dedication to lawmaking, which took him away almost every day; in fact, he spent so much money on tickets to fly back to Michigan that she began to worry about their financial well-being. And despite his love for her, she could not fail to note that attractive women turned his head. As one of her biographers pointed out, starting a family offered her some stability, and by the end of 1952, the Fords had two sons: Michael and Jack. To help take care of the children, the Fords hired a woman named Clara Powell, who became an honorary family member. Needing a larger place, they had moved from their apartment on Q Street to a larger residence in the Fairfax Park neighborhood of Alexandria, Virginia.[26]

The Fords did not stay there long. They wanted more children, and their apartment was not big enough. Having paid down their debt and settled in Washington, they found some property in Alexandria in 1954 and located a design for a home they desired to build. Once again taking advantage of the GI Bill, they borrowed money to help pay the $28,000 cost. The two-story, three-bedroom home on Crown View Drive offered a living room, dining room, kitchen, and garage. Another bedroom, built over the garage, became the master. A few years later, Ford went to a doctor with back spasms and was told he needed to exercise, prompting him to spend another $7,500 on a 40-foot-by-20-foot swimming pool; swimming laps became a daily habit. Additionally, the Fords finished the basement, bringing the entire cost of the home to about $40,000. Son Jack Ford recalled the neighborhood being "very normal, very middle American. We used to walk to school every day. You'd jump on your bike and go riding down the street, and your parents didn't worry about you."[27] It would be the family residence until Jerry had the title "president of the United States" before his name.

Sitting in the Oval Office was not on Jerry's mind, but climbing up the ladder of power was. With their control over both houses of Congress, the Republicans held both the leadership and the majority on all committees. This included the Appropriations Committee, once again chaired by John Taber. Ford received appointments to two of the committee's key subcommittees: foreign operations, which oversaw the nation's foreign aid program, and Army, which Taber assigned to Ford. Ford was taken aback. "I know more about the Navy," he told Taber. The New Yorker knew this. "All those damn Admirals will be after you, and you won't resist them," he replied. "But if you're with the Army, you will tell the generals to go to hell." Ford admitted that it "was awful good advice."[28]

Ford believed a nation with a strong military was a secure one, yet he remained wedded to his fiscal conservatism, fearing that too much government spending would increase inflation. He developed a reputation on the defense subcommittee as an excellent cross-examiner, taking generals, admirals, and secretaries in the Defense Department to task over the cost of and need for new weapons. Similarly, he refused a request from a group of visiting Grand Rapids businessmen to use his influence to have a military base constructed in his home district. Ford argued that although it would bring money and jobs "during a military buildup or in a war . . . when the buildup ends, or the war is over, everything drops dead. In the end you have more problems than benefits."[29]

Ford also saw how the government spent its tax dollars. In July 1953, an armistice finally brought an end to the Korean War, and he decided to make his first overseas trip to East Asia. At his initial stop, South Korea, he visited U.S. troops and saw American prisoners of war who had been released as part of the agreement ending the conflict. He concluded that while the South had a fine military, it had "no money to fight without our aid." From there, it was off to Indochina. A French colony that is today the independent nations of Vietnam, Laos, and Cambodia, Indochina had fallen under Japanese control during World War II. Following that conflict, Paris had sought to reassert its control. The Vietnamese, desiring independence, resisted, with tens of thousands joining a Communist-led group called the Viet Minh. Ford had joined many others in and out of Congress to encourage both Truman and Eisenhower to offer military aid to the French, and by 1953 U.S. taxpayers were paying for two-thirds of Paris's costs to defeat the Viet Minh. Even with this help, the Viet Minh's use of guerrilla warfare was proving more than the French could handle. Ford was less than convinced by French presentations on how they intended to conquer the insurgents, writing in his diary, "Speeches. Pictures. Bally-hoo."[30]

After Indochina, Ford traveled to Taiwan to meet with Jiang Jieshi,[31] the former noncommunist leader of China who, with the Communist conquest of his country in 1949, had fled with his Nationalist government and many of his supporters. The Beijing regime considered Taiwan to belong to China, and the Communists intended at some point to take the island and unify all Chinese under their leadership. To Jiang, the Communists were

Ford with military personnel in South Korea, 1953. Photo in the Gerald Ford Library, Ann Arbor, Michigan.

usurpers whom he hoped to kick out of power; with them out of the way he could then reassume leadership on the mainland. While the United States had expanded economic and military aid to Taiwan during the Korean War, officials in Washington realized that Jiang had no chance to return to the mainland without U.S. armed support, something neither Truman nor Eisenhower was prepared to offer. Ford shared this sentiment. The Nationalists lacked the capability to take the mainland on their own. Rather, he foresaw Taiwan becoming an independent nation. Making a final layover in Japan to discuss regional military and political affairs, he flew back to Washington. Among the findings he reported to the defense subcommittee was that France was losing its war in Indochina. He was willing, he made clear, to do whatever was necessary to stop "Soviet or Chinese Communist domination" of the world.[32]

More and more Ford made a name for himself. As Phyllis Brown had discovered, he rarely got angry, listened to others' opinions (even if he did not agree with them), and mulled over what he heard before making a decision. His demeanor and work ethic had already caught the attention of key lawmakers such as Taber. Others came to share Taber's sentiment. One was

Melvin Laird, a Wisconsin Republican who had joined Congress in 1952, sat with Ford on Appropriations, and was to become one of the party's most powerful members in the House. Another was Texas Democrat George Mahon, who had served in the House since 1936 and later became chair of the Appropriations Committee. "I was impressed with his calm judgment and steady hand," stated Mahon. "Regardless of the administration in power, he works toward the accomplishment of the attainable. He is a man you can deal with."[33]

Aware of the support he enjoyed, and given his desire to climb the ladder of power, by the middle of his third term Ford had set his sights on what he regarded as the biggest prize: speaker of the House.[34] The most powerful position in the House of Representatives, the speaker acts as the body's presiding officer, enforces House rules, and names the majority of the members of the House Rules Committee, which determines under what rules legislation comes to the floor. Furthermore, under the Constitution, if neither the president nor the vice president is able to perform his (or her) duties, the speaker becomes the country's chief executive. As the speaker is elected by the members of the majority party in the House, Ford would need to remain almost constantly in campaign mode. He would have to continue to win reelection in his district and do what he could to ensure that his party retained control of the House. The workaholic would have to work even harder.

The 1954 Campaign

Ford's first concern was to win another term in Congress. With the GOP in control of the White House and the legislature, Ford realized Republicans had an opportunity to lead the nation in directions they favored. An Eisenhower Republican even before Eisenhower won office, Ford endorsed the president's domestic program, known as Modern Republicanism, which rejected conservative Republicans' desire to curtail the programs of the New Deal and the Fair Deal but also opposed the idea of expanding those programs, as doing so would require greater government spending, increase inflation and the deficit, and interfere with the free market. This is not to say Eisenhower avoided expensive programs. The president in 1954 called for construction of an interstate highway system, insisting it would benefit the country militarily and economically by offering quicker and easier transit of military personnel and equipment, as well as civilians and goods, across the country. Moreover, it would encourage the construction of places for people to eat or sleep during their travels. Economic considerations also stood behind his decision to join with Canada in constructing the Saint Lawrence Seaway, which would link the Great Lakes to the Atlantic Ocean. Ford eagerly endorsed both initiatives, contending they offered numerous benefits to Michigan's industries and port cities. Eisenhower had easily won Ford's Fifth District in 1952,[35] and the largely conservative constituency there had good reason to favor projects that promoted free enterprise (and, in the case of interstate highways, national security). But it was not clear whether that positive feeling would offset the wariness they felt about retaining programs like Social Security, which they regarded as "socialistic."

It was also uncertain how voters in the Fifth felt about Eisenhower's foreign policy. Midwestern isolationists thought the U.S. foreign-aid program was unnecessarily expensive. Shortly after taking office, Eisenhower called for $5.5 billion for the Mutual Security Program (MSP)—which was established in 1951 and provided military and economic aid to foreign nations to help them fight communism—leading to a quarrel among Republicans on the House floor. The internationalist-minded Ford was among those who curried support for the appropriations bill. Ultimately, Congress ended up giving the president nearly everything he wanted. "Dear Gerry," Eisenhower wrote afterward, misspelling Ford's nickname, "I was already confident that your strong arm would be behind the [Mutual Security Agency] appropriation. . . . But, even so, I want you to know that I deeply appreciate your active and helpful approach in Committee and on the Floor."[36]

Ford also bucked a growing Republican trend toward protectionism. He shared Eisenhower's view that the RTAP was necessary for U.S. security. As an example, the president maintained that the spread of communism in Asia threatened to cut Japan off from markets needed to maintain the capitalist-democratic system it had adopted under U.S. guidance following World War II. Hence, American markets had to remain open to Japanese goods. As the president put it, Washington's "trade policy could 'dictate whether these areas remain in the free world or fall within the Communist Orbit.'"[37]

The fact was that Ford had little reason to fear losing his seat, but, ever the determined competitor, he acted like an underdog who had to scrap for every vote. In a move certainly aimed at courting the many citizens of Dutch descent in his district, Ford asked Congress in early 1953 to admit 50,000 Dutch immigrants to the United States so that they could escape flooding then taking place in the Netherlands.[38] The next year, he called for repeal of an excise tax opposed by furniture companies in Grand Rapids. Also in 1954, he endorsed the Communist Control Act, which outlawed the

U.S. Communist Party, and, that same year, the Espionage and Sabotage Act, which imposed a penalty of life in prison or even death for spying on or committing acts of sabotage against the United States. He also required foreign agents to register with Washington. He established a direct line between his Grand Rapids and Washington offices so he could keep up with matters at home. Though he retained a home in Furniture City, in 1954 he began using a mobile trailer that permitted him to travel around the district to canvass opinion during Congress's summer break.[39]

Furthermore, Ford took advantage of a relatively new medium, television, airing on station WOOD in Grand Rapids and on radio a "cross-examination" in which moderators asked him questions about his position on various issues. Some queries concerned Senator McCarthy, who had recently embarrassed himself and the Republican Party during nationally televised congressional hearings prompted by his accusation that the U.S. Army had been harboring Communists. Adopting a position similar to that of many others in his party, Ford said that he did not approve of the Wisconsin senator's methods but that he believed McCarthy "had performed a service in that he had emphasized the serious problem of Communist infiltration in our government and within our continental limits." Shifting his focus to more-local matters, he repeated his opposition to public housing, reminding the citizens of Grand Rapids that they had voted against public housing in two separate referenda. He reminded voters that the Saint Lawrence Seaway would assist in developing Michigan's ports, including Grand Rapids. The cost of living index, which uses a base of 100 to express the price of residing in a city or nation, had "more or less stabilized" under Eisenhower, Ford said, after rising over 10 points under Truman. Finally, while unemployment in Grand Rapids stood at about 6.1 percent, it was several points lower than it had been under Eisenhower's predecessor.[40]

While most of the questions focused on domestic matters, Ford also received a query about "massive retaliation." Early on, the Eisenhower administration had announced that its foreign policy would be based on what it called the "New Look," which emphasized reliance on America's nuclear weapons to deter Communist aggression rather than a combination of atomic and conventional arms. Not only were nuclear explosives more powerful, Eisenhower and his secretary of state, John Foster Dulles, believed, but they were less expensive to maintain, allowing the United States more easily to hold down defense spending. The centerpiece of the New Look was massive retaliation, defined by Dulles in a January 1954 speech:

"Local defenses must be reinforced by the further deterrent of massive retaliatory power."[41] In short, the United States was prepared to use its nuclear weaponry to stop communism's spread.

There is little doubt Ford had prepared himself for a question about massive retaliation. It was the centerpiece of Eisenhower's foreign policy. Furthermore, Ford admitted he saw much in Eisenhower that he liked, including the president's desire to maintain a strong defense while simultaneously holding down government spending. Finally, a couple of weeks before the cross-examination, a new crisis with China had erupted when the Communists began an artillery bombardment of Jinmen and Mazu (also known as Quemoy and Matsu), two small islands off the mainland coast controlled by the Nationalists.

The Eisenhower administration thought Beijing had ordered the assault to soften up the two islands prior to trying to take first them and then Taiwan itself. Concerned that the loss of Taiwan might mean Communist conquest of the rest of Southeast Asia, the White House publicly declared its commitment to protect the Nationalists. The administration was more ambiguous if that commitment might entail the use of nuclear weapons and risk turning a local conflict into a much broader, more destructive one. Thus, when questioned about the Eisenhower-Dulles policy, Ford emphasized that Dulles had spoken of the "capacity" to use the atom. The secretary of state "never said that we were going to use it on every little place where a fire broke out." Whether the cross-examination influenced voter sentiment is not clear, but that November, Ford easily defeated his Democratic opponent, R. S. McAllister.[42] The news was not as good for the Republican Party, which lost control of both the House and Senate.

More Steps Up

Ford's seat was safe for another two years, but keeping it necessitated that he continue doing what he could for his constituents. For instance, a month after winning reelection, he received a letter from a John Schwander, who wrote that his wife's stepfather, a Mr. Harrison, had been involved in an accident in 1951; since the stepfather could not purchase a new vehicle, Schwander bought him one and signed the title over to him. However, Mr. Harrison did not have it notarized and mailed it to Michigan's secretary of state. In June 1952, Harrison hit and injured a pedestrian, who sued. As the title was in Schwander's name, it was he who ended up as the defendant, and a court ordered him to pay more than he could afford. Consequently, he lost his driver's license and car plates. He asked Ford for help. The Michigan representative forwarded the request for assistance to Owen Cleary, Michigan's secretary of state. Cleary replied that the state was obliged to take action against Schwander, and although Schwander had filed an appeal, "we had to return it because there is no appeal under the statute" in question. Ford had more luck helping another constituent, Mort Olds, get a hardship discharge from the U.S. Navy.[43]

More broadly, Ford had to decide what position to take on civil rights. The federal government had taken some measures to help African Americans gain equality, such as Truman's executive order banning segregation in the military. Nevertheless, blacks still faced restrictions, particularly in the South, which treated them as second-class citizens. Eisenhower, himself very conservative when it came to matters of race and worried about losing the votes of southern whites if he took a more activist civil rights stance, favored a gradualist approach that largely left the matter up to the states.

African Americans fought back both through the legal system and through demonstrations. They took their case for school integration to the courts and, in 1954, achieved victory when the Supreme Court in the case *Brown v. Board of Education of Topeka* declared segregation in public schools unconstitutional. The following year, African Americans in Montgomery, Alabama, staged a boycott of the city's segregated bus system. The protest received media coverage throughout the country; made a local reverend, Martin Luther King Jr., nationally famous; and ended with Montgomery agreeing to integrate its buses. But many towns, cities, and states refused to comply with the *Brown* decision or to follow the lead of Montgomery. In early 1956, over 100 southern members of Congress signed the Declaration of Constitutional Principles—or, as it became known, the Southern Manifesto—calling for *Brown*'s reversal. The state of Virginia for its part implemented the Stanley Plan, named after the state's governor, Thomas Stanley, barring state funding to any school district that attempted to integrate even one of its schools.[44]

Ford, in his position on civil rights, was neither as conservative as those who signed the Southern Manifesto nor as racially sensitive as some of his contemporaries. His opposition to public housing, aimed at benefiting the poor—many of whom were minorities—was not progressive. He voted for a bill that included an amendment written by Adam Clayton Powell (D-N.Y.) that would withhold federal moneys from any district failing to comply with *Brown*, only to turn around and vote against it when, he said, Democrats added another provision that would have allowed federal funding to go equally to all school districts, rich or poor, rather than focusing on those with fewer funds.[45]

Yet as a football player he had played alongside African Americans, some of whom became good friends, and Ford considered the resistance exhibited in the Southern Manifesto unconscionable. Therefore, in 1956, he supported giving additional enforcement powers to stop those trying to deprive others of their voting rights, providing federal aid to encourage school desegregation, and establishing and broadening the Commission on Civil Rights. Additionally, he voted for an amendment to a school-construction bill prohibiting financial support for states that failed to comply with the *Brown* decision.[46]

Ford's Eisenhower-like combination of progressivism and conservatism could also be seen when it came to environmental protection. In the early 1900s, the protection of America's natural beauty had drawn interest from some government officials, such as Presidents Theodore and Franklin Roosevelt; Theodore Roosevelt's chief forester, Gifford Pinchot; organizations like the Sierra Club; and naturalists, including John Muir. But environmental protection was largely pushed to the side during the 1940s and 1950s in favor of other matters, including World War II, the Cold War, and postwar economic growth. President Eisenhower was among those who gave the environment short shrift. He preferred economic development over environmental protection. In the name of maintaining a balanced federal budget, he preferred to have state and local governments shoulder the cost of defending the country's flora and fauna. Having spent time as a forest ranger, Ford appreciated the country's natural beauty, and in 1955 he took his first foray into environmentalism by sponsoring a bill to push for a halt to air and water pollution. But that same experience at Yellowstone made him "favor utilization of recreational resources rather than preservation." Additionally, as a fiscal conservative he objected to having the federal government provide money to the states to help them stop pollution.[47]

On foreign policy, Ford steadfastly defended programs beneficial to his country's security and economy. He stood behind GATT. Thanks to the MSP, U.S. allies were able to assume more responsibility for their own defenses, he told his colleagues, permitting Washington "to reduce the personnel of our Armed Forces. The record is clear that we have been able to spend less money for our own United States Armed Forces because of this program. . . . I intend to support this program because it involves the welfare of our citizens."[48]

Indochina, where a decade later the United States was to find itself mired in an apparently never-ending war, was also on Ford's radar. In 1954, the Viet Minh had defeated over 16,000 French troops at the village of Dien Bien Phu, located in what is today northwestern Vietnam, not far from the Vietnamese-Laotian border. Having suffered a total of 94,000 dead and 78,000 wounded trying to regain control of their colony, the French government decided enough was enough.[49] Later that year, French, Soviet, Chinese, Vietnamese, British, and American officials met in Geneva, Switzerland, where they agreed to what became known as the Geneva Accords. The pact granted Vietnam, Laos, and Cambodia their independence; divided Vietnam in two, with the northern half placed under Communist control and the south under a noncommunist regime; and called for elections throughout Vietnam in 1956 to reunify the country. Significantly, the United States was the only attendee not to sign the accords.

Elections were never held. South Vietnam's leader, Ngo Dinh Diem, refused to permit them, and the Eisenhower administration, which had been providing Diem with financial and intelligence support, contended it had no obligation to force his hand, as it had not formally endorsed the agreements reached at Geneva. Ford later called the lack of elections "amply justified if only because the kind of election envisaged by the Geneva Agreement of 1954—a free election—could not have been held. Anyone who thinks that a free election was possible in Communist North Vietnam knows little of how Communists operate and could have fallen in a Moscow-Peiping trap."[50]

Ford also stood behind Eisenhower's handling of the 1956 Suez Crisis. A year earlier, the United States had expressed its preparedness to help Egypt's leader, Gamal Abdel Nasser, construct the Aswan Dam in the hope of keeping Nasser from turning to the Soviet Union for economic support. However, when Nasser made disparaging comments about the West, the Eisenhower administration withdrew the offer. Great Britain also decided against assisting Cairo. Angered, Nasser nationalized the Suez Canal Company, in which the British and French had a sizable interest. Ford praised the White House's handling of the burgeoning crisis, said he opposed using force to make sure the canal remained open, and rejected Democrats' charges of vacillation on the part of the White House.[51]

As it turned out, 1956 proved a particularly important year for Ford, both personally and politically. The Fords welcomed a third son, Steve. Politically, Ford had made enough of a name for himself that Republicans in Michigan approached him to run against the state's governor, G. Mennen Williams, but Ford, determined on climbing the ranks of the House, declined. What he did accept was an offer by the new head of the Appropriations Committee, Clarence Cannon (D-Mo.), to take a seat on that body's subcommittee for intelligence. The very fact that Cannon had approached Ford was evidence of the respect the Michigan congressman had achieved in the House, including among Democratic Party leaders. Furthermore, the post allowed Ford to add to an already-impressive knowledge of some of the country's most important secrets, including covert operations undertaken by the Central Intelligence Agency (CIA).[52]

That year, 1956, also meant both national and district elections. Eisenhower, who remained highly popular,[53] decided to run again, but he had second thoughts about Nixon. The report of the slush fund in 1952 made the former NATO commander question whether keeping him on the ticket that year had been a good idea, and afterward, he had kept his vice president at arm's length both professionally and socially. He also worried about his own health. In 1955, Eisenhower had suffered a heart attack; what if something worse happened to him in his second term? "I've watched Dick a long time," he told his speechwriter, "and he just hasn't grown. So I haven't honestly been able to believe that he *is* presidential timber."[54] That said, the president realized that dropping Nixon might cost him votes among conservatives. Hence, Eisenhower publicly equivocated about retaining him.

Eisenhower's uncertainty convinced a number of liberal Republicans it was time to dump the vice president. One was Harold Stassen, the president's special assistant for disarmament, who called for replacing Nixon with Massachusetts governor Christian Herter. The conservative magazine *National Review* and numerous Republicans protested, with nearly every GOP member of the House expressing his or her support for Nixon, and twenty of them, including Ford, calling for Stassen's resignation. The uproar convinced Eisenhower, albeit reluctantly, to keep his vice president on board. Nixon wrote Ford a letter expressing his appreciation for the latter's "fine gesture of confidence and loyalty."[55] Stassen took a temporary leave of absence from the administration and, in 1958, resigned his post.

Nixon's place on the Republican ticket came up as well in another cross-examination Ford conducted during his bid for a fifth term on Capitol Hill. He believed the vice president had "done a fine job" and had proven "an invaluable aid and asset to the President in his relations with the Congress." He challenged those who said Nixon had used "smear tactics" to win a seat in Congress. The truth was, he continued, that Nixon had run in 1946 against a liberal contender, Jerry Voorhees, and all Nixon had done was to point to Vorhees's liberal record. He also disputed those individuals in the GOP who believed Nixon was too conservative, noting that members of the party who were not conservative had endorsed him as Eisenhower's running mate. Indeed, when it came down to it, said Ford, Nixon was a moderate. Questioned about Nixon's nickname, "Tricky Dicky," Ford again took issue, blaming it on people who were "supporters of Alger Hiss."[56]

Ford also brought up Hiss's name in connection with Adlai Stevenson, whom Democrats again chose to challenge Eisenhower for the presidency. During Hiss's trial, Stevenson had been asked to answer questions regarding what he knew about Hiss's character, and he replied that from what he knew, it was "good." Nixon had brought up Stevenson's statement during the 1952 campaign, forcing the Illinois governor to defend himself. Now, in 1956, Ford insisted it was fair to link Stevenson to Hiss on the grounds that the governor had chosen to stand behind the ex–State Department official. "I think there's nothing wrong with a man's coming to the defense of an individual if he is qualified to make such comment," said the Michigan congressman, "but when you get to the political arena what you've done in the past under any circumstances is exposed to the public view."[57]

Having defended Nixon, Ford turned to his own Democratic opponent, George Clay, who called for tax cuts for low-income groups. Although the deficit of $1.2 billion in 1955 had turned into a $1.75 billion surplus in 1956, Ford rejected the idea of cutting taxes when, in his words, the nation was "running in the red." Most of Ford's constituents agreed. In November, he won 67 percent of the vote.[58] Voters also reelected Eisenhower. To Ford's chagrin, those same voters decided to retain a Democratic-dominated Congress.

Combating Communism on Land and in Space

After lawmakers returned to the capital from their 1956–1957 winter break, Eisenhower called for a joint session of Congress. The crisis involving the Suez Canal had erupted in October 1956, with Israeli, British, and French forces attacking Egypt. The United States reacted by sponsoring a resolution in the United Nations calling for an end to hostilities and then using economic coercion to force the three attackers to withdraw their troops. The Suez Crisis created enormous strains among the Western allies and demonstrated that the United States no longer planned to rely on its European friends to maintain stability in the Middle East. Fearful of a vacuum of power that might entice the Soviets, Eisenhower felt the need to act. Hence, at the joint session in January 1957, he announced what became known as the Eisenhower Doctrine, calling for economic and military aid, along with the authority to have the United States reply militarily if necessary, to defend that oil-rich region of the world.

Some lawmakers took issue with giving the president such power, but Ford was not among them. To him, the Soviets' designs on world domination were little different from the enemy powers he had helped combat during World War II. Failure to stand up to Moscow would mean Communist conquest of the Middle East and, eventually, the planet. Consequently, it was important to grant Eisenhower the powers he asked for to prevent more dominoes from falling.[59]

To combat communism, Eisenhower presented to Capitol Hill a record $73.3 billion budget for fiscal year (FY) 1958, with over half of it devoted to the Department of Defense. Abiding by Modern Republicanism, he devoted other moneys to social programs, such as health care, Social Security, and help for the unemployed. In trying to get this budget passed, the president made two significant errors. The first was to imply that his Treasury secretary, George Humphrey, opposed such a high amount of spending on the grounds that it would cause an economic slowdown. The president then made matters worse by telling lawmakers to see where they might find places to cut. Conservative Republicans took advantage of the opening. They had from the start disparaged Modern Republicanism for permitting the continuation of the liberal, "socialistic" New Deal that undermined an American character built on self-reliance and replaced it with dependence on the government. Their emerging movement found national expression thanks to William F. Buckley, an editor and founder of the *National Review* in 1955. Ford, loyal to the president and his moderate conservative values, stood behind Eisenhower.[60]

One of the biggest fights over the FY 1958 budget between the executive and legislative branches was over the MSP. Once again, conservatives called the program a waste of taxpayer money. Some businesspersons joined these lawmakers, worried that the appropriations might be used to promote socialism in other nations and thereby undermine the ability of U.S. corporate interests to gain access to those markets. For FY 1954, Eisenhower had asked for $5.8 billion for the MSP, or $1.8 billion less than Truman had wanted, but had been forced to cut it back to $5.5 billion, and then by another $1 billion because of conservative resistance. Each year afterward, he had had to accept more cuts, to the point that for FY 1957 and FY 1958, he requested $3 billion. Even that was too much for conservatives. "Every time another year comes around, the Mutual Security Program is compelled to engage in a life-and-death struggle for its very existence," exclaimed the frustrated president. "The attack is based, not on the record, not on the facts. It is based on slogans, prejudices, penny-wise economy." To him, detractors of the MSP were "ostrich-like opponents of mutual security."[61]

It was ironic to Eisenhower that he found more support for the MSP among Democrats than among members of his own party. One of the exceptions in the GOP was Ford, who shared Eisenhower's belief that the MSP was needed to protect America's global interests from communism. "I think we have gotten our dollar's worth out of assistance we have made available to those who were joined with us in this battle against communism," Ford explained to his colleagues. Nations like Pakistan and Turkey spent far less per soldier than the United States, thereby saving Washington money as it sought to contain communism. Indeed, it made far more sense to spend money on military programs than nonmilitary ones, such as the "United Nations . . . the technical cooperation program for the Organization of American States, the U.N. refugee program, the escapee program and the like," for they had no relevance to U.S. security. Unfortunately for both the president and the Michigan lawmaker, Congress ended up cutting the MSP by another $1 billion, and also slashing $2.4 billion from what Eisenhower had asked for defense.[62]

While Ford favored spending what was necessary to protect the nation's security interests, he was not willing to endorse every military-related proposal. In May 1957, the Appropriations Committee's defense subcommittee called for cutting $2.6 billion in military spending while ordering $1 million a year to continue operating two hospitals, one in Massachusetts and the other in Arkansas, even though the subcommittee called them "useless." The hospitals, noted the *New York Times*, had "at least three times more employees than patients," and even the Pentagon favored closing them. Ford wanted to kill the stay-open order, but he faced powerful resistance from influential Massachusetts lawmakers in both the House and Senate, including Democrat and House Majority Leader John McCormack; the Republicans' minority leader in the House, Joseph Martin; and Senator Leverett Saltonstall, a Republican who chaired the Senate Armed Services Committee. Asking her fellow congresspersons to "look into your hearts," Republican representative Edith Nourse, also of Massachusetts, explained that if the hospital in her home state closed, then "[the] wives of servicemen, who 'might have to die in Indo-China,'" would have to travel 14 miles to have their children at the U.S. Army base at Fort Devens. Ford admitted the futility of his cause: "I will say that the potency of the opposition I face—to be very realistic—is overwhelming." The Appropriations Committee proved more willing to reject another funding request, this one from the U.S. Air Force Academy for $97,500 to build a home for that school's superintendent. Ford was among those who declined the petition, calling the $75,000 earlier approved by Congress "more than adequate."[63]

Just how much the United States should devote to defense became an even more poignant question in the fall of 1957. In September, Moscow launched the world's first intercontinental ballistic missile (ICBM), a nuclear weapon capable of traveling from the Soviet Union to the United States in a matter of minutes. Put another way, the Kremlin no longer had to station military forces near the U.S. border to strike American cities. The Soviets followed their coup in October by launching Sputnik, humankind's first unmanned space satellite. These two events shook the American psyche. Americans had long viewed the Soviet Union as a threat, but one that was technologically and scientifically far behind the United States. Now it seemed the Soviets were winning the arms race, the science and technology race, and the Cold War itself. "It appears likely that the effect [of Sputnik] in unsophisticated countries will be to create the impression of Soviet technological and military superiority over the United States," wrote Arthur Larson, the director of the U.S. Information Agency. "[In] more sophisticated areas such as Europe, the impression may be that the USSR is at least equal."[64]

Ford blamed these setbacks on the Democratic Truman administration. In 1947, he claimed, the White House had canceled a contract signed with Convair Company to build an intercontinental missile. That contract was not renewed until 1951, after the Korean War began "and then only on a limited or study basis." Had it not been for such decisions, he asserted, the United States would have had an ICBM capability by 1953. He quoted Eisenhower, who had testified in 1947: "In the field of guided missile electronics and supersonic aircraft, we have no more than scratched the surface of possibilities which we must explore in order to keep abreast of the rest of the world. Neglect to do so could bring our country to ruin and defeat in an appalling few hours." Yet Ford admitted during questions and answers that Eisenhower in June 1946 had approved the reduced budget requested by the Truman administration for national defense, calling it "'the rock bottom' and 'the very least we need.'"[65]

Whatever the cause for Washington's recent reversals, it was essential to restore Americans' confidence in their nation and the global prestige of the United States. One way of doing this was to reassert U.S. scientific and technological prowess. The country for some time had been developing its own rocket, called Vanguard, to launch a satellite into space. Several tests had taken place prior to the Soviets' launch of Sputnik, though none had put a satellite into orbit. Matching Moscow's feat became essential, and on 6 December 1957, following enormous fanfare, the United States attempted to do so. The Vanguard reached four feet off the ground when it exploded. Senate Majority Leader Lyndon B. Johnson (D-Tex.) called it "one of the best publicized and most humiliating failures in our history." Ford seconded Johnson, asserting that the media had played up the rocket so much that "the advance build-up had put 'overemphasis on a minor technical defeat.'" To him, the press was partially to blame for the sense of ignominy.[66] It would be almost two months before the United States launched its first satellite, followed by an ICBM later that year.

Reestablishing U.S. scientific and technological dominance also required augmenting American brainpower. On this score, Eisenhower proposed, and lawmakers, including Ford, passed, the National Defense Education Act to beef up federal funding for science, math, and foreign-language classes at the primary and secondary levels and to provide financial aid for college students. The president also decided it was time to transform the National Advisory Committee on Aeronautics into the National Aeronautics and Space Administration (NASA). Ford saw great value in the new agency. "Our existence is threatened," he told members of the House, "unless we can: First, bring our missile deterrent up to [the level of the Soviets']; secondly, insure that our space program within the next 5–10 years will forge ahead of theirs; thirdly, continue our superiority in long-range aircraft and other defense programs." Moreover, NASA would create jobs, and the technology used in the space program could assist in "exact forecasting of weather," thereby saving "billions" of dollars and furnishing a means of "transporting people and freight between different points on the earth's surface."[67]

The decision to form NASA meant new responsibilities for Ford. After meeting with Eisenhower, Speaker Rayburn and Majority Leader Johnson established a special committee to write up the legislation to create the space agency, and they asked Ford to join it. Ford gladly accepted and discovered it to be a terrific learning experience. While Rayburn was an able politician, few could match Johnson, who longed to become president and made a failed bid for the Democratic nomination in 1956. "Any compromise that Lyndon made," Ford reminisced, "he got better than fifty percent, because he was a skillful, hard working, hard-driving man." Johnson "wouldn't shout. But he would be very firm. He would be hardline, and then he would give just enough to get what he wanted. . . . When he reached his goal, down came the gavel. On to the next business." Concluded Ford, "Watching Lyndon, I knew I was seeing a master in action."[68]

The Young Turk

Ford's words about Johnson suggest the Texas lawmaker inspired him all the more to push for the House speakership. While that may be the case, he knew he could not ignore affairs closer to home. "Home" for him had two definitions. One was his wife and family. Betty tried to help her husband by showing around constituents visiting her husband and periodically volunteering in his office. But much of her time was spent in Alexandria, where she (and, when she could, Clara) took care of the kids. In contrast, Ford spent most of his time at the office or on the road. He did try to be home for dinner each Sunday; his favorite meal was pot roast or steak, red cabbage, and a scoop of butter-pecan ice cream for dessert. Maybe because he realized how often he was away, around 1957 Jerry began taking his wife and children on what became an annual ski trip. During such family trips, Michael remarked, his father "was 110 percent concentration and attention and you felt you had everything that he could give you. That was wonderful." That same year, Betty inherited some money after her stepfather died, and rather than putting it toward paying off their home, she and Jerry left their kids with Clara and traveled to Europe.[69] The number of residents in their home increased by one shortly after their return when Betty in July bore a daughter, Susan.

"Home" also meant the Fifth District. Ford tried to help constituents, such as an army major named Harry Flowers who had lost his job because of military cutbacks and sought help finding a position with the State Department or the International Cooperation Administration.[70] Ford could point out to voters in Grand Rapids that he remained wedded to conservatism, even if at times it was a moderate, pragmatic form. Additionally, he could argue he was liked among his peers in Congress, as evidenced by the requests of Democrats such as Cannon, Rayburn, and Johnson, that he participate in committees they headed.

But there were good reasons for voters to question whether voting Republican was the correct choice as the 1958 midterm election neared. As Humphrey had warned, the nation slid into a recession in the summer of 1957. By the spring of 1958, production of goods had fallen 14 percent and unemployment had reached 7.5 percent. The resulting reduction in tax revenues created an expected $500 million deficit, as opposed to the $1.8 billion

The Ford family, 1958. Photo in the Gerald Ford Library, Ann Arbor, Michigan.

surplus the White House had originally foreseen.[71] Eisenhower was slow to act, believing the economy would recover on its own. When it did not, the budget he presented to lawmakers in 1958 offered only a small amount of financial stimulus, making voters wonder if he cared about their plight.

In addition to seeming slow to respond on the economy, the president had appeared hesitant in 1957 to confront Arkansas governor Orval Faubus, who refused to comply with a court order to integrate Central High School in Little Rock, and the Soviets' achievements in weaponry and space technology only heightened Eisenhower's embarrassment. Adding salt to the wound was word in the middle of 1958 that the president's chief of staff, Sherman Adams, had accepted gifts from a businessperson in return for political favors. As a result of the scandal, Adams resigned that September. Eisenhower's approval rating during 1957 fell from 79 percent at the start of the year to 57 percent at its end, and then to 52 percent in March 1958; it remained in the 50s for the remainder of the year.[72]

Democrats saw opportunity to curry favor as the 1958 midterm election approached. Whether they believed Republicans' vulnerability extended to Ford's Fifth District is not clear, but they were certainly prepared to make a go at winning it. Their candidate, Richard Vander Veen, held two debates with Ford, challenging the incumbent on a wide variety of issues. Thanks to the recession, 16,000 people were unemployed in Grand Rapids, he said, and the way to provide help to them was through public-works programs. He criticized Ford for voting against both a Community Services Bill that Democrats had supported to fight the recession and legislation introduced in Congress by Senators John F. Kennedy (D-Mass.) and Irving Ives (R-N.Y.) aimed at eliminating corruption in the labor movement. Then there was the deficit, which, while not giving numbers, Vander Veen charged was the largest ever in peacetime. Additionally, he contested the White House's foreign policy, focusing on another crisis involving Jinmen and Mazu that had lasted from August through October 1958. To Vander Veen, U.S. support for the Chinese Nationalist presence on those islands had caused tensions between Washington and its European allies. The best way to prevent another such crisis was to have the Nationalists withdraw from Jinmen and Mazu.[73]

Ford naturally took issue with his opponent. Thanks to Eisenhower, he declared, 4 million more Americans had employment, and the cost of living had gone up by only 8 percent, or a third of what it had risen under Truman. It was true that Michigan was not "quite as fortunate as the rest of the United States," but he was working with the governor to find a means of addressing the problem. Public works was not the answer, he insisted, and he then asked how Vander Veen planned "to pay for all these additional things and at the same time try to balance the federal budget." He defended his vote against Kennedy-Ives, attesting that it did not cover all unions and "would have emasculated the Taft-Hartley Act, which is good legislation." As for foreign policy, on Truman's watch fourteen nations had fallen to communism, and the United States had found itself mired in Korea. Thanks to Eisenhower and Dulles, the United States had extricated itself from Korea and recovered all or parts of four nations that had previously gone communist. Without mentioning Vander Veen by name, Ford charged "some . . . Democrats are preaching the gospel of appeasement—peace-meal [*sic*] surrender."[74]

If Democrats believed Ford was vulnerable, they were wrong: the incumbent won with nearly 64 percent of the vote. He could relish that he now had the top minority position on Appropriations' defense subcommittee. The significant word, though, was "minority." The GOP, already holding fewer seats in Congress, lost 13 more in the Senate and 48 in the House, leaving them with 34 in Capitol Hill's upper house and 153 in the lower. The beating the Republicans took, on top of earlier losses, led to rumblings for changes in the House leadership, particularly as concerned Congressman Martin. Martin "had promised to resign after the 1956 election if he didn't make a major gain in '58," recalled Robert Wilson (R-Calif.), "but he refused to step down." The minority leader also "ran a particularly dictatorial operation," further turning his colleagues against him. Martin ignored reports that his position was in jeopardy and saw no reason to accept a suggestion from a friend and Republican National Committee campaign director, Robert Humphreys, that he protect himself by naming Ford as assistant leader. Although Ford was not among the plotters, he shared their sentiment that change was needed. Eisenhower, for his part, made clear to Congressman Charles Halleck (R-Ind.) that he planned to adopt a "hands-off" stance, which Halleck and others in the House took as an indication that the president himself favored change.[75]

Sharing Ford's desire for new leadership were nearly three dozen younger Republican members of the House. Referred to as the Young Turks, their numbers included Wilson and Thomas Curtis of Missouri. They had reached the conclusion that individuals such as the seventy-four-year-old Martin lacked the vigor and imagination needed to give the party control of Congress. Many of the Young Turks wanted Ford to challenge Martin, but the Michigander exhibited little interest in joining what was likely to be a nasty fight. Therefore, the Turks turned to Halleck, who had been in the House since 1935 and who, like Ford, had visions of becoming speaker. Thus, when lawmakers met in a secret caucus in January 1959, Ford cast his vote for the Indianan.[76] By a close 74–70 vote, Halleck won.

Coming Closer to the Pinnacle

That the Young Turks wanted Ford to seek Martin's post pointed not just to the generational changes taking place in the House but also to the growing power of the Michigan lawmaker. He had gradually climbed the ladder of power, moving from being a relative unknown to a member of the powerful Committee on Appropriations and a post on three of that committee's subcommittees. He proved himself a partisan Republican who endorsed Eisenhower's policies and later came to see the ex-general as one of his "presidential heroes," but the initiatives taken by Truman were not anathema to him. "I have great admiration for Harry Truman's foreign policy actions," he wrote years later. Yet "I must write off his domestic record as one which smacked of scandal and extreme partisanship."[77] That tone hid the fact that he accepted some of the Democratic president's domestic policies. It was such moderate conservatism that set Ford apart from liberals or conservatives in his own party. He rejected liberals' calls for dumping Nixon in 1956 and conservatives' efforts to cut funding for America's military and foreign-aid programs, insisting that such assistance was vital to national security. Nor was he prepared to join those in his party who took issue with Modern Republicanism or colleagues in the GOP or Democratic Party who wanted to turn back the clock on civil rights. Ford did not like public-works initiatives or public housing, had qualms about welfare programs, believed the environment could best be protected by local or state officials rather than the federal government, and was not as progressive as many of his contemporaries when it came to the rights of minorities. Yet he had always believed it important to balance limited government with the well-being of the American people. His positions earned him respect not just among his Republican colleagues but also among Democrats, who saw in him someone with whom they could work.

Ford tried to balance his commitments in Washington with those to his family by adding the annual ski trip to his dinners at home. Still, "The harder you work, the luckier you are" continued to resonate in his mind. There were only so many hours in a day, and he wanted to continue climbing up the ladder of authority in the House. His loyalty to his party and his work appeared to be paying dividends, for by 1959 some of his colleagues had considered putting him up as a candidate for minority leader. Even if Ford was not yet ready to take that step, he planned to at some point, which meant devoting more hours to his job. By 1965 that dedication would have brought him to within one step of the speakership, but it would come at a price for his family.

THREE

A Step Away

In October 1952, the American Broadcasting Company aired a new television comedy called *The Adventures of Ozzie and Harriet.* Originally a radio program, *Ozzie and Harriet* followed the activities of a real family, the Nelsons, as they confronted everyday life. The father, Ozzie Nelson, worked outside the house, and his wife, Harriet, was a homemaker. Their sons, Ricky and David, were twelve and fifteen years old, respectively, when the show first aired. The program remained on TV until 1966, giving viewers the opportunity not just to watch various plotlines supposedly based on the Nelsons' real-life experiences, but also to see Ricky become a rock star and both sons marry. Similar family-based comedies appeared on television later in the 1950s, including *Father Knows Best*—which also had started on radio—and *Leave It to Beaver*, but none had the longevity of *Ozzie and Harriet.*

Whereas in 1950 only 12 percent of Americans had a television in their home, by 1960, nearly 90 percent did,[1] meaning that more and more people could tap into the idyllic world of the white middle-class families portrayed in programs like *Ozzie and Harriet.* Americans saw fathers who were breadwinners, mothers who stayed at home, and children who played and went to school. They watched well-manicured parents and kids who were all happy with their assigned roles and optimistic about tomorrow. Minor difficulties—be they a project at work or school, trying to get a date with a girl, or worrying about a doctor's appointment—were resolved with smiles.

Below the surface, however, was a powerful message: this was how your life was supposed to be, and if it was not, then something was wrong. It was a message that ignored reality. For one thing, it disregarded the poverty and abuse confronted by many in the nation, particularly minorities. Furthermore, it hid the widespread ambivalence, even hostility, toward conformity, which was reflected in contemporary professional studies such as the Kelly Longitudinal Survey,[2] in the beat movement, and in popular culture, including in such books as *The Catcher in the Rye* (1951), *The Man in the Gray Flannel Suit* (1955), *On the Road* (1957), and *Naked Lunch* (1959). Even the real Nelsons were anything but the perfect family. Ozzie ruled his home with a near-dictatorial fist, unwilling to accept criticism and determined to manage his children's lives in the quest for fame and profit. David handled his father better than Ricky, who had trouble figuring out where his TV life began and his real life ended. Making matters harder on him was his interest in rock and roll, which Ozzie used to turn his younger son into a popular rock star. Ricky became dismayed, confused, and unhappy. His short life, marked by a failed marriage and drug use,[3] ended in 1985 in a plane crash.

There were parallels between the Nelsons, on the one hand, and Gerald and Betty Ford, on the other. Like the Nelsons, the Fords were 1950s-style parents, with Gerald the breadwinner and Betty the housewife. Jerry remained as determined as ever to climb through the political ranks of the GOP. He continued to stand behind the overwhelming majority of Dwight D. Eisenhower's initiatives. In 1960, he entertained the possibility of becoming Richard Nixon's vice-presidential candidate, though he was not sure how much of a shot he had. When that bid went nowhere, he returned to his primary goal, that of becoming speaker of the House, and by 1965, with the support of the other Young Turks, he found himself one step away from achieving it. But his ambitiousness meant ever more time away from his family. He would leave the house around seven o'clock in the morning and return very late, get "five or six hours" of sleep, and then start a new day. Both Michael and Steve Ford recalled how difficult it was to have a father who was rarely home, but it appeared to have been particularly painful for Susan. "I love my father, but I didn't know I had a father until I was 10 or 12 years old," she commented. Although Jerry made sure to be with his family for Sunday dinner, "it meant nothing to me. Just a man sitting there at the table."[4] It was hard on Betty as well. She loved her husband dearly, but his aspirations left her feeling ever more alone. Increasingly, like Ricky Nelson, she found solace elsewhere, in her case, in the bottle.

The Pragmatic Loyalist

"From the start," wrote *Grand Rapids Press* columnist William Pyper in May 1959, "his seniors saw in Ford the possibilities of a GOP leader in the House. He served two years on the public works committee, a choice assignment, then was transferred to the appropriations committee. His rise to the top of the defense subcommittee is regarded as meteoric in an organization where seniority is the keyword."[5] Even if one could accuse Pyper of championing one of Grand Rapids' own, he was correct that in a relatively short period of time, Ford had made a name for himself. His calm, cool demeanor, willingness to listen to all views before making a decision, and hard work had drawn praise from both sides of the aisle. At the same time, he remained loyal to his party and true to his moderate conservative convictions, championing free enterprise, a strong defense, and a limited government that would live within its means.

Ford's loyalty and moderate views continued to make themselves apparent during the last two years of Eisenhower's administration. He adhered to the president's belief that states should assume responsibility for defending the environment. He also advocated the White House's position on civil rights. Eisenhower remained unwilling to press resistant states to integrate more rapidly, but he did regard it as necessary for the federal government to do what it could to stop racial violence. In 1958 he began to look at new civil rights legislation, only to meet resistance from southern Democrats. Not until 1960 did the White House try again, submitting a bill whose key provision called for federal courts to name referees to look into cases where blacks were having trouble voting. In May lawmakers, including Ford, sent to Eisenhower what turned out to be a weaker form of what the president had wanted. That only Deputy Attorney General William Rogers and Rogers's aide attended the signing ceremony suggested just how feeble the measure was.[6] That Ford voted for it sent a mixed message of support for civil rights but an unwillingness to demand stronger legislation. His position would cause him problems down the road.

Ford also remained true to Eisenhower's foreign policies. Both of them favored a strong military but within sensible financial limits. The debate over how much the United States needed to spend intensified as a result of a crisis involving the German city of Berlin. In 1958, Nikita Khrushchev, who had succeeded Joseph Stalin as Soviet leader, ordered the West to end its occupation of West Berlin by May 1959, or he would sign a peace treaty with East Germany. Eisenhower believed Khrushchev's ultimatum was simply bluster, but the specter of another European war, one that might involve nuclear weapons, spread fear throughout the United States and prompted calls, particularly from Democrats and the armed forces, for more money for defense. The president resisted. He wanted to keep the budget as balanced as possible, so in January 1959 he proposed spending $77 billion for FY 1960, of which $41 billion would go toward defense. Despite his reputation as a Cold Warrior, Ford fought for Eisenhower's budget. What eventually came out of Capitol Hill was a budget of $79 billion. Eisenhower thanked Ford "for helping to keep the total figure within reasonable bounds."[7]

The May deadline passed without Khrushchev acting on his threat, but any hope that a thaw in the Cold War might ensue dissipated when the Soviets in 1960 shot down an American U-2 spy plane and captured the pilot. The U-2 crisis convinced Eisenhower to ask for $4.2 billion for the MSP. Conservatives called for cutting the program by $1 billion, which, Eisenhower said, would prove disastrous. Ford fought to keep as much of the MSP intact as possible, asserting it did not give recipients a free ride insofar as providing for their own defense and again pointing to how much money it actually saved the United States in advancing containment. Although Ford was not able to keep the Democrats, who had the majority of seats, and conservative Republicans from taking a $500 million chunk out of the MSP, the $3.7 billion approved was still more than the 1959 allotment. The Michigan lawmaker's work earned a letter of gratification from the president. "Your support was, of course, a major factor in achieving this result," wrote Eisenhower, "and I thank you for it, not so much personally but, more importantly, officially because this program is so vital to our security and to the buttressing of freedom throughout the world."[8]

Ford for Vice President

The approval of mutual security assistance came at the height of the 1960 presidential campaign season. Following the untimely death of Franklin D. Roosevelt in his fourth term in office, a movement had begun to limit how long a president could serve. The resulting Twenty-Second Amendment restricted the country's chief executive to no more than two terms, meaning Eisenhower was ineligible to run again.

One possible choice to carry the Republican banner was Vice President

Nixon. Though he had a reputation as a conservative, Nixon identified himself with Eisenhower's moderate Modern Republicanism. For that reason not all GOP faithful were enthused about his candidacy. Party liberals preferred Nelson Rockefeller. Born in 1908 into a prominent and wealthy family, he had served in every administration since that of Franklin Roosevelt. He developed a reputation as an anticommunist hawk and pro–New Dealer. After winning the governorship of New York in 1958, he expanded the state university system, signed one of the country's most liberal abortion-rights laws, increased the number of state parks, and oversaw an aggressive building program that included new highways, hospitals, and housing units. He also favored Republicans taking a stronger stand on civil rights.

Moderates were not enthralled by Rockefeller, and conservatives were even less so. The latter preferred Barry Goldwater. Handsome and a terrific orator, the fifty-one-year-old Arizonan was in his second term in the Senate. In earlier years, he had run a small business during the Great Depression, and he disparaged the New Deal as being antibusiness. He saw Eisenhower's Modern Republicanism as little different from the New Deal, referring to it as "the siren song of socialism" and "squanderbust government." While he had presidential aspirations and had a number of delegates willing to commit to him, he realized that if he sought the nomination, he would split the party, to the benefit of the Democrats. Thus, he asked his supporters to endorse the vice president. With Goldwater urging his delegates to vote for Nixon, and lacking his own presidential endorsement, Rockefeller decided to withdraw from the race, but not before convincing the prospective GOP nominee in July to call for more spending for defense and for enhanced efforts to defend civil rights. The move enraged conservatives, including Goldwater, who, in his speech officially withdrawing from the race, told his followers, "Let's grow up, conservatives. If we want to take this party back, and I think we can someday, let's get to work." It was a cryptic statement aimed not just at Rockefeller but also at Nixon,[9] and an indication of the direction the GOP was about to head.

With the nomination in Nixon's hand, the obvious question was who would share the ticket. Early on, Ford's name was floated. He had been loyal to Eisenhower, voting 83 percent of the time in favor of the White House's initiatives. "It seems that Rep. Gerald R. Ford, Jr., of Grand Rapids may be the Michigan Republican most affected by the withdrawal of Gov. Nelson A. Rockefeller from the presidential nomination contest," wrote Pyper. It appeared that "Nixon [would have] the top of the ticket without contest," and selecting Ford as a running mate made sense. He had eleven years of service in the House, including on the Appropriations Committee, and was well liked. True, Ford had shown a desire to remain in Congress, but "he never has said positively that he would refuse to accept nomination for senator or governor, if he could be convinced that his party needed him. Presumably, under similar circumstances, he would feel that he must interrupt his house [*sic*] career to make the run for vice president, if the demand were evident." Ford himself was not entirely averse to running for the country's number-two spot. He wrote a friend in April that he wanted to stay on Capitol Hill. "However, if there is one exception, it would be the vice presidential nomination as the running mate with my good friend Dick Nixon."[10]

Republicans in Michigan began to rally behind the potential candidate. In April, the state party's Central Committee endorsed Ford for the vice presidency. A month later, Paul Goebel, the mayor of Grand Rapids and a friend of the Fords, formed the Ford for Vice President Committee and asked for help in promoting the representative. Ford was willing to support the committee's efforts, but the Republican lawmaker admitted his chances were slim.[11]

That is, until July. At Nixon's suggestion, Raymond Moley, a columnist with the national weekly magazine *Newsweek*, wrote a highly complimentary piece on Ford. The magazine had polled fifty Washington, D.C., correspondents on possible vice-presidential candidates; Ford and the House's Republican whip, Les Arends of Illinois, had tied for second behind the minority leader, Charles Halleck (R-Ind.). "The expression of appreciation for Ford, who holds no office in the House except ranking member on a subcommittee, is especially noteworthy," Moley observed. Ford, he continued, would make a good match for Nixon: he sat on the Appropriations Committee's defense subcommittee, would meet Nixon's call for "a man who would be entirely in sympathy with his policies," was energetic, and had "an abundance of colorful background," including as a star football player, a Yale Law School graduate, and a World War II veteran. Buoyed even more that he might receive the nod, Ford opened a campaign headquarters in Grand Rapids on 22 July, two days before the Republicans held their national convention in Chicago. Jerry and Betty arrived the next day in the Windy City to loud applause from the Michigan delegation,[12] who hoped to see his name as Nixon's running mate.

It was not meant to be. Nixon's first choice was Rockefeller—a move that further infuriated conservatives—who said he was not interested. With Rockefeller out, Nixon's options were, in order, Henry Cabot Lodge, the

Mr. and Mrs. Gerald Ford, circa 1950s. Photo in the Gerald Ford Library, Ann Arbor, Michigan.

U.S. ambassador to the United Nations; Kentucky senator Thruston Morton; and then Ford. Nixon confirmed that Ford was not a top choice when, during a meeting in Chicago, he made clear that if he won, he believed the Michigander could do him the most good by remaining in the House. Asked for his recommendation for a running mate, Ford said Morton, only to find out shortly thereafter that Nixon had chosen Lodge. Ford found the process very confusing. "If Nixon had made up his mind, why would he go through the sham of asking for our advice?" he wondered. "That wasn't the way to play the game. . . . I was very disappointed. Making up his mind and then pretending that his options were still open—that was a Nixon trait that I'd have occasion to witness again."[13]

A couple of weeks prior to the GOP convention, Democrats had met in

Los Angeles and selected as their candidate Massachusetts senator John F. Kennedy. Kennedy's running mate was the Senate's majority leader, Lyndon B. Johnson of Texas. Ford knew both men well. Kennedy's office had been across from Ford's when he first entered Congress, and Ford had served alongside Johnson on the committee that developed legislation to create the National Aeronautics and Space Administration. Although he considered Kennedy a friend and had been impressed by Johnson's leadership in committee, Ford's loyalty was to his party and his longtime pal, Nixon. Knowing his own seat in Congress was safe, Ford became a member of Nixon's "Truth Squad," a group of three Republican congressmen who followed Kennedy around the country, explaining why voters should shy away from the Democratic nominee.[14]

In many ways, Kennedy and Nixon shared similarities, such as endorsing welfare programs and the containment of communism. Nixon had the advantages of experience and a reputation as a hard-line anticommunist, but Kennedy had his own trump cards. Both had served in World War II, but only Kennedy had a combat record, including saving members of the crew of his PT boat after a Japanese warship rammed it. The Democratic nominee assailed the incumbent administration's record on civil rights, welfare programs, and the economy. Moreover, he declared, a "missile gap" had emerged, leaving the United States behind the Soviet Union technologically and militarily. To rebut this last argument, Ford led a task force of fifteen House Republicans that concluded in June that the Democrats' claim was false. "Our striking power, by the hardening and dispersal of bases and warning systems," the group reported, "is now largely indestructible. It is only by exercises of science-fiction fantasy that critics can say Russia might destroy our retaliatory power. These critics are not, in fact, able to say that Russia actually possesses such power."[15]

Despite Ford's efforts, the Republicans were largely on the defensive. Nixon could not announce what he knew to be true—that there was no missile gap—because it would mean divulging top-secret information. He failed to make greater use of Eisenhower on the campaign trail, for if he won, he wanted as much of the credit as possible. An atmosphere in which television made one's appearance more important than before also hurt the GOP nominee. Now it was vital not just to say something meaningful but to look good doing it. Probably no event demonstrated just how essential visuals were than the candidates' initial presidential debate on 26 September. It was the first such give-and-take aired nationally. A tanned Kennedy appeared calm and confident, whereas Nixon, who had been fighting an illness, was pale and sickly looking. According to reports, those who heard the two men speak on radio believed the vice president won. But the 74 million Americans who watched the debate regarded Kennedy as the victor.[16]

Nixon did well in the candidates' three other debates, though it was not enough to keep Kennedy from winning by a razor-thin 118,000 votes. As Lodge, like Kennedy, hailed from Massachusetts, Nixon believed his choice of running mate would force the Democratic nominee to divert time and resources to hold onto his home state. Of the vice-presidential nominees, though, Johnson proved the more effective asset. Although he did not campaign in every state, Johnson was a vocal, vigorous, and aggressive promoter of his party and its plans for the nation. He used his political contacts to rally support for Kennedy in states such as Georgia; gave speeches in California, New York, and Illinois; and, on the suggestion of former president Harry Truman, conducted a 3,500-mile whistle-stop tour that took him to eight southern states. Lodge was no Johnson. Wrote one Nixon biographer, "Henry Cabot Lodge's lethargic run for the vice presidency, and unilateral promise to create a black cabinet seat, [struck] political ineptitude in contrast with the effectiveness with which Lyndon Johnson read the riot act to wary southern Democrats." James Cannon, who worked for President Ford, commented, "A friend of mine was [Lodge's] advance man and he said the son of a bitch wouldn't work. He just wouldn't do anything. He looked at movies in the afternoon. He would go watch television." Ford seconded Cannon, calling Lodge "a lousy campaigner. . . . I used to read about his taking naps every afternoon. Really did a terrible job. Terrible job."[17]

Ford could take pleasure in winning another landslide at home, defeating his Democratic opponent, William Reamon. Republicans also picked up some seats in both houses of Congress. Yet Democrats retained a sizable majority, having eighty-seven more seats in the House and twenty-eight more in the Senate than the GOP. It was another disappointment for the Michigan representative who longed to become speaker.

Kennedy, Ford, and Foreign Policy

The 1960 election may have given the nation a president of a different party affiliation but not one with less commitment to containing communism. Twenty years earlier Kennedy had published his senior thesis, entitled "Why England Slept." Great Britain, Kennedy argued, had foolishly tried to appease Nazi Germany prior to World War II, only to see the Nazis attempt to conquer Europe. After World War II, the Soviet Union replaced Germany as the threat to world peace. The United States had to do what Great Britain did not, which was to stand up to aggression. Kennedy applied that lesson to his inaugural address, telling the audience, "Let every nation know, whether it wishes us well or ill, that we shall pay any price, bear any burden, meet any hardship, support any friend, oppose any foe to assure the survival and the success of liberty."

Ford was not dismayed by the Oval Office's new occupant. "I knew Kennedy, and his ability," he commented, "so I had no apprehension at all about the future of the country. And I was in a position in Congress where I could have some influence. Every President respects the Appropriations Committee, and I thought Kennedy would need me more than I needed him." Ford was correct, as the Kennedy administration tried to court the Michigan lawmaker. The new president's congressional liaison, Lawrence O'Brien, commented that Ford had "vocally supported Eisenhower aid bills, especially military and related defense support. Not as strongly for economic. . . . Deserves special attention as able Member and as ranking minority member of Defense Subcommittee." Hence, when Ford complained that a Grand Rapids company had failed to secure a defense contract, O'Brien tried to help, though to no avail. When Ford made clear he was highly interested in having an icebreaker moved from its port in Wisconsin to Grand Haven, Michigan, which was in Ford's district, O'Brien made sure that it happened.[18]

Ford did stand behind parts of the Kennedy administration's foreign policy. During the 1960 campaign, the Massachusetts senator had proposed the Peace Corps, by which volunteers would travel to impoverished countries to help improve living conditions there. In turn, the people of those nations would view the United States in a better light and would have less desire to turn toward communism. The president established the corps through an executive order in March 1961, and Congress gave its endorsement via the Peace Corps Act, passed that September. Ford was among those who championed the agency's creation, regarding it as yet another means of containment.[19]

Kennedy had considered, but decided against, having the Peace Corps fall under the purview of several government agencies, including the Agency for International Development, which had been established under the Foreign Assistance Act of 1961. The act supplanted the 1951 Mutual Security Act by separating U.S. humanitarian and military aid. Getting the Foreign Assistance Act through the halls of Congress proved to be a battle for the president. When the bill was proposed, Kennedy had asked for $1.7 billion in foreign aid, but the proposal was attacked from all sides: liberal Democrats disliked giving taxpayer dollars to nondemocratic governments; conservative Democrats believed the money went into the pockets of corrupt officials abroad; and conservative Republicans questioned the program's expense and tried to link riders to it, such as a requirement that "recipient nations cease all commerce with the Soviet bloc." When the Appropriations Committee significantly cut Kennedy's request, Ford went to the House floor to demand restoration of the entire amount. How, he asked, was the United States to defend its interests "with less money, which, of course, means less guns, less tanks, less ammunition, less military equipment across the board"? He was not fully successful, but he did see Congress pass a bill that gave the president all but $100 million of what he had wanted.[20]

This is not to say that Ford agreed with Kennedy's foreign policy in its entirety. As a member of Appropriations' intelligence subcommittee, Ford was aware of plans initiated in the Eisenhower administration to get rid of Fidel Castro, a Communist who had seized control of Cuba in 1959. Kennedy learned of these preparations, one of which called for using CIA-trained Cuban exiles to overthrow the new Cuban leader. The new president gave the go-ahead for that operation, which took place in April 1961 at the Bay of Pigs. It was a fiasco. Within days, all of the 1,400 attackers were dead or in Cuban custody. Though sympathetic to Kennedy's designs, Ford joined those who criticized the administration, citing a lack of U.S. air support. When Kennedy later invoked the right of executive privilege to keep his military aide, General Maxwell Taylor, from testifying before Congress about the Bay of Pigs operation, Ford angrily told his colleagues, "Nothing is said in the Constitution about any Executive right to keep Congress in the dark, and I seriously doubt that this was the intention of the framers."[21]

Another complaint of Ford's concerned the way the Department of Defense (DoD) conducted business. In April 1962 a debate erupted when the House unanimously passed and sent to the Senate a defense appropriations bill of $47.8 billion, a record amount for peacetime. A divisive issue in the legislation was a 15 percent limit on what universities could charge for management expenses for research projects they conducted for the DoD. Many university officials charged that the DoD made them subsidize such projects, but Ford replied that the purpose of the limit was "to establish uniform expense allowances throughout the Government." He admitted, though, that attempts to get officials at the DoD "'to cooperate' with Congress" proved impossible, "and 'in our feeling of frustration, we just decided to set this arbitrary figure.'" Two months later, he sounded off to Defense Secretary Robert McNamara that Democrats were notified first about Defense procurement contracts, which allowed them to get their names into the newspapers before Republicans. He understood that politics were behind this, but he was bothered by the fact that military personnel were asked to use their time to type, sign, and deliver the letters of notification.[22]

Alongside other House Republicans, Ford indicted the White House for trying to influence their vote by threatening to curtail defense contracts in districts whose lawmakers refused to back a requested $8 billion increase in the national debt ceiling. "I have consistently supported every debt limitation increase," Ford told his colleagues, but he had changed his mind for two reasons. One was that Kennedy's proposed budget for FY 1963 was nearly $18.5 billion more than Eisenhower had requested in 1961 for FY 1962. More galling to Ford, however, was that some of the largest augmentations in appropriations went to departments other than Defense, including Agriculture and Health, Education, and Welfare. He refused to be "blackmailed" by the administration to endorse a larger debt. It was the administration, though, that came out on top, winning Congress's approval to raise the ceiling to $308 billion.[23]

Kennedy, Ford, and the New Frontier

Ford had complaints about how the White House and Defense conducted business, but he had even more with Kennedy's domestic policies. "The fundamental difference between the Republicans and Democrats on social policy is not that we don't recognize the problems of poverty, housing, and education, but in how we deal with those problems," commented Ford. "Democrats believe the Federal government is the best instrument for the solution of these problems. Republicans believe these problems can best be served by state government, local government, the private sector, or a combination of the three."[24]

Prior to taking office, Kennedy had spoken of a "New Frontier" for America. It had elements related to foreign policy, including promoting peace and combating poverty abroad, but much of it addressed domestic issues, such as helping Americans living in impoverished conditions, promoting education, and ending prejudice. To achieve his vision of a better America, Kennedy considered five pieces of legislation essential: housing, medical insurance for the elderly, aid to public schools, funding for parts of the country hurting economically, and a higher minimum wage.[25]

Not surprisingly, Ford took issue with some of these proposals. A good example concerned medical insurance for the aged, which soon became known as Medicare. In February 1961, Kennedy, working with Representative Cecil King (D-Calif.) and Senator Clinton Anderson (D-N.M.), introduced legislation to add 0.25 percent to the Social Security payroll tax to help America's older folks pay their hospital bills, and public opinion surveys evinced support for the idea. But Kennedy encountered strong opposition from Representative Wilbur Mills (D-Ark.) who chaired the influential House Ways and Means Committee. Mills, along with Senator Robert Kerr (D-Okla.), had sponsored legislation passed in 1960 that sought to address the health needs of the elderly by making benefits available only to those who would otherwise not be able to pay their bill, leaving it up to the states to determine both the benefits and the standards by which to judge who should receive them and providing funding solely via grants-in-aid rather than taxes. Ford liked Kerr-Mills—he admitted it could use some revising, even if he did not say where or how—for it left aid to the elderly in the hands of the states and without taxes on income. Although the Kennedy proposal died in the Senate, there is little doubt that the president would have had a tough time getting it past the resistance it faced in the House.[26]

Ford also disliked Kennedy's plan to raise the minimum wage. The president saw the economy as still weak and thought it could be gotten out of its doldrums by increasing the federal minimum by a quarter, to $1.25 an hour, and by having it cover additional employees, including laundry workers (many of whom were African American women) and truck drivers. Southern laundry operators, represented by their legislators in Congress, successfully fought to have their employees removed from the bill. Other workers also were excluded, meaning that over 350,000 people Kennedy had intended to cover were not. Ford joined the opponents, favoring a substitute bill that reduced the wage increase. When a House-Senate conference committee approved legislation calling for $1.15 in 1961, to go up to $1.25 in 1963, Ford voted against the conference report.[27] The Michigan congressman, though, was in the minority, and the bill passed.

Ford's position on the minimum wage suggested a lack of concern for America's minorities, but from the Michigan lawmaker's point of view, the issue was not minority rights but the rights of private enterprise. Increasing the required federal salary, he believed, meant greater costs for employers, who would have the choice of earning lower profits (and possibly facing financial failure) or passing on their additional expenses to consumers in the form of higher prices. That, in turn, would cut into Americans' purchasing power, which too would hurt the economy.

There was, in fact, evidence pointing to Ford's desire to help minorities.

A good example was his vote in 1962 to eliminate the poll tax that southern states used to deny blacks their right to vote. In this respect, he was ahead of Kennedy, who, much like Eisenhower, favored a go-slow approach vis-à-vis civil rights. The president knew his slim victory in 1960 was anything but a mandate, and polls showed that most Americans favored achieving integration gradually. Additionally, Kennedy believed that if he pushed hard on civil rights, he might lose support for other programs that affected minorities as well, including the minimum wage and medical care for the aged.[28]

Though Ford and Kennedy were not necessarily of the same mind on the minimum wage and civil rights, they saw eye-to-eye when it came to education policy. While running for president, Kennedy had called for providing federal assistance to education, but only for public schools. Parochial institutions were infuriated. To please Catholics, the Kennedy administration offered to amend a bill to extend the National Defense Education Act's life, which would provide loans to parochial institutions. Viewing the issue through the lens of national security, Ford approved the measure, but opponents in the House, led by a New York Catholic and Democrat, Jim Delaney, succeeded in shelving the bill for the remainder of the year. Kennedy and Ford had more luck in seeing an expansion in 1962 of the school-lunch program, thereby guaranteeing another 700,000 children a hot lunch at school.[29]

A "Political Widow"

In January 1962, Ford learned from his stepsister-in-law Janet that his stepfather had died. Gerald Sr. had slipped while walking on some ice, hit his head, suffered a concussion, and passed away less than two days later. Ford immediately went back home to console his mother and remember the person who had always treated him as a son. "Here was a man who never got past the eighth grade," he observed, "but he was widely recognized as an outstanding citizen and good businessman, a man with an impeccable record of integrity and honesty." Following the funeral, Dorothy Ford and her sons read the will and learned that Gerald Sr. had left his wife enough money to permit her to live "in modest comfort for the rest of her life."[30]

Dorothy was now a widow; Betty, for her part, was "a virtual political widow." For her, life in Washington had become a double-edged sword. She liked some aspects of being in the capital, including invitations to the White House for dinner, time spent with the wives of other lawmakers, and, periodically, trips with her husband. She and Jerry managed their money well.

She later reminisced that although her husband had a "tough work schedule while our children were little, I had a good life."[31]

In fact, it was not all good. The demands of his job meant Jerry was rarely home. He woke up early enough to swim laps in his pool and then headed into the capital, arriving in his office by 8:00 a.m. He traveled extensively, spending 280 days on the road in one year alone, and he consistently missed his wedding anniversary because it took place during the height of the campaign season. "I had to bring up four kids by myself," Betty glumly wrote. "I couldn't say, 'Wait till your father comes home'; their father wasn't going to come home for maybe a week." She did not mention Clara Powell, but Powell could not be there every minute, and she was not Betty's husband. If he was home on a Saturday, Jerry would take the kids with him to the Capitol Building, where they would be left on their own to play (and sometimes cause mischief in their father's office). But the majority of the responsibility for raising the children fell on Mrs. Ford, and she began to resent the fact that her spouse was around so rarely. "I was feeling terribly neglected," she recalled. "The loneliness, the being left to yourself at night, is what makes marriages crack, makes liquor more attractive."[32]

Betty's father and first husband had suffered from alcoholism, and she had begun down the same path. At first, she shared a drink with Jerry prior to dinner to get "him to loosen up." With him away so often, the bottle turned into her safety net. She would have a drink while on the phone, preparing dinner, watching television in the evening, or spending time with a neighbor. She even began to put a small amount of vodka into her morning tea, which gave her "a warm, mellow feeling." She later admitted that "alcohol became too important in my life." Her family was aware she had health problems, but, commented Michael Ford, "No one really wanted to admit that we were watching our mother change. . . . We were in denial." Jerry was of like mind. Tom Ford later said his brother, who "had a guilt complex" regarding Betty's well-being, would "inconvenience himself and stay home from speaking engagements, he'd bring her gifts and pitch in to help in every way he could." Yet Jerry remained so wedded to his goal of moving up the political ladder on Capitol Hill that he was largely blind to what was happening to her. Hence, when he talked with her about whether he should seek the chairmanship of the Republican Conference and all the additional responsibility it would entail, she concluded he wanted the post and told him she would stand behind whatever he chose to do.[33]

Another Rung

Ford's decision to become Republican Conference chair was a direct result of the 1962 midterm election. He did not foresee Republicans winning control of the House, but he did anticipate a gain of twenty seats for the GOP. That was before the superpowers came to the brink of war. Taking heed of rumors of Soviet troops putting nuclear missiles in Cuba, the Kennedy administration in October sent U-2 spy planes over the island, which brought back evidence confirming the reports. Knowing that more missiles were on the way via ship, the president imposed a naval blockade of Cuba (or "quarantine," as he called it) and prepared for both an air strike on and an invasion of the island if the Soviets did not remove the missiles there. On 22 October, he made public the presence of the missiles and America's countermeasures, threatening a nuclear strike on the Soviets if any of the weapons on Cuba were launched "against any nation in the Western Hemisphere." Within a week, the crisis came to an end with an agreement by which the United States would not invade Cuba in return for a Soviet withdrawal of the missiles. Ford was impressed with the president's handling of the crisis: "He was calm. He was firm. He was on top if it."[34] Many Americans agreed. Thus, on Election Day, voters gave the Republicans only one additional House seat, leaving the Democrats with an overwhelming eighty-two-person advantage. The news was even worse in the Senate, where the Democrats won three more seats, giving them a total of sixty-six.

The disappointing outcome of the 1962 midterm vote convinced the Young Turks, who had earlier played a part in ousting Joseph Martin (R-Mass.) as minority leader, that it was time once again for change. They also felt the GOP leadership had to match the youth and vigor in the White House personified by Kennedy and many of his advisers. "Compared with youthful President Kennedy," wrote James Reston of the *New York Times*, "Senator Everett McKinley Dirksen and Representative Charles Halleck looked like a veteran Shakespearean actor and W. C. Fields." Following the 1960 election, the two men, on Eisenhower's suggestion, had formed the Joint Senate-House Republican Leadership to get the GOP's message out to the press. As part of that effort, they held periodic televised news conferences that the media called the "Ev and Charlie Show." That program "has been the principal channel from the G.O.P. to the nation for the last two years," wrote Reston, "and it has become the joke of the capital. It was, however, no joke to the young Republicans. They know the power of television in modern politics," and they were worried about the their party's image.[35]

Leading the way among the more youthful party members were Melvin Laird of Wisconsin, Michigan's Robert Griffin, New York's Charles Goodell, and Donald Rumsfeld, the last of whom had just been elected to the House from Illinois but who disliked the idea of his party being led by people "who seemed to accept, or at least not be uncomfortable with, a state of permanent minority status." The term "Young Turks" was appropriate, for with the exception of Laird, who had turned forty two months before the November elections, the others were in their thirties. Rather than targeting Halleck, who had only recently become the Republicans' leader in the House, they went after sixty-seven-year-old Charles Hoeven of Iowa, the head of the Republican Conference and the third-most-powerful individual in the GOP's House membership. The job of the Republican Conference "was to convert party philosophy and ideas into practical programs and campaign debating points." To the Young Turks, "Hoeven was a do-nothing leader and the conference itself was moribund." But the Turks could not find anyone to challenge Hoeven, except for Ford who, Rumsfeld reminisced, "was a workman and very well liked."[36]

To Ford, the conference chairmanship was another step up the ladder to House speaker. Quietly, the Turks rallied support for the Michigan lawmaker. They did their job so well that Hoeven was not even aware of what was going on until 7 January, a day before the House Republicans voted. By an 86–78 vote, Ford was elected as the new Republican Conference leader. The Turks, reported the *New York Times*, said the change "was in no sense a revolt against Mr. Halleck but an attempt to give him younger and better men to work with at the leadership level."[37] Yet, Reston presciently observed, "it is not at all out of the question that Mr. Halleck, after another national Republican defeat at the polls, could be the victim of the secret vote he used to defeat Mr. Martin." Hoeven certainly felt that way, cautioning Halleck that Ford had "just taken my job and the next thing you know, he'll be after yours."[38]

From Kennedy to Johnson

For the time being, though, Ford's main concern was to press forward with an agenda that met his moderate conservative views. He continued to rail against those parts of Kennedy's domestic program that he regarded as expensive and unnecessary. The same was true with the president's foreign policy. After the missile crisis he consistently charged the administration with "underestimating the military power of the Soviets in Cuba" and called for resuming spy-plane flights over the island. He also took issue with the Kennedy administration's plan to remove U.S. Jupiter nuclear missiles from Turkey, a nation that bordered the Soviet Union. The White House held that Polaris missiles could cover the same area and, because they were launched from submarines, would be less vulnerable to a Soviet strike. Ford charged that the Jupiters were a deterrent to Soviet aggression and that it would cost too much financially to take them out.[39] (Despite the opposition, the White House went forward with its plans, removing the last of the Jupiters in the spring of 1963.)

Ford complained too about McNamara's policy of mutual assured destruction (MAD)—sometimes called "mutual deterrence." The United States had about 18,000 nuclear warheads in 1960, eight times what the Soviets had, and an estimated 33,000 at the end of 1963. Of those 33,000, 550 were ICBMs, as opposed to the Kremlin's 100. To the defense secretary, the arsenals of the two superpowers had become so enormous that neither could survive an atomic exchange between them. Accordingly, it made little sense to him to continue large funding for America's atomic stockpile. Ford praised McNamara for trying to hold down spending, but in this case, he said, U.S. security was at stake. "I want the record perfectly clear," he informed his colleagues. "In my judgment, we are adopting the wrong attitude, a bad frame of mind, when we concede that we are inevitably in a period of mutual deterrence, regardless of what we do programwise and dollarwise."[40]

Most surprising was the Michigan lawmaker's position on foreign aid. The alliance among liberal and conservative Democrats and liberal Republicans that had opposed funding for the Foreign Assistance Act back in 1961 had by 1963 grown more potent. Most damaging to the president's plans was a report by General Lucius Clay, a World War II veteran who had overseen the Berlin Airlift. Realizing he faced the likelihood of not getting all he wanted for foreign aid, Kennedy had appointed Clay to head a special committee that would endorse the program. Instead, Clay's committee advised cutting $500 million from the White House's $4.5 billion foreign-assistance request. The House Foreign Affairs Committee chopped off another $420 million. Then the House, including most Republicans, added an amendment cutting spending by $585 million more. While the Senate restored some of the money, the bill that President Lyndon B. Johnson signed—Kennedy had been assassinated a month earlier—gave the executive $3.6 billion, or a quarter less than Kennedy had wanted.[41]

As a hard-core Cold Warrior who had fought to give Kennedy what he desired in 1961 for foreign assistance, one might have expected that Ford would have wanted to restore as much of the $4.5 billion as possible. But he did not. For one thing, he tended to be less supportive of economic-aid programs than of military-assistance ones. He endorsed the creation of the Development Loan Fund, which provided loans to foreign nations. But in 1961 he decried the Kennedy administration's call for having the Treasury offer long-term financing for such loans as "back-door financing" and an effort to limit congressional oversight of the U.S. economic-aid program. Additionally, he appears to have joined those lawmakers impressed by Clay, who as a general was not likely to call for cuts on programs designed to protect U.S. security unless it was possible to assure the nation's defense at lower funding levels. Furthermore, Ford believed that spending reductions opened the door to a cut in federal taxes, which he favored.[42]

As before, Kennedy and Ford agreed on some matters. Kennedy sympathized with the civil rights movement and understood that the oppression facing African Americans was of great propaganda value to the Soviet Union. Yet he did not want to anger southern voters or conservatives in his own party who opposed black rights. Only after intense prodding from civil rights activists did the president in 1963 offer legislation to protect African Americans' right to vote. However, Kennedy failed to follow up, permitting southerners in Congress to kill the measure.[43]

Although Ford endorsed Kennedy's 1963 bill, he too offset what compassion he felt with other considerations. In April, he joined others on the Appropriations Committee to eliminate funding for a public-works program that would have helped the unemployed, many of whom were minorities. Likewise, Ford stood behind Goldwater's position on race. The Arizona senator had voted for the 1957 and 1960 Civil Rights Acts, but he was first and foremost a supporter of states' rights who refused to force the states to comply. By 1961, the Arizonan had reached the conclusion that there was no way Republicans could "outpromise the Democrats," to whom African Americans remained loyal, "so," he said, "let's quit trying specifically to get them." Instead, the party needed to focus on the Midwest, the Far West, and, in the South, whites. Louisiana resident Peter Feringa approved, writing Ford, "It is generally conceded that the Republican Party can win in '64 only if it can garner the Southern vote. This . . . can be done . . . only by adopting as basic strategy Goldwater conservatism and not Kennedy Civil Rights." Ford replied, in language reminiscent of Goldwater's, "You are so right in insisting that the Republican Party make no attempt to imitate or out-promise the Kennedys on civil rights, or spending schemes or on any of the other New Frontier specialities."[44]

The communication between Feringa and Ford came on the heels of weeks of marches in Birmingham, Alabama, led by Martin Luther King Jr., which culminated with nationally televised scenes of city officials unleashing fire hoses and police dogs on the peaceful protestors. The national uproar forced Kennedy to call for new civil rights legislation. From that point on, no issue drew more of the administration's time than civil rights.[45]

Whether Kennedy could have overcome southern resistance to blacks' rights and seen his bill become law will never be known, for on 22 November, gunman Lee Harvey Oswald assassinated the president, who was in Dallas, Texas, to raise funds for his planned reelection bid. The Fords were driving home from a parent-teacher conference when they heard the news over the car radio. Both were in shock. "I just couldn't believe it," Jerry later wrote. "I sped to the office to find out more details." Betty recalled that both she and her husband "seemed to move through a haze of pomp." The next day, they went to the White House to meet with Kennedy's family, and to kneel and pray next to the casket holding the president's body.[46]

Following the events in Dallas, the new president, Lyndon B. Johnson, decided to form a commission chaired by Supreme Court Chief Justice Earl Warren to investigate Kennedy's murder. On McNamara's recommendation, he asked Ford to serve on it. Ford was reluctant, given the time he had to devote to his congressional responsibilities, but the president, who had a reputation for not taking no for an answer, all but ordered him to do so on the grounds of "national duty." Although Ford was concerned about finding the time to devote to his new post, he got help from his old friend, Jack Stiles, and from former New York congressman John Ray, who prepared questions for him to ask at the congressional hearings into the murder and looked for discrepancies in the transcripts. Additionally, Ford traveled with Warren both to question Jack Ruby, a nightclub owner who had shot and killed Oswald two days after Kennedy's assassination, and to visit the Texas School Book Depository Building, from which Oswald had fired his rifle at the president.[47]

The ten-month investigation took its toll on Ford. It was not just the hours spent questioning witnesses, which included people who had been in Dallas on that fateful day and scientists who had determined that the rifle used by Oswald was the murder weapon. It was the evidence, which included photographs and X-rays of Kennedy. "It was shocking to see a friend with, literally, his brains blown out," Ford later commented. "It really hit me inside." The final conclusion of the commission, issued in September 1964, was that Kennedy's death was the work of one man, Oswald, who had felt dejected about the direction his life had taken, hated authority, and sought "a place in history."[48]

Ford's role on the Warren Commission remains a subject of some controversy. According to the commission's report, a single bullet hit Kennedy, who was riding in the rear seat of his vehicle, in the neck, passed through it, and then entered the back of Texas governor John Connally, who was in the vehicle's front seat. Conspiracy theorists have argued that in fact there was more than one bullet, thus opening the door to the possibility of more than a single shooter. Advocates for multiple shooters contend that the draft of the Warren Commission's findings pointed to a bullet hitting Kennedy just above his right shoulder; in that case, it would have been impossible for that shot to make the change in trajectory necessary to puncture Connally's back where it did. Ford, therefore, argue the conspiracy advocates, moved the wound to the neck to protect the single-bullet finding. A second charge has to do with the book *Portrait of the Assassin*, an account of the commission's findings authored by Ford and Stiles. Henry Hurt, an investigative reporter, later claimed that the authors violated federal law by including top-secret information in their manuscript.[49]

Despite the time he devoted to the Warren Commission, Ford could not ignore his work as a congressman. How supportive he would be of the Johnson administration's foreign policy initiatives was not clear to the White House. "Gerald Ford is the fourth man on the Republican side of the House Appropriations committee," O'Brien wrote the new president. "He and Silvio Conte are the only Republican members of the committee who consistently through the years have voted against cuts in Foreign Aid." But in more recent years, O'Brien continued, Ford had begun to demonstrate less resolve in protecting the foreign-aid program. O'Brien suggested that that was because he was considering seeking the vice presidency or the House speakership. As if to confirm that analysis, Ford voted to cut foreign assistance by $585 million. Johnson fought back with an intense lobbying effort. With the help of twenty-three House Republicans, the president convinced Congress to give him $3.25 billion, or only 8 percent less than what he had originally desired. It was, in the words of the *New York Times*, "the lowest percentage cut in the 17-year history of the program."[50]

Ford's desire to cut foreign aid did not mean he had become a dove. The Communist threat was still real, and the Cold War was "a basic prerequisite for both preparedness and the preservation of economic freedom and strength." The problem in his mind was that too many Americans, including those in power, had come to see communism as no longer posing a danger.

In fact, the superpowers had begun to improve their relations following the close call of the Cuban Missile Crisis. In October 1963, along with the United Kingdom, they had signed the Limited Test Ban Treaty (LTBT), which banned all above-ground and underwater nuclear testing. The following February, U.S. and Soviet officials began talks about preventing the proliferation of nuclear technology. Regarding it necessary to remind the U.S. public what it was facing, Ford joined a dozen other Republicans in June in putting a twist on the "missile gap," charging that the Kennedy and Johnson administrations had permitted "American military superiority to slip away" by not devoting enough dollars to research and development. They also accused the White House of "misjudging Soviet intentions," taking issue particularly with the LTBT. While the Kennedy administration had maintained that Washington had the technology to determine whether the Soviets had violated the pact, Ford and his colleagues asserted that the White House had "sacrificed a principle of international inspection." For their part, the nonproliferation negotiations endangered NATO, Ford charged. What was needed instead was "nuclear sharing" among NATO's members. McNamara called the Republicans' accusations "a partisan attack" that failed to take note of how strong America's armed forces were.[51]

Ford also remained adamant the United States had to do something about Cuba. Despite the debacle that had taken place at the Bay of Pigs, he insisted that the White House reimpose the naval blockade of Cuba, resume aerial surveillance of it, "and encourage the Cuban patriots to overthrow Castro." Certainly events in Panama made Ford all the more certain that Castro endangered U.S. hemispheric interests. Panamanians had grown resentful of U.S. control of the Panama Canal Zone, considering it a violation of their country's sovereignty. That frustration bred a four-day riot in 1964 that left twenty-four Panamanians and four U.S. soldiers dead. To President Johnson, this clash was the work of Communist agents sponsored by Castro, a conclusion Ford echoed: "I hope and trust that this Administration will take a strong and effective position in the Panama Canal to protect every American's right and to defeat the purpose of the Castro regime and its Communist cohorts."[52] It was one of the Michigan lawmaker's first forays into a subject that would come back to haunt him during his presidency.

What would become an even more troublesome foreign-policy matter for the United States and eventually for Ford as president was Vietnam. The refusal of the United States and South Vietnam's president, Ngo Dinh Diem, to hold elections throughout Vietnam in 1956 as called for by the Geneva Accords, combined with Diem's corruption and repression, had fomented widespread opposition to his rule, led by a North Vietnamese–supported guerrilla organization called the Viet Cong (VC). The United States responded by sending both economic and military aid, including by 1963 thousands of military advisers, but it was not enough to quell anti-Diem sentiment. A coup in November 1963 left Diem dead and South Vietnam as unstable as ever. Himself a Cold Warrior, Johnson continued to give Saigon more aid and advisers. His administration also prepared a draft resolution to submit to Congress permitting direct U.S. military action to stop the VC.

Ford became increasingly vocal about Vietnam as the U.S. commitment to the South deepened. In June 1964, he joined twelve Republican colleagues in censuring the U.S. government's role in Diem's overthrow, calling it "in many ways the most tragic blunder of the past four years." That same month, unaware of the White House's plans, he said he shared the view of other members of the Appropriations Committee's defense subcommittee that the United States had to send more aid to Saigon. He and a number of his Republican colleagues even endorsed Washington's assuming "operational control of the war," an appeal both the newly appointed ambassador to Vietnam, Maxwell Taylor, and his predecessor, Henry Cabot Lodge, rejected.[53]

Following an attack in August by North Vietnamese gunboats on U.S. warships stationed just off the North's coast in the Gulf of Tonkin, the president ordered air strikes on the gunboat bases and got Congress to approve the so-called Gulf of Tonkin Resolution, which provided him with the authority to "take all necessary measures to repel any armed attack against the forces of the United States and to prevent further aggression." Ford joined the entire House in passing what was essentially a blank check to use military force, commenting that such a move "affecting our own ground forces on prior occasions in Vietnam might have turned the tide our way much sooner."[54] With only two votes in opposition, the Senate followed suit.

Ford's mixed feelings about Johnson's foreign policy matched his sentiments regarding the president's domestic initiatives. Johnson envisioned himself as another Roosevelt, who had used the federal government to aid Americans in dire straits. Speaking in March 1964 at the University of Michigan, the president talked of a vision for the country that included "abundance and liberty for all . . . [and] an end to poverty and racial injustice." Johnson referred to this vision as "the Great Society."

Roosevelt's New Deal had cost the U.S. government billions of dollars, and the Great Society required the same. The question was how to pay for it. With a few exceptions, the United States had run a budget deficit since

World War II. In 1962 it stood at $7.1 billion dollars. For much of his term in office, Kennedy had considered a tax cut to stimulate the economy. Influenced by Keynesian economic theory, in 1963 he proposed slicing taxes across the board by $11 billion. Although the GOP, including Ford, balked, the bill passed the House in September 1963. Before the Senate could consider it, however, Kennedy was killed.[55]

Johnson intended to push through the tax cut. He knew that the chairman of the Senate Finance Committee, Harry Byrd (D-Va.), would permit no tax bill to reach the floor of the Senate without a promise to keep the budget below $100 billion. The president met that requirement by calling for $97.9 billion in outlays for the next fiscal year. With Johnson's cajoling and Byrd's support, the Senate in February 1964 passed the legislation by an overwhelming 77–21 vote. In the House, though, Ford opposed the bill on the grounds that "there was no assurance that spending would be reduced." He bemoaned to a constituent, "We are spending more, not less."[56]

Ford's desire to check federal expenditures and his faith in relying on the private sector rather than the government to solve the nation's problems led him to vote against many of Johnson's other domestic initiatives, including food stamps, the Community Action Program to help cities combat poverty, a domestic form of the Peace Corps called Volunteers in Service to America, and the Economic Opportunity Act, which sought to eradicate poverty through a variety of programs, including Head Start and Job Corps. He also resisted Johnson's plan to revive Medicare, which the Senate had rejected in 1962. To Ford's chagrin, the Economic Opportunity Act passed the Senate in July and the House in August 1964. The Food Stamp Act, which established a program to help families with little or no income purchase food, made it out of Capitol Hill around the same time. Interestingly, Ford endorsed a Senate amendment that would make Medicare part of a bill to increase Social Security benefits. But this did not mean he wanted to see Medicare passed. Clearly he knew that Mills would do all he could to prevent any legislation including Medicare from getting through the Ways and Means Committee.[57] Put another way, Ford could court votes from those who wanted to see Medicare become law while making sure it did not. The fight for insurance for the aged would have to wait until after the 1964 elections.

Ford was more supportive of Johnson's civil rights initiative. More resolute than Kennedy about protecting African Americans' rights, the new president insisted that his predecessor's bill get through Congress. Public opinion polls showing mounting support for doing more for blacks heartened him. Johnson made public appeals, privately brought intense pressure to bear on members of Congress—especially fellow southerners—and massaged the ego of key senators, particularly Dirksen. Through those efforts, he saw Congress pass the Civil Rights Act of 1964 in June. The landmark legislation banned discrimination based on race, ethnicity, gender, or religion in the workplace and in federal programs, at the voting booth, and in public facilities. Ford voted for the bill in the House and then accepted a Senate amendment that emphasized having local authorities try to work out any violations of the law before the federal government stepped in.[58] To add teeth to the bill, Congress passed, and the states quickly approved, the Twenty-Fourth Amendment to the Constitution, prohibiting poll taxes.

Ford also endorsed Johnson's environmental initiatives. The general lack of attention given to environmental protection after World War II had begun to break down as a result of growing concern over radioactive fallout caused by above-ground nuclear testing. But it was the publication of Rachel Carson's *Silent Spring* in 1962 that brought the issue to the forefront of American attention. Carson detailed how the pesticide DDT caused mutations and death among birds, fish, and other fauna and poisoned water used by humans for drinking. The ensuing public outcry demanded more federal protection for the environment, a crusade that the first lady, Lady Bird Johnson, made her own. Ford, who had shown an interest in the environment prior to 1962, joined the cause. In 1963, he had voted for the Clean Air Act to control air pollution. While he continued to lean in favor of the development of America's natural resources rather than their preservation, in 1964 he endorsed the National Wilderness Preservation System (NWPS), which assured that federally protected lands would remain untouched by developers.[59]

By the time Johnson signed the NWPS into law, Ford had clearly made a name for himself among his peers and in his party. Eisenhower was among those who took notice. "Maybe a lot of us ought to be touting [Ford] to our friends more often and more emphatically than in the past," he told a friend in April 1961. A few months later, he even suggested to another friend that the Michigan congressman was a possible presidential candidate.[60] Ford's name would come up in 1964, but the GOP would choose someone else as its nominee, with disastrous short-term but significant long-term results for the party.

A New Minority Leader

The New Right had the most influence in choosing the nominee in 1964. Tracing its origins to the end of World War II, it opposed the labor movement, higher taxes, negotiations with the Soviets, and any "socialist" initiatives that threatened the individualism, self-reliance, morality, capitalism, and democracy that had made America great. Its members did not fully agree on the direction their movement should take, but they found unity in Barry Goldwater, who became the party's presidential nominee in 1964. Goldwater favored canceling the farm-subsidy program, making Social Security voluntary, and bombing North Vietnam. He even joked about dropping a nuclear warhead "into the men's room of the Kremlin." Democrats went after Goldwater, changing the GOP candidate's slogan, "In your heart, you know he's right," to read on bumper stickers, "In your guts, you know he's nuts" and "Stamp out peace—vote Goldwater."[61]

Ford's name had come up as Goldwater's running mate but, according to the *New York Times*, he was regarded as "not an especially warm or skillful platform speaker." Instead, the Arizonan chose New York's Representative William Miller, the chair of the Republican National Committee and someone whom conservatives saw as one of their own.[62] With Goldwater focused on his conservative base, Johnson was able to move to the political center, taking positions that favored civil rights, assistance for the elderly, and anticommunism. He also ran attack ads on Goldwater, including the famous "Daisy Ad" that depicted the Republican candidate as a madman willing to risk a full-fledged nuclear war with the Soviet Union. The ad ran only once, but it created a nationwide stir, and the major TV networks aired it again on the news.

The outcome on Election Day surprised few, with the possible exception of Goldwater ideologues. In a landslide Johnson won every state except Arizona and five southern states, 61 percent of the popular vote, and 486 electoral votes to Goldwater's 52. The outcome carried into Congress, where the Democrats gained 37 seats (for a total of 297) in the House, and two more in the Senate (giving them 68). Forty of the Republicans who ran for reelection that year lost, and nearly half of them had been in Congress for a decade or longer.[63]

If Ford had gotten his way, George Romney would have been the top name on the Republican ticket in 1964. The former governor of Michigan, Romney had had doubts about Goldwater's appeal to voters. But following the Republican National Convention, Ford endorsed the Arizonan, telling a constituent that while he had "differences" with the senator, they were "small compared to the vast differences I have with President Johnson and the members of the Democratic Party in Congress." Indeed, he praised the Republican platform, calling it "a blueprint for a better America and the Free World. It is a strong contrast to the policies of the Johnson Administration which have been unsuccessful in so many areas."[64]

Losing yet another congressional election frustrated Ford's Republican colleagues, who once again believed a leadership change was in order. Just as Hoeven had warned, this time the target was Halleck. In fact, resentment had been building against Halleck for some time. After the Indianan became minority leader in 1959, the party had picked up twenty seats in the House in 1960 but only two in 1962, and it had remained in the minority throughout. Furthermore, in trying to rally the party against the Kennedy and Johnson programs, the right-wing Halleck had a tendency to take on positions not unlike those of southern Democrats and gave GOP liberals and moderates the impression that if they did not endorse what he wanted, they were not loyal to the party. In addition to his politics and his abrasive personality, Halleck had another disadvantage: his status as minority leader meant he had less ability than would the House speaker in giving choice committee assignments to party members. Liberals, and even moderates, in the party believed that the 1964 GOP platform had been "rammed down [their] throats," thereby allowing the Democrats to capture the political center rather than the Republicans. Finally, television built sentiment in favor of someone who was more physically appealing than the heavyset and aging Indiana lawmaker. "Let's face it," commented one GOP congressman, "that face isn't getting any younger. Every time Charlie Halleck appears on TV it gives the party a bad image."[65]

Talk of a leadership change appeared in the press as early as August, but it was after the Election Day results that the Young Turks began quietly mobilizing, with Griffin, Goodell, and Rumsfeld sending out feelers to determine support for replacing Halleck. Ford was aware of the Turks' activities but did not consider himself a likely candidate to take Halleck's place. Missouri's Tom Curtis, also cognizant of the Turks' machinations thanks to a phone call he had received from Rumsfeld, decided to bring the matter into the open and sent his colleagues a lengthy letter on 18 November. "I am tired of behind the scenes maneuverings when it comes to establishing Party machinery and policies," he wrote. He pointed out that he had spoken with both Ford and Halleck, who had agreed to a meeting of the Republican Conference. "I am dissatisfied with our leadership in the House," he conceded, "not necessarily our leaders, however. . . . I'm not arguing for a change of leaders, but I am arguing for a change in the techniques of leadership."[66]

Though Curtis had worded his letter cautiously, the Turks took it as an indication that there was indeed a desire in the GOP for new leadership. "Mr. Halleck pretty well demonstrated that he is going to be the same kind of leader," explained Griffin. "There was no indication of any changing directions. . . . He wasn't providing any leadership. He resisted the establishment of task forces to come to grips with issues such as Medicare and so on." While Rumsfeld said he was neither anti-Halleck nor pro-Ford, he considered it "dangerous for our two party system to continue with this disproportionate advantage for the Democratic Party over the past 30 years." The Turks lobbied anyone willing to listen, discovering that it was mostly younger moderates who showed an interest, with a few conservatives and liberals willing to join them. Additionally, they made clear that their target was not just Halleck but others in the House leadership, including the whip, Leslie Arends, himself of the older generation. Upon hearing of the planned Republican Conference, the press reported that some observers viewed it "as a slap at the leadership of Representative Charles A. Halleck of Indiana" and a test of his ability to remain leader. A number of House members, including Laird, and journalists reported Ford might vie for Halleck's seat, but the Michigan lawmaker kept his distance, insisting that he had yet to decide whether he planned to run.[67]

Laird himself was a possible contender for Halleck's post as minority leader. Now in his eleventh year in Congress, and nine years younger than Ford, he had a reputation for vigorousness and a preparedness to be tough with people, whereas, commented one Republican House member, "Ford was too good-natured, too affable." Yet Laird's toughness also turned some individuals off. Furthermore, he had chaired Goldwater's platform committee, which, in the eyes of many Republicans, tied him too closely to the candidate who had cost them dearly in November. Too, Laird realized that if Ford ran for Halleck's post, it made sense for him to endorse his colleague from Michigan. The two of them sat on the Appropriations Committee, were members of the Chowder and Marching Society, and had become close friends.[68]

Griffin, Goodell, and Minnesota's Albert Quie were optimistic that the winds favored a leadership change and certain that the moderate-minded Ford was the man to head the effort. Ford talked with some business friends, who encouraged him to oust Halleck. Finally, after further thought, he decided to throw his hat into the ring. "I believe the basic Republican position we must regain is the high middle road of moderation," he noted in declaring his candidacy on 19 December. He then went after Halleck. "We welcome into the party Republicans of every reasonable viewpoint. But we must firmly resist the takeover of our party by any elements that are not interested in building a party, but only in advancing their own narrow views. . . . We must stake out our positions independently of any preplanning with the southern Democratic leadership" so that the GOP was not seen as in cahoots with the Dixiecrats. Ford was not worried about his chances. If he defeated Halleck, then he would be minority leader. If he did not, he would still have his ranking position on the Appropriations Committee, a position he very much enjoyed. With that, he departed for the annual Christmastime ski trip with his family,[69] leaving it up to the others in his cabal during that period to campaign for him.

The response to Ford's decision was mixed. "I think you are about to take . . . an erroneous jump!" penned Harry Sherrill of El Paso, Texas. "Your problem is not one of dumping Halleck. . . . I'll tell you the people who should be dumped: Whoever planned Goldwater's campaign and wrote his speeches." Harry Joseph of Springfield, Ohio, felt otherwise. To him, the GOP had "failed to adjust itself to changing conditions as well as the thinking of the average citizen in such areas as education, employment opportunities, the right to bargain collectively, civil rights, foreign aid, fiscal responsibility, local autonomy and etc." A number of Halleck's constituents joined the chorus, angry that the minority leader had voted against the Indian Dunes National Lakeshore bill. The legislation was designed to protect the dunes, but Halleck said it would prevent industrial development within his district.[70]

Halleck, who had been vacationing in Florida, returned to Washington to try to stop the insurrection. Particularly important were the votes of twenty freshmen, who knew that once they chose sides, they put at risk the possibility of receiving choice committee assignments. There were two additional complicating factors. One was Ford himself who, after returning from his trip, appeared to be somewhat unenergetic about rallying supporters. Goodell recalled having to convince Ford one night not to go home for dinner but to stay and make calls to colleagues. The second was Laird's decision to run for Ford's post as chair of the Republican Conference. Some of the Wisconsinite's opponents believed his announcement was part of a Ford-Laird alliance aimed at taking over the GOP leadership in the House. In response, they nominated a third candidate, Peter Frelinghuysen of New Jersey. In-

Senate Minority Leader Everett M. Dirksen celebrates the election of Gerald Ford as House minority leader, 1965. Photo in the Gerald Ford Library, Ann Arbor, Michigan.

stead of challenging Halleck and Ford, Frelinghuysen decided to compete against Laird for head of the Republican Conference.[71]

Throughout, Halleck was confident of victory. He was the party's leader in the House, had influence over committee assignments, had used his position to provide favors to his GOP colleagues, and had the backing of lawmakers who did not favor change. His campaign, though, was not invincible. He failed to ask people to help him. Many of his supporters were lame ducks who had lost on Election Day, and the contest would be determined by secret ballot. Moreover, the Ford camp had taken the step of neutralizing Eisenhower, whom the Michigander's supporters feared might declare in favor of Halleck. Instead, they persuaded the popular ex-president to remain quiet. The Ford team also had aces up its sleeve. As an example, the Turks got Ohio's delegation behind a leadership change by reminding its members that if Ford won, he would have to step down as the ranking Republican on the Appropriations Committee, leaving it open for Ohio's Frank Bow, who was next in line for that seat. Rumsfeld helped convince Kansas's representatives to champion Ford by turning for help from his (Rumsfeld's) friend, Robert Dole. The lobbying worked. By a vote of 73–67, Ford and Laird emerged the winners.[72] The ex–football player and lawyer who dreamed of a life in politics was now the Republicans' leader in the House.

A Step Away

"The Congress got a new Minority Leader, and I lost a husband," Betty penned years later. As one of her biographers pointed out, her comment was only half-true. Mrs. Ford "never had a full-time husband, and her children never had a full-time father." She did have help from Clara Powell. Powell, said Ford's youngest son, Steve, was "just like a second mother" who "could certainly chase you with a slipper and get you back in line." For example, when Steve threatened to drop his sister down the laundry chute of the family home, he could expect to be sent to his room. There was even the possibility of the children being punished once their father returned home, though, added Steve, "by the time he got there a day later, everybody had cooled off, and he didn't want to come in and be the bad guy."[73]

What Betty's comment reflected was a realization that with his new responsibilities, she could anticipate seeing her husband, and her children seeing their father, even less than before. To make matters worse, Betty in 1964 was diagnosed with a pinched nerve. It refused to go away, and the therapy she undertook to relieve the pain developed into osteoarthritis. She began to take painkillers, which turned into an addiction. As the year progressed, she found herself mixing alcohol with her medication. But she kept her pain hidden from Jerry, devoting herself to her husband and his aspirations and trying to continue on with her duties as she had before.[74]

Though Betty was less than happy, Ford was exhilarated. The GOP might have lost the presidential election and failed to capture the House, but he was now one step away from his goal, that of becoming speaker. He had made it that far by holding firm to his moderate-conservative values. He sought to cut government spending, opposed what he considered unnecessary and expensive social-welfare programs, favored tax cuts if economically viable, and endorsed civil rights and environmental initiatives while leaving their implementation wherever possible up to local and state governments. Although his position on foreign assistance seemed to suggest that his resolve to contain communism had weakened, he remained in fact as committed as ever to that policy. He tended to stick to partisan positions, praising Eisenhower while criticizing Kennedy and Johnson. Yet he was a pragmatist who was prepared to reach across party lines in those cases where he believed Democrats might endorse initiatives he favored. In the process, he ruffled some feathers among his colleagues, but he was well respected on both sides of the aisle, and the Young Turks liked him enough to encourage him to run for Republican Conference chair and then minority leader. All the while, he was oblivious to what was happening in his own household.

FOUR

High Expectations . . . Unrealized

"What the hell is going on? I thought we were winning the war!" So asked CBS news anchor Walter Cronkite when he learned on 31 January 1968 that the North Vietnamese Army (NVA) and Viet Cong (VC) had attacked over 200 locations throughout South Vietnam, including the U.S. embassy in Saigon. It took weeks for South Vietnam's army, the Army of the Republic of Vietnam (ARVN), and U.S. troops to turn back what became known as the Tet Offensive, at the cost of 1,100 American and 2,300 South Vietnamese military lives.

That question, "What the hell is going on?," could have referred to the general state of affairs in the United States by early 1968. Like Cronkite,[1] many Americans had assumed there would be a relatively quick victory in Vietnam, only to find their country mired in what seemed to be a never-ending war that cost far more in lives and money than the White House had anticipated. President Lyndon B. Johnson had suggested that the United States could afford both Vietnam and the "Great Society," the name given to his domestic programs that would use federal power to eradicate poverty, promote civil rights, protect the environment, and help Americans get an education. Many voters and members of Congress initially shared that vision. But they began to wonder if the Great Society was achievable as they watched antiwar protests, race riots, and a rising crime rate grip the country.

For the GOP's new minority leader, Gerald Ford, America was in its mess because the Johnson administration was prosecuting the Vietnam War incorrectly and refused to assume a more conservative course in its domestic initiatives. The president's idea that he could afford both guns and butter was wishful thinking. From the time he assumed the minority leadership until the 1968 elections, Ford chastised the Johnson administration for not relying more heavily on air and naval power in Southeast Asia and for excessive spending on the Great Society. Americans began to express doubts about Johnson's foreign and domestic policies in the elections of 1966 and 1968. Republicans gained seats in both those years and won control of the White House in 1968, yet for Ford the House speakership remained out of reach.

He Had It All but . . .

Ford's career as minority leader did not start out auspiciously. He had wanted New Jersey's Peter Frelinghuysen to serve as whip in place of Leslie Arends of Illinois, who had favored retaining Charles Halleck as minority leader. Arends was also part of the older generation the Young Turks sought to remove. Frelinghuysen, in the words of Representative Silvio Conte of Massachusetts, would have drawn support for the new leadership from liberals, but the New Jerseyite was "inclined to be snobbish." Arends was also helped by a desire within the party, which had witnessed two leadership changes in less than a decade, to end the "bloodshed" and by his personality. His colleagues described him as "a nice guy with no real enemies" and as someone who "believes in loyalty above all." To prove he was a team player, Arends publicly promised his "loyalty to [Ford] and to our Party position [that] will be as firm as it was to Joe Martin and Charlie Halleck." Ford apparently appreciated what he heard and what his whip had said, telling William Springer (R-Ill.) that he was convinced of Arends's "complete loyalty to me or what is best for the Republican cause."[2]

Working alongside Senate Minority Leader Everett Dirksen (R-Ill.), Ford had more luck in removing Barry Goldwater's loyalists from the party's hierarchy. Ford and Dirksen replaced Dean Burch as the GOP's national chairman with Ray Bliss. They also removed from positions of influence members of right-wing groups such as the John Birch Society, an organization that, they believed, had adopted views out of tune with those who represented Republicans in Congress, took "its orders from the top," and prevented the party from adopting a centrist tone that could draw in wider support. One exception to this housecleaning was Representative John Rhodes (R-Ariz.). Ford held two transgressions against the Arizonan: he had endorsed Goldwater in 1964, and, like Arends, he preferred to keep Halleck on as minority leader, because, in Rhodes's words, the Michigander was "trying to move [up] a little too fast." The Arizonan wanted to head the party's Policy Committee, a body that offered GOP alternatives to Democratic proposals. As its chair, Rhodes would hold the number-four spot in the House leadership. Because of Rhodes's questionable loyalty, Ford suggested that he become chair of a new Research and Planning Committee and that policy planning be handed over to the minority leader's Young Turk ally, Charles Goodell of New York. When Rhodes refused and found enough votes among House Republicans to get the position he wanted, Ford named Goodell as head of Research and Planning, which oversaw some dozen task forces that would provide "long-range policy planning" and would have status equal to that of the Policy Committee.[3]

By early 1966, Ford appeared to have consolidated his power around a small core group consisting of himself, Republican Conference chairman Melvin Laird, Goodell, Arends, and Rhodes. In truth, the inner circle was even smaller and reflected Ford's determination to move the party toward moderation. Rhodes was one of the casualties, as Ford favored Goodell over the Arizonan. Shortly after becoming minority leader, he asked his colleagues to work with Laird and the Republican Conference in developing "a sound legislative program for 1965" that would address civil rights, poverty, environmental degradation, and the conflict in Vietnam. Goodell commented a year later, "The Policy Committee has largely turned out to be a meeting in which we ratify policy already made by the committees themselves" and expressed his pleasure that he himself had not held Rhodes's post.[4]

Arends was also on the outs. "The Republican Conference under Laird's direction has become the center of power from which other things relate," Goodell continued. "Gerry has completely cooperated and agreed to this approach. . . . Arends has been largely eclipsed." William Brock, a Young Turk from Tennessee who had joined the House in 1963, similarly witnessed "a gradual erosion of participation in the leadership group by Les." Hence, what observers saw was a party led predominantly by Ford and Laird.[5]

Ford and Laird were an impressive match. The two had first met in 1948, when Laird was a state senator. Ford referred to the Wisconsinite as an excellent planner, "an idea man" who had "a long-range view of what's going to happen, and knows what he wants to do." Their temperament could not have been more unalike. Ford was patient, listening to all sides before pursuing a course of action. He made sure, recalled Representative Bob Dole (R-Kans.), that "his door was always open. You didn't have to get an appointment, you'd just walk in if he wasn't busy." Consequently, he successfully courted representatives of each of the GOP's wings, including liberals who had feared he planned to move the party in a more conservative direction. Laird was restive, determined to move ideas into policy proposals as quickly as possible. "You had to kick him in the ass usually to get him to do anything," Laird later said of Ford. "You had to keep prodding him to meet with the newspaper people to tell them about our alternatives, to sell our programs." What to Ford was cautious consideration of alternatives was to Laird a lack of vision: "Jerry doesn't catch on as rapidly as he should to the political significance of an event or issue. Once he understands it, there's no problem—but it does take him time." Despite their differences, and some intraparty speculation that Laird might one day do to Ford what Ford did to Halleck, the two men shared respect and confidence in the other.[6]

The new GOP leadership was seeking to refashion the party's image. As Ford put it, "We simply had no right to shout 'No, no, no' unless we had come up with better solutions to the problems at hand." Furthermore, he wanted to dissociate Republicans from the conservative coalition with southern Democrats. Although Republicans tended to agree with southern Democrats on matters relating to the economy and the size of government, members of the GOP tended to hold more progressive views regarding race. More broadly, Ford wanted to avoid the impression that his party was in any way beholden to southerners from across the aisle. What he favored was an unconstrained GOP that remained true to its pro–free enterprise, pro–limited government, pro–states' rights values as it sought to cure the nation's ills, even if that at times meant endorsing the initiatives of the Johnson administration. Indeed, he admitted that in promoting the Republican agenda, "it was necessary to have some Liberals" side with the GOP.[7]

Hence, within a matter of months, Ford appeared to have it all. He had become minority leader, had removed or at least sidelined Goldwater's allies, and had surrounded himself with a coterie of legislators ready to move the party down a moderate path that, it believed, could repair the damage done to Republicans in 1964. His position in the House guaranteed him more media attention than before, and the "Ev and Charlie Show," now renamed the "Ev and Jerry Show," further got his name before voters. He was still a lackluster speaker, but he had a reputation among journalists for getting right to the point and for speaking with them cordially. At home, he was unbeatable. "Jerry Ford," commented the *Grand Rapids Press*'s Neil

Munro, "is one of those rare politicians who has lived the Great American Success Story": football star, lawyer, veteran, and a politician who had become minority leader. "And he hasn't let his political fences sag. He has the reputation in Grand Rapids of being a man who does his political homework and knows the problems of his constituents," one who "annually makes the rounds in his mobile-home office" and who made each person he spoke with feel that that individual's "problem is the only one [he] has to worry about in Washington." Indeed, Ford responded to all sorts of letters, from adults and children, ranging from matters of public policy to issues of employment and adoptions and even information on geraniums, and he personally signed each letter. He matched his work ethic with a regimen that included laps in his pool, a game of golf when possible, an occasional drink, a pipe, and an annual visit with his family to the ski slopes at Vail, Colorado. Physically, the 198-pound, 6-foot-tall Ford looked like a man substantially younger than his fifty-three years.[8] He seemed fit, happy, and ready to make a strong run at the speakership of the House in 1966.

Ford's ambitions, however, continued to take their toll on his family, especially Betty. He continued to be an absent husband and father, admitting years later, "As Minority Leader, I was making about two hundred speeches a year, most of them out of town. Still, I thought they were in a worthy cause," because events by then had led him to believe that he and his party could win the House and he himself, the long-desired speakership. Betty loved her husband and regarded her marriage and children as more important than her own well-being. Underneath, though, she was fighting a sense of abandonment and a lack of "self-worth." She was already addicted to alcohol and painkillers. The pressure became so much that in 1965 she suffered a mental breakdown. When Susan found her mother crying uncontrollably, she called on the family housekeeper, Clara Powell, who immediately contacted Jerry. At the time, the minority leader was meeting with President Johnson and members of Congress about the Vietnam War; he rushed home, where he found a doctor tending to his wife. Even Betty recognized she needed psychiatric help. "[I] felt as though I were doing everything for everyone else, and I was not getting any attention at all," she later wrote. "Up until then," she added, she had not wanted to tell her husband about her physical and mental anguish, for "I'd thought I should be strong enough to shoulder my own burdens, not carry them to somebody else." Jerry promised to do whatever was necessary, including traveling with her to the psychiatrist. She replied that she wanted to go on her own, and she responded well to the twice-weekly treatment. She remembered the doctor telling her "to take time out to do some things for myself. . . . I had to believe that I was important, and that if I went to pieces I wouldn't be of much value to Jerry or the children." Secretly, however, she continued abusing alcohol.[9]

Guns . . .

Assuming all was well now at home, Ford returned to his workaholic ways in his quest to become House speaker. He had two goals. First, he continued to seek a bipartisan consensus on defeating communism. Second, he sought to limit federal domestic spending. With regard to the former, he focused increasingly on the Vietnam War. Although Johnson denied during the 1964 presidential campaign that he had any intention of sending U.S. combat troops to Vietnam, the Gulf of Tonkin Resolution had given him that authority. Moreover, he regarded the conflict in Southeast Asia as a test of American will. In language reminiscent of the domino theory, Johnson had said in 1947 that "human experience teaches me that if I let a bully of my community make me travel the back streets to avoid a fight, I merely postpone the evil day. Soon he will try to chase me out of my house."[10]

Johnson cashed in the blank check afforded him by the Tonkin resolution after the Viet Cong attacked a U.S. air base at Pleiku, South Vietnam, in February 1965, killing nine Americans. The president retaliated by authorizing Operation Rolling Thunder, a program of air attacks on the North. He also ordered 3,500 U.S. marines to defend the U.S. air base at Danang. The commander of the U.S. Military Assistance Command, Vietnam—General William Westmoreland—argued it was not enough. The result was a gradual increase in the number of U.S. troops in the South, which reached 184,000 by the end of 1965 and 385,000 as 1966 came to a close.[11]

Despite the widening commitment, the White House was confident. It assumed a limited war could stop the North's offensive and allow U.S. troops to come home by the middle of 1967. According to a Lou Harris poll, 65 percent of Americans endorsed what Johnson was doing, and a September *Washington Post* survey reported that 75 percent of respondents wanted the president "to hold the line or carry the war north." Lawmakers reflected that sentiment, rapidly endorsing Johnson's request in May for $700 million to pay for America's military activities in Vietnam. "If we as a legislative body are to err in providing military hardware for those who are serving on the frontlines for the defense of freedom and our own country," Ford told his House colleagues, "we should err on the side of generosity." Such language displeased what was then a small but growing antiwar movement, particularly among college students. Ford saw the antiwar movement as no different from those who had tried to appease Adolf Hitler in the months prior to World War II. "We should warn the young people of the serious consequences," he commented, "if their demonstrations and their irresponsible actions do lead to miscalculation on the part of the Communist[s], whether in the Kremlin or Peiping."[12]

Though Ford agreed with Johnson on combating communism in Vietnam, he did not accept the president's tactics. He recalled his own military experience as well as events at Dien Bien Phu in 1954, when the French had asked the United States for help against the Viet Minh. President Dwight D. Eisenhower had offered only air power, preferring to leave it up to Washington's allies to provide ground forces. Now, in 1965, Ford echoed Eisenhower, urging the White House to avoid miring U.S. ground troops in a war in Southeast Asia. Rather, Ford and Laird convinced the Republican Coordinating Committee (RCC)—which included all members of the party in Congress, the Republican governors, and those who might seek the presidency—that the United States should make "maximum use" of its air and naval power against the North.[13]

To Ford's chagrin, Johnson adopted a different course. He used the draft to raise the requisite forces and, not wanting to create a replay of the Korean War by provoking a Soviet or Chinese military response,[14] kept a tight rein on the bombing campaign. He rejected requests from the Joint Chiefs of Staff (JCS) to hit industrial and petroleum facilities in the North Vietnamese cities of Hanoi and Haiphong. Receiving word from Moscow that Hanoi might talk if the bombing stopped, Johnson agreed in late 1965 to a bombing pause. Ford did not outwardly criticize the pause in the aerial assault, but he was happy to see it resume in early 1966 after the North refused to come to the negotiating table. In a white paper entitled "Vietnam: Some Neglected Aspects of the Historical Record," House Republicans expressed their criticism of the administration's handling of the war, charging both John F. Kennedy and Johnson with sending mixed signals to the Communists in Vietnam. The report drew an angry retort from the president, who suggested the GOP "was playing politics with national security." Ford refused to back down, telling reporters, "We shouldn't be muzzled. We shouldn't be smothered. We shouldn't be muted."[15]

It is too simplistic, however, to depict the executive-legislative spat on Vietnam as one between the president and a unified Republican Party. Oregon's liberal Republican governor, Mark Hatfield, called for a negotiated settlement in Vietnam, while Dirksen, who was a good friend of the president's, favored giving Johnson wide latitude in prosecuting the war. "Let us be crystal clear," Dirksen commented. "Viet Nam is not our war. But we pledged ourselves to help a small nation. Our word was given. We are there to keep our word."[16]

Ford had no intention of permitting his differences with fellow Republicans to divert him from challenging Johnson's handling of the Communist threat. He thought that events in the Dominican Republic, where a military coup had overthrown a reformist government led by Juan Bosch, were part of communism's drive for world domination. Bosch's supporters rose up against the new regime, leading to a civil war. The leftist leanings of those who backed Bosch convinced the Johnson administration that Communists were behind the insurrection, and in April 1965, the president sent 20,000 U.S. troops to that country.

Although Ford stood behind Johnson's dispatch of combat forces to the Dominican Republic, he continued to believe that the real threat was Fidel Castro. "We will not prevent this arsonist," Ford remarked, "this fire starter, from creating one problem after another, until we prevent his exporting communism to other nations in the Caribbean." He voted for a resolution introduced in September that endorsed any action the president might take "to prevent in a timely manner Communist subversion in the hemisphere," yet he expressed the reservation that "those of us on the minority side of the aisle must reserve independent judgment as to the precise way in which the challenge to subversion is undertaken."[17]

Johnson's Panama policy was also disconcerting to Ford. Following the unrest in that country in 1964, the president had agreed to "review every issue which now divides" the two countries and indicated a willingness to revise the 1903 treaty that had granted the United States control of the Canal Zone. Negotiations with the Panamanians began later that year. Ford told a constituent that while the Constitution prohibited the House of Representatives from voting on any agreement signed with Panama, "no revision of the treaty should in any way impair the interests of the United States."[18]

. . . and Butter

Ford was even more critical of the Great Society than he was of Johnson's foreign policy. For conservatives, the president's domestic program was another example of government waste that, like the New Deal and the Fair Deal, made Americans rely on the federal dole. It also meant too much intrusion by Washington into Americans' lives. "A government big enough to give us everything we wanted," Ford later wrote, "would also be big enough to take away from us everything we had." This is not to say he rejected every Great Society program. Having been raised in an impoverished part of Texas, President Johnson wanted to see that everyone had the opportunity to receive a good education as a first step toward a better life. In March, the House passed the Elementary and Secondary Education Act (ESEA) to provide money to schools in poor districts of the nation. Ford backed the legislation, having voted earlier in favor of the National Defense Education Act in 1958 and the 1963 Higher Education Facilities Act, which offered federal aid to build or improve academic buildings at colleges and universities. The minority leader charged that Democrats had refused to permit a full debate on the ESEA, but he joined the 268 members who voted for it. The Senate followed suit the next month,[19] and the act became law.

Of Johnson's Great Society proposals in 1965, one that Ford particularly criticized was Medicare. In April the House voted 313–115 in favor of the plan's creation. Ford was among the 115, denouncing "the regressive payroll tax methods of financing hospital care for the aged." The Senate followed with its endorsement, and the bill went to a House-Senate conference committee before being reported to both houses of Congress. Ford joined the 116 representatives who voted against the conference bill, but 307 others endorsed it in the House, followed by a majority in the Senate, and Medicare became law in July. That same month, Ford was among the minority who voted against $1.9 billion for the Office of Economic Opportunity, which oversaw the War on Poverty.[20]

Ford also registered differences with Johnson's civil rights legislation. Despite the Civil Rights Act of 1964, African Americans in the South had continued to face restrictions on their right to vote. Continued violence in that part of the country against blacks, including police use on 7 March of tear gas and batons against peaceful protestors in Selma, Alabama, forced the president's hand. A week after the upheaval in Selma, Johnson submitted to Congress a Voting Rights Bill of 1965. Efforts by southern senators to weaken the measure failed, and the legislation went to the House in May.

Sharing the disgust at what had happened in Alabama, Ford had wanted Johnson to "take immediate steps to protect the basic rights of our citizens." However, he disliked the administration's bill, for it focused only on the southern states and stepped too much, in his view, on states' rights. What he and other Republicans favored was an alternative that would endorse civil rights while not treating the South too harshly. Ford therefore cosponsored with William McCulloch (R-Ohio) a substitute that applied to all states and authorized the use of federal examiners only after twenty-five or more people in a district complained. William Tuck (D-Va.) urged those who opposed civil rights to vote for the Ford-McCulloch substitute. Not wanting to be seen as endorsing discrimination, Ford joined numerous Republicans and the majority of Democrats in voting 215–166 against the very bill he had originally cosponsored and for the White House's legislation, which passed overwhelmingly in July.[21]

Ford's willingness to support civil rights did not extend to the growing radicalization and militarization taking place within that movement. It was a trend that dismayed many Americans, including civil rights activists such as Martin Luther King Jr., who had always encouraged the use of civil disobedience as the means to achieve equal rights. More and more blacks, believing that civil disobedience had failed to break down the barriers to equality, proposed more-aggressive methods, including the use of violence. One such was Malcolm X, who referred to the March on Washington as the "Farce on Washington." Another, Stokely Carmichael, coined the term "Black Power," which many whites associated with violence. When a white police officer arrested a black man in Watts, a predominantly African American neighborhood of Los Angeles, on suspicion of drunken driving, blacks took to the streets and rioted for five days. The violence came to an end only after the arrival of 16,000 police officers and National Guardsmen.

Prentiss Walker, a Mississippi Republican, blamed the Watts Riot on the Great Society's failure to make good on its promises of help for minorities. Appearing on *Face the Nation* shortly thereafter, Ford refused to go that far, but he did state that the solution to such disorder was jobs and education for African Americans. He also blamed a "radical element" in the civil rights movement for the unrest. His comments elicited a mixed reaction from viewers, with some approving of his "forthright and intelligent reaction" and others charging him with not taking a firm, antiadministration stand. In one particularly racist rant, a woman from Michigan called for sending blacks "back to Africa[,] spend the money we are spending for illegitimate children and those who refuse to work. We have them, many of them, and send them back."[22]

Republicans came to see the Watts Riot and, more generally, a rising crime rate as something they could attribute to the Democrats. Criminal activity had increased during the 1950s, but not until Barry Goldwater made it an issue during his 1964 presidential bid did it draw national attention. In response, in March 1965 Johnson announced a "war on crime" and in the summer established a commission headed by Attorney General Nicholas Katzenbach to understand what led to lawbreaking and to look at how the police and courts tried to prevent it. But Johnson thought that the key was to eliminate the conditions that bred crime in the first place and that the answer there was the Great Society. It would attack lawbreaking's "root causes" by providing employment, education, and the expectation of a better tomorrow. Conservatives mocked that solution, favoring a crackdown and jail for those who broke the law. Ford, whose views on combating crime were as hawkish as his views on winning the war in Vietnam, questioned "a soft social theory" that held that "the man who heaves a brick through your window or tosses a firebomb into your car is simply the misunderstood and underprivileged product of a broken home."[23] It was a difference of opinion that those to the right of center continued to play on through the remainder of Johnson's term.

Fine-Tuning the Message

Johnson's legislative victories were proof to Robert Hartmann that Republicans had to work harder to win in 1966. On Laird's suggestion, Ford had appointed Hartmann as his chief speechwriter. Prior to World War II, he had worked for the *Los Angeles Times*. After serving in the navy during the war, he returned to the *Times*, eventually landing a position as the newspaper's Washington Bureau chief. Stocky and hard-headed, Hartmann was as suspicious of others as Ford was trusting, and he had a reputation of rubbing others the wrong way. "The fact is he's just plain damned offensive," said one Ford associate. He was also highly intelligent and capable of writing a good speech, which could help a minority leader not known for giving inspiring speeches or for having big visions. As Hartmann put it, "Ford was not inarticulate. He was very intelligent, but almost tone-deaf to a felicitous combination of words. . . . He was better at talking specifics than concepts." Additionally, he added, "to get the flow of words right so that anyone would remember what he said, he had to work at it, all the time." As Ford's speechwriter he was able to produce addresses that espoused common sense in simple phraseology. Ford was impressed enough with his new aide that he also began to use him as a political adviser.[24]

In March 1966 Hartmann wrote a lengthy memo to his boss detailing a path to the House speakership. He suspected the public and press wanted Republicans to do "political battle" with the Democrats. To do so, he asked for daily meetings with Ford and to use a news ticker and Xerox machine to keep track of events and to disseminate the party's message. Through such forums as responses to the president's State of the Union addresses and press conferences, that message would focus on "a very few political priorities," among them Vietnam, inflation, taxes, and credibility. The GOP could also engage in "covert political warfare" similar to the Democrats' use of the charge of a "missile gap" during the Eisenhower years. "Terrific," Ford wrote at the end of the memo. "This is what we needed and more of. Talk with me pronto."[25]

Ford was optimistic of success in 1966, for as the year progressed, Johnson became politically weaker. The president still refused to discuss openly the war's escalation. While increases in federal spending on the war and on the Great Society had so far generated strong economic growth without inflation, some economists (and even some of Johnson's own advisers) began to warn by the end of 1965 that higher prices were likely. The president himself had started quietly to look into wage and price controls as a way to curb inflation. Even Senate Majority Leader Mike Mansfield (D-Mont.) and Harry McPherson, one of Johnson's aides, urged him to cut back on new legislative initiatives. The president knew Mansfield and McPherson had a valid point. Saying that he could no longer vigorously pursue the Great Society, however, would infuriate liberals. Rather, he wanted to reassure Americans from all political spectra that it was possible to fund both guns and butter, without raising taxes. Hence, in his 1966 State of the Union address, he admitted that Vietnam needed to become America's key concern; he could not achieve all he wanted at home. By improving government efficiency, restraining inflation, avoiding labor unrest, and continuing an exceptionally high rate of economic growth, the nation could still achieve the Great Society.[26]

Johnson was wrong on all fronts. Relying heavily on statistics to determine how the war was going, including the infamous "body count," the White House assured voters that the nation was on the road to victory in Vietnam. But as 1966 progressed and the United States appeared no closer to ending the war, polls found a growing number of Americans questioning the president's handling of it. The Great Society was not doing much better. During the year, Congress passed 97 of the 113 bills related to Johnson's domestic program, but only two matched the importance of such legislation as Medicare and the Voting Rights Act: the creation of a new Department of Transportation to make travel safer and to oversee and improve the nation's transportation infrastructure, and a "Model Cities" program that would attempt to prevent another Watts Riot by sending federal money to rundown urban areas. That Model Cities passed by a relatively close vote—with Ford among those opposed—and at a time when most members of Congress were away campaigning was an indication of how little excitement it generated. Furthermore, the influx of dollars into the economy thanks to Vietnam and the Great Society began to push up both inflation and the deficit.[27]

Throughout, Johnson refused to acknowledge what had become apparent to Americans: that he had begun to restrain spending on antipoverty programs in the hopes of holding down the deficit and inflation. The disconnect between what the White House said about Vietnam and the Great Society and what the evidence suggested took its toll on the president's popularity. His approval rating by the spring of 1966 had fallen to below 50 percent, and charges of a "credibility gap" became increasingly commonplace.

Taking advantage of Johnson's weakness and Hartmann's blueprint, Republicans went on the attack. Who thought of the idea of responding to Johnson's State of the Union speeches is unclear,[28] but the first of the rejoinders appeared before Hartmann wrote his March 1966 memo. Two months earlier, Ford and Dirksen had received a half hour of TV time on the three major networks to deliver their own "State of the Union" address. Speaking before about 100 GOP lawmakers and their spouses, Dirksen spoke predominantly about Vietnam, endorsing the Johnson administration's effort to achieve victory there. Turning his attention to the home front, Ford rejected any idea of taxing Americans to pay for Vietnam and the Great Society. Rather, he said, it was possible to finance the war if the White House got rid of "'low priority' domestic programs," such as the War on Poverty, which he said was full of "waste, controversy, and the bad odor of political bossism."[29]

The Republican leaders' statements, though, set the stage for more spats between them. Ford's remarks received acclaim; not a single hand clapped for Dirksen. "There I was waiting for the chance to applaud," said an unnamed Republican senator from New England, "and I'll be damned if I could hear one thing Ev said that was worth applauding." On the Ev and Jerry Show in April, Ford charged the White House with "shocking mismanagement" of the war. The Pentagon, he announced, lacked merchant vessels, had not provided the U.S. military in Vietnam with enough bombs, and had done poor logistical planning, at the cost of additional American lives. "What mismanagement?" asked Dirksen afterward. "I don't know that there has been shocking mismanagement. I don't deliver a judgment like that unless I have some very hard facts." An acknowledgment from Defense Secretary Robert McNamara that the Defense Department had purchased back from U.S. allies bombs it had sold them and an RCC report that the Soviets had more and newer merchant ships than the United States appeared to give salience to Ford's statements and forced Dirksen to backtrack. "Jerry's followed this thing a lot more closely than I have," said the senator, "and he has a lot more information."[30]

The Ford-Dirksen quarrel continued after Johnson made another go at peace, pledging to support Saigon but telling Hanoi that if it withdrew its troops from the South, the United States would follow suit within six months. Ford called the overture a "gimmick," one aimed at courting votes for Democrats in the next month's election. Another white paper critical of the administration infuriated Dirksen even more. The continued intraparty bickering between the two minority leaders left many in the GOP troubled. "We have to learn to live with it," replied Ford.[31]

Notwithstanding his disagreement with Dirksen, Ford had no intention of dropping his criticism of Johnson's handling of the war. If anything, the minority leader intensified his opposition. Adopting Hartmann's recommendation of developing some key themes, Ford began to focus on prestige. Few nations, including many of Washington's closest allies, supported America's military involvement in Vietnam, wrote Hartmann in July. Public-opinion polling showed that Americans believed international respect for their country was falling. But what made prestige particularly useful, he penned, was that if the war turned in America's favor—which would benefit the Johnson administration and the Democratic Party—Republicans could still contend that because of "his preoccupation with a tiny peninsula in Southeast Asia, LBJ has let the U.S. position of leadership in the rest of the Free World go to pot." In October, Ford used similar language. Others in the party followed suit. Senator Thruston Morton of Kentucky reported that polling in five Western European nations found that a plurality of respondents concluded that the world was farther from peace thanks to Johnson's policies. Even fewer believed U.S. prestige since the early 1950s had risen more under Johnson than during the Eisenhower or Kennedy presidencies.[32]

Ford also challenged the president's proposal in October 1966 to improve superpower ties. Although Richard Nixon is oftentimes credited with the establishment of détente between the United States and Soviet Union, its germination began under Johnson, who thought better relations between Washington and Moscow might lead the Kremlin to force Hanoi to discuss peace. Consequently, the president curbed long-standing restrictions on commerce with the Soviet Union and sought to augment cultural contacts. Ford rejected such revisions to America's Soviet policy, asserting it would "result in Communist encouragement, growth and enrichment." Likewise, he remained suspicious of the ongoing nuclear nonproliferation talks with the Kremlin. Any treaty that resulted from those meetings, he averred, had to offer "bonafide, legitimate inspection" to make sure Moscow did not cheat.[33]

Like a growing number of Americans, Ford also questioned how forthcoming the president had been about peace in Vietnam. He stated that Johnson had not been "candid" when he claimed in 1965 that Hanoi had shown no interest in a peace agreement. What the GOP's Planning and Research Committee had discovered, declared the minority leader, was that in 1964 the White House had passed on a "peace feeler" from the North arranged by UN Secretary General U Thant. In making this claim, Ford was being disingenuous. In light of the differences between them on key issues, particularly that of South Vietnam's independence, a peace agreement between Hanoi and Washington was highly unlikely. Additionally, at the time Johnson was in the midst of his presidential campaign, and he had no intention of incurring the wrath of voters and lawmakers, who would use the talks to charge him with abandoning the South.[34] But for a public questioning the administration's credibility, Ford's charge had the potential to resonate come the 1966 midterms.

Members of the GOP tied the credibility gap to a new message, one that *Atlantic* magazine credited Ford and Laird with being among the first to elucidate: the slogan "guns versus butter." Quite simply, they turned against Johnson his unwillingness to be straight with the American people about how he planned to pay for Vietnam and the Great Society without raising taxes or accepting a large deficit. Whereas President Harry Truman's motto had been "The buck stops here!," said the minority leader, Johnson's was "Slip, slide and pass the buck!" Ford also accused Johnson of wanting a Congress that would rubber-stamp whatever came out of the Oval Office. When confronted with queries about his initiatives, he continued, the president's fallback was to play fast and loose with the numbers. For instance, the administration claimed in March that unemployment had fallen by nearly 4 percent, but the key reason was that hundreds of thousands of men who might have looked for jobs at home had instead been drafted into the military. Moreover, the Great Society was poorly managed and unnecessarily expensive. The Head Start program was "moderately successful despite administrative bungling but that program threatens now to grind to a halt"; Job Corps was much more fiscally wasteful. Meanwhile, inflation had started to rise. "Food prices have climbed 3.7 percent in one year," Ford commented in February 1966. "The housewife's $10 in 1961 now buys only $9.14 at the grocery store." When, in September, the president announced inflation-cutting measures, including reductions in federal spending "to the fullest extent consistent with the well-being of our people," Ford called it too little, too late.[35]

So what was the solution to the guns-versus-butter conundrum? One was increasing income taxes. Johnson remained convinced it was unnecessary. Ford was equally certain that the president was biding his time and would ask for one after the election. Despite his own opposition to a tax hike, he was prepared to accept one if necessary to win in Vietnam. Even then, he worried that raising taxes would ultimately cause serious harm to the economy. Borrowing more money was another option, but as Dirksen pointed out, the United States was already paying $13 billion in interest annually on the debt. This left what Ford regarded as the best alternative, that of reducing "nonmilitary, nonessential spending," such as spending for antipoverty programs. In so doing, the country could stop the Communists in Vietnam and simultaneously hold down inflation.[36]

Republicans realized that an attack on the Great Society by way of spending cuts could cost them politically, so in 1966 they came up with a solution, called the "Opportunity Crusade," a term that Vice President Hubert Humphrey had ironically suggested to Johnson as an alternate moniker for the Great Society. The Opportunity Crusade would take the keystone of the Great Society, the War on Poverty, out of the hands of the federal government and have state and local governments oversee the effort. It would also generate more money, said the GOP, with the funds coming predominantly from state and local officials, and especially from the business sector.[37]

Johnson realized he was in trouble. Republicans and Democrats might disagree over the Vietnam War, but he alone had to take the blame for America's failure to bring an end to that conflict. Paying for Vietnam and the Great Society had begun to push up inflation, which could wreak havoc on the economy. Apathy and anger with Johnson's handling of the economy convinced political observers that Republicans were likely to gain seats in Congress. Johnson feared that the GOP could win as many as sixty seats in the House and eight in the Senate. Dirksen anticipated seventy-five in the House, while Ford expected forty.[38]

As usual, Ford used both the media and stump speeches in his home district. Knowing his seat was safe, however, he took to the road to campaign for other Republicans, giving hundreds of speeches and traveling 58,000 miles during the first six months of 1966. Cognizant of complaints regard-

Representative Gerald R. Ford, Senator Everett M. Dirksen, Ray Bliss, and Thruston Morton watch election returns, 8 November 1966. Photo in the Gerald Ford Library, Ann Arbor, Michigan.

ing the amount of time he spent on the road, wrote one Grand Rapids reporter, Ford "whip[ped] out a card with figures to show his rollcalls and votes: 88.5 percent for the first session of Congress, 87.3 for this one." Ford easily won reelection,[39] and the overall outcome for the GOP was slightly better than he had anticipated. Republicans gained 47 seats in the House, giving them a total of 187; in the Senate, they won 3, bringing their number up to 36. Republicans were still a minority, and Ford remained minority leader, but the outcome suggested that Johnson's problems and the GOP's message had resonated at the voting booth.

'68 on His Mind

The news for Johnson only got worse over the next two years. The hope for an end to the war by mid-1967 proved ill-founded. Spending on the conflict continued to go up, as did the number of troops who went to Vietnam and of those who came home in body bags. Support for the war continued to flag. Senator Robert Kennedy (D-N.Y.), the brother of the slain president, joined those who called for an end to the fighting. A "dump Johnson" movement emerged in the summer among liberals who hoped for someone within the Democratic Party to run against the president in 1968. Antiwar protests continued and grew increasingly violent. One, held in Washington in October 1967, drew some 100,000 people and ended with federal officers using tear gas and batons against the protestors.[40]

The antiwar protests exemplified a breakdown of the Cold War consensus that communism posed a threat to the United States. They also were one facet of a growing sense that the country was falling apart. Counterculturalists rejected societal norms in favor of drugs, rock music, "free love," and a communal lifestyle. Militants in the civil rights movement, among them Carmichael, H. Rap Brown, and Huey Newton, made news for advocating the use of violence or, in the case of Newton, participating in a shootout with police that left one officer dead. Predominantly minority-populated and impoverished neighborhoods in Newark and Detroit witnessed rioting similar to the one that had taken place in Watts. The unrest, alongside the machinations of Carmichael, Brown, and Newton, further turned whites against the civil rights movement and gave the impression to a significant segment of the voting public that there was a connection between color and crime. By mid-August, Johnson's approval rating had fallen to 39 percent, its lowest point yet.[41]

The president realized he had to be more honest with voters about guns and butter. In his January 1967 State of the Union speech, he pointed to numerous accomplishments, but he made clear that he had no intention of pushing the Great Society with the vigor he had previously. The theme was no longer expansion of the Great Society or the federal government's assumption of responsibility for helping those in need; now it was taking what already existed and making it better in cooperation with local and state officials. Johnson's rhetoric on Vietnam changed as well. The anticommunist tone of previous State of the Union speeches disappeared. While committed to South Vietnam's independence, he indicated a preparedness to accept a coalition government in the South that would include members of the VC. He estimated a $126.7 billion budget for FY 1967. To help cover it, he asked for a two-year, 6 percent hike in personal and corporate income taxes—exempting single people with an annual income of $1,900 or less and married couples with children who made less than $5,000.[42]

Johnson's curatives pleased neither Republicans nor southern Democrats. In their State of the Union response, Dirksen continued to demand "a hard-line on Vietnam," while Ford again called for the president to curtail domestic spending and to rely more heavily on the private sector. As the year wore on, even Johnson realized his solutions were not enough. The White House estimated it could expect a $29 billion deficit for the 1968 fiscal year. In August, the president asked for another tax increase of 4 percent (for a total of 10 percent). The new taxes were opposed by 85 percent of Americans, and nearly 75 percent preferred reductions in government spending. The president's approval rating, which had received a boost because of his candor in January, sank to 40 percent in September, 8 points higher than the number of Americans who endorsed his job performance. Southern Democrats in Congress joined the critics, with both Representative Wilbur Mills of Arkansas and Senator Russell Long of Louisiana questioning the need for more taxes. Knowing any tax bill would have to come through the Ways and Means Committee, which he chaired, Mills made clear he would support a tax increase only if Johnson matched it with cuts for Great Society initiatives.[43]

Ford could smell political blood in the water. The elections of 1968 were a little more than a year away, and in light of how well Hartmann's strategy had paid off in 1966, he saw no reason to change it. Throughout 1967, he challenged Johnson. The numbers the president offered in his State of the Union speech were "budgetary gimmickry"; the Great Society was "a runaway locomotive with a wild-eyed engineer at the throttle," one that cost enormous sums of money and had led to a "ruthless extension of federal authority, financing and control." The president needed not to raise taxes but to reduce nondefense spending, including on the War on Poverty. Trying to end the Vietnam conflict by curtailing restrictions on commerce with the Soviet Union was nothing less than self-deception. "Trade can be an instrument for world peace but only when applied to the hard-nosed tradition of the Yankee trader," he declared, "not with the soft-headed hope that it will somehow sway dedicated Communist governments from their stated international goals." Alongside the rest of the House and Senate GOP leadership, he endorsed a resolution introduced by Laird in March calling for making commerce with the Soviets contingent on "demonstrable evidence that their actions and policies with regard to Vietnam have been redirected toward peace and an honorable settlement."[44]

Ford launched his strongest attack on the president's conduct of the Vietnam War. In a lengthy address on the House floor in August, he challenged Johnson's call for higher taxes. "I believe everyone in this House would willingly vote any level of taxes and the American people would willingly pay them if they were convinced it would bring the Vietnam war to an end," but the White House refused to change its strategy or tactics, which had already cost the United States so dearly in both dollars and lives. It was time for Johnson to do what Ford had been trying to persuade him to do since 1965: unleash American naval and air power. Impose a naval blockade of the North and expand the air war further, he insisted. "Americans wonder why North Vietnam has not been totally destroyed," as had been the case with cities like Berlin and Tokyo during World War II. Then, using the refrain "Would the American people believe," he raised the credibility gap, charging the administration with denying the armed forces authority to hit military targets in the North. Nearing the end of his remarks, he proclaimed, "I for one am running short of patience. . . . I believe that ending the war in Vietnam must have the very highest of national priorities, now. . . . Neither more men, nor more money, nor more material will do any good unless there is more will and more courage at the top."[45]

Ford was a hawk when it came to Vietnam, for the war there was part of the broader effort to contain communism. His speech, though, was meant to appeal to both hawks and doves. By using World War II as a reference point, he sought to remind those voters who wanted to prosecute the war to its end of their country's history of military victory. His strategy, he assured them, would guarantee yet another success over America's enemies. Simultaneously, he sought to convince those who wanted to see the conflict come to an end that he shared their desire.

Yet it was a speech with a number of flaws. First, comparing North Vietnam to the Axis powers of World War II was a false analogy. North Vietnam's industrial and transportation infrastructure was nothing like that of Germany, Japan, or Italy. While it had a few paved roads and railroads and some industry, the North was a predominantly agricultural nation, linked together by a network of dirt roads and paths dug through its thick jungles.

Furthermore, Ford's formula risked widening the war rather than ending it. Johnson had authorized the U.S. military to hit 95 percent of targets in the North. The remainder were off-limits because of their proximity to civilian homes or the Chinese border. Removing those restrictions, and imposing a naval blockade, could lead to disaster. "What happens when Soviet ships bringing supplies to Haiphong are intercepted by our warships?," asked the *New York Times*'s James Reston. If those vessels did not turn around, "do we blow them out of the water?" And even if the blockade became effective, Moscow and Beijing would open up new land routes, requiring an expansion of the list of targets the United States would have to bomb.[46]

Even if the Soviets and Chinese respected the blockade, could another expansion of the air war do the damage necessary to bring Hanoi to the negotiating table? This was clearly Ford's assumption, and it was a highly dubious one. The Strategic Bombing Survey that had looked at the effectiveness of the Allied aerial campaign during World War II found that it had failed to destroy the military might of the Axis or to demoralize the people of Germany and Japan. Furthermore, the North Vietnamese had dug hundreds of miles of tunnels in which to hide or to transport goods, and they had a force of approximately 500,000 people (most of them women and children) whose job it was to repair bridges and railroads and to fill craters; they were assisted by members of the Chinese armed forces, whose numbers had reached 320,000 by 1968. Communist troops and supplies also entered South Vietnam by way of the Ho Chi Minh Trail, a logistical system that connected North and South Vietnam via the neighboring countries of Laos and Cambodia. The Chinese and Soviets continued to replace equipment lost. Much of the ammunition that did not come from the North's allies was produced in the South or captured from the ARVN. U.S. officials knew just how ineffective the widened air campaign was, admitting that North Vietnamese infiltration into the South rose nearly 300 percent between 1965 and 1967.[47]

Additionally, the minority leader ignored South Vietnam's political and military deficiencies. Its government was infused with corruption, and its army, which on paper stood at 800,000 men at the end of 1967—nearly 300,000 more than in 1965—was poorly commanded. U.S. officers complained that the ARVN did not fight well and were derelict in adopting American combat methods. Stated one U.S. soldier, "I am sure that if Saigon were left to fend for itself . . . in 20 years this place would be all rice paddies again." The ARVN's troubles meant U.S. troops assumed ever more of the burden of combat. Ford was aware of the problems. He admitted to reporters later that month that Americans wanted "the South Vietnamese army to do a better job than they have been doing in the last 2 or 3 years." Yet given the growing frustration within the United States over the war, he also knew it made political sense to fault President Johnson for America's troubles in Vietnam.[48]

Ford was mindful that not everyone in his party shared his solution to ending the war. Hatfield, who had just joined the U.S. Senate in January, told union workers in April that the White House "has lost the capacity" to win the war and that it was time to find a way to end it. Even Laird had begun to doubt the possibility of victory. In July, eight Republican lawmakers, led by Bradford Morse of Massachusetts, offered a five-step plan that would extricate the United States from Southeast Asia, starting with a sixty-day pause in bombing. Ford neither endorsed nor rejected the Morse proposal. "I feel if you are going to initiate a bombing pause program," he said on *Issues and Answers*, "the preferable way to do it is the plan suggested several weeks ago by Congressman Brad Morse, a Republican, and others, which would call for a step-by-step bombing pause. . . . This would, I think give [North Vietnam and the VC] and us an opportunity to show our good faith."[49]

Although Dirksen remained adamant that Republicans stand behind Johnson, widespread disagreement existed among Republicans over how best to disengage from Southeast Asia. Even those who questioned Johnson's conduct of the war still voted for money for the conflict: when Congress in March 1967 agreed to another $12.2 billion for Vietnam, only one Republican, Ohio's Charles Mosher, was in the "no" column. Finally, Ford and Laird reminded Dirksen that the presidential election was coming up, and the GOP should adopt its own position, even if it meant not following Johnson. Forced to stand down, in December Dirksen, in a joint news conference, joined Ford in implying that the Johnson administration could do more to reach a negotiated settlement in Vietnam.[50]

Ford's frustration with the Johnson administration extended beyond the Vietnam War. He was unhappy with the White House's handling of U.S. policy toward China. It was not just that Beijing was helping Hanoi. In 1964, China had tested its first nuclear weapon, making it the fifth country (after the United States, the Soviet Union, the United Kingdom, and France) to acquire the bomb, and in June 1967 it exploded its first hydrogen device. Those tests, proclaimed Ford, had "evidenced more rapid technological progress and greater sophistication than most U.S. experts had predicted." It was time, therefore, for Washington to proceed with deployment of an antiballistic missile (ABM) system as soon as possible, "which, the Defense Department estimates, might save millions or tens of millions of American lives." Unfortunately, Ford continued, the Johnson administration had refused to budget for one, permitting the Soviets time to develop their own and leaving the United States vulnerable to Chinese and/or Soviet nuclear assault. "Time, unlike money, cannot be recovered," said Ford. "Wasting time is therefore a far more serious matter than wasting funds." When McNamara announced in September that the United States would develop a limited ABM system called Sentinel, a pleased Ford pointed out that a Republican president would have made such a move sooner.[51]

And if U.S. military and diplomatic troubles were not enough to convince voters of the need for change, then affairs at home might. Antiwar protestors, already scorned by those who supported the war or who saw the demonstrators as spoiled middle-class brats, faced a new charge: they were at the very least Communist dupes, who encouraged the North Vietnamese and the Viet Cong to continue fighting. It was an indictment that came from the White House and members of Congress, including Ford. Speaking on the House floor in November, the minority leader announced that there was evidence that the October protest in Washington had been orchestrated by Americans who were in direct contact with North Vietnam (even if there was no solid proof of that). Other Republicans, such as Arends and Ohio's Frank Bow, seconded him. Democratic senator Frank Lausche of Ohio also drew attention to a "superior force" behind protests that had taken place in Indiana.[52]

Matching the growing opposition to the war was the unrest taking place in American cities, as witnessed by the riots in Detroit and Newark. Ford publicly reprimanded Johnson for taking too long to send federal troops to Detroit and accused the president of using the disorder to rap Congress for not doing more for the Great Society. The War on Poverty was not the solution to urban unrest, insisted Ford. It was the Opportunity Crusade and punishment for those who broke the law that would solve the problem. "When Rap Brown and Stokely Carmichael are allowed to run loose, to threaten law-abiding citizens with injury and death, it's time to slam the door on them and any like them, and slam it hard," he told reporters.[53]

Working with southern Democrats, Republicans in the House attacked key pieces of Johnson's domestic legislation. In January the president had asked for a Safe Streets and Crime Control Act that would outlaw the use of wiretapping and provide federal grants to the states via the office of the U.S. attorney general. Katzenbach's commission seemed to reinforce the need for a federally run effort, reporting in March that crime originated from "limited social and economic opportunities for the poor and for racial minorities." Its solutions included guaranteeing that such opportunities became available, making the criminal justice system fairer to those charged with lawbreaking, and using parole and probation rather than incarceration as the means of punishing offenders. Republicans and southern Democrats balked. They were upset with additional restrictions the U.S. Supreme Court had placed on law enforcement, among them the 1966 *Miranda v. Arizona* decision requiring police to inform a suspect that he or she had the right to remain silent and to have legal representation. Consequently, they took the money out of the hands of the executive branch and sent it directly to state governments. They also added a provision aimed at preventing riots like those that had taken place in Detroit and Newark. That same month, they altered another of Johnson's proposals, a new civil rights law, whose key clause banned discrimination in the sale or rental of any home nationwide. The president thought that open housing would remove a major cause of racial unrest. In a shot at militants in the civil rights movement, Republicans and southern Democrats added a rider suggested by James Wright (D-Tex.), that would criminalize any interstate activity designed to "incite violence." In August, Ford voted for both pieces of legislation,[54] neither of which the Senate had acted on prior to Congress's Christmas break.

About the only domestic issue on which Ford and Johnson saw eye-to-eye following the 1966 midterms was pollution control. More extensive use of coal as a power source had generated an increasing problem of smog, and it was in the 1950s that Los Angeles received the nickname "smog capital of America." In 1967, Ford joined the majority of lawmakers who voted for the Air Quality Act, the first federal bill to restrict emissions of lead from cars. Ironically, although the public liked the bill, many Americans were less than pleased that the changes to gasoline caused by the legislation affected the performance of their vehicles.[55]

As the year ended, Ford touted his party's accomplishments. Thanks to voters who had given him nearly four dozen more Republicans in the House and several more GOP senators, Congress had cut appropriation for initiatives unrelated to defense, passed an antiriot bill, and endorsed a clean-air act, among other pieces of legislation. This record was certain to please the growing number of Americans favoring reduced federal spending, tougher crime-prevention efforts, and environmental protection.[56] While he did not mention it, Ford believed his proposed route to victory in Vietnam might resonate as well among voters.

There were dangers for Republicans, though. Their record of joining forces with southern Democrats, who had a history of opposing civil rights legislation, suggested a lack of empathy for racial and ethnic minorities, if not outright racism. It would be wrong to call Ford a racist; he believed that all Americans, irrespective of creed, color, or ethnicity, could achieve the American dream if they applied themselves. What he rejected was the idea of relying on the government dole, which wasted taxpayer money and gave recipients no incentive for self-improvement. Furthermore, his desire to limit the power of the federal government convinced him that the promotion of civil rights should remain in the hands of the states. Ford's views, which had become increasingly mainstream as the 1960s progressed, set him apart from those who stressed that removing obstacles to equality required an active federal hand.

Not wanting to taint Republicans with charges of indifference or hatred toward nonwhites, Ford had declared upon becoming minority leader that the conservative coalition with southern Democrats needed to end. That is exactly what he did, commented the *National Review*, which also maintained that Ford wanted to portray southern Democrats as liberals who should be replaced with Republicans. Poppycock, wrote *Newsweek*'s Emmet John Hughes. Republicans' promise "to shun alliance in the House with southern Democrats has earned the kind of credibility that Laird commonly extends to Soviet peace proposals." Likewise, the *New York Times* editorialized, "The pattern of voting in the House of Representatives during the first session of the Ninetieth Congress reveals that the traditional coalition of Republicans and Southern Democrats has returned to power. . . . The alliance with the Southern Democrats has always been a practical comfort but a propagandistic concern for the House Republicans," for the latter had "to prove that the Southern tail was not wagging the Republican dog. . . . An identification with them can scarcely be helpful to the G.O.P. in the big cities and their suburbs, where the Presidency and most Senate seats are won or lost."[57] Ford certainly had to wonder what the undeclared partnership with southern Democrats meant for him and his party come 1968.

1968

The election year began like others. On 17 January, Johnson gave his State of the Union address, asking for $186 billion for FY 1968—$10 billion more than the previous year—to fund the war, combat crime and discrimination in housing, and help the poor, and he resubmitted his request for a 10 percent tax increase. He believed some of his proposals, such as open housing, would cost little and could elicit the endorsement of the private sector. Taking a page from the GOP, he asked U.S. business interests to do more to address poverty in the nation's cities. The hour-long GOP response included not just Ford and Dirksen but fifteen other conservative and moderate members of the GOP. According to the *New York Times*'s John Herbers, this was because of "complaints in the party's ranks that the Dirksen-Ford performances had little public appeal." Taking what Herbers referred to as a "tone . . . of toughness toward the administration, tougher than the Republicans have been in the recent past," Senator John Tower of Texas renewed the call for a naval blockade of Vietnam and lauded what he saw as the White House's greater determination to win in Vietnam. Ford called attention to the nation's growing crime problem, while Laird again pressed for the Opportunity Crusade. How effective the effort was is questionable. Tennessee senator Howard Baker argued that the Republicans' response played well in his home state. Yet both he and Goodell concluded that the party's representatives could have done a better job of presenting "a positive message" to the country.[58]

But 1968 became anything but a normal year. In January, North Korea seized the U.S. spy ship *Pueblo*. Johnson responded with a combination of a naval show of force and negotiations, though it took nearly a year of talks before the North Koreans released the *Pueblo*'s crew. Then came the Tet Offensive later that month. In February, disaffected voters nearly handed victory in the New Hampshire primary to the darling of the "dump Johnson" movement, Senator Eugene McCarthy of Minnesota. With the president clearly politically weak, Senator Robert Kennedy threw his hat into the ring. Realizing he stood virtually no chance of cinching the Democratic nomination, and concerned about his own health, Johnson announced on 31 March that he was withdrawing from the presidential race.

Four days later, Martin Luther King Jr. was assassinated. Rioting broke out throughout the nation. Johnson pressed lawmakers to finish passage of his civil rights bill, and the Senate agreed, but only after adding an antiriot amendment directed at individuals such as Carmichael and Brown. Upon receiving the Senate version of the legislation, Ford played both sides of the coin. Along with the majority of Republicans and southern Democrats, he first asked to send it to a conference committee. When that failed, Ford voted for what became the 1968 Civil Rights Act. He had long opposed open housing, but in the highly charged atmosphere following King's death, he did not want to be seen as opposed to civil rights. Yet to court southerners, he made clear on the House floor that once Johnson submitted a request to pay for the bill, he and his fellow Republicans "will do everything we possibly can to prevent any funding whatsoever for those programs."[59]

Barely two months after King's assassination, a gunman took Robert Kennedy's life. The New York senator had appeared to be a shoo-in to win the Democratic nomination, having beaten McCarthy in all but one primary. Ford called the loss of Kennedy "a great tragedy in the history of the United States" and tied it to the national problem of crime: "Surely there are things that we must do in this legislative body to help avoid a recurrence of such an incident such as the immediate approval of the anti-crime bill which has been approved in different versions by both the House and Senate."[60]

Less than two weeks after Kennedy's death, Congress passed the Omnibus Crime Control and Safe Streets Act. The legislation was much unlike that which Johnson had favored. The Senate held fast to providing grants to the states, and appended riders permitting wiretapping—which represented a slap at Johnson—and barring the interstate shipment of handguns. The president disliked the provisions regarding grants and wiretapping, but the bill did offer funding to fight crime. Taking into account the politically charged environment following Kennedy's murder, the president signed the bill on 20 June. Ford was among those who voted for the bill. He was a strong supporter of the right to bear arms but believed that the restrictions on interstate shipments of handguns would prevent criminals from getting them.[61]

Johnson was also disappointed with congressional action on his 10 percent tax surcharge. Inflation had reached 6 percent, but a Gallup survey found that 79 percent of respondents opposed raising taxes to bring down prices. A plurality preferred a wage-and-price freeze. Such numbers reinforced the determination of Mills, Ford, and others in the Republican–southern Democrat coalition to stand up to the president and demand that any increase in funding for the Vietnam War that came from a tax hike be met with cuts in domestic spending. In June, Congress endorsed the Revenue and Expenditure Control Act, which included the tax increase and called for $6 billion in domestic spending reductions; Ford was among those who voted for the bill, saying it was a needed step to control spending. Johnson was unhappy with Capitol Hill. Nevertheless, he believed that in the end lawmakers would in fact cut less than they had demanded. As it turned out, Congress ultimately reduced domestic spending by about half of what it had planned.[62]

As lawmakers debated on Capitol Hill, negotiations were underway in Paris to end the Vietnam War. To the White House's surprise, Hanoi had accepted the president's request for talks. Ford praised this turn of events but argued against a rapid withdrawal of the U.S. military presence in the South; doing so, he warned, would be analogous to the efforts of Neville Chamberlain, then Britain's prime minister, to appease Hitler a year before World War II began in Europe.[63]

Ford's determination to resist communism also continued to make him wary of Moscow. A reformist movement in the Soviet satellite nation of Czechoslovakia bred worries in the Soviet Union and other Eastern European nations that Prague intended to move away from communism and out of the Kremlin's orbit. In August, Soviet premier Leonid Brezhnev used military force to crush the reformists' efforts and reassert Moscow's authority, justifying his action on the grounds that as leader of the socialist world, the

Soviet Union had the right to intervene in the affairs of other socialist countries. The attack was proof, said Ford, "that the Soviet Union is unwilling to tolerate any evolution toward individual liberty in the countries of East and Central Europe, lest the yearning of man for freedom might infect various parts of the Soviet Union herself. It also shows that the Soviet Union is still not a law-abiding member of the international community." As evidence, he pointed to the Kremlin's machinations in the Middle East, telling a Jewish audience that Moscow posed a direct threat to America's regional ally Israel. The Soviets were no different from the Nazis, he commented, except that they wanted to "turn the Mediterranean into a Russian lake." Dangerous as well was the Soviets' nuclear missile program, which jeopardized America's military superiority over its Cold War rival.[64]

August was also the month of the two parties' national conventions. As the presidential campaign season began in earnest, four Republicans appeared as contenders for their party's nomination. Three were governors: California's Ronald Reagan, Michigan's George Romney, and New York's Nelson Rockefeller. The fourth was Richard Nixon. Rockefeller never officially declared his candidacy, and his liberal leanings drew him the enmity of conservatives. Reagan, a former Hollywood actor and a favorite of the Far Right, had made a name for himself by giving a rousing speech at the 1964 Republican National Convention and then winning California's top post in 1966. However, he had little appeal outside conservative ranks. Romney attracted moderates and seemed to have a strong chance at securing the nomination. In August 1967, though, he remarked that his previous support for the Vietnam War had been the result of "brainwashing." That comment, in the words of one historian, "mortally wounded his promising presidential campaign."[65]

This left Ford's longtime friend Nixon. For years, he had been in political exile. He had failed to win the presidency in 1960 or California's governorship in 1962. Afterward, he began to revitalize his political career. He moved from California to New York, where he made numerous political connections; courted the media—which he had long seen as an enemy; and traveled widely. In a well-received article he wrote for *Foreign Affairs* magazine in 1967, he said that the United States was "a Pacific power." But Vietnam had created enormous social, economic, and political tension in America and highlighted Washington's limited military resources in the region. Hence, the United States would have to rely more heavily on its allies to defend the West's interests there. Americans also had to come to grips with China's growing power, and he foresaw the possibility of negotiating with Beijing once its leaders realized the benefits of ending their country's isolationist policies. While Nixon stood behind the talks with North Vietnam and behind South Vietnam's independence, it was clear that he thought U.S. policy in the Far East needed to move in new directions. He wooed conservatives of all stripes, playing on the increasing distrust of liberalism—the Great Society and big government, higher taxes, the counterculture, overly lenient courts and coddled criminals, and radical antiwar protestors—and he asked for votes from "the silent center, the millions of people in the middle of the political spectrum who do not demonstrate, who do not picket or protest loudly" and who disliked "the ever-higher piling of Federal tax on state and local tax."[66]

Following in Barry Goldwater's footsteps, Nixon gave particular emphasis to what became known as his "southern strategy." Following the *Brown v. Board of Education* decision, southern school districts had decided to permit students to choose which school to attend rather than forcing them to go to an all-black or all-white institution. In 1968, the Supreme Court decided that such "freedom-of-choice" rules had failed to go far enough in promoting integration and called for seeking other methods to comply with *Brown*. The Court did not mention busing children to schools outside their districts, but that was one possibility. Nixon made clear that he did not condone the use of busing to achieve integration and derided interference by federal judges in local schools.[67] Having wide appeal and no serious challenge, Nixon won the party's nomination on the first ballot.

The question now was with whom he would share the ticket. Nixon made clear he intended to run a national campaign, so it was important that his choice be acceptable to as many voters as possible. Rhodes suggested Bob Griffin and Ford. Nixon asked the minority leader if he was interested, but Ford, believing that Republicans had an excellent shot at winning the House and that he would become speaker, declined. When Nixon asked Ford whom he might suggest, he offered the name of John Lindsay, New York City's mayor. Handsome, a good speaker, a member of the party's liberal wing, and a resident of a politically important state, Lindsay would offer a nice balance to the ticket. California's Robert Wilson seconded the suggestion.[68]

Nixon's solicitation of suggestions for a running mate, though, was simply pro forma, as he knew already whom he wanted. Rather than accept any of the names offered, Nixon selected Maryland governor Spiro Agnew. Originally from the party's liberal wing, Agnew had become more conservative, particularly on race. Because of that, he stood to draw southern support. He was also a political unknown, whose choice shocked many observers, including Ford. "I couldn't believe it," he later wrote. "Here was a man who had risen from total obscurity a few years earlier to become governor of a border state. . . . I shook my head in disbelief. This was the reaction of many of my House colleagues."[69]

Later that month, Democrats gathered to choose their nominee. McCarthy was still in the race, but his liberal, antiwar record was likely to turn both conservatives and moderates against him. Following Johnson's decision not to run, Vice President Humphrey had thrown his hat into the ring, and with Kennedy's assassination, he became the front-runner. But he had little support among rank-and-file Democrats. Opponents of the war and the Great Society charged that he was just another Lyndon Johnson. A newcomer to the race was George Wallace, the pro-segregationist former governor of Alabama who, knowing he had no chance to get the Democratic nomination, ran as the candidate for the American Independent Party. He hoped that he could take enough votes away from both the eventual Democratic nominee and Nixon to throw the race into the House of Representatives, where he and southerners could work together to scrap recent civil rights legislation.

The Democrats held their national convention in Chicago and selected Humphrey. Outside the convention hall, antiwar protestors railed against the party that they accused of miring the country in a deadly and unpopular war. Chicago's mayor, Richard Daley, who had no intention of allowing the demonstration to get out of hand, had prepared by putting the city's 12,000-man police force on duty and calling in 13,500 National Guardsmen and regular-army troops. Instead, violence reared its head, with police and National Guardsmen beating demonstrators, who fought back with fists. Ford blamed the turmoil on Daley and on the Democratic National Committee chairman, John Bailey, who he said "'gave the orders' that resulted in demonstrators, newsmen and convention delegates being beaten and manhandled."[70] For many viewers who watched it all on TV, the brawl was yet another example of the instability in the country and more evidence of the need for someone who would bring law and order back.

Election Day proved a mixed bag for Ford. Not wanting "to take sides" until he was sure who the candidate was and hopeful of becoming the Republican convention's permanent chairman, he held off endorsing Nixon until it was obvious the former vice president was going to get the nomination. Once that happened, he threw his resources behind Nixon, who helped make him the convention's permanent chair. In November, Nixon defeated Humphrey in a relatively close race, winning all the South (minus five states that went for Wallace) and virtually the entire Midwest and Far West. With one of their own in the Oval Office for the first time in eight years, Ford and Dirksen canceled the "Ev and Jerry Show."[71]

The congressional elections were a different story. Republicans had seemed poised to do well there too. The backlash against the Johnson administration and the Democratic Party had been good for the GOP's coffers. By mid-September the Republican House Campaign Committee had over $2 million on hand and was ready to spend anywhere from $10,000 to $15,000 in districts where it appeared the GOP had a chance of victory. As in 1966, Ford knew his seat was safe, so he spent much of 1968 on the road, traveling over 103,000 miles to twenty-seven states and giving 180 speeches to approximately 61,000 people. He told reporters that he expected Republicans to gain forty seats in the House, giving them a majority and Ford his long-desired speakership.[72] Instead, Republicans gained a mere five seats in the House, and the same number in the Senate, leaving them in the minority and Ford without the title of speaker.

Unrealized Dreams

Why did Republicans fail to gain control of the House? The minority leader cited several reasons: the split among Democrats at the national level did not affect state or district campaigns, Nixon's coattails proved short, it appeared the Vietnam War might be on the verge of ending, and Wallace might have had an impact on local races. How much an effect Wallace had is questionable. He took more votes from Humphrey than from Nixon. That said, the other two candidates adopted his law-and-order plank, thus taking that popular issue away from the Alabaman; Wallace's initial appeal to union workers dissipated when labor realized that his record as governor showed little concern for their interests; and his racism did not play well outside the South. Nixon indeed had short coattails. In 1960, he had campaigned in every state, which wore him out and contributed to his poor appearance in his first debate with John F. Kennedy. Not willing to make a similar mistake this time, the Republican candidate restricted his efforts to winning the same states he had taken in 1960, along with the eight largest industrial states. The Vietnam War also had an effect. The media began to report that a breakthrough was imminent in the talks to end the conflict, and a decision by the Johnson administration to halt the bombing on 31 October seemed to confirm that suspicion. The possibility the war was on the verge of ending gave Humphrey a large bump in the polls. (The Democrat's numbers, though, began to flag when Saigon refused to participate in any negotiations with Hanoi.) Finally, the vice president successfully retained the backing of the coalition that had supported Democrats since the 1930s. African Americans disliked Wallace and did not see Nixon as much better, unions fled Wallace for Humphrey, the poor liked what Johnson and the Democrats had tried to do for them, and urban voters, whose political views tended to be more liberal than those of people living in rural areas, stood behind the Democratic Party. Hence, while voters expressed a willingness to see new leadership in the White House, they had little desire to kick out the incumbents who had been representing them on Capitol Hill.[73]

Despite not getting the speakership, Ford could look forward both to an occupant in the Oval Office whom he considered a political ally and friend and to the end of what had been a difficult relationship with Johnson. It was not just that the two men had disagreed on so many political matters; it was also that their personalities were very dissimilar. Ford was thoughtful, considerate, and well liked, even by those who did not agree with his politics. Johnson was often overbearing and crass. He was known to meet members of his staff while he defecated in the toilet, insisted they swim with him nude in the White House swimming pool, and was proud of "Jumbo," the nickname he gave his penis. He frequently used the "Johnson treatment" on rivals and allies alike, taking advantage of his physical size to coerce them to do his bidding. He also ridiculed those who disagreed with him, including Ford. "Jerry played football too many times without a helmet," the president said of the minority leader. "Jerry Ford is so dumb he can't walk and fart at the same time." Urged to respond, Ford refused. "I never retaliated," said the Michigander. "I knew he was wrong. I just made up my mind I was not going to let it bother me."[74]

But there was a compassionate side to Johnson as well. He truly wanted to help African Americans and the poor, and the loss of life in Southeast Asia took an emotional toll on him. In September 1967, Dorothy Ford, Jerry's mother, passed away while attending church. The loss of his only surviving parent was hard on the minority leader. "It was the first time I saw my father cry," said his son, Michael. "It was very hard for me. I cried more for him than I cried for her death, because I knew he was in pain." Johnson promptly sent Ford a letter of condolence. "Please let me know if I can be helpful to you in any way," he penned.[75]

Furthermore, there is evidence that the two men admired one another, even if it took until the 1968 election for them to admit it. Shortly after voters cast their ballots, Ford recalled a meeting with Johnson during which they "forgot all the conflicts of the past and started a new era of friendship." Evidence of their new relationship came in a letter Johnson sent Ford three days before Nixon's inauguration: "Before I leave the Presidency, I want to have one last word with a man who has sometimes been an adversary, sometimes a supporter, but always a respected legislator. No man knows better than I the value of different opinions in a democratic society and no man more admires an independent spirit. I know you will continue to provide a strong and clear voice in the halls of Congress."[76]

What Ford could not have known was that no matter how difficult his relationship had been with Johnson, the one with Nixon would be even more of a problem, confounding members of Congress—including fellow Republicans—and drawing the nation into a constitutional crisis unlike any it had ever seen.

FIVE

Not Speaker, but President

It appeared at first to be an odd but relatively unnewsworthy event. On Saturday, 17 June 1972, Washington, D.C., police arrested five men who had broken into the Democratic Party's national headquarters, located in the Watergate building. Within a day, the Associated Press had learned that one of the burglars, James McCord, had ties to President Richard Nixon's reelection campaign fund, and by the following Tuesday, the *Washington Post* had linked another, Howard Hunt, with the White House. The Federal Bureau of Investigation (FBI) began looking into the incident, finding additional information that raised more questions about the administration's complicity. Yet the break-in received little attention during the summer and fall, as reporters were more interested in the Vietnam War, the economy, and the presidential race, which pitted Nixon against South Dakota's Senator George McGovern. The apparent lack of public interest pleased Nixon, who unknown to all but his closest confidants had committed violations of the law to hide his role in the scandal. Washington, D.C., attorney Richard Bishop did not share Nixon's confidence that Watergate would remain off the front pages. "I realize that there are many facts undisclosed to me and others in the public sector," he wrote the GOP's minority leader in the House, Gerald Ford, that October. "However, the fact remains that the White House has made no move to clarify a situation that worsens on a daily basis as the Federal Bureau of Investigation releases information obtained by its agents."[1]

Bishop's observation was more prescient than he could have realized. Ford had become minority leader while Lyndon B. Johnson was still in office, hoping that he might achieve his goal of become House speaker. Attaining that objective, though, had proven elusive. Nixon's victory in 1968 had brought a Republican into the Oval Office, which heartened Ford, who did his best to support the president, even if it meant at times taking positions that contradicted those he had adopted previously. Although voters returned Nixon to the Oval Office in 1972, they kept Democrats in control of Congress throughout the president's tenure. Disappointed that the speakership remained out of reach, Ford decided to retire from public life in 1976, a notion his wife, Betty, strongly supported. Instead, a scandal involving Vice President Spiro Agnew and then Watergate catapulted Ford into the vice presidency and then into the Oval Office itself.

Early Omens

Ford knew that with his friend and Republican ally in the Oval Office, his job was no longer to offer alternatives to White House proposals but instead to see to it that legislation favored by the administration made it through the House of Representatives. He was aware as well that in so doing, he might have to assume positions he had once rejected, but that was the nature of politics. What he did not realize was how troublesome coordinating policy with the White House was going to be.

Ford's difficulties can largely be attributed to the personality of the new president. Raised in a dysfunctional family, Richard Nixon's life before and during his political career was marked by disappointment and embattlement. He was highly intelligent and desired to attend one of the nation's top colleges after graduating high school, but his parents could not afford it. He ended up going to Whittier College for his undergraduate studies, followed by Duke University, where he received a degree in law. Though a fine school, Duke lacked the connections available to graduates of Ivy League institutions, which made it difficult for Nixon to land a good job. Returning to California to practice law, he fell in love with Patricia Ryan, who initially failed to reciprocate his attention; it took two years of courting for her finally to agree to marry him. During World War II, he served in the U.S. Navy as a lawyer and came home lacking the combat record of Ford or John F. Kennedy. He won a seat in the U.S. House of Representatives in 1946 and became nationally famous for his role in the Alger Hiss case. Conservatives admired him, but eastern liberals did not. Nor, he believed, did the eastern media. He became Dwight D. Eisenhower's vice-presidential nominee, only to see Eisenhower consider dropping him from the ticket in both 1952 and 1956. In 1960, Nixon tried himself to become president, only to have, in his mind, the eastern establishment deny him victory.

Compounding Nixon's sense of disappointment and deep-seated suspicions was his social awkwardness. Shy and introverted, he had a hard time speaking with others in person, preferring instead to hold conversations via the telephone. Unable to trust those outside his family and a very few aides, he admitted to a reporter his inability to "let my hair down with anyone." Reporters who wrote, or whom he suspected might compose, stories critical of him or his administration could find themselves denied access to the Oval Office. Nor did he enjoy press conferences, holding the fewest of any president between Herbert Hoover and Jimmy Carter.[2]

Nor did Nixon care for the Washington bureaucracy. He thought the executive branch departments concerned themselves more with protecting their turf than with defending the administration's interests. Since he could not anticipate that the cabinet would do his bidding, and mistrustful of others anyway, Nixon transferred much of policy making into the hands of what essentially became a kitchen cabinet, consisting of himself and a select group that included National Security Adviser Henry Kissinger, presidential aide Charles Colson, domestic adviser John Ehrlichman, and, above all, Chief of Staff H. R. Haldeman.[3]

In a government of coequal branches, particularly one in which the executive needs to work closely with the legislative to get bills passed, limiting access to the Oval Office poses a problem. It created complications for Nixon's congressional liaisons, Bryce Harlow and Harlow's successor, William Timmons. Timmons had a better personal relationship with Nixon than Harlow. Both Harlow and Timmons were respected on Capitol Hill. But they had to contend with Haldeman. A longtime friend of Nixon whose relationship with him dated to Nixon's time as Eisenhower's vice president, Haldeman had joined with Ehrlichman in creating what became known as a "Berlin Wall" around the Oval Office, determining who did or did not get access to a president who desired minimal personal contact with others. Harlow bitterly complained about Haldeman's "imperious manner," a sentiment shared by many of the lawmakers with whom Harlow met.[4]

Ford was one of them. He liked Kissinger, a German-born émigré who had fled to the United States to escape Nazism. Kissinger saw combat in

World War II and went to Harvard afterward. A brilliant student, he received a PhD from Harvard in 1954 and then taught there. He supported the presidential bids of New York's Governor Nelson Rockefeller in the 1960s before serving in Nixon's administration. Ford considered the national security adviser to be "an extremely competent and dedicated public servant who is interested only in serving the President and the American people." His opinion of the others was a different matter. At first, the minority leader was "very optimistic" about having a good working relationship with the White House. Within two weeks after Nixon's inauguration, he and Harlow had worked out an arrangement by which the congressional liaison would check out all the administration's legislative proposals with the Republican Party leadership in Congress. The White House planned to provide "personnel to Congressional staffs" and advance texts of presidential communications to each member of the GOP on Capitol Hill.[5] As a result, Ford and other Republicans would know before Democrats what the president wanted from them. For example, they would receive advance notice of nominations to federal positions in their states and districts and could take credit at home for any aid provided by Washington.

In fact, the president's top aides had little understanding of how Washington operated—and there is question as to whether they even cared—and, having devoted so much time to winning the election, neither they nor Nixon had given much thought to developing a clear line of communication with Capitol Hill. Add to that the problems Harlow had in getting Nixon's ear, and it is not surprising that Republicans in Congress began to lodge complaints about their treatment. One of the first was North Dakota's Thomas Kleppe, who told Ford in February that the state's only Democrat in Congress, Senator Quentin Burdick, continued to get notification of federal grants to the state before Kleppe did, thereby allowing Burdick—who planned to seek another term in 1970—to receive recognition for them. Pennsylvania's Lawrence Williams wrote that he had not received word that a Raymond Winch had been assigned to the U.S. Postal Service's regional office in Philadelphia, which was in Williams's district. Lawrence Hogan of Maryland issued a similar grievance about lack of notification. "The Johnson Administration always gave my predecessor this courtesy," he protested. Although Nixon aide John E. Nidecker attributed the complaints to "shaking down in the various departments" and assured Ford's assistant Robert Hartmann that most of the problems had been addressed, some Republicans continued to charge the White House with giving them the cold shoulder. Ford complained, but how much of an impact he had in the Oval

President Richard M. Nixon meets with Senate Minority Leader Hugh Scott, House Minority Leader Gerald R. Ford, and Representative John Rhodes in the Cabinet Room, 1971. Photo in the Gerald Ford Library, Ann Arbor, Michigan.

Office is questionable. To him, the central problem was Nixon's key aides. "Until he got tied in with some of the people, like Haldeman, Ehrlichman, Colson," he commented, "I felt good." He did not like any of them, calling Ehrlichman "arrogant and difficult" and Colson "no genius."[6]

In truth, these individuals only reflected the way Nixon felt about Capitol Hill. Granted, it was not unusual for a president to grumble about trying to get lawmakers to do what he considered best for the nation, particularly in those cases where one or both houses of Congress were in the hands of the opposition. Nixon, though, felt that the House of Representatives and the Senate were, like the media, simply in the way. He "spoke with feeling about the inadequacy of Congress, indeed he spoke of Congress with contempt," Nixon's counselor, Arthur Burns, wrote in his diary. "No leaders—none. Not [Senate Majority Leader Mike] Mansfield, not [Senate Minority Leader Hugh] Scott, nor Ford, not anyone in fact. Two or three good senators—all from the South." Whereas Johnson had considered it an obligation to meet with lawmakers and enjoyed the give-and-take involved, Nixon, who was averse to face-to-face meetings anyway, did not. At first, the president held biweekly Tuesday meetings with the GOP leadership from 8:30 to 10:00 a.m., but he did not find them particularly "productive and informative." It appears he decided they took up too much of his time, for in November 1970, his special assistant, Dwight Chapin, asked that Ford and Scott—who had become Senate minority leader upon Dirksen's death in September 1969—have those meetings end "at 9:30 a.m., precisely," or "at least give the President the option to leave the session."[7] It was not the best of attitudes for a president to take to get his legislation passed.

The New Federalism

Although Nixon had a record as a hard-core anticommunist and equally tough critic of Democrats, he was not a right-winger like Barry Goldwater. Quite the opposite. "There is only one thing as bad as a far left liberal and that's a damn right wing conservative," he once said. If anything, he was a moderate and a pragmatist, and his domestic record proved more progressive than one might have anticipated in 1968.[8]

Nixon's domestic program, called the New Federalism, offered evidence of his approach to governance. He had run for the presidency against the Great Society, which he saw as an example of wasteful spending that granted Washington too much authority in determining how federal moneys were spent and encouraged Americans to live off the government dole rather than find work. His slim victory over Hubert Humphrey might have given the impression that a sizable percentage of the voting public did not share those conclusions, but polling suggested otherwise. For instance, 84 percent of those surveyed agreed that "there are too many people receiving welfare money who should be working" and that many welfare recipients "are not honest about their needs." Nixon planned to curb funding for, or to eliminate, those antipoverty programs he considered inefficient or unnecessary. He also favored "revenue sharing," by which state and local governments would have a greater say in how federal money provided them was used. Proposed at least as far back as 1958 by Representative Melvin Laird, revenue sharing had gained popularity among many in the GOP, including liberals such as Nelson Rockefeller and moderates like Ford.[9] The New Federalism would combine a less costly, more efficient effort to fight poverty by apportioning dollars.

Aside from appealing to those in and out of Washington who disliked the Great Society, the New Federalism allegedly would reduce inflation. At the time Nixon took office, unemployment stood at approximately 3.5 percent, and inflation was about a point higher. The number of those without a job was disconcerting, but prices were even more so to the president, and he was prepared to reduce inflation by cutting federal spending, even if it meant less money for programs designed to give people jobs and or to assist those looking for work.[10]

Nixon's pragmatism became evident in April 1969 when he announced his anti-inflation initiative. He asked that the 10 percent tax surcharge Johnson had requested and Congress had passed in 1968 be maintained until January 1970 and that about 13 million low-income families be removed from the tax rolls. Moreover, he wanted to eliminate an "investment tax credit" that President John F. Kennedy had signed into law in 1962. The purpose of the tax credit was to give corporations more money to spend on themselves so they could expand and, in turn, promote economic growth. Ford called Nixon's proposals "sound policy" that would bring in more revenue for the government, reduce inflation, and provide tax relief for Americans. While pro-business, he had opposed the tax credit in 1962 (although he did not explain why), and he endorsed its revocation. "There is always risk involved in actions taken to dampen down the economy," Ford conceded. "But we must take such risks carefully and judiciously, if we are to bring inflation under control."[11]

At first, the House appeared unlikely to pass the surtax extension. An alliance of conservative southern Democrats and liberal northern Democrats opposed the measure, the former believing the surcharge permitted too much government spending, and the latter demanding proof that the Nixon administration favored tax reform. The House's Democratic leadership decided to delay any action on the measure. Nixon intervened, promising "meaningful tax reform" later in the year, and Ford guaranteed that the overwhelming majority of Republicans would vote for the surtax. With that, the bill went to the House floor, where it passed by five votes. (Ford was among those in favor.) The Senate followed suit in July, and Nixon signed it into law the following month.[12]

Nixon had promised tax reform, but lawmakers had already begun to act on it. Just before the president's inauguration, outgoing Treasury Secretary Joseph Barr had warned of a growing "taxpayer's revolt," motivating the House Ways and Means Committee the following month to hold hearings on the issue. With Ford among those in support, the House passed the Tax Reform Act in August. The Senate followed suit in December. The new law augmented both Social Security benefits and the individual income-tax exemption, established the alternative minimum tax to make sure high-wage earners paid their fair share of taxes, extended Johnson's tax surcharge at a rate of 5 percent until 30 June 1970, and took off the tax rolls numerous people who lived below the poverty line. While not everything Nixon had wanted, the bill contained some measures he liked, and it had wide appeal to voters. The president therefore signed it into law on 30 December.[13]

As Congress debated tax reform, administration officials looked at reforming the country's welfare system in a manner consistent with the New Federalism. After months of discussions among his aides, the president in August 1969 proposed a Family Assistance Plan (FAP) that would guarantee all families an annual income of $1,600 (or about $10,900 today) and expand the food stamp program. For a president who had pledged to dismantle the Great Society because it encouraged dependence on federal aid, FAP appeared to go in the opposite direction by increasing welfare rolls by 13 million people. Realizing conservatives would balk, he added provisions that would provide more federal revenue to the states, encourage those welfare recipients able to work to find a job, and tie FAP to the elimination of the Office of Economic Opportunity (OEO)—the government agency that had overseen the War on Poverty and one that Nixon and conservatives regarded as an example of federal waste.[14]

Once again, Ford set aside his own fiscal inclinations in favor of party unity and urged FAP's passage. That was easier said than done. For one thing, Harlow had exhorted Nixon to consult with Capitol Hill before presenting the plan, but the president had refused. Hence, lawmakers were upset that they had received no opportunity to vet FAP. Moreover, the proposal drew the ire of conservative Republicans, who disliked what they saw as essentially a continuation of the Great Society. Liberal Democrats considered the $1,600 base too low. In April 1970, the House passed FAP, but it never made it out of the Senate. In subsequent years, Nixon tried, with Ford's help, to resuscitate FAP, but the program had become a nonstarter. Ford saw its demise as "a 'Congressional failure to the American people.'" Nor did Nixon have any luck in eliminating the OEO, which had strong support in a Democratic-controlled Congress, though he did, with Ford's support, shift some of its functions to other departments or local governments, reducing its size significantly. Additionally, he succeeded in eventually killing Model Cities, a program both he and Ford agreed was another prodigal government program.[15]

The attack on the Great Society tied into Nixon's war on crime. Conservatives believed that Johnson had wrongly concluded that it was possible to use federal money to address the cause of crime, and liberal-minded courts made matters only worse. One of the most dramatic examples of criminal activity was bombings: there were 600 actual or attempted bombings in 1969, and the number increased to nearly 1,600 the following year. The way to curb crime was not to discover its roots but to impose harsh punishments on lawbreakers, said those on the political right. The outcome of the 1968 election seemed to prove that many Americans felt similarly. Publicly, the president promised to go after those who violated the law. Privately, he had the CIA, the FBI, and the National Security Agency (NSA) conduct clandestine surveillance and harassment of "radicals."[16]

Ford repeatedly defended the administration's crime-control measures. When, in March 1970, House Majority Leader Carl Albert (D-Okla.) noted that crime had gone up by 11 percent the year before, Ford called it "the lowest increase in the last 4 years." Furthermore, the minority leader said, the White House had proposed spending over $1.2 billion for FY 1971 to fight crime, "the first time in history that any administration has sought more than $1 billion in new obligational authority for the Justice Department." That same year, Ford voted for the D.C. Court Reform and Criminal Procedure Act, which permitted wiretapping to fight crime and created both a superior court and an appeals court for the nation's capital to speed up the process of trying people charged with violations of the law. As it turned out, these efforts had no appreciable impact on the crime rate, prompting Democrats, as Republicans had done to Johnson, to charge that Nixon was "soft on crime."[17]

Conservatives saw a relationship between crime and drugs. For much of the 1960s, drugs had been touted as a way to replace the oftentimes disturbing realities of everyday life with happiness and "feeling good." The use of heroin, cocaine, LSD, and speed all saw dramatic increases. By the start of the 1970s, Americans had drawn a link between illicit narcotics and an increase in organized crime, the spread of venereal disease, and the untimely deaths of the musicians Janis Joplin, Jimi Hendrix, and Jim Morrison. President Johnson had signed some laws aimed at stopping drug abuse and rehabilitating addicts, but Nixon was the first president in the postwar era to make drug control a key initiative. He started in September 1969 with Operation Intercept, which was less an interdiction program than it was a public-relations campaign. The following year, the president signed the Organized Crime Control Act (OCCA)—a portion of which created the Racketeer Influenced and Corrupt Organization (RICO) Act—the Comprehensive Drug Abuse Prevention and Control Act, and the Drug Abuse Education Act.[18]

Whether under Johnson or Nixon, Ford endorsed these measures to combat drug use and, not surprisingly, gave particular credit to his long-time friend. He said that the OCCA was "long overdue" and that Nixon's "sweeping approach" would help the country "cope effectively with this most complex problem of drug addiction and its rise and spread." The administration's effort achieved mixed results. RICO's provisions were complex, and it took time for the nation's justice system to determine how best to use it, so its effectiveness was limited at first; over the long term, it proved successful in curbing organized crime. The war on drugs was another matter. Despite a doubling in the number of people arrested for drugs by 1973, cocaine use remained prevalent, and by 1974, the availability of heroin had risen.[19]

Nixon had made the Great Society's abolition and fighting crime central parts of his platform in 1968; he had said nothing, however, about the environment and had received few questions on the subject during his run for the White House.[20] Whether he had an interest in environmental protection is a matter of debate,[21] but there is no doubt that a series of events in 1969, including an oil spill off the coast of California and Ohio's Cuyahoga River catching fire, made it a subject he could not ignore. That *Time* magazine found only three of Lake Erie's beaches to be "completely safe for swimming" also captured public attention. Whereas in 1965 only about one-quarter of Americans were concerned about air pollution and one-third about water pollution, those numbers by 1970 respectively had grown to 69 and 74 percent. Also on Nixon's mind was Ehrlichman, who supported environmental protection, and Democratic senators Edmund Muskie of Maine and Henry Jackson of Washington, both of whom were likely contenders for the presidency in 1972 and shared Ehrlichman's environmental sentiments.[22]

The president and lawmakers realized they had do something about protecting the environment. There was little doubt which way Ford would vote. He had long shown an interest in environmental protection, his hometown sat on one of the Great Lakes, the Grand River had become so polluted that people refused to eat the fish caught in it, the air in Grand Rapids ranked among the dirtiest in the nation, and he was loyal to the Oval Office's new occupant. As he put it, "The Federal Government should be setting an example for the States, localities, and private industry in our effort to restore and preserve our environment." Asked by the White House to do more to defend the environment, Congress put together what became known as the Water Quality Improvement Act, which made oil companies liable for cleaning up oil spills, added restrictions on thermal pollution generated by nuclear power plants, and established an Office of Environmental Quality. Ford was among the 392 members of the House who voted for the law in 1969, which Nixon signed the following year. Ford also voted for Senator Jackson's brainchild, the National Environmental Policy Act (NEPA) of 1970, which established a Council on Environmental Quality and required government agencies to submit statements on the potential impact a proposed activity would have on the environment. That same year, 1970, the president established the Environmental Protection Agency (EPA) to coordinate the executive branch's environmental programs. Ford called the EPA necessary "to provide clear-cut consistent standards for enforcement in the area of industrial pollution and a single Federal agency to which State and local pollution control officials can go for financial support and technical help."[23]

Ford versus Douglas

Ford's endorsement of Nixon's domestic initiatives demonstrated his personal and political loyalties, but his fealty to Nixon took him to the edge of impropriety when he sought to impeach Supreme Court Justice William Douglas. Appointed to the Court during President Franklin D. Roosevelt's second term, Douglas had developed a reputation as a liberal. A strong believer in civil liberties, in 1953 he had granted a stay of execution for Julius and Ethel Rosenberg—who had been sentenced to die for giving top-secret information on the U.S. nuclear weapons program to the Soviet Union—on the grounds that they had been sentenced without a jury trial. He dissented in *Roth v. United States* (1957), in which the Court declared that material appealing to the "prurient interest" could be banned under the First Amendment; this was a more limited definition of what constituted obscenity than had been the case previously. To Douglas, the majority view in *Roth* made no sense, as "the arousing of sexual thoughts and desires happens every day in normal life in dozens of ways." In 1969, the Court heard the case *Goldwater v. Ginzburg*, in which former senator Goldwater sued magazine editor Ralph Ginzburg for libel. Douglas refused to recuse himself from the case even though he had received money for publishing an article in a magazine owned by the defendant. A year later, in his book *Points of Rebellion*, he pointed out that violence had occurred periodically in American history; while what he actually wrote was a warning that the unrest of the 1960s could lead to another such episode, conservatives took his words as designed to incite violence. Prior to publication, portions of the book appeared in the April 1970 edition of *Evergreen Review*,[24] a magazine that also included photographs of nude women.

Ford's decision to target Douglas was tied to Nixon's effort to find a replacement for Associate Justice Abe Fortas, who had resigned in May 1969 after being accused of ethics violations. Desiring to continue his "southern strategy," Nixon wanted a person from the South who held to a strict constructionist interpretation of the Constitution: that is, someone who favored tight reins on federal authority. His first choice was a South Carolinian who sat on the Fourth Circuit Court of Appeals, Clement Haynsworth Jr. But Haynsworth's positions on civil rights and unions drew fire, and the Senate rejected him in November. Digging in his heels, Nixon chose G. Harrold Carswell, a Georgian who sat on the Fifth Circuit Court of Appeals. The reaction was even more hostile, as Carswell's past comments and decisions showed little concern for minorities. Publicly condemning those who had said no to his first two nominees, Nixon went outside the south, nominating Judge Harry Blackmun, who sat on the Eighth Circuit Court of Appeals. He was a midwestern jurist who favored strict limits on federal power, which Nixon believed would play well in the South. While Blackmun's strict constructionism did not please liberals, he was highly respected, and in May the Senate approved his nomination by 94–0 vote.

The Senate's rejection of Haynsworth, though, still rankled. Enter Ford, who in the summer of 1969 had begun looking into impeaching Douglas. "Impeachment," he later wrote, "*resembles* a regular criminal indictment but it is *not* the same thing. It is a proceeding of an entirely *political* nature," one based on whether the officeholder targeted had engaged in "good behavior." In considering what constituted good behavior, history demonstrated the importance of holding federal judges to "a higher standard . . . than [expected] of any other 'civil Officers' of the United States."[25] In Ford's mind, Douglas had not met that standard. Aside from the *Ginzburg* case and the *Evergreen* article—the latter of which Ford appears to have found personally offensive—Douglas had received payment for speaking engagements "from sources outside the government," including "from a foundation that had received some of its money from Las Vegas gambling interests."[26]

There is some question as to whether Ehrlichman convinced Ford to begin these proceedings against Douglas at Nixon's behest.[27] Ford denied it. "Ehrlichman has no credibility on anything," he told an interviewer in 2003. "I was close enough to Dick to pretty much ignore Ehrlichman and those guys, who were evil influences on him." Rather, Douglas's conflicts of interest and record on the Court had come to his attention at almost the same time as Fortas's resignation, and from sources outside the administration. Whatever actually occurred, it was perceptions that mattered. Ford had tried to keep his intentions "under wraps," but when the *Washington Post* discovered in November 1969 what he was up to, the conclusion was that he had targeted Douglas on Nixon's behalf to get back at liberals' opposition to Haynsworth.[28]

Ford defended himself, telling a constituent that it made no sense to charge Haynsworth for impropriety while permitting Douglas, who in his mind was guilty of the same, to sit on the nation's highest court. But a backlash developed over his efforts to impeach Douglas, even among Ford's own constituents. One charged him with engaging in a "slimy vendetta," and another accused him of "persecuting" the justice. In December 1970 the *New York Times* joined the chorus of opposition: "It is time for President Nixon and Representative Ford to call a halt to this squalid campaign," its editors wrote, "which threatens the integrity and the independence of the Supreme Court."[29]

Ford dropped his pursuit of Douglas at around the same time. Earlier in the year, he had submitted a bill to proceed with the investigation and found support from over 100 members of the House. His intention was to establish a special committee to investigate Douglas, but Representative Andrew Jacobs (D-Ind.), one of the justice's allies in Congress, submitted an impeachment resolution, knowing that it was certain to fail and, in turn, embarrass the White House. As Jacobs had intended, the case went to the House Judiciary Committee, headed by Emanuel Cellar (D-N.Y.), another of Douglas's champions, which delivered a report finding that the justice had done nothing wrong. Furthermore, with Blackmun's appointment in May, the administration decided not to continue its crusade against Douglas.[30]

Even though Ford's pursuit of Douglas was over, the affair tarnished him. John Osborne, who wrote for the liberal *New Republic,* called it "savage and shoddy," and James Cannon, who worked for President Ford and later wrote a laudatory biography of the Grand Rapids native, admitted that trying to remove Douglas from the Court "damaged Ford's reputation for leadership and fairness." Even Ford conceded, "It was a mistake."[31]

Trilateralism

Of greater interest to Nixon than domestic affairs was foreign policy. No diplomatic matter was more pressing when he took office than Vietnam. By early 1969, negotiations with the North Vietnamese to end the war were underway in Paris, and the United States had started the process of "Vietnamization," gradually removing its military forces from South Vietnam while building up the ARVN so that it could defend itself. Détente—the improvement in relations between the United States and the Soviet Union—had also begun.

Nixon and Kissinger, however, saw even greater opportunity than simply improving ties with Moscow. Relations between the Soviet Union and the People's Republic of China (PRC) had so deteriorated by 1969 that the once-allies had become enemies, so much so that each wanted a closer association with the United States. The president and his national security adviser intended to engage in "trilateralism," by which they would play off the two Communist powers against one another, thereby further dividing the Communist bloc. As part of trilateralism, they would use "linkage," making a price of America's friendship the preparedness of Beijing and Moscow to convince Hanoi to end the Vietnam War on terms acceptable to Washington.

Knowing his history protected him from charges of being soft on communism, Nixon felt free to signal his intentions to both the Soviets and the Chinese. The Johnson administration had been the first to consider strategic arms limitation talks that would reduce the superpowers' nuclear arsenals but had not pursued them. In February 1969, Nixon suggested to the Soviet ambassador to the United States, Anatoly Dobrynin, the need to revive the strategic arms limitation talks, and he linked those discussions to reducing tensions in hot spots such as Vietnam. To pressure the Soviets, he asked Congress to fund the development of an antiballistic missile (ABM) system called Safeguard and the testing of multiple independently targetable reentry vehicles (MIRVs)—missiles with more than one warhead, each of which could hit a different target. Ford did not address MIRVs, but he endorsed Safeguard. With it, Washington would have a bargaining chip to use against Moscow. Without it, "the United States enters into negotiations naked [and] will come out of those negotiations naked." When the Soviets showed no preparedness to accept linkage, a chagrined Nixon accepted moving forward with the strategic arms limitation talks alone. He also pursued Safeguard, urging both Republicans and hawkish Democrats in Congress to side with him. The Senate voted for the system in September, and Ford was among the majority of members of congress who followed suit the next month.[32] In November, the negotiations opened in Helsinki, Finland.

What all of this meant for Vietnam was anyone's guess. Moscow had rejected linkage, and there was no way of knowing if China had any intention of offering help in ending the war. Nixon understood he could not wait and see what the Soviets and the PRC might do, and accordingly he moved on several fronts. During a visit to Guam in 1969, he issued what became the Nixon Doctrine, calling for America's allies to do more to defend themselves. In so doing, he placed Vietnamization within a broader framework that recognized the limits of U.S. power. He had Kissinger continue the Paris negotiations with Hanoi's representative, Le Duc Tho. Finally, he intensified the air campaign and had U.S. aircraft bomb North Vietnamese safe havens in Cambodia. He had intended to keep the attacks secret, but to his anger, the *New York Times* reported on them shortly after they began.

Nixon's expansion of the war into Cambodia revived an antiwar movement that had been flagging since the 1968 Democratic National Convention. Peace activists held "moratoriums" in October and November, calling for an end to the war. But the indignation of the war's opponents reached new heights when Nixon announced on 30 April 1970 that he had sent U.S. and ARVN forces into Cambodia to destroy North Vietnamese and Viet Cong sanctuaries there. By 1 July, when those troops returned to South Vietnam, they reported having killed 2,000 enemy soldiers, eliminated 8,000 bunkers, and seized 7,000 tons of rice and millions of rounds of ammunition. Nixon proclaimed the mission had "crippled" the North Vietnamese. In fact, the North Vietnamese had pulled deeper into Cambodia to avoid contact with the U.S. military and the ARVN; once the Americans and South Vietnamese withdrew, they returned to their bases near the South Vietnamese border.[33]

At home, the response was largely one of outrage. The president had told few members of Congress of his intentions vis-à-vis Cambodia, and he made sure that those in the know were people who would back him. Senate Minority Leader Scott was furious that he had not received advance notice but, in the name of party unity, declared his support. Most of his colleagues felt differently and voted to nullify the Gulf of Tonkin Resolution. Senators George McGovern and Mark Hatfield (R-Oreg.) went even further, proposing an amendment (which did not pass) that would have forced the president to withdraw all U.S. troops from Vietnam by the start of 1972.[34] Protests broke out throughout the country, most famously at Kent State University in Ohio, where National Guardsmen shot and killed four students.

Ever the loyal Republican, and a friend of the man who now sat in the Oval Office, Ford stood behind the president. He praised the Nixon Doctrine and Vietnamization, repeatedly citing how many troops had come home thanks to the president. To Nixon's credit as well, he said, the number of Americans killed and wounded had fallen, declining from a peak of 61,000 in 1968 to 19,400 in 1970. The Cambodian operation had been a success, one that would enhance the South's security, save U.S. soldiers' lives, and make it possible for Washington to continue its military drawdown. Those who recommended a route other than that favored by Nixon were deceiving themselves. When Representative Charles Vanik (D-Ohio) suggested the United States offer a "cease-fire by region or by military unit" to test Hanoi's desire for peace, Ford replied that such a unilateral move on Washington's part meant "exposing a number of defenseless Americans to be shot by the enemy." Anyone who favored a rapid withdrawal from South Vietnam only "encouraged" Hanoi and the VC to resist a peace agreement. Ford accused the media of exaggerating the number of people who participated in the first moratorium, asserted that those who called for the protest were "working for the communist conspirators," and denied reports that the second moratorium was peaceful. In truth, he said, police had to use tear gas on the protestors, property was damaged, and over 350 people were arrested, with a total cost to taxpayers of over $1.8 million.[35]

Election, Environment, Education, and the Economy

For the first time since 1948, it looked as if Ford's seat might be vulnerable. The *Grand Rapids Press* reported in June 1970 that the number of people signing petitions to nominate Ford were not "filling . . . up as fast as they have in the past," and college students in the region were "embittered by what they call the House Minority Leader's 'me tooism' on the Vietnam War policies of Presidents Nixon and Johnson, his attacks on anti-poverty legislation, support of Nixon's 'southern strategy,' and his failure to take a leadership role in the fight against pollution." His Democratic opponent was Jean McKee, an attorney and mother of three who favored a deadline for withdrawing from Vietnam. She charged that Ford was little more than a mouthpiece for the president, said if anyone deserved credit for fighting crime it was President Johnson, and accused Ford of doing far too little to protect the environment. Ford retorted that he would do a better job than McKee to safeguard America's security interests, praised Vietnamization, and defended his record on crime and the environment. Realizing that McKee had the support of a large number of younger and African American voters, Ford ran TV commercials showing him with both groups. By October, it was clear even to McKee that Ford's name recognition and incumbency guaranteed him another term in office, and the following month, he won with 61 percent of the vote.[36] Once again, though, the news was not as good for the Republican Party. Democrats lost four seats in the Senate but gained twelve in the House and retained control of Congress.

Despite his victory, Ford could not but take notice of the growing criticism. Stung by the charge that he was not pro-environment enough, in 1971 he introduced two antipollution bills, though neither made it out of committee. He was less certain about the Environmental Pesticide Control Act, aimed at amending a 1910 law and giving the EPA the authority to regulate the sale, distribution, and use of pesticides. Ford called himself "a layman in this field" who, "like a lot of other legislators . . . are unconvinced by the evidence presented on both sides of this issue." Although he was not present for the vote in which the House passed the bill, he did favor it, and in 1972, the Environmental Pesticide Control Act became law. Finally, he voted for overriding Nixon's veto of the 1972 Clean Water Act. The act was designed to restrict the discharge of pollutants into water and set water-quality standards, but Nixon had refused to sign it because of its expense.[37]

Ford took a different track than he had in the past when it came to education. The minority leader had long demonstrated himself willing to endorse bills meant to help students, whether proposed by Democrats or Republicans. "We must open higher education to all of our qualified young people," he stated in 1971. "America must truly be the land of opportunity." Nevertheless, in 1972, he took issue with the Education Amendments to the Higher Education Act of 1965. The most controversial amendment was Title IX, which banned gender discrimination in educational institutions that received federal aid. Ford cited unspecified "reservations" regarding the conference report and voted against it. However, when the amendments passed Congress, Ford touted them as "a landmark higher education bill."[38]

Without a doubt, the "reservations" to which Ford referred concerned forced busing. The Michigander had at times shown himself a progressive on civil rights, but at other points in his legislative career, he had taken the position that states, not the federal government, should take the lead in promoting racial equality. By the late 1960s, the idea of busing students outside their districts to get schools to comply with the 1954 *Brown v. Board of Education* decision had become a major topic of discussion. Nixon in

1968 had declared himself opposed to forced busing, and Ford seconded the president. He favored integration, yet he believed that making people leave their neighborhoods to comply with *Brown* did not guarantee a better education and infringed on individual freedom. In 1971, Ford had endorsed an amendment to the Higher Education Act that would suspend court orders favorable to forced busing, and, the next year, he called for a constitutional amendment to prohibit the use of busing as a means of achieving racial equality. The Education Amendments did include a provision, Title VIII, which restricted the use of federal moneys for forced busing, but the language was not as strong as Ford favored.[39] Certainly politics was also on Ford's mind, for his position would appeal to white southerners and allow Nixon to repeat his southern strategy come Election Day.

The most serious concern for the administration and most Americans, though, was the economy. In 1970, the nation entered its first recession in more than a decade. The causes were complex. President Johnson's determination to have both guns and butter pushed up inflation. U.S. companies invested their profits into improving production methods and increasing workers' wages; consequently, per capita productivity fell while salaries remained high, meaning the products coming out of American factories became more expensive. And they were not built well. Meanwhile, Japan and West Germany, having recovered industrially from World War II and offering goods similar to those of the United States—such as steel, automobiles, and electronics—but at lower cost, were able to cut into America's global economic dominance. In 1971, for the first time since the late 1800s, the United States imported more products than it exported, setting the stage for years of trade deficits. Inflation had reached 6.1 percent by the end of 1969 and was still at 5.3 percent at the beginning of 1971. Having trouble competing, U.S. companies laid off workers, driving unemployment up to 6 percent by 1970; it stayed there through the remainder of the year and into 1971. The nation began to confront something new called "stagflation," marked by high inflation and little or no economic growth.

Nixon had little interest in domestic politics and found economics boring, but he would not permit the economy to go into free fall. By early 1971, he and his Treasury secretary, John Connally, began to talk about doing something that no president had done since World War II: impose wage and price controls. The year before, Congress had given Nixon the authority to do just that; the free-market-minded Ford had resisted, saying that it was an effort "to cripple the American economy by bureaucracy." Lawmakers, though, believed no Republican would ever agree to such controls.[40]

For a time, they were correct. In 1971 Nixon instead implemented an economic stimulus program that violated the Republican Party's long-held support for balanced budgets. Yet that initiative too did little to curb rising prices and joblessness, and in August the president offered the New Economic Policy (NEP). He asked Congress to pass what became known as the Revenue Act—which would do away with the excise tax on automobiles in order to boost sales and would restore the investment tax credit—and to levy a 10 percent tax on imports. Additionally, he removed the United States from the gold standard. Since 1944, the U.S. dollar had been pegged to gold. That system had worked well enough, but it had become problematic by the early 1970s, for it kept the price of American exports high. By leaving the gold standard, the dollar would "float," allowing Nixon to depreciate its value and, in doing so, make U.S. products more attractive to foreign buyers. Finally, he imposed a ninety-day freeze on wages and prices. Over the next three months, the White House reached agreements with its European allies and the Japanese by which they accepted the dollar's devaluation and promised to remove restrictions on U.S. imports in return for the White House dropping the 10 percent import tax and a provision of the investment tax credit designed to encourage Americans to buy U.S.-made products. Once again, Ford's partisanship came to the surface. Whereas he had opposed the investment tax credit when first introduced in 1962, he now endorsed its restoration and voted for the Revenue Act.[41]

At first, these measures appeared to work. The U.S. trade deficit and inflation began to fall. What Nixon did not consider was what might happen when the wage and price freeze ended, so in October he announced "Phase II," and set up a Price Commission and a Pay Board that would not freeze prices and wages but instead would restrict how high they went. Phase II lasted until just after Nixon's reelection in 1972, and it had some success in restraining inflation and salary hikes. However, it had only a limited impact on unemployment, which stood at 5.6 percent.[42]

Publicly, Ford stood behind the president. When Phase II was announced, he called it "an effective method of stimulating the economy" and justified it to a constituent on the grounds that "the inflationary forces which were built up from 1966 through mid-1969 were more powerful than could be cured by the traditional methods of a change in monetary and fiscal policy." He appeared to contradict his earlier claim that wage and price controls meant bigger government, telling his colleagues in August 1972 that they were "working despite the fact that they are limited in nature and that enforcement does not require a huge bureaucracy." Privately, though, he was uneasy. He had endorsed wage and price controls during the Korean War in the name of national defense, but they had hit retailers hard by forcing them to limit increases in what they charged for goods while spending more to restock. Hence, he later said, those controls "were a mistake. And we suffered until we got rid of them." Now, it was not national defense but partisanship that overcame his personal qualms. Still, he would admit years later that "the idea of wage and price controls . . . was one of Nixon's few mistakes."[43]

Foreign Policy Breakthroughs

Ford not only had to swallow his dislike of wage and price controls, but he was also rethinking his foreign-policy views. Nixon had signaled to the Soviet Union that he was open to better relations; he had made similar gestures aimed at the PRC. China had reciprocated. Then, in July 1971, Nixon shocked the world when he announced he had accepted a PRC invitation to visit Beijing. Fearful that the United States and China would develop close ties, the Kremlin asked Nixon to come to the Soviet Union as well. The president accepted, visiting Beijing in February 1972 and Moscow three months later.

In combination, the two trips were monumental. Nixon, accompanied by Kissinger and State Department officials, became the first president to visit the PRC. Sixty million Americans watched on national TV as the president landed in Beijing. The key discussions, held among Nixon, Kissinger, and the Chinese premier, Zhou Enlai, addressed a wide range of issues, including Sino-Soviet relations, Indochina, and Taiwan. Significantly, Zhou exhibited no preparedness to force North Vietnam's hand. He also wanted the United States to stop providing economic and military support to Taiwan.[44] On 27 February, the U.S. and Chinese leaders signed in Shanghai a carefully worded and sometimes vague communiqué in which Washington promised to withdraw its military presence from Taiwan at some point and, for the first time, recognized Taiwan as part of China. Furthermore, they pledged to improve their cultural and commercial relationship, preparing the stage for what appeared to be an early normalization of relations.

The results of Nixon's visit to the Soviet Union were even more significant. The president and Soviet premier Leonid Brezhnev agreed to cooperate on matters relating to science, the environment, and space exploration. The capstone, however, was the signing of the Strategic Arms Limitations Treaty (SALT I). SALT I consisted of two agreements. The Treaty of Anti-Ballistic Missile Systems, which required Senate ratification, restricted each country to two ABM systems each (later reduced to one); consequently, each superpower received some protection from an attack by the other but not enough to relieve them of the danger of mutual assured destruction. The Interim Agreement on Limitation of Strategic Offensive Arms, an executive agreement that did not require Senate approval, restricted until 1977 the number of intercontinental and submarine-launched ballistic missiles to what existed at the time of SALT I's signing. While the Soviets had advantages in both categories, SALT I did not address long-range heavy bombers or missiles with multiple warheads—in both cases, the United States had the upper hand—or new weapons systems.

By visiting Beijing and Moscow and by signing the Shanghai Communiqué and SALT I, Nixon had significantly shifted U.S. Cold War policy, established détente with the Soviet Union, and put Washington on the road toward normalization of relations with the PRC. Journalist James Reston referred to Nixon's junkets "as the bravest diplomatic initiative of the postwar generation." Reston reflected broader sentiment at home. Upon learning of Nixon's acceptance of Beijing's invitation to visit, Mansfield said he was "flabbergasted, delighted, and happy," while Scott called it "an extremely important step in producing world peace." Seventy-eight percent of respondents to a Harris poll favored Nixon's trip to China, and the president's approval rating, which was at 53 percent in March, rose 8 points as the Moscow Summit came to an end.[45]

There were, of course, detractors. Just as Nixon's announcement shook the Soviets, so it did for Taiwan, which feared abandonment by the United States. Japan was also displeased, for Nixon had promised advance notice of such a move. In Congress, conservatives took issue with the president's opening to Beijing, and the decision of the United Nations in October 1971 to boot out Taiwan in favor of the PRC caused additional alarm among those on the political right. According to the John Birch Society, Nixon's junket "humiliated the American people and betrayed our anti-Communist allies."[46] Joining those on the political right were individuals on the left who later received the moniker "neoconservatives." Liberal on social and economic matters, they were hawks when it came to foreign policy. In particular, they believed that America's problems in Vietnam encouraged Soviet adventurism in other parts of the world and that Washington could keep Moscow in check only by maintaining a powerful U.S. defense.

Ford shared the neoconservatives' desire for a strong U.S. military but sided with Nixon's actions vis-à-vis the Communist powers. In so doing, he had to backtrack on long-held positions. He had been a critic of the Soviet

Union and of its treatment of its people—particularly its refusal to permit Jews to emigrate to Israel—and he had been wary of arms-control agreements with Moscow, such as the Limited Test Ban Treaty and the nuclear-nonproliferation talks, the latter of which had culminated in the Nuclear Nonproliferation Treaty of 1968. Those pacts, though, had been negotiated and signed under Democratic administrations. Now, in mid-June 1972, he expressed his endorsement of SALT I, saying that it would restrain "the Russians' headlong rush into nuclear superiority." He admitted the agreement would restrict the U.S. nuclear arsenal, but said, "We can still maintain the quality of our nuclear weapons." Furthermore, he encouraged passage of a House resolution supporting SALT I, reminding his colleagues that their negotiation required Nixon to take into account Congress's position.[47]

Ford also revised his stand on China. Once critical of the PRC, he now told a constituent that despite his opposition to its membership in the UN, "I do think that it is good to review and re-evaluate our positions from time to time," and he justified the rapprochement with Beijing as helping lead to an end to the Vietnam War: "If we could get the cooperation of the communists in China in resolving the Vietnamese problem we will all be grateful." Similarly, he felt that the Shanghai Communiqué was "an encouraging first step [that] enhances the prospects for world peace." As for Taiwan's expulsion, he angrily wrote that Washington should "re-evaluate its financial contribution to the United Nations and to those countries in the United Nations who voted out Taiwan," only to change his mind on the grounds that doing so would damage U.S. credibility.[48]

Ford was also upset by news at the end of February 1972 that the PRC had invited the Senate leadership to come for a visit. It was not fair, he stated, for the House was "a co-equal branch of Congress" and had been more supportive of the White House's diplomacy than had the Senate. The administration tried to explain that the invitation came from Beijing, not Washington, but that did not mollify either Ford or Carl Albert, who was now House speaker. Following further Sino-American discussions, the PRC at the end of March asked Ford and House Democratic leader Hale Boggs to come for a visit.[49]

Ford's constituents split over the trip. The junket offered "great promise," said one. Another called the minority leader a "cry baby," charged him with going on a "vacation" to the PRC, and asked why Ford did not instead use taxpayer money for "visiting ghettos areas, run down nursing homes, or even your own city of Grand Rapids." A particularly incensed individual accused Ford of "fraternizing and collaborating with the Chinese," adding,

"I do not want to wish you any bad luck but I hope your air craft falls into the middle of the Pacific Ocean for stabbing the American people in the back. It was this same kind of fraternizing, collaborating and double-cross that helped the Nazis overtake the Netherlands in 1941." Although Ford attempted to mollify his detractors by saying it was not a vacation, that the Chinese would foot the bill, and that an improvement in Sino-American ties would "increase international goodwill and lessen the possibility of future wars,"[50] it was clear that many voters in his conservative-minded district were displeased with him.

Boggs, Ford, and their wives and aides traveled to China in late June. Their talks with Zhou and Vice Minister of Foreign Affairs Qiao Guanhua rehashed many of the same topics addressed in February, with much of the conversation focusing on commercial, cultural, and political contacts. Upon returning home, the two lawmakers reported to Nixon that they found the country "'frightening' as well as fascinating." On the one hand, they were impressed by the Chinese people, who seemed happy and healthy. On the other, the Americans were disturbed by the degree to which Beijing forced its citizenry to accept communist ideas from a young age. "We sensed that ultimately China could become vastly dangerous in the international arena," they wrote, "should these millions of bright-eyed children reach maturity with a deeply-implanted hostility toward other societies at the same time that China reaches a technologically advanced stage."[51]

The improvement of ties with the Soviets and the Chinese might have been ends in themselves, but they were also means to another goal, that of concluding the Vietnam War. The pressure at home to terminate the conflict had continued to grow. In 1971 Representatives Charles Whalen (R-Ohio) and Lucien Nezdi (D-Mich.) proposed an amendment to end the war which, though rebuffed, was the first time a majority of Democrats in the House had endorsed such a proposal.[52] The problem was that neither Beijing nor Moscow, competing with one another for influence in North Vietnam, showed any willingness to put undue pressure on Hanoi. For their part, the U.S.–North Vietnamese talks remained stalled. In May 1971, Kissinger made a major concession by giving up Washington's demand that the North pull its forces out of the South as a condition for U.S. forces to leave. But Hanoi continued to insist on the removal from power of the South Vietnamese president, Nguyen Van Thieu.

Believing a major offensive might force the Nixon administration to make further concessions, Hanoi launched a massive attack on South Vietnam at the end of March, using 120,000 troops supported by tanks. At first, the invasion set the ARVN back on its heels, but the South Vietnamese successfully counterattacked thanks to U.S. air support. It appears that the outcome of the so-called Easter Offensive influenced Hanoi's approach to the war. Although the attack exposed the ARVN's weaknesses, the North had suffered some 100,000 casualties. Furthermore, Nixon's hard-line response had received widespread approval in the United States. By the fall, it was clear that the incumbent would win another term as president, thereby giving North Vietnam all the more reason to negotiate.

1972 Election

The election of 1972 pitted Nixon against McGovern. The South Dakota senator was a dove who wanted to withdraw from Vietnam, and Hanoi hoped that if he won, the United States would pull out on the North's terms. But McGovern's campaign was a disaster from the start. Senator Scott called him "The candidate of the 3 A's: acid, abortion, and amnesty," a description that turned off even many Democrats. The Democratic convention was a mess, with delegates recommending over three dozen people for the vice presidency, including Chinese leader Mao Zedong. By the time McGovern had selected his running mate, Missouri's Senator Thomas Eagleton, it was 2:45 a.m. on 15 July, meaning that virtually no one saw the candidate give his acceptance speech. Worse, McGovern had failed to vet Eagleton, and as a result he was not aware that the Missourian had been treated for a mental breakdown. With his own poll numbers not looking good, McGovern had no choice but to remove Eagleton, replacing him with the former head of the Peace Corps and the OEO, Sargent Shriver. Reporters, who liked McGovern as a person, felt obliged to be as unbiased as possible, reporting extensively on his campaign problems. Cognizant that he had a clear path to reelection, Nixon spent most of his time at the White House and rarely met with journalists.[53]

If McGovern's terrible campaign was not enough of a blessing to Nixon, the Vietnam War looked to be on the verge of ending. By October, Kissinger and Le Duc Tho had reached a tentative agreement that called for a ceasefire, an end to the U.S. bombings, the return of American prisoners of war (POWs), and the right of the North to keep its troops in the South. In a concession on their part, Hanoi no longer insisted on Thieu's removal from office. Instead, the draft called for a "council of national reconciliation" that would work out a political settlement in the South acceptable to all sides. "Peace is at hand," Kissinger excitedly told an equally jubilant voting public just before the election. In a landslide, Nixon took forty-nine of the fifty states and 520 electoral votes to McGovern's 17.

Despite the anger within his own district over his changed position on China, Ford had the advantages of incumbency in a conservative district. Once again, his opponent was Jean McKee, who tried to distance herself from McGovern but found it impossible to do so. Ford made sure to emphasize that connection, saying that the "McGovernites" sought to promote "welfarism at its worst—a new brand of socialism which would bankrupt our middle class and destroy Middle America!" Once again, Ford easily won, taking 61 percent of the vote.[54]

The Nixon and Ford victories did not reflect the fate of the GOP in the congressional elections. One would have expected the rebellion against the McGovernites to benefit Republicans, but as in 1968 and 1970, voter sentiment at the national level did not necessarily transfer to states or districts. As Nixon stayed close to home rather than going on the stump, moreover, Republican candidates found it hard to use the president's coattails to their advantage. The GOP gained twelve seats in the House but ended up *losing* two seats in the Senate, and Democrats preserved their majority in both houses. The results left Ford dejected. "I said to myself, if we couldn't get a majority in 1972 against McGovern, and with a Republican winning virtually every state, I couldn't see any Republican candidate coming down the road in '76 that would give us a majority." Nor was he optimistic about 1974. And he had grown weary of Nixon's aides, who "seemed to think that we in the Congress were their patsies."[55]

Nixon's attitude did not help. One telling instance took place in early 1973, when Ford and Scott met with Nixon, expressed their concern about low morale in the party, and said there needed to be better liaison with the White House. Nixon exploded. "Bring them down for cookies?" he asked. "Our Senators are nothing but a bunch of jackasses. . . . We can't count on them. Fuck the Senate!" Although the House had been less problematic for him than the Senate, Nixon asked what Ford and his colleagues could do for him, as opposed to vice versa.[56]

This was all actually good news for Betty. She still enjoyed some of the benefits of being the minority leader's wife, such as the opportunity to travel with her husband to China. She found the trip "fascinating." She was particularly taken with an operation Jerry and she watched in which the doctor used acupuncture instead of anesthesia. But she was ready for him to leave the capital and go into retirement. The two of them decided that he would run one more time in 1974 and then call it quits in 1976. They would keep their home in Alexandria, but Betty also hoped that they would find another place near their children, who at the time were living in different parts of the country.[57] Neither of them knew what the Watergate break-in had in store for their future.

Unraveling Watergate

With his reelection behind him, Nixon turned his attention back to Vietnam. Thieu had rebuffed the October draft agreement on the grounds that it permitted North Vietnamese troops to remain in the South and opened the door to Communist participation in his government. In early January 1973, a frustrated Nixon sent his troublesome ally an ultimatum: Sign the agreement and, if the North violated it, expect the United States to "respond with full force." Do not sign, and the United States would withdraw anyway, leaving the South vulnerable to the "gravest consequences." Thieu relented, and on 27 January—the same day Nixon formally ended the unpopular draft—the United States and the two Vietnams signed the Paris Peace Accords. All sides instituted a cease-fire, Washington promised the withdrawal of its remaining forces within sixty days, Hanoi pledged to return American POWs, and the North was allowed to retain its forces in the South. The settlement could not have come at a better time. Polls showed the overwhelming majority of Americans wanted to end the war, and, reflecting that sentiment, Democrats on Capitol Hill used their majority to end all funding for military action in Southeast Asia.[58]

Congress had begun to turn against what the historian Arthur Schlesinger Jr., referred to as the "imperial presidency,"[59] the idea that the executive branch had expanded its powers so far beyond its constitutional limits that it was all but out of control. It was up to Capitol Hill to rein it in. Hence, in October, lawmakers passed the War Powers Resolution. Under its provisions, the president had to let the legislature know within forty-eight hours if, without a congressional declaration of war, he sent U.S. forces into combat abroad. If Capitol Hill did not approve of his decision, the president had sixty days to end the deployment. Ford had voted against the resolution, commenting, "If the Congress does not want a military conflict continued it 'ought to have the guts and will' to vote against the action, rather than expressing disapproval by doing nothing."[60] Nixon called the bill unconstitutional and vetoed it, but lawmakers easily overrode him.

Nothing, though, had an impact on Nixon comparable to Watergate. Determined to plug leaks of information from the White House and to gather information on political enemies, he had had Ehrlichman establish a group called the "plumbers." Their number included E. Howard Hunt and G. Gordon Liddy, two of the men connected to the Watergate burglars. In its inquiry, the FBI discovered evidence of White House complicity. On 23 June, Nixon made the fateful decision to have Haldeman order the CIA to impede the FBI investigation. Consequently, the president had involved himself in a conspiracy, one that entailed obstructing a federal investigation.

Nixon's hope to stop the investigation failed. The CIA found Nixon's request without cause, a federal grand jury in September 1972 indicted the five Watergate burglars, and the Senate in February of the following year established its own committee of inquiry, cochaired by Sam Ervin (D-N.C.) and Howard Baker (R-Tenn.). Gradually, the cover-up fell apart. In April, Nixon fired his counsel, John Dean, who was involved in the conspiracy and had told Nixon the White House was in trouble. Furthermore, he announced the resignations of Haldeman, Ehrlichman, and Attorney General Richard Kleindienst—who had warned Nixon that prosecutors had enough information to indict the president's chief of staff and domestic adviser. To replace Kleindienst, Nixon nominated Defense Secretary Elliot Richardson. The Senate Judiciary Committee, though, questioned how much independence Richardson would have and made his appointment contingent on appointing an independent prosecutor. The new attorney general did just that, naming Archibald Cox to investigate Watergate.

Not Speaker, but Vice President

Two days after the Watergate break-in, Ford met with John "Jack" Marsh, a friend and lawyer who worked in the capital. By that time, the *Washington Post* had reported McCord's involvement. "I know this fellow McCord," Marsh told the minority leader, "and I know he works closely with John Mitchell. . . . In light of McCord's position, and who he works for, it seems to me that someone at a very high level was bound to have some knowledge or association with this break-in at the Watergate." Maybe, thought Ford, but he wanted to be sure, and he happened to have a meeting later that day with Mitchell, who headed Nixon's campaign fund, called the Committee to Reelect the President (CREEP). Ford asked whether Mitchell or CREEP had any involvement in Watergate, and Mitchell adamantly replied, "Absolutely not!" Having long believed in the goodness of people and trusting that his old friend Nixon would never have involved himself in such a stunt, Ford did not question CREEP's head further.[61]

Assured of Nixon's innocence, Ford did everything he could to defend the president. Wright Patman (D-Tex.), the chair of the House Banking Committee, sought shortly after Nixon's reelection to look more closely at CREEP's role in Watergate. Nixon, Haldeman, and Ehrlichman agreed to have Ford kill Patman's investigation. By the time Ehrlichman passed on the White House's request, the minority leader had already intervened with Republicans on the Banking Committee, telling them that what Patman wanted was to engage in a partisan "campaign fishing expedition," one that would resonate well for Democrats come Election Day. Alongside six Democrats, all but one of the Republicans voted against Patman's plan.[62]

Patman might have been out of the way, but suspicion regarding what Nixon knew and when he knew it continued to grow. As the leader of Nixon's party in the House, Ford naturally became the target of reporters, who wanted his thoughts on the growing scandal. Feeling himself embattled, the minority leader finally spoke out, telling an audience in Michigan that the best way for the White House "to clear up Watergate is for John Mitchell, Bob Haldeman, John Dean, and any others . . . [to] go before the Senate Committee, take an oath," and declare themselves innocent. His comments received national attention, convincing Nixon to ask Ford to come to the Oval Office. There, the president again denied any involvement, blaming the scandal on the Democrats and stressing his preoccupation with other matters, including the rapprochement with China and the SALT I talks. "You have to believe the President, and I did believe him," Ford later commented. Indeed, he called Nixon's April announcement regarding Dean, Haldeman, and Ehrlichman "a necessary first step by the White House in clearing the air on the Watergate affair. . . . I have the greatest confidence in the President, and I am absolutely positive he had nothing to do with this mess."[63]

Ever fewer Americans agreed. With the end of the draft and the Vietnam War, Nixon's approval rating hit 62 percent as 1973 got underway. But by May, when a grand jury indicted Mitchell and the Senate Watergate Committee began its hearings, it had fallen to 45 percent. Millions of Americans watched on television as McCord, Haldeman, Ehrlichman, Dean, and Mitchell appeared before the committee. Dean's testimony was especially important. Not only did he bring with him a voluminous body of documents, but he recalled in detail discussions he had had with Nixon about Watergate.[64]

The bombshell came in July. Numerous presidents had recorded their conversations, including Kennedy and Johnson, and Nixon had kept a system in the Oval Office that audiotaped his meetings with visitors. One of the few people who knew of its existence was Nixon aide Alexander Butterfield. Dean had suggested that his conversations in the Oval Office had been taped, so the Senate Watergate Committee asked Butterfield whether a taping system existed. It did, he responded. The Senate and Cox quickly introduced subpoenas asking for the tapes, but the president refused, citing executive privilege.

In October 1973, as the president and Congress battled over the tapes, Egypt and Syria launched a military offensive on Israel to retrieve land they had lost to Tel Aviv in a war six years earlier. In what came to be known as the Yom Kippur War, the Israelis used American-provided arms to turn the tide against the attackers. Under pressure from their Soviet ally, Cairo and Damascus agreed to a cease-fire. Kissinger traveled to Israel and got Tel Aviv to follow suit. Infuriated by U.S. support for Israel, the Organization of Petroleum Exporting Countries (OPEC), a cartel of oil-producing nations that included a number of Arab members, imposed an embargo on petroleum exports to the United States and its Japanese and western European allies.

For a nation that imported about one-third of its oil, the embargo hurt an economy already in trouble. Phase II of Nixon's economic program had not done much good in addressing inflation and unemployment, and Phase III, which eliminated the Price Commission and Pay Board, saw food prices skyrocket. Therefore, in July 1974, the president had announced Phase IV, which attempted but failed to control the price of food. The oil embargo compounded matters, raising oil imports from four dollars per barrel to twelve dollars. The price of fuel went up from 38.5 cents per gallon in May 1973 to 55.1 cents a year later, and that assumed there was any to be had, for the embargo also caused shortages at gas stations. Nixon accordingly announced "Project Independence," a program to end U.S. dependence on foreign energy sources by 1980. He reduced the speed limit on highways to 55 miles per hour—before this, the states decided how fast drivers could go, with some setting speed limits as high as 80 miles per hour—encouraged power plants to use coal rather than oil, called for the construction of new nuclear-power plants, and cut back by 15 percent the amount of heating oil available to consumers. These steps, however, were not enough to prevent inflation from rising to an annual rate of 14.5 percent and the gross national product from seeing its worst decline in sixteen years. Ford did not comment on Phase IV, but he probably endorsed its measures, having commented earlier that Phase III stood "a good chance of success."[65]

If the embargo was not bad enough for Nixon, October also witnessed the resignation of Vice President Spiro Agnew. In August, the media reported that he was the target of a federal investigation on several charges, among them bribery and tax evasion. It turned out that while serving the state of Maryland, both when he was a county official and when he was governor, he had taken kickbacks from contractors, and he then did the same thing as vice president. Nor had he paid taxes on the money he had received. The investigation had begun in February, but Agnew was not aware of it until it became public. Already facing scrutiny himself, Nixon refused to devote political capital to saving his vice president. The evidence against Agnew proved overwhelming. Given a choice between resignation and a fine or jail time, he selected the former in October, paying $10,000 for tax evasion and giving up the vice presidency.[66]

For the first time in its history, the U.S. government would invoke the Twenty-Fifth Amendment to the Constitution, added in 1967. Article II, Section I of the Constitution addressed the question of presidential and vice-presidential succession, but it left some questions unanswered. For instance, what if the vice president died and the president proved unable for mental or physical reasons to perform his duties, or him- or herself passed away? The Kennedy assassination and the accession to the presidency of Lyndon B. Johnson, who had a history of health problems, made it appear all the more essential to offer clarification. The result was the Twenty-Fifth Amendment, which stated that if the president died or resigned, the vice president took his place. In a case when the vice president resigned or passed away, the president would nominate someone, with both houses of Congress deciding by majority vote whether the nominee deserved the post.

Nixon sought to find someone to replace Agnew who met what for him were four criteria: party loyalty, qualification to become president, an ideology similar to his own, and acceptability to Congress. Although there were many in the party who assumed that Nixon, as he had before, already had someone in mind,[67] numerous lawmakers offered their suggestions, with many listing Ford as their number one or two choice.[68]

For his part, Ford suggested John Connally, followed by Laird and either Rockefeller or Reagan. Nixon preferred Connally, but the Treasury secretary had infuriated Democrats by leaving that party to join the GOP. Laird did not want the post—and his abrasiveness would have been a negative anyway—and Rockefeller and Reagan were out, as they might use the vice presidency as a stepping stone to run for the GOP presidential nomination in 1976, something Nixon wanted Connally to have. That left Ford. Despite the minority leader's belief that he and Nixon were good friends, the

Secretary of Defense Melvin Laird and House Minority Leader Gerald R. Ford on the steps of the U.S. Capitol, July 1969. Laird was among those who encouraged President Richard Nixon to nominate Ford to replace Vice President Spiro Agnew. Photo in the Gerald Ford Library, Ann Arbor, Michigan.

president did not think much of the Michigander. "Can you imagine Jerry Ford sitting in this chair?" he reportedly asked. Butterfield commented that to the White House, Ford was "like a puppy dog. They used him when they had to—wind him up and he'd go 'Arf, Arf.'" Still, Harlow, Laird, and Albert made clear to Nixon that only Ford met all four requirements. As a bonus, the minority leader told Nixon he had no intention of running for the presidency in 1976, thereby permitting Connally the opportunity to seek the office that year.[69]

Two days after Agnew resigned, Ford, on Nixon's instruction, got a call from Laird. His erstwhile Young Turk ally had resigned his post at Defense in 1973 as part of a larger White House shake-up that saw fifty-seven people resign, among them Secretary of State William Rogers, whose title Kissinger assumed on top of his existing position as national security adviser. Laird, though, maintained contact with Nixon and had been among those who told the president that nominating Connally would infuriate the Democratic-dominated Congress. His choice was Ford. Believing Nixon was leaning in that direction, he wanted to know if the minority leader would accept the vice presidency if offered. Before answering, Ford said he wanted to talk with Betty first.[70]

Later that day, the Fords considered the pros and cons of accepting. There were good reasons to say no. Ford wondered if he would even like the job. As the vice president and his family had a Secret Service detail assigned to them, Betty worried about the impact on their children. At the same time, Ford had reached the conclusion that he would not become speaker. Moreover, he planned to retire from politics in 1976, so the vice presidency would mean "a nice cap for my career." Finally, he had always agreed to a request by the president, Republican or Democrat, to take on an important job, whether it be joining the committee to write up the legislation to form the National Aeronautics and Space Administration or to sit on the Warren Commission. With Betty supporting his decision, Ford called Laird back. "We've talked about it and agreed that, if I were asked, I'd accept. But I won't do anything to stimulate a campaign. I'm not promoting myself."[71]

Ford had just finished a swim at his Alexandria home prior to dinner when the phone rang. Answering it, he heard Nixon, who then put Haldeman's successor, Alexander Haig, on. "I've got good news for you," Haig said. "The President wants you to be the Vice President," and he then suggested Ford put Betty on the line. Ford was shocked. He admitted later that he had missed hints that Nixon had given suggesting he was the top choice. At one point, the president had told congressional leaders during the nominating process, "I'd like to be in the shape with the American public that Jerry Ford is." During a one-on-one meeting between Ford and the president, Nixon had called in a photographer. "Take this picture," the president commented. "It may be historic." But Ford had no idea he was Nixon's selection until the call came. In a case of somewhat comedic timing, Betty was unable to get on the phone, as she was on the house's other line speaking with one of the Fords' sons. Haig had to call back a few minutes later so that both Fords could hear the offer.[72]

After accepting, the Fords traveled to the White House for the formal announcement. Betty was not happy. She had been looking forward to her husband's retirement, which would mean that his days as an absent spouse and father would come to an end. Taking the country's second-most-powerful position threatened that dream. "Mother was ready to go through the roof," commented Steve Ford. "Betty, just don't worry," Jerry assured her. "Vice presidents don't do anything." Whether she believed him is questionable, for she did not want to go to the swearing-in ceremony. Afterward, when Nixon shook hands with the Fords and congratulated them, she asked, "Congratulations or condolences?"[73]

Upon returning home, the Fords were met by neighbors who offered their congratulations, numerous phone calls, and Secret Service agents who had put a command center on the front lawn. Considering it unfair to have the agents stuck outside, Mrs. Ford offered them a spare bedroom, but they declined. (Eventually, the garage was converted for the Secret Service's use.) The agents urged the Fords to continue as they had before, which was impossible. Jerry had to give up his congressional seat, could no longer go anywhere without a Secret Service detail, and could not fly on commercial airlines as he once had. Yet there were perks. Waiting in line at airports was over, and he was honored at Red Flannel Day, an annual celebration he attended in Cedar Springs, Michigan. His new title also offered potential benefits at home. Susan had made a five-dollar bet with her mother that her father was Nixon's choice, and having been proven right, she tied up one of the phone lines to inform her friends. Ford asked an aide to tell her to free up the line, but realizing that might not have an impact on a teenager, he upped the ante: "Tell her the Vice President told her to get off."[74]

In Congress, the nomination received praise from both parties. Ford's penchant for partisanship did not bother most people on Capitol Hill, where one was expected to stand behind his or her party. Despite his effort to impeach Douglas, the minority leader remained popular. Colleagues called him a "low-pressure personality," and younger House members had particular affection for him, as he was "approachable and willing to take time to counsel them." Albert stated, "I think it will be easier to get Jerry Ford confirmed than any other Republican I know." Similarly, Senator Frank Church (D-Idaho) observed, "It's a very good thing for the country we're not likely to have a protracted struggle."[75]

Sixty-six percent of Americans endorsed the nomination, and only 7 percent were opposed. The media was less enthusiastic. *Time* praised the nomination and pointed to Ford's "corruption-free reputation." The liberal-minded *Nation* was not so kind. In language that pointed to the possibility that Watergate could bring down Nixon, its editors wrote, "Gerald Ford has none of the qualifications which the people have a right to look for in a man who just might succeed to the Presidency." He was "a mediocrity" but someone who, unlike the other possible nominees, "will not make Nixon feel uneasy nor will he overshadow him." Even the conservative *Wall Street Journal* was critical, accusing the president of thinking about the short term, nominating someone whom Congress would confirm, rather than considering the long term and choosing a candidate who could reverse Americans' distrust of government.[76]

The media reaction may have pointed to a final reason why Nixon chose Ford. According to Kissinger, Nixon saw in Ford someone so poorly versed in foreign affairs that few if any members of Congress, no matter how much they liked the minority leader, would want to see him become president. If that was the case, it was a serious miscalculation on Nixon's part. "It was more tempting for Democrats to remove Nixon if his successor seemed to be someone they thought they could beat in the Presidential election of 1976," Kissinger wrote. Even Republicans recognized that the president had probably shortened his tenure. As Arizona's Representative John Rhodes put it, by picking Ford, Nixon "probably signed his own death warrant."[77]

Resignation

With Ford's nomination out of the way, Nixon turned his attention to Cox and the subpoenaed tapes. A federal appeals court had set an October deadline for turning over the tapes, and the president offered the special prosecutor a deal: summaries of the nine tapes, with Senator John Stennis (D-Miss.) to retain the originals and vouch for the accuracy of what Cox had received. When Cox rebuffed Nixon's proposal, the president decided to get rid of the troublesome prosecutor, and on 20 October he ordered Richardson to fire him. Richardson said no and resigned. The president then turned to Richardson's deputy, William Ruckelshaus, who followed the lead of his boss and quit as well. It was Solicitor General Robert Bork, the third-ranking person at Justice, who gave Cox his walking papers. The Saturday Night Massacre, as it became known, gave the impression of a president desperate to conceal his guilt. A Gallup poll found that Nixon's approval rating had fallen to 17 percent.[78] Albert announced his intention to ask the House Judiciary Committee to begin looking into Nixon's impeachment.

With it appearing ever more likely that Nixon's political future was short, Representative Bella Abzug saw an opportunity. A liberal Democrat from New York, Abzug hated Nixon and encouraged others in her party to delay the hearings to confirm Ford's nomination. Her hope was that in the meantime, Nixon would be forced out of office, and with no vice president in place, the Oval Office would, under the Constitution, fall to Albert. "Get off your goddamned ass," she told the House speaker, "and we can take the presidency." The lobbying group Americans for Democratic Action and others in the House and Senate, including members of the Congressional Black Caucus, also had little interest in seeing Ford confirmed because of his positions on civil rights, social programs, the environment, and Vietnam. Albert, however, had no intention of holding up the confirmation hearings. He did not want to be president,[79] and he knew that to achieve the presidency through what would appear to be a Democratic conspiracy would undermine his credibility with the American people.

With the majority of lawmakers determined to press ahead, in October Ford went before both houses on Capitol Hill to testify in his confirmation hearings. In one of the most extensive background checks in American history, 350 FBI agents had spoken with over 1,000 people and turned over to lawmakers 1,700 pages of material. Now, with the possibility that Nixon himself might be removed from office, members of the House and Senate knew they were deciding whether to confirm the person who would probably become the country's next president. To help prepare himself for what he knew would be intense questioning, Ford turned to his former law partner, Philip Buchen. He also received help from Benton Becker, a law professor at the University of Miami, and Hartmann, whom he now appointed as his chief of staff.[80]

Appearing before the Senate Judiciary Committee and then its equivalent in the House, Ford defended himself against charges that he had hidden over $11,000 in campaign contributions in 1970. When asked how he avoided having a mortgage despite owning a home in Virginia and a condominium in Vail, Colorado, Ford replied that he had used a combination of personal savings, money from an inheritance, a bank loan, and his children's savings accounts. The most potentially damaging testimony came from lobbyist Robert Winter-Berger, who claimed that Ford had received psychotherapy treatment and had taken money in return for making sure the president of International Mining Company, Francis Kellogg, received an ambassadorship. Ford denied both charges, and the Senate Rules Committee found enough inconsistencies in Winter-Berger's statements that it considered charging him with perjury. Finally, when asked about Watergate, Ford cautiously expressed his independence of mind, telling his examiners that early on Nixon should have made an offer to turn over the tapes. Asked whether Nixon at any time had a right to lie to the U.S. public, Ford said no; nor, he said, did the president have the right to defy a court order. As for impeachment, "I don't believe there are grounds," he commented, "but that's a personal judgement."[81]

Ford's statements drew praise from both parties. "I think your answers have been open-handed and frank," said West Virginia's Robert Byrd, one of the top Democrats in the Senate. "You have met some tough questions head-on, and I want to commend you."[82] Both Judiciary Committees voted overwhelmingly for confirmation. The full Senate did the same on 27 November, as did the House on 6 December.

Nixon sought to hold his new vice president's swearing-in ceremony in the White House's East Room, which would allow him to control the affair and share the spotlight. Ford would have none of it, insisting that it occur on Capitol Hill: "That would be a much better place for my relations with the Congress and for yours as well." The president concurred, and on 6 December, Chief Justice Warren Burger oversaw the ceremony, using a Bible provided by the Fords' son Michael, who was then in divinity school. As his family watched, Ford took the vice presidential oath and then delivered a short address. Comparing himself to America's sixteenth president, he told those in attendance, "I am a Ford, not a Lincoln." He admitted he was not as good a speaker as Abraham Lincoln, "but I will do my best to equal his brevity and plain speaking." Further, he promised both "to uphold the Constitution . . . and, within the limited powers and duties of the vice presidency, to do the very best that I can for America."[83]

All the while, Nixon made clear he had every intention of retaining his post, telling a television audience in November, "I am not a crook." But he knew he was in trouble. He faced growing calls for his resignation; Cox's successor, Leon Jaworski, determined to get to the bottom of Watergate; the House Judiciary Committee began its hearings; and Nixon's lead attorney,

Fred Buzhardt, told the Senate Watergate Committee that two tapes were missing. A third, the administration announced about a week later, had an eighteen-and-a-half-minute erasure, reinforcing the belief that the president had something to hide. The following spring, the Judiciary Committee and Jaworski subpoenaed dozens of additional tapes. Rather than release them, Nixon at the end of April provided the committee with edited transcripts, which he made public. Americans were shocked at the number of times "expletive deleted" appeared, while John Sirica, chief judge of the U.S. district court in Washington who oversaw the trials of individuals involved in Watergate, insisted he had to have the tapes themselves. For his part, Jaworski demanded that the U.S. Supreme Court decide whether the president had to comply with the demand made of him by the House and the special prosecutor.

Ford found himself pulled in different directions. As Betty had feared, his absences grew, in part because the White House expected him to act as Nixon's "principal public defender." He traveled around the nation giving speeches defending the administration's policies—so many speeches that writer Norman Mailer suggested someone "take his airplane away from him." Occasionally, he represented the administration in talks with foreign officials. One of his first meetings was with the Soviet ambassador to the United States, Anatoly Dobrynin, during which they discussed the Middle East, SALT I, and Nixon's desire to grant the Soviet Union most-favored-nation (MFN) trading status. Nixon thought that granting MFN status to Moscow would promote détente. What stood in the way was Soviet restrictions on emigration. In an effort to persuade the Soviets to loosen their restrictions, the House in December passed a trade bill that included an amendment introduced by Vanik that required the Soviets to allow free emigration in return for MFN. Ford expressed his desire that the House vote not prevent Congress from offering a "favorable" bill that included MFN.[84]

Even more than before, Ford also had to assume positions he had once rejected. A particularly telling example is the change in his statements on the Panama Canal. Negotiations between the United States and Panama over the waterway's future had made little progress, but in February 1974, Kissinger announced that he had worked out an agreement for a new treaty abrogating that of 1903, ending U.S. "jurisdiction over Panamanian territory" and, over time, giving Panama full control of the waterway. As late as October 1973, Ford had written to a constituent, "The Panama Canal is an essential part of our transportation system, and the United States must maintain control over the Canal and the surrounding area." Now, six months later, he expressed to Panama's ambassador to the United States, Nicolas Gonzalez-Revilla, his pessimism that a new treaty could get through the Senate, but he added that if both nations pursued one, it should not leave any matters unresolved.[85]

Getting such a treaty through the Senate needed Nixon's help, but Watergate consumed ever more of his time. The same was the case for Ford, who tried to remain loyal to his boss. He went too far down that path in January, though. He permitted the president's speechwriters to prepare an address he was to give the American Farm Bureau Federation. The language sounded less like his and more like the president's. "A few extreme partisans," he proclaimed, including labor unions and Americans for Democratic Action, sought to use "the ordeal of Watergate for their own purposes" and defeat both the president and "the policies for which he stands." The speech appeared out of order for Ford, who, though partisan, had so far avoided such strongly worded attacks on specific persons or groups. Even some conservatives were surprised, and they worried that Ford risked hurting his reputation and further damaging that of the GOP. Admitting he had caused himself "considerable embarrassment," Ford made certain from that point on that Hartmann wrote all his speeches.[86]

Hartmann later said that Ford did not want to be "Nixon's boy," and the vice president began to distance himself from his boss. A group of midwestern Republicans lauded him in March when he told them that "the political lesson of Watergate is this. Never again must America allow an arrogant, elite guard of political adolescents like CREEP to bypass the regular party organization and dictate the terms of a national election." In Hartmann's view, Ford's words made him "the *de facto* head of the Republican Party," a point reaffirmed when Reagan, Rockefeller, and Senator Charles Percy of Illinois echoed him. Further proof that Ford wanted to loosen his ties to Nixon came in April, when he told John Osborne of the *New Republic* that if he became president, he would keep Kissinger but remove both Defense Secretary James Schlesinger and White House Press Secretary Ron Ziegler. Ford said his comments, which infuriated the president, were supposed to be off the record, but he declined to deny their accuracy.[87]

An embattled Nixon left the country in June, heading first to Israel and then to the Soviet Union. Three weeks after he returned home, the Supreme Court issued its decision: he had to turn over the tapes. By then, it was almost certain that Nixon would not survive impeachment. Sixty-six percent of Americans called for his removal from office, and during the last week of July, the House Judiciary Committee—including all of the Democrats and some of the Republicans who sat on it—approved three articles of impeachment, including obstruction of justice and contempt.

Nixon knew his tenure was nearing its end. Included on the tapes released to Congress was the conversation he had had with Haldeman on 23 June, proving his complicity. Even his staunchest defender on the Judiciary Committee, Charles Wiggins (R-Calif.), publicly announced that the evidence proved Nixon's tenure "must be terminated."[88]

Early on the morning of 1 August, Nixon informed Haig that he intended to resign. He asked the chief of staff to make sure Ford was ready to become the country's chief executive. Afterward, Haig called the vice president and requested to see him as soon as possible. "Come over now," Ford replied and then told Hartmann of the phone call. Not one to trust Haig, Hartmann insisted that he, Marsh, or the two of them be in the office when Haig arrived. "Okay, Bob, you sit in," Ford told him. Arriving at 9:00 a.m., Haig told Ford that Nixon was in serious jeopardy; one tape was "very damaging," though Haig said he himself had not heard it. Asked by the vice president how Nixon was doing, Haig said the president could not decide whether to fight the charges or resign. The meeting lasted forty-five minutes—Haig did most of the talking—after which Ford told Haig to keep him informed and Hartmann to keep the meeting secret.[89]

Because Haig disliked Hartmann as much as Hartmann did him, he had not been as open as he wanted, and he decided to see Ford again that day, but alone. First, though, he met with Buzhardt to ask what Nixon's options were. Buzhardt offered several, including resigning, facing impeachment, pardoning himself, or having his successor pardon him. The last suggestion intrigued Haig, who asked if it was possible for a president to pardon someone who had not yet been charged with a crime. Absolutely, Buzhardt responded. With that, he called Ford, requesting once again to see him, but strictly one-on-one. Ford agreed and told Hartmann and Marsh, the latter of whom did not know of the meeting that morning. Again, Hartmann suggested someone else be present, but this time Ford refused, promising to let his two aides know afterward what transpired.[90]

At 3:30 that afternoon, Haig arrived at the Executive Office Building. "Are you ready, Mr. Vice President, to assume the Presidency in a short period of time?," he asked. "If that happens, Al, I am prepared," Ford replied. His experience as a lawmaker who had worked on financial, intelligence, defense, and foreign-aid matters assured him that he could assume the reins of power. With that, Haig apprised the vice president that in the intervening hours between their meetings, he had seen a transcript of the "smoking-gun" tape. It was clear that Nixon had the choice of resigning or facing impeachment, but he was not certain which alternative the president might select. Asked if Nixon had any chance of avoiding conviction by the Senate if the House voted to impeach him, Haig said no. He then offered Ford the various options open to him, including a pardon. "What is the extent of a President's pardon power?" the vice president queried. He could pardon someone who had not yet been convicted of a criminal offense, Haig answered. "I will need some time to think about this. I want to talk to [Nixon counsel James] St. Clair. I want to talk to my wife before giving any response," said Ford. With that, Haig departed.[91]

Ford was in shock. He had always believed there was good in people, and he had naively assumed that his old friend Nixon, who had a history of misleading others, would be straightforward with him about any role he had played in Watergate. It was clear that the president had lied to him. "The hurt was very deep," recalled Ford. Returning home that evening, he told Betty to cancel a planned trip to New York "because we're probably going to move in to the White House."[92]

Betty had mixed feelings about what was in store for them. She later wrote that had she foreseen the events that would lead her husband from the vice presidency into the White House, "I think I probably would have sat down and cried." Yet she also concluded that "Jerry . . . had no choice. And I had such belief in my husband I never doubted he could do it."[93]

Realizing the path their lives were about to take, the two of them sought support from a higher power. Commented son Steve, the Fords did not express their faith in the same way that "other Christians live out their faith." His parents said grace before every meal and attended church weekly, but their devotion to God was more private than public. Son Michael, who went into the ministry, recalled that his father was "very committed to God" but "not outspoken or vocal about his commitment." That commitment, though, was very strong, and with a new and challenging phase in their lives before them, the Fords prayed, hoping He might provide them guidance.[94]

What the vice president had not considered was whether Haig's meeting with him was another of Nixon's schemes. It was certainly on Hartmann's mind, though. After Haig left, Ford told Hartmann about the conversation, including his comment that he had to think about a pardon. "You what?" asked an incredulous Hartmann. "That's almost the worst answer Haig could take back to the White House. You told Haig you were willing to entertain the idea of a pardon if he resigns—that's probably all Haig and Nixon want to know." The president would never have asked his chief of staff to raise a pardon if he did want insight into Ford's position on the matter. By not saying no to a pardon, Ford had left that option open, Hartmann continued. Stubbornly, Ford insisted that was not the case. Ask Marsh what he thinks, Hartmann urged, but Ford demurred, preferring to wait until the next day.[95]

The next day, 2 August, Ford met with St. Clair, who assured him that there was enough on the tape to convict Nixon. Surer than ever that he was going to become the next president, Ford did as Hartmann asked and called in Marsh to talk about his conversation with Haig. Like Hartmann, Marsh insisted that by not discounting the possibility of a pardon, Ford had suggested that route was available. Ford stood firm, insisting that he had done nothing wrong, so Marsh asked him to talk with Harlow, whom he knew Ford trusted. Speaking with the vice president that afternoon, Harlow seconded Marsh and Hartmann: "I cannot for a moment believe that all this was Al Haig's own idea, or that the matters he discussed originated with 'the White House staff.'" Without a doubt Haig met with Ford on Nixon's instructions. What Nixon wanted was "to hear your recommendations and test your reaction to the pardon question." Finally convinced that Nixon had to get out of office but without any promises of help, Ford called Haig and emphasized that their conversation in no way was a recommendation as to what Nixon should do or a suggestion of what he, Ford, might do. "You're absolutely right," stated Haig.[96]

Nixon continued to waver over whether to fight. There was no doubt that the House would impeach him, and the Senate would find him guilty. At a cabinet meeting on 6 August, Republican National Committee chairman George H. W. Bush "all but told Nixon he had to retire." Haig concurred, as did House Judiciary Committee chair Peter Rodino. "If he resigns," Rodino asked a colleague to inform Nixon, "we can drop this, the impeachment, the threat of criminal proceedings. If he quits, that's the end of it."[97] With that, the president decided on 8 August to announce his resignation and so informed the Republican leadership on Capitol Hill.

The Unelected President

At 9:00 p.m. on 8 August, Nixon announced his resignation, effective the next day. He conceded "some of my judgments were wrong," but he refused to admit any criminal wrongdoing. After a sleepless night, he said goodbye to the White House staff and then joined his wife, as the now president and Mrs. Ford escorted them to a helicopter that would take the Nixons to

Chief Justice Warren Burger swears in Gerald Ford as the thirty-eighth president of the United States as Mrs. Ford looks on, 9 August 1974. Photo in the Gerald Ford Library, Ann Arbor, Michigan.

California. Jerry then headed to a limousine that would drive him about two blocks to the Executive Office Building, where the vice president's office was located. "I stared ahead at the car, and I wanted the agents to open the door as soon as possible so I could climb inside. I needed to be alone."[98]

Ford took the oath of office that evening and then joined his family at their Virginia home. While preparing dinner, Betty told him, "Jerry, something's wrong. You just became president of the United States, and I'm still cooking." Amazingly, Ford had been so certain Nixon would hold onto the presidency that, even after becoming the nation's number-two official, he had retained the family's home telephone number, which was available to anyone who took the time to look it up in the white pages. He had justified that decision on the grounds that it made him accessible to those who might seek his help. Now that he was president, he got a new, unpublished phone number.[99]

It had been a roller-coaster ride for the new president. One historian referred to Ford as a "foot soldier for Nixon,"[100] and it is not an inaccurate description. Ford, like Nixon, had demonstrated that he was a pragmatist who was willing to buck the stand taken by many in his own party, but when push came to shove, he was a Republican partisan. With Nixon's accession to the presidency in 1969, it had appeared that the Republicans' political fortunes would soon give the party the majority of seats in the House and let Ford achieve his dream of the speakership. The minority leader had repeatedly defended the president, even assuming positions on taxes, wage and price controls, and foreign policy that contradicted his previous stands on those issues. He had also made the potentially dangerous mistake of demanding Justice Douglas's impeachment and was lucky it did not cause him lasting damage.

Ford also stood behind Nixon as the Watergate scandal unfolded, despite the evidence and the president's known penchant for duplicity. It took months for the minority leader and then vice president to begin to distance himself from his longtime friend. Yet it was not until the revelation of the smoking-gun tape that Ford realized Nixon was not innocent. Having longed to become House speaker, upon Nixon's resignation he now found himself president of the United States. Whether he intended to continue Nixon's policies or seek a new course for himself was the question.

SIX

Honeymoon and Hardship

One day after he assumed office, Gerald Ford was due to deliver his first speech as president. He had asked his top aide and speechwriter, Robert Hartmann, to compose it. Starting late the night before, Hartmann put together what he considered a good address. Ford read it and came to one line he did not like. "Bob," the new president commented, "I think we better leave it out." Hartmann refused. "Don't you see," he implored, "that's your whole speech! That's what you have to proclaim to the whole country—to the whole world. That's what everybody *needs* to hear, *wants* to hear, has *got* to hear you say." Ford yielded in the face of such emphatic resistance: "O.K., I guess you're right. I hadn't thought about it that way."[1]

Ford's family, including all the children, were there to witness the event. Steve and Susan were still in high school and living with their parents, but Mike and Jack were already on their own. Mike had married Gayle Brumbaugh only a month earlier and had just returned to Boston from Washington when Secret Service agents handed them airline tickets for their flight back to the capital. Jack was in Yellowstone National Park working as a ranger. He was out on patrol when he received a call to head back to camp and fly to Washington. They were a few of the millions of Americans who watched Ford deliver a short inaugural speech of only 850 words. He asked for Americans' prayers and reminded viewers that he had not sought either the vice presidency or the presidency. That said, he offered a fresh start. His administration would be open, honest, and not bound by the past. To reinforce that last point while simultaneously offering a tribute to the love of his life, he made clear, "I am indebted to no man, and only to one woman—my dear wife—as I begin this difficult job." As further proof of his intention to lead the country down a new path, he delivered the line he originally had sought to delete: "My fellow Americans, our long national nightmare is over." He continued, "As we bind up the internal wounds of Watergate, more painful and more poisonous than those of foreign wars, let us restore the golden rule to our political process, and let brotherly love purge our hearts of suspicion and of hate." Asking for the goodwill of the American people, the country's thirty-eighth president concluded, "God helping me, I will not let you down."[2]

It was a powerful address, one aimed at establishing a clear break with the Nixon administration and Watergate and at reassuring Americans that they could expect their new chief executive to adopt a path based on transparency, truthfulness, and respect for the law. "The simplicity with which Gerald R. Ford addressed the nation as he took the oath of office in the White House yesterday reflects the nature of this unpretentious man," reflected the *New York Times*. "It also suggests the straightforwardness and the humility which may be expected to characterize Mr. Ford's approach to the great office he now will occupy." The *Washington Post*'s William Greider declared that Ford's "level gaze and Midwestern voice seemed more dramatic than the loftiest rhetoric," and *Newsweek* magazine praised the new president's "gripping eloquence. . . . The promises were accordingly modest, the tone positively deferential."[3]

The word "simplicity," as used by the *New York Times*, could have easily referred to more than the language Ford adopted. It also could have meant the image the new president wanted to convey. It was not that he was simpleminded or unintelligent. Rather, unlike the "imperial" President Nixon, he was an average American. He cooked his own breakfast, preferring a relatively simple meal consisting of an English muffin, melon, orange juice, and tea, and, reported *Time* magazine, he "worked in his shirtsleeves." To reinforce his common-man status, Ford had the White House band stop playing "Hail to the Chief" and instead asked for the University of Michigan fight song, "The Victors." He urged close friends to call him by his first name as opposed to "Mr. President." Unlike Nixon, who as president retreated to secluded homes in California and Florida, Ford's Vail chalet was near the abodes of others in town, and both townspeople and reporters could watch him as he tackled the slopes.[4]

Ford was also warmhearted. Nixon had the reputation of being a liar and crook, but in addition he was introverted and uncomfortable in large groups, he spurned those with alternate points of view, and he held grudges against anyone he believed had offended him. The gregarious Ford was willing to listen to others' opinions, even if he disagreed with them. Even those who were critical, such as speechwriter John Casserly—who wrote an embittered memoir after leaving the Ford administration—commented, "[Ford] tells the truth when he speaks. He is good-natured, even-tempered, and extraordinarily calm for a man with such responsibility. . . . If there appears to be a conflict between what is convenient and what is decent or honorable, Mr. Ford will inevitably choose what is decent." Among his first actions as president was to meet with members of the Congressional Black Caucus and with labor-union leader George Meany, all of whom had received a cold shoulder from Nixon. An even firmer indication that Ford intended to stake out a new course was during a dinner he and Betty hosted for Jordan's king and queen. Though the dinner had originally been planned by the Nixons, the Fords' guest list included a number of persons who had been persona non grata at the White House, including journalist Eric Sevareid and former defense secretary Robert McNamara. "My God, you know things have changed when they let *you* in here," commented Senator Mark Hatfield and Secretary of State Henry Kissinger upon seeing McNamara. Observed one secretary who had worked under Nixon, "I haven't seen so many smiles around here in a long, long time."[5]

The optimism Ford tried to communicate to the country did not last long. By early 1975 he had become the target of critics. His programs to address the energy crisis and the weak economy appeared moribund; his proposal for a clemency program for those who had evaded the Vietnam draft received a cool response; his decision to nominate Nelson Rockefeller as vice president infuriated the right wing of his party; negotiations aimed at curbing the arms race, achieving peace in the Middle East, and resolving a crisis over Cyprus were not going as smoothly as hoped; and members of Congress showed little desire to assist South Vietnam. But more than anything else, the president's decision to pardon Nixon a mere month after taking office brought a swift and angry end to the goodwill Ford had received on 9 August and cost Republicans heavily in the 1974 midterm elections. "At a stroke," wrote *Newsweek* a week after the pardon, the president “not only ended his political honeymoon but called his own good faith into question.”[6]

The Transition

The term “presidential transition” evokes the period during which an outgoing president and his staff ready their departure and the president-elect prepares to enter the Oval Office. Until 1937, this was an interval of four months, starting with Election Day in November and ending on 4 March. Improvements in communications, travel, and vote-counting technology, as well as a desire to cut down the period of time the president was a lame duck, led Congress and the states to add the Twentieth Amendment to the U.S. Constitution in 1933, moving Inauguration Day up to 20 January. During those weeks, the outgoing president and his aides have time to complete any unfinished business and to clean out their offices. In the meantime, the president-elect appoints or, if senatorial approval is required, nominates his top aides and gets set to move into the White House.

At least, that was the way presidential transitions were supposed to take place. Though no president before Nixon had resigned, eight had died while in office. In those cases, the White House became the home of the former vice president, who had to wait for the executive mansion to be readied for him and his family. It was not always a quick process. When Zachary Taylor passed away in July 1850, his vice president, Millard Fillmore, told Margaret Taylor she could take her time in arranging her affairs before vacating the White House; three days later, immediately following her husband’s funeral, the distraught first lady left Washington, never to return. James Garfield, shot by an assassin in July 1881, lingered for over two months, and the White House was transformed into a makeshift hospital. During those weeks, the mansion did not receive much in the way of upkeep, requiring the vice president, Chester A. Arthur, to wait for the building to be renovated before he could occupy it.[7]

The Fords did not have to bide their time nearly as long as did Arthur, but it took the Nixons a week to clear out of the executive mansion. In the meantime, the Ford family home in Alexandria became the White House for all practical purposes. Reporters and the Secret Service “took over the whole damn neighborhood,” the president recalled, and “our poor neighbors went through hell.” Ford did his best to continue life as normal, using his pool—which he admitted he hated to give up—speaking with neighbors, and signing autographs, but journalists could not help but notice when, on the morning after taking the oath of office, the president appeared on his front porch in pajamas to pick up his copy of the *Washington Post.* (One media outlet pointed out that the newspaper arrived late, and a Secret Service agent passed it into the Fords' house.)[8]

No one could have known the transition period would require Ford to operate from his Virginia home, but it had been clear to many observers months before the resignation that Nixon's days were probably numbered. One such observer was Phil Buchen, Ford's former law partner and longtime friend. Realizing the need to prepare for a presidential transition, Buchen in May 1974 approached Clay Whitehead, a Harvard graduate and former employee of the RAND Corporation who had worked in the Bureau of the Budget under President Lyndon B. Johnson and as director of the Office of Telecommunications Policy (OTP) during Nixon's last four years in office. Loyal to Nixon, Whitehead was not eager to join Buchen, but he changed his mind when Buchen assured him their work would be secret. They lined up three more people to join them: Brian Lamb, who had served as Whitehead's OTP assistant; Larry Lynn, who had worked on the National Security Council; and Jonathan Moore, an aide to New York's former governor, Nelson Rockefeller.[9]

The Buchen-Whitehead transition team reached two conclusions. The first was to suggest a spokes-in-the wheel approach to decision making. Instead of having a chief of staff who would determine who had access to the president, the spokes-in-the-wheel plan assumed an egalitarian system in which all the president's top advisers had the same access to him. It was a concept that made sense for a former congressman and vice president who preferred to leave his door open to anyone who wished to see him rather than receive a memo or have a gatekeeper determine who got through the door. Second, they agreed that Al Haig, Nixon's overbearing chief of staff, would have to go.[10]

Believing Ford would have been furious had he been aware of this unauthorized transition team, Buchen had quietly kept it from him. Word of the smoking-gun tape in early August, though, made it clear that Nixon's presidency was going to end, and it behooved Buchen to make his friend aware of what he had been doing. Not willing to leave transition planning up to a group about whose members, except for Buchen, he knew little, Ford asked his former law partner to add five more individuals with whom he had been close: Interior Secretary Rogers Morton, Senator Robert Griffin (R-Mich.), Representative John Byrnes (R-Wisc.), U.S. Steel Corporation lobbyist William Whyte, and Nixon's congressional liaison Bryce Harlow.

Instead of Buchen and Whitehead becoming the principals of a team of ten, the two groups acted independently of each other. They also reached different conclusions, with the second team, headed by Whyte, arguing that a pure spokes-in-the wheel approach would prove harmful because it established no clear line of authority. Instead, it suggested giving all of Ford's top staff equal access to the president but having a single person act as overseer. That person would not receive the title "chief of staff" but would have similar authority. The Whyte group proposed retaining Haig, assuming he would leave of his own accord. It even offered Ford some names of people who might take Haig's place when that happened. From that list, the vice president selected his erstwhile Young Turk ally, Donald Rumsfeld.[11]

It made sense to both the Whyte team and Ford to keep Haig in his post—minus the title "chief of staff"—because of his experience, which would be essential once Ford assumed the presidency. Haig was "the only one who knows how to fly the plane," commented Hartmann. "We're not going to shoot him in the cockpit before we learn to fly the plane or design a new plane." Indeed, Ford felt that way about the entire White House staff, asking them just before he took the presidential oath of office "to stay on long enough to assure a steady and informed transition of the Presidency." He repeated that request at his first cabinet meeting, held on 10 August.[12]

Retaining Haig and other Nixon staffers was a recipe for trouble. There was no love lost between those who had served the outgoing president and the man who was about to take his place. "Goddammit," commented one Ford aide, "this President is not going to be mean. He doesn't feel anybody should be punished for doing his duty as ordered." Certainly the fiercest animosity was that between Hartmann and Haig. Hartmann might have agreed that Haig had to stay on, but he disliked having his position challenged by someone he considered a usurper. Had Hartmann had his way, he would have removed not just Haig but all the Nixon holdovers, thereby allowing Ford to separate himself from the Nixon administration and create his own presidency. Instead, those who had served Nixon, whom Hartmann in his memoir sarcastically called the "Praetorian Guard"—a reference to the bodyguards who protected Roman emperors—prevented Ford from becoming his own man. That the media early on got wind of this infighting did not help matters.[13]

Nor did Ford ease the tense relations between old and new staff. As minority leader, he sought to achieve consensus by allowing those representing different points of view have their say. In this way, he also hoped to avoid a replay of Watergate. Accordingly, he endorsed the spokes-in-the-wheel style of decision making.[14] But there was a key difference between being minority leader and being president. Americans looked to the president to enunciate a vision of where he planed to take nation. They also expected that he would not only seek to get the American people and Congress behind his vision but also make sure that his staff were aware of his plans so that they could ensure that their respective departments and agencies spoke with one voice. Ford, however, never offered a clear vision, and his desire for collegiality permitted bureaucratic infighting that further complicated his presidency.

Reaction from the Right

Adding to the president's difficulties was the right wing of his own party. Republicans might have praised Nixon for selecting Ford as vice president, but those on the GOP's far right did not see the more moderate Michigander as one of their own. Two of Ford's early decisions gave them all the more reason to question the president.

One had to do with Vietnam. What bothered the GOP's conservative wing was not Ford's commitment to Saigon; a day after taking the oath of office, he had assured South Vietnamese president Nguyen Van Thieu that Washington would stand behind his government. A few days later, the new president made a similar pledge before a joint session of Congress.[15] Rather, it had to do with draft-age Americans who had avoided combat in Vietnam. Some had refused to register, others had fled to foreign nations, and still others had joined the military but had then gone AWOL or had decided to seek asylum outside the United States. No matter their motive or how they evaded combat, all were seen as draft dodgers.

Nixon's desire to achieve "peace with honor" had raised the question of whether those who had shunned military service should receive amnesty. Neither the president nor then congressman Ford countenanced the idea, but now president Ford began to reconsider. All his sons favored some form of protection from prosecution for those who had refused to fight, but more important to the president were political considerations. Both Defense Secretary James Schlesinger and Ford friend (and former Defense secretary) Melvin Laird argued that finding a solution to Vietnam evaders would establish a new tone for the country, one aimed at healing the wounds of America's "nightmare." In so doing Ford would separate his presidency from Nixon's. His decision made, Ford chose to announce it on 19 August at a most unlikely place. Before the annual convention of the Veterans of Foreign Wars, he reminded the veterans and reporters in attendance of his opposition to amnesty, but he also "acknowledged a Power, higher than the people, Who commands not only righteousness but love, not only justice but mercy." Therefore, to the shock of those in the convention hall, he announced his intention to offer clemency to those who had evaded service; that is, those who admitted they had violated the law could anticipate a lesser punishment than if they refused to come forward. Because it was not amnesty, which would have immunized anyone who turned himself in, the veterans had no reason to boo. Because Ford was prepared to show leniency to those who had refused to serve their country, though, they had no reason to cheer, either. Congress was also divided. Senate Majority Leader Mike Mansfield (D-Mont.) and Representative Bella Abzug (D-N.Y.) supported the clemency program. Conservatives, among them Representative Felix Hébert (D-La.) and Senator J. Strom Thurmond (R-S.C.), vigorously disapproved.[16]

Despite the voices of protest, Ford proceeded with the clemency program. Each eligible person had to turn himself in, and then, depending on whether or not he had been convicted of desertion, his case would go before the Department of Defense, the Department of Justice, or a new Presidential Clemency Board (PCB). The agency in question then passed on a recommendation to Ford regarding punishment, with the president determining the person's fate. The PCB continued its work until September 1975, with Justice deciding any outstanding cases. Only about one-fifth of those who qualified for clemency requested it from the PCB, but the board processed almost 13,600 cases, with Defense and Justice taking care of another 6,250.[17]

Conservatives were unhappy with the clemency program, but they were even more so with Ford's choice for vice president. Ford's accession to the country's highest office necessitated naming someone to fill the number-two spot. At his first cabinet meeting, he said he planned to employ the same process Nixon had used when Spiro Agnew resigned: he would solicit recommendations. Of some 300 Republicans surveyed by the White House, Republican National Committee chairman George H. W. Bush received the most votes, followed by Rockefeller. Disqualifying Bush was a recently released story in *Newsweek* showing that in his unsuccessful bid for a U.S. Senate seat in 1970, he had received money from a secret White House fund designed to help candidates who President Nixon believed would be loyal to him.[18]

Hence, Ford turned to Rockefeller, but whether the ex-governor would accept was questionable. In the words of one observer, he was "a shrewd and enormously ambitious man with a natural impulse to take control."

That description did not harmonize well with a job that was seen as one with little power. John Nance Garner, who had held the position during President Franklin D. Roosevelt's first two terms, called the vice presidency "a spare tire on the automobile of government." Rockefeller himself had referred to it as "stand-by equipment" and insisted, "I don't think I'm cut out to be a No. 2 guy." When Haig informed him on 16 August that Ford planned to phone him, though, the New Yorker knew what was in the offing. That call came the next day, and the two men spoke for an hour. Ford asked about Rockefeller's physical well-being, whether he would undergo the required background checks, and if there was anything unseemly in his past that could endanger his nomination. To allay any concerns the former governor had about his role in the administration, Ford proffered him a domestic-policy role similar to the one that Secretary of State/National Security Adviser Henry Kissinger had over the nation's diplomatic affairs. Assured that his position would be one of real authority and realizing that to say no would create serious problems for a president who had not been elected in his own right yet was in the midst of trying to extricate the country from one of its most serious constitutional crises, Rockefeller accepted.[19]

"The selection was not well received by the Republicans," said Representative Lee Hamilton (D-Ind.), particularly those on the right. Rockefeller was a well-known member of the GOP's liberals, and his reputation for womanizing only added to the uproar. "You can kiss the Republican Party goodbye," commented Senator Barry Goldwater, who had competed with Rockefeller for the party's presidential nomination in 1964. "I can live with him but I can't support him. . . . Frankly, I don't know how I can go home to Arizona now." Senator Marlow Cook (R-Ky.) called the nomination "a mistake. . . . He's worse than the last President . . . any way we can get Nixon back?" Legislative affairs aide Bill Timmons reported to Ford that, coming on top of the clemency program, the Rockefeller nomination had generated a "mini-revolt among congressional conservatives" and "funny-farm rumors that you will come out soon for busing, gun control and abortion."[20] That revolt, however, became far more widespread when Ford decided to pardon his predecessor.

The Pardon and the Papers

The idea of a pardon had been raised by Haig even before Nixon's resignation, and it had taken some effort by Hartmann, Harlow, and presidential counselor John Marsh to convince then vice president Ford to shut the door on any consideration of the idea. Even so, both Hartmann and Paul Miltich—who had served as Ford's press secretary when Ford was vice president—warned him to expect questions during his first press conference, scheduled for 28 August, on whether Nixon might avoid trial. The president pooh-poohed their advice and presumed he would receive inquiries regarding the economy, "reorganization of the White House staff," or foreign-policy matters.[21]

From the point of his nomination as vice president, Ford held weekly prayers with Billy Zeoli, a friend and spiritual counselor. Just before the press conference, he joined Zeoli, read from the Bible, and prayed. He then headed to the White House East Room to meet with the journalists. Of the twenty-nine questions asked, fewer than a quarter had to do with Nixon, but Ford came away feeling that the ex-president's fate was the only thing about which the press cared. "Was I going to be asked about Nixon's fate every time I met with the press?," he later mused.[22]

Ford determined that he "had to get the monkey off my back," and he made as much clear during a 30 August meeting with Buchen, Hartmann, Haig, and Marsh. He intended to grant a pardon, he told them. He could not envision Nixon in prison, believed his predecessor could not receive a fair jury trial, and asserted that a pardon could get Watergate behind the administration. Marsh questioned the timing, but Ford wondered, "Will there *ever* be a right time?" Hartmann cautioned that the White House would be the target of "a firestorm of angry protest"; indeed, a Gallup poll found that 56 percent of Americans favored putting Nixon on trial. Ford brushed him aside. "I don't need to read the polls to tell me whether I'm right or not," he insisted, and though he admitted some people would be upset, "most Americans will understand."[23]

During the next week, Ford debated in his mind how to proceed. He had asked Buchen to look into his ability to offer a pardon, to find out what charges Nixon would face in a trial, and to determine whether the ex-president stood any possibility of getting a fair hearing. Furthermore, he wanted to figure out how to dispose of Nixon's presidential papers and to get a "statement of contrition" from his predecessor. After seeking the assistance of Benton Becker, a lawyer for the Department of Justice whom Ford had called on to work on the case, on 3 September Buchen informed Ford that the president's power to offer a pardon was "absolute." Citing a case during the administration of Woodrow Wilson, he said that a pardon, once accepted, "carries an imputation of guilt, acceptance, a confession of it." The following day, Buchen met with Watergate special prosecutor Leon

Jaworski, who explained that the list of charges facing Nixon included obstruction of justice, wiretapping, and misuse of federal agencies. As for a fair trial, Jaworski admitted it would take a significant amount of time to put together "an open-minded jury."[24] Knowing that he could offer the pardon, believing that Nixon's acceptance of it was tantamount to an acknowledgment of guilt, and persuaded that a trial would continue to draw attention away from what he considered more important matters, Ford leaned ever more toward protecting his predecessor from prosecution.

Ford, though, did not want to grant a pardon without determining the disposition of Nixon's papers and getting a statement of contrition from the ex-president. Both were difficult matters to resolve. Based on tradition and legal precedent, a president's papers and tapes were his property, and they were supposed to be returned to him. Nixon had all the more reason to possess those materials: he had been subpoenaed to appear at the trials of several Watergate conspirators, including those of his former domestic adviser, John Ehrlichman, and his ex–chief of staff, H. R. Haldeman; he also wanted them to help him write his memoirs, from which he hoped to earn millions of dollars and to absolve himself of any wrongdoing. Jaworski, though, also demanded the papers and tapes, as did the Watergate defendants. Almost certainly on Nixon's instructions, Haig had made an attempt to sneak those materials out of the capital a few days after Ford became president but before he was able to move into the executive mansion. Haig's intention was to load the papers stored in the White House's West Wing and the tapes, which were held next door in the Executive Office Building (EOB), onto air-force trucks and have them taken to nearby Andrews Air Force Base, from which they would be flown to Nixon in California. While doing some work at the EOB, Becker witnessed the process underway at the executive mansion and successfully convinced Secret Service agents to order the air-force personnel to return the documents and recordings and leave. Afterward, Nixon's attorney, Fred Buzhardt, instructed Jerry Jones, one of Haig's top aides, to box up the tapes and make sure they remained under lock and key.[25] A statement of contrition was also problematic, for it would require the former president to admit to wrongdoing, something Nixon was unlikely to do.

Finding a resolution to the disposition of the papers and tapes became possible when Nixon hired attorney Herbert Miller to represent him. Working with Buchen and Becker, Miller arranged to store the materials in a federal warehouse near Nixon's office in California. Opening the room would require two keys, one of which would remain in the former president's hands and the other in the possession of the General Services Administration. Nixon would hold title to all the documents and tapes and would retain the right to determine who could listen to the recordings. Finally, he could order the destruction of any tapes he chose after September 1979.[26]

Nixon, however, would have to sign off both on the arrangement worked out for the papers and tapes and on a statement of contrition. The former would be tricky enough. The latter would be even more difficult, for, without Ford's knowledge, Haig had been keeping the ex-president informed of the discussions for a pardon, giving Nixon the upper hand in discussions with whoever represented Ford. The president would have sent Buchen, but his old friend's childhood bout with polio limited him physically. Buchen was also well-known, so if reporters saw him going to Nixon's residence, they might interpret the visit as indicating that Ford planned to pardon his predecessor. Hence, the president chose Becker, who flew with Miller to California. Ron Ziegler, Nixon's press secretary and now his personal assistant, represented his boss in the negotiations. Through Ziegler, Nixon signed off on Miller's draft agreement regarding storage of the materials in California and the two-key system. Convincing the former president to admit guilt was another matter. After several drafts, the parties adopted language by which Nixon accepted a pardon but never expressed any suggestion that he had broken the law. Rather, he admitted that he had been "wrong in not acting more decisively and more forthrightly in dealing with Watergate" and apologized for the "anguish my mistakes over Watergate have caused the nation."[27]

Before Becker had left for California, Ford had asked him to see how Nixon looked, and the former president granted his successor's representative an audience. He found the former president sitting at an empty desk in an office with bare walls. "My first impression was unhappily one of freakish grotesqueness," Becker recalled. Nixon's "arms and body were so thin and frail as to project an image of a head size disproportionate to a body." The former president looked like a man of eighty-five. Sometimes "he was alert, at times he appeared to drift."[28] The possibility that Nixon might not survive much longer gave Ford all the more reason to lean in favor of a pardon.

Following a round of golf with Melvin Laird—to whom he had said nothing about a pardon—Ford called together the aides with whom he had first discussed absolution for Nixon. This time, he asked press secretary Jerald terHorst to join them. Ford had purposely kept terHorst out of the loop so that his press secretary would not taint his relationship with reporters by

President Ford announces his decision to pardon Richard Nixon, 8 September 1974. Photo in the Gerald Ford Library, Ann Arbor, Michigan.

lying to them. TerHorst, who had been telling reporters up to that point that Ford had made no decision regarding a pardon, was "stunned." He decided he could no longer serve in the administration,[29] and he prepared a letter of resignation.

The next day, Ford went to church and then had a meeting with Rockefeller and several congressional leaders, during which he informed them of his intention to pardon Nixon. All were shocked. "I'm telling you right now," House Speaker Thomas "Tip" O'Neill (D-Mass.) warned, "this will cost you the election. I hope it's not part of any deal." Ford assured him there had been no quid pro quo. "Then why the hell are you doing it?" wondered O'Neill. "Tip," replied Ford, "Nixon is a sick man. And Julie keeps calling me because her father is so depressed." The House speaker could see the president's point of view, but he remained intransigent: "I know you're not calling for my advice, but I think it's too soon." The president was just as adamant. "I can't run this office while this [Nixon] business drags on day after day," said Ford. "There are a lot more important things to be spending my time on."[30]

Just after 11:00 a.m. on 8 September, Ford announced the pardon. A few media outlets praised the president. The *Wall Street Journal* remarked,

"From the nation's standpoint . . . it is better not to have the aftermath of the impeachment crisis dragging on indefinitely," and the *New Orleans Times-Picayune* called it "a course courageously chosen," adding that Nixon "has already been penalized far beyond the bounds of the sternest of judges and juries." Some Americans and lawmakers joined that sentiment, including Representative Joseph Waggonner (D-La.) and Ford's Young Turk friend, Senator Robert Griffin. Without saying he fully agreed with the decision, Griffin publicly suggested that he did, and he urged Americans to "look forward instead of backward [and] get on with the urgent business that really needs the attention of Congress and the country."[31]

The overwhelming response, however, was indignation. "This blundering intervention is a body blow to the President's own credibility and to the public's reviving confidence in the integrity of its Government," seethed the *New York Times*. The *Washington Post* proclaimed that Ford's action represented "nothing less than the continuation of the cover-up," an opinion shared by Ford's hometown newspaper, the *Grand Rapids Press*. For every one telephone call to the White House endorsing the pardon, eight railed against it, and irate letters poured into Washington. "Talk about rip-off, cover-up, secrecy in government and unequal justice—in pardoning President Nixon, you are the worst offender of all," wrote one individual. "I say put Nixon behind bars! Don't let Ford get away with this cover-up!," an infuriated caller told Representative Jim Wright (D-Tex.). Congressman Paul McCloskey (R-Calif.) favored having allowed the legal process to run its course; his Democratic colleague, Jerome Waldie, offered a stronger response, likening Ford's "abuse of the law" to his attempt to impeach Supreme Court Justice William Douglas. Senator Frank Moss (D-Utah) seconded Waldie, telling his constituents, "President Ford has flouted the nation's most fundamental principle, equal justice before the law."[32]

Of particular concern to Republicans was how the pardon might play in the upcoming midterm elections. "Doesn't he have any sense of timing?," asked Cook. "There are a bunch of us in the middle of election campaigns." One of them, aside from Cook, was Senator Robert Dole (R-Kans.) who contacted Ford "to thank him for throwing me an anchor with the Nixon pardon." Another was Indianapolis mayor Richard Lugar, who was then seeking a seat in the U.S. Senate and who recalled that with the pardon, "I saw my fortunes of trying to get elected . . . going downhill very rapidly." An angry Senate passed by a 55–24 vote a resolution demanding no more pardons of anyone involved in Watergate until all the trials had ended. Ford later admitted that the response to his decision was "more vigorous" than he had anticipated, but he remained steadfast: "I am convinced it was right in the national interest, and I would do it again."[33]

The ramifications of the pardon were multifold. Ford had asked at his first cabinet meeting, "Who knows how long the honeymoon will last?," and the pardon provided the answer. His approval rating, which had stood at 71 percent before his 8 September announcement, nose-dived 22 points immediately afterward, and a month later stood at 32 percent.[34]

The pardon also played a role in several resignations. One was Jaworski's. The special prosecutor had not been keen on charging Nixon and had asked an aide, Henry Ruth, to look at ten areas where Nixon might face an indictment, including obstruction of justice, misuse of the Internal Revenue Service, and illegal wiretaps. On 3 September Ruth had found no evidence to "prove even a probable criminal violation by Mr. Nixon." It was that conclusion that led Jaworski to tell Buchen the following day that trying the former president would take a significant amount of time. Despite lacking evidence that Jaworski opposed a pardon, Richard Ben-Veniste, who served on Jaworski's team, concluded that Ford would probably not have made his announcement had he any reason to believe the special prosecutor might stand in the way. "Well," said Ben-Veniste years later, "I knew [Jaworski] wouldn't challenge it." James Doyle, who also worked for the special prosecutor, seemed to echo that assessment, writing that Jaworski was "relieved" upon hearing of the pardon.[35]

Haig too called it quits. He had grown fed up with the laid-back tenor of the new administration, and he did not get along with some of members of Ford's staff, particularly Hartmann. There were also those in the new administration who believed that Haig, who was known to have been in contact with Nixon, had convinced Ford to pardon the ex-president. Although Ford realized that Haig and Hartmann were both prickly personalities, it was Hartmann on whom he relied the most. With the pardon accomplished, the Nixon holdover had all the more reason to depart.[36]

Ford himself had not intended to keep Haig on for the long term anyway and had planned instead to name him to another post. One possibility was to appoint him as army chief of staff to replace General Creighton Abrams, who had passed away in early September 1974. To do so, though, would mean promoting Haig from colonel to four-star general and moving him from a political post to a military one, and in this case, one necessitating congressional approval; in turn, Ford could anticipate strong resistance from the army and from lawmakers. A more acceptable alternative was to appoint Haig as commander of the military forces of the North Atlantic

Treaty Organization, an important post in itself but one not requiring Capitol Hill's endorsement, and one that the army regarded as less significant than chief of staff. Ford accepted the recommendation, and Haig left for Europe later in September.[37]

To take over Haig's responsibilities, Ford selected Rumsfeld. It was not an auspicious decision. Rumsfeld had known Ford since their days together in Congress, had experience working in the Nixon administration, including as director of both the Office of Economic Opportunity and the Cost of Living Council, and had a clear grasp of how to get things done in Washington. In that respect, his appointment boded well for the administration. Indeed, by the start of the new year, he had cut the White House staff to 480, or 60 fewer than when Ford took office, and he insisted on "strict organizational discipline." But appointing Rumsfeld failed to end the infighting. He had no faith in the spokes-in-the-wheel concept, for it endangered a clear line of authority to the president. Hence, although Rumsfeld, like Haig, had the title "coordinator," he assumed responsibilities that might as well have made him a chief of staff, including overseeing the Presidential Personnel Office, the Office of the Staff Secretary, and the Office of the Cabinet Secretary. Because he had worked for Nixon and because he desired so much authority, Rumsfeld found himself on a collision course with Hartmann, who regarded Rumsfeld as just another member of the Praetorian Guard. But whereas Haig decided after a while to leave the White House rather than fight Hartmann, Rumsfeld intended to take on the longtime Ford aide. That included participating in speechwriting, which Hartmann had long considered one of his key duties.[38]

The other departure was Jerald terHorst. An easygoing individual who got along well with the press corps, terHorst understood the need to break down the skepticism that Vietnam and Watergate had engendered toward the executive branch, including among journalists. He thus made changes in the White House press room to indicate that Ford's administration would be an open one. He sat reporters closer to the podium from which the president delivered his statements and answered questions. He removed a blue curtain that had hung behind Nixon and opened the doors that connected the press room to the grand entrance hall, thereby emphasizing that Ford had nothing to hide. "It feels like someone threw open the window of the White House to let in light and air," remarked the *Chicago Daily News*'s Peter Lisagor. Other reporters shared that observation, and the result had been good media-presidential relations, at least until the pardon. Both Ford and Marsh had tried to convince the press secretary to stay on, but terHorst could not do it. There was nothing wrong with a press secretary and the president disagreeing, he explained, yet to pardon Nixon "flew in the face of my own understanding of the Constitution and its credo of equal justice for rich and poor, strong and weak. I had no choice but to resign."[39]

TerHorst's successor was Ron Nessen. A graduate of American University, he had worked at United Press International and NBC News. In the latter post, he spent a year as a White House reporter before taking on several foreign assignments, including in Vietnam. Returning to Washington, he covered Vice President Spiro Agnew and then Gerald Ford prior to receiving the president's request to join the administration. Nessen suggested upon his introduction by Ford that he would continue the laid-back atmosphere established by terHorst: "I am a Ron, but not a Ziegler," he said in a joking reference to Nixon's despised press secretary. In truth, though, the workaholic Nessen was thin-skinned and, like Hartmann, easily angered. Unlike the relaxed meetings journalists had had with terHorst, gatherings with the new press secretary, commented his successor at NBC, Tom Brokaw, were like being in a "cock-fighting pit." Nevertheless, Ford found in Nessen someone he could trust and who could serve as a sounding board.[40] Yet in an age when the press had become increasingly skeptical of those in positions of leadership in Washington, Nessen's presence did not augur well for White House–media relations.

Still another consequence of the pardon was something that had not happened in over a century: testimony by a sitting president before a congressional committee. What motivated the pardon became the topic of resolutions of inquiry submitted by several lawmakers, including Representative Abzug. Those resolutions went to Congressman William Hungate (D-Mo.), the head of the House Judiciary subcommittee on criminal justice, who forwarded the questions to the White House. Of particular interest, he wrote, was whether Ford knew of the criminal charges facing Nixon, whether there was a deal, and who was involved in discussions prior to the pardon. Possibly without reading it, Ford signed a reply written by Buchen that simply repeated the president's rationale for the pardon. Hungate regarded the letter as nonresponsive; he insisted that Ford answer each of the questions submitted to him and that someone from the White House testify before his subcommittee on the events surrounding the pardon.[41]

Ford decided he should be the one to testify. It would not have been the first time a president testified before Congress; both George Washington and Abraham Lincoln had done so. Mansfield thought it a good idea, but Buchen, Hartmann, House Whip Les Arends (R-Ill.), and Representative

Charles Sandman (R-N.J.) all expressed reservations. The Hungate committee's "motives are purely political," wrote Sandman, and the president's presence before that body would draw media attention, commence a replay of all the events surrounding Watergate, and "cause a devastating loss in the House of Representatives." Ford refused to reconsider. Only he could quell the storm caused by the pardon. The midterm elections may also have been on his mind, for some in the cabinet argued that there were many voters who had yet to make their decision in the upcoming midterms, and the president's appearance might cool the public's fury, which could help Republicans come November.[42]

Ford appeared before the Hungate committee on 17 October. His rationale for the pardon, he told those seated before him, was just what he had said it was a month earlier, which was "to change our national focus. I wanted to do all I could to shift our attentions from the pursuit of a fallen President to the pursuit of the urgent needs of a rising nation." He detailed the meeting he had had with Haig shortly before assuming the presidency in which Nixon's chief of staff had listed Ford's six options vis-à-vis Nixon, adding that Haig had not recommended any of them. Furthermore, explained the president, he had called Haig to make it clear that their conversation in no way represented an endorsement of any course of action Nixon might take or what decision he (Ford) might make upon assuming the presidency. Quite simply, there was no deal. With the single exception of Elizabeth Holtzman (D-N.Y.), the members of the Hungate committee found Ford's answers reasonable and straightforward. The president did "the right thing," Representative Peter Rodino (D-N.J.) later commented. Had Ford refused to appear, "it would have left . . . a serious doubt in the minds of those who wanted him to come up as to whether or not he was going to withhold something."[43]

The same day Ford appeared before the Hungate committee, he vetoed a law passed by Congress to strengthen the Freedom of Information Act. First passed in 1966, it gave Americans the right to federal information. There were exceptions, such as when it came to documents related to national security or individual privacy, but the purpose of the law was to make the government more transparent. In the aftermath of Watergate, Capitol Hill added provisions designed to hasten the declassification process. Convinced by the State and Defense Departments, as well as by the nation's intelligence organizations, that the law posed a danger to American security, Ford refused to sign it, only to have lawmakers override him. While Watergate was without doubt the key reason for Congress's determination, the pardon, so intricately linked to that scandal, gave the House and Senate all the more reason to see its passage.[44]

The pardon had one final repercussion for executive-legislative relations, which materialized on Election Day. Hartmann later commented that Ford should have waited until Nixon ended up in the hospital, thereby permitting the president to justify a pardon as an "act of compassion" and, in turn, to offer some protection to Republicans in November. John Rhodes (R-Ariz.) believed that Ford should have delayed until after the New Year, which would have allowed the GOP time to mentally prepare voters for the pardon. "This approach," he wrote, "could have saved many Republican seats in the House." In light of the anger felt toward Republicans as a result of Watergate, there is little doubt that the GOP would have suffered in November 1974, but it is equally clear that coming on the heels of that scandal, the pardon had a multiplier effect. Despite Ford's stumping for his party's candidates, Republicans lost forty-eight seats in the House and four in the Senate, leaving Democrats with veto-proof majorities of 291 seats in the lower house and 60 in the upper. (Cook and Lugar were among those defeated.) Even in his home district in Michigan, voters rejected the Republican nominee (and Ford favorite) Robert VanderLaan and chose instead the Democratic nominee, Richard Vander Veen. The outcome served to emphasize Ford economic adviser William Seidman's conclusion that "the Nixon pardon so destroyed [Ford's] image it was hard for him to talk about anything."[45]

The Economy, Energy, and a First Lady

The "anything" that Ford desired to discuss included numerous pressing issues, among them the economy. Inflation, driven in large part by higher oil prices, continued to plague the country, so much so that the *Washington Post* called it the new president's "first and most urgent concern." At the time of Nixon's resignation, most families where both adults worked earned $10,000 to $25,000 annually. The cost of living, though, for an "average" nuclear family was $9,000 to $14,000, leaving "precious little room for maneuver but plenty of scope for anxiety." Prices rising at an annual rate of 12 percent further curtailed standards of living for people of all economic classes, made it harder to purchase basic necessities, and precipitated over 6,000 strikes, the most for any year in the post–World War II era. Normally higher prices indicate an economy in overdrive, which creates jobs, but in Ford's case, as had been true for Nixon, unemployment remained high, at

5.4 percent. Stagflation continued to afflict the country, which economic experts warned was teetering toward another recession.[46]

For economic advice, Ford could turn to the members of his cabinet, the Council of Economic Advisers (CEA), and the Domestic Council. However, none of them had done a good job in anticipating or offering solutions for the country's economic ills. Moreover, the new president had not had a chance to get to know the CEA's chair, Alan Greenspan, whom Nixon had appointed to that post only a month before resigning. Seidman proposed establishing a new executive-branch agency to propose, coordinate, and implement U.S. economic policy. Ford liked the idea, and at the end of September he signed an executive order establishing the Economic Policy Board (EPB), whose members included the heads of every cabinet-level department except Defense and Justice as well as the chairs of the CEA and the Council on International Economic Policy. To lead the EPB, Ford appointed Treasury Secretary William Simon.[47]

Ford's economic advisers concurred that inflation posed the greatest threat to the nation's well-being. It was true that unemployment was expected to reach 6 percent in 1975, but, declared Simon, rising prices were even more worrisome. It was key, therefore, to reduce the money supply, and here the U.S. government could help by curbing spending. The proposed budget for FY 1975 was $305 billion, and Ford hoped to trim that by $5 billion to $10 billion. As a bonus, reduced spending would also slice into the deficit, expected to be about $3 billion in 1974 but likely to rise to $9.6 billion the following year. Granted, even a $10 billion cut was only about 3 percent of the entire budget and would not have an appreciable impact on the deficit, but it would signal the administration's longer-term intentions.[48]

Cuts in spending were not likely to resonate well with liberals in Congress, so Ford adopted a proposal made to him by Mansfield to hold a series of summits that would bring together the president's economic advisers, key lawmakers, and experts in fields such as agriculture and industry to consider the best means of tackling the country's domestic ills. The largest was held in the capital at the end of September. Attending it were some 800 people, including the president.[49]

In the middle of that September meeting, Ford suddenly had to rush to Bethesda Naval Hospital in Maryland. The reason was not his health, but his wife's. Even before she had become first lady of the United States, Betty Ford had made a name for herself, meeting with the press over 200 times during her husband's vice presidency. Suddenly thrust into the position of first lady, she faced new responsibilities, such as hosting state dinners, including the aforementioned one for Jordan's royal couple. Putting together such events had traditionally been one of the duties of the first lady, and Mrs. Ford proved herself a capable hostess. However, she was also known for her plainspokenness and willingness to take positions on issues that were certain to raise eyebrows, particularly among conservatives, as evidenced in a press conference she gave on 4 September. She declared herself a proponent of the Equal Rights Amendment, which had first been proposed in the 1920s but had yet to become part of the Constitution. More significantly, she said that she favored a woman's right to an abortion. Her comment infuriated conservatives and set her apart from her husband, who opposed the Supreme Court's decision in the 1973 case *Roe v. Wade* that granted women the right to terminate a pregnancy. The uproar might have continued for longer than it did had the nation's attention not turned to the president's decision to pardon Nixon.[50]

Mrs. Ford was back in the news only a few weeks later. On 26 September, she joined a friend, Nancy Howe, who was to receive a breast cancer exam at Bethesda Naval Hospital. Howe persuaded Betty to have herself checked out, and during her exam, the doctor discovered a lump in her right breast. Two other physicians, including Ford's doctor, William Lukash, corroborated the finding. That evening, Lukash called the president, who met with him and Dr. Richard Thistlehwaite of Bethesda Naval, and learned of the diagnosis and the plan to have her come back to the hospital the next evening; the following morning, her doctors would determine if she needed a mastectomy. The Fords returned to the White House and "that evening, when we went to bed," remembered the president, "we held hands and prayed."[51]

As planned, Mrs. Ford returned to the hospital the next day. Her surgeon, Dr. William Fouty, determined that she needed a mastectomy and removed a small tumor that was later found to be malignant. Ford had been working on a speech he was to deliver to the attendees of the economic summit that evening when Lukash called to tell him about the surgery. In the emotion of the moment, the president cried: "All my tensions and fears poured out in a brief flood of tears," he wrote. Mike and Gayle, who had come in from Massachusetts where the Fords' oldest son was attending seminary, hurried with Ford to Bethesda, where Mrs. Ford, with Susan at her side, was in recovery. Later that day, the president returned to the summit to give his speech, which he started off by telling the attendees that his wife's surgery had been successful. His comments earned him a standing ovation.[52]

The events of September also netted praise for Betty. Breast cancer killed more women in their early forties than any other disease, yet fewer than

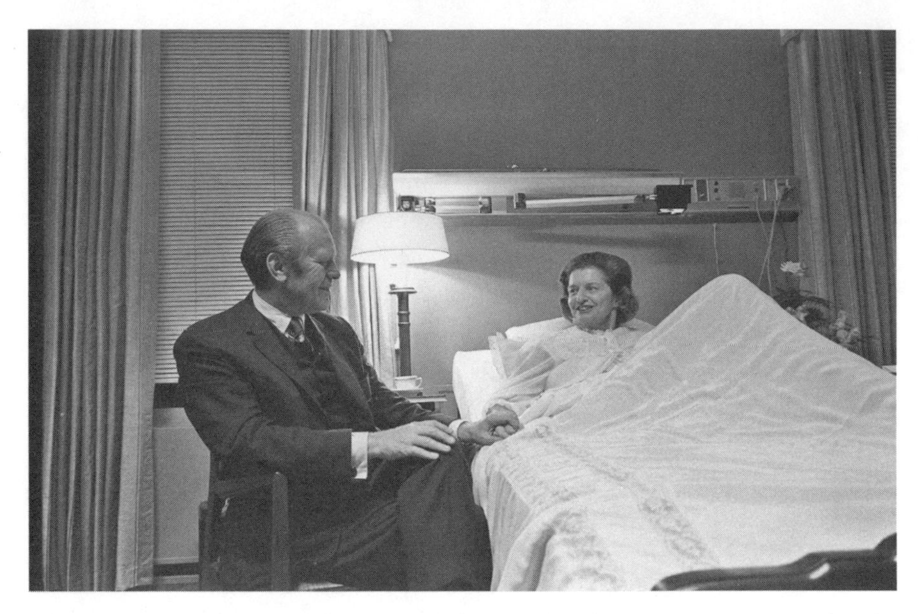

Gerald Ford joins his wife, Betty, following her breast surgery at Bethesda Naval Hospital, October 1974. Photo in the Gerald Ford Library, Ann Arbor, Michigan.

one-fifth of women examined their breasts for lumps, and only about one-half visited their doctors each year. It was an illness that received little public attention until the first lady told a reporter about her hospitalization. Her candor elicited tens of thousands of letters and cards, many of them from women who themselves had suffered from cancer or had had mastectomies, and she herself became an outspoken advocate encouraging women to conduct self-exams and have mammograms. "For all intents and purposes," wrote one of her biographers, "Betty Ford started the breast cancer awareness movement in the United States."[53]

Knowing his wife's treatment had gone well, Ford was able to turn his attention back to the economy. How useful the September summit had been is debatable. On the one hand, rather than coming up with new ideas for addressing the nation's economic ills, the attendees spent most of their time arguing among themselves. On the other hand, the meeting gave critics of the administration's approach a chance to express their grievances. Furthermore, there was a general consensus that if they could not concur on a solution, the nation's economic outlook was gloomy, with some even foreseeing a recession on the horizon.[54]

Searching for a cure, Ford in early October gave his first major economic speech before a joint session of Congress. He promised help for farmers, called for a public works program in the event unemployment exceeded 6 percent, proposed increasing the investment tax credit for businesses from 7 to 10 percent, and implored Congress both to limit spending to $300 billion for the next fiscal year and to impose a one-year, 5 percent surtax on the incomes of corporations and of married couples who made more than $15,000 annually—the equivalent of $78,400 in 2017. He encouraged deregulation of industry, arguing that regulations stifled the free market, unnecessarily expanded the federal bureaucracy, and drove up prices. He then unveiled a voluntary anti-inflation program he called Whip Inflation Now (WIN). "We can share burdens as we can share blessings," he told those on Capitol Hill and at home. Accordingly, he urged Americans to conserve and, in turn, to cut oil and gas prices by turning down home thermostats, driving to work less, and carpooling. He also encouraged listeners to reduce "the food that you waste by 5 percent." Yes, he conceded, sharing such burdens was not easy, and "I am sure that 5 percent more is not nearly enough to ask, so I ask you to share everything you can and a little bit more."[55]

Reaction to the speech was tepid. *Time* called Ford's nonvoluntary prescriptions "more balm than bite," while the *New York Times* referred to them as "weak, flaccid and generally disappointing." Those on the political left split over deregulation. Consumer advocate Ralph Nader charged that federal regulations were necessary for humans' safety and for the environment. Massachusetts senator Edward Kennedy saw at least the idea of curtailing the power of the Civil Aviation Board, which regulated the airline industry, as offering a means of bringing down the price of air fares. On the surtax, Democrats were more unified, with Congressman Henry Reuss of Wisconsin calling it "a rip-off of the middle class." Fifty-eight percent of Americans joined Reuss in declaring themselves unwilling to give more of their salaries to the government. Even Seidman admitted that the surtax "was stillborn."[56]

It was WIN, though, that received the most attention. The idea of a voluntary campaign came from one of Ford's speechwriters, Paul Theis, and newspaper columnist Sylvia Porter, and it was endorsed by some of those who attended the economic summits. This is not to say that it was universally accepted among the president's advisers. Greenspan, Simon, and Paul O'Neill, the deputy director of the Office of Management and Budget, were among those who were unenthusiastic about the program,[57] but Ford liked it and proceeded with it.

The media had little faith in WIN, and journalists ranging from James Reston to George Will were critical of it. One must wonder as well how smart it was for Nessen to wear a WIN button upside down and explain that "NIM" stood for "No Instant Miracles." Yet for all the doubt, the public response appeared positive. Numerous companies, ranging from Rite-Way drugstores to Southern Airways participated by incorporating WIN in their advertising or products. Others froze prices or rescinded plans to increase the cost of their commodities. Americans sent ideas to the White House to curb inflation, and companies produced items with "WIN" printed on them. Most popular were the Whip Inflation Now buttons, which Ford first wore during his October speech. Similarly, proposals poured into the executive mansion suggesting ways to save energy, ranging from cutting down on the use of household lights to respecting the speed limit, and even a suggestion to raise the minimum age for a driver's license to eighteen so as to force teenagers to use buses.[58]

The apparent excitement, however, hid some serious shortcomings. Determined to hold down government spending, Ford planned for WIN to receive funding from private sources, but within two weeks of his October announcement, the EPB reported the program was in trouble for want of money. WIN's staff, made up of chairman Russell Freeburg, two full-time volunteers, and two-part time employees, was unable to keep up with the thousands of letters and phone calls that poured in weekly. By late November, Freeburg groused about "a complete lack of follow through by the White House. I've been unable to get any help or funding. I don't think [the administration] had any idea of the staff such an undertaking should have right at the start. Most days I've been juggling a dozen balls at one time." Frustrated, he left the administration in December.[59]

Nor was a voluntary program likely to matter much to those who had lost jobs. No longer the economic powerhouses they once were thanks to their failure to modernize their plants and in the face of competition from Japanese and West German firms, U.S. companies began to shut down or shift their factories to places with lower labor costs. In the steel industry alone, 100,000 people lost their jobs between the middle of 1974 and the spring of 1975. One example was Bethlehem Steel, which began to give workers their pink slips starting in November 1974. For the plant workers who made $240 a week, being reduced to $89 per week in unemployment benefits hurt. Said one who had hoped to buy gifts for his family that Christmas, the holiday instead would "just have to be another day."[60]

Likewise, a voluntary energy-conservation program was unlikely to work in a country that was so wedded to a lifestyle built around the ubiquitous automobile. One in three Americans lived in the suburbs in 1970—compared to one in five, thirty years earlier—and 84 percent of American families owned a car by 1974. U.S. drivers, who had long purchased heavy, fuel-inefficient vehicles, began to trade in their cars for smaller imports that offered more miles per gallon. Others took to carpooling or to using public transportation. While these measures helped conserve fuel, the United States still used 17 million barrels of petroleum daily, and demand had been increasing at an annual rate of 4.5 percent.[61]

Both Simon and the Federal Energy Administration head John Sawhill believed the federal government had to take actions of its own to curtail Americans' dependence on oil, and they favored a hike in the gas tax. Since 1959, that tax had stood at four cents per gallon, and Simon wanted it raised to twenty-four cents. Simon, however, offered his advice quietly, while Sawhill publicly encouraged the higher tax, which drew protests from members of Congress. Ford declared himself against increasing the tariff on gas. When Sawhill continued to insist publicly that that was the wrong solution, Ford forced his resignation in October and replaced him with Frank Zarb, a former business executive who in 1973 had become an associate director in the Office of Management and Budget.[62]

Cyprus, Vietnam, and Congressional Opposition

Ford also encountered congressional resistance in the realm of foreign policy. Events in Vietnam had made lawmakers determined to have a greater say in their country's diplomacy, as became evident during the new president's first foreign-policy crisis. It was not in Southeast Asia or Eastern Europe but in the Mediterranean. In 1960, Great Britain had awarded the island of Cyprus its independence. Located east of the Greek island of Crete and just south of Turkey, Cyprus was inhabited by both ethnic Greeks, who made up the overwhelming majority of the population, and Turks. The two sides accepted a power-sharing agreement, but a desire by each to unite with their home country meant tensions between them remained high.

In 1973, General Dimitrios Ioannidis seized control of Greece's government and called for *enosis*, a union between Greece and Cyprus. In July of the following year, he staged a coup that ousted Cyprus's president, Archbishop Makarios III, and put in his place Nikos Sampson, a Greek nationalist who also favored *enosis*. Determined to prevent Cyprus from coming under the control of Athens, Turkish prime minister Bülent Ecevit ordered an invasion five days later, landing 30,000 troops on the island's northern side and establishing a corridor to Cyprus's capital, Nicosia. Disgraced, Sampson resigned, and the Greek junta fell from power. The Greek people elected Constantine Karamanlis as their new leader, and Glafkos Clerides became the head of a new Greek Cypriot government. Peace talks commenced between Ankara and Athens, with the former demanding the departure of Greeks from Turkish enclaves on Cyprus, control of 30 percent of the island, and the establishment of a federal Cypriot government that would oversee separate, autonomous Greek and Turkish administrations.[63]

A day after Ford took the oath of office, Kissinger explained to the president where things stood on Cyprus and suggested he begin an effort to "get a compromise." The president gave his secretary of state the go-ahead.[64] But on 14 August, concluding that the Greek government was stalling, Turkey invaded again. In a matter of two days, Ankara had control of the northeastern part of the island, and Greek Cypriots had fled to the southern portion of Cyprus. Its goals achieved, Turkey declared a cease-fire. Both Greece and Greek Cypriots presumed that the United States was somehow involved in the Turkish invasion. In protest, Athens withdrew from NATO, and on Cyprus, ethnic Greeks forced their way into the U.S. embassy in Nicosia and killed Washington's ambassador, Rodger Davies.

The crisis placed the Ford administration in a difficult situation. Like Greece, Turkey was a NATO member, and the White House did not want to see the alliance further weakened. Moreover, in launching the invasion, Turkey had used U.S.-supplied weapons which, according to the U.S. Foreign Assistance Act, could only be used in the name of self-defense. The Turks argued that they had acted to protect their citizens. The Ford administration was prepared to give Ankara, with which the United States historically had good relations, a pass.[65]

Not so Congress. Greek Americans were furious with the White House and put pressure on their representatives on Capitol Hill. On 19 September, charging the Turks with violating the Foreign Assistance Act, the Senate passed a resolution calling on Ford to stop providing military assistance to Turkey; the House followed suit five days later. Unwilling to anger the Turks, Ford vetoed the bill. Hoping to keep lawmakers at bay, Kissinger told Capitol Hill's bipartisan leadership on 26 September that Athens was willing to give Ankara 20 percent of Cyprus, but the Turks wanted 33 percent. The secretary of state believed it would be possible to find a middle ground. He realized that "leverage on Turkey" might be necessary, "but if we cut off aid ahead of time we will lose that leverage. If we are tough beforehand, the Greeks—who will be tough negotiators anyway—would have leverage over us" and would expect U.S. concessions. "These restrictions," he continued, "would lose us the Turks without helping the Greeks." Turkey might even leave NATO, he warned. Unmoved, Congress passed another resolution on 17 October cutting off aid unless Ford could prove "substantial progress" had been made toward achieving peace in Cyprus. The president again issued a veto, but a day later he signed on to a compromise that would postpone the stoppage in assistance until December 10. Negotiations with Congress over an amended Foreign Assistance Act, which Ford signed at the end of December, pushed that deadline back to 5 February 1975.[66]

Congressional resistance also appeared with regard to U.S. policy toward Vietnam. By the time Ford took office, the Paris Peace Accords signed between North and South Vietnam had become worth no more than the paper they were printed on. The North Vietnamese Army (NVA) infiltrated more forces and matériel into the South, and both it and the National Liberation Front (NLF)—better known in the United States as the Viet Cong—prepared to launch another assault on the South that might finally unify all of Vietnam under a Communist government. South Vietnamese president Nguyen Van Thieu had 1.1 million soldiers to defend his country, far more than the 285,000 North Vietnamese troops who were now in the South. Yet only 150,000 of Thieu's forces were combat troops. North Vietnam's soldiers were far better trained, and whereas Thieu had thinly spaced his army around the country and tried to support it with long, vulnerable supply lines, North Vietnam's military units could rely on a well-designed logistics system. Increasing Thieu's problems were a loss of American dollars caused by the U.S. withdrawal, which had led to rampant inflation; a capital city, Saigon, whose population had exploded over the past decade from 1 million to 4 million as people looked for work or a place to live; and widespread corruption.[67]

Ford might have assured Thieu of continued U.S. support, but a more assertive Capitol Hill had other ideas. The White House had requested $1.45 billion in military aid for South Vietnam for FY 1975. Lawmakers, determined to rein in the executive branch's control over foreign-policy making and unwilling to pump large sums of money into what they regarded as a losing cause, cut it to $700 million. Such a small amount, an angry Kissinger wrote Ford in early September, "will drastically reduce the effectiveness of South Vietnam's forces." Sharing that assessment, the president asked for a supplemental $500 million for Saigon, only to have lawmakers rebuff him.

Caught between his desire to help Thieu and a Congress that was certain to overturn any veto, Ford had the U.S. ambassador in Saigon, Graham Martin, pledge to the South Vietnamese leader that the White House would do all it could to provide the South with the full aid request. In October, Ford signed the appropriations legislation, which became part of the amended Foreign Assistance Act that he endorsed two months later. However, he proclaimed that the amount would be "inadequate to provide for all of [Saigon's] critical needs, if South Vietnam's enemies continue to press their attacks."[68]

In the meantime, Kissinger took it on himself to do everything possible to save South Vietnam. Invoking trilateralism, he urged Ford, who was about to travel to the Soviet Union, to ask that country's premier, Leonid Brezhnev, to insist that Hanoi comply with the Paris Accords. Meanwhile, the national security adviser approached the Chinese vice premier, Deng Xiaoping, urging him to do the same. There is no evidence that Ford raised the matter with Brezhnev, and Deng held fast to the Chinese line of not involving itself in Vietnam's affairs. In truth, trilateralism would have been about as successful as it had in the past. Historically, relations between Vietnam and China had not been close, and with the withdrawal of the U.S. military from the South, in combination with the Sino-American rapprochement, Sino-Vietnamese tensions had reappeared. With an opportunity for greater influence in North Vietnam before them, the Soviets expanded their assistance to Hanoi.[69]

As in the past, Kissinger sought to combine trilateralism with a buttressing of South Vietnam. The day after Christmas, the NVA launched an attack against South Vietnamese units near the Cambodian border, both to test the South's army and to see if or how the United States responded. Thieu sent only minimal reinforcements to stop the assault, and the United States offered no military support. Consequently, Hanoi realized it could launch a major offensive without fear of retaliation by Washington. To the U.S. intelligence community, Saigon's future was bleak if it did not receive an infusion of more cash.[70]

The ominous signs prompted Kissinger to hold a meeting of the Washington Special Actions Group (WASAG), a committee of high-level diplomatic, military, and intelligence officials whose job it was to offer solutions to international crises. On the suggestion of Deputy Secretary of Defense William Clements and the chairman of the Joint Chiefs of Staff, General George Brown, Kissinger decided to ask Ford to request $300 million in assistance for the South. There was far greater dissension over what steps the United States might take to discourage further aggression by the North.

Brown suggested sending a U.S. aircraft carrier into the Gulf of Thailand or F-4 fighter-bombers to the Philippines, whereas Kissinger offered the option of flying in B-52 heavy bombers. Clements, Assistant Secretary for East Asian and Pacific Affairs Philip Habib, and CIA Director William Colby warned that Thailand was about to have elections and that any option involving Bangkok would embolden political parties there that wanted to see U.S. bases removed from Thai soil. Furthermore, all the proposals on the table would upset Congress and make it more difficult to win approval of the $300 million supplement. Kissinger remained steadfast. He planned to put all the military options before Ford and took issue with the idea that a show of force would alarm Capitol Hill: "They (Congress) are certainly not going to give us the money if we act like a bunch of pacifists." He also expressed frustration with what he regarded as too much legislative influence in foreign-policy making, asking, "What, have we lost our ability to move carriers around without being questioned?"[71]

As WASAG conferred, conditions in Cambodia too had begun to worsen. On New Year's Day 1975, the Khmer Rouge, strengthened thanks to help from both China and North Vietnam, began its final offensive against the beleaguered noncommunist government of Lon Nol. Determined to shift the blame for any failures in Cambodia and Vietnam to Congress, Ford on 28 January asked for a total of $522 million in additional military aid for both Vietnam and Cambodia, including the $300 million for Saigon. The administration believed that the supplemental assistance would give Thieu's government the ability to purchase enough ammunition to defend itself through the next fiscal year and would raise the chances that Lon Nol would hold out through the dry season, when it would face the greatest pressure from the Khmer Rouge. Equally, if not more important, congressional approval of the White House's request would defend America's credibility. "The consequences of refusing them this assistance will reach far beyond Cambodia's borders and impact severely on prospects for peace and stability in that region and the world," Ford explained to lawmakers. The president used similar language in a cabinet meeting the next day, telling those present, "Our global relationships are very important. It is necessary for people around the world to know that we will stand by our allies." Additionally, it was essential to show nations such as the Soviet Union and Communist China that statements coming out of the White House were "backed by the American people, and the American Congress. It will impair our international negotiating ability if it always hinges on the domestic question of whether or not Congress will approve."[72]

Détente Disintegrating?

In criticizing Congress's effort to have a say over U.S. foreign-policy making, Ford also had in mind another diplomatic concern, that of continuing détente with the Soviet Union. By the time he took office, détente showed clear signs of disintegration. Part of the problem was one of definition. To the Soviets, détente did not mean that competition between the superpowers would end; rather, it meant that they needed to make sure their rivalry with the United States did not degenerate into armed conflict. The Nixon administration saw détente as requiring the Kremlin not to shake up the status quo. SALT I provided evidence of what Moscow could achieve if it played by the rules. Moreover, the Soviets faced growing economic troubles, particularly an inability to meet a domestic demand for food, and desired access both to U.S. grain products and to sophisticated industrial equipment from the West. As long as the Soviets showed a preparedness to continue cooperating with Washington, Nixon was willing to offer concessions, including granting most-favored-nation (MFN) status to Moscow.

Neoconservatives adopted a different message. The Vietnam War and Brezhnev's statements were evidence that the Soviets could not be trusted to abide by U.S.-desired standards of conduct. Concessions to the Kremlin, whether commercial or military, signified American weakness and, hence, gave Brezhnev all the *less* reason not to shake things up on the global scene. The Soviet Union only understood power, contended neoconservatives, and what the United States had to do was adopt a more confrontational stance and augment its military might.

Complicating matters for the Nixon administration was a growing interest in human rights. Realpolitik, insisted Kissinger and Nixon, required that Washington be prepared to work with repressive governments. That did not sit well with lawmakers like Representative Donald Fraser (D-Minn.). As chair of the House Foreign Affairs Committee's subcommittee on international organizations and movements, Fraser held a series of hearings that resulted in a 1974 report calling for giving greater emphasis to human rights in American foreign-policy making.[73] The United States did not provide military aid to the Kremlin, and the subcommittee's pronouncement clearly applied to both right- and left-wing regimes. But neoconservatives viewed the emphasis on human rights as advantageous, for they could cite the Soviets' treatment of their own people as justification not to pursue détente.

Finally, there was Watergate. No matter how much Nixon desired to pursue détente, his political survival demanded ever more of his attention. With the president focused on troubles at home, Kissinger largely found himself overseeing the country's foreign policy. He could not consummate any further agreements without Nixon's signature, though, nor was it likely Congress had the desire or time to endorse any pact that required its approval.

Enter Ford. On his first day in office, he wrote Brezhnev of his intent to sustain Nixon's policies, and he repeated that during a meeting with Soviet Foreign Minister Andrei Gromyko. To emphasize the point, he announced his intention of keeping Kissinger as secretary of state. As a further reassurance to the Kremlin, he explained that he had long been "a hard-liner" when it came to superpower ties, but "as I became acquainted with the benefits of [détente] to our two countries and to the whole world, I changed my views." SALT I was set to expire in 1977, and his goal was to see a SALT II agreement signed before then. In that case, timing was of the essence, Kissinger commented. The superpowers had to have "an agreement in principle in November," for otherwise it would be impossible to sign a final pact in 1975. And, realized Ford, signing SALT II in 1976 was out of the question, for it was an election year.[74]

Muddying the situation were the questions of trade and emigration. In October 1972, the United States and the Soviet Union had signed an agreement that would grant Moscow MFN status, thereby eliminating discriminatory commercial policies between them. The pact required congressional approval, but Watergate soured executive-legislative relations and deflected Capitol Hill's attention elsewhere. Doubting the benefits of détente, and taking advantage of the new emphasis on human rights, neoconservatives such as Senator Henry Jackson (D-Wash.) charged the Kremlin with repression, citing particularly its refusal to permit Jews to emigrate, and, in conjunction with Representative Charles Vanik (D-Ohio), wrote an amendment tying any commercial agreement with Moscow to a more liberalized Soviet emigration policy. With the easy passage of the Jackson-Vanik Amendment in the House in December 1973, attention turned to the Senate, where Jackson knew he had enough votes to see his legislation become part of the trade bill. Although the Washington-state senator's political ambition to become president played a part in his push for the amendment's passage, his reputation could not be ignored in the U.S. capital or Moscow. As evidence, the number of Soviet émigrés had risen from 400 in 1968 to 35,000 five years later.[75]

The rub was the statistics. Ford had intended to pursue Nixon's policies, including the trade agreement, and the Soviets had offered to increase the number of emigration visas to 45,000. Jackson, though, wanted 75,000. Senators Jacob Javits (R-N.Y.) and Abraham Ribicoff (D-Conn.), both from states with large Jewish and immigrant populations—and both of whom, unlike Jackson, were up for reelection in 1974—convinced their Washington state colleague to split the difference, at 60,000 emigration visas. The president made clear to the three senators when he met with them on 15 August that he wanted to avoid any quotas. Kissinger suggested that the way to handle the situation was a process by which the Soviets would promise to allow greater emigration, the White House would pass Moscow's vow on to Capitol Hill via a letter, and Congress's leadership would reply in writing that it understood that the number of emigrants would "rise promptly." Jackson found this exchange of letters acceptable, as did Gromyko, when Kissinger passed on the proposal to him in September.[76]

The arrangement worked out between the White House and the three senators fell apart the following month. On 18 October, Jackson, Ribicoff, and Javits arrived at the White House for an exchange of the letters and, afterwards, a press conference arranged by Ford. Jackson, determined to gain political points for his planned presidential run, told the reporters in attendance that 60,000 constituted "a benchmark—a minimum standard of initial compliance . . . and we understand the president proposes to use the same benchmark." The comment infuriated Ford and the Kremlin's ambassador in Washington, Anatoly Dobrynin. Dobrynin recalled that the president commented that Jackson had "behaved like a swine." Dobrynin himself emphasized to Kissinger that the Kremlin would never accept such a quota, an observation sustained during a visit by the secretary of state to Moscow later that month. While there, Gromyko gave Kissinger a note declaring that his government "categorically rejected" the planned exchange of letters.[77]

The visit to the Soviet capital illustrated to Kissinger "the wide and still growing gulf that had opened up between" the superpowers, but he remained focused on achieving progress on SALT II. The original SALT agreement had focused on "launchers" with intercontinental capability, specifically, underground silos that contained land-based intercontinental ballistic missiles (ICBMs), submarines armed with ballistic missiles (SLBMs), or long-range heavy bombers capable of penetrating deep into Soviet or U.S. territory. SALT I was also asymmetrical, giving the Soviet Union advantages in some areas and the United States the upper hand in others. In terms of total numbers, SALT I capped the Soviet Union at 2,498 launchers and the United States at 2,225. Among its 2,498 launchers, the Soviets had 1,618 ICBMs and 740 SLBMs, or 564 more ICBMs and 84 more SLBMs than America. Additionally, the Soviets' nuclear arsenal retained greater "throw weight," or explosive power measured in tons of TNT equivalent.[78]

While it therefore appeared that SALT I gave the Kremlin atomic supremacy, the treaty failed to address long-range strategic bombers, missiles with multiple independently targetable reentry vehicles (MIRVs), and forward-based systems (FBS), where the United States had numerical or technological advantages. America's armed forces had 525 heavy bombers to 140 for the Soviets and planned to replace its aging B-52s with B-1s, which were faster and carried a heavier payload. Washington was ahead of Moscow in MIRVing its missiles and had more of them armed with MIRVs. "Forward-based systems" referred to weapons systems without an intercontinental capability but placed close enough to an adversary that they could penetrate deeply into its territory. Thanks to its NATO membership, Washington had missiles it could launch from western Europe to hit Soviet targets; Moscow had no such capability. Additionally, SALT I imposed no prohibitions on the development of new weapons systems. This meant the United States could continue its work on the Trident submarine and the cruise missile. The Trident could carry two dozen SLBMs. The cruise missile was a pilotless guided drone that, as planned, could hit targets from as much as 1,500 miles away.[79]

The questions were over what to replace SALT I with and how long that new agreement might last. One school of thought favored a permanent agreement, yet that appeared unlikely in light of the news that the Soviets had begun to test new MIRVed missiles. The United States feared that if it was unable to control Moscow's MIRV program, the Kremlin could replace existing weapons armed with only one warhead with new ones that could hit numerous U.S. or allied targets. Washington tried to convince the Soviets in March 1974 to limit themselves to 1,000 MIRVs, or 100 fewer than the United States, but Moscow balked. With a permanent agreement that included MIRVs unlikely, the two countries had, by the time Ford became president, agreed to consider a new, interim agreement that would last until 1985.[80]

On 14 September and 7 October, the National Security Council (NSC) met to determine the U.S. negotiating position, focusing on two options. One was to seek an agreement that, like SALT I, permitted inequalities. The other was a symmetrical treaty requiring parity (also referred to as "equal aggregates") in the number of launchers or the amount of throw weight. Schlesinger shared Jackson's desire for symmetry and wanted to focus on throw weight. In light of Soviet MIRVing, he insisted that "limiting MIRV throw weight is the most important." Turning to launchers, Schlesinger discounted FBS, pointing to the large number of shorter-range missiles and medium bombers the Soviets had to offset the forward systems of the United States and its allies. He felt that an asymmetrical agreement that left the United States with inferior numbers "would not have much Congressional support." He and Clements admitted that to achieve a SALT agreement with equal aggregates might require boosting the defense budget, a proposition that made Ford queasy. Though a hawk, the president was a realist who pointed out to those in attendance that lawmakers had just cut the defense budget by $4.5 billion as a means of combating inflation. He could not see why Capitol Hill would suddenly reverse itself and accept a large spending increase.[81]

Schlesinger left Ford perturbed. The defense secretary was "inflexible," he told Kissinger. Moreover, the defense secretary was kidding himself if he believed that the Soviets would accept a treaty based on equal throw weight, for it would require them to destroy their larger ICBMs. Following another NSC meeting on 18 October at which Kissinger offered four possible approaches—two based on symmetry and two on asymmetry—Ford instructed the secretary of state to go to Moscow and propose an agreement based on launchers as opposed to throw weight. Under the American plan, the superpowers would be permitted no more than 2,200 launchers each by 1984, meaning the Soviet Union would face greater cuts than the United States; of that 2,200, no more than 1,320 could be MIRVed. Cruise missiles launched from aircraft (ALCMs) would be permitted a range of no more than 1,800 miles. Finally, the superpowers would cap the deployment of new heavy bombers, ICBMs, and SLBMs at 175 annually. Just before Kissinger departed for the Soviet capital, the White House announced that Ford would hold a summit with Brezhnev in Vladivostok, a port city on the Soviet Union's Pacific coast.[82] The significance of that meeting would depend on the outcome of Kissinger's trip.

Ford had anticipated that Kissinger would run headlong into hard-nosed Soviet resistance to the U.S. proposals. And the secretary admitted to the president following his talks at the Kremlin that no "set of principles can be worked out before your meeting with [Brezhnev] in November." The Soviet premier called the 2,200-launcher limit unfair, for it would require his country to make significant cuts in its nuclear-strike capability while leaving the United States and its FBS intact. Instead, he wanted equal aggregates of 2,400 by 1985, with Washington limited to 2,200 and the other 200 coming from British-based SLBMs. He found 1,320 MIRVs acceptable, insisted that the United States restrict itself to ten Trident submarines, and was mum about bombers. His offer left the White House uncomfortable. Counting the

President Ford and General Secretary Leonid I. Brezhnev sign a joint communiqué following talks on the limitation of strategic offensive weaponry, November 1974. Photo in the Gerald Ford Library, Ann Arbor, Michigan.

British missiles was something the Ford administration wanted to avoid; not counting them would smack of asymmetry, which Jackson and his ilk would rail against; getting to 2,200 launchers would require the United States to retain some older weaponry, like B-52s (which were expensive to maintain), or to build more Trident submarines and B-1 bombers (which too were costly); and the omission of bombers was something détente's opponents would certainly find unpalatable. Kissinger, however, saw the cup as half full, calling the Kremlin's offer "a major step forward toward a SALT agreement in 1975, and perhaps a significant announcement at Vladivostok." Still, he knew that people like Jackson were ready to pick apart Brezhnev's proposal, and he urged Ford to keep it quiet.[83]

A month later, Ford arrived in Vladivostok. At a personal level, he and Brezhnev got along well, finding common interest in their love of the outdoors and sports. Once they got down to business, however, their differences became evident. Brezhnev insisted on the 2,400/2,200 split on launchers, but Ford made clear that politically he could not submit to Congress anything other than equal aggregates. After two days of intense negotiation, the delegates adopted a framework for a decade-long SALT II agreement. It would limit the total number of launchers to 2,400, including the 1,320-sublimit on MIRVed weaponry. Rather than insisting on counting FBS against the 2,400-launcher cap for the United States, the Soviets accepted the American position that Washington would make up the difference by retaining older systems, like the B-52. If a B-52 or any other long-range bomber carried ALCMs with a range of less than 600 kilometers (about 375 miles), the aircraft would count against the 2,400-launcher limit.[84]

It appeared that Ford could return home and sell SALT II as an agreement that even neoconservatives could accept. Schlesinger, who had disliked the idea of a pact based on launchers rather than throw weight—and complained enough that Ford told Kissinger, "If he won't be a team player, I don't want him"—hesitatingly endorsed it. Not so Jackson. In part, it was the result of the senator's playing politics. For instance, he insisted on a 1,700-launcher limit, which the Soviets clearly would spurn. Ford and his aides had erred as well, though. In their haste to create a framework, they left unresolved some key issues, and an aide-mémoire issued by the superpowers on 10 December offered little clarification. One such issue had to do with ALCMs. While there had been agreement on counting ALCMs with a range of less than 600 kilometers, there had been no resolution as to how to account for those with a greater range. The Soviets had proposed that in such a case, *each missile* (as opposed to each aircraft) was to be counted against the 2,400 aggregate. The United States, however, wanted that condition applied only to ballistic missiles, meaning missiles launched from a land- or sea-based platform (such as a submarine or an underground silo), and not an aircraft. Assuming that Moscow understood that, the Ford administration permitted the removal of the word "ballistic." The other issue in dispute was the Tu-22M "Backfire" bomber, an aircraft that was in use by the Soviet Union by the time of the Vladivostok Summit and that some—including Jackson—claimed had an intercontinental capability. Brezhnev insisted the Backfire lacked the range to reach the United States and return home, and Ford considered the plane out of date anyway. Hence, the aide-mémoire only referred to heavy bombers without clarifying what types of aircraft fell into that category. The end result was that the White House had given the appearance of weakening America's striking capability while permitting the Soviets to enhance theirs. Jackson himself called the summit's outcome "a severe disappointment," one that benefited Moscow to the detriment of American security.[85]

The entangled issues of emigration and trade further confused matters. Following its passage by both the House and the Senate and after further consideration by a joint House-Senate committee, the 1974 Trade Act, including the Jackson-Vanik Amendment, passed Congress on 20 December. Ford had reason to consider vetoing the legislation, but on 3 January 1975, he signed it. Though he considered it discriminatory, he found some of its provisions attractive. It gave the president the power to negotiate lower tariffs and to conclude commercial agreements with other nations, and it enabled him to institute countermeasures against countries that engaged in unfair trade practices. For another thing, the Trade Act had passed by such overwhelming margins that Ford realized he could expect Congress to override a veto. A week later, the Soviets publicly rejected the trade bill. Commercial relations continued: for instance, in October Washington had agreed to $400 million in grain sales to Moscow. The handling of the legislation, however, had infuriated the Kremlin and embarrassed both Ford and Kissinger, and the Soviets retaliated by imposing new restrictions on emigration. The number of Jews permitted to leave the Soviet Union fell to 13,000 in 1975, 8,000 fewer than in 1974 and 22,000 less than in 1973. Détente had been dealt a serious blow.[86]

Middle East

Nor did the signs look good with regard to U.S. policy toward the Middle East. The end of the Yom Kippur War in October 1973 had given Kissinger the opportunity to work toward a broad Middle East peace agreement. Soviet activities during the 1973 conflict had convinced Nixon and Kissinger that détente had its limits; if the United States could achieve a regional peace on terms agreeable to the interested countries of the Middle East, it could simultaneously reduce Soviet influence in the region, protect Israel, and bring about stability in a strategically vital part of the world.

Deciding that it was impossible to get all the parties to agree to peace at once, Kissinger adopted a dual-track approach. One course was a conference in Geneva, hosted by the United States and the Soviet Union, that would bring the contending countries of the Middle East—and potentially the Palestine Liberation Organization (PLO)—to the bargaining table. In truth, Kissinger did not want to have such a meeting, for he knew that Israel would refuse to attend if the PLO was present, that the Soviets would do all they could to influence the gathering's direction, and that, therefore, a multilateral gathering was certain to fail. The other route was the one

Kissinger favored: a step-by-step process, in which the United States would hold bilateral meetings with each Middle East nation. In so doing, he could control the negotiations. And by keeping the threat of Geneva hanging over the heads of the other parties involved, they might offer the concessions necessary that would permit the broader peace he sought.

All went well at first. The Israeli leadership, as well as the heads of states of numerous Arab nations, accepted the idea of a meeting in Geneva, which took place on 21 December. The event was more symbolic than substantial. During the one-day event, the Israeli and Arab delegates threw barbs at one another. Moreover, although Washington and Moscow jointly sponsored the conference, it was the former that largely acted as overseer. The two superpowers agreed to have permanent representatives remain behind to meet with Arab or Israeli officials if asked, but no request from Tel Aviv or any of the other Middle Eastern parties was forthcoming. Having taken the lead in getting the conference arranged, Kissinger was now free to turn his attention to step-by-step diplomacy.[87]

The initial steps were to reach disengagement agreements between Israel and Egypt, followed by agreements between Israel and Syria. The first proved relatively easy. In wars with Cairo in 1967 (the so-called Six-Day War) and in 1973, Tel Aviv had captured from Egypt the Sinai Peninsula, portions of the eastern and western banks of the Suez Canal, and the Gaza Strip; the West Bank from Jordan; and Syria's Golan Heights. Logistically, Israel could not maintain those positions. Working with Anwar Sadat, Egypt's moderate and pragmatic president, Kissinger was able to work out a disengagement agreement, called Sinai I, by which Israel pulled back to a position just west of the strategically significant Mitla and Gidi Passes, located on the western side of the Sinai. To keep the peace, a UN military force stationed itself between the Egyptians and Israelis.[88]

In May 1974, Kissinger worked out a similar disengagement agreement between Syria and Israel. However, Tel Aviv retained control of the Golan Heights. Moscow complained about being left out of the peacekeeping process, but that was Kissinger's intent all along. Equally impressive, Kissinger stipulated the lifting of the Arab oil embargo as the price for his mediation between Syria and Israel, a demand that succeeded in restoring the flow of petroleum from the Middle East.[89]

Shortly after Ford's inauguration, Kissinger brought him up to speed on his step-by-step approach. His intention was to use the disengagement agreements as the start of a process that would eventually lead Israel to return the territories it had occupied since 1967 to their original owners. Of those territories, the secretary said, it would be easiest to find a permanent solution for the Sinai Peninsula, followed by the West Bank and then the Golan Heights, which the secretary admitted was "the most impossible."[90] The president was more than willing to let the secretary of state, whom he had long admired, proceed.

With Israeli-Egyptian and Israeli-Syrian talks begun, the next logical move was to bring Israel and Jordan to the negotiating table. That was easier said than done, for the West Bank was the home of eastern parts of Jerusalem, the city that Palestinians had long claimed as the capital of an independent homeland they hoped to create. Further muddying the waters were tense Jordanian-Palestinian relations. King Hussein of Jordan had grown upset with the PLO's use of his country as a staging ground from which to launch attacks on Israel. Therefore, in 1970, he used his army to force the PLO to flee into Lebanon. In so doing, he turned much of Arab opinion against him.[91] Consequently, it was crucial for him to get the West Bank back to prove his ability to stand up to Israel and restore his legitimacy in the Arab world.

Kissinger did not help himself by pinning his hopes on an Arab summit in Rabat, Morocco, planned for October 1974. He had come to the conclusion that the most intractable of the disputes in the Middle East was that between Israel and Jordan. Therefore, he intended to address what he considered the easiest of the problems confronting him, that of Egypt and Israel, and see if the Rabat summit might open the door to Israeli-Jordanian talks.[92]

The secretary later admitted that he had erred. To his (and Hussein's) dismay, the heads of state who met in Rabat at the end of October 1974 recognized the PLO as the representative of the Palestinian people and declared that it had sovereignty over the West Bank. Accordingly, Hussein wrote, he could not "negotiate for the West Bank unless authorized by the Arab leadership in council, including the P.L.O." It was, commented Kissinger, "the worst possible outcome." He lamented to Schlesinger in mid-November that what happened at Rabat could have been avoided had the Israelis been willing to give up just four kilometers of the West Bank.[93]

Kissinger, though, could not dwell on his mistake. His focus was on a second Israeli-Egyptian disengagement agreement, even if getting it would not be easy. Israeli prime minister Golda Meir had resigned in the middle of 1974, paving the way for a new government, led by Yitzhak Rabin. Rabin and his aides wanted to divide Egypt and Syria, hoping that in so doing they could prevent another unified attack on Israel. Hence, they demanded that Sadat offer a statement of nonbelligerency—in short, end the state of war with Israel—that any agreement be valid for a lengthy duration, and that Cairo not demand that Israel give up the Mitla and Gidi Passes. Tel Aviv also wanted to retain control over oil fields in the Sinai Peninsula. Sadat knew that declaring nonbelligerency would make him a pariah among his fellow Arab leaders. The best he could do was to offer "specific elements of non-belligerency in return for a further substantial second stage withdrawal of Israeli forces from the Sinai." To Sadat, "substantial" meant the Israelis would back off from the two passes and the oil fields. Kissinger had suggested to Ford using a recent Israeli request for military aid as a lever for concessions on Tel Aviv's part. Ford did just that, explaining to Israeli foreign minister Yigal Allon in January 1975, "I couldn't go to the Congress without results." He told Max Fisher, a highly respected leader of the U.S. Jewish community, that as a first step, "Israel has to give up the passes and the oil fields."[94] That was a big step, however, and one the Israelis were certain to resist.

Omens?

If there was any good news for the administration as the new year began, it was that Congress had confirmed Nelson Rockefeller as vice president. The process had been long and arduous. The Senate had begun its hearings on 23 September, and after four days of testimony aired on national TV, Rockefeller appeared to be well on his way to an easy confirmation. But he was hurt by leaks regarding his financial largesse, including some $2 million in payments to twenty different people—including $50,000 to his then aide Kissinger—and by news that he owed some $1 million to the Internal Revenue Service. He had to defend himself before both the Senate Rules Committee and the House Judiciary Committee, insisting that the payments he had made were not intended to "corrupt . . . either the receiver or the giver." Further, he promised to put his money into a trust and to pay what he owed the government. Even then, his confirmation was not assured. The House Judiciary Committee's Edward Mezvinsky (D-Iowa) had wanted Rockefeller to divulge the property and financial holdings of every member of his family, but the nominee refused, for to do so would have revealed that he had promised each of his children different amounts of financial support upon his death, a revelation that would, he told his aides, "destroy the family." The Congressional Black Caucus also had qualms about Rockefeller, who, as governor in 1971, had ordered the use of force to put down a riot in New York state's Attica Prison, an overcrowded and particularly repressive facility populated predominantly by African Americans and guarded by an all-white staff that reportedly engaged in racist acts. By the time state officers had retaken the prison, thirty-nine inmates and ten guards lay dead. Behind the scenes, Ford urged Tip O'Neill and House Speaker Carl Albert (D-Okla.) to push his nominee's confirmation. On the advice of the House majority leader, White House staffers courted the Black Caucus and New York's House delegation, both of which were made up largely of Democrats. On 11 December, the Senate confirmed the nomination 90–7, and that same day, the Judiciary Committee followed suit. Eight days later, the full House gave its endorsement by a vote of 289–128, and Rockefeller took the oath of office.[95]

Initially, Ford appeared to abide by his promise to give Rockefeller real power. The vice president had wanted to head the Domestic Council, only to encounter resistance from Buchen and Rumsfeld. Neither felt Rockefeller should have a staff position. Ford saw merit in their argument; he decided to keep a Nixon holdover, Kenneth Cole, as the council's executive director. Yet he appointed Rockefeller as vice chairman, thereby granting his vice president substantial influence. Furthermore, he gave Rockefeller additional responsibilities, including sitting in on all National Security Council meetings, assisting in recruiting staff, and offering suggestions for the nation's upcoming bicentennial celebrations.[96]

Rumsfeld remained wedded to reining in the vice president. By the end of the year, he had completed a plan to reorganize the administration, replacing the spokes-in-the-wheel approach with one that made him little less than chief of staff, even if he did not have the title. This placed him on a collision course with Rockefeller. The Domestic Council had been established by the Nixon administration to assist with policy making, but it proved less effective than envisioned. Rockefeller wanted it to have significant influence and foresaw it serving as a "White House think tank" that would seek outside advice and then independently offer policy recommendations. Rumsfeld, however, thought the Council should function as a more conventional agency, one that had such responsibilities as preparing briefing memorandums for the president and serving as a liaison with members of Congress. Moreover, thought Rumsfeld, if the council did attempt to offer policy recommendations, it needed to have those suggestions vetted by other members of the White House staff before arriving on the president's desk. Put another way, Rumsfeld wanted to make sure he controlled the flow of paper and did not want to allow the Domestic Council to challenge his authority. Having discovered that the spokes-in-the-wheel system took too much of his time,

Ford accepted Rumsfeld's logic with regards to the paper flow: "A President needs one person who at least coordinates people."[97]

There were other portents of trouble. About a week after the midterm elections, the White House finally admitted that the country was in a recession, forcing Ford to declare in December that he had to reevaluate the economic proposals he had put before the country two months earlier. He planned to use his annual holiday vacation in Vail to figure out how best to address the country's economic and energy woes, only to receive criticism for using 14,000 gallons of fuel to get there. Then, while on the way to Colorado, he learned that the *New York Times* was about to run a story attesting to a CIA operation to spy on Americans. The article, which appeared in the *Times*'s 22 December edition, relied on an internal report in which the agency admitted to tracking over 10,000 U.S. citizens. "Sniffing a potential Watergate," recalled Ford, "reporters bore down hard on the story, and there was pressure on Congress to establish committees to investigate the agency's misdeeds."[98]

Popular culture reflected the feeling of dismay with the government, the state of the country, and a desire for escape. Three of the ten highest-grossing films of 1974 were the disaster flicks *Airport 1975*, *Earthquake*, and *The Towering Inferno*. A sequel to the 1970 film *Airport*, *Airport 1975* dramatized the lives in jeopardy of the crew and passengers on a Boeing 747. *Earthquake*, which opened in theaters in November (a month after *Airport 1975*), depicted an earthquake registering a 10 or 11 on the Richter scale that devastated Los Angeles. December's *The Towering Inferno* had the world's tallest building, standing a full 138 stories, catch on fire and threaten to bring it down and kill everyone inside. Americans wanted to break away from such portents of doom in favor of a better future, a sentiment that ironically was reflected in the past. There was no better evidence of such nostalgia than in the popularity of *Happy Days*, a television comedy series that began its decade-long run in 1974 and, by its very title, depicted the 1950s as "a golden age of happiness and simplicity."[99]

That desire for a better future was reflected in January 1975 in the inauguration of the new Congress. Ninety-two new faces joined Capitol Hill, of whom seventy-five were Democrats. Called the "Watergate babies," these first-term congresspersons were determined to change the way business was conducted in Washington. "Insistent, assertive, suspicious of authority, and determined to change things in the name of *reform*, the group was like molasses in Carl Albert's hair," wrote Representative Jim Wright. There were twenty-two committees in the House, and thirteen of them had chairs who were more conservative than most of their peers. They also could be overbearing. Pat Schroeder (D-Colo.), who entered Congress in 1973, recalled that Felix Hébert sent her "a book that he had written, and he had autographed it, saying, 'The Lord giveth, the Lord taketh away, I am the Lord.'" Those in Congress who shared the babies' desire for reform succeeded in curtailing the power of committee chairs and in removing from their positions not only Hébert but also Ways and Means's Wilbur Mills (D-Ark.) and Agriculture's William Poage (D-Tex.).[100]

Ford was probably correct that waiting to pardon Nixon would have diverted the country's attention from more pressing issues, and he had acted bravely in absolving his predecessor when he did. Furthermore, there was no guarantee that waiting until after Election Day would have stemmed the losses suffered by the Republican Party. Yet there is no doubt that by pardoning Nixon so early in his administration, Ford was at least partially responsible for the election of a Congress where younger, liberal, reformist-minded individuals insisted on altering power relationships in Washington. It was not a situation that augured well for a president whose views were of a more conservative nature. He had yet to come up with a program to address America's thirst for energy, and his inflation-fighting campaign appeared to be in jeopardy. He already faced congressional challenges to his foreign policy, particularly with regard to Indochina, Cyprus, and the Soviet Union, and it was likely that this new coterie of lawmakers would be even less amenable to his goals than were those who sat on Capitol Hill prior to November 1974.[101] Nor could he anticipate making headway toward a comprehensive Middle East peace settlement.

Most significantly, by early 1975 the president had not provided a vision for the country that indicated the broader purpose of his initiatives. In a sense, this was not surprising. James Cannon, who in 1975 replaced Cole as executive director of the Domestic Council and later wrote a biography of Ford, commented that the president lacked a vision because "he was unelected. He came in under the 25th Amendment, thinking he would serve out Agnew's term and move into private life. That was his plan and he had no reason to think of, 'This is what I would do if I were President.'" Because "Ford had no [presidential] campaign and only 24 hours notice he was going to be President, he obviously had no agenda."[102]

As December came to an end, though, Ford had had nearly five months to explain what his vision was, yet it remained unclear. To Douglas Bennett, Ford's special assistant for legislative affairs starting in January 1975, Ford did have an overarching goal, which was to "restore integrity, confidence in the office of the President, in the White House, and in the leadership of the country." If that was the case, the pardon did not help. William Seidman, Paul O'Neill, and Robert Goldwin, an academic who served as a White House adviser, thought Ford's intention was to restrain spending. That might be fine for a lawmaker who, in Goldwin's words, was "very good at legislative detail," but not for a president whose job it was to put those details, whether domestic or foreign related, into an overarching concept for where his administration planned to take the country. Hence, it is understandable that the *New York Times*'s John Herbers wrote that when Ford returned from his Vail vacation, he would "face the same challenges that confronted him on Aug. 9—developing the policies and leadership that the country expects of him." Whether Ford could do so was uncertain. In prescient language that suggested the president's common-man image had started to wear thin, Representative Barber Conable (R-N.Y.) penned, "Increasing doubts are arising as to whether Gerald Ford can administer the government. The impression he has created so far is that of a nice man struggling manfully in the deep water far over his head."[103]

SEVEN

Confronting Crises

On 15 January 1975, President Gerald Ford entered the Capitol Building to deliver his first State of the Union address. As dictated by protocol, he slowly made his way to the Speaker's rostrum, greeting members of Congress on the way and then handing copies of his speech to House Speaker Carl Albert and Vice President Nelson Rockefeller. Reaching the podium, he briefly recollected his own career as a lawmaker and then entered the substance of his speech. "I must say to you," he told the audience watching in person and on television, "that the state of the Union is not good: Millions of Americans are out of work. Recession and inflation are eroding the money of millions more. Prices are too high, and sales are too low. This year's federal deficit will be about $30 billion; next year's probably $45 billion. . . . Our plant capacity and productivity are not increasing fast enough. We depend on others for essential energy."[1]

What was the solution? At the suggestion of his chief speechwriter, Robert Hartmann, Ford had given the answer two nights before. Knowing his boss was not good at orating from behind a podium, Hartmann had suggested Ford give a fireside chat to the nation. The idea appealed to the president, and Hartmann wrote the speech. What Hartmann put together "was awful," remembered Press Secretary Ron Nessen, "ten minutes too long, full of clichés, flowery, with the major points blurred." To the speechwriter's chagrin, Nessen and White House Coordinator Donald Rumsfeld wrote their own version, and Ford, finding parts from each that he liked, accepted a mixture of the two.[2]

Planned for 8:00 p.m. on 13 January, the White House pushed the fireside chat back an hour to avoid competing with the Smothers Brothers, a popular musical-comedy duo who had scheduled a comeback on national television at that time. Using a teleprompter for the first time, dressed in a suit and tie, and speaking from the White House library with a warm flame in the fireplace behind him, Ford told the American people that it was time to "shift our emphasis from inflation to recession," and he proposed "a simultaneous three-front campaign against recession, inflation, and energy dependence" that included raising the fees on imported petroleum by one dollar per barrel over each of the following three months; returning a large portion of $30 billion raised through those fees to individuals and to state and local governments to curb unemployment; lifting price controls on domestically produced oil and, because that would mean enormous profits for petroleum companies, levying a windfall-profits tax on those firms; making automobiles more fuel efficient; promoting the development of alternative energy sources; and implementing a $16 billion tax cut that would further increase Americans' spending power, encourage business investment, and reduce joblessness. To avoid the political ramifications of an unlimited tax break that would benefit the wealthy, the maximum a person could expect returned was $1,000. He made clear that, save for those initiatives related to energy, he would hold firm against new spending programs and vowed to veto any such bills sent to him by Congress.[3]

Two days later, Ford delivered his State of the Union address. Like the fireside chat, Hartmann had written his own version, only to have Rumsfeld offer a competing one. The infighting between the two men disturbed Nessen, who called it "wasteful and divisive" and who considered Ford "too much Mr. Nice Guy" to put an end to it. Ford reproved his staff, and, working until 4:00 a.m. the following morning, he finished revising the speech, leaving him with only three hours' sleep before he had to begin that day's schedule of events. After offering the same list of proposals he had set out forty-eight hours earlier, he turned his attention to foreign-policy matters. Pleased with "significant achievements in recent years in solving problems and crises," he expressed at the same time discomfort with unrest in the Middle East, the state of the international economy, the conflict in Vietnam, the U.S. relationship with the Communist world, and congressional restrictions on the president's freedom to lead the country's diplomacy. He pledged to work closely with lawmakers on both foreign and domestic policy matters,[4] but clearly he wanted Capitol Hill to give him leeway in both areas.

As with his October 1974 speech, press reaction to the State of the Union was mixed. Conservatives, including both Ford's own Treasury secretary (and Richard Nixon holdover), William Simon, and former California governor Ronald Reagan, privately (in the case of Simon) and publicly (in Reagan's case) argued that Ford had rejected conservative values and failed to give the fight against inflation an opportunity. Among media outlets, the *New York Times* and the *Washington Post* praised him for his honesty, while *Newsweek* believed Ford "had at last discovered and tapped one of the real wellsprings of Presidential authority—the power to define the issues and to set the terms in which they are debated." Yet tempering the laudatory rhetoric was the *Times*'s conclusion that the president had "misfired in his attempt to rally the nation behind a new program to meet the many-sided economic emergency." A more serious charge came from *Newsweek*, which accused him of being a flip-flopper. The criticism was fair, for Ford had gone from talking of a surtax to advocating a tax cut. Furthermore, the tax cut, in combination with the recession, would mean a trade deficit of almost $35 billion for FY 1975 and of over $51 million for FY 1976. Finally, it would be those in the upper crust of American society making $50,000—about $230,000 in 2017—or more a year who would receive the maximum $1,000 credit; a couple earning $5,000 annually would get $12. Americans might like Ford as a person—78 percent of respondents to a Harris poll felt he was "a nice guy"—but a plan that appeared to benefit the rich convinced 86 percent of those surveyed by Harris to doubt Ford's ability to handle the economy. Even though the media paid little attention to the foreign-policy portions of the State of the Union speech, it too was on Americans' minds. Six in ten of respondents to a Gallup survey were uncertain about Ford's ability to handle the nation's diplomacy and believed that 1975 would be "a troubled year with much international discord."[5]

Coming to grips with the unsettled domestic and international environments proved to be a difficult challenge for the president. Congress repeatedly forced Ford's hand on both economic and energy matters, generating further charges that the president had no idea how to find a solution to the country's problems. A charge of flip-flopping also applied to his response to a financial crisis involving New York City. On foreign policy, the administration received kudos for its handling of a crisis involving the U.S. merchant ship *Mayaguez* and for reaching a disengagement agreement between Egypt and Israel. But lawmakers refused to endorse the president's desire to assist South Vietnam and Turkey. He was also criticized for not seeing Soviet dissident Aleksandr Solzhenitsyn, and arms-control talks with Moscow had stalled. As a result, by the end of 1975, Ford looked vulnerable enough to convince Reagan to challenge him for the Republican nomination for president.

Clashing with Congress

By the time Ford returned from Vail to give his two January speeches, the country was in the worst economic downturn since the Great Depression. Detroit automakers had only just begun to shift production from large vehicles to the smaller cars Americans now wanted. Housing too suffered, with new construction showing a precipitous decline. An inflation rate of nearly 12 percent and an unemployment rate of 7.1 percent only compounded the nation's economic decline, so much so that economic growth was a negative 5 percent. Further complicating the country's economic woes was the continued flight of affluent persons out of downtown areas and into the suburbs, reducing the tax base of America's urban areas.[6]

Those on the political left wanted to fight the recession through increased government spending, which would create jobs. Ford, however, thought that option would mean a larger deficit, higher interest rates and higher inflation, and less incentive for the private sector to invest in the economy. The alternative was a tax cut. It might offer more appeal to Americans, believed Ford, but he realized that route also offered perils, some of them the same as more spending. After intense discussions that saw the president's advisers disagree over how much of a tax break to offer, the White House came upon the formula announced in the president's two speeches.[7]

Two months later, Ford participated in a golf tournament, his putts missing left and right. Perturbed by his performance, a reporter asked if the president was doing "about as well as you are doing with Congress?" Ford insisted, "I'm going to do better with both." That, however, appeared unlikely, for Democrats had taken issue with the president's economic and energy initiatives. Ways and Means Committee chairman Al Ullman (D-Oreg.) began the assault, calling for a hike in expenditures on domestic programs and a $19.4 billion reduction in taxes, with far more of the cuts going to families in the middle and on the lower end of the socioeconomic spectrum and with a maximum rebate of $300 rather than $1,000. Congressional Democrats in both houses voted for an even larger tax cut of $22.8 billion sans cuts in spending, with those reductions again going toward the lower and middle classes and with a rebate cap of $200. The Democrats' bill also offered an earned-income credit to help working-class Americans, tax breaks for those purchasing new homes, and a bonus of $50 to those receiving Social Security.[8]

Ford's advisers split over whether the president should sign the bill. Simon urged a veto on the grounds that the bill would create a deficit, make the recession worse, and increase unemployment. Better to sign it, argued most of Ford's advisers, among them Hartmann, Rockefeller, Secretary of Housing and Urban Development James Lynn, and Deputy Director of the Domestic Council Richard Dunham. Otherwise the Democratic-controlled Congress would accuse Ford of favoring only his version of tax cuts. In retaliation, lawmakers might demand even more spending. In return, they urged the president to insist on fiscal restraint. Ford accepted the advice from the majority, signing the Tax Reduction Act on 29 March and cautioning, "I will resist every attempt by the Congress to add another dollar to the deficit. I will make no exceptions."[9]

Ford's energy program also caused controversy. Among a group of forty governors, twenty-eight railed against the tariff on oil imports. The strongest reaction came out of New England, a region that, unlike others in the nation, relied almost entirely on imported oil for energy. Both Senators Henry Jackson of Washington and Edward Kennedy of Massachusetts joined the furor, declaring that Ford had exceeded his authority, and they introduced a resolution calling for a ninety-day freeze on the tariff on oil imports. Congress passed the Jackson-Kennedy measure by an overwhelming vote of 309–114 on 5 February, four days after the first dollar-per-barrel increase went into effect. The Senate followed suit two weeks later, voting 66–28 in support of the House measure. Ford vetoed the bill in early March, but knowing that his opponents had enough support to override it, and having been told by energy czar Frank Zarb that Congress would only accept a phased-in decontrol program, he offered to delay the next two one-dollar tariffs and the removal of controls on domestically produced petroleum until 1 May, thereby permitting Capitol Hill an opportunity to offer a counterproposal to his energy program. The Senate did just that in April, passing legislation that favored federal and state intervention rather than decontrol to promote conservation. The House acted more slowly, though, with two separate bills stuck in committee as of the start of May. In an attempt to push the House to act, Ford ordered a phased-in decontrol of petroleum over a twenty-five-month period and warned Albert that if the House did not move quickly, he would impose the next one-dollar tariff within a month.[10]

As May neared its end and the House temporized, Ford decided to turn up the pressure. Numerous observers commented that it was rare for the president to exhibit his temper, but, admitted congressional liaison Max Friedersdorf, when Ford "felt like he'd been misled or he was in the right, he could get very, very aggressive." Congress's lollygagging on energy was one such case, and it pushed the president to his breaking point. Appearing on national television, he delivered what was the angriest address of his tenure. Sitting at his desk, he reminded viewers that he had submitted a plan in mid-January to protect the United States from another energy crisis; failure to act would make the country all the more vulnerable to another oil embargo. Then, picking up a large calendar sitting next to him, he asked, "Now, what did the Congress do in February about energy?" Ripping that month's page from the calendar, he answered, "Congress did nothing." He then asked similar questions with regard to March, April, and May. Finally, he announced that he intended to tack on the next one-dollar tariff on imported oil.[11]

Ford's speech failed to have its desired effect. Democrats in Congress assailed it as "a childish act" and called Ford a "demagogue," and even Republican senator Charles Percy of Illinois referred to it as "amateurish." Americans were also less than impressed. A Gallup survey discovered that 60 percent of Americans considered the cost of living their greatest concern, with another 20 percent worried about unemployment. Only 7 percent of respondents regarded the energy crisis as the country's most pressing problem. If anything, the energy crisis appeared to be over. By 1975 the supply of oil and gas had increased, and the price of gasoline had fallen to fifty-three cents per gallon. It made no sense, the U.S. public believed, to pay more for energy, particularly in a time of recession. Knowing their constituents had little desire to devote more dollars to necessities, a large number of congresspersons resisted Ford's plan.[12]

The makeup of Congress also played a part in the lawmakers' obstinacy. Congressional reforms instituted as a result of the 1974 midterms reduced the influence of Capitol Hill's leadership, including both Albert and Mansfield, and the large number of freshmen meant that there were many people in the House and Senate who lacked experience in the art of policy making. Regional differences compounded matters. For example, the Northeast had an extensive public-transportation system, few oil wells, and a significant number of residents who relied on oil for heating; hence, the oil-import fee was among the most pressing matters to congresspersons from that part of the country. To those from the West, where a larger percentage of people commuted by car and where there was much more locally produced petroleum, gas prices were the number-one concern.[13]

In June, an energy bill failed to make it out of the Senate. Taking advantage of the opening, the Ford administration proposed a program that would extend the decontrol period from twenty-five to thirty months, only to have the House reject it in July. The White House tried again, offering thirty-nine months to eliminate controls, but the House again said no and then passed its own program, which offered to continue controls for six months. Ford issued another veto, adopting instead a forty-five-day controls extension. "The United States endangers not only its own interests but its leadership of the free world by this Congressional paralysis," deemed the *New York Times*. Once the forty-five-day period came to an end, Ford would "probably impose his will. Such action would be a travesty of democratic government, but it may be the only way to start the United States toward the critical conservation of energy that the vital interests of the nation—and the world—demand."[14]

Ford's proposals for resolving the country's economic and energy ills did not sit well with those who favored federal efforts to protect the environment. The rise in energy prices as a result of the oil crisis generated a backlash from individuals who argued that federal environmental regulations hampered efforts to lower energy prices. As a congressman, Ford had not opposed measures to protect the environment—particularly if encouraged by a Republican president—but he preferred to leave their formulation up to the states. Now, as a chief executive overseeing a nation that was in a recession and had yet to fully emerge from an energy crisis, he contended that federal environmental restrictions stifled economic growth and efforts to promote America's energy independence. Ford failed to overcome resistance to expanding the country's use of nuclear power: he had wanted atomic power plants to provide 20 percent of Americans' electricity—or about twice what it was when he took office—but for a variety of reasons, including problems with plants breaking down and questions about where to place the facilities and to store the waste, he made no headway.[15]

Ford had more luck with coal. One-third of the world's known reserves of coal were in the United States, but there was opposition to expanding its use. Mining was physically dangerous to humans, the smoke emitted by coal-fired plants caused air pollution, and strip-mining—by which the top soil and surface rock were removed to expose the coal beneath—destroyed the topography. For those reasons Congress passed bills in December 1974 and again in the spring of 1975 to restrict strip-mining, only to have Ford veto them both. The legislation, he later wrote, would have cost "thousands of jobs" and limited access to an important source of energy. Both times, lawmakers failed to secure the votes to overcome the vetoes. Thanks to Ford's efforts, the federal government loaned $750 million to coal companies. Coal production reached an all-time high in 1976 of 670 million tons. But Ford's determination to prioritize the economy cost him among environmentalists. Congressman Morris Udall (D-Ariz.) charged Ford with endorsing "grossly deficient environmental standards," and the Environmental Policy Center declared that the president had launched "an assault on water and land resources."[16]

Crises in Beantown and the Big Apple

Ford sought to match his desire to restrict federal intervention in the environment with his response to crises in Boston and New York. In the former, education was the issue; in the latter, it was economics. The president held firm to letting Boston resolve its problems on its own. He tried to do the same with regard to New York, but eventually he relented.

Despite the Supreme Court's 1954 *Brown v. Board of Education* decision requiring the integration of schools, state and local governments did not always comply. This was not just true in the South. By the mid-1960s, Boston had few African American teachers, no black principals, and schools that failed to meet the standards demanded by *Brown*. In 1974, U.S. District Court Judge Arthur Garrity Jr. found Boston in violation of *Brown* and ordered the city to institute a busing plan to integrate schools. When the Boston School Committee refused, Garrity prepared his own plan, prompting a divide in Boston between those for and those against the proposal. Violent incidents began to occur as black students entered what had been white schools. White parents at times refused to send their children to schools ordered to integrate.

The stabbing of a white student at South Boston High on 11 December 1974 prompted white parents to surround the school, threaten the lives of African Americans inside, and smash police cars. Although the black students were whisked away to safety with the help of volunteers, the danger signs convinced Representative Charles Rangel (D-N.Y.) to urge Ford to do what Dwight D. Eisenhower had done during a similar crisis in Little Rock in 1957 and send in the National Guard. As a lawmaker, Ford had opposed the use of busing to force school integration, preferring to leave the process of desegregation up to local and state governments. Holding firm to that position, he rejected Rangel's entreaty.[17]

In January, the Boston School Committee finally adopted a desegregation plan based on freedom of choice, but it left important questions unanswered, such as what constituted a "segregated" school. Violent outbursts persisted, and numerous white families took their children out of the city's schools rather than accept the concept of racial equality. What happened in Boston further convinced Ford that busing was the wrong way to proceed. In August, he signed a busing bill, but he did so reluctantly, commenting that "forced busing . . . does not lead to better education and it infringes upon traditional freedoms in America." Members of the administration, including the only African American in the Ford cabinet, Transportation Secretary William Coleman, and Domestic Council member Richard Parsons, privately took issue with Ford's stance. Meanwhile, the U.S. Commission on Civil Rights publicly denounced the president for taking an "equivocal" position on the matter rather than one clearly favorable toward busing.[18]

Staying out of New York City's affairs proved far more difficult for the president. New York had 7,566,000 residents in 1974, 329,000 fewer than in 1970. As tax revenues were declining, the city had been increasing spending by about 12 percent annually since 1965 to pay for hikes in wages and benefits for city workers and for a city university system that accepted, tuition free, anyone who graduated from a New York state high school. To cover its bills, the city sold municipal and short-term bonds—so many of them that by the mid-1970s 18 percent of municipal bonds and almost 40 percent of short-term bonds in the United States came from New York. Even that was not enough. By 1973, when Abe Beame became the city's mayor, it faced a $3 billion deficit that was likely to grow as the tax base declined further.[19]

By the spring of 1975, New York City was in serious trouble. It had sought to save itself by offering more bonds but found no takers. Nor would the city's major banks offer any assistance. Needing $1.4 billion to pay the city's workforce and to cover its existing debts, Beame and New York state's recently elected governor, Hugh Carey, met with Treasury Secretary William Simon and Federal Reserve Chairman Arthur Burns and asked for a $1 billion bailout. Neither Simon nor Burns was willing to help. They understood that without the assistance, New York City might have to default on its debts, but they agreed it would not have a major effect on the country's financial system or on the stock market. Ford shared their sentiment. The president, a fiscal conservative who disliked interfering in what he regarded as local or state matters, felt that New York had to do a better job of balancing its budget and had to "stop promising more and more services without knowing how [to] cover their costs." And if the city was to ask for help, it needed to turn to Albany.[20]

The New York State Legislature agreed to step in, offering $800 million in assistance and establishing the Municipal Assistance Corporation (MAC) to refinance some of the city's debt. Yet it was clear that MAC could not cover all the city's bills, meaning that by the end of FY 1975, it could anticipate a shortfall of more than $1 billion. Both Domestic Council head James Cannon and Simon warned that if the federal government bailed out the city, it would "create a precedent" by which other urban areas would call on Washington to help them rather than balancing their books. To save money, Beame laid off about 25 percent of the city's employees, including emergency and sanitation workers. Carey, though, appeared to be unwilling to accept further spending cuts, requesting instead $1.6 billion from New York City's banks—an entreaty that was rejected. "Carey has not responded adequately to his responsibilities," Simon wrote Ford. If anything, "avoiding a default is less important to the Governor than his own political future." Specifically, in the event the city defaulted, Carey could blame either the city's banks or Washington and "absolve himself of responsibility."[21]

By October, New York City's financial situation looked dire. The state had sold some bonds by using money in its pension fund, but the city still faced a significant shortfall. Rockefeller, who had initially stood behind the president's hard-line position, began to have second thoughts. He urged the White House to help New York, but Ford declined. Frustrated, and without asking first for authorization from the president, Rockefeller on Columbus Day publicly insisted Congress step in. Ford, though, remained adamant, telling the National Press Club two days later that he intended "to veto any bill which has as its central purpose the Federal bailout of New York City to prevent a default."[22]

The response to the president's speech varied. The *New York Daily News* made its feelings clear through a front-page story with the headline "Ford to City—Drop Dead." House speaker Tip O'Neill, who faced pressure from Democrats in the city to offer help, called again for providing "aid of some type. Ford should forget about politics for a few minutes. This is a national problem." New Yorkers in the House, including Republicans Hamilton Fish IV and Peter Peyser, joined the speaker. The GOP's whip in the House, Bob Michel of Illinois, called Ford's speech "Damn good. Right on target," and Senator Robert Griffin (R-Mich.) deemed it "the right course—a course that ultimately will serve the best interests of New York City and the country as a whole." For their part, most Americans shared the sentiment of the *Daily News* and took offense to what they regarded as an overly harsh attitude. Prior to Ford's address, 49 percent of Americans opposed helping the city, 7 points more than favored assistance. Afterward, 69 percent wanted to offer funding to the city, 50 percent more than opposed it. The president, however, stood firm.[23]

A breakthrough occurred in the middle of November, when New York state and the city reached an agreement with the latter's banks. Albany promised $6.8 billion in aid and the passage of a bill to allow it to borrow over $2 billion more from its pension fund; the city agreed to a tax increase to raise $200 million, a reduction in its contribution to the employee pension fund, and a balanced budget by the end of FY 1977. The banks approved the refinancing of the city's loans. Ford declared himself pleased with the accommodations made by all sides and promised to approach Congress about legislation to offer a loan to the city, which he did shortly thereafter. Lawmakers quickly endorsed the loan, and Ford signed it into law on 9 December.[24]

How wise Ford was to stand pat against helping New York City was questionable. On the one hand, Ford was a fiscal conservative who wanted states and cities to live within their means, just as he desired the federal government to do. Certainly those who wanted New York City to control its spending were pleased when voters there replaced local officials identified with labor unions and the welfare state with individuals who were more favorable to big business and smaller government.[25] On the other hand, the president could have taken a stance that at least appeared to be sympathetic to the plight of America's largest city. And in light of the fact that Ford himself had announced in July that he intended to run for the presidency, it was not politically smart to engage in rhetoric that stood the chance of turning the voters of one of the most electoral-rich states against him.

Investigating Intelligence

Domestic politics converged with foreign policy when the *New York Times* accused the Central Intelligence Agency at the end of 1974 of conducting domestic surveillance. Established in 1947, the CIA had the mandate to collect intelligence outside U.S. borders. Its ability to collect information within the United States was severely circumscribed. Yet there was very little public or congressional oversight of the agency, and those members of Congress responsible for keeping track of it tended not to ask many questions. That included Ford, who had served from 1956 to 1965 on the House Appropriations Committee's intelligence subcommittee.[26] Hence, with the endorsement of presidents, the CIA was able to expand its operations quietly to include the toppling of foreign governments in Iran and Guatemala during the Dwight D. Eisenhower administration, attempts to assassinate foreign leaders during the tenures of both Eisenhower and John F. Kennedy, and, starting under Lyndon B. Johnson, efforts to link antiwar activists to foreign "radicals." When Director of Central Intelligence (DCI) Richard Helms refused to use his agency to help President Richard Nixon cover up the Watergate scandal, Nixon reassigned Helms as ambassador to Iran and appointed James Schlesinger in his place. Schlesinger learned about the CIA's illegal activities and ordered his agents to report to him any activities he believed violated the agency's charter. The result was a nearly 700-page report, which became known as the "Family Jewels," detailing all the CIA's unlawful doings. Within a few months, Nixon had reappointed Schlesinger as secretary of defense and named William Colby as the new DCI.

Any hope of keeping the CIA's machinations secret fell apart when someone in Congress leaked information on the Family Jewels report to *New York Times* reporter Seymour Hersh. After getting confirmation from Colby, Hersh published his story. Shocked by what he read, Ford immediately demanded an explanation from Colby. The DCI admitted his agency had kept tabs on over 9,900 Americans and that he had ended the surveillance program in March 1974, but he insisted that Hersh had exaggerated the full extent of the operation. With the 1976 election on his mind, Ford knew he could not have another potential scandal hanging over his head or permit the more assertive Congress to take the lead on the matter. Hence, on 4 January 1975, he ordered Nelson Rockefeller to head a special President's Commission on CIA Activities to assess whether the agency had violated its mandate and, if so, to recommend changes to keep it from doing so in the future. The seven-man committee included former University of Virginia president Edgar Shannon, former Treasury secretary Douglas Dillion, AFL-CIO secretary-treasurer Lane Kirkland, and Ronald Reagan. That Kirkland and Reagan were on the committee suggests that Ford was looking toward the 1976 campaign. Labor leaders such as AFL-CIO president George Meany were upset with Ford's pardon of Nixon and with the administration's prioritization of fighting inflation over fighting unemployment,[27] and

Reagan's presence would please the party's right wing, who had from early on questioned how much Ford favored its positions.

Lawmakers, however, had no intention of being preempted. Both the House and the Senate established their own committees to look into the CIA's activities. Leading the Senate Select Committee to Study Governmental Operations with Respect to Intelligence Activities was Frank Church, a liberal Democrat from Idaho. Having served in the upper house since 1957, he was a highly moralistic individual who had long opposed the use of covert operations. He also had plans to run for the presidency in 1976 and saw his committee as an opportunity to gain national notoriety. A few months later, the House established a Select Committee on Intelligence, headed by New Yorker Otis Pike, a moderate Democrat known for his biting personality.

Ford added to the furor. In mid-January, he had imparted to some visitors from the *New York Times* his surprise at what Colby had told him. "If you knew what they were doing," the president explained, "it would curl your hair." When *Times* editor Abe Rosenthal asked, "Like what?," Ford replied, "Like assassinations." The *Times* decided not to run the story, but CBS reporter Daniel Schorr, who had been told about the president's comments from someone who had been present, pursued it. Getting confirmation from none other than Colby that the agency had indeed been involved in attempts to assassinate foreign leaders, Schorr at the end of February informed a national audience, "Colby is on the record saying, 'I think that family skeletons are best left where they are, in the closet.' He apparently had some literal skeletons in mind." Helms was furious. "You killer! You cocksucker!" he later yelled at Schorr before a group of journalists.[28] But the cat was out of the bag. It was clear that the CIA had been involved not just in spying on Americans but also in at least attempting to murder foreign officials.

Just how much to divulge to Church and Pike became a matter of contention between the White House and the two congressional committees. Rockefeller made sure his commission kept its hearings closed, and reporters could not take notes of witnesses' testimony. Nevertheless, there is reason to believe that the commission disregarded evidence about matters it felt should remain confidential. Church and Pike insisted that the executive branch turn over to them secret materials so they could assess the CIA's violations of its mandate (and of U.S. law). Though Ford realized that a claim of executive privilege had gotten Nixon into trouble during the Watergate scandal, he used that rationale to resist giving either of the congressional committees what they wanted, and almost every member of the administration seconded him. One significant exception was Colby, who contended that some cooperation was needed. Otherwise lawmakers might demand even more far-reaching reforms. Consequently, the DCI appeared before the Church Committee twice in May to discuss his agency's covert operations and the assassination plots.[29] From that testimony, and the little documentation it had received from the White House and the Rockefeller Commission hearings, Church obtained a fairly good understanding of the extent of the assassination attempts.

The executive and legislative branches also fought over what to divulge to the public. The first of the three reports was Rockefeller's, which was disclosed during the second week of June. For the most part, it was favorable toward the CIA. Yes, the Rockefeller Commission admitted, the agency had engaged in untoward behavior, including domestic espionage, and "some of these activities were initiated or ordered by presidents." But it offered little in the way of suggestions for reform. Further undermining the commission's credibility was its deliberate failure to fully reveal what it knew of the CIA's attempts to assassinate foreign leaders. Questions posed during a press briefing on the commission's findings reflected, said one news outlet, "suspicion of a whitewash or a cover-up."[30]

The Church Committee sought to publish what it knew, generating a fight with the White House. At the end of October Ford urged the Idaho senator not to release his body's findings, for doing so risked "serious harm to the national interest and may endanger individuals." Church refused and asked the full Senate to endorse the report's release. Following a heated debate, the upper house decided not to take any action. Resolute in his determination, Church gave the report to journalists; in December, the committee published its findings, detailing transgressions not just by the CIA but also by the FBI and the NSA, among them the assassination attempts and an effort to overthrow the government of Chile in 1970. Calling the CIA "a rogue elephant," it offered over 180 recommendations aimed at giving Congress greater oversight of the agency "to assure that in the future our intelligence community functions effectively, and within the framework of the Constitution." With Watergate still vividly in the minds of Americans, the report further weakened confidence in Washington and intensified demands that the government disassociate itself from unscrupulous activities, whether domestic or foreign.[31]

The fight between the Pike Committee and the White House was even more intense. In a sense, that was surprising. In contrast to the Senate, which focused on what the CIA had done wrong, the Pike Committee intended to detail what the agency had done correctly. What neither it nor the White

House had anticipated was the publication of *Inside the Company*, a book by Philip Agee, a former CIA operative who had become disillusioned with his job. In the book, Agee revealed the names of a number of agents, including that of Richard Welch, who was then working in Greece. Two days before Christmas in 1975, Greek terrorists murdered Welch, raising the specter of other CIA employees suffering the same fate if the Pike Committee's report became public. Both for that reason and in the name of defending U.S. security, the White House insisted on the suppression of the committee's findings, and the full House by a 2-to-1 margin concurred in early 1976.[32]

Welch's murder also hurt Church. Even before the agent's death, Americans had questioned whether the Idaho senator was driven more by his own political ambitions than by the welfare of the country. Indeed, even before Welch was killed, only 38 percent of respondents to a public opinion survey had a positive appraisal of the Church Committee. After news of the agent's murder, the backlash grew even more intense, severely damaging the senator's desire to win the Oval Office.[33]

Cyprus

Welch's assassination took place in the midst of ongoing efforts by Ford to bring an end to the Greco-Turkish dispute over Cyprus. The greatest concern of the administration was the impending embargo on military aid to Turkey. Colby had warned Kissinger that enactment of the embargo would not only have dangerous ramifications for NATO but might "jeopardize a number of intelligence facilities located in Turkey . . . which would be difficult if not impossible to replace." Not wanting to see the Western alliance against the Soviets fray further, Kissinger urged members of Congress in early February to rescind the aid cutoff, but he had no effect. Representative Benjamin Rosenthal (D-N.Y.) told the secretary, "If we wipe out this action, there will be a reaction in the American Congress because there is a deep-seated principle involved, and it does not favor a pragmatic solution." John Brademas (D-Ind.) joined his colleague, warning, "If you try to get this overturned, you will be clobbered and it will not contribute to a Cyprus solution and it could worsen your relations with the Congress." Four days later, the ban on aid to Turkey began. "A suspension of military aid to Turkey is likely to impede the negotiation of a just Cyprus settlement," a frustrated Ford told the nation. "Furthermore, it could have far-reaching and damaging effects on the security and hence the political stability of all of the countries of the region."[34]

Over the next several months, the White House continued its pressure on Congress. Kissinger had been in the midst of negotiations with Chinese officials aimed at normalizing relations between the two countries, and he warned lawmakers that the embargo made Beijing question why it should seek better ties with Washington when the U.S. government cut off aid to Turkey, "a country that stands between the Middle East and the USSR." The next month Ford approached lawmakers, but he made no progress. In April, he warned publicly that the embargo prevented "progress towards reconciliation" on Cyprus and, by angering Turkey, endangered America's national security.[35]

The administration finally saw a ray of light in May, when Mansfield joined Senate Minority Leader Hugh Scott (R-Pa.) in pushing for a bill that would resume most military assistance to Turkey if Ankara maintained the cease-fire and if Ford offered monthly reports to Congress on the progress of the talks. It was "not improbable," warned Mansfield, that if the embargo were to continue, Turkey might swing its allegiance from NATO to Moscow. Furthermore, restoring aid offered a chance to bring the Greco-Turkish negotiations vis-à-vis Cyprus to a successful conclusion. Leading the opponents of the Mansfield-Scott bill, Senator Thomas Eagleton (D-Mo.) declared that the proposed legislation would constitute an endorsement of Turkey's invasion and undermine legal restrictions on the use of American arms. The Senate passed the measure on 19 May, and a hopeful White House turned its attention to the House. The discussions did not go well, leading Ford to state at the end of a meeting with congressmen on 23 June, "I think we unfortunately have reached an impasse. I think the consequences will be tragic." For their part, Greek Americans pushed just as strongly for retention of the aid cut.[36]

On 24 July, the House voted against Mansfield-Scott. Ankara retaliated by ordering the United States to stop operating American bases on Turkish soil, including four intelligence stations Washington used to gather information on the Soviet Union. The Senate drew up a new bill, which it passed on 31 July, containing language similar to that in the bill the House had just rejected, and Ford once again sought to get the House to endorse it. One difficulty for the administration was Rangel's insistence on tying any restoration of aid to Turkey to Ankara's assistance in stopping the world's heroin trade. Turkey had decided in 1974 to permit cultivation of the opium poppy, which was used to make heroin. Rangel had joined with the other fifteen members of the Congressional Black Caucus (CBC) in voting against Mansfield-Scott on the grounds that Turkish poppy production was directly linked to narcotics abuse within the African American community. Having received word from Rangel that "if some positive direction were taken regarding the narcotics situation in this country and its relationship to Turkey," the CBC might vote for the new military aid bill, Ford assured the Rangel that he had spoken with Turkey's prime minister, Süleyman Demirel, about opium production. "I know that you will be pleased as I was to hear how strongly the Prime Minister believes in the most effective control on the production of opium poppies," the president wrote. Additionally, commented Ford, he wanted it understood that he believed "the illicit export of opium to this country [is] a threat to our national security." Rangel found the letter "helpful," and some of his colleagues began to worry about the impact of the embargo on U.S. security interests in the eastern Mediterranean.[37]

On 2 October the House voted for the partial lifting of the embargo. Included in the House bill was an amendment proposed by Rangel asking Ford to begin negotiations with Turkey to "prevent the diversion of Turkish opium into illicit channels" and to keep Congress informed of those talks. After signing the bill, Ford tried to convince Greek prime minister Constantine Karamanlis that the partial lifting of the embargo gave the United States leverage over Turkey, but Karamanlis was not convinced. "Nothing," he replied, "absolutely nothing, has happened . . . to justify a reappraisal of the Greek position."[38]

Indochina

The sparring between the White House and Congress also continued over policy toward Indochina. In Cambodia, Lon Nol's army was down to about 60,000 troops by early March, or half what he had had three months earlier, and the Khmer Rouge pushed ever closer to Phnom Penh, where some 2.7 million Cambodians had fled to escape the fighting. At about the same time, the North Vietnamese began their final offensive against the South, with the intention of cutting the country in half in preparation for moving on Saigon. On 18 March, Deputy Assistant for National Security Affairs Brent Scowcroft declared that the South was "in deep trouble" and said, "[It] cannot survive without American military aid as long as North Vietnam's war-making capacity is unimpaired and supported by the Soviet Union and China."[39] Making matters worse for the White House was Capitol Hill. Despite an intense lobbying effort by the administration to get $522 million for Vietnam and Cambodia approved,[40] the foreign-aid bill that came out of Capitol Hill provided no money for either.[41]

Shortly before Ford took office, the U.S. government had received warnings that inflation, corruption, and deterioration of the ARVN's morale had placed Saigon's future at risk. Yet just how fast the South began to collapse surprised even officials in North Vietnam. The ancient Vietnamese capital of Hue, a focal point of the 1968 Tet Offensive, fell to the Communists on 25 March. That same day, South Vietnamese president Nguyen Van Thieu asked Ford to order U.S. air strikes on the attackers, but the president realized that Congress would never agree to such a move. Rather, he promised the South Vietnamese leader that he would do all he could to see that Capitol Hill provided additional military aid. Moreover, he had decided to send the U.S. Army's chief of staff, General Frederick Weyand, to Vietnam to assess the situation.[42]

Weyand arrived on 29 March. It just so happened that that same day Ford was in Palm Springs, California, on vacation playing golf. To Americans, scenes of the president on the links when South Vietnam appeared to be on the verge of destruction gave the impression that he did not care about the fate of the U.S. ally. In fact, Ford remained just as determined as ever to do what he could to assist Saigon. Returning to the United States on 4 April, Weyand reported that the South was "on the brink of a total military defeat" but said that with U.S. assistance, it could hold out. He recommended $722 million in aid for Saigon and, as Thieu had requested, air strikes on the attackers. He knew, though, that there was strong congressional opposition to U.S. military intervention or to spending more money to protect the South, and for those reasons, he also suggested preparing plans to evacuate a large number of both American citizens and Vietnamese.[43]

The White House had already undertaken measures to start evacuating U.S. nationals and ordered its ambassador in Saigon, Graham Martin, to provide a categorized list of those South Vietnamese whom Washington should help escape. A military response was out of the question, for it would infuriate members of Congress, risk a violation of the War Powers Resolution, and probably spawn unrest comparable to that following Nixon's announcement of the invasion of Cambodia. That left the $722 million aid request. Martin called "the military situation . . . grim . . . but not that hopeless" and encouraged approval of the money. David Kennerly, Ford's White House photographer who had gone with Weyand to South Vietnam, took an equally forceful but opposing stance: "Mr. President, Vietnam has no more than a month left, and anyone who tells you different is bullshitting."[44]

Kissinger later commented that Weyand's aid request "was preposterous. Vietnam was likely to collapse before any equipment at all could arrive."

But U.S. credibility was at stake; what Weyand had asked for represented "the minimum amount with which something might still be salvaged, the one [action] most likely to give the South Vietnamese the shot in the arm with which to gain time for evacuation." As before, if Congress declined the request, then the White House could blame lawmakers for America's defeat. Therefore, Kissinger told the National Security Council (NSC) on 9 April that he wanted not just the $722 million but additional funds for humanitarian purposes—namely, to assist refugees and evacuate U.S. nationals, their dependents, and Vietnamese who wanted to leave. Schlesinger was less sanguine. "We must recognize that it is gone," he said in reference to South Vietnam, and he added that what the United States should do was focus on extricating itself.[45]

Ford shared both concerns. The following day, he told a joint session of Congress that "the free nations of Asia . . . must not think for a minute that the United States is pulling out on them or intends to abandon them to aggression." Accordingly, he requested the $722 million in military assistance and another $250 million for humanitarian and economic aid for South Vietnam. He also chided lawmakers for not doing more to help Cambodia. Two members of Congress walked out during the president's speech,[46] an indication not just of how strongly they opposed continuation of the war but also of lawmakers' determination to rein in the "imperial presidency."

A day after giving his speech, Ford approved Operation Eagle Pull, the code name for the withdrawal of U.S. personnel and allied Cambodians from Phnom Penh. The operation had been developed in 1973 as a contingency in case Cambodia appeared to be on the verge of falling to the Communists. With the Khmer Rouge tightening its stranglehold on the Cambodian capital, Lon Nol had fled on 1 April. What remained of his military was in no position to hold back the Communist onslaught. Seeing the inevitable, three dozen U.S. helicopters operating from warships in the Gulf of Thailand safely extricated 270 people, including just over 80 Americans and nearly 160 Cambodians.[47] On 17 April, the Khmer Rouge marched into the capital and began a three-year reign of terror during which about 25 percent of Cambodia's population died from starvation, disease, or execution.

That same day, in a vote reflecting the opinions of the 78 percent of Americans who opposed more aid to South Vietnam, the Senate Armed Services Committee refused to endorse the $722 million in military aid. On 22 April, its corresponding committee in the House did the same. Once again, Ford was irate. "Those sons of bitches," he seethed. It was the first time, recalled Nessen, that he had heard the president curse.[48]

The White House's attention now turned to evacuating American nationals and friendly Vietnamese from Vietnam and to winning approval for the request for humanitarian and economic assistance. The sheer number of potential evacuees was enormous. Divided into eight categories of importance, the first five, which included "American citizens and their relatives," U.S. diplomats, and American employees and their dependents, totaled nearly 200,000 people. When added to the other three categories—Vietnamese related to American citizens, senior South Vietnamese officials, Vietnamese employed by the United States, and their dependents—the total was approximately 1.7 million. Ford instructed Martin to draw down the American presence to no more than 1,250, but the ambassador, who seemed oblivious to the true nature of the situation he faced, was reluctant to do so for fear of causing a panic. It took a direct order from Kissinger to get his ambassador to agree to have dependents of U.S. nationals leave, thereby reducing the total number of Americans to about 2,000. Over the next several days, Martin accepted cutting the U.S. presence to about 1,100, equivalent to what could "be evacuated in one helo lift."[49]

Saigon was to be the epicenter of the evacuation. Ford hoped to forestall any effort by North Vietnam to take the city until the United States had completed its effort. On 19 April, Kissinger asked the Soviet ambassador in Washington, Anatoly Dobrynin, to have his government urge Hanoi to accept a two-week cease-fire. Without declaring a cease-fire, the North Vietnamese promised both in public statements and through Moscow not to stand in the way of the evacuation. In truth, the North was not yet ready for the assault on the South's capital and wanted to have all its pieces in position before launching its attack, which was planned for the end of the month.[50] Realizing that his government's days were numbered, Thieu resigned on 21 April, turning power over to his vice president, Tran Van Huong.

Ford too saw South Vietnam's fate. As it was, he had planned to speak at Tulane University's convocation on 23 April, and there seemed no better crowd to hear about the war's impending end than college students, the people who had been most affected by and who had most strongly protested events in Vietnam. "America can regain the sense of pride that existed before Vietnam. But it cannot be achieved by refighting a war that is finished as far as America is concerned," the president announced. The words generated thunderous applause from the crowd and infuriated Kissinger. Normally, the national security adviser saw copies of foreign-policy speeches before Ford delivered them; in this case, he had not. The following morning, Kissinger expressed his anger to the president, but Ford held firm. It had

President Ford discusses the American evacuation of Saigon with Secretary of State Henry Kissinger and Vice President Nelson Rockefeller, 28 April 1975. Photo in the Gerald Ford Library, Ann Arbor, Michigan.

become clear to the president that no matter how much the United States wanted to avoid reality, it could no longer duck the fact that it would not play a role in Vietnam's future.[51]

When Ford gave his speech at Tulane, the evacuation had been under way for two days. On 27 April, the NVA began its final assault on Saigon. Tan Son Nhat Airport, which had been used by the United States to fly fixed-wing planes out of the city, came under fire, and although the North Vietnamese halted the bombardment of the airfield, the White House decided on 28 April that it was no longer safe to use it. Washington now implemented Operation Frequent Wind, which used helicopters operating from ships in the South China Sea as the means of transportation. Some helicopters went to Tan Son Nhat, but others landed on the roof of the U.S. embassy. Schlesinger objected to the fact that the evacuation proceeded during the night, which he believed unnecessarily put U.S. pilots at risk. Martin asked for more time, and Kissinger agreed, giving him until 3:45 in the morning of 30 April (Saigon time) to get himself and any remaining Americans out.[52]

Martin did not depart from the embassy until almost 5:30 a.m. Assured that all Americans had been taken to safety, Ford, Nessen, and Kissinger announced the end of the evacuation. To his surprise, the secretary of state then learned that 130 U.S. marines had accidentally been left behind, forcing helicopters to return to the embassy to get the marines out. Nessen suggested saying nothing, but Rumsfeld insisted on being forthcoming with the American people: "This war has been marked by so many lies and evasions that it is not right to have the war end with one last lie." Ford concurred, and the White House issued a correction. Kissinger was embarrassed and blamed Schlesinger for the miscommunication. "So," Rumsfeld later wrote, "the war in Vietnam ended in much the way it had been carried out—with recriminations and regret."[53]

Frequent Wind helped 1,400 Americans and 5,600 Vietnamese escape to safety, a small proportion of the 86,000 evacuated by the United States. Another 41,000 Vietnamese fled by boat. Even though some were able to get out without incident, many others did not. Indeed, it was video and pictures of frightened Vietnamese trying to escape, some of them jumping for the landing gears of the last departing helicopters, that came to symbolize a war that had not gone as planned. Approximately 2.6 million Americans had served in the conflict; over 150,000 had suffered serious injury and another 58,000 had been killed. For Ford, who from the beginning had seen Vietnam as a test of American resolve against communism, watching the evacuation "was probably the saddest time of my political career and certainly in the White House from a government point of view." Adding salt to the wound was the decision of the House of Representatives on 1 May to reject the request for humanitarian aid on the grounds that South Vietnam's surrender and the evacuation made the dollars unnecessary and that if the aid were approved, it would end up in Communist hands. To Ford, the denial was another example of who was at fault for America's defeat. Yes, he admitted years later, voters had grown weary of the war, but he placed the blame primarily on the shoulders of a resistant Congress.[54]

Ford could console himself knowing that he would receive credit for formally ending U.S. involvement in Vietnam. Furthermore, he considered it important to help Cambodian and Vietnamese refugees who were in the Philippines, Taiwan, Wake Island, Guam, or other locales and who desired to settle in the United States. There were two interrelated issues. One was to convince lawmakers to provide funding for the resettlement of these individuals. That, wrote L. Dean Brown, a career Foreign Service officer who had helped organize the evacuation from Saigon, would require "a strong Presidential statement." Then there was their sheer number. In April, Ford, after consulting lawmakers, had agreed to parole 130,000 refugees so they could enter the United States, and established an Interagency Task

Force to oversee the evacuation process. Early the following month, though, Kissinger warned the number could be as high as 150,000. To avoid any difficulties with Congress, the secretary suggested that any funding request reflect resettling 130,000 of them, with the remainder to find homes in other countries.[55]

In mid-May, Ford established the President's Advisory Committee on Refugees, with the purpose of helping the refugees settle in the United States, and began lobbying for Congress's assistance. He made clear that of those who wanted to come to the country, only 35,000 were heads of households, meaning there would be far fewer vying with Americans for jobs than the 130,000 number suggested. He also had the endorsement of labor unions, including the AFL-CIO, which had had powerful influence among workers in Vietnam, and of the American Jewish Committee and several governors. With widespread support for helping the refugees and assurances that the newcomers would not create economic problems for their constituents, lawmakers passed the Indochina Migration and Refugee Act. The law, which Ford signed later that month, allocated $400 million to provide assistance to those who had escaped Vietnam and Cambodia. In December 1975, the last of the refugees passed through a receiving center, and the Interagency Task Force ceased operations.[56]

The *Mayaguez*

The United States may have believed it could now close the door on the former Indochina, but events less than two weeks after the last helicopter left Saigon proved otherwise. On the morning of 12 May, the 10,500-ton American container ship *Mayaguez*, with a crew of thirty-nine and loaded with nonlethal military equipment, was sailing from Hong Kong to Singapore by way of Thailand. Just after 2:00 a.m., Cambodian patrol boats fired across the ship's bow and ordered it to stop. As the *Mayaguez* came to a halt, the ship's radioman sent an emergency message in the clear. A few minutes later, Cambodian sailors boarded and seized the ship, claiming that it had illegally strayed into Cambodian waters. The action of the Khmer Rouge government could not have come at a worse time. In addition to having ordered the last Americans to leave Vietnam, the Ford administration was not making progress in its effort to resolve tensions in the Middle East. The president was also taking heat for refusing to help New York City address its financial crisis. If handled poorly, the *Mayaguez* crisis could further sully the White House. That said, the *Mayaguez* offered an opportunity. White

House officials knew that they could not sit by and let the Cambodians push the United States around the way the North Vietnamese had done. If handled adeptly, this new crisis could demonstrate both to Americans and to the world that the United States and its president were resolved to stand up to aggressors.[57]

It did not take long for the White House to learn of what had happened. An employee of the Delta Exploration Company in Indonesia had first picked up the distress signal and forwarded it to the U.S. embassy there. Less than two hours later, the information was in Scowcroft's hands. Ford recalled receiving a phone call from his deputy national security adviser at 5:30 a.m. regarding a "rumor" of the incident. At about 7:40, he received confirmation. Thirty minutes later, Kissinger's staff debriefed the secretary of state. Not only had the Cambodians commandeered the ship, he learned, but an intelligence report had them taking it to the coastal city of Kompong Som (today, Sihanoukville). "Now goddamn it," the secretary of state roared. "We are not going to sit here and let an American merchant ship be captured at sea and let it go into the harbor without doing a bloody thing about it." He then relayed what he knew to Ford, who ordered a noontime meeting of the NSC.[58]

At that gathering the administration set forth its plan of action. As Washington did not have direct diplomatic contact with the Khmer government, Kissinger suggested sending a strongly worded protest note via China. Further, he recommended "some show of force." Fearful of a replay of the 1968 *Pueblo* incident, Rockefeller strongly favored "a violent response. . . . The world should know that we will act and that we will act quickly." What resources the United States had in the area was the question. There were B-52s, F-4 and F-111 fighter jets, AC-130 gunships, and helicopters in Thailand and two aircraft carriers in the region; of them, the *Coral Sea* was closest, but it was on its way to Australia and would need time to turn around and get within striking distance of Cambodia.[59]

Ford agreed with the need to demonstrate American resolve and to rescue those he believed were the victims of a "clear act of piracy." He decided to have the *Coral Sea* steam toward Cambodia, have reconnaissance keep track of the *Mayaguez*'s movements, transmit a protest to Phnom Penh via Beijing, issue a public statement decrying Cambodia's actions, and prepare an amphibious force in the Philippines to engage in ground operations, if necessary. He realized the War Powers Resolution could restrict his freedom of maneuver. Accordingly, he told his advisers not to say "we will do anything militarily since we have not decided." However, he had not favored the resolution at the time it was passed, and now, with American lives at risk, he made clear that "irrespective of Congress, we will move." Ford's calm but firm demeanor impressed all those present. "I'll tell you," commented Kennerly, "if ever a man was in control of the situation, he was it. [It] firmly established him in my mind as the President of the United States."[60]

Reconnaissance of the *Mayaguez* began shortly after Ford's instructions. Nessen issued a statement in which he called the ship's seizure "an act of piracy," and Deputy Secretary of State Robert Ingersoll delivered a protest note to China's liaison office in Washington for transmission to Cambodia. Naval elements started toward the Cambodian coastline even before the president's orders reached them. Mike Rodgers, commander of the guided-missile destroyer *Henry B. Wilson*, was on his way to the Philippines after providing protection for evacuees leaving South Vietnam when he heard about the *Mayaguez* over his personal shortwave radio. He immediately turned his ship around and headed for the Cambodian coastline. Similarly, Admiral Maurice Weisner, commander of the U.S. Pacific Fleet, ordered the *Coral Sea*, its escorts, and the frigate *Harold E. Holt* to move at top speed toward Kompong Som.[61]

Several wrinkles soon appeared. The first was the *Mayaguez*'s destination. The assumption on the morning of 13 May was that the ship was on its way to the Cambodian mainland, but word then arrived that it had turned for Koh Tang, an island off the Cambodian coast. By 7:15 a.m., Ford had confirmation that the vessel had anchored off Koh Tang and that the crew had been taken to the island. Then there was the protest note. The chief of the American liaison office, George H. W. Bush, had numerous contacts in China, but none of them knew to whom in the new Cambodian government to transmit the U.S. message. (Beijing later returned the note as undeliverable, but Bush believed it had in fact been sent to Phnom Penh.) Finally, Thailand posed a potential problem. Between January and March, that country had gone through three governments, the last of which was headed by Prime Minister Kukrit Pramoj. Kukrit did not want to do anything that might threaten his incumbency, such as having American aircraft based in Thailand take part in the *Mayaguez* operation.[62]

The White House had no intention of letting Thai officials determine its plan of action. Ford later wrote that "until the *Mayaguez* and her crew were safe, I didn't give a damn about offending their sensibilities." Over the next two days, the NSC met three more times, during which the president and his advisers honed their plan of action. They would not permit the Cambodians to take the *Mayaguez* crewmen, who were all believed to be on Koh Tang, to the mainland, and U.S. aircraft monitoring the situation received orders to destroy any Cambodian boats that tried to leave Koh Tang for the mainland. Additionally, Ford and his top aides concurred that the United States needed to have enough ground forces to hold off the estimated 100 defenders on Koh Tang while retaking the *Mayaguez* and freeing the Americans. There were 125 U.S. marines at the American air base at Utapao, Thailand. The administration ordered reinforcements from Okinawa and the Philippines to bring the number of marines at Utapao to 1,000. The plan called for those troops to land on Koh Tang by helicopter. As the eleven choppers at Utapao could bring in no more than 270 marines at a time, the entire contingent would have to arrive in waves. In light of the four-hour round trip,[63] the first group of Americans would have to wait some time for help if it came under heavy fire.

There was disagreement, however, over how fast to act and over the use of naval resources. Colby estimated that there were 2,000 Khmer soldiers at Kompong Som, with another 400 on their way, and the Cambodians had enough shipping at Kompong Som to take all 2,400 of them to Koh Tang at one time when the marines landed. Kissinger wanted to move rapidly, retake the *Mayaguez,* and attack Kompong Som and Koh Tang "all at once." Doing so would give "the impression that we are potentially trigger-happy" and, in turn, send a message to North Korea, the Soviet Union, and other adversaries. Vice President Rockefeller echoed that sentiment. "Many are watching us, in Korea and elsewhere," he commented. "I think we need to respond quickly. The longer we wait, the more time they have to get ready." Moreover, he suggested sinking the Cambodian navy. Schlesinger warned that such heavy-handed measures might lead the Khmer government to destroy the *Mayaguez* and would put the lives of the ship's crew in danger. Furthermore, explained Scowcroft, it was best to wait until the U.S. warships had arrived, which would not be until the following day. The *Holt* could station itself between the *Mayaguez* and Kompong Som, thus preventing the Cambodians from taking the U.S. vessel to the mainland. Additionally, Schlesinger pointed out, the *Holt* and the *Coral Sea*, once they were in position, could provide cover for the marines landing on Koh Tang.[64]

Nor did Ford's aides see eye-to-eye on the use of air power. Kissinger and Rockefeller wanted to have B-52s participate in the bombing of the mainland, while Deputy Secretary of Defense William Clements, Schlesinger, and Rumsfeld all expressed caution. "I think dropping a lot of bombs on the mainland will not help us with the release of the Americans," commented

Clements. Schlesinger warned that using B-52s would raise "a red flag on the Hill." Rumsfeld seconded the defense secretary. The B-52 was "associated with damage inflicted across Vietnam and had caused negative reactions in the region and in America," he explained to the president. It made more sense to use aircraft from the *Coral Sea*, which "could strike with precision and reduce the potential of civilian casualties."[65]

The White House also had to take into account the War Powers Resolution, which required notice within forty-eight hours of the use of U.S. combat forces abroad. On 13 May, as the NSC deliberated, the White House received word that three Cambodian boats had tried to leave Koh Tang. Scowcroft told the president that one had been sunk, another had returned to Koh Tang, and the third, a fishing vessel escorted by patrol craft, was trying to get to the mainland. It was unclear if the third boat was carrying crew from the *Mayaguez*, but after weighing the issues, Ford ordered its sinking. "If we don't do it," he explained, "it is an indication of some considerable weakness."[66]

There are discrepancies in the reports of what happened next. Schlesinger claimed later that he refused to pass on the order, which is what kept the pilots of the U.S. aircraft from attacking the vessels. According to the evidence, though, Scowcroft relayed the order to shoot via his military aide, General John Wickham; Wickham reported a little more than an hour later that one of the pilots was reluctant to shoot because he had seen what he believed to be Caucasians on board. (In fact, this boat was carrying the *Mayaguez* crew.) Not sure what to do, Scowcroft contacted Ford. Worried about the public reaction if he gave an order that led to the death of Americans, he changed his earlier instructions and called for the pilot to do all he could to prevent the boat from reaching the mainland without destroying it. The point was that American planes had fired on Cambodian vessels, said White House Counsel Philip Buchen, and hence Ford needed to let the congressional leadership know of his orders. Rumsfeld worried about the president "being crimped by Congress," a position echoed by Kissinger, who recommended telling Capitol Hill's leaders of the operation without saying when the marines would actually land on Koh Tang.[67]

Harassment of the third boat failed to keep it from reaching Kompong Som. Unbeknownst to the White House, the Cambodians had already offered the *Mayaguez* crewmen their freedom. Initially, the Khmer soldiers told the *Mayaguez*'s captain, Charles Miller, that he could take a gunboat to his ship, where he could radio U.S. authorities that he and his crewmates would be freed if U.S. planes stopped flying over Cambodia's airspace. Fearful that any armed vessel would be a target of American aircraft, Miller refused and asked for a fishing boat. The Cambodians had none on hand at that moment but promised to put the crew on such a vessel the next morning so they could head to the *Mayaguez* and go home.[68]

Assuming that the *Mayaguez* crew had become hostages and that the United States was on the verge of replaying the *Pueblo* crisis, the president gave his final instructions in the late afternoon of 14 May. He agreed with those who preferred not to use the B-52s. Otherwise, he favored Kissinger's all-at-once response. He therefore ordered attacks on the mainland and on Koh Tang, and the recapture of the *Mayaguez*, all to take place the next day. The timing would give the U.S. warships then on their way the opportunity to get into position. At 6:30 p.m. on 14 May he and Kissinger briefed the bipartisan congressional leadership, with the president offering details of the three-part operation. Mansfield questioned bombing the mainland, but Ford replied that it was essential to "prevent [Cambodian] forces from interfering with our operations." Albert pointed out that some lawmakers believed the president had violated the law by not telling them immediately of the military's actions, prompting a testy response from Ford: "I have the right to protect American citizens." Senator Robert Byrd (D-W.Va.) wondered why no one in the executive branch had informed the congressional leadership in advance so that lawmakers could have had "a chance to urge caution." Ford responded that he had chosen what he considered "the prudent course of action. Had we put the Marines' lives in jeopardy by doing too little, I would have been negligent. It is better to do too much than too little." Byrd pressed his case, yet Ford remained firm. "We have a separation of powers," said the president. As commander in chief of the country's armed forces, "I exercised my power under the law and I complied with the law. I would never forgive myself if the Marines had been attacked by 2400 Cambodians."[69]

About forty minutes after Ford and Kissinger began their meeting with Congress's leaders, the first wave of marines landed on Koh Tang. For reasons that remain unclear, the military officers stationed in Thailand who planned the operation had not received two highly accurate reports, one from the Commander Intelligence Pacific and the other from the Defense Intelligence Agency, stating that the Cambodians had as many as 150 to 250 troops on Koh Tang armed with machine guns, a mortar, and rocket-propelled grenade launchers. Because of this lack of intelligence, the operation did not proceed as planned. Three of the eleven helicopters that departed Utapao transported their marines to the *Holt*, which pulled alongside

President Gerald R. Ford with senior staff members as they learned of the recapture of the SS Mayaguez *and its crew, May 1975. Photo in the Gerald Ford Library, Ann Arbor, Michigan.*

the *Mayaguez*. After using tear gas, the troops boarded the ship but found no one aboard. Matters went far less smoothly for the other eight helicopters, which took marines to Koh Tang itself. Coming under heavy fire, three of them were shot down and four others suffered damage; one of the aircraft from the *Mayaguez* operation, which flew in to rescue a contingent of marines who had been pinned down by the defenders, was also put out of action. This left three helicopters to bring in reinforcements.[70]

A few minutes before the first wave arrived, the Cambodian government announced that it intended to release the *Mayaguez* crew. Ford questioned whether he should proceed with the air strike on Kompong Som, but Kissinger convinced him to do so. At 9:24 p.m., after hitting the port town, Nessen announced that the United States would cease its operations once Cambodia announced the crew's release. In fact, the Cambodians had already done just that. Two hours later, a U.S. aircraft spotted the boat carrying the *Mayaguez*'s men, who were picked up by the *Wilson*.[71]

There was jubilation when Washington learned the *Mayaguez*'s crew was safe. Hartmann recalled that Ford "let out an old-fashioned Indian war whoop. 'Thank God! We got 'em all! They're all safe!'" Scowcroft asked about ending the military operation, but Kissinger convinced Ford to proceed with the fourth bombing raid. "Let's look ferocious!," he exclaimed.

"Otherwise they will attack us as the ship leaves." The decision made, the president also commanded extraction of the marines and then announced the successful recovery of the *Mayaguez* crew.[72]

Getting the marines out was easier said than done. Not only were they under heavy fire, but prior to receiving the disengagement order, a second wave of them had arrived. U.S. warships and warplanes provided cover as the few remaining helicopters extricated the marines over a period of several hours. The Khmer government announced that it had suffered 125 casualties, including 55 killed, but it remains unclear how accurate that figure is.[73] Fifteen Americans died; in addition, twenty-three were killed when what would have been a twelfth helicopter crashed on the way to Utapao. Forty-nine others were wounded, and three more were missing in action.

In the short run, the rescue of the *Mayaguez* crew was a political windfall for the president. Ford saw his approval rating jump 11 points, and much of the media praised him. *Newsweek* asserted that the operation was "a daring show of nerve and steel . . . swift and tough—and it worked." The *New York Times*'s C. L. Sulzberger wrote that the president's "resolute and skillful leadership" had destroyed "a polluting American image of lassitude, uncertainty and pessimism." Most members of Congress also were laudatory. Byrd congratulated Ford for his "firmness," and Representative Carl Curtis (R-Nebr.) called Ford's decision making "courageous and decisive."[74]

Yet the crisis could have turned out much worse. The determination of the president to look tough in the face of aggression had risked the lives of the *Mayaguez* crew. It was only Schlesinger's refusal to pass on the order to fire and the concern of an unnamed pilot that prevented more Americans' names from being added to the list of casualties and saved the White House from suffering a public-relations disaster.

Furthermore, events surrounding the *Mayaguez* once again revealed dissension among Ford's top aides. Schlesinger found himself at odds more than once with Kissinger (and Rockefeller) over such matters as the B-52 strikes. Even if he was not alone in that sentiment, it was he who, as the secretary of defense, set the tone for a Pentagon position that appeared to be out of line with what the president and the secretary of state favored. Resentment toward Schlesinger increased when Nessen learned that the Defense Department had informed reporters of the rescue of the *Mayaguez*'s crew before he had a chance to announce it himself. Ford shared Nessen's anger when he discovered that the fourth bombing run never took place. The president tried to find out who in the Defense Department "had contravened my authority," but he never did. "I let the matter drop," he later wrote,[75] but subsequent events made clear that the issue remained on his mind.

In the longer run, the *Mayaguez* crisis paid fewer political dividends than hoped. Kissinger had wanted to display American strength following the evacuation of Saigon, but even he admitted in an interview on 23 May that what had happened in Cambodia "could not alter the reality that we had entered Indochina to save a country, and that we had ended by rescuing a ship." The General Accounting Office (GAO), which conducted its own investigation of the crisis, concluded in a 1976 report that while the aims of the rescue operation and the rapidity with which U.S. military forces reacted were commendable, the White House could have done a better job in finding out where the crew was and in gathering more accurate intelligence on the strength of Koh Tang's defenders. The GAO determined as well that it was not U.S. military action that obtained the release of the crew but approaches from China. Simply put, it wondered if the United States could have achieved the same outcome without the loss of American lives. Finally, and most important, both the evacuation of Saigon and the rescue of the *Mayaguez* crew showed that the administration could, albeit haphazardly, handle a crisis. What the two events had failed to demonstrate was whether the White House was able to offer a vision for its broader foreign-policy goals.[76]

Solzhenitsyn, the Summit, and SALT

One of those foreign-policy goals was signing and achieving the ratification of a second Strategic Arms Limitation Treaty (SALT II), but Capitol Hill's passage of the Trade Act threatened to derail the agreement. Determined to stay on course, Ford reassured Soviet premier Leonid Brezhnev a few days after signing the legislation that he remained committed to pursuing the arms-control pact. Resolved to avoid another setback that might affect SALT II, Ford deferred a meeting with the famous Soviet dissident and author, Aleksandr Solzhenitsyn. Imprisoned for a time for his views, he had been thrown out of the Soviet Union in 1974 and had had his citizenship revoked by the Kremlin. Those who opposed détente, demanded Soviet respect for human rights, or both rallied around the dissident. One such was George Meany, who called détente "appeasement" and "a giveaway in the search of profits for our corporations through a combination of American capital and Soviet slave labor."[77]

Meany planned to have a banquet in Solzhenitsyn's honor and invited

Ford to attend, as did two right-wing GOP senators, Strom Thurmond of South Carolina and North Carolina's Jesse Helms. Presidential Counselor Jack Marsh, Rumsfeld, and Deputy White House Coordinator Richard Cheney all suggested that Ford go, whether to please conservatives or to shield the reputation of a president willing to speak to anybody. But Kissinger urged the president to forgo the event and instead invite Solzhenitsyn to the White House. Ford disliked either alternative. He expected that if he were to go, he would hear the author denounce détente; additionally, Ford's presence would risk infuriating the Soviets. Bringing the author to the White House would also be symbolically dangerous, and anyway, Ford regarded Solzhenitsyn as "a goddamned horse's ass." The president thus announced that his schedule prohibited either the dinner or a one-on-one visit.[78]

Unmoved, Helms and Thurmond publicly exhorted Ford to meet with Solzhenitsyn on 4 July. There was no way the president could have done so, even had he wanted to, in light of a long-planned and long-publicized multicity tour in honor of the nation's bicentennial. Ford was outraged by this clear effort to paint him into a corner, but he understood that an outright rejection would upset the conservative wing of his party. As a result, he issued an open invitation for Solzhenitsyn to visit him, but only after an upcoming summit in Helsinki. The two men ultimately never met, and the whole affair left the antidétente coalition irate. "If Kissinger and Ford had met with Solzhenitsyn rather than cowering in fear of the Soviet reaction to such a meeting," stated Henry Jackson, "they would have learned that all Solzhenitsyn is asking for is a detente without illusions, for an American-Soviet relationship that promotes the cause of human rights and a genuine peace." In even harsher language, the conservative columnists Rowland Evans and Robert Novack accused Ford of "Snubbing Solzhenitsyn."[79]

The summit in Helsinki, arranged to formalize agreements reached at the Conference on Security and Cooperation in Europe (CSCE), further riled the GOP right wing and neoconservatives. The surrender of the Axis in World War II had not been followed by a formal end to the state of war in Europe. Moreover, the years after the last global military conflict had witnessed important changes to national boundaries in Europe, as well as Soviet domination of the eastern part of that continent. As early as 1954, Moscow had suggested a conference that would give international sanction to those borders and, by extension, to the Kremlin's European sphere of influence. In the name of détente, President Richard Nixon had reluctantly agreed to such a meeting,[80] which opened at the foreign-minister level in

1973, among the United States, Canada, the Soviet Union, and more than thirty other European countries.

By 30 July, when the Helsinki Summit took place, the CSCE participants had concluded its Final Act and made it available for signing by their respective nations' leaders. Its provisions fell into three "baskets." Basket I confirmed the existing borders in Europe and called for the peaceful resolution of disputes, respect for human rights, and self-determination. Basket II centered on international cooperation on scientific, environmental, technological, and commercial matters. Basket III affirmed the free transfer of people, information, and ideas among the signatories. In the United States, détente's critics assailed the Final Act. Reagan, who was considering a run against Ford for the GOP nomination, made clear his opposition. "I am against it, and I think all Americans should be against it," he remarked. The *National Review* described the Final Act's message to the people of Eastern Europe as "Abandon hope, all ye who read our words."[81]

Kissinger, however, convinced Ford of the need to attend Helsinki and speak with Brezhnev, who was also slated to attend. Progress on SALT II had been exceedingly slow. In addition to the disagreements over the Backfire bomber and cruise missiles, the two countries' delegations faced new complications, such as how to count the number of MIRVed missiles—namely, if one missile of a type was MIRVed, should all missiles of that type be counted as MIRVed?—and how to verify compliance with the agreement. Furthermore, détente had begun to fray. A meeting with the Soviet premier would be "a crucial encounter for several reasons," the secretary of state wrote. "First, it will largely determine the future course of the SALT talks . . . ; second, and equally important, it will be the opportunity to reestablish a mutual commitment, at the highest level, to improve Soviet-American relations as the basic policy of both sides." Moreover, Kissinger said, it would prove important "to maintain Alliance cohesion," the Final Act was a nonbinding statement of principles, and, in a reference to the act's human-rights provisions, "*the philosophy which permeates most of the CSCE's declarations is that of the West's open societies*" (emphasis in the original).[82]

The meetings in Helsinki among Ford, Brezhnev, and their aides did little to make headway either toward achieving a SALT II or toward reinvigorating détente. The two sides could not get beyond their differences over cruise missiles and the Backfire bomber or on policy toward the Middle East, with the Soviets rejecting the step-by-step process favored by the United States and calling for another Geneva Conference. Brezhnev also used Helsinki to denounce U.S. pressure to increase emigration from the Soviet Union, commenting that there had been a falloff in the number of Soviets requesting to leave, that some people could not be permitted to leave for security reasons—a policy that he said Washington ascribed to as well—and that to meet the numbers demanded by individuals like Jackson would mean forcing Soviet nationals to depart against their will. It was on this last score that the Washington senator, who had announced his bid for the presidency in February 1975, derided Helsinki, calling the portions related to human rights "so imprecise and so hedged as to raise considerable doubt about whether they can and will be seriously implemented." An angry Kissinger afterward mused to Japanese foreign minister Kiichi Miyazawa, "Senator Jackson is a fool. If we followed his policy, we would be attacked within a year for not pursuing peace."[83]

Middle East

Peace was at the heart of yet another target of the Ford administration, the Middle East. Acting on Ford's instructions to continue the peace process begun under Nixon, Kissinger sought as his immediate goal an Israeli-Egyptian disengagement agreement. During the early months of 1975, he shuttled between those two nations as well as Syria, keeping Ford apprised of his efforts throughout. He wanted to assure Syrian president Hafez al-Assad that he was not ignoring Syria's interests, but Assad knew that Israel wanted to split Cairo from Damascus. Another problem was the Soviets, who continued to complain they were being ignored and insisted on reconvening the Geneva Conference.[84] Both Kissinger and Ford ignored Moscow, and despite Assad's protests, the secretary held to his course, gradually working through a number of the issues separating Tel Aviv and Cairo.

In early March, Egyptian president Anwar Sadat, while not using the word "nonbelligerency," offered a public "no-war pledge" in return for Israel's withdrawing its military presence from the two passes and the Sinai oil fields. Furthermore, Egypt would abide by any pact reached with Israel "until superseded by another agreement." The Israelis had offered some concessions of their own, but they insisted that Sadat pledge nonbelligerency. Additionally, they wanted to keep control over an intelligence facility at Umm Khisheiba, located on the western side of the Gidi Pass. Kissinger grew angry, for Prime Minister Yitzhak Rabin's government had indicated that it would accept alternate language. Frustrated, he wrote Ford on 14 March, "Either by neglect or design the Israeli government encouraged us to engage our full prestige in this exercise and led us to believe that a formula less than nonbelligerency would be acceptable."[85]

Throughout his career, Ford had defended Israel's interests, but he had come to share his secretary of state's exasperation with Tel Aviv's intransigence. "The failure to achieve an agreement is bound to have far-reaching effects in the area and on our relations," he informed Rabin on 21 March. To show he was serious, he told the prime minister that he had "directed an immediate reassessment of U.S. policy in the area, including our relations with Israel." Kissinger departed Israel that same day, and upon his return, Ford publicly announced his intention of reconsidering Washington's ties with Tel Aviv. The president followed up by placing a hold on Israel's request for $2.5 billion in military assistance.[86]

"I don't think I have ever been so disappointed as when I heard Henry was coming back without a settlement," Ford told U.S. Jewish leader Max Fisher a few days later. "It was as low as I have been in this office." Clearly, the president hoped that Fisher might prod the Israelis to budge, and he was pleased to have Mansfield and Albert express Democratic support for taking a harder line with the Rabin government. For the next month, Kissinger and Ford met with their aides, a group of foreign policy "wise men"—including former secretary of state Dean Rusk and former secretary of defense Robert McNamara—and American ambassadors and academics. The administration concluded it had three options. The first was to call for a reconvening of the Geneva Conference and seek a regional settlement. The second was to return to the step-by-step process. The third was to seek an interim Israeli-Egyptian agreement that would not demand a complete withdrawal of the two countries' military forces or require a statement of nonbelligerency.[87]

If the administration hoped its reassessment would force Israel to budge, it was wrong. If anything, Tel Aviv appeared more intransigent, Jewish organizations in the United States lobbied Congress, and lawmakers, who had originally stood behind the White House, began to rethink their position. The House of Representatives withdrew consideration of a Senate resolution lauding Kissinger's work to achieve a Middle East peace, and in May seventy-five senators urged the president to accept both Israel's request for $2.5 billion in aid and its desire for "'defensible' frontiers." To Ford, this was another example of congressional interference in foreign-policy making. The letter from the senators "really bugged me," the president later wrote. "The Senators claimed the letter was 'spontaneous,' but there was no doubt in my mind that it was inspired by Israel." Yet it was also clear to Ford and Kissinger that the only viable alternative was to return to the step-by-step process. Both the Ford administration and Sadat had invested heavily in it,[88] and the other two options offered far greater dangers to America's regional interests than a second Israeli-Egyptian disengagement pact.

Ford devoted even more attention to the peace process, holding discussions with Sadat and Rabin during the first two weeks of June. He had not met the Egyptian president before they got together in Salzburg, Austria, on 1 June. At a personal level, the two men hit it off, but geopolitically, Sadat held firm to his position on the passes, oil fields, and nonbelligerency. The same was true for the Umm Khisheiba facility, but he was willing to have Americans man it. The talks with Rabin went little better. Ford suggested that the idea of Americans manning the monitoring station was Washington's own. The Israeli prime minister seemed prepared to make some concessions to get beyond his current spat with the United States. The Israeli cabinet, though, remained unyielding. To an exasperated Kissinger, Israel's leaders were "the world's worst shits," "a bloody minded bunch," and "SOBs," whose goal it was, he told Ford, to make sure the president did not win the 1976 election.[89]

Having reached the conclusion that its impasse with the United States did Israel more harm than good, the Rabin government made a new offer on 24 June. Israel would draw back its military presence to the eastern side of the Gidi and Mitla Passes and give Egypt the right to use a portion of a road on the Sinai so that Cairo would have access to the Abu Rudeis oil field. Additionally, Tel Aviv asked for an agreement of only three to four years' duration. Finally, UN peacekeepers would maintain their presence between the Israeli and Egyptian lines. In return, Israel expected the United States to provide it with the military and economic aid it desired, as well as with a guarantee of petroleum to make up for the oil it would lose by giving up Abu Rudeis. Sadat disliked the proposal and threatened to call for a reconvening of the Geneva Conference, which he knew would ultimately lead to a failure of the peace process. Ford decided to keep up the pressure, telling Rabin that his government had acted disingenuously. As far as he, Ford, was concerned, "Israel's position is forcing the evolution of negotiations toward an outcome which runs counter to the interests of the United States and the world."[90]

The Israelis began to recognize that their stubbornness and their attempts to use the U.S. political system against the Ford administration had not worked. If anything, they had begun to jeopardize Israeli security. In early July, Tel Aviv's ambassador to Washington, Simcha Dinitz, repeated his country's request for over $2 billion in military aid, only to have Ford make clear that such assistance was contingent on a "satisfactory" disengagement agreement. Pushed into a corner, the Israelis showed a preparedness to make more concessions. For six weeks, Kissinger had stayed out of the Middle East, as the Ford administration had seen no reason to send him there if a disengagement agreement appeared unlikely. The atmosphere having changed, Ford on 17 August instructed his secretary of state to return to the region.[91]

Over the next two weeks, Kissinger whittled down the differences between Tel Aviv and Cairo, and on 1 September, he worked out the final details of what became the Sinai Interim Agreement, Sinai II. Israel would withdraw from the Gidi and Mitla Passes and from the Abu Rudeis oil field, thus returning 2,000 square miles of land to Egypt. Egypt promised to permit nonmilitary hardware to pass through the Suez Canal to Israel and to curb anti-Israeli propaganda. Both Cairo and Tel Aviv pledged themselves not to use force against the other (nowhere did Cairo declare nonbelligerency); Israel would retain the Umm Khisheiba station, which it would jointly man with American technicians; and the United States would help Egypt construct a similar station. U.S. personnel would join Egyptians at that facility, and Americans alone would oversee several more stations. In returning to agreeing to these terms, Israel expected from the United States the military aid it demanded as well as oil to replace what Tel Aviv would lose once Abu Rudeis was turned over to Cairo. Furthermore, the United States would not negotiate with the PLO until the PLO accepted Israel's right to exist. Washington also guaranteed that the terms of any talks with Syria regarding disengagement had to guarantee Israeli retention of the Golan Heights. Finally, the United States would consult with Israel if Israel was threatened by the Soviet Union.[92] Three days later, Sadat and Rabin separately signed the accords.

Sinai II was a major achievement for the Ford administration. The president called it "one of the greatest diplomatic achievements of this century." America's allies in Europe and Japan praised the results. One official in Tokyo commented that it raised the "prospect for the progress of future peace negotiations." Still, *U.S. News & World Report* observed that the price paid was "very stiff," including $2.2 billion in military aid for Israel, around $650 million more in assistance for Egypt, and the presence of at least 100 Americans to man the monitoring stations.[93]

Most members of Congress, such as Representative Howard Baker (R-Tenn.), appeared willing to accept those conditions, but a few, including Senators Jackson and Mansfield, expressed anxiety about Americans being placed in such a dangerous area and the possibility that the United States could find itself dragged into yet another Vietnam-style war. Not surprisingly, the Soviets denounced the agreement as pro-Israeli. More disconcerting were the loud cries of anger from Arab opinion: Assad fumed over both U.S. acquiescence to Israeli retention of the Golan Heights and his being cut out of the disengagement process. Many Arab leaders, including moderates such as Jordan's King Hussein, condemned Sadat for accepting peace with Israel.[94] As significant as Sinai II was, it proved to be the last step in Kissinger's step-by-step approach to Middle East peace prior to the 1976 election.

The Candidate and the Conservatives

Certainly the election was on Ford's mind by the time Sinai II came to fruition. The president had told his wife that he intended to call it quits in Washington in 1976, and at first he appeared to hold to that promise, privately telling Kissinger early on of his disinclination to seek the presidency in his own right come the next election. The secretary "was very upset," Ford reminisced, and cautioned that to make such an announcement public would cost the president "all influence domestically and internationally." Ford found Kissinger's reasoning compelling. But Ford had an additional incentive to seek the presidency in own right. His ambition had been to become House speaker. Instead, he found himself in the nation's most important political office. And for all its frustrations, he enjoyed the job. Hence, in November 1974, he had Nessen quietly indicate that he intended to run for the Republican nomination come 1976.[95] Ford formalized his plans in July of the following year when he himself announced his candidacy.

There were already indications that Ford faced an uphill battle. The outcome of the 1974 midterms convinced Democrats he was vulnerable. Moreover, organized labor, the poor, African Americans, Jews, and other traditional Democratic constituencies had little reason to bolt to the Republicans in light of Ford's policies. More ominous was a possible revolt among GOP conservatives, who were angered by the president's positions on Rockefeller's nomination, the economy, and policy toward the Soviet Union.

The Right's ire piqued in August 1975, not because of anything Ford himself had done but because of his wife. Betty's support of the Equal Rights Amendment and of abortion displeased conservatives, and an interview on the popular television news show *60 Minutes* added to their vexation. Questioned by veteran journalist Morley Safer, the first lady talked about

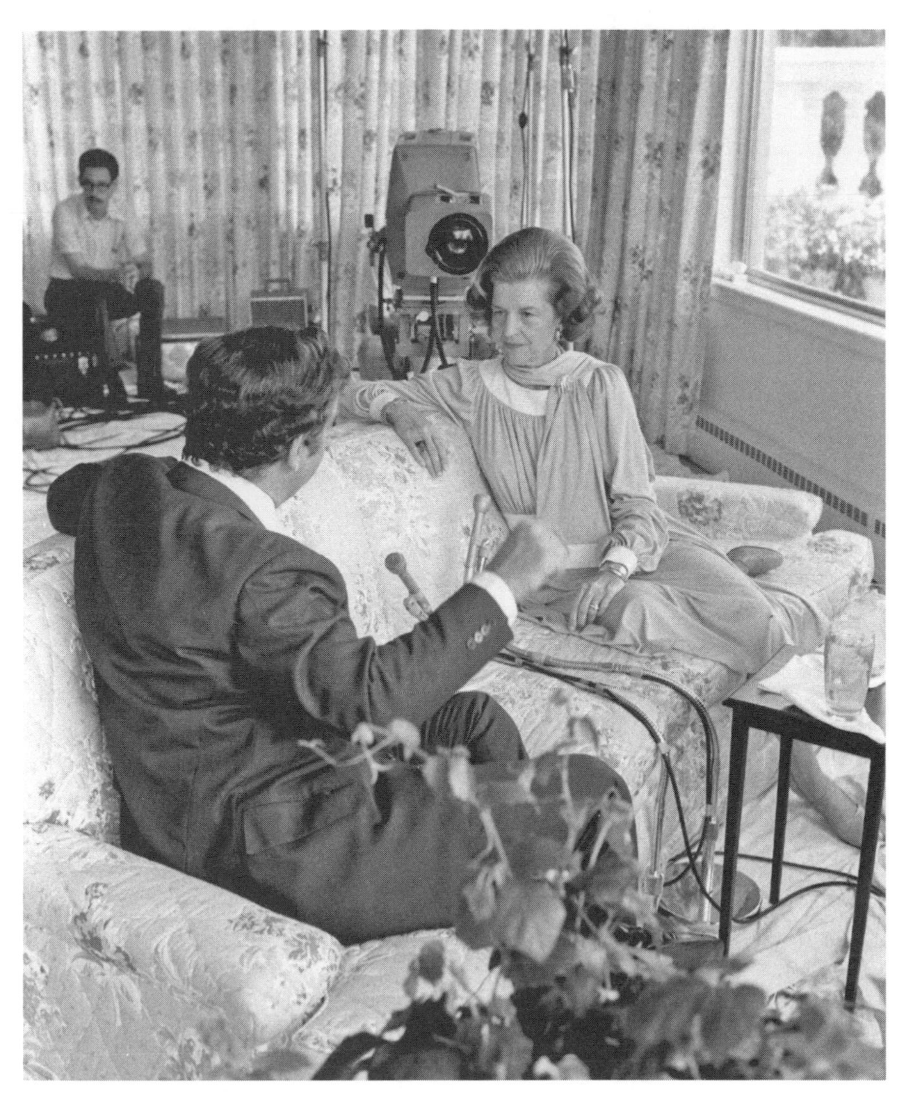

First Lady Betty Ford interviewed by Morley Safer of CBS's 60 Minutes, *21 July 1975. Photo in the Gerald Ford Library, Ann Arbor, Michigan.*

her responsibilities in the White House, called *Roe v. Wade* a "great, great decision," and admitted to visiting a psychiatrist. Betty had clearly been prepared for such queries, but she appeared to be surprised when Safer asked if younger individuals should live together prior to marriage. "Well, they are, aren't they?," she replied. When he asked how she would respond if she learned her daughter Susan was "having an affair," the first lady rejoined,

"I wouldn't be surprised. . . . If she wanted to continue it, I would certainly counsel and advise her on the subject." Safer also wondered whether any of the Ford children might have tried marijuana and whether she herself might have experimented with it in her younger years. Yes, she said, it was likely that her children had smoked it, and she too would probably have done the same.[96]

The interview at first embarrassed Susan, but she quickly came to the first lady's defense. There was "nothing wrong" with what her mother had said, she insisted. Conservatives, though, were outraged. New Hampshire's *Manchester Union Leader* wrote that "the immorality of Mrs. Ford's remarks is almost exceeded by their stupidity. . . . Coming from the first lady in the White House, it disgraces the nation itself." About 28,000 letters poured into the White House, many expressing similar sentiments. Wrote a proclaimed lifelong Republican, "As long as we have people like *Mrs. Ford* [emphasis in the original] living in the White House and shooting off her mouth with irresponsible remarks on such poor standards of morals, showing little concern with the principles of right conduct, then I say, who needs her or her husband living in the White House." Penned another, "Morals have not changed, and that mistaken belief of some people such as yourself, is what is contributing to the decadence of our country. . . . If you were looking for a platform to express your liberated views, you did get it . . . *but* [emphasis in the original] at the expense of losing a lot of votes for your husband."[97]

Privately, President Ford discounted their warnings. Sheila Weidenfeld, the first lady's press secretary, recalled the president "jokingly" throwing a pillow at his wife and proclaiming, "You just cost me 10 million votes. . . . No, you just cost me 20 million votes." Yet Betty's comments were not a joking matter. "I believe it is a mistake to continue to shrug off the public controversy over Mrs. Ford's remarks as harmless and without political effect," Nessen wrote. Ford tried to explain away his wife's statements as a "misunderstanding." Although the controversy eventually died down,[98] the firestorm of protest was another indication that the administration could not ignore an increasingly outspoken right wing.

A month later, it was not the Right that went after Ford but two women who sought to kill him—literally. While in California to give a speech on crime on 5 September, Ford shook hands with several individuals, one of whom, he remembered, pointed a gun at him. "I ducked," he wrote, and a Secret Service agent grabbed the weapon before the would-be assassin, Lynette "Squeaky" Fromme, could fire it. A follower of Charles Manson, who was then serving a life sentence on murder charges, Fromme herself would spend over thirty years in prison before being released in 2009.[99]

Back in California on 22 September, Ford had just left a hotel where he had met with union officials. As he waved to onlookers standing across the street, Sara Jane Moore pulled out a pistol and shot at the president. Thanks to the intervention of another person in the audience, who hit her arm, the bullet missed its intended target. Moore claimed that she wanted to create "chaos, and that chaos would be the catalyst for the winds of change."[100] She would spend the next thirty-two years in jail.

Ford had commented in the past that luck had intervened in his life, and no doubt he had been lucky to avoid any physical injury from two attempts to kill him. Whether that luck would continue to play out politically for him was another matter, particularly following a series of decisions he made in early November. Although Reagan had yet to announce whether he intended to challenge Ford for the Republican nomination, the president and his campaign team were well aware that it was a possibility. Also on Ford's mind were the views of Bo Callaway, a conservative from Georgia who headed the president's reelection campaign and who considered Rockefeller a political liability. The president was further concerned over the brouhaha created by investigations into the intelligence community, criticism that Kissinger had too much authority in the administration, clashes between Defense Secretary Schlesinger and Ford and others on his staff, and leaks to the press regarding Schlesinger's opposition to the SALT talks.[101]

Feeling the pressure, on 31 October Ford instituted a major shake-up of his administration. He asked Rockefeller not to seek reelection, which the vice president formally did the following Monday. On 2 November, the president requested that Schlesinger and Colby leave the administration and that Kissinger turn his responsibilities as national security adviser over to Kissinger's deputy, Scowcroft. The president then nominated the U.S. ambassador to China, George H. W. Bush, to assume Colby's job and Donald Rumsfeld to take Schlesinger's place. Richard Cheney took over his boss's old post. Finally, Ford named Nixon's former attorney general, Elliot Richardson, to replace Secretary of Commerce Rogers Morton.[102]

Morton had been in ill health, and so leaving Commerce would give him a chance to recuperate. The others asked to resign were less than pleased. A disappointed Rockefeller believed Rumsfeld had convinced Callaway to push him off the ticket—a charge Rumsfeld vehemently denied. Rockefeller subsequently told an interviewer that Ford "never really understood that I was only there to help him and the country." Schlesinger resisted leaving

Defense. When asked to quit, he made it clear to the president, "I haven't resigned, sir. You're firing me." Kissinger was also upset and raised with Ford the issue of submitting a letter of resignation from the administration. After a conversation that lasted more than an hour, the president convinced Kissinger to stay on as secretary of state.[103]

Ford had planned to disclose that Rockefeller was off the ticket before announcing the other staff changes later. But *Newsweek* magazine got wind of the fact that Schlesinger was going to be let go, so on 3 November (a Monday), the White House revealed all the changes. *Newsweek* described what it called the "Halloween Massacre" as "hastily planned, badly timed, and clumsily executed," and it questioned whether Ford really was "in control of his unelected Presidency and his uncertain political fortunes." *Time* understandably charged the president with giving "the impression that he was bumbling and dominated by political motives."[104]

Compounding the charge of political buffoonery in the media was the failure of the purge to rally Republican support. Betty told her husband that he was "a damn fool" to let Rockefeller go. Moderates and liberals in the party shared that appraisal. And if the president believed he would win support from conservatives, he erred there as well. "I am not appeased," commented Reagan upon hearing of the decrease in Kissinger's titles. If anything, the Right was infuriated, predominantly because of Schlesinger's firing. The defense secretary had the endorsement of conservatives because of his opposition to détente, and they saw removing him from his post as further evidence that Ford was anything but an ally. Polls indicated just how much damage the Halloween Massacre had caused. Two weeks earlier, a Gallup survey of GOP voters had Ford leading Reagan by 22 points; after the purge, NBC found Reagan ahead of Ford, 44 percent to 43 percent.[105]

Also troubling was Ford's failure to explain exactly what his broader vision was. John Casserly, a member of the White House's speechwriting staff, recalled a meeting in March 1975 at which a number of Ford's aides expressed unease that the president wanted to avoid a catchphrase—like the "Great Society" or "New Federalism"—that might stimulate voters. His speechwriters told the president that he left the impression of being an "indecisive" leader. An internal administration analysis from May that looked forward to the 1976 election shared that impression: "The facts are that the public does not know what Ford stands for. The Administration's energy program is a melange; the budget issues are unclear; the economic policy is confused; and foreign policy is in disarray." The left-leaning *Nation* joined the chorus. Two days before Ford announced the changes to his administration, it had referred to Ford's presidency as "vacuous," one "bereft of any sign of inspirational leadership in either foreign or domestic policy." That lack of vision was "the real source of the difficulty Ford faces from within the Republican Party, rather than any grass-roots groundswell of support for the only potential challenger who has emerged thus far, the former actor and ex–California Governor, Ronald Reagan."[106]

Reagan took the media and public reaction as evidence of Ford's vulnerability. He also was aware that in 1972 the GOP had altered the nominating process by increasing the number of state primaries that would select delegates to the party's national convention, making for a more open contest than ever before. On 19 November, he called Ford to let the president know he planned to enter the race for the Republican nomination. He had no intention of dividing the party, he insisted, but Ford knew better. "How can you challenge an incumbent president of your own party and *not* be divisive?," he wondered. *Newsweek* realized that that was a possibility. Reagan's "open declaration for Ford's job . . . could bloody their common party, ensnarl the President for months in the politics of survival, and conceivably drive Ford out of the race before next spring is out," the magazine remarked.[107] If that assessment were to prove true, Ford would become the first nonelected president in over ninety years who failed to win his party's nomination.

EIGHT

Image and the Election

"Live, from New York, it's *Saturday Night!*," shouted comedic actor Chevy Chase on the premier of a new late-night television program, NBC's *Saturday Night Live*. The creation of producer Lorne Michaels, the show first aired on 11 October 1975 and starred a cast of seven actors, comically referred to as the "Not Ready for Prime Time Players," who participated in live skits parodying contemporary politics and culture. It became an immediate hit, and despite numerous changes to the cast, it retains a loyal audience to the present day.

President Gerald Ford became a butt of jokes on the show. In June 1975, after landing in Salzburg, Austria, where he was to meet Egyptian president Anwar Sadat, the U.S. head of state slipped down the rain-soaked stairs of Air Force One. Afterward, the now-more-attentive media began to latch on to any slip on the ski slope, any poor swing on the golf course, any trip on the sidewalk, developing the caricature of Ford-as-klutz. That he had been a star athlete in high school and college and continued to exercise, including swimming laps in a pool he had installed in the White House, received little or no attention.[1] And Chase piled on, portraying a bumbling Ford on the 8 November episode of *Saturday Night Live*.

Chase's burlesque of Ford became a recurrent theme on the show, and neither an appearance by the president opposite Chase at a correspondents' dinner at which Ford lampooned himself nor one by Press Secretary Ron Nessen on *Saturday Night Live* diminished the impression that the country's leader was an oaf. Nessen's appearance proved particularly damaging. He had grown concerned that *Saturday Night Live*'s parody might derail Ford's bid to win the Republican nomination, let alone the 1976 presidential election. When Al Franken, one of *Saturday Night Live*'s writers, asked Nessen to host an episode, the press secretary agreed, believing it would demonstrate that the White House viewed the program as a joke but had a sense of humor about it. Airing on 17 April 1976, the show included one skit with Nessen speaking to a bumbling Ford (played by Chase) about *Saturday Night Live*; while that skit was relatively inoffensive, other sketches were risqué and included references to "presidential erections" and a "carbonated douche" called Autumn Fizz that had "the effervescence of uncola." Both President and Mrs. Ford watched the program, finding some of the skits funny but others "a little distasteful." More disconcerting, numerous media outlets and some viewers took offense. One person wrote the *Washington Post* that if the president had given Nessen the go-ahead to host *Saturday Night Live*, "I don't see how I can vote for a man who could be so dumb."[2]

That comment reflected a doubt about Ford's intelligence that had begun to appear within months after he took office. In truth, the president was anything but empty-headed. He had finished in the top third of his law-school class at Yale, understood how Washington worked well enough to rise quickly up the Republican Party ranks, and became well-versed in U.S. economic and defense policy. As president, he supplemented his daily news summary by reading at least ten newspapers, including the *Washington Post*, the *New York Times*, the *Los Angeles Times*, and the *Grand Rapids Press*. Still, it was not uncommon for observers to equate klutziness with deficient brainpower. President Lyndon B. Johnson had done just that in his comment about then minority leader Ford's ability to walk and pass gas simultaneously. Columnist Richard Reeves, who had followed Ford around in 1974, reached a similar conclusion; in 1974, for *New York* magazine, he detailed "Ford's speech errors and blunders," and the following year, he authored *A Ford, Not a Lincoln*, in which he called the chief executive "slow . . . unimaginative and not very articulate." Numerous jokes appeared to confirm what Johnson and Reeves had concluded—for example,

> Question: What is the President Ford tongue twister?
> Answer: Hello

and

> The Secret Service has already ruled out any possibility that Ford will toss out the first ball of the baseball season next spring. Says a Secret Service spokesman: "There is too much danger of his being beaned."

It is therefore not surprising that a Harris survey in January 1976 discovered that a plurality of Americans believed Ford lacked the "intelligence and qualifications to be a first-rate President."[3]

The claims that he was physically unsteady and intellectually vacuous reflected a far broader problem that plagued Ford as he fought first for his party's nomination and then for voters' endorsement on Election Day: image. Americans liked Ford as a person, and his down-to-earth family reinforced the perception that the president himself was an average Joe. Characterizing him as a "genial oaf" allowed voters to escape from bad memories left by Vietnam and Watergate and from the battle with stagflation.[4] Yet what Americans wanted was not a kindly buffoon but a chief executive who seemed to be in charge and who could offer them a vision of where he wanted to take the country. Individual successes such as Sinai II and the *Mayaguez* crisis were offset by the Nixon pardon, the Whip Inflation Now campaign, and the Halloween Massacre. They also served to reinforce the image of a president who made poor decisions and did not know which way was up. As the presidential campaign got into full swing, Ford made further errors. He discounted the threat posed to his ambitions by former California governor Ronald Reagan until it was nearly too late. He repeatedly changed his campaign manager, appeared to be trying to hide U.S. involvement in Angola, seemed to be grasping at straws over the country's newfound interest in human rights, ran headlong into new economic troubles at home, and made a major gaffe during one of the debates with the Democratic nominee, Jimmy Carter. His actions all served to reinforce the image of a president who was incompetent, indecisive, and unorganized and who had no idea where he wanted to take the country. Nevertheless, Ford came close to winning the presidency in his own right.

The All-American Family

Despite the knocks on his image, there was reason to see Ford in a positive light. His decision to pardon Richard Nixon and Nessen's acerbic personality had turned a once-fawning press against the president, but Ford remained wedded to developing a good relationship with journalists. During his 895 days in the White House, he held twenty-nine press conferences, an average of just over one per month, or twice as many as Nixon and even more than the "great communicator," Ronald Reagan. Polls in 1975 and 1976 found that most Americans regarded Ford as a nice person who ran "an open Administration and listen[ed] to people." Similarly, while Betty was also criticized, particularly for her comments in her August interview, a Harris survey taken three months later discovered that the majority of Americans stood with her on the Equal Rights Amendment and on her desire to offer counsel if she learned her daughter was having an affair.[5] Indeed, there was much about her to like beyond her outspokenness: she loved to dance, made a cameo appearance on the television comedy *The Mary Tyler Moore Show*, happily declared her affection for the soap opera *The Young and the Restless*, and outwardly expressed her love for the president. They might have their naysayers, but there was much about the Fords to like.

And their kids were endearing. The Ford children shared their parents' good looks. The Fords took their kids to church each week and prayed for their children each night, and they inculcated in their sons and daughter the quiet but powerful spirituality in which they believed. Jerry involved his boys in sports, and prior to becoming president, each summer he took one of his sons on a trip that built in them a love of the outdoors. And for the most part, the Ford children, like Betty, were willing to speak their minds. Michael, who was twenty-four when his father entered the Oval Office, had begun his college career as a political science major but then felt a calling from God that led him to divinity school. He tended to avoid the spotlight, but if pressed, he offered his opinions; as an example, he made clear that he disliked his father's decision to pardon Nixon. Jack, two years younger than Michael, had developed an interest in nature, received a degree in forestry from Utah State University in 1975, and in 1976 began working for a travel company. He was more outspoken and more interested in politics than Michael, expressing his concern about his father becoming president; admitting, following his mother's *60 Minutes* interview, that he had smoked marijuana; and, behind the scenes, encouraging his dad to do more to curb unemployment among youth. Steve, an eighteen-year-old senior in high school at the time his father assumed the presidency, also had been influenced by his father's outdoors experiences and desired to help animals. He spent summers working on an Alaskan ranch, began but did not complete a college degree in animal science, and worked both as a professional rodeo roper and for the National Geographic Society. His unique career path attracted a fair amount of press coverage, but he himself sought to remain below the radar.[6]

As the first presidential daughter to live in the White House since the popular Caroline Kennedy, Susan attracted the greatest attention from journalists. Her childhood prior to her father's presidency had been typical of many girls' lives, consisting of attending public school, having friends over—who enjoyed the fact that the Fords had a pool—and playing with dolls. She joined Girl Scouts. As first daughter, she refused to give up blue jeans (despite her father's urging her to do so), became an avid photographer, took her mother's place as administration hostess while Betty recovered from breast cancer, began writing a column for *Seventeen* magazine on her life in Washington, and, in 1975, had her high school prom at the White House. Her eighteenth birthday party, held in Vail, consisted of hot dogs, hamburgers, and dancing—not unlike a party any "normal" American teenager might have. Reporters continued to follow her after she graduated and began her freshman year in the nation's capital at Mount Vernon College for Women.[7]

The appealing qualities of the Fords stood to generate an alternate image to that of the president as unintelligent buffoon: that of a chief executive who was part of an "average," all-American family. He and Betty were good-looking, fun-loving, devoted, "average" parents who had raised four well-rounded, "average" children. As a family, the Fords were open, honest, and God-fearing; they loved sports and enjoyed spending time outdoors. The problem for Ford was that for as much as the public liked him and his family, it found reason to separate his personal and professional image from that of his wife and children.

Trying to Prove Himself

The challenges Ford faced in proving himself a capable chief executive were compounded by the state of the country. There was reason for optimism, for the rate of inflation had continued to fall, dropping from nearly 12 percent when 1975 began to 7.4 percent that October. The unemployment rate never fell below 8 percent, however, and the president had made little progress in his efforts to deregulate industry.

Ford also had to address the energy crisis. In a blow to what he considered a necessary means of tackling that problem, in August 1975 the U.S. Court of Appeals for the District of Columbia declared unconstitutional his two-dollar oil-import fee. Then, in November, following weeks of wrangling among themselves, members of Congress sent to Ford's desk the Energy Policy and Conservation Act (EPCA), the first attempt to provide a national energy policy for the country. The bill was far different from what Ford had favored. It called for imposing more, not fewer, controls on oil prices, followed by a phased-in decontrol program that would permit petroleum prices to rise, but not more than 10 percent per year. It did not include an oil-import fee or the tax credits that the president had desired to encourage conservation. Yet there were provisions in the legislation Ford found acceptable. He could recommend increasing the annual rate hike on oil to more than 10 percent. The EPCA included measures to promote energy conservation, such as requiring states to submit plans to reduce energy consumption if they wished to receive federal money. It called for home appliances to have labels denoting how energy efficient they were, established a strategic petroleum reserve, and required new cars to meet mandatory standards for fuel economy.[8]

Ford was of two minds over what to do. On the one hand, Treasury Secretary William Simon, along with many Republicans, including Reagan, opposed the bill. Moreover, signing it could cost the president votes in oil-producing states. On the other hand, both energy czar Frank Zarb and Alan Greenspan, the chair of the Council of Economic Advisers, argued that the benefits of endorsing the EPCA outweighed the costs. Lawmakers might attempt to force the president's hand, they warned, and if Ford failed to sign the EPCA, members of Congress could claim that the nation's leader preferred higher prices to the well-being of consumers. He also had to consider the sentiment of voters in the northeastern states, including in New Hampshire, whose citizens were to go to the polls early the following year and where opposition was strong to any bill that meant higher prices for energy.[9]

High energy prices threatened to slow down economic growth, but in Ford's mind, so did high taxes and the power posed by unions. In October 1975 Ford had called for a $28 billion cut in taxes, matched by $28 billion in spending cuts. The president believed his plan would stimulate the economy and win him votes come 1976, but lawmakers passed legislation that only cut taxes, eliciting a White House veto. Unable to override Ford, Congress endorsed the Revenue Adjustment Act, which would reduce taxes by $9 billion. Ford also disliked a common-situs-picketing bill that was before him. That legislation faced strong resistance from the Right, as it would amend the 1947 Taft-Hartley Act by permitting a union to picket, and potentially shut down, an entire construction project even though the target of the protest was a single subcontractor at that site. Ford wanted to veto both bills, but if he were to do so on top of refusing to sign the EPCA, it might, warned his aide, Robert Hartmann, create the impression that he "lack[ed] the ability to move the country forward." Weighing all the pros and cons, Ford signed the EPCA and the Revenue Readjustment Act and vetoed the common-situs bill. The president believed his decisions would please both moderates and conservatives in his own party and voters in key states. Whether that was the case was questionable. Simon, who reflected the view of conservatives, called the EPCA "the worst error of the Ford administration." Meanwhile, Labor Secretary John Dunlop resigned in protest of the common-situs veto.[10] Although unions tended to lean Democratic, the president could expect them to intensify their efforts to prevent him victory on Election Day—assuming he could get past Reagan first.

Getting past Reagan would not be easy. One roadblock was money. In 1971, Congress had passed the Federal Election Campaign Act, enhancing the requirements for candidates for federal office and political action committees to disclose their finances and introducing the use of public funds for federal campaigns. Abuses by Nixon during his bid for the presidency a year later moved Capitol Hill to amend that legislation in 1974. Signed into law by Ford, those additional provisions would in 1976 restrict presidential candidates' spending to $10.9 million as they sought their party's nomination and to approximately $22 million during the general campaign. Furthermore, a presidential candidate could not begin fund-raising until he had established a presidential committee, and contributors could donate no more than $1,000 each to a candidate seeking federal office. Finally, the 1974 amendments created the Federal Election Commission to enforce the act. Consequently, Ford had to wait until he announced the formation of the President Ford Committee (PFC) to oversee his campaign, and he could only spend so much on advertising to get his message to voters.[11]

The difficulty of getting the message out was compounded by Ford's poor performance as a speaker. Having a background in acting, Reagan was an expert at using the camera; the president had far more trouble giving a rousing oration, particularly via television. Whereas Reagan had sought for and won a statewide office and had made a bid for the Oval Office in 1968, Ford had only run within a single district in a single state. Moreover, the president's campaign chairman, former army secretary Bo Callaway, had never overseen a national campaign and had little idea how to organize or coordinate one.[12]

It would be not Callaway but Richard Cheney who became the key figure in Ford's drive for a full term in the Oval Office. Cheney had served in the Nixon administration under Donald Rumsfeld, who was then the head of the Office of Economic Opportunity. After Rumsfeld left to become the U.S. ambassador to NATO, Cheney spent time with an investment firm, and then again became Rumsfeld's deputy when Ford asked Rumsfeld to serve as White House coordinator. When Rumsfeld moved to the Department of Defense, Cheney took his place as coordinator. Not only did he prove himself highly capable as an administrator, but his likable personality also helped him avoid getting into the feuds with other staff members for which his predecessor had a penchant. Now, as Ford's campaign got underway, Cheney began to serve as liaison to the PFC. Along with Stuart Spencer, who had overseen Reagan's gubernatorial bid in California in 1964, and pollster Robert Teeter, Cheney sought to make Ford appear "decisive" and "presidential."[13]

Ford had the opportunity to do just that on 19 January—the same day that residents of Iowa declared their choice for the GOP's presidential candidate—when he delivered the annual State of the Union address. The process of writing it had precipitated yet another battle among Ford's staff. Hartmann had put together a draft of the speech, but Cheney found it wanting and had one of his aides, David Gergen, pen an alternative. The president liked parts of each and met with both groups of speechwriters on 17 January, only to have the three-hour meeting marked by further squabbling. Angered by the inability of his aides to work together, Ford pounded his "hand on the table" and demanded "a final draft by noon tomorrow." He got it and made some revisions prior to appearing before Congress. Recalling that a year earlier he had called the state of the country "not good," he now said it had since shown some improvement. Inflation, which stood at nearly 12 percent in January 1975, had fallen, but unemployment remained high. The numbers proved that the United States could not "be a policeman abroad and an indulgent parent at home," as it had during the Johnson years, and so it was time for a "new realism," one that balanced the government's ability to address the nation's economic troubles with its duty to provide for defense. Hence, Ford proposed shaving about $14 billion from social programs and offsetting the pain caused by that reduction with $10 billion in tax cuts, a $2.5 billion public-service initiative to fund just over 300,000 jobs, and, to assist those who might otherwise face high medical bills because of "a serious and extended illness," expanding Medicare to include "catastrophic health insurance"—with the money for that insurance program coming from a hike in short-term-care fees. Furthermore, he wanted to combine over a dozen federal health-care programs and to provide additional state funding for low-income families. His only request for a significant spending boost was for the military, which would receive $101 billion, or an increase of $8 billion over 1976. His administration foresaw spending $395 billion for FY 1977, which would mean a deficit of $43 billion. But that was $10 billion less than would have been the case without constraints on spending.[14]

Though Ford's budget requests cut into social-welfare programs, he considered that subordinate to the need for a strong defense. His budget was also a response to the challenge from the Far Right and Reagan. The former governor and his supporters thought that those in positions of authority in Washington had failed to devote enough money to defense, gave too many dollars to social initiatives, and were responsible for the burgeoning deficit. By offering more to the Pentagon, cutting expenditures on social programs, and emphasizing the ways he was eating away at the deficit, Ford could appeal to conservatives. In doing so, though, he risked turning away Republican moderates and liberals.[15]

To reinforce in voters' minds his command of the issues and to rebut those who considered him intellectually weak, Ford decided to do something no president since Harry Truman had done: lead a press briefing on the budget. It was a risk. The budget was nearly 1,000 pages long, chock-full of details regarding spending for every government agency and program. But Ford was confident in his abilities, having served for years on the House Appropriations Committee. After some short opening comments, the president took more than fifty questions, including questions on specific line items, such as catastrophic insurance under Medicare and federal support for housing construction. "I felt that my appearance had done more to convince members of the press of my competence to be president than almost anything else I had done," wrote Ford.[16]

Yet the president failed to take advantage of an opportunity to offer a vision of where he wanted to take the country. The Domestic Council's Henry Perritt Jr. proposed using "the new realism" as the slogan for that vision, a phrase Ford had employed in his most recent State of the Union address. It would point to Ford's desire to move toward a more sensible fiscal program. It was also broad enough to imply that it was time to reconsider what America's foreign responsibilities should be. Ford, however, never used the term again. Maybe he feared a replay of the WIN campaign, which had failed to get off the ground. Certainly he disliked catchphrases, arguing later, "Those are nice for speeches, but I'm always one who believes in substance, not in labels."[17]

The CIA and the Soviets

Despite the hope that the January 1976 State of the Union address and the press briefing would prove Ford's abilities and set him on the path to victory on Election Day, events overseas promised trouble. The same month Reagan announced his bid for the Republican nomination, Americans learned of covert U.S. support for anticommunist forces in Angola. A Portuguese colony that was on the road to independence, in 1975 it was the scene of a civil war that pitted three groups against one another: the openly Marxist and Soviet- and Cuban-funded Popular Movement for the Liberation of Angola (MPLA), commanded by Agostinho Neto; the National Liberation Front of Angola (FNLA), led by Holden Roberto; and the National Union for the Total Independence of Angola (UNITA), headed by Jonas Savimbi. The FNLA had the support of the United States, China, and Zaire. UNITA too received some money from Washington, but most of its bankrolling came from South Africa.

Fearful of permitting Angola to fall to communism, Henry Kissinger asked the CIA to put together a plan to give covert aid to Roberto via Zaire and convinced the 40 Committee—a body that had been established during the Nixon administration to recommend individual covert operations and that Kissinger chaired—to endorse the idea of such assistance. Then defense secretary James Schlesinger questioned the value of helping Roberto, whom he did not think had "the tenacity to win," but Ford, sharing Kissinger's fears, dismissed that sentiment: "It seems to me that doing nothing is unacceptable." Knowing that the president had deferred to his judgment, Kissinger met again with the 40 Committee, which put together a $14 million covert-aid program. Ford approved the plan on 18 July.[18]

Kissinger believed that approval of what became known as Operation IA Feature could not have come at a better time. The MPLA had recently driven the FNLA and UNITA from Angola's capital, Luanda, and the surrounding area, and it appeared to be on the verge of further advances. Now facing enemies armed with American weapons and reinforced with two companies of paratroopers from Zaire, Neto turned to Cuba for help. In August, Havana sent nearly 500 military advisers. The Soviets assisted him as well, shipping arms and armored cars. The South Africans, in turn, escalated their aid, including sending advisers to UNITA and 1,000 troops into southern Angola.

For the Ford administration, the news from Angola grew worse as the fall progressed. With Cuban help, the MPLA continued to make gains. The Chinese cut their ties to the FNLA, and the MPLA on 11 November declared itself the leader of an independent Angola. Kissinger wanted to proceed with IA Feature, but DCI William Colby—who was on his way out of the administration as part of Ford's shake-up—told the 40 Committee on 21 November that the CIA was "fresh out of money" and that the only alternative was to have the Defense Department reprogram funding for his agency. Since that route would require "the consent of the appropriations committees" on Capitol Hill, it would divulge the operation. The administration felt the risk was worth taking and prepared a request for $28 million from Congress. To keep prying eyes away, Ford insisted on having the petition receive consideration during a closed hearing.[19]

Within days, the public became aware of what was happening in Angola. The *Washington Post* on 23 November reported the presence of South African troops in Angola, which Savimbi confirmed a few days later. Then, in mid-December, *New York Times* reporter Seymour Hersh offered particulars on IA Feature, including its provision of $300,000 in arms to Savimbi and other aid to Roberto. The reports generated a furor on Capitol Hill. Dick Clark (D-Iowa), a Watergate baby and the chair of the Senate Foreign Relations Committee's Africa subcommittee, and Senator Clifford Case (R-N.J.) presented a resolution to the upper house barring further aid for Angola. Senator John Tunney (D-Calif.) took matters a step further by attaching a rider with similar language to a defense appropriations bill that was about to come up for a vote. The Senate passed the appropriations legislation, with the Tunney Amendment, on 20 December, and the House followed suit in January. Ford considered vetoing the bill, but he was told by his aides that he could anticipate Congress overriding him, and he signed it on 9 February. A frustrated president declared that Capitol Hill had "lost its guts."[20]

Ford's vexation grew when, the same month he signed the appropriations bill, New York City's alternative newspaper, the *Village Voice*, published the Pike Committee report on the CIA's past activities. Whereas bodies headed by Senator Frank Church (D-Idaho) and Vice President Nelson Rockefeller that had investigated the CIA had revealed their findings to the public, the House of Representatives had quashed release of the Pike Committee's findings. However, CBS reporter Daniel Schorr had obtained a copy of the committee's report. Angered when CBS refused to publish it, Schorr gave it to the *Village Voice*. What Americans learned was that there was no oversight of how the CIA spent its budget and that the agency itself had done a poor job of using its money. Most important, the CIA was not the "rogue elephant" depicted by the Church Committee. The president had approved every covert action in which it had been involved, including those in Chile, Iraq, and Angola.[21]

In combination, the revelation of the CIA's operations in Angola and its past actions prompted Ford to abolish the 40 Committee and replace it with the Operations Advisory Group (OAG). Whereas under the 40 Committee covert operations were addressed at a subcabinet level, the OAG required they be discussion by the cabinet. In turn, it circumscribed the power of the director of the CIA to oversee covert operations. Moreover, the president banned the use of assassinations.[22] Not reassured by such edicts, lawmakers set up a half dozen oversight committees of their own, including both a House and a Senate Select Committee on Intelligence.

There were also reverberations that could affect Ford's presidential bid. Even if most Americans saw Ford as a decent president who ran an "open administration," they saw it as unbecoming in the post-Watergate era for a president to stand behind covert operations that in the past had been used to kill foreign leaders and prop up unsavory regimes elsewhere. Other observers took note of his inability or unwillingness to stop Congress from usurping his power or to stand up to Soviet aggression abroad. That the South Africans pulled out of Angola not long after Ford signed the appropriations bill and that the Cuban- and Soviet-reinforced MPLA succeeded in crushing its rivals only seemed to underscore the weakness of a president reluctant to defend America's interests worldwide.

Reagan emphasized what he judged to be Ford's feebleness when, in his first major speech on foreign policy in 1976, he tied Angola to the Ford administration's determination to pursue détente, including the SALT II talks. If the United States was to negotiate with the Soviet Union, it would have to do so "from a position of military strength," the former governor insisted. Instead, the White House had placed Washington in a weaker position. Referencing Kissinger's recent trip to Moscow to discuss SALT II, Reagan asked, "If you were a Russian official and you heard the American Secretary of State deliver stern warnings to you for trying to dominate the situation in Angola, but all the time you knew he was packing his bags to come to Moscow to negotiate a new arms limitation agreement, would you really take him seriously?" The next month, he insisted that both Ford and Kissinger "be held accountable to history" for letting America "slip behind the Russians in military power."[23]

Reagan was not alone in his criticism of SALT II. Neoconservatives, including Senator Henry Jackson (D-Wash.) and two former top aides to President Johnson, Walt Rostow and Paul Nitze, joined the chorus, as did right-wing think tanks and committees, including the Coalition for a Democratic Majority and the Committee on the Present Danger. And members of Ford's own administration, including his new defense secretary, Donald Rumsfeld, added their voices. A neoconservative himself, Rumsfeld had serious doubts about Soviet adherence to the SALT I agreement and, consequently, questioned whether Moscow could be trusted to abide by SALT II. Moreover, he knew that the United States had the upper hand in cruise-missile technology and opposed any agreement that jeopardized that edge. Unlike Schlesinger, Rumsfeld had the advantages of having been Ford's friend since their days in Congress together, and he had a far better grasp of how the Washington bureaucracy functioned and how to use it. He also had political ambitions. Some observers, such as longtime colleague Ken Adelman, thought Rumsfeld's goal was to replace Rockefeller as Ford's running mate in 1976.[24]

Just before Ford delivered his State of the Union address, Rumsfeld called for another $8.9 billion in defense spending, for a grand total of $100 billion—the largest ever requested in the country's history. Furthermore, neither he nor the Joint Chiefs of Staff (JCS) were willing to give on either cruise missiles or the Backfire bomber. "The Chiefs [*sic*] view is that we should give up as little cruise missile capability as we can," JCS chairman George Brown commented at an NSC meeting in February 1976. "It is one point of our leverage on the Soviets." Nor did Brown want to see an agreement that would permit unrestricted production of the Backfire. Sharing those views, Rumsfeld at the same meeting recommended deferral of a solution to the superpowers' differences over cruise missiles and the Backfire. Kissinger rejected the idea, for he had tried that very maneuver with both Soviet ambassador to the United States Anatoly Dobrynin and Moscow's foreign minister Andrei Gromyko, only to have them nix it.[25]

Deciding that he could not stand against Defense and the Joint Chiefs of Staff, Ford accepted Rumsfeld's recommendation and a few days later informed Soviet premier Leonid Brezhnev of his decision. In his reply, Brezhnev dealt another blow to Kissinger's standing in the administration by blaming the failure for progress on the United States. But to Ford, whose greatest concern was Election Day, it made the most sense to return to SALT II after voters had cast their ballots.[26]

The Reagan Message Resonates

Whether Ford would make it through the political storm was up in the air. Desiring to make him seem "presidential," Ford's campaign handlers had him run a "Rose Garden strategy," by which he would remain in the capital and have proxies stand in for him at campaign events. Neither he nor Reagan campaigned in Iowa, where voters instead held a straw poll that Ford won by a narrow margin. Attention instead focused on the next prize, New Hampshire. Betty, who had remained popular nationally despite her comments on marijuana use and abortion, became the prime stand-in for the president. It was a risky gambit. New Hampshire was a conservative state, and the first lady's positions on the issues, particularly abortion, set her apart not only from voters there but from her husband: whereas she was pro-choice, he declared that he opposed abortion and also regarded the issue as one that should be left up to the states.[27]

Yet it was not just Betty who campaigned in New Hampshire. After Nessen made the mistake of telling reporters that the president did not like to ski in New Hampshire—a state that prided itself on its ski resorts—because its slopes were "too icy," Susan Ford found herself called into action. Sent to that state, she took to its powder, in Mrs. Ford's words, "to pacify any New Hampshire voters who might have been offended by Ron Nessen's" comment.[28]

In a further attempt to influence New Hampshire voters, Cheney, Spencer, and Teeter hired a New York advertising firm to produce a series of TV spots that showed Ford hard at work and that were intended to make him appear more "presidential." They also went after Reagan, pointing out that in September 1975 the former California governor had proposed cutting federal spending by $90 billion. Ads aired in New Hampshire showed the ways those cuts would require states to raise taxes; this would be especially difficult for New Hampshirites, who paid neither a sales tax nor a state income tax. Reagan found himself on the defensive, and his pollster, Richard Wirthlin, believed it was vital for the ex-governor to return to New Hampshire prior to the primary. He said as much to Reagan's campaign chair, John Sears. Instead, to Wirthlin's surprise and dismay, Sears had Reagan head to his birth state of Illinois the weekend before New Hampshire voters went to the polls. As Wirthlin had feared, the president won the state on 24 February with 51 percent of the ballots. He followed that triumph with victories in Massachusetts and Vermont on 2 March. With Betty joining him in the field, and using the power of the incumbency to offer lucrative contracts, Ford won Florida on 9 March and Illinois a week later.[29] It looked like the president was well on his way to winning the 1,130 delegates he needed to secure the nomination.

Ford had other reasons to be optimistic about the election. The administration expected the economy to grow at an annual rate of 6 to 6.5 percent, driven by corporations' building up inventories of products, replacing outdated equipment, and investing anticipated greater-than-normal profits. All that activity led forecasters to expect unemployment to fall nearly 1 percent during the year. Determined to avoid any shocks that might derail this optimistic prediction, the White House decided to avoid any measures aimed at economic fine-tuning. That uneasiness on the part of the executive branch appeared not to concern voters, who liked the good news coming out of Washington. By early March, the president's approval rating had climbed to 50 percent, or 11 points higher than at the end of 1975.[30]

Hanging over the Ford administration, however, was the policy of détente. The White House had warned the Kremlin that the latter's machinations in Angola could jeopardize an improvement in relations, but to no avail. In early March, Reagan charged that Ford had "neither the vision nor the leadership necessary to halt and reverse the diplomatic and military decline of the United States." That same month, on the TV show *Meet the Press*, he called détente "a one-way street. We are making the concessions. We are giving [the Soviet Union] the things they want; we ask for nothing in return. In fact, we give them things before we ask for the return."[31]

Reagan's strategy began to take its toll on the White House. Ford stopped using the word "détente" starting in March. While defending his administration's diplomacy, he also began publicly to downplay the possibility of achieving SALT II in the near term. Some members of Congress who wanted to declare themselves for Ford, such as Maryland congressman Robert Bauman, privately expressed reluctance to do so because there was strong support for Reagan in their states or districts. Then, on 22 March, a day before North Carolina held its primary, conservative columnists Rowland Evans and Robert Novak wrote that State Department Counselor Helmut Sonnenfeldt had spoken in a speech of a "permanent organic union" that existed between Moscow and its Eastern European satellites. In fact, Sonnenfeldt had not used that language, but Reagan took advantage of the report to charge that the White House had given up on resisting Communist domination of Eastern Europe.[32]

Reagan had one more ace up his sleeve: the Panama Canal. As a congressman Ford had firmly resisted any idea of handing that waterway over to Panama, but he had changed his tune after becoming Nixon's vice president. At the time, Kissinger had argued that trying to retain the canal risked continued unrest in Panama, to the detriment of American interests; indeed, the president of Panama, Omar Torrijos, might turn against the United States. The secretary of state had thus continued negotiations with Panama's leadership that had begun during the Johnson presidency, and Ford had accepted Kissinger's rationale for finding some kind of an accord with Panama that both it and the United States might find acceptable.

The White House was well aware that the negotiations with Panama displeased not just conservatives in the Republican Party, such as South Carolina senator Strom Thurmond, but even Democrats, among them Pennsylvania congressman Daniel Flood. "Will the Thurmonds and the Floods go crazy?" Ford had asked Kissinger in May 1975 regarding a treaty that might turn the canal over to Panama. "Yes," his secretary of state replied. "I think there are no terms they would accept."[33]

Jesse Helms was another Republican conservative who rejected the talks with Panama. The North Carolinian had raised his own concerns about the negotiations with Reagan in 1974. He now suggested to Sears that criticizing the dialogue with Panama would please voters in the Tar Heel State. Reagan liked the idea. His campaign was nearly out of money, and he had to find some way to reinvigorate it and draw donations. Moreover, he shared Helms's objections to negotiating with Torrijos. He therefore began giving a series of speeches in which he declared, "We should end those negotiations and tell [Torrijos], 'we bought it, we paid for it, we built it and we intend to keep it.'" Assuming that their string of victories in lining up delegates had all but killed Reagan's campaign, Callaway, Ford, and their aides were slow to realize how effectively the former governor's challenge had riled conservatives. Only after it was too late did the president promise that the United States would make sure it had the right to defend the canal. As Reagan had hoped, his campaign got a new lease on life. He won North Carolina with 52 percent of the popular vote and over half of the state's fifty-two delegates, and the dollars began to pour in. The president, put on the defensive, had no choice but to cease further talks with Panama.[34]

Ford later wrote, "I didn't take Reagan seriously." It was an error that now put him in danger of losing the race for the nomination. Reagan intensified his attacks. At the end of March he delivered a nationally aired speech in which he cited Ford's "establishment" credentials and lambasted the administration for negotiating with Panama, for not meeting with Soviet dissident Aleksandr Solzhenitsyn, and for signing the Helsinki Accords. Consequently, America had become "Number Two in a world where it is dangerous, if not fatal, to be second best." The speech earned dividends, in terms both of fund-raising and of winning endorsements from members of Congress who, up to that point, had not been sure whom to support for the GOP nomination.[35]

In the meantime, Ford's campaign appeared to be in free fall. A few days before North Carolina held its primary, Cheney had forced Callaway to resign after the PFC chair was charged with misusing his post as army secretary to get the right to develop what had been federal land. Although there was no proof behind the accusation, Callaway's ouster added to the impression of an administration that had lost its sense of direction. Memories of Watergate and of Ford's pardon of former president Nixon were revived with the publication of *The Final Days*, a book by Bob Woodward and Carl Bernstein—the two *Washington Post* reporters who helped to unravel Watergate—and the release on 9 April of *All the President's Men*, a movie based on Woodward and Bernstein's 1974 book by the same name that traced their efforts to discover Nixon's part in the break-in at the Democrats' party headquarters in 1972. Then came Nessen's appearance on *Saturday Night Live*, further augmenting the sense among voters that Ford made poor decisions.[36] Despite Ford's victories in Wisconsin and Pennsylvania in April, he suffered a series of defeats in the first two weeks of May, including in delegate-rich Texas. Even with presidential triumphs in West Virginia, Michigan, and Maryland later that month, Reagan still held the lead in the delegate count, 528 to 479.

Foreign Policy to the Rescue?

Between 25 May and 1 June, Ford and Reagan split the nine states that held primaries, but none were as important as the three whose voters went to the polls on 8 June: California, Ohio, and New Jersey. The Ford team knew it would have to concede defeat in California, as it was Reagan's home state. This made winning Ohio and New Jersey of supreme importance. As expected, California went Reagan's way, but in Ohio and New Jersey, voters set aside any concerns they had about the incumbent and concluded that he stood the best chance of winning on Election Day.[37] The primaries were over, yet neither candidate had enough delegates to capture the nomination. Ford was closer, needing 170 to secure his ticket for the general election, whereas Reagan required 270.

A week after the final primaries, the Ford administration had to confront a crisis in the Middle East nation of Lebanon. Despite ethnic and religious divisions, Lebanon had been relatively stable and prosperous. But as the 1970s progressed, tensions between Christians and Muslims in the capital, Beirut, grew. Meanwhile, the arrival of Palestinians from Jordan increased that group's population to about 350,000, and the PLO began to use Lebanon as a staging ground for attacks on Israel.[38]

By 1976, Lebanon had fallen into a state of civil war, with Christians and Muslims fighting one another. Syrian president Hafez al-Assad feared that a breakdown of law and order in Lebanon could strengthen the position of the PLO—whom Assad supported—which in turn might trigger a full-scale Israeli intervention. In that case, Assad could see his prestige in the Arab world nose-diving. Accordingly, in May 1976, he ordered a limited military intervention into Lebanon. Sharing Assad's concerns, both the Ford administration and Israel, in a odd twist, stood behind the Syrian leader, though Tel Aviv warned that it would invade if Syrian regulars entered southern Lebanon.[39] Slowly, the Syrians began to gain control of the situation and, by the fall, had achieved a cease-fire.

All the while, Ford hoped the United States could stay out of the events in Lebanon. The optimism disappeared on 16 June, when the U.S. ambassador to that country, Francis E. Meloy Jr., and Meloy's aide, Robert Waring, were found dead after having been kidnapped in Beirut. There were 1,400 other Americans residing in Lebanon, and the White House decided that it had to get them out. Whether they were in fact in danger was unclear, but at least some in the administration saw an opportunity for political points in a U.S. election year. "Reagan could jump on this and demand that you take strong action," Rockefeller warned Ford that same day. Determined to rescue U.S. nationals and to publicize his own decisiveness, the White House made sure the press was able to witness the navy evacuating 263 people, 116 of whom were American. Reagan asserted that the White House had purposely generated a crisis where there was none, and even America's British ally charged the president with politicking.[40]

Public-opinion polls showed that Americans cared far more about domestic policy, particularly the economy, than they did the nation's diplomacy, and the evidence points to an administration worried primarily about what the Lebanese crisis meant both for peace in the Middle East and for East-West relations. Kissinger sought to restrict the extent of Syria's intervention in Lebanon so as not to provoke Israel. Otherwise, Tel Aviv was likely to send in its military as well, leading to a full-fledged war in the region, one that could precipitate some form of military action by Moscow.[41] Yet it would be wrong to suggest that domestic politics were not on the minds of at least some in the White House, particularly when the president was in a fight for his political life.

The election also played a role in the growing attention the administration gave to human rights. Reagan had clearly touched a nerve by criticizing the effort to promote détente with a repressive Soviet government, but the White House also had to consider the attacks it faced from Democrats, particularly former Georgia governor Jimmy Carter. A dark horse going into the Democratic race for the presidency, Carter had emerged by the spring of 1976 as the candidate most likely to win his party's nomination. The Georgian had first announced his bid for the Oval Office at the end of 1974. By this time he had already put together a well-oiled national machine, and his background and public statements had wide appeal. He came from the increasingly populous and politically powerful South. He was a born-again Christian and a fiscal conservative, which pleased evangelicals and those who believed that the federal government was too big and that it used taxpayers' dollars poorly. His progressive record as governor on civil and women's rights stood to please those on the left side of the political spectrum. Knowing that Americans tied the Washington establishment to Vietnam and Watergate, he promised he would not lie to voters and, like Reagan, he touted his outsider credentials. Finally, he realized that making the promotion of human rights a plank of his campaign could win him political points from those who were upset with past U.S. support for assassinations or for repressive regimes. It could also bind a Democratic Party left divided by the failed 1968 and 1972 presidential campaigns by drawing in neoconservatives who wanted to challenge the Soviet bloc and more liberal-minded Americans who insisted on denouncing right-wing governments. "The question, I think, is whether in recent years our highest officials have not been too pragmatic, even cynical, and as a consequence have ignored those moral values that had often distinguished our country from the other great nations of the world," Carter commented during the campaign.[42]

Americans, in fact, were exhibiting a growing interest in combating repression abroad. Between 1970 and 1976, an average of 10,000 people in the United States joined the human-rights organization Amnesty International, and the spread of news through international travel, satellite transmissions, and direct-mail campaigns served to keep the topic of proper treatment of others before the public. Americans also reacted favorably to comments made by Daniel Patrick Moynihan, whom Ford had appointed as ambassador to the United Nations in 1975. A neoconservative, Moynihan had grown frustrated with the anti-Western critiques delivered by representatives from developing nations and decided that the best way to fight back was to "make human rights the theme" of the UN General Assembly.

Most notably, he denounced Third World dictators for hypocrisy when they repressed their own people while censuring the oppression of other leaders. One public opinion survey found that 70 percent of Americans endorsed his comments. Editorials echoed that sentiment.[43] Reflecting public opinion, lawmakers on Capitol Hill who favored combating repression abroad intensified their effort to incorporate human rights concerns into U.S. diplomacy.

The Ford administration's policies toward Rhodesia and Latin America suggested it intended to devote greater emphasis to human rights. After Rhodesia achieved independence from Great Britain in 1965, its majority-black population lived under an apartheid regime headed by Prime Minister Ian Smith. In 1966, the international community condemned his unwillingness to rescind white minority rule by endorsing a UN embargo on the importation of Rhodesian chrome. The United States joined the embargo, only to rescind it in 1971. Congressman Ford had favored this reversal. In 1975, President Ford showed little interest in endorsing a bid by some lawmakers—a bid that ultimately failed—to reimpose the embargo. Fearful that Carter might use the administration's failure to restore the embargo against the White House, Ford ordered a review of U.S. policy toward Salisbury in April 1976. That same month, Kissinger went on a multicountry trip to Africa, during which he called for black majority rule in Rhodesia. Upon returning home, he urged reimposition of the embargo on chrome. In Latin America, the human rights violations of military governments in countries such as Argentina, Chile, and Uruguay prompted the secretary of state, during a June meeting of the Organization of American States, to criticize governmental repression in that part of the world.[44]

Despite the rhetoric, the White House strongly resisted giving human rights priority status. Kissinger saw Moynihan's comments as a threat to improving ties with developing countries and had the UN ambassador removed from his post in early 1976. Similarly, in an apparent recognition of the desire in and out of Congress to challenge repressive regimes, in 1976 the State Department established the Bureau of Human Rights and Humanitarian Affairs (HA). Yet Kissinger largely ignored HA, and the new agency's head, James Wilson, adopted a low profile. Indeed, he devoted most of his attention not to promoting human-rights policy but to combating congressional efforts to condition assistance to other countries on the recipients' human-rights records.[45]

That Wilson took up arms against Capitol Hill was proof that the White House wanted not only to deemphasize morality as a part of U.S. diplomacy but also to thwart the desire by a more assertive Congress to have a say in Washington's relationship with other countries. Such could be seen in the administration's response to the International Development and Food Assistance Act. Passed by the House of Representatives in December 1975, it included an amendment proposed by Watergate baby and freshman representative Tom Harkin (D-Iowa) that would ban economic aid to human-rights-violating countries unless such assistance would help the needy. The Ford administration fought the amendment in the Senate, only to have the upper house accept it with no opposition; deciding continued resistance was futile, the president signed the bill in May 1976.[46]

The same month he signed the International Development and Food Assistance Act, Ford vetoed the International Security Assistance and Arms Export Control Act. Designed to revise the U.S. military-aid program, it included—at the urging of two of the leading proponents of curbing assistance to repressive nations, Representatives Donald Fraser (D-Minn.) and Stephen Solarz (D-N.Y.)—a provision called Section 502B that barred the sale of military wares to human-rights-violating countries. When the Senate passed the legislation, Ford refused to sign it in part because of Section 502B. Unable to muster the two-thirds majority needed to pass the bill in its existing form, both houses of Congress accepted a weakened version of 502B that required a joint congressional resolution to prevent the allocation of any assistance. Finding that language more acceptable, Ford signed the act on the last day of June.[47]

Finally, the administration sought to calm the fears of those nations that might worry about becoming targets of cuts in aid. South Africa had an apartheid government, yet neither the president nor the secretary of state pushed that country as hard as they pushed Rhodesia, regarding its cooperation as essential to getting Smith to bend. Wanting to maintain cordial ties with Chile's leader, Augusto Pinochet Ugarte, the Ford administration encouraged banks to make loans to his government and approved millions of dollars in military wares to Santiago.[48] In the name of détente and for geopolitical purposes, the White House adopted a cautious approach toward the Soviet Union, South Korea, and other countries. Simply put, the Ford administration hoped to win the war of human-rights rhetoric while trying to limit the damage a strong human-rights policy could pose to realpolitik.

The administration's position did not go unnoticed. Blacks, who had hoped Ford's meeting with their congressional caucus shortly after he became president was an indication that he planned to devote more to their interests, had been pleased when he spoke to the National Association for the Advancement of Colored People's conference in 1975. Yet he said nothing there to suggest that he had the welfare of African Americans in mind. If anything, his record pointed in the opposite direction. Blacks had been disappointed by his position on busing, and his unwillingness to take on apartheid only reinforced the impression of disinterest. More broadly, the downplaying of human rights, believed some observers, was harmful to America's image as the land of liberty. "In Chile, in Brazil, in the Soviet Union and South Korea and many other places," wrote columnist Anthony Lewis, "the American government has appeared insensitive to the grossest inhumanity—a strange contrast to our feelings and legal standards at home."[49]

Celebration and the Convention

Ford hoped to offset such criticism by pointing to the positives in his record as president. The country for the first time since 1965 was at peace. Unemployment still stood around 7.5 percent, but that was less than it had been when 1975 had ended. The rate of inflation was down to 6 percent in June and continued to fall, and both industrial production and housing sales were up. *Business Week* found "there are fewer and fewer pessimists about the business outlook for 1976," while *U.S. News & World Report* commented, "The U.S. economy has now scrambled almost all the way out of the valley of recession and will soon be hitting new peaks of output."[50]

The Bicentennial appeared to build on this sanguine mood. Throughout the country, Americans celebrated 200 years of independence: Philadelphia's Memorial Hall became the home of the globe's biggest birthday cake, tall-masted sailing ships traversed New York and Boston Harbors, Britain's Queen Elizabeth made a visit to the U.S. capital, and consumers had the opportunity to purchase all kinds of products decked out in red, white, and blue. For a country whose people had for over a decade confronted what seemed like nonstop turmoil, the Bicentennial offered the turning of a new page, one marked by stability and hope for a better day. *Time* magazine best captured this sentiment, commenting, "After thirteen consecutive years of assassinations, race riots, youth rebellion, Viet Nam, political scandal, presidential collapse, crisis, and recession, the nation's mood seems optimistic again."[51]

Ford believed that he and his administration played an important part in the "new spirit" he saw appearing in America. To capture that sentiment, he gave numerous speeches in honor of America's fight for freedom and the work of its Founding Fathers. "From this small but beautiful building,"

Ford said at Independence Hall in Philadelphia, "then the most imposing structure in the Colonies, came the two great documents that continue to supply the moral and intellectual power for the American adventure in self-government," the Declaration of Independence and the Constitution. The speech encapsulated the nation's mood and, Hartmann reflected, was "Ford at his very, very best."[52]

The Republican National Convention, which took place in Kansas City from 16 to 19 August, also stood to benefit Ford. As president, he could offer delegates various goodies, whether a trip to the White House to meet with him or other dignitaries, a possible position in government, or a promise to visit a state's party convention, where delegates were divided up among the candidates. As an example, Neal Thigpen, who was part of the South Carolina delegation, recalled Ford's aides flying him and others in his group to Washington, where they ate at a fine restaurant across from the White House and then had a meeting with the president himself. Sears knew Reagan was at a disadvantage. "The incumbent could offer them anything," he recalled. "So we were in a position where if we just stayed and did nothing, we were gonna be beaten."[53]

Playing on an improving economy and American patriotism and, most important, using the power of the presidency, Ford regained the lead in delegates. As the last state convention came to an end, he needed only 28 more votes to achieve the magic number of 1,130. Responding to this crisis situation, Reagan decided to take a chance. Traditionally, candidates for president announced their running mates at the party's national convention, but with Ford drawing ever closer to getting the GOP's nod, the former California governor could not wait until the Republican delegates gathered. Therefore, on 26 July Reagan announced Senator Richard Schweiker of Pennsylvania as his vice-presidential nominee. Schweiker was a liberal Republican who could draw delegates from that wing of the party to Reagan. At the same time, Reagan's aides hoped, he would prove acceptable to the right wing because of his conservative views on such issues as abortion and gun control. Furthermore, Schweiker's presence on the ticket might draw delegates from Pennsylvania and other northeastern states.[54]

Cheney knew otherwise. "We just got the best news we've had in months," he told Ford. He was correct. Conservatives were irate. Choosing Schweiker was "the dumbest thing I ever heard of," commented Ohio's Representative John Ashbrook; his Illinois colleague, Henry Hyde, said that Reagan's selecting Schweiker was akin to "a farmer selling his last cow to buy a milking machine." Worse for Reagan, the overwhelming majority of

Pennsylvania's 103 delegates had committed themselves to Ford and refused to switch their vote. Southern conservatives who had promised to back Reagan started to defect.[55]

With Reagan's chances flagging, Sears made one more attempt to save his boss's campaign by proposing what became Rule 16-C, by which all of the GOP's presidential candidates—including Ford—would have to declare their running mate before the delegates cast their votes. Both Ford and the Republican National Committee objected, and the proposal was successfully shot down. The Reagan team succeeded, however, in changing a plank of the GOP's platform. Referred to as the Morality in Foreign Policy plank, it lauded Solzhenitsyn and censured the Helsinki Accords for "taking from those who do not have freedom[,] the hope of one day getting it." It was a not-so-subtle reference to the growing emphasis on human rights and a clear attack on Ford and Kissinger. Not surprisingly, the president found the plank an infuriating vilification of his foreign policy, but with the exception of Kissinger, all of his key aides, including Spencer, Cheney, and Nessen, urged him to sign, not only to promote party unity but because failure to do so could cost the president the nomination. Ford conceded the plank and, on 19 August proceeded to cinch the GOP nomination, 1,187 to 1,070.[56]

The question now was whom Ford planned to choose as his running mate. He knew that he had to court the conservative wing of the party. Reagan was one possibility, but the former governor made clear to Ford that he had no desire to share the ticket with the president. Political speculation circulated that Ford's top two choices were Tennessee's Senator Howard Baker and former Nixon attorney general William Ruckelshaus. Ford liked them both, but both men were from the moderate wing of the party, and Ruckelshaus lacked name recognition. After further consideration, the president selected someone who had been on few pundits' radars, Kansas senator Robert Dole. It was a risky selection. Presidential candidates generally sought running mates from parts of the country outside their own so as to balance the ticket and expand their base of support; choosing Dole meant selecting a fellow midwesterner. Dole, though, was from the party's conservative wing, and being from Kansas could please farmers, who were angry with Ford's decision in 1975 to suspend temporarily the shipment of grain to the Soviet Union. Additionally, Dole was known as an aggressive campaigner, and he could serve as the Ford campaign's attack dog against Carter, thereby permitting Ford to stay above the fray and appear presidential.[57]

Yet the fight, at least symbolically, was not over. The president had planned to deliver his acceptance speech during prime time, but Reagan's supporters in the convention hall, refusing to acknowledge defeat, loudly chanted for their favorite and, in turn, delayed Ford's appearance. Waiting in his hotel suite to head to the convention hall, a furious Ford recalled using "four-letter words that I almost never use." It was not until 10:40 that evening that he delivered his acceptance speech, one the *New York Times* called "a masterful political performance." Under his leadership, he told the delegates, the country was at peace for the first time since the Eisenhower administration, and the economy was "on the march to full economic recovery." Then, in a line that he had kept secret and that electrified the crowd, he challenged Carter, who had secured the Democratic bid in July, to a one-on-one debate. "We want Ford!" those in attendance repeatedly yelled. The president had only just begun his speech, but he happily found himself interrupted by standing ovations. He reminded voters of his repeated use of the veto to curb government spending and reduce voters' tax burden and warned that a Democratic administration would neither engage in tax reform nor spend the money necessary to defend the nation's security. "My fellow Americans," he concluded, "I like what I see. I have no fear for the future of this great country. And as we go forward together, I promise you once more what I promised before: to uphold the Constitution, to do what is right as God gives me to see the right, and to do the very best that I can for America. God helping me, I won't let you down."[58]

Then, in a show of party unity, Ford, in an unplanned maneuver, invited Ronald and Nancy Reagan to the stage and asked the former governor to say a few words. As Ford stood off to the side of the stage, Reagan extemporaneously delivered a short, six-minute speech, praising the Fords' kindness and the GOP platform and enjoining those at the convention and in the party to stand behind their nominee. "We must go forth from here united, determined," he declared, "that what a great general said a few years ago is true: There is no substitute for victory." Shaking Reagan's hand afterward, Ford was confident he would win on Election Day. That, though, seemed presumptuous, as a Gallup poll gave the Democratic nominee a 15-point lead over the incumbent.[59]

Campaign Strategies

During the lull between the end of the Republican Convention and Labor Day weekend, when the unofficial start of the campaign season began, Carter and Ford prepared their battle strategies. Since both agreed to accept federal financing and no private contributions, they were limited by law to

$21.8 million in campaign funds. One key change took place on the Ford campaign during this time. On 26 August, Rogers Morton, who had replaced Callaway, himself resigned, citing poor health. Taking his place was James A. Baker III. A Texas attorney and friend of George H. W. Bush, he had been active in Republican politics, serving as the party's finance chairman in 1971 and, a year later, on Nixon's reelection campaign. After Nixon's resignation, he had returned to law before heading Ford's effort to round up the delegates he needed to secure the GOP nomination.[60] With Cheney continuing to act as liaison to the PFC, the Ford campaign saw a clear improvement in its professionalism.

For Cheney, his colleagues, and their counterparts on Carter's team, the limited money available for their respective campaigns made it key to determine how to target their efforts. Teeter dejectedly pointed out that Carter had captured the nomination by earning the support of virtually every group in America: gun-control advocates, blue-collar workers, Catholics, Jews, African Americans, environmentalists, the rich, and the poor. Both campaigns knew that Ford was strongest in the central Midwest and the Mountain West, whereas Carter's base was in the Deep South. Hence, the fight for votes would take place in a number of swing states, including California, southern border states, and "northern industrial States" such as Illinois, Ohio, Michigan, New York, and Pennsylvania.[61]

To win those swing states, Carter intended to continue his attack on Washington, pointing to his own outsider status and morality, linking Ford to Watergate and the Nixon pardon, pointing out that Ford was a nice person who was not a competent leader, and emphasizing that voters had the power to bring about positive change for the country. To win as wide a swath of the electorate as possible, he purposely took a vague position on the issues. He opposed abortion but would not endorse a constitutional amendment banning it. He planned to continue détente, yet he believed that Ford had been too soft toward Moscow. He appeared to reject any idea of using nuclear weapons, only to state that he was prepared to use a preemptive atomic strike "if I was convinced that the existence of our nation was threatened."[62]

Ford devised a different line of assault. The incumbent's aides commented that the brawl with Reagan had shown the president's inability "to communicate a vision of what life in America should be, and a well-articulated, logical program to get us there." Hence, the conclusion among voters was that the current occupant in the Oval Office was "indecisive," "not smart," and not "in control of this Administration." The bid by the president to win his party's nod had also led some Americans to question whether he was as open as they had once believed, or whether he instead would say and do whatever it took to win. Therefore, in targeting those swing states, Ford's team planned to focus on suburban middle- and upper-class blue- and white-collar workers and add them to the president's "base of rural and small town majorities." In addition, his strategists hoped to appeal to Catholics and Jews, who, it was anticipated, would be wary of Carter's born-again fundamentalism. The message to these swing voters emphasized Ford as a compassionate, moral, and capable leader who supported national defense, had succeeded in getting the country past Vietnam and Watergate, had turned the economy around, wanted to do more for education than simply stop forced busing, and sympathized with the desire among many Americans to protect the environment. Simultaneously, Ford accused Carter of "fuzziness," raised questions about the challenger's qualifications to be president, and linked the Democratic nominee to liberal, big-ticket programs.[63]

In making these appeals, Ford's team intended not to have him lead the campaign from the front lines. Though he had done some stumping during the primaries, Ford's style was far more wooden, especially before large crowds, than Reagan's. As Spencer told his boss in no uncertain terms, "Mister President, as a campaigner, you're no fucking good." Hence, Ford would continue his Rose Garden strategy—or, as White House aide Michael Raoul-Duval called it, the "no-campaign campaign"—and show voters that their chief executive was hard at work for them. This game plan carried risks. Most notably, by taking the president off the stump, it made it more difficult to present him as not only an intelligent, hard-working president but also as a "nice guy." To circumvent that danger, Cheney and his team planned to have Dole lead the attacks on Carter. Ford's family would join the vice-presidential nominee and, in their own ways, try to draw support away from their challenger by touting Jerry's accomplishments. Despite her views on topics such as abortion, Betty remained highly popular in much of the country, Susan could court younger voters and women, Mike's background in the ministry might appeal to evangelicals, and Steve—whose lifestyle evoked a "cowboy image"—and Jack could stump in the West.[64]

All did not go as planned. Dole made appearances in Iowa and Delaware, Susan Ford went to South Carolina to oversee the opening of her father's campaign headquarters there and participated in a parade in New York City, Steve traveled via motorhome through the Mountain West and the Far West, Jack made appearances in Colorado, and Mike spent time in Ohio.

Betty in her memoir gave the impression that she participated aggressively in the general campaign. In truth she played a much smaller role than she had during the primaries and caucuses. Being out on the stump was hard on her; her arthritis and pinched nerve acted up, and, unbeknownst to her family, she took even more painkillers and continued to drink. But removing from the campaign one of the president's best and most popular champions was unlikely to help him keep his job.[65]

Having others speak for Ford was also part of his campaign's planned advertising blitz, though the emphasis was different. In contrast to the primaries and caucuses, which put Ford's qualities as president at center stage, the new ads initially focused on his character as a good, compassionate family man. Then, having established that foundation, the focus shifted to what the president had achieved and his vision for the future. The strategy of the advertising firm hired by the White House, Bailey/Deardourff, was to let others tout the president's accomplishments. This was an effective way of getting out his message, for it kept off camera a person not known as a compelling orator. While Carter's team put together an advertising strategy similar to Ford's, it placed far greater emphasis on his presidential qualities. The result was an interesting dichotomy, with the challenger planning to portray himself as a moral, upstanding person who was ready to enter the Oval Office, and the person who already held that post trying to convey that he was a good, moral individual.[66]

Errors and the Economy

The Ford campaign's strategy of touting the incumbent's experience while charging Carter with being an inexperienced, big-government liberal began to cut into the Democratic nominee's lead in the polls. Carter then unintentionally handed Ford a gift when an interview the challenger gave to *Playboy* magazine began to leak. Slated for publication in the November issue, the Georgian admitted to having "committed adultery in my heart many times" and made reference to a "guy who screws a whole bunch of women." It is possible the former governor wanted to show he was an average person rather than a religious fundamentalist, but to use such language, let alone in a pornographic magazine, threatened to derail his attempt to characterize himself as upstanding and moral. To avoid appearing mean and to permit Carter's own words to bring the Georgian down, the White House decided to say nothing. Members of the president's party, though, were more than happy to go on the attack, extolling Ford's own religious credentials and, in turn, questioning his challenger's. As Patrick Anderson, one of Carter's speechwriters, commented, the interview "destroyed [Carter's] lead, soured his press relations, threw him on the defensive and his campaign into chaos, and probably cost him the big electoral victory he had expected."[67]

With Carter suddenly in trouble and with Ford's fortunes on the upswing, the presidential debates, the first to receive television coverage since 1960, assumed even more importance. Carter realized his greatest weakness was his lack of a foreign-policy record, and so he had wanted the first of those three meetings to cover domestic matters; indeed, he would have preferred that none of them focus on diplomacy. Ford, knowing he had the upper hand when it came to America's foreign affairs, took the opposite stand. Finally, they agreed to have the first debate address domestic matters and the second foreign relations.[68]

The first encounter, which took place on 26 September in Philadelphia, became famous for a nearly thirty-minute failure of the sound system near the end, during which both candidates stood around, unsure what to do. When the audio did work, it was Ford who most impressed the audience. In the age of television, how one appeared while presenting information mattered as much as substance. On this score, the president's aides had done their homework, having him prep himself in a mock studio and practice his delivery. To viewers, he appeared at ease, and he effectively used the charge of fuzziness against Carter, who seemed rattled and unable to answer key questions, such as offering details as to how he would achieve a promised $60 billion budget surplus within four years. Ford also went after his challenger's outsider credentials, asserting that it was not the White House but Congress that was responsible for antiestablishment sentiment in the country. A poll immediately afterward declared Ford the debate winner, and Carter found himself now only 8 points ahead of the president.[69]

Following the first debate, the Ford campaign began its advertising effort, accentuating the president's "human dimension." In the TV spots, his wife and children told viewers about their husband and father, each of them appealing to particular constituencies. Hence, in one five-minute-long segment, Steve told a gathering of North Dakota voters that his father would not embargo grain, which would please farmers in that state, Michael discussed the president's religious beliefs, Susan told viewers how close she was to her dad, and Betty kissed her husband. "Sometimes a man's family can say a lot about the man," the announcer concluded. The problem with the ad was that it appeared to suggest that the president was running not for another term in office but, in the words of one scholar, "for father of the year."[70]

President Ford and Jimmy Carter in Philadelphia for the first of three presidential debates, 23 September 1976. Photo in the Gerald Ford Library, Ann Arbor, Michigan.

Two news stories involving former Nixon counsel John Dean compounded Ford's problems. In late September the *Washington Post* published excerpts from Dean's memoir, including a claim that then minority leader Ford had successfully stopped an investigation by Congressman Wright Patman (D-Tex.) into Watergate. Then Dean, who now worked as a reporter for *Rolling Stone* magazine, divulged that Ford's agriculture secretary, Earl Butz, had told him and entertainers Sonny Bono and Pat Boone racist jokes while on a flight to California in August. Dean did not name Butz, but the *New York Times* learned who Dean was referring to and notified the agriculture secretary that it intended to publish the story and name him as the offender. Butz informed Cheney, who passed the word on to Ford. The president was reluctant to fire his friend, who could help in rallying votes in farming states, but calls for Butz to quit exploded when the *Times* piece appeared on 1 October. Deciding he had no choice, Ford sacked Butz. While the early indications were that Butz's ouster would not cost Ford support among farmers, the president's failure to cut ties immediately with his problematic agriculture secretary hurt. Allowing the scandal to persist so long turned the media's attention away from Carter's comments in *Playboy*. Furthermore, it impugned the president's image. The Butz affair "sharply undermines the quality of decency and leadership Mr. Ford's campaign is attempting to project," the *Times* commented. Carter joined the attack, tying Ford to the evils perpetrated by the incumbent's predecessor: "The spirit of this country has been damaged by Richard Nixon and Gerald Ford. We don't like their betrayal of what our country is, and we don't like their vision of what this country ought to be."[71]

Carter made sure not to talk outright about the pardon, for fear that doing so could make him look mean. However, his ads referred to the "Nixon-Ford administration," thus making the implication clear. They also allowed the challenger to remind voters of all of Nixon's failures and, in so doing, to accentuate the incumbent's shortcomings, such as his inability to curb unemployment, and to raise doubts in voters' minds as to just how nice and compassionate the president was. Additionally, Carter questioned Ford's ability to handle the reins of leadership while offering in his ads his own "vision of America. . . . I see an America poised not only at the beginning of a new century but at the brink of a long new era of more effective and efficient, and sensitive and competent government." Bailey/Deardourff fought back with a new round of spots that, without doing so explicitly, separated the incumbent from his predecessor and stressed not only his years of experience in Washington but also all he had accomplished since entering the Oval Office, as well as proposals for what he would do if elected in his own right. "He's making us proud again" became the slogan for these new ads. But this strategy had two shortcomings. It reminded voters of what he had "healed," which included Watergate and, by extension, the pardon. It also failed to place Ford's plans within the context of a broader vision. John Deardourff, his firm's vice president, later complained, "I was never sure that the President or anybody else that he had around him had a clear sense of what you did for an encore after you got things back on an even keel." Hence, whereas Carter expressed "a sense of hope and [brought] with him a sense of vision of a different kind of presidency," viewers of Ford's ads got only a list of policy proposals.[72]

Despite his apparent problems, Ford remained only about 8 points shy of Carter. With the next debate, slated for 6 October in San Francisco, to focus on foreign policy, the president had every reason to feel confident that he could cut even further into Carter's lead. His intention was to show the American people that his diplomacy, based on peace through strength, had brought the country dividends, including reduced tensions with the Soviet Union. What he did not anticipate was how well Carter had prepared himself. From the start, the Georgian went on the attack, indicting Ford for allowing Kissinger to run the nation's foreign policy and for failing to make "progress . . . toward a new SALT agreement." Trying to recover, Ford accused his challenger of planning to slash $15 billion from the Pentagon's budget.[73]

Then came a question from the *New York Times*'s Max Frankel, who asked whether the submission of Eastern European countries to Soviet rule was proof that the Soviets were winning the Cold War. Because of the furor following Sonnenfeldt's speech, Ford had prepared for such a question. He had intended to deny that the United States recognized any Soviet sphere of influence in Europe. His aides had suggested several responses, including "To say that my policies accept Soviet domination over Eastern Europe is patent nonsense," or to state that the United States had no intention of "conceding Soviet domination" over Eastern Europe. Instead, Ford remarked, "There is no Soviet domination of Eastern Europe, and there never will be under a Ford administration. The United States does not concede that those countries are under the domination of the Soviet Union." Taken aback, Frankel asked Ford to clarify, thereby giving the incumbent a chance to reword his response. Instead, the president compounded his error. In his mind, the peoples of Yugoslavia, Romania, and Poland did not consider themselves "under the domination of the Soviet Union." Carter immediately pounced. "I'd like to see Mr. Ford convince Polish-Americans and Hungarian-Americans in this country that those countries don't live under the domination of the Soviet Union."[74]

Recalling the gaffe, Rumsfeld commented, "I immediately knew it was a disaster." It was. James Burnham, writing in the conservative *National Review*, called it "so surprising as to be almost inexplicable." The *Los Angeles Times* said Ford's comment was "either a momentary lapse of reason or evidence of a profound misunderstanding of one of the most important world security problems." Surveys afterward had Carter winning the debate by 42 points, and the president only made matters worse by refusing to explain himself. No doubt that was due in part to his well-known stubbornness. But it is also possible that he feared that acknowledging a mistake would add to the image of klutziness. Spencer and Cheney strongly advised Ford that the beating he was taking from Carter and in the polls required some form of clarification, which elicited an admission from him the next day: "I was perhaps not as precise as I should have been." Yet that did little to calm the firestorm. Not until 12 October did he finally concede his error and admit that the "countries of Eastern Europe are, of course, dominated by the Soviet Union."[75]

Ford's refusal to acknowledge his mistake was costly. The debate "left us dead in the water for about 10 days," Teeter commented. Ford conceded later, "[It] was the worst mistake I ever made politically." Eastern European Catholics, one of the group of swing voters whose support the Ford campaign hoped to obtain, turned instead toward Carter. More significantly, it diminished further an image Ford had tried to build. When he heard the president's comment regarding Poland, Carter aide Stuart Eizenstat remarked, "That is the dumbest thing I've ever heard." Many observers shared that sentiment. Columnist David Broder wrote, "Evaluations of Ford's ability in the foreign policy area declined significantly following the second debate." Not only was the president now seen as a klutz who could not even get the facts of international politics correct, but the charges of unintelligence appeared to be true as well, disqualifying him for the post he held.[76]

Bad economic news compounded the president's difficulties. The economy's rebound started to come to a halt by the fall, with slowing auto sales, sluggish housing starts, and indications that inflation was starting to tick up. The cause became a matter of debate; while some observers blamed the Ford administration's determination to rein in spending, the White House claimed it was the result of businesses investing less, including in inventory. By October, many economists predicted the pause would last longer than originally anticipated. In conjunction with Ford's poor performance in San Francisco—about which Carter continued to remind voters—a Gallup poll published in mid-October found a growing number of independents shifting their support to the Georgian, thereby protecting his lead over the president, with slightly more than two weeks to go until Election Day.[77]

Piling on to Ford's problems was the first vice-presidential debate in U.S. history, held on 15 October in Houston. Although Dole was supposed to serve as the Ford campaign's attack dog, he came across as particularly nasty and partisan. The two world wars and the Korean War were, he charged, "Democratic wars." Those conflicts led to 1.6 million American casualties, he continued, "enough to fill the city of Detroit." Minnesota senator Walter Mondale, Carter's running mate, retorted, "Does he really mean to suggest to the American people that there was a partisan difference over our involvement in the war to fight Nazi Germany?" He also reminded viewers of Ford's comment regarding Poland, calling it "one of the most outrageous statements made by a President in recent political history." In addition to emerging victorious in his encounter with Dole and keeping alive questions about Ford's intelligence, Mondale was able to link the "mean" Kansan to the president and, in so doing, further tarnish Ford's image by creating doubt about how much of a "nice guy" the president was.[78]

Given the rancor, Ford had to avoid any further slip-ups in the third presidential debate, which took place in Williamsburg, Virginia, on 21 October. Carter, too, took a cautious tone, desiring to continue the momentum he had gained over the past weeks. The most intense portion of the exchange was on the economy: Ford pointed to continued economic growth and a nation escaping from a recession; Carter responded that unemployment remained high and that the rate of inflation was taking ever more money out of Americans' pockets.[79] In general, however, both men avoided any significant faux pas.

Ford ended his Rose Garden campaign in early October, and with the election less than two weeks away, he stepped up his stumping, focusing particularly on the nation's most populous states. Throughout, he emphasized the danger Carter posed to all that he had accomplished. The challenger, Ford declared, was a traditional liberal who threatened to take the nation down the wrong path. Reminding the country of the doldrums it had faced as a result of Watergate and stagflation, the president exclaimed, "America has turned around. I put the Ship of State on an even keel. . . . Today we are doing much better. The rate of inflation has been cut more than 50 percent. . . . We have added 4 million more jobs in the last 18 months. . . . We have restored confidence and trust in the White House itself, and America is at peace." He supplemented his speeches with a television campaign that included a half dozen thirty-minute spots of him speaking with former baseball player Joe Garagiola about the administration's accomplishments. A day before the election, Ford finally offered a vision for the country based on "limited government and unlimited opportunity." Despite all the gaffes, it looked like the incumbent might just eke out a victory, for by Election Day, the Gallup and Harris polls each showed only a single percentage point dividing the two candidates.[80]

To secure victory, Bailey/Deardourff proposed one more TV ad, a four-and-a-half-minute piece with the theme song "I'm Feeling Good about America" playing in the background. The ad began with Ford delivering a speech at his alma mater, the University of Michigan. During the oration, what sounded like a shot rang out, causing the president to flinch and stop briefly before finishing his comments. Ford then appeared in Dallas, traveling in an open limousine through the city. Making a reference to the assassination of John F. Kennedy, the ad's narrator declared, "When a limousine can parade openly through the streets of Dallas, there's a change that's come over America. After a decade of tension, the people and their president are back together again." Bailey/Deardourff believed the spot would show how much good Ford had done for the country, but the president's campaign aides went ballistic. Baker called the ad "nutty, absolutely screwy. You can't make a reference to Dallas that way without losing the state of Texas." Ultimately, the piece never aired.[81]

On 2 November, Ford cast his vote in Grand Rapids and flew back to Washington to watch the returns. It became evident that the race was extremely close. Finally, at 3:15 a.m., he told an aide, "If I'm going to be worth a damn tomorrow, I'd better go to bed." The next morning, he learned that he had lost, by 50–48 percent in the popular vote and by 297–241 among the electors. Had 8,000 voters in Ohio and Hawaii changed their minds and voted for Ford, the outcome would have been different.[82]

The loss stung. Ford had developed a strong dislike for Carter, who not only avoided direct answers to questions but, in a reference to the chief executive's deference to Kissinger on foreign-policy matters, had referred to the secretary of state during the debate in Philadelphia as the "President of this country." Ford, though, put aside his feelings and called Carter around 11:00 a.m. to congratulate him on his victory. About an hour later, having lost his voice from giving so many speeches, Ford had Betty read his concession speech, in which he called on the American people to give their support to Carter. A day or two later, a dispirited Ford met with his senior staff, who gave him a rousing ovation and whom he thanked for all their service. "There were tears in everybody's eyes," aide Douglas Bennett recalled. "It was an incredibly moving moment. I will never forget that as long as I live."[83]

Ford then turned his attention to other issues. He still had more than two months to go in his presidency, including giving his last State of the Union address. "I can report that the state of the Union is good," he told lawmakers on 12 January. He called for them to pass legislation to cut individual income taxes by $10 billion and to reduce the corporate income-tax rate by 2 percent. After listing all he had done for the country during his short tenure, he ended with an emotional farewell: "It is not easy to end these remarks. In this Chamber, along with some of you, I have experienced many, many of the highlights of my life. . . . I will always treasure those memories and your many, many kindnesses. I thank you for them all."[84]

Two days after delivering his speech, Ford requested that Congress grant statehood to Puerto Rico. Since becoming a commonwealth of the United States in 1952, a debate had erupted on and off the island over its future. In

Mrs. Ford reads President Ford's concession speech to the press, 3 November 1976. Left to right*: Steve, President Ford, Susan, Mike, Gayle. Photo in the Gerald Ford Library, Ann Arbor, Michigan.*

1967, the majority of Puerto Ricans had voted to remain a commonwealth, but they retained hope that their government would receive greater authority over the island's affairs. Ford and his aides had concluded that the U.S. Constitution prohibited granting such power to San Juan. This left three options. One was to retain Puerto Rico as a commonwealth, even though that smacked of colonialism and limited the island's self-determination. The second was to give it independence. The last was statehood. Ford realized that independence was out of the question because of the economic and strategic importance of the island to the United States. This left statehood, which would grant Puerto Rico the same constitutional rights as the other fifty states.[85]

Ford's move shocked Puerto Rico's recently elected governor, Carlos Romero Barceló, Interior Secretary Thomas Kleppe (whose department would have overseen the drafting of any bill to grant statehood), and members of Congress. "The whole thing is crazy," commented an aide on the Senate Interior Committee. When asked why he would make such a proposal, Ford responded, "Because I'm President until January 20." By starting the statehood process, Ford hoped to leave a mark of his presidency.

Instead, the status quo continued. Just how little interest there was in Puerto Rico becoming a state became evident when even Romero Barceló refused to bring the suggestion up in his inaugural address.[86]

Having laid out his list of initiatives, Ford also prepared for the transition to the new Carter administration. Cheney and presidential counselor Jack Marsh headed that effort, working closely with the incoming president's transition leader, Jack Watson. "To my own surprise," Cheney recalled, "I had no trouble at all showing the ropes to [him]." Desiring to offer lessons to the incoming staff, the Ford transition team showed its Carter counterparts a bicycle wheel, spokes and all, that was in the West Wing and explained why such a system of decision making did not work. (It was a lesson Carter would not heed.)[87]

On 20 January, the Fords traveled to the Capitol to hear Carter deliver his inaugural address and then returned to the White House, where they embraced the numerous friends they had made during their nearly three decades in Washington. Afterward, they boarded a helicopter that flew them to Andrews Air Force Base. As the helicopter lifted off, the now ex-president asked the pilot to fly around not the White House but the Capitol. Tears in his eyes, he commented, "That's my real home."[88]

The Importance of Image

Ford's wistful comment reflected the central reason he lost the election. Contemporaries and later scholars pointed to the pardon, the gaffe regarding Poland, and the economy. Other commentators pointed to antiestablishment sentiment among voters, the damage Reagan did to Ford during the primaries, the Helsinki Accords, and Dole's personality and his comments during the vice-presidential debate. Still others have suggested that Ford erred in removing Rockefeller from the ticket and in not helping New York City through its financial crisis—one or both of which may have cost him New York state in 1976. Ford himself accepted many of these explanations.[89] The president's friend, Philip Buchen, and his running mate, Robert Dole, made an additional charge against Reagan, accusing the Californian of refusing to live up to a promise to stump for Ford during the general campaign. Lyn Nofziger, who served as a Reagan campaign consultant, suggested that there was truth to this claim. Ford had made little effort to reach out to his former challenger for the GOP nomination, he commented. Whatever the case, Ford accepted the lack of Reagan's presence as yet another cause of his failure to win on Election Day. "After I had defeated [Reagan], he only made one appearance on my behalf," the former president grumbled. "And that was at a Republican dinner in Los Angeles, I think. He endorsed me. But in a lukewarm way. There was no question in my mind that if he had campaigned for me in Mississippi, Wisconsin, and Missouri, I could have beat Carter." Ford added that Reagan "just wasn't a party player that year. It was all about himself."[90]

That Ford pointed to Capitol Hill as his "real home," however, reflected the key cause of his defeat: image. As much as he enjoyed being president, he was at heart a congressman. Prior to 1974, his entire political career had been on the Hill, where he gradually rose up the ranks to become minority leader. Throughout, he had been a partisan Republican who acted accordingly, seeking to develop as broad support as possible for or against the policies that were the foundation of the president's vision for the country. Once he became president himself, that job description changed in one important way. He still had to garner as many endorsements as possible for each part of his agenda. But he was the one now expected to express that agenda through a vision that would persuade the American people to follow his lead.

Ford failed to satisfy that job description. For one thing, he had to confront changes taking place within Washington. The Republican Party's conservative wing had grown stronger, and Democrats had won an overwhelming majority on Capitol Hill. Initially, neither was a problem for the president. Americans were happy to be rid of Nixon and liked having a "nice guy" in the Oval Office, a man who appeared to be open and transparent. However, as *Time* magazine's Hugh Sidey put it best, "While no one claimed that Ford would provide brilliance or vision, the hope that his soundness would compensate for his failings grew to enormous proportions." Ford had difficulty meeting those expectations, whether because of his own decisions or because of the political resistance he faced, even from fellow Republicans. Consequently, what Americans witnessed was a good-hearted leader who flip-flopped and lacked direction. Even individual successes—such as his handling of the *Mayaguez* crisis, Sinai II, or indications by early 1976 that the economy was escaping from recession—could not offset the perception caused by Ford's positions on the pardon, New York City, inflation, taxes, the Halloween Massacre, détente, Poland, or Panama that he did not understand what was best for the country and was inconsistent, weak, and too deferential to individuals like Kissinger. Questions about Ford's legitimacy to lead the country played not only into the hands of the conservative wing of his own party but into the hands of the

Democrats. The outcome of the election, commented the *New York Times*, "reflects the conviction that the incumbent Administration has proved incompetent to deal with the profound social and economic problems that rack the country—or even to comprehend them."[91]

The *New York Times*'s charges pointed to a more significant Ford shortcoming, which was the doubt Americans felt about his intelligence and even physical ability to lead the nation. "If the press had not systematically presented Gerald Ford as a bumbling fool who bumped his head all the time on the helicopter door, fell down, and bungled things," said J. Robert Vastine, an aide to Senator Carl Curtis (R-Nebr.), "I think he could have won."[92] Instead, Ford came to be seen as a klutz, not only in his personal life but in how he led the country.

Ford did not help himself by refusing to provide a vision for where he planned to take the nation. As Sidey suggested, this part of his job description at first did not matter, for what Americans wanted most was to put behind them the misery of Vietnam and Watergate. Over time, though, voters desired to have an indication of the broader purpose of his individual initiatives. The lawmaker-minded Ford was unable, and indeed unwilling, to offer it. In his last State of the Union address, for instance, he drew attention to nine different foreign-policy topics without connecting them through some theme. Even Ford later admitted, when asked if he should have adopted a catchphrase like the "New Realism," "Well, in retrospect, I guess . . . we probably should have."[93] There is, of course, no way to know if such a slogan would have worked in the highly charged political atmosphere of 1976. But in a campaign where every vote mattered, the failure to try can be called one of Ford's greatest mistakes. Consequently, what Americans saw was a president who was uncertain of himself, unintelligent, and even incompetent. In retrospect, it is surprising that with all the negatives against him, he still came close to winning the Oval Office in his own right.

NINE

Politics, Money, and the Post-Presidency

Losing the 1976 election left Gerald Ford dejected. In early January, during his last flight on Air Force One as president, he told the *New Republic*'s John Osborne "about the hurt that his defeat by Jimmy Carter had done him." He wanted his comments off the record, yet, the journalist wrote, "it was clear that the defeat had inflicted a wound that would never heal."[1] That assessment proved incorrect. Ford did become one of President Carter's most vehement critics, but in the 1980s, the two men became not just good friends but also allies on a wide range of issues, including Middle East peace, the national debt, abortion rights, and gun control. That Ford would develop such a relationship with a former Democratic rival was indicative of the continuing influence of a political career marked by a moderate conservatism and a willingness to reach across party lines. In the process, Ford and Carter established a precedent that continues to the present day.

Ford's commitment to bipartisan politics did not mean he had given up his loyalty to the Republican Party. In 1980, he considered taking on Carter again for the presidency and then, giving up on that idea, joining the GOP ticket as Ronald Reagan's running mate. While worried about the national debt incurred during Reagan's administration, Ford endorsed the incumbent in 1984 and traveled around the country speaking for Republican congressional candidates.

Politics was not Ford's only concern. He had to decide where to live, a question that was tied directly to Betty's well-being. He gave of his time to teach classes and lead seminars at a number of universities, worked on his memoirs, watched football, and played in numerous golf tournaments.[2] Of even greater importance to him, possibly even more than politics, was money. On the one hand, he had to raise dollars to fund construction of the Ford Library and Museum, which, unlike similar facilities for other presidents, would be built in separate cities rather than in the same locale. On the other hand, he wanted to make money for his own financial well-being. It was that desire to earn a good living that garnered Ford a significant amount of criticism and, combined with what other ex-presidents were earning, triggered a desire among some members of Congress to cut federal support for the country's former chief executives. The idea of reducing monetary help for the ex-presidents ultimately went nowhere, and despite the feeling in some quarters that Ford was using his office primarily to make a buck, he remained quite popular. Even if many Americans did not necessarily agree with all the decisions he made as president, by the time Ford passed away in 2006, what many remembered was a decent and honest average Joe who took the nation through one of the most difficult periods in its history.

"Old Habits Are Hard to Break"

Shortly after he took the oath of office at 12:03 p.m. on 20 January 1977, Carter delivered his inaugural address. As the Fords sat on the platform, the new president paid homage to the Oval Office's former occupant: "For myself and for our nation I want to thank my predecessor for all he has done to heal our land." It was an "unexpected [and] gracious thing for him to say," Ford wrote. "I didn't know whether to remain seated or to stand. But when the cheers continued I decided to stand, and I reached over to clasp Carter's hand."[3]

The departing president was as dejected as Betty was elated about leaving the capital. Yes, she told the journalist Barbara Walters shortly before Carter's inauguration, she would have accepted another four years as the country's first lady. But November's outcome meant "I was getting my husband back." She was also excited about "go[ing] to that nice warm weather."[4]

The reference to "warm weather" was a clue to where the jet waiting for them at Andrews Air Force Base was to take the former first couple. The people of Grand Rapids would have happily had the Fords return, but they had decided instead to retire in California. A major reason for their decision was Betty's health. Because she suffered from rheumatoid arthritis, the Fords thought a milder climate might offer her some respite. Betty also worried that returning to their home state would mean too many demands on her and Jerry's time, whether for attending meetings or giving speeches.[5]

The Fords also looked at Florida and Arizona, but they found Florida too damp, and Arizona lacked the friends the Fords had in California. Moreover, the area around Palm Springs offered numerous golf courses, giving Jerry the opportunity to play the sport he so enjoyed. Their decision made, the Fords sold their house in Alexandria and built one on a golf course in Rancho Mirage, a resort town of about 1,300 people located approximately 10 miles from Palm Springs. Numerous wealthy and famous people lived in the area, including Bob Hope, Frank Sinatra, and Lucille Ball. The beauty of the town impressed Betty: "This must have been what the Garden of Eden looks like."[6]

Retirement gave Ford more time to devote to golf. The day after Carter's inauguration, he was on the links with Arnold Palmer, playing in a golf tournament hosted by Bing Crosby (today the Pebble Beach National Pro-Am). "Where were all these people on Election Day?," he joked when he saw the large crowd that greeted him. He played in ten golf pro-ams in 1978, eleven in 1979, and numerous others in 1980. Among those with whom Ford played was Hope, who had founded the Desert Classic golf tournament in 1965 and became one of the former president's closest friends. "Jerry Ford's fame as an erratic hitter, capable of beaning anyone within a range of 260 yards, is richly deserved," Hope later wrote. "The President doesn't really have to keep score. He can just look back and count the walking wounded."[7]

In truth, admitted Hope, Ford was an excellent player, one who retained the competitive spirit he had had in his youth. He played with "fierce determination" and got upset "after missing a shot." Yet such jokes reflected Ford's inability, despite the caliber of his play on the links and his skill on skis at Vail, to escape his reputation for klutziness. For instance, in 1981 the impressionist Rich Little released the LP *The First Family Rides Again,* a collection of skits that targeted Reagan. But in one track depicting a poker game among Ford, Reagan, Carter, and Richard Nixon, Little portrayed the thirty-eighth president as a clumsy, unintelligent oaf who could not locate the White House, fell into a china cabinet, and confused poker with the games go fish and gin. Fifteen years later, the television program *The Simpsons* targeted Ford. In the episode "Two Bad Neighbors," Ford moved into a home across the street from the Simpsons and invited Homer Simpson over to watch football and have nachos. As they walked to Ford's house, the two men tripped and fell, crying in unison Homer's infamous "D'oh!"

The University of Michigan cared less about such characterizations. If anything, there were those on campus who saw in Ford a loyal alum who might join its faculty. As early as 2 November, the day of the election, political science professor Harold Jacobson concluded that the president might not win and proposed to the dean of the College of Literature, Science and the Arts, Billy E. Frye, that Ford receive a visiting professorship. The idea quickly gained traction. "Defeated candidates are weary and have little respite before they face that early and urged media question, 'What are your plans for the next year, Mr. President?,'" Frye's colleague, George Grassmuck, wrote the university's president, Robben Fleming, a day later. There was no doubt Ford would receive other overtures, continued Grassmuck, so it made sense for Michigan to present "an immediate and realistic offer." Fleming too found the suggestion a good one and reached out first to Ford's longtime friend, Philip Buchen, and then to Ford himself, and Grassmuck did the same with presidential adviser Dick Cheney. To try to convince Ford to come, both Fleming and Grassmuck indicated the university's willingness to make the terms of his appointment as flexible as the president favored. Ford liked the idea of returning to his beloved alma mater and imparting his knowledge in the classroom. In April 1977, as an adjunct professor, he offered a series of classes and seminars on governance and foreign policy; it was attended by about 1,500 students and 100 faculty. That November, he returned to lead three more days of classes and seminars. The American Enterprise Institute (AEI), a conservative think tank that he joined shortly after leaving the White House, helped with the financial arrangements for the visits to Michigan and other universities; by 1980, the former president had been on nearly sixty campuses to talk about domestic and diplomatic matters.[8]

Ford enjoyed his time at his old stomping ground, but he had more in mind for his post-presidency. "Old habits are hard to break," he commented at a Republican Party fund-raiser five months after Carter's inauguration. He intended to remain active in the GOP. Politics was part of who he was. "I'll be around to help, not as a candidate but as a party worker," he said in May 1977. "The quiet role of an elder statesman, though comfortable for some of my predecessors, holds little appeal for me." As such, he was disinclined to remain quiet about his successor's initiatives. He intended "to be selectively critical when I think President Carter is wrong and supportive when I think he is right. Somebody ought to have a detached view, as I think I do."[9]

There was reason to believe that Ford would find much about Carter that he liked. Despite their different party affiliations, they were both fiscal conservatives. Furthermore, Carter continued many of the initiatives that had begun during the Ford or Nixon administrations, including deregulating industry, promoting energy independence, achieving SALT II with the Soviet Union, turning the Panama Canal over to Panama, and normalizing relations with China. Ford endorsed the exchange of ambassadors with Beijing, but more significantly, he played an active role in getting the two Panama Canal treaties ratified. Signed in 1977 between Carter and Panama's leader, Omar Torrijos, the first treaty turned the Panama Canal over to Panama at the end of 1999, while the second gave the United States the right to defend the waterway from external threats. Both Republicans and Democrats in Congress opposed the treaties' ratification. Carter engaged in an intense public-relations and lobbying effort to gain ratification. He found allies in Ford and in former secretary of state Henry Kissinger. In the spring of 1978, the Senate ratified the agreements, both of them by the same 68–32 vote. A gratified Carter wrote Ford, "Without your personal help, approval of the treaties would not have been possible."[10]

That said, Ford remained a GOP loyalist who criticized the Carter administration. He played down the significance of the Camp David Accords, which were among Carter's greatest achievements as president. Signed in September 1978 by Carter, Israeli prime minister Menachem Begin, and Egyptian president Anwar Sadat, the agreements established a framework for peace in the Middle East. Specifically, Israel promised to withdraw from the Sinai Peninsula (which it had captured from Egypt in 1967) in return for official Egyptian recognition of Israel, something no Arab state up to that point had done. Furthermore, in vaguely worded language, Egypt, Israel, and Jordan agreed to develop a formula for Palestinian autonomy on the West Bank and in Gaza Strip. Ford insisted that all Carter had done was carry on the "step-by-step policy" that he and Kissinger had adopted.[11]

Ford was far harsher regarding Carter's policy toward Rhodesia. The new president, who had denounced apartheid and promoted human rights during the 1976 campaign, sought to achieve majority rule in both Rhodesia and neighboring South Africa, itself led by an apartheid government. The hawkish Ford denounced Carter's willingness to endorse the agenda of the Zimbabwe African National Union (ZANU), headed by Robert Mugabe, and the Zimbabwe African People's Union (ZAPU), led by Joshua Nkomo. "Mugabe . . . is a Marxist, a dedicated Marxist and an individual who believes in one-party rule," exclaimed the ex-president. "To put it bluntly, I do not comprehend how our government . . . can support Mugabe and Nkomo, who want to win by bullets that which they cannot win by the ballot box. And our administration ought to be condemned." Nor was he supportive of the idea of U.S. corporations cutting ties to South Africa, despite that nation's repressive apartheid regime.[12]

Even more upsetting to Ford was the incumbent's defense policy. Both Ford and Carter favored limits to federal spending, but the former president repeatedly indicated his willingness to support a significant increase in the military budget. To Ford's chagrin, Carter canceled production of the B-1 bomber and construction of a new aircraft carrier and reduced funding for the MX missile system. "The strategic balance is clearly shifting against us," Ford wrote, and the only way to rectify the situation was for the president to reverse those decisions and increase military spending.[13]

Ford also complained about Carter's domestic programs. Rising unemployment and inflation baffled Carter. Like Nixon and Ford, he seemed unable to decide which posed a greater threat to the country's economic well-being. Likewise, he worried about Americans' reliance on foreign sources of fuel as much as his two predecessors had. A shortage of natural gas in some states during the harsh winter of 1976–1977 added to the sense of crisis. In 1978, Congress passed the National Energy Act, which encouraged both energy conservation and the development of new sources of fuel. "The Carter administration and the Democratic Congress are destroying the economy," Ford declared a few days before the 1978 midterm election. Nor did he have much faith in the president's energy policy, which he said was "crumbling."[14]

The best example of Ford's loyalty to his party and his determination to continue playing a political role was his stumping on behalf of GOP candidates. His post-presidential chief of staff, Penny Circle, recalled that her boss traveled six days a week giving speeches. In October 1978 alone, he was on the road twenty-seven days; during a single ten-day stint, he traveled some 15,000 miles and raised $600,000 for about two dozen Republicans seeking office. He also turned over to them as much as $40,000 of what he had left over from his 1976 presidential bid.[15] How much of an impact he had is unclear. Democrats retained control of both houses of Congress but lost seats. Moreover, those lawmakers who were reelected or entered Congress in January 1979 as freshmen tended to have more conservative leanings than those who sat in the House and Senate in the previous session.

Betty was not happy with her husband's continued political activity. At the start of 1977 she had believed she would have her husband back, only to have him once again become absent. Her arthritis made matters only worse. Depressed, she drank even more, took increasing amounts of drugs, and distanced herself from those around her. She recalled using various "gourmet medications. . . . I had pills to go to sleep, pills for pain, pills to counteract the reactions of all the other pills. And each of these, please note, was from a doctor's prescription." The public received a hint that something was wrong in 1977. The former first lady had signed a contract with NBC to narrate a performance of *The Nutcracker Suite* by the Bolshoi Ballet. What Americans saw and heard was a former first lady whose speech was slurred and who appeared to be about to fall asleep. Betty later admitted that the press justifiably criticized her work. By the spring of 1978, she believed she "was dying, and everyone knew it but me."[16]

When they had become aware of Betty's problems previously, the Fords had turned to physicians. This time, they took personal responsibility. Susan started the process. In 1978, she told Dr. Joseph Cruise, the gynecologist who cared for both her and her mother, about the former first lady's behavior. Cruise, who himself had suffered from alcoholism, urged a family intervention. In the presence of the ex-president, one of his aides, and housekeeper Clara Powell, Cruise and Susan confronted Betty. The former first lady, commented Susan, "called me a monster and kicked me out of the house." The incident made Jerry aware of the full extent of his wife's dependencies. On 1 April, the entire Ford family confronted Betty. To everyone's surprise, it was the former president who led the intervention. Each member of the family, as well as Mike's wife, Gayle, pointed out that she was an addict. Gayle went so far as to tell her mother-in-law that she "would not be a fit grandmother." Initially furious with the accusation that she was an addict, Mrs. Ford soon realized that Gayle was right. On 10 April, the ex–first lady checked herself into the Alcohol and Drug Rehabilitation Service at Long Beach Naval Hospital.[17] It was the beginning of a transformation in Mrs. Ford's life that would make her a national leader in the fight against drug and alcohol abuse.

President Ford . . . for Vice President?

The intervention had less of an impact on the former president. To encourage his wife, he stopped drinking, but he could not break himself away from politics and spend more time with her. He continued to assail Carter's policies, expressing reservations about SALT II, which Carter signed with Soviet premier Leonid Brezhnev in June 1979. The agreement capped the number of platforms (whether based on land, air, or sea) used to launch ballistic nuclear missiles to 2,250, limited how many missiles could have more than one warhead, and permitted the Soviets and the Americans to verify that the other was in compliance with the treaty's provisions. In a lengthy article in the *Washington Post*, Ford asserted that the Vladivostok agreement of 1974 had provisions more beneficial to the United States than SALT II because the former had been negotiated by Kissinger and himself from a position of strength. Carter's poor budgetary decisions, though, had weakened America's worldwide defense posture and permitted the Soviets to get a SALT agreement that was far more favorable to them than the Vladivostok agreement had been. Additionally, he expressed doubts that the verification procedure established by SALT II would prove effective.[18]

Ford linked American military strength to the Iran hostage crisis, which began in November 1979 when Iranian militants seized the U.S. embassy in Tehran and took several dozen Americans hostage. "The current crisis in Iran," he commented, "is the most serious, the most potentially volatile, with the widest ramifications of any international challenge that the United States has faced since the end of World War II." In addition, he said, the situation "underscores this country's eroding military might." Ford was insulted that Carter had refused to contact him about what was happening in Iran, "particularly," he claimed, "since I supported the president on so many foreign policy decisions."[19]

Instability in Iran, which had precipitated the hostage crisis, and a decision by OPEC to curtail oil production resulted in shortages at many gas stations and increased inflation. In an attempt to control prices, Carter endorsed initiatives that tightened the money supply and raised interest rates. Yet by February of 1980, inflation had reached nearly 20 percent, stagflation had returned, and the United States had fallen into a recession. "Carter has handled the economy ineptly," Ford told an audience at the University of Michigan in March 1979. A few months later, he used the word "disaster" to describe his successor's economic programs. Even though Ford pointed the finger primarily at Congress for failing to pass an energy program better than the one it had approved in 1978, he did not consider Carter blameless. "We're . . . importing more foreign crude oil today than the day that Carter became president," he remarked in late 1979. "So, from the point of view of reducing our dependence on OPEC, he's also been disastrous."[20]

Both his desire to return to the public arena and his partisanship led Ford to toy with running for the presidency in 1980. Pushing aside his statement in May 1977 that he had no intention of seeking the GOP nomination, he told an audience in October that he wanted to wait until after the 1978 midterms before making a decision. He remained noncommittal after the midterm vote. "I'm not a candidate," he said on the television show *Weekend* in April 1979, but if by the spring of 1980 the GOP seemed to be unable to decide on a candidate, he "would not duck the responsibility." Polls showed that he could defeat Carter. Together with numerous requests that he run as an alternative to Ronald Reagan—who appeared to be on the verge of announcing his candidacy—Ford inched ever closer to throwing his hat into the ring. For party moderates already in the race, such as Ford's former liaison to China, George H. W. Bush, the ex-president's flirtation with the presidency was disconcerting. It was also no doubt worrisome to Betty, who knew that another term in the Oval Office would put enormous pressure on her and her husband and would mean more time away from each other. Still, Ford told *Family Weekly* magazine only two months after Betty sought treatment for her addictions, "If I said I was going to be a candidate—and I emphasize that I am *not* saying that—I think she would be a good team player and be happy for me to do so."[21]

The GOP's moderate wing seemed set to emerge victorious when Bush won the party's first contest, the Iowa caucus, in January 1980. But the new wave of conservatism that had been growing in the country throughout the 1970s had by then taken firm hold of the Republican Party. Following Iowa, Reagan won seven of the next nine primaries, including in the important states of Illinois and Florida. The increasing likelihood of a conservative representing the GOP raised alarm among the party's moderates and liberals. Adding to their nervousness was Carter's rebound in the polls. The president's failure to solve the nation's economic ills had hurt him, and disagreements with Democratic liberals had prompted Massachusetts senator Edward Kennedy to challenge him for the nomination. But the hostage crisis, followed by the Soviets' decision in December 1979 to invade Afghanistan, had generated a "rally around the flag" sentiment that boosted the president's approval ratings to nearly 60 percent. Given that Carter had a greater likelihood of drawing votes from moderates than did Reagan, middle-of-the-road Republicans looked at Ford as an alternative to the California governor. That Ford polled better against Carter than did other GOP candidates added to a sense of urgency. Ford continued to waffle. He told reporters in early March that Reagan had no chance of winning in November and urged Republicans to rally behind himself as the party's nominee.[22]

By then, however, it was too late. Those in the party who had once urged him to run were no longer as excited as before. Ford also realized that seeking the nomination risked splitting his party, and with the GOP's national convention quickly approaching, there was little chance he could grab enough delegates to wrench the party's bid away from Reagan. "I am not a candidate, I will not become a candidate. I will support the nominee of my party with all the energy I have," he announced in March. Those Republicans still in the race were pleased. "It uncomplicates things," said Reagan. The Carter campaign was also happy, viewing the former California governor as posing less of a challenge than Ford.[23]

In May, Reagan won enough delegates to guarantee himself the Republican nomination. Carter followed suit for his party the following month. Increasingly it appeared that the Californian had an advantage over the Georgian. Carter had responded to the Soviet invasion of Afghanistan by imposing an embargo on grain shipments to the Soviet Union, telling the Senate to shelve SALT II, ordering a U.S. military buildup, and boycotting the summer Olympics in Moscow. But those measures had not convinced the Kremlin to withdraw from Afghanistan. An attempt in April to rescue the hostages failed, and the economy remained sluggish. Ford concluded that Carter was "vulnerable" and that Reagan had "an excellent chance" of winning in November. What worried the ex-president was the decision of Representative John Anderson (R-Ill.) to run as an independent. Anderson could take enough votes away from both Carter and Reagan to throw the election into the House of Representatives, where "all kinds of wheeling and dealing in smoke-filled rooms" would take place.[24]

Reagan might avoid the outcome about which Ford warned by putting together a strong ticket. Ford appeared to take his name out of the running for vice president. The Constitution's Twelfth Amendment, he pointed out to the *Wall Street Journal*, prohibited the members of the Electoral College from voting "for a President and a Vice President from the same state. Governor Reagan and I both live in California," and a Reagan-Ford ticket would mean losing California and its "45 electoral votes—8% or 9% of the total electoral vote." Yet on 17 July the *Chicago Sun Times* announced, "Gerald R. Ford has accepted the vice presidential spot on the GOP ticket."[25] While not as big a blunder as the *Chicago Tribune*'s declaration in 1948 that Thomas Dewey had defeated Harry Truman in that year's presidential bout, the *Sun Times* did speak too soon. But the "dream ticket," as some called it, had come close to reality.

The full story of the Reagan-Ford negotiations remains shrouded in some mystery, yet their failure revolved around the question of power sharing. From the point he secured the nomination, Reagan's aides put together a list of possible running mates, including Bush, Senator Richard Lugar of Indiana, and Senator Howard Baker of Tennessee. Ford, however, was also under consideration. He had presidential experience, "superior credibility," and a broad political base, and his nomination was almost certain to receive a strongly positive response from the press.[26]

Who raised the idea of the "dream ticket" is unclear. Richard Allen, who became Reagan's first national security adviser, speculated that Bryce Harlow, a friend of Ford's, brought the idea of a Reagan-Ford ticket to Reagan campaign manager William Casey, who took it to Reagan and the campaign's chief of staff, Edwin Meese. Reagan's campaign strategist, Stuart Spencer, also ascribed the idea to people in the Ford camp, such as the ex-president's national security adviser, Brent Scowcroft, and counselor, Jack Marsh. Reagan attributed it to "a number of party leaders," among them Nevada senator Paul Laxalt. The most compelling version of what happened attributes the origin to Richard Wirthlin, Reagan's pollster. Wirthlin concluded that Ford had the greatest chance of harming or helping the Reagan campaign. It was time, Wirthlin continued, for the two men to set aside their differences. Accordingly, Reagan traveled to Rancho Mirage, where he met with Ford and asked for the latter's help. The two leaders mended fences. Ford indicated he would do what he could to get Carter out of office. Reagan suggested that Ford become his running mate, an offer the former president turned down.[27]

There were indications, though, that Ford's decision was not set in stone. In July, he returned to his home state to participate in the Republican National Convention in Detroit. In his speech endorsing Reagan, he lambasted Carter's record as president. Then he remarked, "Elder statesmen are supposed to sit quietly and smile wisely from the sidelines. I've never been much for sitting. I've never spent much time on the sidelines. . . . So when this convention fields the team for Governor Reagan, count me in." The nominee was taken with the speech, which he construed to mean that Ford had reconsidered his position on sharing the ticket. Reagan therefore headed to the ex-president's suite and again offered him the vice presidency. "Came out of the blue as far as I was concerned," Ford recollected. "George Bush was always my candidate for vice president. In fact, Betty and I went to Detroit with the hope that we could be helpful to him. But Reagan screwed it all up by getting me involved."[28]

Ford's suggestion that Reagan screwed up the former president's plans smacks of insincerity. It is possible that Ford went to Detroit to promote a Reagan-Bush ticket, but he easily could have maintained that course by immediately telling the Republican candidate he had no desire to become his running mate. The truth was that Ford longed to return to public life, and the prospect of doing so, even as vice president, was something he could not pass up. The very suggestion that Ford might run alongside Reagan excited television reporters, who up to that point had found the convention a rather colorless affair. The possibility confounded Wirthlin, Casey, Meese, Allen, and Reagan adviser Michael Deaver, as well as House Minority Leader John Rhodes (R-Ariz.), who questioned its workability and noted that the Republican Party platform Reagan had endorsed was critical of détente, a policy Ford had embraced as president. Allen claimed—though there is a lack of substantiating evidence—that he worked to get Reagan to consider Bush. While not on friendly terms with Reagan, he was a moderate whose Texas residency could be helpful in November. What is clear is that when Ford gave the impression to *CBS News* anchor Walter Cronkite that he favored a "co-presidency," Reagan concluded that such an arrangement was unworkable. The candidate's and ex-president's camps continued their talks for a few more hours, but when Ford became adamant about having greater power in a Reagan administration than normally would be given to a vice president—such as chairing the National Security Council or serving as chief of staff—the talks fell apart. With that, Reagan contacted Bush, who agreed to become the Californian's number two.[29]

One can only speculate as to whether a Reagan-Ford "dream ticket" could have worked. William Brock, the chair of the Republican National Committee, who kept abreast of the talks between Reagan and Ford, concluded, "I don't think that having Ford on the ticket would have changed very much of anything. It certainly would not have changed Reagan in his conduct during or after the election."[30]

Ford certainly could have done what he accused Reagan of doing to him in 1976—offer minimal assistance to the GOP candidate. But he was not one to hold a grudge, and he wanted to do all he could to help his party. He spent fifty-three of the sixty days between Labor Day and Election Day stumping around the country for Reagan, focusing on the same themes of American weakness. "I've tried my best," he commented, "to divorce myself from politics and consider Carter fairly. He has failed. I have seen how badly Carter has handled the White House. Worldwide we are in serious trouble. We have to do something to change the occupant of the White House."[31]

Voters agreed with Ford. Higher inflation and unemployment and a sense that America was unable to defend its interests abroad helped Reagan defeat Carter in a landslide. Following his 1981 inauguration, the new president put his demands for smaller government and a stronger military into action. He succeeded in getting a Democrat-controlled Congress to cut taxes and government spending. To show the Soviets he meant business, he instituted a five-year, $1.7 trillion military spending program; encouraged the development of a space- and land-based ballistic missile system called the Strategic Defense Initiative; placed medium-range nuclear missiles in western Europe; provided military aid both to the rebels combating the Soviets in Afghanistan and to the contras, groups fighting the left-wing government that had taken power in Nicaragua in 1979; and, in 1983, sent U.S. troops to Grenada to overthrow its Marxist government.

Containment was also part of the Reagan administration's thinking vis-à-vis the Middle East. The president strongly supported Israel and its interests, but he was critical of that country's determination to annex the West Bank, Golan Heights, East Jerusalem, and Gaza Strip—all of them territories taken by Israel from its Arab neighbors in 1967. He was also displeased with Israel's decision in 1982 to invade Lebanon, where civil strife permitted the PLO to stage attacks on the Jewish state. Worried that the unrest in Lebanon could lead to a collapse of its government and to an assumption of power by a regime friendly to Moscow, Reagan sent U.S. troops to Beirut as part of a multinational peacekeeping operation.

Reagan's detractors charged that his domestic policies hurt the needy and pushed the United States into a recession that began in the middle of 1981. His diplomatic initiatives, they said, were anti-Israel and increased the likelihood of a third world war. To mollify his critics, the president made clear he was a stalwart ally of Israel and proposed talks with the Soviets that would lead to the Strategic Arms Reduction Treaty (START). By 1983, he could also point to the emergence of the United States from the recession, as inflation had come under control and the economy had rebounded. But the good news at home hid a burgeoning budget deficit, which rose to $336 billion in 1984.

Ford was of two minds about how to react. Party fealty encouraged him to endorse the president's initiatives. "I fully support President Reagan's economic policies," he told a group of businessmen in Brazil. Similarly, he informed an audience at Auburn University that he foresaw the success of

Reagan's plans for the U.S. economy if the president "has the courage to stand firm against any capitulations, which would bring short-term benefits and long-term detriments." Likewise, Ford stated that the United States had to put missiles in western Europe to offset the presence of Soviet weaponry on the eastern side of that continent. He justified the invasion of Grenada to prevent "a further expansion of Cuban influence in the Caribbean." But using sticks alone would jeopardize any hope of reviving détente. It was also possible that the Soviets might want to strengthen superpower ties once they chose someone to replace Brezhnev, who had passed away in November 1982. Hence, to Ford it made sense to offer the strategic arms reduction talks. He joined those critical of Israel's effort to annex the occupied territories and was pessimistic about the chances for a Middle East peace agreement. Finally, he endorsed Reagan's decision to withdraw U.S. troops from Lebanon after a terrorist driving a truck laden with explosives blew both it and himself up in a U.S. Marine barracks in Beirut, killing 241 U.S. military personnel.[32]

Ford, though, had reason for concern. In his mind, Reagan never grasped how the budget worked and "had no interest in learning it." In 1981 the AEI had begun holding an annual World Forum in Beaver Creek, Colorado, where the ex-president planned to build a new home. Ford hosted the second of the forums, which drew former West German chancellor Helmut Schmidt; Valéry Giscard d'Estaing, who had lost a bid for reelection as France's president that year; and James Callaghan, who had served as British prime minister from 1976 to 1979. "In my years," Ford informed both participants and reporters, "when we had a deficit of $65 billion, everybody thought it was the end of the world. Now the deficit is closer to $200 billion, so clearly something has to be done." As one step, he encouraged delaying the delivery of military hardware and spreading spending on the armed forces over a longer period than Reagan favored. In other venues, he explained that he was a hawk, but his recommendations would neither encourage a Soviet attack nor cause serious harm to the U.S. economy. Additionally, he urged the administration and Congress to consider imposing new taxes, including a levy on oil imports.[33]

Despite such misgivings about Reagan, Ford campaigned for him in 1984 and gave a strong speech endorsing his candidacy at the party's national convention. Walter Mondale, formerly Carter's vice president and now the Democratic nominee, wanted Americans to forget about the terrible state of their country in the late 1970s, Ford told the delegates. Through policies promoting smaller government and stronger defenses, Reagan had reduced inflation and unemployment and restored the country's prestige.[34] The ex-president watched as Reagan proceeded to crush Mondale in one of the most lopsided landslides in the country's history.

Reagan's popularity took a hit in his second term with the eruption of the Iran-contra scandal, which involved the illegal sale of weapons to both Iran and the contras; the former was on the list of nations the United States accused of sponsoring terrorism, and in 1982 Congress had forbidden aid to the latter because of reports that the contras were killing innocent civilians. Also disconcerting were the debt, which had reached a record $3 trillion by the time Reagan left office, and the gap between rich and poor. The interest payment on the debt was the third-largest item in the national budget, and the disparity between the wealthy and the indigent had become the widest since the 1920s.

Still, there was reason for Americans to praise the incumbent. The economy was booming by the time Reagan left office. Mikhail Gorbachev had acceded to the Soviet premiership, and many saw his decisions both to withdraw Soviet troops from Afghanistan and to seek arms-control talks with the United States as proof that Reagan's concept of negotiating from strength had succeeded. The two leaders developed a close personal rapport. Their decision in 1987 to sign the Intermediate Nuclear Forces Treaty—under which they agreed to eliminate all their intermediate-range nuclear missiles—was regarded as marking the revival of détente. A resolution to the Middle East's problems remained as elusive as ever, yet that did little to offset a feeling among a large segment of the American public that their nation's greatness had been restored. As 1988 came to an end, Reagan's job-approval rating was 63 percent, or about the same as it had been in 1984.

Throughout, Ford was far more laudatory of Reagan than of Carter, but he grew increasingly worried about the former California governor's initiatives. In 1985 he said that the country economically was doing well but that the rising debt posed a threat to its future well-being. He called for Washington to "better manage our expenditures." On that score, he favored cuts in entitlement programs and even in defense spending. "I was a hawk, I am a hawk, and I expect to always be a hawk," he told an audience in New York state in 1985. That said, he wanted to take Reagan's five-year program of military spending and expand it to six, thereby generating "a better cash flow and a corresponding better picture as far as the deficit is concerned." Moreover, he again expressed a preparedness to see taxes go up. Nor was Ford happy with the Iran-contra affair. The National Security Council had played a central role in that scandal, ending up in "some action areas where they had no authority under the law. . . . That's where they got their ass in a wringer. . . . The president had a fundamental responsibility and they allowed a terrible example of mismanagement."[35]

With Reagan unable to run for a third term, Vice President Bush became the prospective Republican nominee in 1988. Running on Reagan's coattails, he promised to continue his predecessor's policies. At first, it appeared that Bush might face a strong challenge from Ford's running mate in 1976, Kansas senator Bob Dole, but Bush had a well-funded and well-organized campaign that allowed him to clinch the nomination fairly easily. Bush selected as his running mate a young, handsome, forty-one-year-old senator from Indiana, Dan Quayle. He hoped that Quayle's conservative credentials, good looks, youth, and upbringing would strengthen his base within the party and draw him votes from the Midwest. Many in the GOP, however, were shocked that the vice president had selected an unseasoned lawmaker who was only in his second term in the upper house. That Quayle made numerous verbal gaffes during the campaign did not help him. *Time* magazine ranked Quayle among the worst running mates picked by a presidential candidate, and Ford called Bush's pick his "biggest mistake."[36]

Quayle's selection aside, Ford had even more reason to stump for Bush than he had for Reagan. Like himself, Bush was a moderate Republican, and he had served in Ford's administration. The former president, therefore, urged voters to choose the GOP nominee. In what he called "probably the best political speech," Ford touted the Republican Party's recipe of tax cuts and smaller government for having brought peace and prosperity to America since 1980. The Democrats, though, wanted to raise taxes and expand Washington's power. "We believe," he told his audience, "that a government big enough to give you everything you want is big enough to take from you everything you have."[37] Believing Bush would continue the economic growth that had taken place under Reagan, pleased with the nominee's stated promise that he would not raise taxes, and uninspired by the Democrats' candidate, Massachusetts governor Michael Dukakis, 54 percent of Americans voted for Bush, and he won almost three times as many electors as his rival.

Bush's victory came as the Cold War appeared on the verge of ending. Not only was there an improvement in U.S.-Soviet relations, but Gorbachev had also begun to liberalize both the Soviet economy and its political system. Yet no one foresaw the events that began in 1989, when Germans began tearing down the Berlin Wall, a barrier the Soviets had built a generation earlier to divide East and West Berlin. The collapse of the wall started the end of Communist control of Eastern Europe, as one nation after another, including Poland, threw off their leaders in favor of democratic-capitalist regimes. Recalling his comment in 1976 regarding Poland, Ford mused, "Well, seeing what's been happening today over there, maybe I was right all along."[38] The dissolution of the Soviet Union in 1991 marked not only the end of communism in Europe (with the exception of Albania) but also the end of the Cold War.

The year 1991 was also the start of Operation Desert Storm. Following a lengthy war with Iran, Iraq had sought to recoup its financial losses by selling oil, only to have its neighbor, Kuwait, increase petroleum production and push down oil prices. Infuriated, Iraqi president Saddam Hussein ordered an invasion of Kuwait in 1990. Believing that Hussein planned to conquer Saudi Arabia next, Bush, alongside both Western and Arab nations, initiated Operation Desert Shield and sent troops to defend that country. The president then led the United Nations to pass a resolution ordering Hussein to withdraw his forces from Kuwait by mid-January 1991. When the Iraqi dictator did not comply, Operation Desert Storm began, with the purpose of liberating Kuwait. After six weeks, that goal had been achieved, with the loss of fewer than 200 U.S. lives.

As a result of the Persian Gulf War, Bush's popularity soared to over 90 percent. But it began to fall as a recession took hold of the country. That Bush, like Nixon, had little interest in domestic policy did not help. The president's approval rating sank to below 40 percent. Ford was disappointed in Bush. He had done an admirable job in handling Iraq, the ex-president stated, but then "made a big mistake" when "he didn't realize, or his people didn't realize, that the economy was in trouble. The Democrats moved in and took advantage of it. By the time the Bush administration woke up, the Democrats had the issue and Bush never got it back. That was a serious tactical error."[39]

Many Americans shared Ford's sentiment in 1992. That year, Bush faced two challengers for the presidency: the Democratic nominee, Arkansas governor Bill Clinton, and Texas businessman Ross Perot, who ran as an independent. Clinton assailed Bush's handling of the economy, and Perot's populist rhetoric attracted a fairly significant number of voters who believed neither of the country's established parties cared about the well-being of the average American. On Election Day, Perot won 19 percent of the popular ballots, but Clinton won an overwhelming victory.

The Democratic Friend?

Even as Ford criticized Reagan and Bush, he became close friends with his former rival, Jimmy Carter. Ford's attacks on Carter's stewardship during the 1976 election campaign had left the two men feeling bitter toward one another. That mutual sentiment made itself evident in 1981, when the State Department, deciding it was "too dangerous" to send President Reagan or Vice President Bush to represent the United States at Anwar Sadat's funeral, asked Carter, Ford, and Nixon to lead the American delegation. Their transport, an old Boeing 707 jet, was cramped with the former presidents, Secretary of State Alexander Haig, U.S. ambassador to the United Nations Jeane Kirkpatrick, several lawmakers, entertainer Stevie Wonder, and a teenager who had been Sadat's pen pal. As the jet flew across the Atlantic, Nixon could sense that his two successors were ill at ease with one another and broke the ice. "We were all former presidents who served our country well," remembered Ford, "so there was no reason for any residual bad blood between us. Nixon brought us all together." The resentments between the thirty-eighth and thirty-ninth presidents dissipated as they discovered their commonalities. Both of them were religious, both had been rivals of Reagan, both had known Sadat, and they shared a similar perspective on American diplomacy. "We've made an agreement never to discuss domestic policy issues because the gulf between us is so wide," Ford said in 1995. "But on foreign policy our views are similar, so we can work together on joint projects very effectively." Likewise, their wives developed their own friendship and collaborated on such matters as promoting the Equal Rights Amendment (ERA) and health care and combating alcoholism.[40]

Evidence of the budding Carter-Ford friendship appeared on the flight back from Egypt, when they jointly held a press conference where they took turns responding to questions about U.S. policy toward the Middle East. In a shocking statement at variance with the position both had taken while sitting in the Oval Office, the two ex-presidents said that Middle East peace necessitated U.S. diplomatic recognition of the PLO. A perturbed Israel and Reagan administration vigorously rejected the suggestion. Reagan, who began privately to refer to Ford and Carter as "the Bobbsey Twins," stressed that the United States would neither speak to nor recognize the PLO "until they've recognized Israel's right to exist as a nation, which they still have never done."[41]

The two former presidents joined forces again in early 1983 when they wrote an article for *Reader's Digest* critical of Israel. They considered Tel

Aviv's failure to live up to the Camp David Accords of 1978 to be the greatest challenge to Middle East peace. "It [Israel] has continued to confiscate properties in occupied territories and to build settlements as if to create a de facto Israeli ascendancy there," they explained. "It has publicly repudiated the Reagan peace plan, which calls for a freeze on Israeli settlements." After the *Reader's Digest* article, the two men berated Menachem Begin at a conference held at the Ford Library. Ford, who was on crutches after a surgery to repair one of his knees, and Carter accused the Israeli prime minister of purposely dragging his feet in withdrawing Israeli troops from Lebanon and of building more settlements in the West Bank. "Having two former presidents—one Democrat, the other Republican—criticizing Begin for errant behavior created a mild stir in Israel," said Carter. "It put extra heat on him." That November, the Carter Center hosted a conference on the Middle East, with Ford serving as a cochair. The conference came on the heels of the bombing of the marine barracks in Lebanon but Ford and Carter warned against retaliating militarily. As Carter explained, an armed U.S. attack on the assailants would jeopardize ongoing peace talks between the warring Lebanese factions.[42]

The two men collaborated on more than just the Middle East. In November 1982 they warned against protectionism in world trade, and the following year they participated in a dinner honoring former admiral (and Carter hero) Hyman Rickover and his Rickover Foundation, which provided science and technology scholarships to college students. In 1985 the two former presidents served as cohosts of a conference in Atlanta, Georgia, attended by U.S. and Soviet officials aimed at pushing the superpowers toward initiatives aimed at controlling nuclear weapons.[43]

Even during the presidential election of 1988, Carter and Ford joined forces, forming American Agenda, a bipartisan organization whose purpose was to develop proposals for handling the issues that the country's next president was likely to face. Supported by a $500,000 grant from Times Mirror Company and assisted by two dozen experts, the two ex-presidents produced a widely disseminated report entitled *American Agenda: Report to the Forty-First President of the United States*. Carter and Ford urged the Oval Office's next occupant first and foremost to reduce the deficit; otherwise, the nation would have a difficult time addressing its other pressing concerns, including arms control and national security. Though President Bush lauded the report, Ford lamented that he "never implemented any of our recommendations."[44]

In 1993, Ford, Carter, and now ex-president Bush attended the ceremony at which Clinton signed the North American Free Trade Agreement (NAFTA). Encouraging the worldwide elimination of protectionism had been a recurring theme since the 1930s; statutes and agreements intended to promote that end included the Reciprocal Tariff Act of 1934, the 1947 General Agreement on Tariffs and Trade, and the Israel–United States Free Trade Agreement of 1985. During the Bush administration, the United States began negotiations to eliminate trade barriers among the United States, Mexico, and Canada, which resulted in NAFTA. That three ex-presidents and the incumbent, representing both major parties, participated in the signing ceremony demonstrated NAFTA's bipartisan backing. Ford encouraged ratification of the agreement, contending that it would protect those holding jobs in the United States. "If you defeat NAFTA, you have to share the responsibility for increased immigration to the United States, where they want jobs that are presently being held by Americans," he cautioned. "It's that cold-blooded and practical, and members of the House and Senate ought to understand that."[45]

Five years later, Ford and Carter again came to Clinton's defense. In 1996, the incumbent had defeated the Ford-endorsed Republican candidate, Robert Dole,[46] largely because of an improved economy. Even before his reelection, though, Clinton had faced charges of marital infidelity, which bred distrust of him and played a part in Democrats' losing control of Congress in 1994. Then, in 1998, the *Washington Post* reported on an affair Clinton had had with a White House intern, Monica Lewinsky. Both publicly and in a deposition, he denied the claim, only to have Lewinsky turn over a dress with the president's semen on it. Clinton was forced to recant his earlier denial. Smelling blood in the water, House Republicans, with the backing of some Democrats, succeeded in impeaching Clinton on the charge of obstructing justice.

With Clinton's fate now in the hands of the Senate, Ford and Carter stepped in. Ford believed that Clinton lacked integrity, but neither he nor Carter thought the incumbent's actions justified throwing him out of office. Instead, they favored efforts by some in the House who proposed censuring the president. "Impeachment by the full House has already brought profound disgrace to President Clinton," they wrote in a *New York Times* op-ed. A censure resolution would force Clinton "to accept rebuke while acknowledging the very real harm he has caused."[47]

The Ford-Carter piece attracted widespread attention. Clinton called Ford, asking if the former president might help him fight impeachment. "I think you have to admit that you lied," Ford told the incumbent. "If you do that, I think that will help, and I'll help you. If you'll admit perjury, I'll do more." Clinton found both options objectionable and refused. For their part, Democrats on Capitol Hill favored the suggestion of censuring Clinton, while Republicans, particularly those on the Far Right, were incensed with the attempt by Ford and Carter to save the president's job. Representative Tom DeLay of Texas "wrote me the nastiest letter imaginable," Ford recollected. "He was downright rude. But I didn't care. I thought the House impeachment was enough. If I could pardon Nixon then we could certainly censure—not impeach—Clinton in the Senate. It was the centrist position. And it's what was right for the country."[48] The Senate ultimately acquitted the president in 1999, and no censure resolution passed Congress.

Republican in Name Only?

Ford and Carter based their opposition to impeachment on what they considered the need "to put aside political differences and plant seeds of justice and reconciliation." Aside from Ford's pardon of Nixon, they cited as precedent Carter's decision early in his administration to grant amnesty to those who had evaded the draft during the Vietnam War. A trial of the president would not only be long, they wrote, but would "only exacerbate the jagged divisions that are tearing at our national fabric." What Ford and Carter had pointed to was a growing polarization in American politics. It was not uncommon through much of the postwar period for the members of opposing political parties to have heated debates but, at the end of the day, to joke over drinks or food or play a round of golf. Representative Donald Rumsfeld (R-Ill.) recalled that during the 1968 election he and other Republicans would "beat up on" the Democratic nominee, Hubert Humphrey. "But it was always in a gentlemanly, but substantive way—we would disagree with each other, but we were not disagreeable." Likewise, Minority Leader Ford and House Majority Leader Hale Boggs (D-La.) reportedly rode together to the National Press Club and decided what subjects they would debate. Afterward, they would have lunch together before heading back to Capitol Hill.[49] Even Reagan was on friendly terms with House Speaker Tip O'Neill of Massachusetts, who was a member of the Democrats' liberal wing.

That sense of camaraderie had disappeared by the 1990s, replaced by what one sociologist referred to as a "culture war,"[50] a take-no-prisoners, no-holds-barred fight between the two political parties over the direction of the country. Hence, when Clinton refused to accept the harsh budget cuts demanded by Republicans following the 1994 midterms, GOP lawmakers permitted a shutdown of all nonessential federal activities during the winter of 1995–1996 (and subsequently took a lot of heat from an angry American public). Likewise, the effort to impeach Clinton was arguably as much about morality as it was about the law. Harsh rhetoric and talk of left- or right-wing conspiracies aimed at destroying the country became ever more commonplace.

Ford blamed his own, increasingly conservative Republican Party for the ill will on Capitol Hill. The GOP's shift to the right reflected a broader, national transformation, one that had started to emerge by the 1960s. Politically, a growing number of voters had concluded that the nation's elected officials were untrustworthy and incapable of properly using taxpayers' money. But there was also a sense that the country had lost its moral compass, as evidenced in rock-and-roll music, "free love," rampant drug use, the *Roe v. Wade* decision granting women the right to an abortion, secularism, and the burgeoning homosexual-rights movement. Religious fundamentalism, which had not had a powerful role in American politics since the 1920s, witnessed a resurgence. The coalition of Christian conservatives that became the New Right identified closely with powerful evangelists such as Pat Robertson and Jerry Falwell, who urged their followers to endorse lawmakers who they believed would bring morality back to America. To assist this effort, in 1979 Falwell founded the Moral Majority, a national conservative religious organization whose members voted in large numbers for Reagan. Ford felt that groups like the Moral Majority threatened to break down the division between church and state that America's Founding Fathers had demanded. "I have never believed in organized religion getting into the political arena," he said a month after Reagan's inauguration.[51] That was not necessarily true: one could argue that Ford's endorsement of prayer in public schools was itself a political maneuver. The distinction was that groups like the Moral Majority played a role in deciding who would become president, which to Ford was giving organized religion too powerful a voice in determining how the U.S. government would function.

The New Right and political conservatives developed a powerful alliance, one that gradually pushed the GOP away from the political center. "I worry about the party going down this ultra-conservative line," Ford told a reporter in early 1998. Recalling earlier elections, such as that in 1972, he added, "We ought to learn from the Democrats when they were running ultra-liberal candidates, they didn't win." He insisted that Americans in fact were centrists, "and Clinton was smart enough in 1996 to talk like a moderate Democrat." Dole, meanwhile, had lost "because 'the party pushed him too far to the right.'"[52]

If anything, Ford had become more liberal on some issues than he had been previously. During his presidency, he avoided taking a firm stand on affirmative action, a policy dating to the 1960s that sought to combat racial and gender discrimination by giving minorities special consideration when they applied for employment or university admissions. That changed in 1999, when the University of Michigan's law school faced two lawsuits on an admissions policy that included affirmative-action provisions. The use of affirmative action, Ford wrote, had permitted Michigan "to create the finest educational environment for all students" and "produced a student body with a significant minority component whose record of academic success is outstanding." To eliminate affirmative action would destroy inclusiveness, he contended, and turn "the clock back to an era" when racial segregation had existed. Right-wing pundits reprimanded Ford for his "liberal" views,[53] but to Ford's pleasure, the Sixth Circuit Court of Appeals in 2002 upheld the law school's admissions policy.

Ford also demonstrated a change of position on abortion, the Equal Rights Amendment, and homosexual rights. With the exception of Mrs. Ford, no one in the Ford administration had championed the cause of women's rights. As president, Ford had opposed the right to an abortion. During his third debate with Carter in 1976, he had called for a constitutional amendment granting the states the power to outlaw termination of pregnancy. Likewise, he made no effort as president to pass the ERA. In 1998, though, he praised the decision of the Republican National Committee to reject a resolution that would have withheld campaign funds from party members who did not declare themselves opposed to late-term abortions. Nor did he favor the resolution that did pass, which condemned use of the late-term procedure. In 1979 Congress set a deadline of 30 June 1982 for ratification of the ERA, and Jerry joined Betty in supporting the amendment.[54] To their disappointment, the ERA failed to receive the constitutionally required endorsement of three-fourths of the states.

On the rights of homosexuals, the former president shirked the issue in 1976 by stating simply that there was no clear answer. In 2001, though, when asked about homosexuals having the same family and marriage rights as heterosexuals, Ford replied, "I think they ought to be treated equally. Period." The following year he joined the Republican Unity Coalition, an alliance of homo- and heterosexual individuals who called for the GOP to include those whose values were not necessarily in accord with those of traditional political or religious conservatives. He criticized conservatives who denounced others for not adhering to proper "family values." "I'll put mine up to theirs any day," he stated.[55]

Why Ford changed his position on affirmative action, abortion, and homosexual rights remains a matter of speculation. The former president had said in 1978 that it was because he was no longer in an elected office: "You don't have to be quite as precise, quite as restrained." Ford special assistant Richard Wennekamp and *Newsweek* reporter Thomas DeFrank shared that assessment. "I think being out of electoral politics kind of freed him up," said DeFrank. "It just kind of liberated him to say what he really believed. I mean, there were just lots of things he knew he couldn't support as a congressman or vice president or as a president. But, freed from those shackles, he felt more liberated and he didn't care what people thought." Others, including the Fords' longtime friend Peter Secchia and Betty's personal assistant Ann Cullen, gave at least some credit to Betty. "She was a strong influence," said Secchia. "I think she did influence him to a degree," explained Cullen, "you know, particularly with women's rights issues, maybe even gay rights, but I think they both were people who saw people as people."[56]

The "bitterness and acrimony" Ford had cited reached new heights in the 2000 presidential election, which pitted the incumbent vice president and Democratic nominee, Al Gore, against the governor of Texas, George W. Bush. Ralph Nader, a well-known advocate for consumer rights, ran as the candidate of the Green Party. Ford had urged Bush to name a running mate who was pro-choice "or at least . . . more so than some Republicans would like." He was pleased when the GOP nominee selected as his running mate Ford's onetime chief of staff, Dick Cheney. Cheney, Ford and Dole wrote, would promote inclusiveness, had a "distinguished record of leadership in the Pentagon" (having been defense secretary under George H. W. Bush), and had served in the House, where people had "to adopt broader views . . . and see a complex world through unfamiliar eyes."[57]

Yet Bush reflected the rightward drift of the GOP. He was, he said, a "compassionate conservative," one who spoke openly of his commitment to God, opposed abortion and affirmative action, and favored tax cuts, government deregulation of industry, and the partial privatization of Social Security. Gore cited statistics and policy proposals as he took positions opposite Bush on these key subjects, and Nader focused predominantly on protecting the environment. When the votes were tallied, Gore had won the popular vote, and some news outlets declared him the winner of the electoral vote, only to recant when it became clear that neither he nor Bush had won enough electoral votes to be declared the victor.

The outcome depended on who took Florida. The original vote count was so close that state law required a recount. Florida had used a so-called butterfly ballot, in which the voter punched out a chad to record his or her choice. Some chads, however, were not punched through but were hanging or showed nothing more than an indentation. For the next five weeks, Americans waited as election officials (and lawyers) went ballot-by-ballot trying to decide the final tally. Some pundits charged Florida governor Jeb Bush with conspiring to make sure his brother won the election. Gore hinted that he might take the case to court if he lost. Finally, after thirty-six days, the U.S. Supreme Court, along a partisan 5–4 vote, called an end to the recount and gave Bush the electoral votes and the victory. For the next four years, Bush faced charges that he was, like Ford, an unelected president.[58]

Following the election, Carter and Ford joined forces again, this time to head a commission designed to avoid a replay of what had happened in Florida. Their group recommended in the spring of 2001 that winners not be predicted until all polling places in the contiguous forty-eight states had closed, setting a "benchmark" for acceptable errors, and having each state adopt a voter-registration system as well as uniform standards prior to an election to determine what amounted to a vote. Using the commission's recommendations, Congress drafted the Help America Vote Act, which Bush signed into law in 2002.[59] The measure established minimum voter-identification requirements, provided federal money to update old voting equipment, and created an Election Assistance Commission to make sure that states complied with the act.

A few months after Carter and Ford made their recommendations, the terrorist organization al-Qaeda launched an attack on the World Trade Center (WTC) in New York City and on the Pentagon in Washington, using aircraft to destroy the WTC's twin towers, killing more than 3,000 Americans. Ford shared the shock felt by many in the country: "That day, I just cried and cried. Those poor, poor people. Our poor, poor country." Shortly after the 11 September attack, Ford and Carter joined President Bush at the site of the Trade Center's remains, and the two former presidents, as well as ex-president Clinton, were named honorary members of a commission to construct a memorial to the terrible event.[60]

Following 9/11, Bush launched an attack on Afghanistan to oust the Taliban, an Islamic extremist group that had permitted al-Qaeda to establish training bases on Afghan soil. Two years later, he ordered U.S. troops into Iraq in 2003 to oust Saddam Hussein from power, claiming that the Iraqi president was developing weapons of mass destruction and had ties to al-Qaeda. Although it did not take long to overthrow Hussein, U.S. troops began to find themselves fighting both Iraqi and foreign fighters who accused the non-Islamic United States of occupying Iraq. Between May and July, sixty Americans had died in Iraq, about half the number killed between the invasion and Bush's declaration of victory; in July, 42 percent of those polled by Gallup said the war was going badly, a threefold increase since May. Although "convinced that . . . we'll prevail," Ford was anxious about how the U.S. public would react if American casualties continued at the current rate. He refused to second-guess administration personnel regarding the number of troops sent to Iraq or regarding whether the president "misstated intelligence information to build support for the war."[61]

A year later, Ford had changed his mind. He had watched as members of his administration returned to positions of influence in Washington, among them Cheney. Then defense secretary Cheney had justified not ousting Hussein from power during Operation Desert Storm on the grounds that it would require the United States to occupy Iraq, an endeavor that could mire Americans in a long-standing conflict. Now, Vice President Cheney endorsed removing Hussein. Moreover, no incontrovertible evidence—weapons of mass destruction or ties between Hussein and al-Qaeda—had been found in Iraq. The Bush administration therefore rationalized the war on the grounds that bringing democracy to Iraq would have a snowball effect and spread throughout the Middle East. Ford found such reasoning illogical. "I just don't think we should go hellfire damnation around the globe freeing people, unless it is directly related to our own national security," he commented in a 2004 interview that was not released until after his death. Rather than military action, "I would have maximized our effort through sanctions, though restrictions, whatever, to find another answer." Ford specifically called out Cheney, who had been "an excellent chief of staff" but who, as vice president, had "become much more pugnacious" and obsessed with the idea that there was a connection between Iraq and terrorism.[62]

Even if a majority of Americans came to share Ford's opposition to the war in Iraq, the truth was that his moderate Republicanism was falling out of favor with the party he so loved. George W. Bush was the first Republican to secure the presidency without winning the electoral-rich state of California. Indeed, his victory required him to rely more heavily on the South, where the party's right wing had dominated since the 1960s. The inclusiveness endorsed by Ford did not sit well with a GOP that believed minorities were part of a "grand conspiracy" with Democrats aimed at destroying the conservative values that the Far Right contended underpinned American culture. Those Republicans who expressed a willingness to reach across party lines or who adopted policy positions regarded by the right wing as "moderate" or "liberal" were little more than "Republicans in name only" (RINOs).[63] This view was not new, as the John Birch Society had attacked President Dwight D. Eisenhower for being out of touch with conservatism, and in 1964 Barry Goldwater's supporters had made a similar claim about the GOP's moderate and liberal wings. What was new was the power the party's right wing came to hold as the country entered the twenty-first century. Ford himself was never accused of being a RINO, but his brand of Republicanism was now a thing of the past.

The Library and Museum

Ford may have devoted a significant portion of his post-presidential years to politics, but he had another concern, that of raising money for a building or buildings that would house his papers and commemorate his tenure in the White House. Indeed, Ford had begun to give attention to this matter shortly after taking the presidential oath. "It would be premature to outline the University of Michigan's interest in and proposals for your Presidential papers," university historian and archivist Robert Warner wrote Ford less than two weeks after Nixon's resignation. "Suffice to say the matter has been discussed by President Fleming and the Board of Regents and all are most interested in the University's playing a major role in preserving the records and memorabilia of your administration." Ford appeared uncertain. "I made a commitment to the University of Michigan for all of my Congressional papers," he told a reporter for the *Grand Rapids Press* the following August, and though he had yet to decide where to put his presidential papers, Ann Arbor seemed the logical place. Yet he also believed there were "a lot of other things that are interesting and would be, I think, perhaps better displayed in Grand Rapids than at Ann Arbor."[64]

Ultimately, Ford became the only president to place his library and his museum in different locations. He had several reasons for doing this. Ann Arbor was home to one of the most renowned universities in the country, where researchers came from around the world. It was also an easy drive from Detroit, with its large international airport. Grand Rapids, Ford's adopted hometown, faced economic difficulties, and placing the museum there would draw tourists. Finally, there had been grumbling at the cost entailed in building presidential facilities: Lyndon B. Johnson's, which opened in May 1971, had cost $18.6 million, and John F. Kennedy's, which was not dedicated until 1979 because of quarrels over where in Boston to put it, had a price tag of $12 million. By putting Ford's facilities in different locations, stated a Ford Library archivist, the president hoped to avoid complaints that presidential libraries had become too expensive.[65]

Because federal law requires former presidents to raise the money necessary to construct their libraries and museums, it was up to the President Ford Library/Museum Fund—later called the Ford Commemorative Committee—to raise dollars for the two facilities and to determine where in Grand Rapids construction of the museum would take place. Headed by the hypermarket magnate Fred Meijer, by April 1978 the commission had achieved its goal of raising $6 million in private donations. That number soon reached $7 million, with Ford himself turning over honorariums he received from speaking engagements. Thanks in part to lobbying by the former president, the state legislature in July promised another $3 million. Additional donations helped cover the $15 million price tag for the two buildings—$4 million for the library and $11 million for the museum—and the cost of museum exhibits.[66]

Ford also helped in choosing the facility's location. Tourism was the second-most-important industry in Grand Rapids. It made no sense to him to place the museum in the suburbs. Rather, he wanted the museum downtown to draw visitors to that part of the city and selected a site along the west bank of the Grand River, opposite the central downtown district. The building required about seven acres of land for the 44,000-square-foot building, 500 parking places, and surrounding grounds. Since there was no existing site large enough, some of the funds raised would have to go toward purchasing nearby buildings and tearing them down—a prospect that displeased some of the existing property owners. After some further wrangling, including in the courts, the museum's planners had the necessary land.[67]

Construction began in June 1978, and the facility opened its doors in September 1981. The dedication, attended by the Fords, Reagan, Mexican president José López Portillo, and Canadian prime minister Pierre Trudeau, was the highlight of a week of festivities that included rides in hot-air balloons, a picnic where Ford met with disabled adults and children, a party at the civic center, and a $1,000-per-plate black-tie dinner hosted by Bob Hope.[68] By that time, the library, built next door to the Bentley Historical Library at the University of Michigan in Ann Arbor—where Ford had been depositing his congressional papers before they were moved to the Ford Library—had been in business for five months.

Ford sought to raise money for his museum and library, but he wanted even more to make money to secure his own financial future. At the time of his retirement, he and Betty had around $200,000 (approximately $830,000 in 2017) in assets. They still owned their home in Grand Rapids (which they donated to the Ford Commemorative Committee in 1979) and their condo in Vail (which they sold that same year), as well as investments in stocks and income from the congressional pension system.[69] They owed no money on their residences, having bought them using their own savings, loans (which they quickly paid off), money he had earned from speeches as a congressman, and an inheritance Betty had received to cover their bills.

A day after the 1976 election, Ford asked his military aide, Robert Barrett, to serve as his executive assistant. Barrett agreed and quickly found himself having to head off numerous requests for Ford's time, including professorships, paid interviews, positions on corporate boards, and opportunities for investments. Even Ford was shocked by how many people approached him: "I never had that experience before."[70]

One offer that grabbed Ford's attention came from Norman Brokaw, who worked for the country's most prestigious talent agency, William Morris. Brokaw met Ford through one of the latter's speechwriters, Don Penny, who had formerly been one of the agent's clients. "I've got this friend in California named Brokaw who has got tremendous talent," noted Penny. "The bottom line is, after you meet Norman you won't be worth this $300,000 but $9 million, and that's a much better number." Ford considered the offer enticing. He and Betty agreed that California was where they wanted to reside, but they knew they could not afford to live in Rancho Mirage on their current income and investments. Meeting with Brokaw at the home of Ford friend Leonard Firestone, the ex-president made clear that he did not want a long-term post. Rather, he wanted to pick and choose what positions he took. Furthermore, he did not want to be tied to any businesses in case he decided to run for the presidency in 1980. He knew that otherwise he might face embarrassing questions about how much influence the corporate community had over him.[71]

Brokaw, according to one historian, "then put together for Ford the most elaborate money-making plan of any former president." He arranged contracts with Harper and Row and with *Reader's Digest* that included a $1 million advance to publish both Jerry's and Betty's memoirs. The Fords also signed a $2 million, five-year deal with NBC to appear in documentaries and give interviews. Additionally, the ex-president went on the lecture circuit, receiving $10,000 to $15,000 per speech. After deciding in 1980 not to run for the presidency (or vice presidency), Ford regarded himself as a "free agent," and, looking to "make some additional money," he began serving as an adviser or board member in the corporate world. It was a symbiotic alliance: industry magnates saw in the former president a gregarious, well-liked person who from his early days in politics had been a champion of free enterprise and whose expertise and stature could help open doors for them both domestically and abroad; Ford, acting as an adviser or board member, was able to draw on his knowledge of finance and politics and, of course, to add to his personal wealth. His board memberships included the natural resources company AMAX, American Express, Nova Pharmaceutical Corporation, and Twentieth Century Fox. AMAX alone paid him $100,000, and American Express another $120,000, and neither of those salaries included director's fees, such as the additional $16,000 AMAX paid him. By 1980, thanks to these positions, his military, congressional, vice-presidential, and presidential pensions, and his speeches and investments, Ford was earning $500,000 a year. It reached $900,000 as 1981 got under way.[72]

Ford also took advantage of the Former Presidents Act (FPA), a 1958 law that provided a pension for the ex–chief executive and authorized funding for office space and staff. It was amended over subsequent years to include health care and Secret Service protection. In 1978, Ford spent nearly all of his allotment of $302,000 for his twelve-person staff and office supplies, and $30,000 for travel; this did not include the $2.2 million to pay for permanent Secret Service protection for him and his wife, his outside income, or the settlement they got from NBC when the company canceled the contract because of lack of interest in the Fords' appearances. In 1981, Ford's government benefits totaled $5 million, and his outside income had reached $1 million. Thanks to his financial windfall, he was able to build his $692,000 home in Rancho Mirage; to partner with Leonard Firestone to purchase two radio stations in Durango, Colorado, in 1979 for $1.55 million; and, in the early 1980s, to spend $1 million on a penthouse condominium in Vail, even while building a 12,000-square-foot chalet in nearby Beaver Creek.[73]

The first broadside against Ford's use of his office came from his former press secretary, Jerald terHorst. In a 1977 article for the *Washington Post* titled "President Ford, Inc.," terHorst charged his former boss with "huckstering and merchandizing" the presidency and of "robbing the office of something decent." He conceded that a former president was a private citizen who had "as much right as any other American to turn a buck in any legal, legitimate way he can." Yet he had hoped Ford would have "set a higher standard for ex-Presidents." He concluded, "That 'nice guy' image of Jerry Ford is getting harder and harder to see behind that pile of money on his Palm Springs doorstep."[74]

Former president Carter joined in the assault, lamenting that his predecessor "was using the ex-presidency to get rich." In fact, Carter, who faced financial problems upon his departure from Washington, used his post-presidency to make large sums of money as well, a fact that Ford pointed out.[75] While unstated, the difference in Carter's mind was that he devoted time to Habitat for Humanity to build homes for the poor, and his money went to the Carter Center—a nonprofit that engaged in humanitarian programs worldwide—whereas Ford focused solely on material gain.

That certainly was the view of some in the media. The *New York Times*'s Robert Lindsey wrote in 1983 that Ford "has become a kind of one-man academic, business, and political conglomerate" who, his critics pointed out, had three homes, taxpayer-supported benefits, and millions of dollars in assets. An even more pointed attack came in 1989 when Carter, whose work with the Carter Center was helping him rehabilitate his tarnished reputation, and Ford went to Panama to monitor an election there. Ford left on election day to play in a celebrity golf meet in California. Carter stayed behind, saw evidence of fraud in the returns, and reported as much to President Bush. "The Ford former presidency, complete with Secret Service entourage, is available for paid speeches, ribbon cuttings and the endorsement of real estate developments," wrote the *Washington Post*'s Richard Cohen. Then, in a swipe at the ex-president's most controversial decision while in office, Cohen added, "Ford sits on corporate boards and is available as a golf partner for wealthy groupies. Should any of them move the ball, Ford undoubtedly would issue a pardon."[76]

Such criticism offended Ford. He regarded Carter as "a friend," but one who "was acting too big for his britches, constantly foisting his services on the Bush White House as though he were still in office." As for his relationship to the corporate world, "Why should I sit around and play golf seven days a week?" It was not like he took every opportunity that came to him. "I've turned down nine for every one I have accepted. I've been very discriminating, and when you look at the list of the people I've been associated with, they are all first class." He worked hard on each of the company boards on which he sat. As far as he was concerned, "I think I've earned every penny I've made."[77]

In addition to his political and corporate activities, Ford engaged in philanthropy. In 1977 he established the Jerry Ford Invitational, an annual golf tournament held in Colorado that drew professional players and that by the early 1990s had raised over $1 million for charity. He helped save the McCallum Theater in Palm Desert, California, and, with Betty, raised millions of dollars to build the Children's Discovery Gerald R. Ford Elementary School in the neighboring city of Indian Wells.[78] He was a proud supporter of the Betty Ford Center, a nonprofit facility cofounded in 1982 by the former first lady, Dr. James West, and Firestone. The facility has since provided treatment for tens of thousands of individuals with alcohol or drug addiction.

Some members of Congress were unimpressed. With the money ex-presidents had begun to make and the dollars taxpayers spent on them, voices began calling for changing the FPA. Among them were Senator Lawton Chiles (D-Fla.) and Representative David Pryor (D-Ark.), who sought to restrict how much Americans paid for their ex-presidents. "We have entered the era of the imperial former presidency," declared Chiles. Pryor proposed cutting all federal aid if the ex-president's outside income reached more than $1 million annually. The Chiles-Pryor initiative went nowhere, but it did not stop efforts to restrict taxpayer coverage for former chief executives. In 1996, Ford successfully lobbied Congress to remove amendments from an appropriations bill that would have cut money for former presidents' staff and office support. The demand to cut funding for ex-presidents, though, continued. Most notably, in July 2016 President Barack Obama vetoed a bill introduced by Republican representative Jason Chaffetz that had provisions similar to those recommended by Pryor.[79]

Decline and Death

In 2000, Ford attended the Republican National Convention to watch George W. Bush receive the party's nomination. He told the public-service network C-SPAN it would be his last. He felt healthy, but age had begun to take its toll. He had tried during his post-presidential years to keep in shape, doing sit-ups, lifting weights, and swimming. In 1990, he had knee-replacement surgery in his left knee, thereby repairing an injury dating to his years as a high-school football player. Still, he had clearly begun to slow down by the time the second Bush accepted his party's nod. Ford looked infirm and exhausted, and slurred his words during an interview. On 1 August he went to the hospital for what was believed to be a sinus infection, only to return the following morning with the same symptoms, in more acute form.

At that point, doctors determined he had had at least one, and possibly two, strokes. Luckily, he suffered no permanent effects from the event.[80]

Two years later, he was back in the hospital, complaining of dizziness during a round of golf in hot weather. In 2004 he was well enough to attend the funeral of Ronald Reagan, who had died after long suffering from Alzheimer's disease. Moreover, his mind remained sharp. He continued to chastise Washington for the polarization of its politics, seconding Carter in blaming the "stalemate" in the capital on "extreme partisanship." Likewise, the two former presidents joined forces in 2004 to call for renewal of a ten-year-old ban on assault weapons, regarding it as a crime-fighting measure.[81] To their disappointment, Bush permitted the ban to expire.

Physically, however, Ford continued to weaken. He was in the hospital in December 2005 to get treatment for "a horrible cold" and then again a month later for pneumonia. In August 2006, he traveled to Minnesota's Mayo Clinic to have a pacemaker put in; that was followed by a second procedure to place stents into two coronary arteries. On 26 December, with his sons at his side—Susan had left two days earlier to spend Christmas with her family—the former president, who in November had become (and remains) the country's longest-lived president, passed away at his home. Commented Reverend Robert Certain, the pastor of Saint Margaret's Episcopal Church in Palm Desert, California, "I think he deliberately held on until Christmas was over. He didn't want to spoil anyone's holiday." Michael, who had received his ordination as a minister in 1984, performed the last rites.[82] Three days later, Saint Margaret's hosted a private service and a public viewing.

On 30 December, a plane carried the casket with Ford's body to Washington for a two-day viewing in the Capitol Rotunda. A funeral service took place at the Washington National Cathedral on 2 January 2007, with Kissinger, George H. W. Bush, NBC News anchor Tom Brokaw, and President George W. Bush offering eulogies. Immediately afterward, the casket traveled to Grand Rapids; to honor one of their own, Boy Scouts lined the entire route as Ford's remains were taken to the Ford Museum for another viewing. The next day, Ford's body was driven to Grace Episcopal Church for a service remembering the most famous member of its congregation. Cheney, Carter, Rumsfeld, President Bush, Kissinger, Alan Greenspan, Ron Nessen, and Ford Library and Museum director Richard Norton Smith were among those who attended. Finally, Ford's remains were transported to a small plot on the museum's north side, where a small group of family members and friends gathered. A Michigan National Guard unit offered a

Her four children behind her, Mrs. Ford pauses at the casket of her husband of nearly sixty years at the U.S. Capitol, 1 January 2007. Photo in the Gerald Ford Library, Ann Arbor, Michigan.

twenty-one-gun salute in honor of the former naval officer and president, while F-15 aircraft flew overhead. Before leaving town on 4 January, Ford's family gathered at the grave site to offer one final goodbye to their beloved husband, father, and grandfather.[83]

"History Will Treat Him Well"

"Jerry Ford brought closure to our national nightmare," opined Sam Nunn, a former Democratic senator from Georgia, "and history will treat him well."[84] One could argue that Nunn did not want to speak ill of the dead, but his comment did reflect a change of attitude toward the former president. Ford had never faced the criticism in his post-presidential years experienced by Carter, whose own party for a time shunned him. Democrats were not enthused about Carter's appearing at the 1984 National Convention. Mondale did not even seek his former boss's endorsement. Nor did Ford face the opprobrium aimed at Carter, whose writings and travels led to charges that he was anti-Israel and too willing to meet with repressive leaders. Yet the country's thirty-eighth president was criticized by his contemporaries for using his title to make money. And while he was not explicitly called one, his moderate Republicanism had placed him in the category of RINO.

Like Carter, however, Ford had witnessed a rehabilitation of his reputation by the late 1980s. In 1989, Hofstra University hosted a conference on his presidency, attended by academics, former administration officials, and Ford himself. Many of the speakers praised his administration. Stephen Ambrose, then a renowned scholar of Nixon, said Ford reestablished respect for the office of the president, and Patricia Witherspoon of the University of Texas noted that, unlike Carter or Reagan, Ford successfully found a balance between assigning responsibility to others (which Reagan did too much) and micromanaging his administration (as Carter had done). In August 1999, President Clinton awarded Ford the Medal of Freedom; two months later, he and Betty received the Congressional Gold Medal; and in November, the University of Michigan named its school of public policy after its alum.[85]

But nothing better pointed to the reassessment of Ford than views about his pardon of Nixon. Looking back, both Ford's contemporaries and scholars determined that his decision to save his predecessor from prosecution was just, lawful, and wise. Carter, who had used the pardon in 1976 as proof of the dishonesty that ran rampant in Washington, called it in 2005 "the right decision," *New York Times* columnist Anthony Lewis questioned whether his criticism of the pardon in 1976 was correct, and the scholar Mark Rozell referred to the pardon as legal and, "from the standpoint of serving justice . . . justified." Possibly the strongest expression of contrition felt by those who had written critically about Ford came from Richard Reeves. Twenty years earlier he had condemned the pardon, but he apologized in 1996. Ford, he wrote, "did his best and did what he thought he had to do: You have my respect and thanks Mr. President." Ford expressed his gratitude to Reeves for having "the guts to apologize. Most journalists don't do that. His article confirmed my belief that history would judge the pardon favorably." Indeed, in acknowledgment of Ford's belief in putting right ahead of politics, the John F. Kennedy Library in 2001 awarded him its prestigious Profile in Courage Award. Whether the reevaluation of Ford will continue remains to be seen. "Time makes everybody look better," commented Cornell University historian Joel Silbey, "particularly if you really landed on them at the time."[86]

What scholars have devoted less attention to is the significance of the partnership that Ford and Carter developed. Certainly Ford took criticism for spending large portions of his post-presidency playing golf rather than

Caroline Kennedy and Senator Ted Kennedy present President Ford with the John F. Kennedy Foundation's Profile in Courage Award, 21 May 2001. Photo in the Gerald Ford Library, Ann Arbor, Michigan.

engaging in a Carter-like humanitarian agenda. But by working together, the two former presidents from opposing political parties gave credibility to the array of issues to which they brought attention and symbolized the importance of bipartisanship. They also set a precedent for joint presidential initiatives. Bill Clinton teamed up with George H. W. Bush to provide assistance to victims of the tsunami that wreaked havoc in Southeast Asia in 2005; Clinton likewise joined with George W. Bush to establish the Presidential Leadership Scholars program.[87]

These post-presidential partnerships have done much good throughout the world, but they have failed to break through the partisanship that continues to infect Washington. If anything, it has become worse, marked by anger and harsh language. In looking at the GOP specifically, *Time* magazine in March 2016 asked, "What Happened to This Party?"[88] If he was alive today, Gerald Ford no doubt would ask the same.

Conclusion

During his eulogy at Gerald Ford's funeral, the historian Richard Norton Smith commented, "For sixty years he was a patriot before he was a partisan. . . . In contending for the greatest of all freedoms—the freedom to be oneself—he did not hesitate to dissent from party orthodoxy. This, too, should have come as no surprise—for he had first entered politics as a rebel with a cause, a young veteran of World War II who was unafraid to take on the entrenched isolationism of his own party's establishment."[1] There was much truth to that statement. Ford clearly loved his nation. And though it would be wrong to say he was not partisan, he was a pragmatic partisan, one who was loyal to the Republican Party but who did not always agree with the directions it took or the positions staked out by some in its ranks. Nor was he unwilling to reach across party lines and work with Democrats in seeking what he believed was best for the country. It was a standard he adopted long before he entered the White House.

Climbing the Ladder of Power

During a visit to his hometown of Grand Rapids, Michigan, to cast his vote on Election Day in 1976, Ford drove to Kent County Airport for the dedication of a mural that spotlighted important periods in his life. On the mural, one can see Ford as brother, Boy Scout, football player, park ranger, sailor, congressman, president, and parent. But it was the pictures of his parents that drew Ford's attention. Teary-eyed, his voice trembling, he told those at the event, "I owe everything to them, and to the training, the love, the leadership and whatever has been done by me in any way whatsoever—it is because of Jerry Ford, Sr., and Dorothy Ford."[2]

Ford's parents certainly were a powerful influence on him. From his stepfather, he learned to think for himself, to do what he believed was right, to enjoy sports, to work hard, to seek financial well-being with as little government assistance as possible, and to question the need for extensive federal oversight of the economy. His mother personified strength and perseverance in the face of what appeared to be overwhelming odds. Together, the loving couple also inculcated in Jerry the values of honesty, devotion to God, kindness, and patience.

It would be incorrect, however, to see all the future president's personality traits as coming from his parents. Boy Scouts, football, and his naval career were equally central to understanding who he became. The first two reinforced the values of self-restraint and of playing by the rules that his parents had instilled in him. Moreover, they taught him to be a loyal team member, to accept that losing was not the end of the world, to make sure that competition did not breed hate for others, and, when faced with a troop leader or coach who was not happy with him, to listen to criticism and learn from it. He also discovered a love for leadership, whether it be as an Eagle Scout or as captain of the football squad. From his service during World War II, he came to realize the danger aggression posed to the United States and to world peace.

Ford credited luck for his rise to positions of prominence, and there is no doubt that it was important to his career path. But it is equally apparent that Ford had every intention of making a name for himself. Determined to become a lawyer, he gave up the opportunity to play professional football, clawed his way into Yale University, got his degree, and left his first serious girlfriend, Phyllis Brown. During and immediately after World War II, he cozied up to individuals who themselves held powerful posts, including Captain Lester Hundt of the *Monterey* or the lawyer Julius Amberg. Even when facing long odds, such as when he sought to take on the Frank McKay political machine and dethrone Representative Bartel Jonkman, Ford refused to give up, using both his own personal connections and his membership in numerous civic organizations to develop the base of support he needed to enter Congress in 1948.

Thus began a congressional career that lasted a quarter century, a career in which a man who appeared to be lacking in leadership skills repeatedly achieved leadership positions. During his entire professional career, Ford never sponsored a major piece of legislation.[3] Nor was he an intellectual. Even his colleagues admitted he had trouble seeing beyond specific policies. Yet his ultimate goal was to become speaker of the House. He also had the personality of a leader, combining patience and cordiality with a desire to build political coalitions within his own party and with Democrats. Thanks to serendipity and to the connections he developed in the House, as a new member of Congress he gained a seat on the powerful Appropriations Committee. He earned the respect of both Republicans and Democrats, including those who served in the Oval Office. Democrats asked him to join the committee to write up legislation to form the National Aeronautics and Space Administration, John F. Kennedy identified him as someone to court, and Lyndon B. Johnson named him to the Warren Commission. Republicans in the House saw enough in Ford that they liked to encourage him to seek the positions of Republican Conference chair and of minority leader.

Throughout, Ford demonstrated that he was a party loyalist. He sought to curtail the size of government, restrain federal spending and oversight of the economy, and balance the budget. He stood behind Eisenhower 83 percent of the time, and he backed the president's positions as much as 89 percent of the time during Richard Nixon's tenure. He was far less prepared to back Democrats; for instance, in 1966, he endorsed only 40 percent of the proposals sent by Johnson to Capitol Hill.[4]

But those numbers tell only part of the story. Much depended on *what* Ford was voting for. He was particularly favorable toward programs aimed at strengthening national defense and containing communism abroad. Hence, and sometimes despite the discouragement of conservative Republicans, he endorsed the Defense Production Act, the Mutual Security Program, the Reciprocal Trade Agreements Program, the National Defense Education Act, the Foreign Assistance Act, the Peace Corps, the ousting from power of Dominican Republic president Juan Bosch, and the wars in both Korea and Vietnam. Indeed, he favored John F. Kennedy's foreign policy initiatives nearly 75 percent of the time, significantly higher than the average for most Republicans.[5]

Conversely, he took issue with those presidents, particularly Democratic ones, who adopted positions he regarded as detrimental to the global war against communism. He criticized President Harry Truman for not taking stronger measures to end the Korean War, Johnson for relying on ground forces rather than air and sea power to prevent the dominoes from falling in Southeast Asia, and both Kennedy and Johnson for not keeping closer tabs on Cuba. Similarly, he opposed the concept of "mutual deterrence," the Limited Test Ban Treaty (LTBT), the talks that led to the Nuclear Nonproliferation Treaty (NPT), and programs that focused on using economic as opposed to military means to contain communism.

He could also be inconsistent, particularly when Republicans sat in the White House. He accepted Dwight D. Eisenhower's call for restraining military spending in the name of balancing the budget. A congressman who had opposed the negotiations with Panama begun by Johnson, who had long denounced Communist China, and who rejected the LTBT and NPT was also likely to reject the Panama Canal treaty talks, the rapprochement with China, and the Strategic Arms Limitations Treaty (SALT I). But Nixon favored continuing the talks with Panama, sought better ties with Beijing, and signed SALT I, and Ford believed that in the name of party unity he had to support the president. In so doing, he found himself at odds with not just neoconservatives but the far right of the GOP.

That Ford was prepared to challenge members of his own party and stand behind about three-quarters of Kennedy's foreign policy initiatives showed how pragmatic he could be in his partisanship. But an even clearer indication of his willingness to reach across party lines could be seen in his support for environmental protections years before the modern environmental movement appeared. Having served as a park ranger, he came to enjoy the country's natural beauty and sought to curb pollution that imperiled flora, fauna, and humans. He backed the Clean Air Act, the National Wilderness Preservation System, the National Environmental Protection Act (NEPA), and the establishment of the Environmental Protection Agency (EPA). The latter two were endorsed by a fellow Republican, Richard Nixon, but they also had the support of Democrats. Some caution, though, is in order. Ford was not a preservationist who sought to make America's natural resources unavailable to humans; rather, he wanted the American public to enjoy them. Furthermore, he sought to balance federal and state authority, particularly when it came to the use of dollars to protect the environment. Finally, if given the choice between safeguarding the environment and economic growth, he favored the latter. One scholar of the Nixon presidency commented, "The 1970s became known as the 'environmental decade,' even though there was considerable backsliding during the Ford administration."[6]

Ford's desire to balance federal and state power was even more apparent when it came to civil rights. He had grown up with friends who were African American and empathized with the desire of blacks to combat racism in the United States. Hence, he endorsed the Supreme Court's *Brown v. Board of Education* decision and denounced the Southern Manifesto. Yet he was opposed to public housing and forced busing. He also preferred that local governments rather than Washington enforce the Civil Rights Act of 1964 and the Voting Rights Act of 1965.

Ford was most resistant to social welfare programs. He denounced Medicare, Medicaid, and the War on Poverty because he believed they encouraged Americans to rely too much on the government and not enough on their own efforts. They also sapped money that could be used for balancing the budget or for defense. Nor was he favorable toward raising the minimum wage, believing that it would interfere with the free market and hurt the economy. Still, he was not doctrinaire. He stood behind the Family Assistance Plan, no doubt in part because it was a Nixon initiative, but also because in return, the president endorsed proposals Ford favored, such as giving more revenue to the states and encouraging people to get off the welfare rolls and find a job.

Ford's stances on domestic and foreign policy drew him into the very thing he claimed he wanted to avoid: an alliance with southern Democrats. Moderates and liberals within the GOP had cited that relationship as a reason for removing Charles Halleck (R-Ind.) from his position as minority leader. Yet Ford had, reluctantly, stood behind Barry Goldwater in the 1964 presidential election, despite the fact that Goldwater had taken positions in alignment with those of southern Democrats. And even though Minority Leader Ford had called for cutting ties with southern Democrats, that association remained firm. During Ford's tenure as minority leader, Republicans joined with southern Democrats in retaining the U.S. commitment to Vietnam, in rejecting higher taxes to pay for the war and the Great Society, in assailing President Johnson's proposals to combat crime, and in altering the language of a civil rights bill forwarded to Congress by Johnson in 1967. Ford's own positions on civil rights before becoming minority leader and his seeming unwillingness to forgo the Republican relationship with southern Democrats after getting the GOP's top congressional spot may have helped Nixon's southern strategy, but they did little to give minorities and the poor reason to believe the Republican Party had their interests at heart.

The other significant shortcoming of Ford's tenure as minority leader was his naïveté, particularly when it came to his friendship with Richard Nixon. Ford's determination to impeach Supreme Court Justice William Douglas was unwise and smacked of revenge rather than an effort to remove from office someone who had committed a legal transgression. Likewise, both as minority leader and as vice president, he convinced himself that Nixon had no involvement in Watergate, despite increasingly solid evidence that the incumbent had violated the law. In both cases, Ford faced particularly strong criticism from constituents and from the media. Yet playing football, he wrote, "helped me develop a thick hide, and in later years whenever critics assailed me, I just let their jibes roll off my back."[7]

Ford held firm to his desire to become minority leader, despite the impact it had on his family. He was an absent husband and father, one who tried to be home for Sunday dinners and took the family on yearly ski trips, but who otherwise spent most of his day at work or on the road. Betty turned to housekeeper Clara Powell for help in raising four well-rounded children, but it was hard on Mrs. Ford to see her husband so little, and for Michael, John, Steve, and Susan to have a father who was away so often. Betty was even more unhappy when her spouse became vice president of the United States, but at least she could look forward to him retiring come 1976. That was before a series of remarkable events moved him from the vice presidency into the Oval Office in a period of eight months.

A Caretaker President?

Years after his tenure as president ended, Ford said, "I want to be remembered as a . . . nice person, who worked at the job, and who left the White House in better shape than when I took it over." By all accounts, Americans considered him a decent person. Even if he did pardon Nixon, there was a lot more to like about Ford than about his predecessor. The problem was that aside from the pardon, Americans could think of nothing of substance to say about their nation's only unelected president. No better evidence of that were the results of a Gallup poll taken after Ford left office: to the question of what Ford's greatest achievement was, the most common response was "no great achievement."[8]

Arguably, the reason Americans regarded Ford's presidency as lacking accomplishment was the difficulties he encountered in building an agenda reflective of his moderate conservatism. He faced pressure from his party's far right, which criticized both his domestic and foreign policies, including on taxes, inflation, and détente. Simultaneously, he confronted an assertive Congress controlled by Democrats who insisted on reining in the "imperial presidency." And he made matters worse by pardoning Nixon, which, in an environment where anger directed at Washington was already endemic, contributed to a midterm election that brought into power a group of younger Democrats who attacked the existing power structure on Capitol Hill and pushed their party more to the left.

But it would be inaccurate to blame Ford's problems solely on outside forces or bad luck. Ford was comfortable around people who might have large egos, who were highly intelligent and driven, and whose views might not be identical with his. His friendship with Mel Laird, dating from his days in Congress, was proof of that. Likewise, as president, he surrounded himself with people ranging from the more liberal Nelson Rockefeller to conservatives such as Donald Rumsfeld and William Simon.[9] It all reflected Ford's desire to build coalitions and to hear different points of view before making decisions. Where the president ran into trouble was his refusal to get rid of Nixon holdovers. Consequently, it became all the harder for him to separate his tenure from his predecessor's. Moreover, when the press began to publicize the fighting between those holdovers and Ford's team, voters could not but see an administration at war with itself and, hence, unable to accomplish anything significant.

Ford also lacked a vision for the nation. Ford's press secretary, Ron Nessen, found the president's subordinates worrying about that very issue as the winter of 1975 approached. "Did he have an overall plan for governing?," they asked. "What was he trying to accomplish by the end of the year and in the long run?" In a bitter memoir, John Casserly, who worked on Ford's speechwriting team, commented that in early 1976 he tried to get his superiors, Robert Hartmann and Paul Theis, "to offer the country some 'vision,' as well as some idea of what the President stands for, but they have resisted the thought."[10]

Because many of Ford's aides served under Nixon, and because Ford appeared to have neither policies nor a vision to set him apart from his predecessor, the impression developed that he was little more than a caretaker, whose job it was to keep the chair behind the desk in the Oval Office warm until either he won the presidency in his own right or his successor entered the White House. "Appointed rather than elected and elevated to power by freakish circumstances," the *New York Times* commented in February 1975, "Mr. Ford has no democratic mandate. His party was dramatically repudiated in last fall's mid-term Congressional and state elections." Jim Shuman, the associate director of communications during the Ford administration, worried about such assessments. In August 1975, a month after Ford announced his candidacy for the presidency, he asked, "Does the Ford Administration have a vision to carry the country through the 1980's and into the next 100 years? Or is it to be little more than a nuts and bolts caretaker of the machinery of government? These questions, which strike at the heart of what could become a major campaign issue, began to surface in the nation's press even before the President announced he would be a candidate."[11]

The claim that Ford was little more than a caretaker continued into 1976. In a withering critique of Ford's pardon of Nixon, journalist Clark Mollenhoff wrote, "Ford was truly an 'accidental president,' and his only accomplishments were combinations of accidents and non-action." During that year, both Illinois congressman Philip Crane, a member of the GOP's right wing, and Ronald Reagan used the word "caretaker" to describe Ford's tenure.[12] That assessment still resonates among many scholars and in textbooks.[13]

There is reason to assert that Ford was a caretaker. He became president not through an election but by the most unprecedented means following the resignation of both the country's vice president and then president. In turn, he had no mandate to pursue his own agenda. On foreign policy, he adhered to the initiatives begun under his predecessor, such as pursuing Middle East peace, détente, a second Strategic Arms Limitation Treaty, a treaty on the Panama Canal, and a commitment to Vietnam after the last U.S. troops withdrew. Even when facing new diplomatic crises in Turkey and Cambodia, Ford appeared to defer to a Nixon holdover, Henry Kissinger. The steps Ford took to rein in America's intelligence agencies also appeared unremarkable, for he acted under congressional pressure rather than independently. Domestically, he rejected new programs, except for those related to energy, on the grounds that they could increase the deficit. One of his few initiatives, the Whip Inflation Now campaign, was dead on arrival. Otherwise, he acted only when his hand was forced. He rejected environmental legislation, viewing it as harmful to the economy. He flip-flopped on taxes, reluctantly signed a forced-busing bill and offered assistance to New York City, accepted comprehensive energy legislation that was in many ways unlike what he favored, and endorsed the Revenue Readjustment Act even though it cut spending by only about one-third of what he wanted. In the name of his no-new-programs pledge, he employed the veto sixty-six times—twenty-three more than Nixon—during his 895-day tenure. Said one lawmaker, "Jerry Ford uses the veto as if he were still the minority leader voting 'Nay.'" Indeed, he had more vetoes than agenda proposals.[14]

And Ford admitted in his memoir what others said about him, that he was not an intellectual or original thinker: "If 'vision' is to be defined as inspirational rhetoric describing how this or that new government program will better the human condition in the next sixty days, then I'll have to confess I didn't have it."[15] Consequently, what the country saw was an administration that appeared to tackle policy on a case-by-case basis. That Ford seemed unable or unwilling to stop well-publicized infighting among his own appointees and Nixon holdovers, to take a chance on new initiatives, or to have someone other than Kissinger oversee the country's foreign policy convinced many voters that he had little in the way of leadership skills that might set his administration apart from Nixon's.

Even if he was not an intellectual, Ford was highly intelligent. Yet the impression he left with voters was that of a dull-witted klutz. During a visit to Kansas in February 1975, Ford expressed his love as a child for L. Frank Baum's book *The Wonderful Wizard of Oz,* prompting the press corps to come up with a song based on the Scarecrow's song in the 1939 movie. Went one verse,

> I could overcome inflation
> Put gas in every station
> And we would feel no pain
> I could make the Arabs cower
> I could be an Eisenhower
> If I only had a brain.

In one of the many jokes about Ford that he compiled in his 1976 *The Jerry Ford Joke Book*, Max Brodnick linked Ford-as-klutz to Ford-as-caretaker: "Washington insiders aren't surprised by all those accidents the President has been having. After all, he is an accidental President."[16] It proved to be impossible to overcome the image that he was an intellectually lacking buffoon who protected Nixon from prosecution and could not solve the nation's pressing problems, and that image cost him on Election Day.

Yet, as early as 1976, a counterargument came from none other than one of Ford's most hostile early critics, Richard Reeves. In the aftermath of a nation torn apart by the social movements of the 1960s and Vietnam and enmeshed in the doubt in its elected officials left behind by both Vietnam and Watergate, wrote Reeves, Americans favored a mediocre, simpleminded president who did not offer leadership. In that respect, Ford was "not an accident or an anachronism, not some chummy caretaker who stumbled into our highest office. Gerald Ford is the future."[17]

The reappraisal of Ford-as-caretaker continued as more revisionist accounts of his term in office appeared. Numerous individuals, from Ford's contemporaries to scholars, have credited the country's thirty-eighth president with restoring the integrity of the Oval Office. Roger Porter wrote in 1988 that Ford "left to future presidents a legacy of remarkable skill not only in building morale within the executive branch but also in adopting decision-making approaches in the major areas of federal policy that skillfully took into account the strengths of the team he had assembled and the policy realities he had to address." In a laudatory account of his former boss, James Cannon saw Ford as someone who turned the economy around, "put an end to the Vietnam War—albeit a ragged end," and signed the Helsinki Accords. The historian Yanek Mieczkowski seconded Cannon's praise, contending that Ford deserved more credit than he received for turning the economy around, and pointed out that his call for industrial deregulation set a precedent for both Jimmy Carter and Ronald Reagan. If Ford failed to accomplish more, it was not for lack of trying but, rather, the result of a "cynical" public and an assertive Congress dominated by the opposition. To *New York Times* columnist Thomas Friedman, Ford was the country's "first energy president," one who was willing to impose fees on imported crude to curb oil consumption and who could have rejected the Energy Policy and Conservation Act but did not. Former Central Intelligence Agency director Robert Gates wrote that the Helsinki Accords "provided the spark that kindled widespread resistance to communist authority and the organization of numerous independent groups throughout Eastern Europe and even in the Soviet Union determined to bring change." Likewise, historian Andrew Bacevich argued that the outcome of Helsinki "probably made a greater contribution to undermining the Soviet Union than did the reconstitution of U.S. military power in the 1980s."[18] It would take another fifteen years for the Cold War to come to an end, and although the policies of Soviet premier Mikhail Gorbachev must be taken into account,[19] individuals such as Gates suggest the Ford administration deserves credit for its part in the process.

A Legacy Forgotten?

Freed from the constraints of Washington after January 1977, Ford's pragmatic partisanship became all the more apparent. He remained loyal to Republicans who ran for office, even if he did not always agree with their policies, but he began to reach out to Democrats, particularly Jimmy Carter. Moreover, he began to stake out positions that he never would have taken as a lawmaker or president, either because they were not in accord with his values at the time or because they risked political suicide. He became more critical of Israel, endorsed the right to an abortion and homosexual rights, opposed the abolition of the assault weapons ban, and expressed dismay at the continued rightward drift of his own party.

Ford, however, will almost certainly be remembered not for what he did after he left the presidency or even for what he achieved before entering the Oval Office. Rather, it is likely that he will continue to be regarded as America's only unelected president, as a caretaker whose sole accomplishment of any significance was pardoning Richard Nixon. If that is the case, it will be most unfortunate, for Ford personified something much more important, best expressed by a Democrat, Representative John Dingell, during his eulogy for the former president: "I ask that you and my fellow colleagues join me in remembering President Gerald R. Ford, and honoring him by carrying out his legacy of bipartisanship . . . in the years to come."[20] It is an entreaty that has been forgotten in Washington.

Notes

Abbreviations Used in Notes

ANF	Alphabetical Name Files
BHL	Bentley Historical Library, University of Michigan, Ann Arbor
CFP	Carter Family Papers
CGP	Charles Goodell Papers
CQA	*Congressional Quarterly Almanac*
CR	*Congressional Record*
EHP	Edward Hutchinson Papers
FRUS	*Foreign Relations of the United States*
GFL	Gerald Ford Library, Ann Arbor, Michigan
GFMOPL	Gerald Ford Materials from Other Presidential Libraries
GRFCP	Gerald R. Ford Congressional Papers
GRFM	Gerald R. Ford Museum, Grand Rapids, Michigan
GRFS	Gerald R. Ford Scrapbooks
GROHC	Grand Rapids Oral History Collection
GRPL	Grand Rapids Public Library
GVTP	Gordon Vander Till Papers
JCL	Jimmy Carter Library, Atlanta, Georgia
JECF	James E. Connor Files
JFKL	John F. Kennedy Library, Boston, Massachusetts
JGCF	John G. Carlson Files
JKJC	Jacob K. Javits Collection
JMCF	James M. Cannon Files

JMCP	James M. Cannon Papers
JMCRIN	James M. Cannon Research Interviews and Notes
JMF	John Marsh Files
JWML	J. Willard Marriott Library, University of Utah, Salt Lake City
LC	Library of Congress, Washington, D.C.
LLF	Loen and Leppert Files
LWSF	L. William Seidman Files
MLFF	Max L. Friedersdorf Files
MRP	Michael Raoul-Duval Papers
NARP	Nelson A. Rockefeller Papers
NYPL	New York Public Library
OJF	O'Donnell and Jenkins Files
PBF	Philip Buchen Files
PFEM	Papers of Frank E. Moss
PHF	Presidential Handwriting File
PLFO	Papers of Lawrence F. O'Brien
PMLS	Papers of Mary Louise Smith
PPPUS	*Public Papers of the Presidents of the United States*
PRPG	Papers of Robert P. Griffin
RAC	Rockefeller Archive Center, Sleepy Hollow, New York
RBCF	Richard B. Cheney Files
RKWF	Robert K. Wolthuis Files
RLPRIN	Robert L. Peabody Research Interview Notes
RMNL	Richard M. Nixon Library, Yorba Linda, California
RRPL	Ronald Reagan Presidential Library, Simi Valley, California
RTHF	Robert T. Hartmann Files
RTHP	Robert T. Hartmann Papers
SUNY-SB	State University of New York—Stony Brook
UIWA	University of Iowa Women's Archive, Iowa City, Iowa
WESP	William E. Simon Papers
WETF	William E. Timmons Files
WHCF	White House Central File
WHSF	White House Staff Files
YMRI	Yanek Mieczkowski Research Interviews

Preface

1. Edward L. Schapsmeier and Frederick H. Schapsmeier, *Gerald R. Ford's Date with Destiny: A Political Biography* (New York: Peter Lang, 1989); Douglas Brinkley, *Gerald R. Ford* (New York: Times Books, 2007); James M. Cannon, *Gerald R. Ford: An Honorable Life* (Ann Arbor: University of Michigan Press, 2013).

2. For a good overview of the literature on this score, see Jason Friedman, "Just a Caretaker?," in *A Companion to Gerald R. Ford and Jimmy Carter*, ed. Scott Kaufman (Malden, Mass.: Wiley Blackwell, 2016), 196–210.

3. Andrew Dugan and Frank Newport, "Americans Rate JFK as Top American Pres-

ident," Gallup, http://www.gallup.com/poll/165902/americans-rate-jfk-top-modern-president.aspx, accessed 24 March 2016; "Obama Is First as Worst President since World War II, Quinnipiac University National Poll Finds; More Voters Say Romney Would Have Been Better," http://www.quinnipiac.edu/images/polling/us/us07022014_U73jabn.pdf, accessed 24 March 2016; John Dumbrell, "Agendas, Speakers, and Spokesmen," in *A Companion to Gerald R. Ford and Jimmy Carter*, ed. Scott Kaufman (Malden, Mass.: Wiley Blackwell, 2016), 548.

Chapter One: A Ford, Not a King

1. Oral history, Mr. and Mrs. Paul Goebel, 25 January 1980, interviewed by Thomas Soapes, and oral history, Philip Buchen, 18 January 1980, interviewed by Thomas Soapes, GROHC, Box 1; oral history, Gerald Ford, 13 November 1990, interviewed by James Cannon, Ford, Gerald—Interview, 11/13/90, oral history, Gerald Ford, 26 April 1990, interviewed by James Cannon, Ford, Gerald—Interview, 4/26/90, and oral history, Gerald Ford, 22 April 1992, interviewed by James Cannon, Ford, Gerald—Interview, 4/22/92, JMCRIN, Box 1, GFL.

2. James M. Cannon, *Time and Chance: Gerald Ford's Appointment with History* (Ann Arbor: University of Michigan Press, 1994), 2–3; Hendrik Booraem V, *Young Jerry Ford: Athlete and Citizen* (Grand Rapids: William B. Eerdmans, 2013), 3. I want to thank Patricia Rose of the Knoxville Public Library for identifying the name of the college Dorothy Gardner attended. St. Mary's itself no longer exists.

3. Cannon, *Time and Chance*, 1–2, 6; Booraem, *Young Jerry Ford*, 4.

4. Booraem, *Young Jerry Ford*, 5–6; Cannon, *Time and Chance*, 5; U.S. Naval Intelligence Service, "Ninth Naval District Investigation Report," U.S. Department of the Navy, Office of Naval Intelligence, Investigatory records on Gerald Ford, applicant for a commission, 1941–1942, www.fordlibrarymuseum.gov/library/document/0069/2825430.pdf, accessed 4 January 2014; Booraem, *Young Jerry Ford*, 5–7, 9; Cannon, *Time and Chance*, 5–6.

5. Marilyn Coleman, Lawrence H. Ganong, and Kelly Warzinik, *Family Life in 20th-Century America* (New York: Greenwood, 2007), 29–30; Gay C. Kitson, *Portrait of Divorce: Adjustment to Marital Breakdown*, with William M. Holmes (New York: Guilford Press, 1992), 11; Kristin Celello, *Making Marriage Work: A History of Marriage and Divorce in the Twentieth-Century United States* (Chapel Hill: University of North Carolina Press, 2009), 21; Booraem, *Young Jerry Ford*, 7–9.

6. Z. Z. Lydens, ed., *The Story of Grand Rapids* (Grand Rapids, Mich.: Kregel, 1967), 19, 48; Booraem, *Young Jerry Ford*, 21; G. Christian Carron, *Grand Rapids Furniture: The Story of America's Furniture City* (Grand Rapids, Mich.: Public Museum of Grand Rapids, 1993), 27.

7. Booraem, *Young Jerry Ford*, 21–23; Carron, *Grand Rapids Furniture*, 48.

8. Charles W. Dunn and J. David Woodard, *The Conservative Tradition in America*, rev. ed. (Lanham, Md.: Rowman and Littlefield, 2003), 40–41; Booraem, *Young Jerry Ford*, 9; Douglas Brinkley, *Gerald R. Ford* (New York: Times Books, 2007), 148; Lee Hamilton, telephone interview by Scott Kaufman, 3 September 2015; Richard Lugar, telephone interview by Scott Kaufman, 22 July 2015; oral history, David

Frey, 13 May 2010, interviewed by Richard Norton Smith, http://geraldrfordfoundation.org/centennial/oralhistory/david-frey/, accessed 24 December 2016.

9. See George R. Ford, MyRootsPlace: Genealogy, History, Archives & More, http://myrootsplace.com/getperson.php?personID=I151667&tree=MRP, accessed 23 January 2015.

10. Booraem, *Young Jerry Ford*, 9–10, 23.

11. Ibid., 10–11; Gerald R. Ford, *A Time to Heal: The Autobiography of Gerald R. Ford* (New York: Harper and Row, 1979), 44–45; Cannon, *Time and Chance*, 8–9.

12. "Ford Occupied Many Local Addresses," *Grand Rapids Press*, 27 December 2006, insert, 3; James Cannon, *Gerald R. Ford: An Honorable Life* (Ann Arbor: University of Michigan Press, 2013), 43; Ford, *Time to Heal*, 43.

13. Booraem, *Young Jerry Ford*, 12; Ford, *Time to Heal*, 45.

14. Booraem, *Young Jerry Ford*, 12–13; Ford, *Time to Heal*, 44; Hendrik Booraem V, *The Education of Gerald Ford* (Grand Rapids, Mich.: William B. Eerdmans, 2016), 72–73.

15. Booraem, *Young Jerry Ford*, 13.

16. Ibid., 30–31, 32; oral history, Gerald Ford, 25 April 1992, interviewed by James Cannon, Ford, Gerald—Interview, 4/25/92, JMCRIN, Box 1, GFL; Cannon, *Gerald R. Ford*, 43.

17. Blair H. Laackman, *Gerald R. Ford's Scouting Years* (Grand Rapids: West Michigan Shores Council #266, Boy Scouts of America, 1982), 24; oral history, Gerald Ford, 25 April 1990, interviewed by James Cannon, Ford, Gerald—Interview, 4/25/90, JMCRIN, Box 1, GFL; Cannon, *Gerald R. Ford*, 44.

18. Cannon, *Time and Chance*, 10; Ford, *Time to Heal*, 46.

19. Cannon, *Gerald R. Ford*, 44–45.

20. Notes from interview with Betty Ford, 30 April 1990, interviewed by James Cannon, Ford, Betty—Interview, 4/30/90, JMCRIN, Box 1; oral history, Gerald Ford, 24 April 1990, interviewed by James Cannon, Ford, Gerald—Interview, 4/24/90, JMCRIN, Box 1, GFL; Cannon, *Time and Chance*, 12.

21. Cannon, *Time and Chance*, 12; Ford, *Time to Heal*, 46–47; Booraem, *Education of Gerald Ford*, 84.

22. Oral history, Art Brown, 26 January 1980, interviewed by Thomas Soapes, GROHC, Box 1, GFL; Dave Anderson, *The Minnesota-Wisconsin College Football Rivalry* (Charleston, S.C.: Arcadia, 2015), 33; Buzz Thomas, telephone interview by Scott Kaufman, 16 October 2015.

23. Cannon, *Gerald R. Ford*, 45–46, 48; Ford interview, 24 April 1990; "South Places Three Men on Herald's Second All-City Eleven," *Grand Rapids Herald*, 1 December 1929.

24. Booraem, *Young Jerry Ford*, 31, 36, 38.

25. James J. Flink, *The Automobile Age* (Cambridge: MIT Press, 1990), 221; Lydens, *Story of Grand Rapids*, 79–80.

26. Cannon, *Gerald R. Ford*, 46, 48; Booraem, *Young Jerry Ford*, 95; Ford interview, 25 April 1990.

27. Ford, *Time to Heal*, 47–48; Cannon, *Gerald R. Ford*, 46.

28. Ford, *Time to Heal*, 48; Booraem, *Young Jerry Ford*, 18–19.

29. Ford interview, 24 April 1990; oral history, Dick Ford, 4 August 2008, interviewed by Richard Norton Smith, http://geraldrfordfoundation.org/centennial/oralhistory/dick-ford/, accessed 11 May 2015; "1930 All-City Selections," *Grand Rapids Herald*, 30 November 1930.

30. Booraem, *Young Jerry Ford*, 39; U.S. Naval Intelligence Service, "Ninth Naval District Investigation Report."

31. Ford interview, 24 April 1990; Cannon, *Gerald R. Ford*, 48–49; Krause to Kipke, 11 May 1931, on display at GRFM.

32. Ford interview, 24 April 1990; Cannon, *Gerald R. Ford*, 49; Ford, *Time to Heal*, 50–51.

33. Cannon, *Gerald R. Ford*, 49–50; Ford interview, 24 April 1990; Ford, *Time to Heal*, 51.

34. Ford, *Time to Heal*, 52.

35. Ibid., 52–53; Cannon, *Time and Chance*, 20; Ford interview, 24 April 1990.

36. Laurence McQuillan, "Looking Back, Ford Says He Has No Regrets," *USA Today*, 17 July 2000; Cannon, *Time and Chance*, 20; Bud Vestal, *Jerry Ford, Up Close: An Investigative Biography* (New York: Coward, McCann, and Geoghegan, 1974), 45; University of Michigan, Transcript of Gerald R. Ford, Gerald R. Ford Student File, GFL.

37. Ford, *Time to Heal*, 54; Cannon, *Time and Chance*, 24.

38. Ford interview, 24 April 1990.

39. Cannon, *Time and Chance*, 21–22.

40. Ibid., 23.

41. Ford interview, 22 April 1992; U.S. Naval Intelligence Service, "Ninth Naval District Investigation Report"; Cannon, *Time and Chance*, 24.

42. Ford, *Time to Heal*, 55–56.

43. Ibid., 56; Ford interview, 24 April 1990.

44. Ford interview, 24 April 1990; Cannon, *Time and Chance*, 21, 31.

45. Ford interview, 24 April 1990; *PPPUS*, 1975: 1214.

46. Cannon, *Time and Chance*, 24–26; U.S. Naval Intelligence Service, "Ninth Naval District Investigation Report."

47. Cannon, *Time and Chance*, 26–27; Ford, *Time to Heal*, 56.

48. Cannon *Time and Chance*, 27; Ford interview, 24 April 1990; oral history, Phyllis Brown, 28 April 1990, interviewed by James Cannon, Brown, Phyllis—Interview, 11/13/90, JMCRIN, Box 3, GFL.

49. Ford, *Time to Heal*, 56; Brown interview, 28 April 1990; Ford interview, 24 April 1990.

50. Brown interview, 28 April 1990; Ford interview, 24 April 1990; Cannon, *Time and Chance*, 29.

51. Cannon, *Time and Chance*, 28–29; Brown interview, 28 April 1990; Ford interview, 24 April 1990; Ford, *Time to Heal*, 57.

52. Cannon, *Time and Chance*, 30.

53. Ibid.; Lydens, *Story of Grand Rapids*, 94–95.

54. Cannon, *Time and Chance*, 30–31.

55. Ford interview, 13 November 1990.

56. Brown interview, 28 April 1990; notes from interview with Gerald Ford, 21 April 1993, interviewed by James Cannon, Ford, Gerald—Interview 4/21/93, JMCRIN, Box 1, GFL.

57. Cannon, *Gerald R. Ford*, 56; interview with President Gerald R. Ford and Philip W. Buchen, undated [1995], and interview between Walter Russell and Phil Buchen, 18 May 1995, vertical file, "Ford Interview," GRPL; Ford interview, 24 April 1990.

58. Ford and Buchen interview, undated; oral history, Philip Buchen, 15 February 1990, interviewed by James Cannon, Buchen, Philip—Interview, 2/15/90, JMCRIN, Box 3, GFL. Twelve hundred dollars in 1941 would be about $20,130 in 2016.

59. Buchen interview, 15 February 1990; Ford, *Time to Heal*, 57.

60. Notes from interview with Ford, 1 April 1993, interviewed by James Cannon, Ford, Gerald—Interview, 4/21/93, JMCRIN, Box 1, GFL; Cannon, *Time and Chance*, 33–34; Ford, *Time to Heal*, 58.

61. Ford, *Time to Heal*, 58; Ford interview, 13 November 1990; Cannon, *Time and Chance*, 35; Bob Drury and Tom Calvin, *Halsey's Typhoon: The True Story of a Fighting Admiral, an Epic Storm, and an Untold Rescue* (New York: Grove Press, 2007), 154.

62. Ford, *Time to Heal*, 58–59; Drury and Calvin, *Halsey's Typhoon*, 154.

63. Ford, *Time to Heal*, 59–60; Drury and Calvin, *Halsey's Typhoon*, 153, 155, 157; C. Raymond Calhoun, *Typhoon, the Other Enemy: The Third Fleet and the Pacific Storm of December 1944* (Annapolis, Md.: Naval Institute Press, 1981), 86.

64. Cannon, *Time and Chance*, 38.

65. Ibid., 39.

66. Ibid., 40; Ford, *Time to Heal*, 60–61.

67. Cannon, *Time and Chance*, 41.

68. Ibid., 42.

69. Ibid., 42–43.

70. John Robert Greene, *Betty Ford: Candor and Courage in the White House* (Lawrence: University Press of Kansas, 2004), 2; John Pope, "Elizabeth Ann (Betty) Bloomer Ford," in *American First Ladies: Their Lives and Their Legacy*, 2nd ed., ed. Lewis L. Gould (New York: Routledge, 2001), 364.

71. Greene, *Betty Ford*, 3–4.

72. Ibid., 5–10.

73. Cannon, *Time and Chance*, 47; Ford, *Time to Heal*, 65.

74. Cannon, *Time and Chance*, 32–33, 44; William A. Syers, "The Political Beginnings of Gerald R. Ford: Anti-Bossism, Internationalism, and the Congressional Campaign of 1948," *Presidential Studies Quarterly* 20, no. 1 (1990): 131, 132.

75. Cannon, *Time and Chance*, 44–45, 48–49; oral history, Willard B. Ver Meulen, 26 January 1980, interviewed by Thomas Soapes, GROHC, Box 1, GFL.

76. Oral history, Gerald Ford, 30 April 1990, interviewed by James Cannon, Ford, Gerald—Interview, 4/30/90, JMCRIN, Box 1, GFL.

77. Ford, *Time to Heal*, 64, 65–66; Syers, "Political Beginnings of Gerald R. Ford," 133; Cannon, *Time and Chance*, 49.

78. Ford, *Time to Heal*, 66; Cannon, *Time and Chance*, 49, 50.

79. Oral history, Collins C. Clark, 28 January 1980, interviewed by Thomas F. Soapes, GROHC, Box 1, GFL.

80. Ford, *Time to Heal*, 67; oral history, Dorothy L. Judd, 27 January 1980, interviewed by Thomas Soapes, GROHC, Box 1, GFL; Ford interview, 25 April 1990.

81. "Most Incumbents Win in Primaries," *New York Times*, 16 September 1948; Betty Ford interview notes, 30 April 1990.

82. Ford interview, 30 April 1990; Ford, *Time to Heal*, 67; Jeffrey S. Ashley, *Betty Ford: A Symbol of Strength* (New York: Nova History, 2003), 31–32; Edward L. Schapsmeier and Frederick Schapsmeier, *Gerald R. Ford's Date with Destiny: A Political Biography* (New York: Peter Lang, 1989), 30; Cannon, *Time and Chance*, 51; Betty Ford, *The Times of My Life*, with Chris Chase (New York: Harper and Row, 1978), 61.

83. Ford interview, 30 April 1990; Betty Ford interview notes, 30 April 1990; Ford, *Time to Heal*, 67–68.

84. Brinkley, *Gerald R. Ford*, 18.

85. Betty Ford interview notes, 30 April 1990; Betty Ford, *Times of My Life*, ix, 55.

Chapter Two: Climbing the Ladder of Power

1. Andrew E. Busch, *Truman's Trumpets: The 1948 Election and the Making of Postwar America* (Lawrence: University Press of Kansas, 2012), 128, 196–197; David Pietrusza, *1948: Harry Truman's Improbable Victory and the Year That Transformed America's Role in the World* (New York: Union Square, 2011), 362–363.

2. John Pope, "Elizabeth Ann (Betty) Bloomer Ford," in *American First Ladies: Their Lives and Their Legacy*, 2nd ed., ed. Lewis L. Gould (New York: Routledge, 2001), 366; oral history, Gerald Ford, 23 April 1992, interviewed by James Cannon, Ford, Gerald—Interview, 4/23/92, and oral history, Gerald Ford, 30 April 1990, interviewed by James Cannon, Ford, Gerald—Interview, 4/30/90, JMCRIN, Box 1, GFL; Bud Vestal, *Jerry Ford, Up Close: An Investigative Biography* (New York: Coward, McCann and Geoghegan, 1974), 103; Gerald R. Ford, *A Time to Heal: The Autobiography of Gerald R. Ford* (New York: Harper and Row, 1979), 68; Betty Ford, *The Times of My Life*, with Chris Chase (New York: Harper and Row, 1978), 74.

3. Oral history, Gerald Ford, 25 April 1990, Ford, Gerald—Interview, 4/25/90, JMCRIN, Box 1, GFL; James Cannon, *Time and Chance: Gerald Ford's Appointment with History* (Ann Arbor: University of Michigan Press, 1994), 53.

4. Cannon, *Time and Chance*, 53; Conrad Black, *Richard M. Nixon: A Life in Full* (New York: PublicAffairs, 2007), 98; oral history, Gerald Ford, 22 April 1992, interviewed by James Cannon, Ford, Gerald—Interview, 4/22/92, JMCRIN, Box 1, GFL.

5. Ford interview, 22 April 1992; Cannon, *Time and Chance*, 54.

6. Ford interview, 22 April 1992; oral history, Gerald Ford, 22 April 1993, interviewed by James Cannon, Ford, Gerald—Interview, 4/22/93, JMCRIN, Box 1, GFL; Ford interview, 25 April 1990.

7. Gary A. Donaldson, *Truman Defeats Dewey* (Lexington: University Press of Kentucky, 1999), 30.

8. Ibid., 3, 130; David M. Jordan, *FDR, Dewey, and the Election of 1944* (Bloomington: Indiana University Press, 2011), 253, 269, 307; David McCullough, *Truman* (New York: Simon and Schuster, 1992), 669–670, 672–673; Lewis L. Gould, *Grand Old Party: A History of the Republicans* (New York: Random House, 2003), 315, 316, 321.

9. Edward L. Schapsmeier and Frederick Schapsmeier, *Gerald R. Ford's Date with Destiny: A Political Biography* (New York: Peter Lang, 1989), 40.

10. "Gov't May Drop Right to Include Retailers in Bill," *Billboard*, May 21, 1949, 15; "Civil Rights Record of Gerald Ford," 21 June 1976, PHF, Box C42; Library of Congress, Congressional Research Service, "Analysis of the Philosophy and Voting Record of Representative Gerald R. Ford, Nominee for Vice President of the United States," 25 October 1973, Ford—Analysis of Philosophy and Voting Record of Rep. Gerald Ford (1), EHP, Box 89, GFL; Schapsmeier and Schapsmeier, *Gerald R. Ford's Date with Destiny*, 41–42.

11. "Analysis of the Philosophy and Voting Record of Representative Gerald R. Ford"; Judith Resnik, "Federalism(s), Feminism, Families and the Constitution," in *Women and the United States Constitution: History, Interpretation, and Practice*, ed. Sibyl A. Schwarzenbach and Patricia Smith (New York: Columbia University Press, 2003), 134–135.

12. Donald R. McCoy, *The Presidency of Harry S. Truman* (Lawrence: University Press of Kansas, 1984), 174; *CR*, 1950: 2501.

13. *CR*, 1950: 11996, 13737; Schapsmeier and Schapsmeier, *Gerald R. Ford's Date with Destiny*, 46; Chester J. Pach Jr. and Elmo Richardson, *Presidency of Dwight D. Eisenhower*, rev. ed. (Lawrence: University Press of Kansas, 1991), 62–63; Ellen Schrecker, *Many Are the Crimes: McCarthyism in America* (Boston: Little, Brown, 1998), 258; Ford, *Time to Heal*, 71.

14. Cannon, *Time and Chance*, 70; CR, 1952: A777.

15. "Analysis of the Philosophy and Voting Record of Representative Gerald R. Ford."

16. Schapsmeier and Schapsmeier, *Gerald R. Ford's Date with Destiny*, 45; Paul G. Pierpaoli Jr., *Truman and Korea: The Political Culture of the Early Cold War* (Columbia: University of Missouri Press, 1999), 34–36; *CR*, 1951: 454–455.

17. Gould, *Grand Old Party*, 326.

18. Ford interview, 23 April 1992; Jim Newton, *Eisenhower: The White House Years* (New York: Doubleday, 2011), 54; Gould, *Grand Old Party*, 326–327; Peter G. Boyle, *Eisenhower* (New York: Pearson Longman, 2005), 14; Scott et al., to Eisenhower, 22 February 1952, Eisenhower Library: Items from White House Central Files, GFMOPL, Box 1, GFL.

19. Eisenhower to Ford, 10 March 1952, on display at GRFM.

20. Boyle, *Eisenhower*, 14.

21. McCoy, *Presidency of Harry S. Truman*, 279–280; Piers Brendon, *Ike: His Life and Times* (New York: Harper and Row, 1986), 218–222, 226–227; Jeff Broadwater, *Adlai Stevenson and American Politics: The Odyssey of a Cold War Liberal* (New York: Twayne, 1994), 117, 119.

22. Ford, *Time to Heal*, 69; Cannon, *Time and Chance*, 61; "Governor Called Captive," *New York Times*, 20 August 1952; Schapsmeier and Schapsmeier, *Gerald R. Ford's Date with Destiny*, 50–51.

23. Cannon, *Time and Chance*, 59; Schapsmeier and Schapsmeier, *Gerald R. Ford's Date with Destiny*, 33–34, 45; oral history, Mildred Leonard, 15 May 1992, interviewed by James Cannon, Leonard, Mildred—Interview, 5/15/92, JMCRIN, Box 3, GFL; Vestal, *Jerry Ford*, 105.

24. Cannon, *Time and Chance,* 61.

25. Jeffrey S. Ashley, *Betty Ford: A Symbol of Strength* (New York: Nova History, 2003), 35–36; Betty Ford, *Times of My Life*, 57.

26. Betty Ford, *Times of My Life*, 64–65, 81; John Robert Greene, *Betty Ford: Candor and Courage in the White House* (Lawrence: University Press of Kansas, 2004), 21–22; Ashley, *Betty Ford*, 39–40, 46.

27. Ashley, *Betty Ford*, 42; Ford interview, 23 April 1992; Pat Shellenbarger, "Trip to Boyhood Home Stirs Memories for Ford Son," *Grand Rapids Press*, 2 January 2007.

28. Ford interview, 25 April 1990.

29. Cannon, *Time and Chance*, 62.

30. Ibid., 62–63.

31. There are two ways to transcribe Chinese into English, Pinyin and Wade-Giles. While Jiang Jieshi is better known by the Wade-Giles transcription of his name, Chiang Kai-shek, Pinyin has become more commonly used by scholars.

32. Cannon, *Time and Chance*, 63, 64; Robert Accinelli, *Crisis and Commitment: United States Policy toward Taiwan, 1950–1955* (Chapel Hill: University of North Carolina Press, 1996), 67, 117–118; Ford interview, 25 April 1990.

33. Cannon, *Time and Chance*, 62, 64; oral history, John Rhodes, 4 December 1990, interviewed by James Cannon, Rhodes, John—12/4/90, JMCRIN, Box 3; oral history, Gerald Ford, 13 November 1990, interviewed by James Cannon, Ford, Gerald—11/13/90, JMCRIN, Box 1, GFL.

34. Ford interview, 25 April 1990. Ford's first congressional aide, John Milanowski, claimed that Ford in fact had his eye on the speakership almost from the beginning of his tenure in the House. See Vestal, *Jerry Ford*, 100.

35. Schapsmeier and Schapsmeier, *Gerald R. Ford's Date with Destiny*, 51–52; Douglas Brinkley, *Gerald R. Ford* (New York: Times Books, 2007), 21; Cannon, *Time and Chance*, 61.

36. Schapsmeier and Schapsmeier, *Gerald R. Ford's Date with Destiny*, 52.

37. David A. Deese, *World Trade Politics: Power, Principles and Leadership* (New York: Routledge, 2008), 51.

38. "Taft Proposes Aid to Victims of Flood," *New York Times*, 11 February 1953. Congress ultimately rejected this proposal.

39. Schapsmeier and Schapsmeier, *Gerald R. Ford's Date with Destiny*, 35; "Analysis of the Philosophy and Voting Record of Representative Gerald R. Ford."

40. "Cross Examination of Gerald R. Ford Jr. 9-21-54," 1954 Campaign—Cross-Examination of Gerald R. Ford, Jr. 9/21/54, GRFCP, Box G1, GFL. I wish to thank Ford Library archivists Donna Lehman and Elizabeth Druga for tracking down information on where this cross-examination was aired.

41. "Text of Dulles' Statement on Foreign Policy of Eisenhower Administration," *New York Times*, 13 January 1954.

42. "Cross Examination of Gerald R. Ford Jr. 9-21-54"; Schapsmeier and Schapsmeier, *Gerald R. Ford's Date with Destiny*, 53.

43. Schwander to Ford, 9 December 1954, Ford to Cleary, 14 December 1954, and Cleary to Ford, 23 December 1954, Correspondence—December 1954 (2), Owen Cleary Papers, Box 6; Ford to Goebel, 16 May 1956, Correspondence, Mar.–May 1956, Paul Gordon Goebel Papers, Box 1, BHL.

44. J. Douglas Smith, "'When Reason Collides with Prejudice': Armistead Lloyd Boothe and the Politics of Moderation," in *The Moderates' Dilemma: Massive Resistance to School Desegregation in Virginia*, ed. Matthew D. Lassiter and Andrew B. Lewis (Charlottesville: University Press of Virginia, 1998), 43.

45. "Cross Examination of Gerald R. Ford, Jr. 9-16-56," 1956 Campaign—Cross Examination of Gerald R. Ford, Jr. 9/16/56, GRFCP, Box G2, GFL.

46. "Analysis of the Philosophy and Voting Record of Representative Gerald R. Ford"; Schapsmeier and Schapsmeier, *Gerald R. Ford's Date with Destiny*, 56–57.

47. Benjamin Kline, *First along the River: A Brief History of the U.S. Environmental Movement*, 2nd ed. (Lanham, Md.: Acada Books, 2000), 52–60, 64–67; Byron W. Daynes and Glen Sussman, *White House Politics and the Environment: Franklin D. Roosevelt to George W. Bush* (College Station: Texas A&M University Press, 2010), 123–124; Fraser to member of Congress, 16 October 1973, Gerald Ford—Vice President, Martha Griffiths Papers, Box 54, BHL; "Analysis of the Philosophy and Voting Record of Representative Gerald R. Ford."

48. *CR*, 1956: 12353.

49. Spencer C. Tucker, *Vietnam* (Lexington: University Press of Kentucky, 1999), 78.

50. Quoted from *In the Year of the Pig*, videorecording, directed by Emile de Anonio (1969; Oak Forest, Ill.: MPI Home Video, 1987).

51. "Cross Examination of Gerald R. Ford, Jr. 9-16-56."

52. Schapsmeier and Schapsmeier, *Gerald R. Ford's Date with Destiny*, 57; Cannon, *Time and Chance*, 65.

53. Eisenhower was so popular that his average approval rating never fell below 50 percent. See Charles O. Jones, *The Presidency in a Separated System*, 2nd ed. (Washington, D.C.: Brookings Institution, 2005), 150.

54. Boyle, *Eisenhower*, 69.

55. Michael Bowen, "Getting to Goldwater: Robert A. Taft, William F. Know-

land, and the Rightward Drift of the Republican Party," in *Barry Goldwater and the Remaking of the American Political Landscape*, ed. Elizabeth Tandy Shermer (Tucson: University of Arizona Press, 2013), 98, 99; Newton, *Eisenhower*, 216, 217; Schapsmeier and Schapsmeier, *Gerald R. Ford's Date with Destiny*, 51.

56. "Cross Examination of Gerald R. Ford, Jr. 9-16-56."

57. Walter Johnson, ed., *The Papers of Adlai Stevenson*, vol. 4, *"Let's Talk Sense to the American People," 1952–1955* (Boston: Little, Brown, 1974), 165–167; "Cross Examination of Gerald R. Ford, Jr. 9-16-56."

58. "Cross Examination of Gerald R. Ford, Jr. 9-16-56"; Schapsmeier and Schapsmeier, *Gerald R. Ford's Date with Destiny*, 58.

59. Schapsmeier and Schapsmeier, *Gerald R. Ford's Date with Destiny*, 58–59.

60. Pach and Richardson, *Presidency of Dwight D. Eisenhower*, 167–168; Schapsmeier and Schapsmeier, *Gerald R. Ford's Date with Destiny*, 60.

61. Herbert S. Parmet, *Eisenhower and the American Crusades* (New York: Macmillan, 1972), 285–286; Boyle, *Eisenhower*, 108–109.

62. *CR*, 1957: 14929; Pach and Richardson, *Presidency of Dwight D. Eisenhower*, 169.

63. "Budget Paradox Aids 2 Hospitals," *New York Times*, May 26, 1957; *CR*, 1957: 7731, 8067, 12579, 13788.

64. Pach and Richardson, *Presidency of Dwight D. Eisenhower*, 170; Larson to Strauss, 15 October 1957, Fallout, Correspondence, 1957, Atomic Energy Commission Series, Box 26G, Papers of Lewis L. Strauss, Herbert Hoover Library, West Plains, Iowa.

65. Allen Drury, "Truman Accused on Missile Lag," *New York Times*, December 12, 1957.

66. "Capital Dismayed at Test's Failure," *New York Times*, 7 December 1957.

67. "Analysis of the Philosophy and Voting Record of Representative Gerald R. Ford"; *CR*, 1958: 9940.

68. Cannon, *Time and Chance*, 67.

69. Ford interview, 30 April 1990; Ashley, *Betty Ford*, 42–43, 50–51; notes from interview with Michael Ford, 8 February 1991, interviewed by James Cannon, Ford, Michael—Notes on Conversation, 8 February 1991, JMCRIN, Box 1, GFL; Betty Ford, *Times of My Life*, 82.

70. Flowers to Goebel, 8 August 1957, Goebels to Ford, 14 August 1957, Ford to Jones and Ford to Scott, 19 August 1957, Correspondence, July–Aug. 1957, Ford to Scott, 11 March 1958, Correspondence, Mar.–Apr. 1958, Paul Gordon Goebel Papers, Box 2, BHL.

71. Michael S. Mayer, *The Eisenhower Years* (New York: Facts on File, 2010), 196.

72. Pach and Richardson, *Presidency of Dwight D. Eisenhower*, 175–176.

73. "Vander Veen—Ford—Foreign Policy Debate, Oct. 15, 1958," 1958 Campaign—Debate with Richard Vander Veen on Foreign Policy, 10/15/58, and "Debate with Richard Vander Veen on Election Issues, November 2, 1958," 1958 Campaign, Debate with Richard Vander Veen on Election Issues, 11/2/58, GRFCP, Box G3,

GFL; Michael O'Brien, *John F. Kennedy: A Biography* (New York: Thomas Dunne/St. Martin's, 2005), 379–383.

74. "Debate with Richard Vander Veen on Election Issues, November 2, 1958."

75. James J. Kenneally, *A Compassionate Conservative: A Political Biography of Joseph W. Martin Jr., Speaker of the U.S. House of Representatives* (Lanham, Md.: Lexington Books, 2003), 270–271; oral history, Bob Wilson, 7 April 1965, interviewed by Robert Peabody, Apr. 7, 1965—Bob Wilson, RLPRIN, Box 1, GFL; Parmet, *Eisenhower and the American Crusades*, 545.

76. Kenneally, *Compassionate Conservative*, 270, 271; Robert L. Peabody, "Leadership Change in the House of Representatives: The Minority Leadership Contest, 1965," April 1965, Peabody, Robert—Draft Paper on the Minority Leadership Contest, 1965, Melvin R. Laird Papers, Box A12, GFL.

77. Oral history, Gerald Ford, 25 October 1994, interviewed by Yanek Mieczkowski, Ford, Gerald—10/25/94, YMRI, Box 1, and Ford to Pfeiffer, 20 April 1971, Truman Library, GFMOPL, Box 1, GFL.

Chapter Three: A Step Away

1. Andrew J. Dunar, *America in the Fifties* (Syracuse, N.Y.: Syracuse University Press, 2006), 234.

2. See, for instance, Elaine Tyler May, *Homeward Bound: American Families in the Cold War Era*, 20th anniversary ed. (New York: Basic Books, 2008).

3. David Halberstam, *The Fifties* (New York: Fawcett, 1993), 515–520.

4. Bud Vestal, *Jerry Ford, Up Close: An Investigative Biography* (New York: Coward, McCann and Geoghegan, 1974), 117; notes from interview with Michael Ford, 8 February 1991, interviewed by James Cannon, Ford, Michael—Notes on Conversation, 8 February 1991, JMCRIN, Box 1, GFL; Steven Ford, telephone interview by Scott Kaufman and Alissa Warters, 13 August 2015; Betty Ford, *The Times of My Life*, with Chris Chase (New York: Harper and Row, 1978), 10.

5. William T. Pyper, "Ford's Big Day Coming," *Grand Rapids Press*, 31 May 1959.

6. Fraser to member of Congress, 16 October 1973, Gerald Ford—Vice President, Martha Griffiths Papers, Box 54, BHL; Library of Congress, Congressional Research Service, "Analysis of the Philosophy and Voting Record of Representative Gerald R. Ford, Nominee for Vice President of the United States," 25 October 1973, Ford—Analysis of Philosophy and Voting Record of Rep. Gerald Ford (1), EHP, Box 89, GFL; Chester J. Pach, Jr., and Elmo Richardson, *The Presidency of Dwight D. Eisenhower*, rev. ed. (Lawrence: University Press of Kansas, 1991), 156–157.

7. Pach and Richardson, *Presidency of Dwight D. Eisenhower*, 200–201, 202–203; Eisenhower to Ford, 6 June 1959, Eisenhower Library: Items from Other White House Central Files, GFMOPL, Box 1, GFL.

8. Steven Wagner, *Eisenhower Republicanism: Pursuing the Middle Way* (DeKalb: Northern Illinois University Press, 2006), 112; *CR*, 1960: 12912; Eisenhower to Ford, 14 May 1960, Eisenhower Library: Items from Other White House Central Files, GFMOPL, Box 1, GFL.

9. Herbert S. Parmet, *Eisenhower and the American Crusades* (New York: Macmillan, 1972), 565–566; Lewis L. Gould, *Grand Old Party: A History of the Republicans* (New York: Random House, 2003), 342, 344–345, 346; Rick Perlstein, *Before the Storm: Barry Goldwater and the Unmaking of the American Consensus* (New York: Nation Books, 2009), 20–21, 33.

10. Edward L. Schapsmeier and Frederick Schapsmeier, *Gerald R. Ford's Date with Destiny: A Political Biography* (New York: Peter Lang, 1989), 52, 67; William F. Pyper, "Rep. Ford Could Benefit from Rockefeller's Decision," *Grand Rapids Press*, 3 January 1960.

11. "Favorite Son Chosen," *New York Times*, 24 April 1960; Goebel to fellow Republican, 6 May 1960 and 29 June 1960, and Ford to friends, 7 July 1960, Ford for Vice President Committee, Gordon Vander Till Papers, Box 2; and Goebel to Vonk, 3 June 1960, Russell to Ackerman, 9 June 1960, Russell to Ford, 22 June 1960, Ford to Zylsta, 28 June 1960, 1960 Campaign—Ford for Vice President—Correspondence, June, Gerald R. Ford Congressional Papers, Box G6, GFL.

12. James Cannon, *Time and Chance: Gerald Ford's Appointment with History* (Ann Arbor: University of Michigan Press, 1994), 68; Raymond Moley, "Ford for Vice President?," *Newsweek*, 11 July 1960, 96; Austin Wehrwein, "Field for Second Place Widens Despite Hints of Limit by Nixon," *New York Times*, 23 July 1960; "Favorite Son Hailed."

13. Schapsmeier and Schapsmeier, *Gerald R. Ford's Date with Destiny*, 69; Jerald F. terHorst, *Gerald Ford and the Future of the Presidency* (New York: Third Press, 1974), 73; Gerald R. Ford, *A Time to Heal: The Autobiography of Gerald R. Ford* (New York: Harper and Row, 1979), 72–73.

14. Douglas Brinkley, *Gerald R. Ford* (New York: Times Books, 2007), 22.

15. "Criticism of Defense Unfounded, G.O.P. House Study Group Says," *New York Times*, 20 June 1960.

16. Kayla Webley, "How the Nixon-Kennedy Debate Changed the World," *Time*, 23 September 2010, http://content.time.com/time/nation/article/0,8599,2021078,00.html, accessed 6 March 2015; Gould, *Grand Old Party*, 346–347.

17. Robert Dallek, *Lone Star Rising: Lyndon Johnson and His Times, 1908–1960* (New York: Oxford University Press, 1991), 584, 586; Randall Woods, *LBJ: Architect of American Ambition* (Cambridge, Mass.: Harvard University Press, 2006), 365–366; Herbert S. Parmet, *Richard Nixon and His America* (Boston: Little, Brown, 1990), 390; oral history, Gerald Ford, 23 April 1992, interviewed by James Cannon, Ford, Gerald—Interview, 4/23/92, JMCRIN, Box 1, GFL.

18. Cannon, *Time and Chance*, 69; "House Appropriations Committee Subcommittee on Foreign Operations," undated (circa June 1961), Ford, Gerald R., Presidential Papers, WHSF, PLFO, Box 5, JFKL; Schapsmeier and Schapsmeier, *Gerald R. Ford's Date with Destiny*, 71–72.

19. Ford to Essebaggers, 16 January 1963, B6-46, GRFCP, Box B6, GFL.

20. James Giglio, *Presidency of John F. Kennedy*, 2nd ed., rev. (Lawrence: University Press of Kansas, 2006), 157; Stephen W. Stathis, *Landmark Legislation 1774–2012: Major U.S. Acts and Treaties* (Thousand Oaks, Calif.: CQ Press, 2014),

309; Robert David Johnson, *Congress and the Cold War* (New York: Cambridge University Press, 2006), 92; *CR*, 1961: 18140–18141, 18176–18177; Schapsmeier and Schapsmeier, *Gerald R. Ford's Date with Destiny*, 73.

21. Ford interview, 23 April 1992; *CR*, 1964: 15284; Mark J. Rozell, *Executive Privilege: The Dilemma of Secrecy and Democratic Accountability* (Baltimore: Johns Hopkins University Press, 1994), 47; *CR*, 1963: 5817–5819.

22. "House Votes Defense Bill that Provides 47 Billion," *New York Times*, April 19, 1962; Ford to McNamara, 27 June 1962, Ford, Gerald R., Presidential Papers, WHSF, PLFO, Box 5, JFKL.

23. "Debt Bill Brings 'Blackmail' Cries," *New York Times*, 14 June 1962; *CR*, 1962: 10407–10410; John D. Morris, "House Passes Trade Bill; G.O.P. Aids in 298–125 Vote; President Hails Victory," *New York Times*, 29 June 1962.

24. Cannon, *Time and Chance*, 70.

25. Giglio, *Presidency of John F. Kennedy*, 99.

26. Theodore R. Marmor, *The Politics of Medicare*, 2nd ed. (Hawthorne, N.Y.: Aldine de Gruyter, 2000), 27–28, 31–32; Giglio, *Presidency of John F. Kennedy*, 104; Ford to Fitzgerald, 22 January 1963, B5-50, Box B5, and Ford to Zuidema, 27 February 1963, B2-46, Box B2, GRFCP, GFL.

27. Giglio, *Presidency of John F. Kennedy*, 101–102; Michael O'Brien, *John F. Kennedy: A Biography* (New York: Thomas Dunne / St. Martin's, 2005), 564; "Analysis of the Philosophy and Voting Record of Representative Gerald R. Ford."

28. "Analysis of the Philosophy and Voting Record of Representative Gerald R. Ford"; Giglio, *Presidency of John F. Kennedy*, 175.

29. O'Brien, *John F. Kennedy*, 565–567; Giglio, *Presidency of John F. Kennedy*, 103–104; "Analysis of the Philosophy and Voting Record of Representative Gerald R. Ford"; James N. Giglio, "John F. Kennedy and the Nation," in *Debating the Kennedy Presidency*, ed. James N. Giglio and Stephen G. Rabe (Lanham, Md.: Rowman and Littlefield, 2003), 110.

30. Cannon, *Time and Chance*, 72.

31. Schapsmeier and Schapsmeier, *Gerald R. Ford's Date with Destiny*, 37; Cannon, *Time and Chance*, 74; Ford, *Time to Heal*, 71, 72; Betty Ford, *Times of My Life*, 91–92, 96.

32. "Ford and Long: New Leaders in the 89th," *Newsweek*, 18 January 1965, 20; John Pope, "Elizabeth Ann (Betty) Bloomer Ford," in *American First Ladies: Their Lives and Their Legacy*, 2nd ed., ed. Lewis L. Gould (New York: Routledge, 2001), 367; Betty Ford, *Times of My Life*, 96; Cokie Roberts, interviewed by Richard Norton Smith, 19 November 2009, http://geraldrfordfoundation.org/centennial/oralhistory/cokie-roberts/, accessed 20 June 2015; Anne Holkeboer, interviewed by Richard Norton Smith, http://geraldrfordfoundation.org/centennial/oralhistory/anne-holkeboer/, accessed 20 June 2015; Cannon, *Time and Chance*, 74.

33. Cannon, *Time and Chance*, 74–75; John Robert Greene, *Betty Ford: Candor and Courage in the White House* (Lawrence: University Press of Kansas, 2004), 26.

34. Cannon, *Time and Chance*, 73.

35. Ibid.; James Reston, "Republican Leadership Gets a Break," *New York Times*,

9 January 1963; Henry Z. Scheele, "Response to the Kennedy Administration: The Joint Senate-House Republican Leadership Press Conferences," *Presidential Studies Quarterly* 19, no. 4 (1989): 826–827; Henry Z. Scheele, "Prelude to the Presidency: An Examination of the Gerald R. Ford—Charles A. Halleck House Minority Leadership Contest," *Presidential Studies Quarterly* 25, no. 4 (1995): 769.

36. Cannon, *Time and Chance*, 73; Reston, "Republican Leadership Gets a Break"; Donald Rumsfeld, *Known and Unknown: A Memoir* (New York: Sentinel, 2011), 64.

37. Cannon, *Time and Chance*, 75; Dale Van Atta, *With Honor: Melvin Laird in War, Peace, and Politics* (Madison: University of Wisconsin Press, 2008), 64; E. W. Kenworthy, "Southern Senators Plan Fight to Keep Filibuster," *New York Times*, 9 January 1963; James Reston, "Democracy Raises Its Head in the House," *New York Times*, 16 January 1963.

38. Ford, *Time to Heal*, 74.

39. Ford to Zuidema, 27 February 1963, and Ford to Lindlord, 12 February 1963, and Ford to the Maases, 27 February 1963, B2-46, GRFCP, Box B2, GFL; "Minutes of the Fifty-Sixth Meeting of the Joint Republican Congressional Leaders," 28 March 1963, Joint Senate-House Republican Leadership Minutes, 1961–1968, Everett M. Dirksen Papers, Dirksen Congressional Center, http://www.everettdirksen.name/guides_emd/Minutes1961-1968/03_19_1963.pdf, accessed 10 March 2014.

40. Robert J. McMahon and Thomas W. Zeiler, *Guide to U.S. Foreign Policy: A Diplomatic History* (Thousand Oaks, Calif.: CQ Press, 2012), 373; Richard Reeves, *President Kennedy: Profile of Power* (New York: Simon and Schuster, 1993), 555–556; Geir Lundestad, *East, West, North, South: Major Developments in International Politics since 1945*, 6th ed. (Thousand Oaks, Calif.: Sage, 2010), 137; *CR*, 1963: 11466.

41. Reeves, *President Kennedy*, 483–484; Johnson, *Congress and the Cold War*, 94–102; Felix Belair Jr., "G.O.P. Will Seek Foreign Aid Cut of $500 Million," *New York Times*, 19 June 1964.

42. "Analysis of the Philosophy and Voting Record of Representative Gerald R. Ford"; *CR*, 1961: 15812–15815 and 1963: 24731; Ford to Hoople, 13 February 1963, B3-7, GRFCP, Box B3, GFL. Kennedy's congressional liaison, Larry O'Brien, suggested a final possibility: that Ford could not decide if he wanted to be House speaker or vice president. This seems the least likely explanation, however, for although Ford in 1960 toyed with the idea of serving as Nixon's running mate, his heart throughout had been on the House speakership. See O'Brien to president, 10 December 1963, John Library—Watson Files (1), GFMOPL, Box 1, GFL.

43. O'Brien, *John F. Kennedy*, 833–834.

44. "Civil Rights Record of Gerald Ford," undated, Civil Rights Record of Gerald Ford, 1949–1976," Ron Nessen Papers, Box 3, and Feringa to Ford, 1 July 1963, and Ford to Feringa, 3 July 1963, A6-22, GRFCP, Box A6, GFL; Fraser to member of Congress, 16 October 1973; Judith Russell, *Economics, Bureaucracy, and Race: How Keynesians Misguided the War on Poverty* (New York: Columbia University

Press, 2004), 69; Gary Donaldson, *Liberalism's Last Hurrah: The Presidential Campaign of 1964* (Armonk, N.Y.: M. E. Sharpe, 2003), 322n47; Timothy N. Thurber, *Republicans and Race: The GOP's Frayed Relationship with African Americans, 1945–1974* (Lawrence: University Press of Kansas, 2013), 122–123, 172–173.

45. Giglio, *Presidency of John F. Kennedy*, 197.

46. Ford, *Time to Heal*, 74; Betty Ford, *Times of My Life*, 102.

47. Telephone conversation between the president and Congressman Gerald Ford, 29 November 1963, Johnson Library—Selected Telephone Conversations Concerning the Special Commission to Investigate the Assassination of President Kennedy, GFMOPL, Box 1; and oral history, Gerald Ford, 25 April 1990, Ford, Gerald—Interview, 4/25/90, JMCRIN, Box 1, GFL; Cannon, *Time and Chance*, 75–76; Ford, *Time to Heal*, 75.

48. Cannon, *Time and Chance*, 76; Anthony Lewis, "Warren Commission Finds Oswald Guilty and Says Assassin and Ruby Acted Alone; Rebukes Secret Service, Asks Revamping," *New York Times*, 28 September 1964.

49. Michael L. Kurtz, *The JFK Assassination Debates: Lone Gunman versus Conspiracy* (Lawrence: University Press of Kansas, 2006), 85–86; Henry Hurt, *Reasonable Doubt: An Investigation into the Assassination of John F. Kennedy* (New York: Holt, Rinehart, and Winston, 1986), 249.

50. O'Brien to president, 10 December 1963; Johnson Library—Wilson Files (1), GFMOPL, Box 1, GFL; Felix Belair Jr., "House Approves $3.3 Billion Aid, Backing Johnson," *New York Times*, 2 July 1964; Felix Belair Jr., "Congress Votes $3.25 Billion Aid," *New York Times*, 3 October 1964.

51. Hedrick Smith, "G.O.P. Bloc Scores U.S. Defense 'Gap,'" *New York Times*, 30 June 1964.

52. Ford to Moser, 9 March 1964, B11-15, GRFCP, Box B11, and Ford to Peters, 31 January 1964, B13-42, GRFCP, Box B13, GFL; H. W. Brands, *The Wages of Globalism: Lyndon Johnson and the Limits of American Power* (New York: Oxford University Press, 1995), 31–33.

53. Smith, "G.O.P. Bloc Scores U.S. Defense 'Gap'"; Hedrick Smith, "A Wider U.S. Role Opposed by Lodge," *New York Times*, 1 July 1964.

54. *CR*, 1964: 18551.

55. Giglio, *Presidency of John F. Kennedy*, 139–140; *CQA*, 1963: 633.

56. Robert Dallek, *Flawed Giant: Lyndon Johnson and His Times, 1961–1973* (New York: Oxford University Press, 1998), 71–74; Robert A. Caro, *The Years of Lyndon Johnson: The Passage of Power* (New York: Vintage, 2012), 472–475, 552–557; Ford to Gay, 9 March 1964, B12-9, GRFCP, Box B12, GFL.

57. "Analysis of the Philosophy and Voting Record of Representative Gerald R. Ford"; Woods, *LBJ*, 448; Dallek, *Flawed Giant*, 205; Ford to Stenson, 6 April 1964, B13-6, GRFCP, Box B13, and Ford to the Rosemans, 10 September 1964, B13-10, GRFCP, Box B13, GFL; Sean J. Savage, *JFK, LBJ, and the Democratic Party* (Albany: State University of New York Press, 2004), 128; Schapsmeier and Schapsmeier, *Gerald R. Ford's Date with Destiny*, 95.

58. Dallek, *Flawed Giant*, 114, 117–119; Ford to Farmer, 20 December 1963,

B2-8, GRFCP, Box B2, GFL; "Analysis of the Philosophy and Voting Record of Representative Gerald R. Ford."

59. "Analysis of the Philosophy and Voting Record of Representative Gerald R. Ford."

60. Eisenhower to Persons, 19 April 1961, and Eisenhower to Knox, 18 August 1961, Eisenhower Library—Post-Presidential Papers, GFMOPL, Box 1, GFL.

61. Dallek, *Flawed Giant*, 131, 170.

62. "G.O.P. Chairman Picked for No. 2 Spot on Ticket," *New York Times*, 16 July 1964; Perlstein, *Before the Storm*, 389.

63. Robert L. Peabody, "Leadership Change in the House of Representatives: The Minority Leadership Contest, 1965," Peabody, Robert—Draft Paper on the minority leadership contest, 1965, Melvin R. Laird Papers, Box A12, GFL.

64. Perlstein, *Before the Storm*, 357; Ford to Stuart, 27 July 1964, A15-24, GRFCP, Box A15, GFL.

65. Peabody, "Leadership Change"; Brinkley, *Gerald R. Ford*, 26–27; Scheele, "Prelude to the Presidency," 780; Henry Z. Scheele, *Charlie Halleck: A Political Biography* (New York: Exposition Books, 1966), 245.

66. "Restive Republicans," *Wall Street Journal*, 7 August 1964; Peabody, "Leadership Change"; "The Ford-Halleck Race 1964–1965," 7 June 2000, library.rumsfeld.com/doclib/sp/23/06-07-2000%20DR%20-%20The%20Ford-Halleck%20Race%201964-1965.pdf#search+%22Halleck%22, accessed 15 March 2015.

67. Oral history, Robert Griffin, 29 December 1964, interviewed by Robert Peabody, Dec. 29, 1964—Robert Griffin Interview, and oral history, Donald Rumsfeld, 30 December 1964, interviewed by Robert Peabody, Dec. 30, 1964—Donald Rumsfeld Interview, RLPRIN, Box 1, GFL; Peabody, "Leadership Change"; John D. Morris, "House G.O.P. Calls a Special Caucus," *New York Times*, 3 December 1964; "Romney Confers with Eisenhower," *New York Times*, 12 December 1964; John D. Morris, "G.O.P. Caucus Will Test Halleck's House Strength," *New York Times*, 14 December 1964.

68. Peabody, "Leadership Change"; Van Atta, *With Honor*, 65–68.

69. Oral history, Gerald Ford, 24 April 1992, interviewed by James Cannon, Ford, Gerald—Interview, 4/24/92, JMCRIN, Box 1, GFL; Brinkley, *Gerald R. Ford*, 26–27; Ford, *Time to Heal*, 78.

70. Sherrill to Ford, 21 December 1964, Joseph to Ford, 22 December 1964, and Bennett to Ford, Anderson to Ford, and the Owenses to Ford, 31 December 1964, A16-22, GRFCP, Box A16, GFL; Cobb to Ford, 30 December 1964; Gary Elliott, *Senator Alan Bible and the Politics of the New West* (Reno: University of Nevada Press, 1994), 141.

71. Oral history, Charles E. Goodell, 27 November 1978 and 6 June 1979, interviewed by Charles T. Morrisey, Charles E. Goodell, Former Members of Congress., Inc., Oral History Interviews, Box I: 4, LC; John D. Morris, "Ford Challenges Halleck in House Power Struggle," *New York Times*, 20 December 1964; John D. Morris, "House G.O.P. Fight Divides Liberals," *New York Times*, 23 December 1964; John D. Morris, "New. G.O.P. Battle Likely over Laird," *New York Times*, 25

December 1964; Geoffrey Kabaservice, *Rule and Ruin: The Downfall of Moderation and the Destruction of the Republican Party, from Eisenhower to the Tea Party* (New York: Oxford University Press, 2012), 421n53.

72. Peabody, "Leadership Change"; Rumsfeld, *Known and Unknown*, 93–94; Scheele, *Charlie Halleck*, 248–249.

73. Betty Ford, *Times of My Life*, 120; Greene, *Betty Ford*, 23, 24, 25; Steven Ford, telephone interview, 13 August 2015.

74. Greene, *Betty Ford*, 24, 25.

Chapter Four: High Expectations . . . Unrealized

1. Douglas Brinkley, *Cronkite* (New York: HarperCollins, 2012), 341.

2. James S. Fleming, *Window on Congress: A Congressional Biography of Barber B. Conable, Jr.* (Rochester, NY: University of Rochester Press, 2004), 79; Ford to Colleague, 12 January 1965, A30-42, "Statement of Representative Leslie C. Arends, of Illinois," 14 January 1965, and Ford to Springer, 19 January 1965, A30-43, GRFCP, Box A30, and oral history, Robert Griffin and Charles Goodell, 15 January 1965, interviewed by Robert Peabody, 15 January 1965—Robert Griffin and Charles Goodell, oral history, William Pitts, 6 April 1965, interviewed by Robert Peabody, Apr. 6, 1965, and oral history, Silvio Conte, 19 January 1965, interviewed by Robert Peabody, Jan. 19, 1965—Silvio Conte Interview, RLPRIN, Box 1, GFL.

3. Edward L. Schapsmeier and Frederick Schapsmeier, *Gerald R. Ford's Date with Destiny: A Political Biography* (New York: Peter Lang, 1989), 91; "Ford Again Rebuffed by House GOP," *Toledo Blade*, 24 February 1965; Gerald R. Ford, *A Time to Heal: The Autobiography of Gerald R. Ford* (New York: Harper and Row, 1979), 80.

4. John Rhodes, *John Rhodes: "I Was There,"* with Dean Smith (Salt Lake City: Northwest Publishing, 1995), 119; oral history, Charles Goodell, 26 January 1966, interviewed by Robert Peabody, 26 January 1966—Charles Goodell, RLPRIN, Box 1, and Ford to Colleague, 28 January 1965, A30-43, GRFCP, Box A30, GFL.

5. Goodell interview, 26 January 1966; oral history, Charles Goodell, 22 April 1966, interviewed by Robert Peabody, 22 April 1966—Charles Goodell, RLPRIN, Box 1, GFL; "House Republicans—They're Out to Win," *Wall Street Journal*, 14 March 1967.

6. Correspondence, Laird to Kaufman, 21 May 2015; "House Republicans"; James M. Cannon, *Time and Chance: Gerald Ford's Appointment with History* (Ann Arbor: University of Michigan Press, 1994), 90–91; Bill Brock, telephone interview by Scott Kaufman and Alissa Warters, 26 September 2015; Robert Dole, telephone interview by Scott Kaufman, 19 August 2015.

7. Ford, *Time to Heal*, 79, 80; Schapsmeier and Schapsmeier, *Gerald R. Ford's Date with Destiny*, 93–94; "Minutes of the One Hundred and Seventh Meeting of the Joint Senate-House Republican Leadership," 26 August 1965, Everett M. Dirksen Papers, Dirksen Congressional Center, http://www.everettdirksen.name/guides_emd/Minutes1961-1968/08_26_1965.pdf, accessed 22 June 2014.

8. Schapsmeier and Schapsmeier, *Gerald R. Ford's Date with Destiny*, 98–99;

Neil Munro, "GR's Jerry Ford: A Real-Life American Success Story," *Grand Rapids Press*, 10 January 1965; Ford, *Time to Heal*, 83; Koll to Ford, undated (circa 4 June 1963) and Ford to Koll, 24 June 1963, A5-1, GRFCP, Box A5; Anderson to Ford, 10 November 1963, and Ford to Anderson, 15 November 1963, A5-33, GRFCP, Box A5; Eckert to Ford, 12 March 1965, and Ford to Eckert, 16 March 1965, A27-54, GRFCP, Box A27, GFL; Anne Holkeboer, interviewed by Richard Norton Smith, 8 August 2008, http://geraldrfordfoundation.org/centennial/oralhistory/anne-holkeboer/, accessed 21 June 2015; Arthur Edson, "Rep. Ford Sets Whirlwind Pace," *Grand Rapids Press*, 12 June 1966.

9. Ford, *Time to Heal*, 83; Betty Ford, *The Times of My Life*, with Chris Chase (New York: Harper and Row, 1978), 123–124; Cannon, *Time and Chance*, 88; John Robert Greene, *Betty Ford: Candor and Courage in the White House* (Lawrence: University Press of Kansas, 2004), 26.

10. Quoted in Doris Kearns, *Lyndon Johnson and the American Dream* (New York: Signet, 1976), 100.

11. George C. Herring, *America's Longest War: The United States and Vietnam, 1950–1975*, 4th ed. (Boston: McGraw Hill, 2002), 182.

12. Randall Woods, *LBJ: Architect of American Ambition* (Cambridge, Mass.: Harvard University Press, 2006), 616–617; Donald F. Kettl, "Economic Education of Lyndon Johnson: Guns, Butter, and Taxes," in *The Johnson Years*, vol. 2, *Vietnam, the Environment, and Science*, ed. Robert A. Divine (Lawrence: University Press of Kansas, 1987), 60; Robert Dallek, *Flawed Giant: Lyndon Johnson and His Times, 1961–1973* (New York: Oxford University Press, 1998), 290; Herring, *America's Longest War*, 161; Charles Peters, *Lyndon B. Johnson* (New York: Times Books, 2010), 123; *CR*, 1965: 9520, 9537, 27425.

13. Schapsmeier and Schapsmeier, *Gerald R. Ford's Date with Destiny*, 96; Edward L. Schapsmeier and Frederick H. Schapsmeier, *Dirksen of Illinois: Senatorial Statesman* (Urbana: University of Illinois Press, 1985), 205; Dale Van Atta, *With Honor: Melvin Laird in War, Peace, and Politics* (Madison: University of Wisconsin Press, 2008), 105–106.

14. On this score, see Yuen Foong Khong, *Analogies at War: Munich, Dien Bien Phu, and the Vietnam Decisions of 1965* (Princeton: Princeton University Press, 1992); and Victor S. Kaufman, *Confronting Communism: U.S. and British Policies toward China* (Columbia: University of Missouri Press, 2001), 196–197.

15. Woods, *LBJ*, 679–680; Peters, *Lyndon B. Johnson*, 129; Telephone Conversation between Johnson and McNamara, 17 January 1966, and Notes of Meeting, 25 January 1966, *FRUS, 1964–1968*, 4: 75, 141; Andrew Johns, *Vietnam's Second Front: Domestic Politics, the Republican Party, and the War* (Lexington: University Press of Kentucky, 2010), 97; Van Atta, *With Honor*, 104.

16. "The Dirksen-Ford Rumpus: A Split over War 'Mismanagement'?," *U.S. News & World Report*, 2 May 1966; Johns, *Vietnam's Second Front*, 94–95, 104.

17. *CR*, 1965: 9520, 24352.

18. *PPPUS, 1964*: 405; Ford to Drake, 30 November 1965, B28-1, GRFCP, Box 28B, GFL.

19. Ford, *Time to Heal*, 80; Library of Congress, Congressional Research Service, "Analysis of the Philosophy and Voting Record of Representative Gerald R. Ford, Nominee for Vice President of the United States," 25 October 1973, Ford—Analysis of Philosophy and Voting Record of Rep. Gerald Ford (1), EHP, Box 89, GFL; Marjorie Hunter, "House Approves School-Aid Bill; G.O.P. Is Rebuffed," *New York Times*, 27 March 1965; Marjorie Hunter, "Senate Passes School Aid Bill with No Change," *New York Times*, 10 April 1965.

20. *CR*, 1965: 7175; "House Roll-Call Vote on Medicare Bill," *New York Times*, 9 April 1965; *CQA*, 1965: 950; Fraser to Member of Congress, 16 October 1973, Gerald Ford—Vice President, Martha Griffiths Papers, Box 54, BHL; "House Approves Expanded Drive against Poverty," *New York Times*, 23 July 1965.

21. Ford to Winter, 16 March 1965, B17-12, GRFCP, Box B17, and "Civil Rights Record of Gerald Ford," 21 June 1976, PHF, Box C42, GFL; Geoffrey Kabaservice, *Rule and Ruin: The Downfall of Moderation and the Destruction of the Republican Party, from Eisenhower to the Tea Party* (New York: Oxford University Press, 2012), 141–142; Robert Mann, *When Freedom Would Triumph: The Civil Rights Struggle in Congress, 1945–1968* (Baton Rouge: Louisiana State University Press, 2007), 245–246; *CQA*, 1965: 561.

22. Excerpt from *Face the Nation*, 15 August 1965, Wedemeyer to Ford, 16 August 1965, Myers to Ford, 16 August 1965, Hamilton to Ford, 16 August 1965, and Gerould to Ford, 17 August 1965, A23-62, GRFCP, Box A23, GFL.

23. David B. Wolcott and Tom Head, *Crime and Punishment in America* (New York: Facts on File, 2010), 206; Willard M. Oliver and James F. Hilgenberg Jr., *A History of Crime and Criminal Justice in America* (Boston: Pearson, 2006), 284; "Crime: Declaration of War," *Newsweek*, 9 August 1965, 30; Rick Perlstein, *Nixonland: The Rise of a President and the Fracturing of America* (New York: Scribner, 2008), 146.

24. Cannon, *Time and Chance*, 91–92; oral history, Gerald Ford, undated (circa 1979), interviewed by Hugh Morrow, Interview w/GRF Hugh Morrow (1979), JMCP, Box 34, GFL; "Inside the President's Inner Circle," *Newsweek*, 19 August 1974, 29.

25. Hartmann to Minority Leader, 7 March 1966, House Republican Conference, Melvin R. Laird Papers, Box A9, GFL.

26. Dallek, *Flawed Giant*, 284, 299–300.

27. Ibid., 311–322, 329–330.

28. The Schapsmeier brothers attribute it to Ford, but they offer no evidence to support that conclusion. See Schapsmeier and Schapsmeier, *Gerald R. Ford's Date with Destiny*, 104.

29. Val Adams, "Johnson Critics Granted TV Time," *New York Times*, 14 January 1966; David S. Broder, "G.O.P. Urges Cuts at Home for War," *New York Times*, 18 January 1966.

30. "Republicans: State of the Riposte," *Newsweek*, 31 January 1966, 22; "The Joint Senate-House Republican Leadership," 21 April 1966, Ev and Jerry Show, 4/21/66, RTHP, Box 51, GFL; "The Dirksen-Ford Rumpus."

31. Johns, *Vietnam's Second Front*, 124–125.

32. Hartmann to Minority Leader, 15 July 1966, and William McGaffin, "GOP Trying to Build Issue of Declining U.S. Prestige," *Chicago Daily News*, 28 September 1966, Presidential Decline—General (2), RTHP, Box 82, GFL; E. W. Kenworthy, "Europeans Found Critical of U.S.," *New York Times*, 31 October 1966.

33. Frank Costigliola, "Lyndon B. Johnson, Germany, and 'the End of the Cold War,'" in *Lyndon Johnson Confronts the World: American Foreign Policy, 1963–1968*, ed. Warren I. Cohen and Nancy Bernkopf Tucker (New York: Cambridge University Press, 1994), 196–197; Walter LaFeber, *America, Russia, and the Cold War, 1945–2002*, 3rd ed. (Boston: McGraw-Hill, 2002), 267; Republican Leadership of the Congress Press Conference, 13 October 1966, Ev and Jerry Show, 13 October 1966, RTHP, Box 51, GFL. For more on the competition between the Soviet Union and China for influence in Hanoi, see I. V. Gaiduk, *The Soviet Union and the Vietnam War* (Chicago: I. R. Dee, 1996), and Zhai Qiang, *China and the Vietnam Wars, 1950–1975* (Chapel Hill: University of North Carolina Press, 2000).

34. *CR*, 1966: 24642; Stanley Meisler, *The United Nations: A History*, rev. and updated ed. (New York: Grove Press, 2011), 161.

35. "The Joint Senate-House Republican Leadership," 24 February 1966, Ev and Jerry Show—Joint Senate-House Republican Leadership Press Conference, 24 February 1966, and "The Joint Senate-House Republican Leadership," 17 March 1966, Ev and Jerry Show, 3/17/66, RTHP, Box 50; "Address by House Republican Leader Gerald R. Ford, Mid America Gas Dealers Assn. at Kansas City, Missouri," 1966 Campaign—Public Relations Speech Materials and Press Releases, GRFCP, Box G14, "Joint Senate-House Republican Leadership," 3 March 1966, Ev and Jerry Show, 3/3/66, Republican Leader of the Congress Press Conference, 1 September 1966, Ev and Jerry Show, 9/1/66, and Republican Leadership of the Congress Press Conference, 22 September 1966, Ev and Jerry Show, 9/22/66, RTHP, Box 51, and Press Release Issued Following a Leadership Meeting, 28 July 1966, Credibility Gap (3), RTHP, Box 46, GFL; Dallek, *Flawed Giant*, 310.

36. "Address by House Republican Leader Gerald R. Ford, Mid-America Gas Dealers Assn.," 13 September 1966, 1966 Campaign—Public Relations Speech Materials and Press Releases, GRFCP, Box G14, and the Joint Senate-House Republican Leadership, 10 March 1966, Ev and Jerry Show, 3/10/66, RTHP, Box 50, GFL; Ev and Jerry Show, 1 and 22 September 1966.

37. Sidney M. Milkis, "Lyndon Johnson, the Great Society, and the 'Twilight' of the Modern Presidency," in *The Great Society and the High Tide of Liberalism*, ed. Sidney M. Milkis and Jerome M. Mileur (Amherst: University of Massachusetts Press, 2005), 10; Robert R. Korstad and James L. Leloudis, *To Right These Wrongs: The North Carolina Fund and the Battle to End Poverty and Inequality in 1960s America* (Chapel Hill: University of North Carolina Press, 2010), 349; the Joint Senate-House Republican Leadership, 2 June 1966, Ev and Jerry Show, 6/2/66, RTHP, Box 51, GFL.

38. Dallek, *Flawed Giant*, 332, 335–339; Rep Leadership of the Congress Press Conference, 15 September 1966, Ev and Jerry Show, 9/15/66, RTHP, Box 51, GFL.

39. Campaign Scripts re Law and Order, Inflation, and Taxes and Debt, undated (1966), 1966 Campaign—Public Relations Television Advertising (1), GRFCP, Box G14, GFL; Arthur Edson, "Rep. Ford Sets Whirlwind Pace," *Grand Rapids Press*, 12 June 1966; "Table of Votes for the House of Representatives in the Election Last Tuesday," *New York Times*, 13 November 1966.

40. Herring, *America's Longest War*, 204, 209, 211.

41. Woods, *LBJ*, 790–791, 793, 795; Wolcott and Head, *Crime and Punishment in America*, 205; Mark Hamilton Lytle, *America's Uncivil Wars: The Sixties Era from Elvis to the Fall of Richard Nixon* (New York: Oxford University Press, 2006), 234–235, 237, 238.

42. *PPPUS*, 1967: 2–14; Woods, *LBJ*, 748–749.

43. John Herbers, "Republicans Say President Leads U.S. to Failure," *New York Times*, 20 January 1967; Dallek, *Flawed Giant*, 395–396, 398; Woods, *LBJ*, 796–797.

44. Joint Republican Leadership Press Conference, 10 January 1967, Ev and Jerry Show, 10 January 1967, the Republican Leadership of the Congress Press Conference, 2 February 1967, Ev and Jerry Show, 2/2/67, and the Republican Leadership of the Congress Press Conference, 20 April 1967, Ev and Jerry Show, 4/20/67, RTHP, Box 51, and "The Republican Leadership of the Congress Press Release," 25 May 1967, Middle East—General (1), RTHP, Box 73, GFL; *CR*, 1967: 36328; Van Atta, *With Honor*, 118–119.

45. *CR*, 1967: 21897–21899.

46. James Reston, "Washington: The Strategy of Strangulation," *New York Times*, 11 August 1967.

47. James S. Olson and Randy Roberts, *Where the Domino Fell: America and Vietnam, 1945–1995*, 5th ed. (Malden, Mass.: Blackwell, 2008), 147–148; Qiang Zhai, "An Uneasy Relationship: China and the DRV during the Vietnam War," in *International Perspectives on Vietnam*, ed. Lloyd C. Gardner and Ted Gittinger (College Station: Texas A&M University Press, 2000), 7–8; Herring, *America's Longest War*, 178.

48. Olson and Roberts, *Where the Domino Fell*, 158; Herring, *America's Longest War*, 199–200; the Republican Leadership of the Conference Press Conference, 21 September 1967, Ev and Jerry Show, 9/21/67, RTHP, Box 51, GFL; Reston, "Washington."

49. "Hatfield Calls War Unsolvable for U.S.," *New York Times*, 5 April 1967; John Herbers, "Hatfield, Percy and Brooke Delight Senate G.O.P.," *New York Times*, 17 April 1967; Johns, *Vietnam's Second Front*, 158; Neil Sheehan, "8 in G.O.P. Propose Phasing Out War," *New York Times*, 11 July 1967; The Republican Leadership of the Congress Press Conference, 13 July 1967, Ev and Jerry Show, 7/13/67, RTHP, Box 51, and Transcript, *Issues and Answers*, 27 August 1967, Vietnam—General, 1967 (3), RTHP, Box 103, GFL.

50. Johns, *Vietnam's Second Front*, 140–141; Van Atta, *With Honor*, 124–125; John Herbers, "Dirksen, Erstwhile Johnson Ally, Suggests G.O.P. Might End War," *New York Times*, 8 December 1967.

51. *CR*, 1967: 17801–17803; the Republican Leadership of the Congress, 21 September 1967, Ev and Jerry Show, 9/2/67, RTHP, Box 51, GFL.

52. Charles DeBenedetti, *An American Ordeal: The Antiwar Movement of the Vietnam Era* (Syracuse: Syracuse University Press, 1990), 176–178; *CR*, 1967: 33706–33707; Fred P. Graham, "3 in G.O.P. Say Hanoi Organized Capital Protest," *New York Times*, 29 November 1967.

53. *CR*, 1967: 19949; "Analysis of the Philosophy and Voting Record of Representative Gerald R. Ford"; the Republican Leadership of the Congress Press Conference, 3 August 1967, Ev and Jerry Show, 8/3/67, and the Republican Leadership of the Congress Press Conferences, 29 August 1967, Ev and Jerry Show, 8/29/67, RTHP, Box 51, GFL.

54. Wolcott and Head, *Crime and Punishment in America*, 203; John Herbers, "Crime Bill Voted in House, 377–323; Riot Curbs Added," *New York Times*, 9 August 1967; "Crime Bill Roll-Call Vote," *New York Times*, 9 August 1967; John Herbers, "House Approves Civil Rights Bill to Curb Violence," *New York Times*, 17 August 1967.

55. Martin V. Melosi, "Lyndon Johnson and Environmental Policy," in *The Johnson Years*, vol. 2, *Vietnam, the Environment, and Science*, ed. Robert A. Divine (Lawrence: University Press of Kansas, 1987), 136; *CR*, 1967: 30999.

56. *CR*, 1967: 37248.

57. "At Home," *National Review*, 29 August 1967; Emmet John Hughes, "The Wooden Army," *Newsweek*, 25 December 1967; "Return to Normalcy," *New York Times*, 21 December 1967.

58. *PPPUS*, 1968–1969: 25–33; John Herbers, "Johnson Program Indicted by G.O.P.," *New York Times*, 24 January 1968; Goodell to Gustafson, 1 February 1968, and Baker to Goodell, 13 February 1968, Republican State of the Union Address, CGP, Box 45, NYPL.

59. Dallek, *Flawed Giant*, 533–534; "Analysis of the Philosophy and Voting Record of Representative Gerald R. Ford"; *CR*, 1968: 23688.

60. *CR*, 1968: 16044, 16227.

61. See, for instance, Ford to Bohn, 24 January 1967, B-63-7, and Ford to Schulmeyer, 25 March 1967, B63-13, GRFCP, Box B63, GFL; *CQA*, 1968, 225–237.

62. Ford et al. to James Stuart Olson, *Historical Dictionary of the 1960s* (Westport, Conn.: Greenwood, 1999), 465; "Gallup Poll Finds Opposition to Tax Surcharge," *New York Times*, 24 January 1968; President, 25 April 1968, Tax and Spending Cuts (1), RTHP, Box 102, GFL; "Analysis of the Philosophy and Voting Record of Representative Gerald R. Ford"; Dallek, *Flawed Giant*, 535–536.

63. Herring, *America's Longest War*, 254–255; Schapsmeier and Schapsmeier, *Gerald R. Ford's Date with Destiny*, 113–114, 116.

64. *CR*, 1968: 28395; "Address before Jewish Men's Club at East Rockaway, N.J., Wednesday, Feb. 29, 1968," www.fordlibrarymuseum.gov/library/document/0054/4526093.pdf, accessed 3 October 2016.

65. Johns, *Vietnam's Second Front*, 163, 167–168.

66. Richard M. Nixon, "Asia after Viet Nam," *Foreign Affairs* 46 (October

1967): 111–125; Lewis L. Gould, *Grand Old Party: A History of the Republicans* (New York: Random House, 2003), 376.

67. Elizabeth Drew, *Richard M. Nixon* (New York: Times Books, 2007), 19–20; Gould, *Grand Old Party*, 377–378.

68. Confidential Memo re Nixon Meeting to Discuss Vice Presidential Nomination, 8 August 1968, papers.rumsfeld.com, accessed 9 March 2014; Ford, *Time to Heal*, 85–86.

69. Gould, *Grand Old Party*, 378; "The Name Is Agnew," *Newsweek*, 19 August 1968, 31; "Flare-Up over Agnew—Its Meaning," *U.S. News & World Report*, 19 August 1968, 6; "Vice-Presidential Choice," *New York Times*, 9 August 1968; Richard Lugar, telephone interview by Scott Kaufman, 22 July 2015; Ford, *Time to Heal*, 86.

70. "Ford Suggests House Inquiry into the Disorders in Chicago," *New York Times*, 1 September 1968.

71. Schapsmeier and Schapsmeier, *Gerald R. Ford's Date with Destiny*, 114–115, 117.

72. Ibid., 116; John Herbers, "Politics: House Republican Leaders Stress a Drive for Seats in Marginal Areas," *New York Times*, 19 September 1968; "G.O.P.'s Quarterback," *New York Times*, 7 August 1968; "Ford Says G.O.P. Will Win House," *New York Times*, 4 July 1968.

73. Richard Steven Conley, *The Presidency, Congress, and Divided Government: A Postwar Assessment* (College Station: Texas A&M University Press, 2003), 112; Stephen E. Ambrose, *Nixon*, vol. 2, *The Triumph of a Politician, 1962–1972* (New York: Simon and Schuster, 1989), 221; Lewis L. Gould, *1968: The Election that Changed America* (Chicago: Ivan R. Dee, 1993), 146–161; "The Anatomy of the Vote," *Newsweek*, 11 November 1968, 35.

74. Richard H. Growald, "Ford as Mr. Nice Guy," *Grand Rapids Press*, 13 February 1975; Peters, *Lyndon B. Johnson*, 139; Cannon, *Time and Chance*, 93; Dominic Sandbrook, *Mad as Hell: The Crisis of the 1970s and the Rise of the Populist Right* (New York: Knopf, 2011), 25; Richard Reeves, *A Ford, Not a Lincoln* (New York: Harcourt Brace Jovanovich, 1975), 25n. Historians later inaccurately changed "fart" to "chew gum."

75. Cannon, *Time and Chance*, 94; Sanders to Ford, 18 September 1967, Johnson Library—WHCF Name File (1), GFMOPL, Box 1, GFL.

76. Mike Lloyd, "Face to Face with Ford," *Grand Rapids Press*, 7 January 2007; President to Ford, 17 January 1969, Johnson Library—WHCF Name File (3), GFMOPL, Box 1, GFL.

Chapter Five: Not Speaker, but President

1. Richard Reeves, *President Nixon: Alone in the White House* (New York: Simon and Schuster, 2001), 502–503, 507–508, 519, 525–526; Bishop to Ford, Campaign, 17 October 1972, 1972 (3), RTHP, Box 39, GFL.

2. Melvin Small, *The Presidency of Richard M. Nixon* (Lawrence: University Press of Kansas, 1999), 215, 217, 228.

3. Conrad Black, *Richard M. Nixon: A Life in Full* (New York: PublicAffairs, 2007), 624; Small, *Presidency of Richard M. Nixon*, 42.

4. Small, *Presidency of Richard M. Nixon*, 43, 46; Elizabeth Drew, *Richard M. Nixon* (New York: Times Books, 2007), 35; Karen M. Hult and Charles E. Walcott, *Empowering the White House: Governance under Nixon, Ford, and Carter* (Lawrence: University Press of Kansas, 2004), 120.

5. Ford to Osmer, 15 February 1972, B227-41, GRFCP, Box B227, oral history, Gerald Ford, 24 April 1992, interviewed by James Cannon, Ford, Gerald—Interview, 4/24/92, JMCRIN, Box 1, and Ford to Ranking Republican Member, 3 February 1969, House—Ranking Republican Committeemen Meeting, 1/30/69, RTHP, Box 67, GFL.

6. Oral history, William F. Hildenbrand, 8 and 15 April 1985, interviewed by Donald A. Ritchie, William F. Hildenbrand, U.S. Congress, Senate Historical Office, Oral History Interviews, Box 3, LC; Kleppe to Ford, 24 February 1969, Williams to Ford, 4 March 1969, and Hogan to Harlow, 15 April 1969, Bitch File (1), RTHP, Box 37; Nidecker to Hartmann, 23 April 1969, Bitch File (2), RTHP, Box 37; and Mayer to Ford, 22 September 1969, Nixon—Misc., RTHP, Box 78, GFL; Timmons to Butterfield, 2 August 1971, 1971 [3 of 4], WHCF, ANF: Ford, Gerald, RMNL; Ford interview, 24 April 1992.

7. Hildenbrand interview, 15 April 1985; "Transcript of Arthur F. Burns' Handwritten Journals, January 20, 1969–July 25, 1974: Journal II," 50, www.fordlibrarymuseum.gov/library/document/0428/Burnstranscript2.pdf, accessed 14 June 2014; Hult and Walcott, *Empowering the White House*, 122; Timmons to Ford, 10 July 1970, 7/1/70–9/30/70, and Chapin to Timmons, 30 November 1970, 10/1/70–12/31/70, WHCF, ANF: Ford, Gerald, RMNL.

8. John C. Whitaker, "Nixon's Domestic Policy: Both Liberal and Bold in Retrospect," *Presidential Studies Quarterly* 26, no. 1 (1996): 131.

9. Small, *Presidency of Richard Nixon*, 186, 194; *CR*, 1969: 23835.

10. Small, *Presidency of Richard Nixon*, 205.

11. Ibid.; *CQA*, 1962: 603; *CR*, 1969: 9686, 10247.

12. *CQA*, 1969: 205, 209–210, 27H; "House Approves Keeping Surtax; Vote is 210 to 205," *New York Times*, 1 July 1969.

13. *CQA*, 1969: 589, 39H; Small, *Presidency of Richard Nixon*, 205.

14. Small, *Presidency of Richard Nixon*, 188.

15. Ibid., 188–189, 190, 191–192; Library of Congress, Congressional Research Service, "Analysis of the Philosophy and Voting Record of Representative Gerald R. Ford, Nominee for Vice President of the United States," 25 October 1973, Ford—Analysis of Philosophy and Voting Record of Rep. Gerald Ford (1), EHP, Box 89, GFL.

16. Small, *Presidency of Richard Nixon*, 157–158.

17. Nancy E. Marion, *A History of Federal Crime Control Initiatives, 1960–1993* (Westport, Conn.: Greenwood, 1994), 72–73; "Analysis of the Philosophy and Voting Record of Representative Gerald R. Ford"; *CR*, 1970: 7953.

18. Mark Hamilton Lytle, *America's Uncivil Wars: The Sixties Era from Elvis to*

the Fall of Richard Nixon (New York: Oxford University Press, 2006), 337; Small, *Presidency of Richard Nixon*, 160; Larry E. Sullivan, gen. ed., *Encyclopedia of Law Enforcement* (Thousand Oaks, Calif.: Sage, 2005), 834.

19. *CR*, 1969: 19329; *CR*, 1970: 35308; "Analysis of the Philosophy and Voting Record of Representative Gerald R. Ford"; Small, *Presidency of Richard Nixon*, 160.

20. Small, *Presidency of Richard Nixon*, 197.

21. On this score, see ibid.; Black, *Richard M. Nixon*, 682; and Jonathan Aitken, *Nixon: A Life* (London: Weidenfeld and Nicolson, 1993), 397.

22. Thomas R. Wellock, *Preserving the Nation: The Conservation and Environmental Movements, 1870–2000* (Wheeling, Ill.: Harlan Davidson, 2007), 172–173; Hal K. Rothman, *Saving the Planet: The American Response to the Environment in the Twentieth Century* (Chicago: Ivan R. Dee, 2000), 127–128; "The Cities: The Price of Optimism," *Time*, 1 August 1969, 41; Small, *Presidency of Richard M. Nixon*, 197; Rick Perlstein, *Nixonland: The Rise of a President and the Fracturing of America* (New York: Scribner, 2008), 460–461; Joan Hoff, *Nixon Reconsidered* (New York: Basic Books, 1994), 21.

23. Ellen Arlinsky and Mary Ed Kwapil, *In Celebration of Grand Rapids* (Northridge, Calif.: Windsor, 1987), 29; "Analysis of the Philosophy and Voting Record of Representative Gerald R. Ford"; "Voting Record of Rep. Gerald R. Ford on Pollution and Environmental Legislation 1965–1970," undated (circa 1972), Congressional Campaign, 1972—Campaign Information (1), GVTP, Box 1, GFL; Robert G. Kaufman, *Henry M. Jackson: A Life in Politics* (Seattle: University of Washington Press, 2000), 202–204; *CR*, 1970: 23532.

24. James C. Duram, *Justice William O. Douglas* (Boston: Twayne, 1981), 112, 118, 120; Edward L. Schapsmeier and Frederick Schapsmeier, *Gerald R. Ford's Date with Destiny: A Political Biography* (New York: Peter Lang, 1989), 123.

25. Gerald R. Ford, "Impeachment—A Mace for the Federal Judiciary," *Notre Dame Law Review* 46 (1971): 669, 673, 674.

26. Gerald R. Ford, *A Time to Heal: The Autobiography of Gerald R. Ford* (New York: Harper and Row, 1979), 90–91; John Robert Greene, "'A Nice Person Who Worked at the Job': The Dilemma for the Ford Image," in *Gerald R. Ford and the Politics of Post-Watergate America*, vol. 2, ed. Bernard J. Firestone and Alexej Ugrinsky (Westport, Conn.: Greenwood, 1993), 640; Small, *Presidency of Richard Nixon*, 170.

27. John Robert Greene states that there is "no solid evidence . . . that Ford was working under White House orders." See John Robert Greene, *The Presidency of Gerald R. Ford* (Lawrence: University Press of Kansas, 1995), 7. Douglas Brinkley raises the possibility that Ehrlichman did get Ford to move against Douglas, but Bruce Allen Murphy writes that Ehrlichman found Ford unwilling to act. Therefore, continues Murphy, Nixon's domestic adviser started to make comments about Douglas's impeachment "to light a fire under Ford." See Douglas Brinkley, *Gerald R. Ford* (New York: Times Books, 2007), 39; and Bruce Allen Murphy, *Wild Bill:*

The Legend and Life of William O. Douglas (New York: Random House, 2001), 430. Benton Becker claims it was Will Wilson, who worked as an assistant to Attorney General John Mitchell, who put Ford on to Douglas, but Wilson never provided Ford with any evidence to justify impeachment. See Benton Becker, interview by Richard Norton Smith, 9 June 2009, http://geraldrfordfoundation.org/centennial/oralhistory/benton-becker/, accessed 20 June 2015; Ehrlichman later said he was not sure if Ford understood what Nixon wanted. See John Ehrlichman, *Witness to Power: The Nixon Years* (New York: Simon and Schuster, 1982), 122.

28. Brinkley, *Gerald R. Ford*, 39; Ehrlichman, *Witness to Power*, 122; Ford, *Time to Heal*, 90–91, 92.

29. Ford to Lewakowski, 11 November 1969, B152-51, GRFCP, Box B152; Bagger to Ford, May 1970, Clarke to Ford, 7 May 1970, and Fielder to Ford, 7 May 1970, Correspondence, 5/1/70–7/31/70, and Kirk to Ford, 13 December 1970, and Mills to Ford, 13 December 1970, Correspondence, 12/9/70–12/31/70, GRFCP, Box R14, GFL; "The Campaign against Douglas," *New York Times*, 16 December 1970.

30. Schapsmeier and Schapsmeier, *Gerald R. Ford's Date with Destiny*, 124; Greene, *Presidency of Gerald R. Ford*, 8.

31. James M. Cannon, *Time and Chance: Gerald Ford's Appointment with History* (Ann Arbor: University of Michigan Press, 1994), 101; John Osborne, "The Nixon Watch: Nightmares," *New Republic*, 27 October 1973, 11.

32. John Prados, "Prague Spring and SALT: Arms Limitation Setbacks in 1968," in *The Foreign Policies of Lyndon Johnson: Beyond Vietnam*, ed. H. W. Brands (College Station: Texas A&M University Press, 1999), 33–34; Small, *Presidency of Richard M. Nixon*, 101–102; *CR*, 1969: 28137; *CQA*, 1969: 49H.

33. James S. Olson and Randy Roberts, *Where the Domino Fell: America and Vietnam, 1945–1995*, 6th ed. (Malden, Mass.: Blackwell, 2014), 220–221; George C. Herring, *America's Longest War: The United States and Vietnam*, 4th ed. (Boston: McGraw Hill, 2002), 292.

34. Herring, *America's Longest War*, 293–295.

35. Ibid., 267; *CR*, 1969: 19616, 29941–29942, 30882, 31195–31196, 35540, 39753; *CR*, 1970: 4068, 12560, 14422, 22189; Ford to Berrios, 29 October 1969, B138-54, GRFCP, Box B138, GFL.

36. Gordon VanderTill, interviewed by Richard Norton Smith, 10 August 2009, http://geraldrfordfoundation.org/centennial/oralhistory/gordon-vandertill/, accessed 4 July 2015; "Democrats Pose Serious Threat to Ford's Seat," *Grand Rapids Press*, 24 June 1970; "Jean McKee Says Ford Serves Nixon Not People," *Grand Rapids Press*, 6 October 1970; and Steve Aulie, "Combat Yanks Soon to Be out of Viet, Ford Says in Debate with Jean McKee," *Grand Rapids Press*, 15 October 1970; 1970 Campaign—Campaign Issues (1), GRFCP, Box G18, GFL; "McKee Wants Deadline for Pullout in Vietnam," *Grand Rapids Press*, 12 October 1970; Saul Friedman, "Gal Gives Gerald Ford His Toughest Race in Years," *Detroit Free Press*, 28 October 1970; Maury de Jonge, "Don't Weaken Defenses, Ford Warns," *Grand Rapids Press*, 12 October 1970.

37. "Analysis of the Philosophy and Voting Record of Representative Gerald R. Ford"; Ford to Ruhl, 28 December 1971, B209-21, GRFCP, Box 109, GFL; *CQA*, 1971: 934, 94H; *CQA*, 1972: 708, 98H.

38. "Analysis of the Philosophy and Voting Record of Representative Gerald R. Ford."

39. Lawrence J. McAndrews, *The Era of Education: The Presidents and the Schools, 1965–2001* (Champaign-Urbana: University of Illinois Press, 2006), 72–73; David R. Rosenbaum, "Antibusing Plea Is Signed by Ford," *New York Times*, 26 January 1972; *CQA*, 1972: 40H.

40. Small, *Presidency of Richard Nixon*, 207; "Analysis of the Philosophy and Voting Record of Representative Gerald R. Ford."

41. Small, *Presidency of Richard Nixon*, 209–210; "Analysis of the Philosophy and Voting Record of Representative Gerald R. Ford."

42. Small, *Presidency of Richard Nixon*, 210–211.

43. Ford to Sawyer, 10 April 1972, Congressional—Gerald Ford Jr., Philip A. Hart Papers, Box 73, BHL; *CR*, 1972: 26519; Paul G. Pierpaoli Jr., *Truman and Korea: The Political Culture of the Early Cold War* (Columbia: University of Missouri Press, 1999), 101–102; Oral history, Gerald Ford, 30 March 1994, interviewed by Yanek Mieczkowski, Ford, Gerald—3/30/94, YMRI, Box 1, and oral history, Gerald Ford, 1 September 1989, interviewed by James Cannon, Ford, Gerald—Interview, 9/1/89, JMCRIN, Box 1, GFL.

44. "60 Million Saw Nixon Arrive," *New York Times*, 25 February 1972; Chris Tudda, *A Cold War Turning Point: Nixon and China, 1969–1972* (Baton Rouge: Louisiana State University Press, 2012), 183–190.

45. James Reston, "Cheers for the President," *New York Times*, 2 June 1972; John W. Finney, "Congress Chiefs Pleased; Taiwan Lodges a Protest," *New York Times*, 16 July 1971; "78% in Poll Favor Trip," *New York Times*, 25 February 1972; George H. Gallup, *The Gallup Poll: Public Opinion, 1972–1977* (Wilmington, Del.: Scholarly Resources, 1978), 1: 27, 37.

46. "Birch Society Denunciation," *New York Times*, 1 March 1972.

47. Ford to Wein, 25 October 1972, B227-47, GRFCP, Box B227, and Ford to Boraks, 15 January 1973, B249-22, GRFCP, Box B249, GFL; "Analysis of the Philosophy and Voting Record of Representative Gerald R. Ford."

48. Ford to Staal, 21 July 1971, B189-9, GRFCP, Box B189, and Ford to the Thedes, 30 November 1971, B189-14, GRFCP, Box B189, GFL; David E. Rosenbaum, "Congress Leaders Put Off Comment," *New York Times*, 28 February 1972; "Analysis of the Philosophy and Voting Record of Representative Gerald R. Ford."

49. Cook to President, 29 February 1972, and MacGregor to President, 7 March 1972, 1/1/72–6/31/72 [1 of 2], WHCF, ANF, Ford: Gerald, RMNL; John W. Finney, "House Leaders, Indignant, Want to Go to China, Too," *New York Times*, 2 March 1972; "Peking Invites Boggs and Ford," *New York Times*, 30 March 1972.

50. Wright to Ford, undated, and Ford to Wright, 4 April 1972, B129-25, Windemuller to Ford, 18 May 1972, Goff to Ford, 29 May 1972, and Ford to Goff, 3 June 1972, B129-26, GRFCP, Box B129, GFL.

51. Boggs and Ford to President, 20 July 1972, China—Ford/Boggs Trip—Report to the President, RTHP, Box 43, GFL.

52. Robert David Johnson, *Congress and the Cold War* (New York: Cambridge University Press, 2006), 181.

53. Small, *Presidency of Richard M. Nixon*, 258–259.

54. Schapsmeier and Schapsmeier, *Gerald R. Ford's Date with Destiny*, 129.

55. " . . . and Empty Landslide," *New York Times*, 9 November 1972; oral history, Gerald Ford, 26 April 1990, interviewed by James Cannon, Ford, Gerald—Interview, 4/26/90, JMCRIN, Box 1, GFL.

56. Reeves, *President Nixon*, 576.

57. Betty Ford, *The Times of My Life,* with Chris Chase (New York: Harper and Row, 1978), 140–143; Ford interview, 26 April 1990.

58. Olson and Roberts, *Where the Domino Fell,* 227–228.

59. Arthur M. Schlesinger Jr., *The Imperial Presidency* (Boston: Houghton Mifflin, 1973).

60. "Analysis of the Philosophy and Voting Record of Representative Gerald R. Ford."

61. Cannon, *Time and Chance*, 104–106.

62. Ibid., 128–130; Marjorie Boyd, "The Watergate Story: Why Congress Didn't Investigate until after the Election," *Washington Monthly*, April 1973, 41.

63. Cannon, *Time and Chance*, 152, 159.

64. Gallup, *Gallup Poll,* 1: 79, 124; Small, *Presidency of Richard Nixon*, 284–285.

65. Natasha Zaretsky, "In the Name of Austerity: Middle Class Consumption and the OPEC Oil Embargo of 1973–1974," in *The World the Sixties Made: Politics and Culture in Recent America*, ed. Van Gosse and Richard Moser (Philadelphia: Temple University Press, 2003), 140; Small, *Presidency of Richard Nixon*, 212–213; *CR*, 1973: 839.

66. Brinkley, *Gerald R. Ford*, 50–51.

67. "A Good Lineman for the Quarterback," *Time*, 22 October 1973, 16.

68. See, for instance, Clancy to President, Carter to President, Veyser to President, Treen to President, and Clawson to President, 11 October 1973, Nixon Presidential Materials Project: Materials re Selection of Gerald R. Ford and His Role as Vice President, GFMOPL, Box 1, GFL.

69. Ford to President, 11 October 1973, www.archives.gov/education/lessons/ford-nixon-letter/ford-nixon-letter.pdf, accessed 26 June 2014; "Good Lineman for the Quarterback," 17; Dale Van Atta, *With Honor: Melvin Laird in War, Peace, and Politics* (Madison: University of Wisconsin Press, 2008), 454–455; "Letter from Washington," *New Yorker*, 22 October 1973, 142; Cannon, *Time and Chance*, 275; Seymour Hersh, "The Pardon," *Atlantic*, August 1983, 21; Stephen Ambrose, *Nixon*, vol. 2, *The Triumph of a Politician* (New York: Simon and Schuster, 1989), 236–237; Richard Nixon, *RN: The Memoirs of Richard Nixon* (New York: Grosset and Dunlap, 1978), 925–926.

70. Small, *Presidency of Richard Nixon*, 270; Van Atta, *With Honor*, 455; Cannon, *Time and Chance*, 206.

71. Cannon, *Time and Chance*, 206–207.

72. "Good Lineman for the Quarterback," 16–17.

73. Steve Ford, interviewed by Richard Norton Smith, 7 March 2011, http://geraldrfordfoundation.org/centennial/oralhistory/steve-ford/, accessed 3 July 2015; Robert T. Hartmann, *Palace Politics: An Inside Account of the Ford Years* (New York: McGraw-Hill, 1980), 27.

74. Oral history, Betty Ford, 20 July 1990, interviewed by James Cannon, Ford, Betty—Interview, 7/20/90, JMCRIN, Box 1, GFL; Schapsmeier and Schapsmeier, *Gerald R. Ford's Date with Destiny*, 140; "Good Lineman for the Quarterback," 18.

75. "Good Lineman for the Quarterback," 17; "With Agnew Out—Why Nixon Picked Ford," *U.S. News & World Report*, 22 October 1973, 17; "Gerald Ford: A 'Team Player' Gets the Call," *U.S. News & World Report*, 22 October 1973, 20.

76. "The President Should Resign," *Time*, 12 November 1973, 19; "Nixon's Wheel Horse," *Nation*, 29 October 1973, 418; "Squandered Opportunity," *Wall Street Journal*, 15 October 1973.

77. Henry Kissinger, *Years of Upheaval* (New York: Simon and Schuster, 2011), 514; oral history, John Rhodes, 4 December 1990, interviewed by James Cannon, Rhodes, John—Interview, 12/4/90, JMCRIN, Box 3, GFL.

78. Small, *Presidency of Richard Nixon*, 290.

79. Alan H. Levy, *The Political Life of Bella Abzug, 1920–1976: Political Passion, Women's Rights, and Congressional Battles* (Lanham, Md.: Lexington Books, 2013), 196–197; Cannon, *Time and Chance*, 219; Fraser to Member of Congress, 16 October 1973, Gerald Ford—Vice President, Martha Griffiths Papers, Box 54, BHL; Ford interview, 26 April 1990; oral history, Carl Albert, 24 July 1990, interviewed by James Cannon, Albert, Carl—Interview, 7/24/90, JMCRIN, Box 3, GFL.

80. "Ford Gets the Twice-Over," *Newsweek*, 12 November 1973, 41; Schapsmeier and Schapsmeier, *Gerald R. Ford's Date with Destiny*, 141–142.

81. "Ford Gets the Twice-Over"; Cannon, *Time and Chance*, 242.

82. "Growing in Stature," *Time*, 19 November 1973, 26–27.

83. Schapsmeier and Schapsmeier, *Gerald R. Ford's Date with Destiny*, 144–145; Brinkley, *Gerald R. Ford*, 53.

84. "The New Veep's Real Mission," *Newsweek*, 17 December 1973, 26; John Robert Greene, *Betty Ford: Candor and Courage in the White House* (Lawrence: University Press of Kansas, 2004), 29; Memoranda of Conversation, 11 December 1973, www.fordlibrarymuseum.gov/library/document/0023/002302707.pdf, accessed 29 June 2014; Small, *Presidency of Richard Nixon*, 115.

85. David N. Farnsworth and James W. McKenney, *U.S.-Panama Relations, 1903–1978: A Study in Linkage Politics* (Boulder, Colo.: Westview, 1983), 145–146; Ford to the Tillinghasts, 11 October 1973, B254-5, GRFCP, Box B254, and Memorandum of Conversation, 26 April 1974, PHF, Box C1, GFL.

86. Schapsmeier and Schapsmeier, *Gerald R. Ford's Date with Destiny*, 149–150; Ford, *Time to Heal*, 115; Cannon, *Time and Chance*, 265.

87. Oral history, Robert Hartmann, 19 June 1991, interviewed by James Can-

non, Hartmann, Robert—Interview, 6/19/91, JMCRIN, Box 3, GFL; Seth S. King, "Ford Calls Campaign Unit 'An Arrogant, Elite Guard,'" *New York Times*, 31 March 1974; Hartmann, *Palace Politics*, 114; John Osborne, "Ford's Future," *New Republic*, 13 April 1974, 10–12.

88. J. Anthony Lukas, *Nightmare: The Underside of the Nixon Years* (New York: Viking, 1976), 557.

89. Cannon, *Time and Chance*, 290–291.

90. Ibid., 291–292.

91. Ibid., 292–294.

92. Ibid., 294; Ford interview, 26 April 1990.

93. Betty Ford, *Times of My Life*, 148, 157.

94. Ford interview, 26 April 1990; Steve Ford interview, 7 March 2011; Susan Ford, interviewed by Richard Norton Smith, 25 July 2010, http://geraldrfordfoundation.org/centennial/oralhistory/susan-ford-bales/, accessed 3 July 2015; "The Ford in Our Future," *Christianity Today*, 7 December 1973, 50.

95. Cannon, *Time and Chance*, 295–296.

96. Ibid., 300–302, 306–307.

97. Black, *Richard M. Nixon*, 976; Small, *Presidency of Richard Nixon*, 295.

98. Cannon, *Time and Chance*, 335, 336; Ford, *Time to Heal*, 30.

99. Matt Vande Bunte, "My Dad, the President," *Grand Rapids Press*, 16 April 2011; Hartmann interview, 19 June 1991.

100. Brinkley, *Gerald R. Ford*, 30.

Chapter Six: Honeymoon and Hardship

1. Oral history, Gerald Ford, 25 April 1990, interviewed by James Cannon, Ford, Gerald—Interview, 4/25/90, JMCRIN, Box 1, GFL; Robert Hartmann, *Palace Politics: An Inside Account of the Ford Years* (New York: McGraw-Hill, 1980), 159–160.

2. Doug Wead, *All the Presidents' Children: Triumph and Tragedy in the Lives of America's First Families* (New York: Atria, 2003), 264; oral history, Gerald Ford, 27 April 1990, interviewed by James Cannon, Ford, Gerald—Interview, 4/27/90, JMCRIN, Box 1, GFL; *PPPUS, 1974*: 1–2.

3. "President Ford" *New York Times*, 10 August 1974; William Greider, "Plain-Spoken Promises and a Level Gaze," *Washington Post*, 10 August 1974; "The Once and Future Ford," *Newsweek*, 19 August 1974, 23, 27.

4. Yanek Mieczkowski, *Gerald Ford and the Challenges of the 1970s* (Lexington: University Press of Kentucky, 2005), 30, 43; Richard W. Waterman, Robert Wright, and Gilbert St. Clair, *The Image-Is-Everything Presidency* (Boulder, Colo.: Westview, 1999), 29.

5. John Casserly, *The Ford White House: The Diary of a Speechwriter* (Boulder: Colorado Associated University Press, 1977), 81; Richard H. Growald, "Ford as Mr. Nice Guy," *Grand Rapids Press*, 13 February 1975; "'The Sun Is Shining Again,'" *Newsweek*, 26 August 1974, 18.

6. "Was Justice Done?," *Newsweek*, 16 September 1974, 23.

7. Elbert B. Smith, *The Presidencies of Zachary Taylor and Millard Fillmore* (Lawrence: University Press of Kansas, 1988), 167; Thomas H. Appleton Jr., "Margaret (Mackall Smith) Taylor," in *American First Ladies: Their Lives and Their Legacy*, ed. Lewis Gould (New York: Garland, 1996), 151; George Frederick Howe, *Chester A. Arthur: A Quarter-Century of Machine Politics* (New York: Frederick Ungar, 1966), 165–166.

8. Ford interview, 27 April 1990; Paula Burkes, "Former President's Son Revisits Father's Decisions," *Oklahoman*, 17 September 2011; "The Transition: Enter Ford," *Time*, 19 August 1974, 14.

9. John Robert Greene, *The Presidency of Gerald R. Ford* (Lawrence: University Press of Kansas, 1995), 23–24.

10. Ibid., 21, 24.

11. Buchen to the Vice President, 8 August 1974, Transition—General (1), PBF, Box 62, GFL; James M. Cannon, *Time and Chance: Gerald Ford's Appointment with History* (Ann Arbor: University of Michigan Press, 1994), 324.

12. Ron Nessen, *It Sure Looks Different from the Inside* (Chicago: Playboy Press, 1978), 31; Vice President to White House Staff, undated (circa 9 August 1974), Transition—General (1), PBF, Box 62, GFL; Memorandum for the Record, 10 August 1974, http://www.fordlibrarymuseum.gov/library/document/0314/1552745.pdf, accessed 10 June 2014.

13. "The New Broom at Work," *Newsweek*, 16 September 1974, 34; Greene, *Presidency of Gerald R. Ford*, 27. Hartmann refers to the "Praetorian Guard" throughout his memoir, *Palace Politics*; "Who's Minding the New Store," *Newsweek*, 30 September 1974, 28.

14. Gerald R. Ford, *A Time to Heal: The Autobiography of Gerald R. Ford* (New York: Harper and Row, 1979), 132.

15. Nguyen Tien Hung and Jerrold L. Schecter, *The Palace File* (New York: Harper and Row, 1986), 240; *PPPUS*, 12 August 1974: 11–12.

16. Barry Werth, *31 Days: Gerald Ford, the Nixon Pardon, and a Government in Crisis* (New York: Anchor Books, 2006), 106–107; *PPPUS*, 19 August 1974: 22–28; Greene, *Presidency of Gerald R. Ford*, 38–40; Memorandum of Conversation, 16 September 1974, http://www.fordlibrarymuseum.gov/library/document/0314/1552790.pdf, accessed 15 March 2014; "The Shape of Amnesty," *New Republic*, 31 August 1974, 9.

17. Greene, *Presidency of Gerald R. Ford*, 40–42.

18. Ibid., 30; Memorandum for the Record, 10 August 1974; "A Natural Force on a National Stage," *Time*, 2 September 1974, 14.

19. "Rocky's the One," *New Republic*, 31 August 1974, 8; "Making the Best Use of Rockefeller," *Time*, 2 September 1974, 18; "A Natural Force on a National Stage," *Time*, 2 September 1974, 14; Greene, *Presidency of Gerald R. Ford*, 30; Richard Norton Smith, *On His Own Terms: A Life of Nelson Rockefeller* (New York: Random House, 2014), 644–645.

20. Lee Hamilton, telephone interview by Scott Kaufman, 3 September 2015; Timmons to the President, 21 August 1974, http://www.fordlibrarymuseum.gov

/library/document/0047/phw19740822-08.pdf, accessed 22 March 2014; Timmons to the President, 22 August 1974, memoranda—Timmons to the President, August 1974 (2), WETF, Box 5, GFL.

21. Ford, *Time to Heal*, 158.

22. Ibid., 157–158; Werth, *31 Days*, 213–214, 221; James Cannon, *Gerald R. Ford: An Honorable Life* (Ann Arbor: University of Michigan Press, 2013), 222.

23. Ford, *Time to Heal*, 159; Cannon, *Time and Chance*, 373–375; "The Pardon That Brought No Peace," *Time*, 16 September 1974, 11.

24. Cannon, *Time and Chance*, 373, 374, 377–379.

25. Ibid., 359–360; Werth, *31 Days*, 281–282; Ford, *Time to Heal*, 164–165.

26. Nixon to Sampson, 6 September 1974, Nixon Papers: Agreement, 9/6/1974, PBF, Box 28, GFL.

27. Cannon, *Time and Chance*, 379–380; Joan Hoff, *Nixon Reconsidered* (New York: BasicBooks, 1994), 327.

28. Cannon, *Time and Chance*, 381; Werth, *31 Days*, 304.

29. Werth, *31 Days*, 308, 312–313, 315.

30. Cannon, *Time and Chance*, 382–383.

31. "Mr. Nixon Pardoned," *Wall Street Journal*, 10 September 1974; "Pardon Commendable," *New Orleans Times-Picayune*, 10 September 1974; Alexanders to Moss, 12 September 1974, No. 19—White House (Pardon) 93rd Congress 1974, Box 497, PFEM, JWML; Waggonner to Ford, 13 September 1974, letter on display at GRFM; Remarks by U.S. Senator Robert P. Griffin re the pardon, 9 September 1974, Ford's Pardon Decision, PRPG, Box 277, CHL.

32."The Failure of Mr. Ford," *New York Times*, 9 September 1974; "The Presidential Pardon," *Washington Post*, 10 September 1974; "The Nixon Pardon," *Grand Rapids Press*, 9 September 1974; Douglas Brinkley, *Gerald R. Ford* (New York: Times Books, 2007), 68; Kunkel to President, 9 September 1974, No. 15—White House (Pardon) 93rd Congress 1974, and Moss to Constituents, 23 September 1974, No. 18—White House (Pardon) 93rd Congress 1974, Box 497, PFEM, JWML; Jim Wright, *Balance of Power: Presidents and Congress from the Era of McCarthy to the Age of Gingrich* (Atlanta: Turner Publishing, 1996), 225; Stanley I. Kutler, *The Wars of Watergate: The Last Crisis of Richard Nixon* (New York: Knopf, 1990), 565–566; Jerome R. Waldie, "Playing Politics with Justice," *Nation*, 28 September 1974, 264.

33. Korologos to Timmons, 10 September 1974, www.fordlibrarymuseum.gov /library/exhibits/pardon/004700549-002.pdf, accessed 10 July 2014; Andrew Downer Crain, *The Ford Presidency: A History* (Jefferson, N.C.: McFarland, 2009), 64; Richard Lugar, telephone interview by Scott Kaufman, 22 July 2015; Gerald Ford, 1 September 1989, interview by James Cannon, Ford Gerald—Interview, 9/1/89, JMCRIN, Box 1, GFL; Brinkley, *Gerald R. Ford*, 74.

34. Memorandum for the Record, 10 August 1974; Crain, *Ford Presidency*, 63.

35. Greene, *Presidency of Gerald R. Ford*, 51–52; Cannon, *Time and Chance*, 379; James Doyle, *Not above the Law: The Battles of Watergate Prosecutors Cox and Jaworski* (New York: Morrow, 1977), 373.

36. Crain, *Ford Presidency*, 64–65.

37. Callaway to the President, 6 September 1974, http://www.fordlibrarymuseum.gov/library/document/0047/phw19741012-05.pdf, accessed 12 July 2014; Greene, *Presidency of Gerald R. Ford*, 64.

38. Greene, *Presidency of Gerald R. Ford*, 64–66; Crain, *Ford Presidency*, 68–69.

39. Greene, *Presidency of Gerald R. Ford*, 35; terHorst to President, 8 September 1974, terHorst Resignation as Press Secretary, JECF, Box 19, GFL; "'Off to a Helluva Start,'" *Time*, 26 August 1974, 52; Cannon, *Time and Chance*, 383–384; Jerald F. terHorst, *Gerald Ford and the Future of the Presidency* (New York: Okpaku Publishing, 1974), 240.

40. Greene, *Presidency of Gerald R. Ford*, 63–64; "Taking the Heat on Nixon Pardon," *Time*, 30 September 1974, 30.

41. Crain, *Ford Presidency*, 65; Cannon, *Time and Chance*, 387–388; Hungate to Ford, 17 September 1974, Nixon Pardon—Hungate Subcommittee: Correspondence (1), PBF, Box 33, GFL, and Buchen to Hungate, 24 September 1974, and Hungate to the President, 25 September 1974, Nixon Pardon—Hungate Subcommittee: Correspondence (2), PBF, Box 33, GFL.

42. Crain, *Ford Presidency*, 65; Cannon, *Time and Chance*, 388; Sandman to the President, 1 October 1974, and President to Sandman, 4 October 1974, http://www.fordlibrarymuseum.gov/library/document/0047/phw19741004-01.pdf, accessed 12 July 2014; Cabinet Meeting: 11 October 1974, Cabinet Meetings—Campaign 1974, Dean Burch Files, Box 1, GFL.

43. Cannon, *Time and Chance*, 390–391; Peter Rodino, 28 September 1990, interviewed by James Cannon, Rodino, Peter—Interview, 9/28/90, JMCRIN, Box 3, GFL.

44. *CQA*, 1974: 654.

45. Robert Hartmann, June 19, 1991, interview by James Cannon, Hartmann, Robert—Interview, 6/19/91, JMCRIN, Box 3, and L. William Seidman, 18 October 1994, interview by Yanek Mieczkowski, Seidman, L. William—10/18/1994, YMRI, Box 1, GFL; John Rhodes, *John Rhodes: "I Was There,"* with Dean Smith (Salt Lake City, Utah: Northwest Publishing, 1995), 179.

46. Mieczkowski, *Gerald Ford*, 105, 106–107; Dominic Sandbrook, *Mad As Hell: The Crisis of the 1970s and the Rise of the Populist Right* (New York: Knopf, 2011), 32; Brinkley, *Gerald R. Ford*, 76; Greene, *Presidency of Gerald R. Ford*, 68.

47. Greene, *Presidency of Gerald R. Ford*, 69–70.

48. Crain, *Ford Presidency*, 76–77.

49. Ibid., 77; *PPPUS, 1974*: 9.

50. "Betty Ford Will Set a Different Style," *U.S. News & World Report*, 19 August 1974; John Robert Greene, *Betty Ford: Candor and Courage in the White House* (Lawrence: University Press of Kansas, 2004), 38–39, 43–44, 87–90.

51. Greene, *Betty Ford*, 45–46; Ford, *Time to Heal*, 190.

52. Greene, *Betty Ford*, 47–49; Ford, *Time to Heal*, 191; Marjorie Hunter, "Mrs. Ford Faces a Breast Biopsy," *New York Times*, 28 September 1974; Marjorie Hunter,

"Ford's Wife Undergoes Breast Cancer Surgery," *New York Times*, 29 September 1974; *PPPUS, 1974*: 205.

53. Greene, *Betty Ford*, 49–51, 121.

54. "Summing Up the Summit," *Time*, 7 October 1974, 37.

55. *PPPUS, 1974*: 237.

56. Mieczkowski, *Gerald Ford*, 122–124; Seidman interview, 18 October 1994.

57. Mieczkowski, *Gerald Ford*, 133–135; Paul O'Neill, telephone interview by Scott Kaufman, 21 October 2015.

58. Mieczkowski, *Gerald Ford*, 137–138, 217; Mark J. Rozell, *The Press and the Ford Presidency* (Ann Arbor: University of Michigan Press, 1992), 65.

59. Mieczkowski, *Gerald Ford*, 140–141.

60. Sandbrook, *Mad as Hell*, 33.

61. Joseph A. Gusfield, *The Culture of Public Problems: Drinking-Driving and the Symbolic Order* (Chicago: University of Chicago Press, 1981), 121; James Ciment, *Postwar America: An Encyclopedia of Social, Political, Cultural, and Economic History* (New York: Routledge, 2006), 99; David Howard Davis, "Energy Policy and the Ford Administration: The First Year," in *The Politics of Policy Making in America: Five Case Studies*, ed. David A. Caputo (San Francisco: W. H. Freeman, 1977), 40.

62. Mieczkowski, *Gerald Ford*, 218–219. The Federal Energy Administration had been created by Nixon in 1974 to combat the energy crisis.

63. Telephone conversation between Ford and Kissinger, 10 August 1974, *FRUS, 1969–1976*, 30: 419.

64. Ibid., 420.

65. Crain, *Ford Presidency*, 47.

66. Memorandum of Conversation, 26 September 1974, *FRUS, 1969–1976*, 30: 691, 693; Rifat N. Bali, *Model Citizens of the State: The Jews of Turkey during the Multi-Party Period* (Lanham, Md.: Fairleigh Dickinson, 2012), 198.

67. George C. Herring, *America's Longest War: The United States and Vietnam*, 4th ed. (Boston: McGraw-Hill, 2002), 324–325, 329–330; James S. Olson and Randy Roberts, *Where the Domino Fell: America and Vietnam, 1945–2006*, 5th ed. (Maplecrest, N.Y.: Brandywine, 2006), 240.

68. Kissinger to the President, 9 September 1974, *FRUS, 1969–1976*, 10: 556–557; *PPPUS, 1974*: 244.

69. Kissinger to the President, 23 November 1974, *FRUS, 1969–1976*, 10: 577–578; Memorandum of Conversation, 28 November 1974, *FRUS, 1969–1976*, 18: 627–628; Crain, *Ford Presidency*, 147–148.

70. Olson and Roberts, *Where the Domino Fell*, 241; Interagency Intelligence Memorandum, 7 January 1975, *FRUS, 1969–1976*, 10: 594–595.

71. Minutes of Washington Special Actions Group Meeting, 7 January 1975, *FRUS, 1969–1976*, 10: 582–593.

72. Greene, *Presidency of Gerald R. Ford*, 135; *PPPUS, 1975*, 119–123; Memorandum of Conversation, 11 March 1975, *FRUS, 1969–1976*, 10: 674; Crain, *Ford*

Presidency, 150; Cabinet Meeting Notes, 29 January 1975, 1975/01/29 Cabinet Meeting, James Connor Files, Box 4, GFL.

73. David P. Forsythe, ed., *Encyclopedia of Human Rights* (New York: Oxford University Press, 2009), 1: 271.

74. Ford to Brezhnev, 9 August 1974, and Memorandum of Conversation, *FRUS, 1969–1976*, 16: 7, 102–106.

75. Raymond L. Garthoff, *Détente and Confrontation: American-Soviet Relations from Nixon to Reagan*, rev. ed. (Washington, D.C.: Brookings Institution, 1994), 347, 461; Crain, *Ford Presidency*, 95–96.

76. Memorandum Concerning the Interpretative Response and Other Issues, 14 August 1974, Jackson Amendment—1974, Series 4, Subseries 2, JKJC, Box 58, SUNY-SB; Kissinger to Ford, 9 August 1974, and Memoranda of Conversation, 15 August and 18 September 1974, *FRUS, 1969–1976*, 16: 9, 39–44, 91; Henry Kissinger, *Years of Renewal* (New York: Simon and Schuster, 1999), 258–259.

77. Crain, *Ford Presidency*, 96, 97; Ford, *Time to Heal*, 139; Anatoly Dobrynin, *In Confidence: Moscow's Ambassador to America's Six Cold War Presidents* (New York: Times Books, 1995), 335.

78. Kissinger, *Years of Renewal*, 267; Thomas G. Paterson et al., *American Foreign Relations: A History*, 2 vols. (Boston: Houghton Mifflin, 2006), 2: 256; Kissinger to Ford, undated, *FRUS, 1969–1976*, 16: 51, 52, 53.

79. Paterson et al., *American Foreign Relations*, 2: 256; Kissinger to Ford, undated, *FRUS, 1969–1976*, 16: 52.

80. Kissinger to Ford, undated, *FRUS, 1969–1976*, 16: 54–55.

81. Minutes of National Security Council Meeting, 14 September and 7 October 1974, *FRUS, 1969–1976*, 33: 295–317, 321–337; *CQA*, 1974: 41.

82. Memorandum of Conversation, 8 October 1974, Note from the United States to the Soviet Union, undated, Kissinger to the President, 18 October 1974, and Minutes of National Security Council Meeting, 18 October 1974, *FRUS, 1969–1976*, 33: 339–340, 346–367; Garthoff, *Détente and Confrontation*, 494.

83. Ford, *Time to Heal*, 200; Scowcroft to the President, 25 and 27 October 1974, and Kissinger to Ford, undated, *FRUS, 1969–1976*, 33: 368–377.

84. Crain, *Ford Presidency*, 99; Memoranda of Conversation, 23 and 24 November 1974, *FRUS, 1969–1976*, 16: 325–358.

85. Garthoff, *Détente and Confrontation*, 497–499; Greene, *Presidency of Gerald R. Ford*, 125–126; Memorandum of Conversation, 21 October 1974, www.fordlibrarymuseum.gov/library/document/0314/1552832.pdf, accessed 12 July 2014; Anne H. Cahn, *Killing Detente: The Right Attacks the CIA* (University Park: Pennsylvania State University Press, 1998), 61.

86. *FRUS, 1969–1976*, 31: 776; Greene, *Presidency of Gerald R. Ford*, 123; Garthoff, *Détente and Confrontation*, 509, 512–513, 514.

87. Burton I. Kaufman, *The Arab Middle East and the United States: Inter-Arab Rivalry and Superpower Diplomacy* (New York: Twayne, 1996), 89.

88. Ibid., 89–90.

89. Ibid., 90–91.

90. Memorandum of Conversation, 12 August 1974, and Minutes of National Security Council Meeting, 18 October 1974, *FRUS, 1969–1976*, 26: 402–405, 444.

91. Kaufman, *Arab Middle East and the United States*, 51, 53; H. W. Brands, *Into the Labyrinth: The United States and the Middle East, 1945–1993* (New York: McGraw-Hill, 1994), 126–127.

92. Kaufman, *Arab Middle East and the United States*, 94.

93. Ibid., 94–95; Walter Isaacson, *Kissinger: A Biography* (New York: Simon and Schuster, 1992), 630–631; Memorandum of Conversation, 14 November 1974, www.fordlibrarymuseum.gov/library/document/0314/1552853.pdf, accessed 16 July 2014.

94. Kaufman, *Arab Middle East and the United States*, 95; Memoranda of Conversation, 5 October and 9 December 1974, and 16 and 22 January 1975, and Scowcroft to Ford, 10 October 1974, *FRUS, 1969–1976*, 26: 426, 429, 466, 496, 498–499.

95. Greene, *Presidency of Gerald R. Ford*, 31; Smith, *On His Own Terms*, 647–651.

96. Crain, *Ford Presidency*, 103; Greene, *Presidency of Gerald R. Ford*, 83; Smith, *On His Own Terms*, 654.

97. Michael Nelson, ed., *Guide to the Presidency*, 2nd ed. (New York: Routledge, 2015), 1123; Smith, *On His Own Terms*, 654–655; Ford, *Time to Heal*, 147; Samuel Kernell and Samuel L. Popkin, eds., *Chief of Staff: Twenty-Five Years of Managing the Presidency* (Berkeley: University of California Press, 1986), 230.

98. Ron Nessen, *Making the News, Taking the News: From NBC to the Ford White House* (Middletown, Conn.: Wesleyan University Press, 2011), 140; William Colby and Peter Forbath, *Honorable Men: My Life in the CIA* (New York: Simon and Schuster, 1978), 392–393; Crain, *Ford Presidency*, 115; Ford, *Time to Heal*, 229.

99. David Cook, "Movies and Political Trauma," in *American Cinema of the 1970s: Themes and Variation*, ed. Lester D. Friedman (New Brunswick, N.J.: Rutgers University Press, 2007), 124, 127; Mieczkowski, *Gerald Ford*, 213; Douglas T. Miller, "Sixties Activism in the 'Me Decade,'" in *The Lost Decade: America in the Seventies*, ed. Elsebeth Hurup (Aarhus, Denmark: Aarhus University Press, 1996), 136.

100. Wright, *Balance of Power*, 235–236; Julian E. Zelizer, *On Capitol Hill: The Struggle to Reform Congress and Its Consequences, 1948–2000* (New York: Cambridge University Press, 2004), 162, 163–169; Pat Schroeder, telephone interview by Scott Kaufman and Alissa Warters, 3 November 2015.

101. Paul Charles Light, *The President's Agenda: Domestic Policy Choice from Kennedy to Carter* (Baltimore: Johns Hopkins University Press, 1982), 121.

102. Oral history, James Cannon, interviewed by Yanek Mieczkowski, 19 October 1994, Cannon, James—10/19/1994, YMRI, Box 1, GFL.

103. Oral history, Douglas Bennett, interviewed by Yanek Mieczkoswki, 19 October 1994, Bennett, Douglas—10/19/1994, and oral history, Robert Goldwin, interviewed by Yanek Mieczkowski, 3 March 1994, Goldwin, Robert—3/3/94, YMRI, Box 1, GFL; Seidman interview, 18 October 1994; O'Neill telephone interview, 21

October 2015; John Herbers, "Critical Tests for Ford" *New York Times*, 2 January 1975; Mieczkowski, *Gerald Ford*, 47.

Chapter Seven: Confronting Crises

1. *PPPUS, 1975*: 36–37.

2. Oral history, Ron Nessen, interviewed by Yanek Mieczkowski, 29 January 2002, Nessen, Ron—1/29/02, YMRI, Box 1, GFL; Ron Nessen, *It Sure Looks Different from the Inside* (Chicago: Playboy Press, 1978), 80–82.

3. Richard H. Growald, "Ford as Mr. Nice Guy," *Grand Rapids Press*, 13 February 1975; *PPPUS, 1975*: 30–35; Yanek Mieczkowski, *Gerald Ford and the Challenges of the 1970s* (Lexington: University Press of Kentucky, 2005), 159.

4. Nessen, *It Sure Looks Different,* 85, 161; oral history, L. William Seidman, interviewed by Yanek Mieczkowski, 18 October 1994, Seidman, L. William—10/18/1994, YMRI, Box 1, GFL; *PPPUS, 1975*: 43.

5. John Robert Greene, *The Presidency of Gerald R. Ford* (Lawrence: University Press of Kansas, 1995), 75; "Not Good," *New York Times*, 16 January 1975; Haynes Johnson, "President Had Bad News," *Washington Post*, 16 January 1975; "Ford Makes His Move," *Newsweek*, 27 January 1975, 18–19; "Mr. Ford's Flawed Plan," *New York Times*, 22 January 1975; "A Race to Prime the Pump," *Newsweek*, 20 January 1975, 16; "Ford's Grand Canyon Budget," *Time*, 10 February 1975, 12; "Go on Taxes, Slow on Energy," *Time*, 3 March 1975, 10; Mieczkowski, *Gerald Ford*, 163; "Nixon, Ford Viewed in Poll as Opposites," *New York Times*, 21 February 1975; George H. Gallup, *The Gallup Poll: Public Opinion, 1972–1977* (Wilmington, Del.: Scholarly Resources, 1978), 1: 405–406.

6. Mieczkowski, *Gerald Ford*, 148, 151–153.

7. Ibid., 146–148.

8. Ibid., 165–166, 168; "Trying to Avert a Collision," *Time*, 10 March 1975, 11; Greene, *Presidency of Gerald R. Ford*, 76.

9. Simon to President, 28 March 1975, http://www.fordlibrarymuseum.gov/library/document/0047/phw19750329-16.pdf, accessed 28 June 2015; Hartmann to the President, 28 March 1975, http://www.fordlibrarymuseum.gov/library/document/0047/phw19750329-12.pdf, accessed 28 June 2015; Rockefeller to the President, 28 March 1975, http://www.fordlibrarymuseum.gov/library/document/0047/phw19750329-13.pdf, accessed 28 June 2015; Lynn to the President, 28 March 1975, http://www.fordlibrarymuseum.gov/library/document/0047/phw19750329-15.pdf, accessed 28 June 2015; Dunham to the President, 28 March 1975, http://www.fordlibrarymuseum.gov/library/document/0047/phw19750329-19.pdf, accessed 28 June 2015; Greene, *Presidency of Gerald R. Ford*, 76; *PPPUS*, 1975: 409.

10. "Go on Taxes, Slow on Energy," 10; Mieczkowski, *Gerald Ford*, 232, 233–235; Jackson and Kennedy to Colleague, 21 January 1975, Energy—Oil Import Fees, OJF, Box 4, GFL; Greene, *Presidency of Gerald R. Ford*, 78.

11. Oral history, Philip Buchen, interviewed by James M. Cannon, 15 February 1990, Buchen-Philip—Interview, 2/15/90, JMCRIN, Box 3; oral history, Max Friedersdorf, interviewed by Yanek Mieczkowski, 14 August 2001, Friedersdorf, Max—

8/14/2001; oral history, Ron Nessen, interviewed by Yanek Mieczkowski, 29 January 2002, Nessen, Ron—1/29/2002, YMRI, Box 1, GFL; *PPPUS, 1975*: 729–732.

12. Mieczkowski *Gerald Ford*, 236–238, 240; Gallup, *Gallup Poll*, 1: 443.

13. Mieczkowski, *Gerald Ford*, 243–244.

14. Greene, *Presidency of Gerald R. Ford*, 78–79; "Abdication by Congress," *New York Times*, 13 June 1975.

15. Benjamin Kline, *First along the River: A Brief History of the U.S. Environmental Movement*, 2nd ed. (Lanham, Md.: Acada Books, 2000), 95; Mieczkowski, *Gerald Ford*, 267.

16. Mieczkowski, *Gerald Ford*, 268–269; Gerald R. Ford, *A Time to Heal: The Autobiography of Gerald R. Ford* (New York: Harper and Row, 1979), 226; "Ford's Strip Mining Bill Termed Unsatisfactory," *Lawrence (Kans.) Journal-World*, 7 February 1975.

17. Greene, *Presidency of Gerald R. Ford*, 89.

18. U.S. Commission on Civil Rights, "School Desegregation in Boston," June 1975, https://www.law.umaryland.edu/marshall/usccr/documents/cr12sch618.pdf, accessed 25 May 2017; Andrew Downer Crain, *The Ford Presidency: A History* (Jefferson, N.C.: McFarland, 2009), 188–189; *PPPUS, 1975*: 35–37; Lawrence J. McAndrews, "Missing the Bus: Gerald Ford and School Desegregation," *Presidential Studies Quarterly* 27, no. 4 (Fall 1997): 795–796; John Kifner, "U.S. Study Assails Officials on Boston Integration," *New York Times*, 21 August 1975.

19. "Summary of Vital Statistics 2010: The City of New York: Population and Mortality," http://www.nyc.gov/html/records/pdf/govpub/6551as_2010_final_population_&_mortality.pdf, accessed 1 November 2015; Greene, *Presidency of Gerald R. Ford*, 90; Crain, *Ford Presidency*, 189.

20. Crain, *Ford Presidency*, 189–190; President to Beame, 14 May 1975, New York City Finances—Meeting with the President, Vice President, Beame, and Carey, 13 May 1975, JMCF, Box 23, GFL.

21. Parsky to Economic Policy Board, undated (circa 21 June 1975), New York City, May–October 1975 (1), and Cannon to Simon, undated (circa July 1975), New York City, May–October 1975 (2), LWSF, Box 78, Simon to the President, 8 September 1975, 32: New York City, WESP, Box 24 (microfiche), and Simon to the President, 28 August 1975, 9: President—Memoranda to and from W.E.S., WESP, Box 25 (microfiche), GFL; Crain, *Ford Presidency*, 190–191.

22. Greene, *Presidency of Gerald R. Ford*, 92–93; *PPPUS, 1975*: 645.

23. Loen to Friedersdorf, 29 October 1975, New York City Financial Crisis (1), JMF, Box 22, GFL; *CR*, 1975: 34346, 34459, 34971, 34983; Crain, *Ford Presidency*, 192.

24. Crain, *Ford Presidency*, 191–192; Greene, *Presidency of Gerald R. Ford*, 94.

25. Kim Phillips-Fein, "The Legacy of the 1970s Fiscal Crisis," *Nation*, 6 May 2013, https://www.thenation.com/article/legacy-1970s-fiscal-crisis/, accessed 8 January 2016.

26. Kathryn Olmsted, "U.S. Intelligence Agencies during the Ford Years," in *The Companion to Gerald R. Ford and Jimmy Carter*, ed. Scott Kaufman (Malden, Mass.: Wiley, 2016), 116.

27. James Cannon, *Gerald R. Ford: An Honorable Life* (Ann Arbor: University of Michigan Press, 2013), 321; Colby to the President, 24 December 1974, Intelligence—Colby Report, LLF, Box 13, GFL; Memorandum of Conversation, 4 January 1975, http://www.fordlibrarymuseum.gov/library/document/0314/1552900.pdf, accessed 12 June 2014; Greene, *Presidency of Gerald R. Ford*, 107; Archie Robinson, *George Meany and His Times: A Biography* (New York: Simon and Schuster, 1981), 335–337.

28. Kathryn S. Olmsted, *Challenging the Secret Government: The Post-Watergate Investigations of the CIA and FBI* (Chapel Hill: University of North Carolina Press, 1996), 59–61; Daniel Schorr, *Clearing the Air* (Boston: Houghton Mifflin, 1977), 147.

29. Greene, *Presidency of Gerald R. Ford*, 107, 110; Olmsted, "US Intelligence Agencies during the Ford Years," 122.

30. Greene, *Presidency of Gerald R. Ford,* 108; "CIA and Assassination Plots—Rockefeller Report Stirs Furor," *U.S. News & World Report*, 16 June 1975, 33.

31. Ford to Church, 31 October 1975, President 9/75–12/75, JMF, Box 87, GFL; Olmsted, "US Intelligence Agencies during the Ford Years," 123; Greene, *Presidency of Gerald R. Ford*, 112; "CIA Murder Plots—Weighing the Damage to U.S.," *U.S. News & World Report*, 1 December 1975, 13.

32. Loch K. Johnson, *A Season of Inquiry: Congress and Intelligence* (Lexington: University Press of Kentucky, 1985), 182; Ford to Pike, 19 November 1974, Intelligence Investigations: Pike Committee, RKWF, Box 2, GFL.

33. Leo Ashby and Rod Gramer, *Fighting the Odds: The Life of Senator Frank Church* (Pullman: Washington State University Press, 1994), 485.

34. Colby to Kissinger, 20 November 1974, Scowcroft to Ford, 12 December 1974, and Memorandum of Conversation, 1 February 1975, *FRUS, 1969–1976*, 30: 584–586, 589, 697; *PPPUS, 1975*: 467.

35. Memorandum of Conversation, 28 February 1975, *FRUS, 1969–1976*, 38: 272–273; Memorandum of Conversation, 21 March 1975, http://www.fordlibrarymuseum.gov/library/document/0314/1552995.pdf, accessed 25 June 2014; *PPPUS, 1975*: 467.

36. *CQA*, 1975: 327–329; Memoranda of Conversation, 19 and 23 June 1975, *FRUS, 1969–1976*, 10: 746–765.

37. Bennett to Marsh, 28 July 1975, Turkey—Military Aid Embargo (3), JMF, Box 41, and Ford to Rangel, 31 July 1975, Turkey—Military Aid Embargo (4), JMF, Box 42, GFL; "Ford Asks Black Caucus Aid in Turkey Embargo Fight," *Afro-American*, 9 August 1975; Memoranda of Conversation, 31 July and 25 September 1975, *FRUS, 1969–1976*, 30: 772, 792–793.

38. *CQA*, 1975: 327, 329–331; Kissinger to U.S. Embassy, Athens, 4 October 1975, http://www.fordlibrarymuseum.gov/library/document/0351/1555810.pdf, accessed 27 July 2014.

39. Crain, *Ford Presidency*, 149; James S. Olson and Randy Roberts, *Where the Domino Fell: America and Vietnam, 1945–2006*, 5th ed. (Maplecrest, N.Y.: Brandywine, 2006), 242; Scowcroft to the President, 18 March 1975, *FRUS, 1969–1976*, 10: 682–683.

40. See, for instance, Memorandum of Conversation, 28 February 1975, *FRUS, 1969–1976*, 38: 271–272; Memoranda of Conversation, 4 and 6 March 1975, *FRUS, 1969–1976*, 10: 657–673.

41. Bartholomew Sparrow, *The Strategist: Brent Scowcroft and the Call of National Security* (New York: Perseus, 2015), 139.

42. Stanley Karnow, *Vietnam: A History*, 2nd rev. and updated ed. (New York: Penguin, 1997), 675; Memorandum of Conversation, 24 March 1975, Ford to Thieu, 25 March 1975, and Lehmann to Scowcroft, 26 March 1975, *FRUS, 1969–1976*, 10: 688, 696–698; Crain, *Ford Presidency*, 151.

43. Crain, *Ford Presidency*, 151; Greene, *Presidency of Gerald R. Ford*, 137; J. Edward Lee and H. C. "Toby" Haynsworth, *Nixon, Ford, and the Abandonment of South Vietnam* (Jefferson, N.C.: McFarland, 2002), 119.

44. Minutes of Washington Special Actions Group, 2 April 1975, and Martin to Scowcroft, 7 April 1975, *FRUS, 1969–1976*, 10: 731; Greene, *Presidency of Gerald R. Ford*, 137; David Hume Kennerly, *Shooter* (New York: Newsweek Books, 1979), 174.

45. Henry Kissinger, *Ending the Vietnam War: A History of America's Involvement in and Extrication from the Vietnam War* (New York: Simon and Schuster, 2003), 538; Minutes of National Security Council Meeting, 9 April 1975, *FRUS, 1969–1976*, 10: 770–771, 777.

46. *PPPUS, 1975*: 462–464; Cokie Roberts, interviewed by Richard Norton Smith, 19 November 2009, http://geraldrfordfoundation.org/centennial/oralhistory/wp-content/uploads/2013/05/Cokie-Roberts.pdf, accessed 6 June 2015.

47. Kenton Clymer, *Troubled Relations: The United States and Cambodia since 1870* (DeKalb: Northern Illinois University Press, 2007), 158.

48. Douglas Brinkley, *Gerald R. Ford* (New York: Times Books, 2007), 92; *CQA, 1975*: 306, 308; Nessen interview, 29 January 2002.

49. Minutes of National Security Council Meeting, 9 April 1975, Martin to Kissinger, 15 April 1975, and Kissinger to Martin, 17 April 1975, *FRUS, 1969–1975*, 10: 823–824, 826, 830–831; Kissinger to Martin, 19 April 1975, *FRUS, 1969–1976*, 10: 774, 823–824, 826, 830–831, 848; Crain, *Ford Presidency*, 154.

50. Anatoly Dobrynin, *In Confidence: Moscow's Ambassador to America's Six Cold War Presidents* (New York: Times Books, 1995), 343–344; Crain, *Ford Presidency*, 155.

51. *PPPUS, 1975*: 569; Greene, *Presidency of Gerald R. Ford*, 140.

52. Crain, *Ford Presidency*, 157–158.

53. Ibid., 158–159; Nessen, *It Sure Looks Different*, 113; Donald Rumsfeld, *Known and Unknown: A Memoir* (New York: Sentinel, 2011), 209.

54. Greene, *Presidency of Gerald R. Ford*, 140–141; "Evacuation and Resettlement of Indo Chinese Refugees," undated (circa May 1975), Refugees—Indochina: General (3), Philip Buchen Files, Box 58, Gerald Ford, interviewed by James Cannon, 1 September 1989, Ford, Gerald—Interview, 9/1/89, and Gerald Ford, interviewed by James Cannon, 27 April 1990, Ford, Gerald—Interview, 4/27/90, JMCRIN, Box 1, and Friedersdorf to the President, 1 May 1975, Presidential Handwriting, 5/1/1975 (2), PHF, Box C20, GFL; *CQA, 1975*: 302, 40-H.

55. Dean to the Secretary, 1 May 1975, and Kissinger to the President, 2 May 1975, Refugees—Indochina: General (3), Philip Buchen Files, Box 58; and "The Ford Presidency: A Portrait of the First Two Years," undated (circa August 1976), President—Report: Two Years (1) (2) (3), RTHF, Box 16, GFL.

56. *PPPUS, 1975*: 641–652; Memorandum for the Record, 6 May 1975, http://www.fordlibrarymuseum.gov/library/document/0314/1553061.pdf, accessed July 11, 2014; "Ford Presidency: A Portrait."

57. Greene, *Presidency of Gerald R. Ford*, 143–144; John F. Guilmartin Jr., *A Very Short War: The* Mayaguez *and the Battle of Koh Tang* (College Station: Texas A&M University Press, 1995), 26.

58. Ford interview, 27 April 1990; Crain, *Ford Presidency*, 164; Minutes of the Secretary of State's Regional Staff Meeting, 12 May 1975, *FRUS, 1969–1976*, 10: 974; Greene, *Presidency of Gerald R. Ford*, 144.

59. Minutes of National Security Council Meeting, 12 May 1975, *FRUS, 1969–1976*, 10: 979; Guilmartin, *Very Short War*, 39, 49.

60. Minutes of National Security Council Meeting, 12 May 1975, *FRUS, 1969–1976*, 10: 977–985; Greene, *Presidency of Gerald R. Ford*, 145.

61. Joint Chiefs of Staff to Commander in Chief, Pacific Command, 12 May 1975, and Ingersoll to Liaison Office in China, 13 May 1975, *FRUS, 1969–1976*, 10: 979n2, 985–986; Greene, *Presidency of Gerald R. Ford*, 145; Guilmartin, *Very Short War*, 47.

62. Greene, *Presidency of Gerald R. Ford*, 145–146; Brinkley, *Gerald R. Ford*, 101; Masters to Department of State, 13 May 1975, and Bush to Department of State, 15 May 1975, *FRUS, 1969–1976*, 10: 987–989, 1037.

63. Ford, *Time to Heal*, 276; Minutes of National Security Council Meeting, 13 May and 13–14 May 1975, *FRUS, 1969–1976*, 10: 996, 998, 1008; Guilmartin, *Very Short War*, 51.

64. Minutes of National Security Council Meeting, 13 and 14 May 1975, 10: 996–998, 1006, 1022.

65. Minutes of National Security Council Meeting, 13 May 1975, 10: 1012–1014; Rumsfeld, *Known and Unknown*, 211.

66. Telephone Conversation between the President and Scowcroft, 13 May 1975, *FRUS, 1969–1976*, 10: 1002; Guilmartin, *Very Short War*, 55–56.

67. Telephone Conversation between the President and Scowcroft, 13 May 1975, Minutes of National Security Council Meeting, 13–14 May 1975, and Minutes of National Security Council Meeting, 14 May 1975, 10: 1003–1006, 1033–1036.

68. Crain, *Ford Presidency*, 166.

69. Memorandum of Conversation, 14 May 1975, http://www.fordlibrarymuseum.gov/library/document/0314/1553074.pdf, accessed 15 July 2014.

70. Guilmartin, *Very Short War*, 60–61, 87–89, 95–96, 100–101.

71. Ibid., 99; Greene, *Presidency of Gerald R. Ford*, 149.

72. Guilmartin, *Very Short War*, 99–100; Robert T. Hartmann, *Palace Politics: An Inside Account of the Ford Years* (New York: McGraw-Hill, 1980), 328; Nessen, *It Sure Looks Different*, 128–129.

73. Guilmartin, *Very Short War*, 99–100, 113–114, 126.

74. Brinkley, *Gerald R. Ford*, 103; Greene, *Presidency of Gerald R. Ford*, 151; Friedersdorf to the President, 16 May 1975, Mayaguez Situation—General (2), Philip Buchen Files, Box 25, GFL.

75. Nessen, *It Sure Looks Different*, 127–128; Ford, *Time to Heal*, 284.

76. Henry Kissinger, *Years of Renewal* (New York: Simon and Schuster, 1999), 575; Comptroller General of the United States, *The Seizure of the* Mayaguez*—A Case Study of Crisis Management*, 11 May 1976, http://archive.gao.gov/f0302/a02828.pdf, accessed 4 March 2014; Greene, *Presidency of Gerald R. Ford*, 151.

77. Ford to Brezhnev, 9 October 1975, *FRUS, 1969–1976*, 16: 435–436; Anne Hessing Cahn, *Killing Detente: The Right Attacks the CIA* (University Park: Pennsylvania State University Press, 1998), 36.

78. Greene, *Presidency of Gerald Ford*, 151; Walter Isaacson, *Kissinger: A Biography* (New York: Simon and Schuster, 1992), 658; Rumsfeld, *Known and Unknown*, 181; Richard B. Cheney, *In My Time: A Personal and Political Memoir,* with Liz Cheney (New York: Threshold Editions, 2011), 87.

79. Cahn, *Killing Detente*, 32–33; Rowland Evans and Robert Novak, "Snubbing Solzhenitsyn," *Washington Post*, 17 July 1975.

80. Edward H. Judge and John W. Langdon, *A Hard and Bitter Peace: A Global History of the Cold War* (Upper Saddle River, N.J.: Prentice Hall, 1996), 224.

81. James M. Naughton, "Ford Sees 35-Nation Charter as a Gauge on Rights in East Europe," *New York Times*, 26 July 1975; "Helsinki: What's in It for the West?," *National Review*, 11 July 1975, 97.

82. Memoranda of Conversation, 20 May and 10 July 1975, and Kissinger to the President, 19 July 1975, *FRUS, 1969–1976*, 16: 580–585, 625–628, 681; Note from the United States to the Soviet Union, undated, *FRUS, 1969–1976*, 33: 419–421; Kissinger to the President, undated, *FRUS, 1969–1976*, 39: 932–933.

83. Memoranda of Conversation, 30 July and 2 August 1975, *FRUS, 1969–1976*, 16: 694–695, 697, 699–701, 706–714; Robert G. Kaufman, *Henry M. Jackson: A Life in Politics* (Seattle: University of Washington Press, 2000), 293; Memorandum of Conversation, 8 December 1975, https://history.state.gov/historicaldocuments/frus1969-76ve12/d215, accessed 6 February 2014.

84. Memorandum of Conversation, 14 February 1975, Scowcroft to Ford, 10 March 1975, *FRUS, 1969–1976*, 26: 509–510, 529–530; William B. Quandt, *Peace Process: American Diplomacy and the Arab-Israeli Conflict since 1967*, rev. ed. (Washington, D.C.: Brookings Institution, 2001), 160–161.

85. Scowcroft to Ford, 9, 14, and 18 March 1975, *FRUS, 1969–1976*, 26: 527, 535–536, 545; Quandt, *Peace Process*, 163.

86. Ford to Rabin, 21 March 1975, *FRUS, 1969–1976*, 26: 553; Quandt, *Peace Process*, 163; Burton I. Kaufman, *The Arab Middle East and the United States: Inter-Arab Rivalry and Superpower Diplomacy* (New York: Twayne, 1996), 95–96.

87. Memorandum for the Files, 24 March 1975, and Memorandum of Conversation, 27 March 1975, *FRUS, 1969–1976*, 26: 570, 577; Memoranda of Conver-

sation, 31 March, 3 April, and 14 April 1975, *FRUS, 1969–1976*: 30: 606–620, 635–641; Quandt, *Peace Process*, 165.

88. Quandt, *Peace Process*, 163, 165; Kaufman, *Arab Middle East and the United States*, 96; Greene, *Presidency of Gerald R. Ford*, 154; Ford, *Time to Heal*, 287.

89. Quandt, *Peace Process*, 166, 167; Memoranda of Conversation, 1, 2, 11, 12, 13, 14, and 21 June 1975, *FRUS, 1969–1976*, 26: 650–664, 672–683, 684, 686, 696, 734.

90. Terence Smith, "Israel Offers Compromise to Egypt on Sinai Accord," *New York Times*, 25 June 1975; Quandt, *Peace Process*, 167; Eilts to Secretary of State, 23 June 1975, Eilts to Kissinger, 25 June 1975, and Ford to Rabin, 27 June 1975, *FRUS, 1969–1976*, 26: 740n4, 744n2, 747–778.

91. Memoranda of Conversation, 1 July 1975 and 8 July 1975, *FRUS, 1969–1976*, 26: 752, 775; Memorandum of Conversation, 16 August 1975, http://www.fordlibrarymuseum.gov/library/document/0314/1553211.pdf, accessed 10 August 2015; Quandt, *Peace Process*, 167; James M. Naughton, "Kissinger Mission for Mideast Pact Begins This Week," *New York Times*, 18 August 1975.

92. Kaufman, *Arab Middle East and the United States*, 96–97; "Brokered Peace," *New Republic*, 13 September 1975, 4; "Kissinger's Costly Triumph," *Newsweek*, 15 September 1975, 32.

93. Isaacson, *Kissinger*, 635; "For U.S.—A Mideast Success, a Bigger Role . . . and Pitfalls," *U.S. News & World Report*, 15 September 1975, 32; "High Cost to U.S. of an Agreement in the Mideast," *U.S. News & World Report*, 1 September 1975, 19; "Breakthrough in the Middle East—U.S. Takes on Controversial Role," *U.S. News & World Report*, 8 September 1975, 15; "Trying to Sell the Deal," *Time*, 22 September 1975, 33.

94. "For U.S.—A Mideast Success, a Bigger Role . . . and Pitfalls"; "The Road to Peace," *Newsweek*, September 8, 1975, 28; Kaufman, *Arab Middle East and the United States*, 97–98; "Kissinger's Costly Triumph," 33–34.

95. Gerald Ford, interviewed by James M. Cannon, Ford, Gerald—Interview, 9/1/89, JMCRIN, Box 1, GFL; "Ford's Low-Key '76 Decision Is No Surprise," *Grand Rapids Press*, 16 November 1974.

96. John Robert Greene, *Betty Ford: Candor and Courage in the White House* (Lawrence: University Press of Kansas, 2004), 76–78; Greene, *Presidency of Gerald R. Ford*, 33.

97. "Fascination with First Family Put Spotlight on Children," *Grand Rapids Press*, 27 December 2006; Greene, *Betty Ford*, 78–79; Wells to Gentlemen, undated (circa 14 August 1975), and Clayton to Ford, 24 August 1975, Betty Ford—Criticism, August 1975, PMLS, Box 61, UIWA.

98. Greene, *Betty Ford*, 79–80; Greene, *Presidency of Gerald R. Ford*, 33.

99. Greene, *Betty Ford*, 81.

100. Ibid., 81–82.

101. Greene, *Presidency of Gerald R. Ford*, 161; Cannon, *Gerald R. Ford*, 393.

102. Greene, *Presidency of Gerald R. Ford*, 161.

103. Ibid., 159, 160; Anthony J. Bennett, *The American President's Cabinet:*

From Kennedy to Bush (New York: Palgrave Macmillan, 1996), 66; Crain, *Ford Presidency*, 195; Isaacson, *Kissinger*, 671–672.

104. "Ford's Big Shuffle," *Newsweek*, 17 November 1975, 24; "Scenario of the Shake-Up," *Time*, 17 November 1975, 17; "Ford's Costly Purge," *Time*, 17 November 1975, 9.

105. Cannon, *Gerald R. Ford*, 400; Greene, *Presidency of Gerald R. Ford*, 161; "Reagan: 'I am Not Appeased,'" *Time*, 15 November 1975, 22.

106. John J. Casserly, *The Ford White House: The Diary of a Speechwriter* (Boulder: Colorado Associated University Press, 1977), 65; "Campaign 1976—Preliminary Analysis," 8 May 1975, Rockefeller, Nelson, RBCF, Box 19, GFL; James Weighart, "The Vacuous Presidency," *Nation*, 1 November 1975, 422.

107. Robert Shogan, *None of the Above: Why Presidents Fail—and What Can Be Done about It* (New York: NAL Books, 1982), 200; Ford, *Time to Heal*, 333; "Can Reagan Stop Ford?," *Newsweek*, 24 November 1975, 30.

Chapter Eight: Image and the Election

1. Yanek Mieczkowski, *Gerald Ford and the Challenges of the 1970s* (Lexington: University Press of Kentucky, 2005), 49–50.

2. Doug Hill and Jeff Weingrad, *Saturday Night: A Backstage History of "Saturday Night Live"* (New York: Beech Tree, 1986), 178–188.

3. "'Off to a Helluva Start,'" *Time*, 26 August 1974, 52; John Robert Greene, *The Presidency of Gerald R. Ford* (Lawrence: University Press of Kansas, 1995), 62; Richard Reeves, *A Ford, Not a Lincoln* (New York: Harcourt Brace Jovanovich, 1975), 26; "The Ridicule Problem," *Time*, 5 January 1976, 33; "A Dose of 'Common Sense,'" *Newsweek*, 26 January 26, 1976, 16.

4. David Farber, "The Torch Had Fallen," in *America in the Seventies*, ed. Beth Bailey and David Farber (Lawrence: University Press of Kansas, 2004), 14.

5. Greene, *Presidency of Gerald R. Ford*, 63; Michael A. Genovese, ed., *Encyclopedia of the American Presidency*, rev. ed. (New York: Facts on File, 2010), 409; "Go on Taxes, Slow on Energy," *Time*, 3 March 1975, 10; William E. Leuchtenburg, *The American President: From Teddy Roosevelt to Bill Clinton* (New York: Oxford University Press, 2015), 554; "Ford's Popularity Dips in Gallup Poll," *New York Times*, 4 July 1976; John Robert Greene, *Betty Ford: Candor and Courage in the White House* (Lawrence: University Press of Kansas, 2004), 83.

6. "The Ford in Our Future," *Christianity Today*, 7 December 1973, 50; Greene, *Betty Ford*, 84–85; "Steven Ford Drops Out of University of Utah," *New York Times*, 31 December 1975.

7. Greene, *Betty Ford*, 85–86; Doug Wead, *All the Presidents' Children: Triumph and Tragedy in the Lives of America's First Families* (New York: Atria Books, 2003), 270; "Susan Ford: On the Go in the White House," *Ladies Home Journal*, January 1975, 109; "Susan Ford: White House Hostess at Age 17," *U.S. News & World Report*, 21 October 1974, 47.

8. Mieczkowski, *Gerald Ford*, 249, 251–252.

9. Ibid., 252–254.

10. Ibid., 254; Greene, *Presidency of Gerald R. Ford*, 79–80, 96–97; William E. Simon, *A Time for Truth* (New York: Reader's Digest, 1978), 79.

11. Anthony Corrado et al., eds., *Campaign Finance Reform: A Sourcebook* (Washington, D.C.: Brookings Institution, 1997), 53–54; Robin Kolodny, "The 1976 Republican Nomination: An Examination of the Organizational Dynamic," in *Gerald R. Ford and the Politics of Post-Watergate America*, ed. Bernard J. Firestone and Alexej Ugrinsky (Westport, Conn.: Greenwood, 1993), 2: 588–589; Kathleen Hall Jamieson, *Packaging the Presidency: A History and Criticism of Presidential Campaign Advertising*, 2nd ed. (New York: Oxford University Press, 1992), 331, 345.

12. Douglas Brinkley, *Gerald R. Ford* (New York: Times Books, 2007), 134; Kolodny, "1976 Republican Nomination," 591.

13. Greene, *Presidency of Gerald R. Ford*, 162–163; Michael Medved, *The Shadow Presidents: The Secret History of the Chief Executives and Their Top Aides* (New York: Times Books, 1979), 336, 338.

14. Gerald R. Ford, *A Time to Heal: The Autobiography of Gerald R. Ford* (New York: Harper and Row, 1979), 349–350; *PPPUS, 1976–1977*: 31–42; "State of the Union: 'I'm an Optimist,'" *Time*, 26 January 1976, 9–10; "Drawing the Battle Lines," *Time*, 2 February 1976, 9–10.

15. Brinkley, *Gerald R. Ford*, 122; "State of the Union," 10.

16. James M. Naughton, "The President's Gamble," *New York Times*, 22 January 1976; *PPPUS, 1976–1977*: 50–75; Ron Nessen, *Making the News, Taking the News: From NBC to the White House* (Middletown, Conn.: Wesleyan University Press, 2011), 193.

17. Perritt to Cannon, 19 May 1976, Presidential Campaign, May 1976, JMCF, Box 41, GFL; oral history, Gerald Ford, 25 October 1994, interviewed by Yanek Mieczkowski, Ford, Gerald—10/25/1994, YMRI, Box 1, GFL.

18. Andrew Downer Crain, *The Ford Presidency: A History* (Jefferson, N.C.: McFarland, 2009), 215, 216; Minutes of National Security Council Meeting, 27 June 1975 and Memorandum of Conversation, 18 July 1975; *FRUS, 1969–1976*, 28: 267–269, 286.

19. Memorandum for the Record, 21 November 1975, *FRUS, 1969–1976*, 28: 347, 348; Crain, *Ford Presidency*, 223; Walter Isaacson, *Kissinger: A Biography* (New York: Simon and Schuster, 1992), 678.

20. Crain, *Ford Presidency*, 223–224; Daniel Spikes, *Angola and the Politics of Intervention: From Local Bush War to Chronic Crisis in Southern Africa* (Jefferson, N.C.: McFarland, 1993), 302; Seymour Hersh, "Angola-Aid Issue Opening Rifts in State Department," *New York Times*, 14 December 1975.

21. Daniel Schorr, *Staying Tuned: A Life in Journalism* (New York: Pocket Books, 2001), 281–282; Kathryn Olmsted, "U.S. Intelligence Agencies during the Ford Years," in *The Companion to Gerald R. Ford and Jimmy Carter*, ed. Scott Kaufman (Malden, Mass.: Wiley, 2016), 126.

22. William J. Daugherty, *Executive Secrets: Covert Action and the Presidency*

(Lexington: University Press of Kentucky, 2004), 177; Greene, *Presidency of Gerald R. Ford*, 115.

23. Jon Nordheimer, "Reagan Bids U.S. Exploit Missile," *New York Times*, 11 February 1976; Jon Nordheimer, "Reagan, in Direct Attack, Assails Ford on Defense," *New York Times*, 5 March 1976.

24. Donald Rumsfeld, *Known and Unknown: A Memoir* (New York: Sentinel, 2011), 229, 231; Robert G. Kaufman, *Henry M. Jackson: A Life in Politics* (Seattle: University of Washington, 2000), 288–289; Bradley Graham, *By His Own Rules: The Ambitions, Successes, and Ultimate Failures of Donald Rumsfeld* (New York: PublicAffairs, 2009), 126–127, 128–129.

25. Graham, *By His Own Rules*, 131–132; Scowcroft to Ford, 21 January 1976, National Security Council Minutes, 21 January and 11 February 1976, *FRUS, 1969–1976*, 33: 554, 595, 599–603.

26. Note from the United States to the Soviet Union, undated, and Brezhnev to Ford, 17 March 1976, *FRUS, 1969–1976*, 33: 607–610; Ford, *Time to Heal*, 358.

27. Greene, *Betty Ford*, 91–94; John C. Skipper, *The Iowa Caucuses: First Tests of Presidential Aspirations, 1972–2008* (Jefferson, N.C.: McFarland, 2010), 51.

28. Betty Ford, *The Times of My Life*, with Chris Chase (New York: Harper and Row, 1978), 258.

29. Greene, *Presidency of Gerald R. Ford*, 163; Lou Cannon, *Governor Reagan: His Rise to Power* (New York: PublicAffairs, 2003), 413–414; Jacob Weisberg, *Ronald Reagan* (New York: Times Books, 2016), 55; Roy Reed, "Betty Ford Greeted on Trip to Florida," *New York Times*, 27 February 1976; photograph, *New York Times*, 13 March 1976; Ford, *Time to Heal*, 368, 370.

30. "The Nation's Economy Is Back on Track," *U.S. News & World Report*, 2 February 1976, 51; "Gallup Finds 11-Point Gain in President's Popularity," *New York Times*, 11 March 1976.

31. Note from the Department of State to the Soviet Leadership, undated, and Note from the Soviet Leadership to the Department of State, undated, *FRUS, 1969–1976*, 16: 860–862; Cannon, *Governor Reagan*, 420; Julian E. Zelizer, *Governing America: The Revival of Political History* (Princeton, N.J.: Princeton University Press, 2012), 331.

32. Zelizer, *Governing America*, 331; Loen to Morton, 5 March 1976, and Friedersdorf to Cheney, 9 March 1976, Campaign, Aug. 1975–April 1976, MLFF, Box 3, GFL; Greene, *Presidency of Gerald R. Ford*, 166–167.

33. Memorandum of Conversation, 12 May 1975, https://www.fordlibrarymuseum.gov/library/document/0314/1553073.pdf, accessed June 8, 2014.

34. Adam Clymer, *Drawing the Line at the Big Ditch: The Panama Canal Treaties and the Rise of the Right* (Lawrence: University Press of Kansas, 2008), 21, 22, 34; Ford, *Time to Heal*, 294; Garry Wills, *Reagan's America: Innocents at Home* (Garden City, N.Y.: Doubleday, 1987), 334.

35. Ford, *Time to Heal*, 294; Greene, *Presidency of Gerald R. Ford*, 166; Cannon, *Governor Reagan*, 426.

36. Greene, *Presidency of Gerald R. Ford*, 163; Philip Shabecoff, "Ford, Nixon and 1976," *New York Times*, 9 April 1976; "37% Approve President," *New York Times*, 17 April 1976.

37. James M. Naughton, "Electability, Not Issues," *New York Times*, 9 June 1976.

38. Burton I. Kaufman, *The Arab Middle East and the United States: Inter-Arab Rivalry and Superpower Diplomacy* (New York: Twayne, 1996), 100; Greene, *Presidency of Gerald R. Ford*, 168–169.

39. Kaufman, *Arab Middle East and the United States*, 100.

40. Greene, *Presidency of Gerald R. Ford*, 169–170; Memorandum of Conversation, 16 June 1976, *FRUS, 1969–1976*, 26: 1033.

41. George H. Gallup, *The Gallup Poll: Public Opinion, 1976–77* (Wilmington, Del.: Scholarly Resources, 1978), 2: 655, 760–761, 913; Memoranda of Conversation, 27 March and 7 April 1976, *FRUS, 1969–1976*, 26: 981, 984, 1017.

42. Goodwin Berquist, "The 1976 Carter-Ford Presidential Debates," in *Rhetoric Studies of National Political Debates*, 1960–1992, 2nd ed., ed. Robert V. Friedenberg (Westport, Conn.: Praeger, 1994), 35; Joshua Muravchik, *The Uncertain Crusade: Jimmy Carter and the Dilemmas of Human Rights Policy* (Lanham, Md.: Hamilton Press, 1986), 2–4; Barbara Keys, *Reclaiming American Virtue: The Human Rights Revolution of the 1970s* (Cambridge, Mass.: Harvard University Press, 2014), 236; "Address by Jimmy Carter," 8 September 1976, *FRUS, 1977–1980*, 1: 42.

43. Keys, *Reclaiming American Virtue*, 178–179, 216, 218–219; William Michael Schmidli, *The Fate of Freedom Elsewhere: Human Rights and U.S. Cold War Policy toward Argentina* (Ithaca, N.Y.: Cornell University Press, 2013), 91.

44. *CQA*, 1975: 353; Address by Secretary of State Kissinger, 27 April 1976, and Janney and Ahern to Eagleburger, 21 July 1976, *FRUS, 1969–1976*, 38: 416–418, 456; NSC Memorandum 241, 21 April 1976, *FRUS, 1969–1976*, 28: 197–198; Memorandum of Conversation, 9 May 1976, *FRUS, 1969–1976*, vol. E-6, https://history.state.gov/historicaldocuments/frus1969-76ve06/d42, accessed 10 April 2016; Juan de Onis, "Kissinger Assails Chile over Curbs," *New York Times*, 9 June 1976.

45. Keys, *Reclaiming American Virtue*, 219; Jeffrey D. Merritt, "Unilateral Human Rights Intercession—American Practice under Nixon, Ford, and Carter," in *The Diplomacy of Human Rights*, ed. David D. Newsom (Lanham, Md.: University Press of America, 1986), 45; Lars Schoultz, *Human Rights and United States Policy toward Latin America* (Princeton, N.J.: Princeton University Press, 1981), 125.

46. Schoultz, *Human Rights and United States Policy toward Latin America*, 281–282.

47. Ibid., 253–254.

48. Jack Anderson and Les Whitten, "Hidden Funds for Chile," *Washington Post*, 8 May 1976; "Human Rights, Chilean Wrongs," *Washington Post*, 27 June 1976.

49. Jeremy D. Mayer, *Running on Race: Racial Politics in Presidential & Campaigns, 1960–2000* (New York: Random House, 2002), 125–126; Carl Watts, "'Dropping the F-Bomb': President Ford, the Rhodesian Crisis, and the 1976 Election," paper presented at the Society for Historians of American Foreign Relations Conference, Lexington, Kentucky, 2014; Anthony Lewis, "Words and Deeds," *New York Times*, 20 November 1975.

50. "Spring Brings a Note of Cheer," *U.S. News & World Report*, 5 April 1976, 17; "The Optimists Take Over," *Business Week*, 5 April 1976, 24; "A Size-up of the Economy Now," *U.S. News & World Report*, 24 May 1976, 24.

51. "The Big 200th Bash," *Time*, 5 July 1976, 8.

52. *PPPUS, 1976–1977*: 1966, 2626; Brinkley, *Gerald R. Ford*, 138.

53. Greene, *Presidency of Gerald R. Ford*, 170; Neal Thigpen, interviewed by Scott Kaufman, 6 August 2015, Florence, South Carolina.

54. Cannon, *Governor Reagan*, 429–430.

55. Mieczkowski, *Gerald Ford*, 318–319; Greene, *Presidency of Gerald R. Ford*, 171; Mieczkowski, *Gerald Ford*, 319.

56. Greene, *Presidency of Gerald R. Ford*, 171–172; Cannon, *Governor Reagan*, 431.

57. Mieczkowski, *Gerald Ford*, 320–321.

58. Ibid., 322, 325; Greene, *Presidency of Gerald R. Ford*, 173; *PPPUS, 1976–1977*: 2163.

59. Adam Wren, "'It Was Riotous': An Oral History of the GOP's Last Open Convention," http://www.politico.com/magazine/story/2016/04/1976-convention-oral-history-213793, accessed 19 January 2017; "Transcript of Reagan's Remarks to the Convention," *New York Times*, 20 August 1976; Mieczkowski, *Gerald Ford*, 325.

60. Crain, *Ford Presidency*, 259.

61. David W. Moore, *The Superpollsters: How They Measure and Manipulate Public Opinion in America* (New York: Four Walls Eight Windows, 1992), 228; "The Democratic National Convention," undated (circa mid-1976), Memorandum—Hamilton Jordan to Jimmy Carter, General Election," CFP, Box 39, JCL; Reichley to Cheney, 25 June 1976, Campaign Strategy—Suggestions (2), MRP, Box 13, and "I—Background," Book on 1976 Election, undated (circa August 1976), Campaign Plan—Final Copy 4 of 4, MRP, Box 13, GFL.

62. Burton I. Kaufman and Scott Kaufman, *The Presidency of James Earl Carter, Jr.*, 2nd ed. (Lawrence: University Press of Kansas, 2006), 12–13, 16; Scott Kaufman, *Plans Unraveled: The Foreign Policy of the Carter Administration* (DeKalb: Northern Illinois University Press, 2008), 16.

63. "I—Background," Book on 1976 Election, undated (circa August 1976), Campaign Plan—Final Copy 4 of 4, MRP, Box 13, GFL; Burton I. Kaufman, *Presidential Profiles: The Carter Years* (New York: Facts on File, 2006), 184; Samuel L. Popkin, *The Reasoning Voter: Communication and Persuasion in Presidential Campaigns*, 2nd ed. (Chicago: University of Chicago Press, 1991), 113.

64. Greene, *Presidency of Gerald R. Ford*, 176–177; "Repub Ldrship," 31 Au-

gust 1976, Congressional Meeting Minutes—8/31/76, JGCF, Box 2, and "GOP Conversations," Ford, Gerald—Campaign, JGCF, Box 3, GFL.

65. Douglas E. Kneeland, "Embargoes at Issue; Dole Asserts that Carter Misled Farmers," *New York Times*, 27 August 1976; Douglas E. Kneeland, "Dole Predicts Carter Losses in the South," *New York Times*, 1 September 1976; "Daughter Opens Ford Offices," *New York Times*, 17 September 1976; Pranay Gupte, "Miss Ford Likes Steuben Parade, Sees President Doing Well Here," *New York Times*, 19 September 1976; "Steven Ford Campaign Plans," *New York Times*, 18 September 1976; Jules Witcover, *Marathon: The Pursuit of the Presidency* (New York: Viking, 1977), 438; *PPPUS, 1976–1977*: 2757; Betty Ford, *Times of My Life*, 258–261; John Pope, "Betty (Elizabeth Ann Bloomer) Ford," in *American First Ladies: Their Lives and Their Legacy*, ed. Lewis L. Gould (New York: Garland, 1996), 550; Greene, *Betty Ford*, 98–99.

66. Greene, *Presidency of Gerald R. Ford*, 178; Darrell M. West, *Air Wars: Television Advertising and Social Media in Election Campaigns, 1952–2012*, 6th ed. (Thousand Oaks, Calif.: CQ Press, 2014), 58–59; L. Patrick Devlin, "Contrasts in Presidential Campaign Commercials of 1976," *Central States Speech Journal* 28 (1977): 241–242, 246; Jamieson, *Packaging the Presidency*, 346.

67. J. Brooks Flippen, *Jimmy Carter, the Politics of Family, and the Rise of the Religious Right* (Athens: University of Georgia Press, 2011), 99; Jamieson, *Packaging the Presidency*, 363; Mulliken to Vice President, 21 September 1976, Folder 13, Series 2: Richard Allison, Subseries 1: Campaign, Box 3, NARP, RAC; Patrick Anderson, *Electing Jimmy Carter: The Campaign of 1976* (Baton Rouge: Louisiana University Press, 1994), 113.

68. Moore, *Superpollsters*, 229.

69. Greene, *Presidency of Gerald R. Ford*, 181–182.

70. Jamieson, *Packaging the Presidency*, 348–349.

71. Greene, *Presidency of Gerald R. Ford*, 182, 183; John Osborne, "Ford, Ruff and Butz," *New Republic*, 16 October 1976, 9; "The Butz Insult," *New York Times*, 4 October 1976; Witcover, *Marathon*, 589.

72. Jamieson, *Packaging the Presidency*, 357–361, 376–377.

73. Greene, *Presidency of Gerald R. Ford*, 184.

74. Ibid., 184–185; Mieczkowski, *Gerald Ford*, 332.

75. Rumsfeld, *Known and Unknown*, 235; James Burnham, "What the Gaffe Said," *National Review*, 26 November 1976, 12813; Leo P. Ribuffo, "Is Poland a Soviet Satellite? Gerald Ford, the Sonnenfeldt Doctrine, and the Election of 1976," *Diplomatic History* 14 (1990): 401–402; Greene, *Presidency of Gerald R. Ford*, 186.

76. Lev E. Dobriansky, "The Unforgettable Ford Gaffe," *Ukrainian Quarterly* 3 (1977): 368; James Cannon, *Gerald R. Ford: An Honorable Life* (Ann Arbor: University of Michigan Press, 2013), 434; Ribuffo, "Is Poland a Soviet Satellite?," 396, 399, 403.

77. "More Signals on the Slowdown," *Time*, 25 October 1976, 51; "A Longer

Pause Than Expected," *Business Week*, 18 October 1976, 36; James M. Naughton, "Carter Assails Ford on 'Serious Blunderer,'" *New York Times*, 8 October 1976; R. W. Apple, "Carter, Focusing on Ford Record, Gains among Independents in Poll," *New York Times*, 15 October 1976.

78. Glenn Fowler, "In Earlier Vice-Presidential Debate Dole and Mondale Tangled Bitterly," *New York Times*, 11 October 1984; Brinkley, *Gerald R. Ford*, 143; Mieczkowski, *Gerald Ford*, 335; Sarah B. Snyder, "Through the Looking Glass: The Helsinki Final Act and the 1976 Election for President," *Diplomacy and Statecraft* 21 (2010): 99.

79. Mieczkowski, *Gerald Ford*, 335–336.

80. Cannon, *Gerald R. Ford*, 434–435; *PPPUS, 1976–1977*: 2821; Mieczkowski, *Gerald Ford*, 336–337; Jamieson, *Packaging the Presidency*, 369–370.

81. Michael Beschloss, "A 'Nightmare' Presidential Campaign Ad That Stayed in the Vault," *New York Times*, 3 September 2016, http://www.nytimes.com/2016/09/04/business/a-nightmare-presidential-campaign-ad-that-stayed-in-the-vault.html?smprod=nytcore-iphone&smid=nytcore-iphone-share, accessed September 4, 2016.

82. "A Long Goodbye," *Newsweek*, 15 November 1976, 27; Greene, *Presidency of Gerald R. Ford*, 187.

83. "Jerry Ford's Blues," *Newsweek*, 6 December 1976, 23; Cannon, *Gerald R. Ford*, 442; oral history, Douglas Bennett, 19 October 1994, interviewed by Yanek Mieczkowski, Bennett, Douglas—10/19/1994, YMRI, Box 1, GFL.

84. *PPPUS, 1976–1977*: 2916, 2926.

85. Ronald Fernandez, *The Disenchanted Island: Puerto Rico and the United States in the Twentieth Century*, 2nd ed. (Westport, Conn.: Praeger, 1996), 221, 232–236.

86. "Jerry Shows, 'I'm Still President,'" *Time*, 17 January 1977, 21.

87. Dick Cheney, *In My Time: A Personal and Political Memoir*, with Liz Cheney (New York: Threshold Editions, 2011), 107.

88. Ford, *Time to Heal*, 442.

89. Oral history, Robert Goldwin, 3 March 1994, interviewed by Yanek Mieczkowski, Goldwin, Robert—3/3/1994, oral history, Paul MacAvoy, 2 May 2002, interviewed by Yanek Mieczkowski, MacAvoy, Paul—5/2/2002, oral history, Ron Nessen, 29 January 2002, interviewed by Yanek Mieczkowski, Nessen, Ron, 1/29/2002, and oral history, James Cannon, 19 October 1994, interviewed by Yanek Mieczkowski, Cannon, James—10/19/1994, YMRI, Box 1; and oral history, Gerald Ford, 29 April 1990, interviewed by James Cannon, Ford, Gerald—Interview, 4/29/90, JMCRIN, Box 1, and oral history, Philip Buchen, 15 February 1990, interviewed by James Cannon, Buchen, Philip—Interview, 2/15/90, and oral history, John Rhodes, 4 December 1990, interviewed by James Cannon, Rhodes, John—Interview, 12/4/1990, JMCRIN, Box 3, GFL; Marjorie Hunter, "Ford Isn't Running but Won't Bar Race," *New York Times*, 22 April 1979; Laurence McQuillan, "Looking Back, Ford Says He Has No Regrets," *USA Today*, 17 July 2000; David Gergen, "Can This Relationship Be Saved?," *New York Times*, 29 August 2004; "Ford Keeps Door

Open for '80," *Newsweek*, 3 September 1979, 25; Berquist, "The 1976 Carter-Ford Presidential Debates," 39; Farber, "Torch Had Fallen," 17.

90. Oral history, Philip Buchen, 25 February 1994, interviewed by Yanek Mieczkowski, Buchen, Philip—2/25/94, YMRI, Box 1, GFL; Robert Dole, telephone interview by Scott Kaufman, 19 August 2015; Jonathan Moore and Janet Fraser, eds., *Campaign for President: The Managers Look at '76* (Cambridge, Mass.: Ballinger, 1977), 151; Brinkley, *Gerald R. Ford*, 140.

91. Hugh Sidey and Fred Ward, *Portrait of a President* (New York: Harper and Row, 1975), 36; "President-Elect Carter," *New York Times*, 4 November 1976.

92. Oral history, J. Robert Vastine, 10 September 1993, interviewed by Donald A. Ritchie, J. Robert Vastine, U.S. Congress, Senate Historical Office, Oral History Interviews, Box 10, LC.

93. Farley Yang, "Turning a Runaway into a Race: The Role of Foreign Policy Issues in the 1976 Republican Primaries," *Michigan Journal of Political Science* 7 (1986): 120; Ford interview, 25 October 1994.

Chapter Nine: Politics, Money, and the Post-Presidency

1. John Osborne, "The Unhealing Wound," *New Republic*, 29 March 1980, 7–8.

2. "Jerry Ford's 'Big' Impact on Golf," *Palm Springs (Calif.) Desert Sun*, 8 January 1980.

3. Gerald Ford, *A Time to Heal: The Autobiography of Gerald R. Ford* (New York: Harper and Row, 1979), 441–442.

4. John Robert Greene, *Betty Ford: Candor and Courage in the White House* (Lawrence: University Press of Kansas, 2004), 101.

5. Oral history, Betty Ford, 20 July 1990, interviewed by James Cannon, Ford, Betty—Interview, 7/20/90, JMCRIN, Box 1, GFL.

6. Paul Hendrickson, "Jerry Ford Likes His Leisurely Life," *Detroit News*, 6 March 1983; Betty Ford interview, 20 July 1990; John Nordheimer, "Ford Ready to Approve 15-Room Retirement Home," *New York Times*, 10 March 1977; Greene, *Betty Ford*, 101.

7. Don Van Natta Jr., *First Off the Tee: Presidential Hackers, Duffers, and Cheaters from Taft to Bush* (New York: Public Affairs, 2003), 98; Blackie Sherrod, "Ford Finds Contentment on the Fairway," *Dallas Times Herald*, 8 May 1980, May 1980 (1)—Clippings, GRFS, Box 27, GFL; Bob Hope, *Confessions of a Hooker: My Lifelong Love Affair with Golf* (Garden City, NY: Doubleday, 1985), 161.

8. Jacobson to Frye, 2 November 1976, Grassmuck to Fleming, 3 November 1976, Fleming to Rhodes et al., 11 November 1976, Fleming to Ford, 7 December 1976, Grassmuck to Fleming et al., 13 December 1976, Fleming to Rhodes, 4 February 1977, Grassmuck to Ford, 8 March 1977, and Jacobson to Ford, 14 April 1977, Gerald R. Ford Presidential Library, President Records, Box 62, BHL; "Ford to Teach Again," *New York Times*, 23 October 1977; Burton I. Kaufman, *The Post-Presidency from Washington to Clinton* (Lawrence: University Press of Kansas, 2012), 436.

9. Nancy Dunn, "Ford Wants to Keep Active in GOP, 'Not as Candidate, But as Worker,'" *Grand Rapids Press*, 25 May 1977; Peer J. Oppenheimer, "Gerald Ford on His Family and Future," *Family Weekly*, 25 June 1978, 7.

10. Adam Clymer, *Drawing the Line at the Big Ditch: The Panama Canal Treaties and the Rise of the Right* (Lawrence: University Press of Kansas, 2008), 49; Carter to Ford, 1 May 1978, [Ford, President Gerald R.], Name File, JCL.

11. "Supplementary Material," *New York Times*, 10 October 1978.

12. "Keynote Address by the Honourable Gerald R. Ford at the South African Foreign Trade Organisation Economic Summit," 29 June 1978, June 1978—Programs, etc., GRFS, Box 22, GFL.

13. "Gerald Ford Takes His Stand on SALT," *Washington Post*, 26 September 1979.

14. Jerry Arthur Siddon, "Jerry Ford on Campaign Trail for GOP," *Chicago Tribune*, 3 November 1978; "Ford Urges U.S. to Fight Communism in Europe," *St. Louis Globe-Democrat*, 31 October 1977.

15. Oral history, Penny Circle, 5 December 2008, interviewed by Richard Norton Smith, http://geraldrfordfoundation.org/centennial/oralhistory/penny-circle/, accessed July 11, 2015; Siddon, "Jerry Ford on Campaign Trail."

16. Greene, *Betty Ford*, 103.

17. Ibid., 104.

18. Ibid., 106; "Gerald Ford Takes His Stand on SALT."

19. Dave Montgomery, "Ford: Crisis in Iran Worst since WWII," *Dallas Times Herald*, 20 November 1979, November 1979—Clippings, GRFS, Box 26, GFL; "A Visit with Ford," *Palm Springs (Calif.) Desert Sun*, 13 December 1979.

20. Erwin C. Hargrove, *Jimmy Carter as President: Leadership and the Politics of the Public Good* (Baton Rouge: Louisiana State University Press, 1988), 86; Peter C. Gavrilovich, "U.S. Should Flex Military Muscle, Gerald Ford Says," *Detroit Free Press*, 2 March 1979; Tom Dammann, "Ford Calls Policy of Carter Disaster," *Grand Rapids Press*, 10 August 1979; "A Visit with Ford."

21. "Ford Urges U.S. to Fight Communism in Europe"; Marjorie Hunter, "Ford Isn't Running but Won't Bar Race," *New York Times*, 22 April 1979; "Why Ford May Hurt the GOP," *Business Week*, 8 October 1979, 130; Adam Clymer, "Ford Rules Out Active Candidacy; Calls on Supporters to Back Others," *New York Times*, 20 October 1979; Hedrick Smith, "Ford Seems to Soften His Stand against a 1980 Race," *New York Times*, 20 November 1979; Oppenheimer, "Gerald Ford on His Family and Future," 8.

22. Hedrick Smith, "Reagan's Recovery: Nervous Moderates Cock Ears for 'Ford Rumblings,'" *New York Times*, 28 February 1980; Adam Clymer, "Ford Declares Reagan Can't Win; Invites G.O.P. to Ask Him to Run," *New York Times*, 2 March 1980.

23. Adam Clymer, "Ford Declines Race for the Presidency to Avoid G.O.P. Split," *New York Times*, 16 March 1980.

24. Charles Wheeler, "Carter Candidacy Vulnerable, Ford Says," *Winston Salem*

Journal, 15 April 1980; Lynn Sweet, "Ford Calls 3rd Party Bid by Anderson 'Mistake,'" *Chicago Sun Times*, 23 April 1980, April 1980—Clippings, GRFS, Box 27, GFL.

25. "An Interview with Gerald Ford," *Wall Street Journal*, 23 June 1980; "It's Reagan and Ford," *Chicago Sun Times*, 17 July 1980. In 2000, presidential nominee George W. Bush and his running mate, Dick Cheney, both claimed Texas as home. To avoid any charges of violating the Constitution, Cheney changed his residency to Wyoming, the state he had represented in Congress.

26. Richard J. Allen, "The Accidental Vice President," *New York Times Magazine*, 30 July 2000, 38; "Vice Presidential Selection," undated, Convention—VP Selection (2 of 2), Ed Meese Files, Ronald Reagan Presidential Campaign Papers, 1964–1980, Box 139, RRPL.

27. Allen, "Accidental Vice President," 38; Ronald Reagan, *An American Life* (New York: Simon and Schuster, 1990), 215; Lou Cannon, *Governor Reagan: His Rise to Power* (New York: PublicAffairs, 2003), 471; Stuart Spencer, 3 April 2007, interviewed by Yanek Mieczkowski, Spencer, Stuart—4/3/2007, YMRI, Box 1, GFL; Joseph E. Persico, *Casey: From the OSS to the CIA* (New York: Viking, 1990), 186; Nancy Gibbs and Michael Duffy, *The Presidents Club: Inside the World's Most Exclusive Fraternity* (New York: Simon and Schuster, 2012), 329–330.

28. Oral history, Gerald Ford, 24 January 2002, interviewed by Yanek Mieczkowski, Ford, Gerald—1/24/2002, YMRI, Box 1, GFL; Cannon, *Governor Reagan*, 473; Thomas M. DeFrank, *Write It When I'm Gone: Remarkable Off-the-Record Conversations with Gerald R. Ford* (New York: Putnam, 2007), 116.

29. Gerald M. Pomper, "The Nominating Contests," in *The Election of 1980: Reports and Interpretations*, ed. Gerald M. Pomper (Chatham, N.J.: Chatham House, 1981), 20; Edwin Meese III, *With Reagan: The Inside Story* (Washington, D.C.: Regnery Gateway, 1992), 44; John Rhodes, *John Rhodes: "I Was There,"* with Dean Smith (Salt Lake City: Northwest Publishing, 1995), 208–209; Allen, "Accidental Vice President," 38–39; Michael K. Deaver, *Behind the Scenes*, with Mickey Herskowitz (New York: Morrow, 1987), 93; Reagan, *American Life*, 215–216.

30. William Brock, telephone interview by Scott Kaufman and Alissa Warters, 26 September 2015.

31. Hugh Sidey, "The Ford View of Carter: Let Me at Him," *Miami Herald*, 5 October 1980.

32. "Ford Says US Positive on Brazilian Economy," *Latin America Daily Post*, 7–8 June 1981, June 1981—Clippings (1), GRFS, Box 31, and *This Week with David Brinkley*, 28 August 1983, September 1983—Clippings, GRFS, Box 38, GFL; Rick Harmon, "Reagan Should Stick to Economic Guns, Ford Says at Auburn," *Birmingham (Ala.) News*, 5 April 1982; Edward L. Schapsmeier and Frederick Schapsmeier, *Gerald R. Ford's Date with Destiny: A Political Biography* (New York: Peter Lang, 1989), 250; David Shribman, "3 Ex–U.S. Presidents Assert Death Marks End of an Era," *New York Times*, 12 November 1982; Godfrey Sperling Jr., "Gerald Ford on Reagan, Watergate, and the State of the Presidency," *Christian Science Monitor*, 11

October 1983; Elinor J. Brecher, "Demonstrators Greet Former President," *Louisville Courier-Journal*, 16 December 1981; James Reston, "Jerry Ford at 70," *New York Times*, 14 August 1983; Steve Moore, "Ford Hails Reagan's Move in Grenada as 'Exactly Right,'" *Tampa Tribune*, 5 November 1983.

33. Oral history, Gerald Ford, 25 April 1990, interviewed by James Cannon, Ford, Gerald—Interview, 4/25/90, JMCRIN, Box 1, GFL; Terence Smith, "5 Leaders Emeritus Take a Look at the World," *New York Times*, 29 August 1983; Adam Clymer, "Ford Bids Reagan Trim Arms Outlay," *New York Times*, 2 April 1982; Marjorie Hunter, "Ford Says Reagan Is Moving toward Political Center," *New York Times*, 23 November 1982; Nancy Nall, "Ford Favors Wait in Arms Spending," *Columbus Dispatch*, 24 May 1983, May 1983—Clippings, GRFS, Box 37, GFL; "To Deal with Soviets, We Must Be Realistic," *USA Today*, 6 September 1983.

34. "Excerpts from Ford's Remarks Extolling the Reagan Record," *New York Times*, 22 August 1984.

35. Gary Kriss, "President Ford Speaks at Purchase," *New York Times*, 31 March 1985; DeFrank, *Write It When I'm Gone*, 91.

36. Oral history, Gerald Ford, 27 April 1990, interviewed by James Cannon, Ford, Gerald—Interview, 4/27/90, JMCRIN, Box 1, GFL.

37. Oral history, Gerald Ford, 29 April 1990, interviewed by James Cannon, Ford, Gerald—Interview, 4/29/90, JMCRIN, Box 1, GFL; Claudia Luther, "Ex-President Responds to Democrats' Attacks: Bush 'at Center of Action,' Ford Declares," *Los Angeles Times*, 17 August 1988, http://articles.latimes.com/1988-08-17/news/mn-451_1_republican-national-convention, accessed 22 July 2015.

38. E. J. Dionne, "New Image Is Surfacing for Ford's Presidency," *New York Times*, 8 April 1989.

39. Mike Lloyd, "Face to Face with Ford," *Grand Rapids Press*, 7 January 2007.

40. Gibbs and Duffy, *Presidents Club*, 342; Douglas Brinkley, *The Unfinished Presidency: Jimmy Carter's Journey beyond the White House* (New York: Viking, 1998), 66, 67, 68–69.

41. "Recognition of PLO Backed by Carter, Ford," *Los Angeles Times*, 12 October 1981; Larry Speakes, *Speaking Out: The Reagan Presidency from Inside the White House*, with Robert Pack (New York: Scribner's, 1988), 103; David Wood, "Reagan Rules Out Talks with PLO," *Los Angeles Times*, 13 October 1981.

42. "Carter and Ford Criticize Israelis," *New York Times*, 18 January 1983; Brinkley, *Unfinished Presidency*, 103, 118.

43. Brinkley, *Unfinished Presidency*, 103; Jimmy Carter, *Beyond the White House: Waging Peace, Fighting Disease, Building Hope* (New York: Simon and Schuster, 2007), 18.

44. Brinkley, *Unfinished Presidency*, 251.

45. Gwen Ifill, "Clinton Recruits 3 Presidents to Promote Trade Pact," *New York Times*, 15 September 1993.

46. Jerry Gray, "Dole Campaigns in Midwest, Opening November Offensive," *New York Times*, 19 March 1996.

47. Lloyd, "Face to Face with Ford"; Gerald Ford and Jimmy Carter, "A Time to Heal Our Nation," *New York Times*, 31 December 1998.

48. DeFrank, *Write It When I'm Gone*, 130–131; Douglas Brinkley, *Gerald R. Ford* (New York: Times Books, 2007), 157.

49. Ford and Carter, "Time to Heal our Nation"; oral history, Donald Rumsfeld, interviewed by Richard Norton Smith, 31 March 2009, geraldfordfoundation.org /centennial/oralhistory/don-rumsfeld, accessed July 7, 2015.

50. James Davison Hunter, *Culture Wars: The Struggle to Define America* (New York: Basic Books, 1991).

51. Nancy Skelton, "Ford Voices Disapproval of Religion in Politics," *Los Angeles Times*, 11 February 1981.

52. Richard L. Berke, "Ford Urges G.O.P. to Drop Abortion Issue and Shift Center," *New York Times*, 20 January 1998; Laurence McQuillan, "Looking Back, Ford Says He Has No Regrets," *USA Today*, 17 July 2000.

53. Samuel Walker, *Presidents and Civil Liberties from Wilson to Obama: A Story of Poor Custodians* (New York: Cambridge University Press, 2012), 344; Gerald R. Ford, "Inclusive America, under Attack," *New York Times*, 8 August 1999; Brinkley, *Gerald R. Ford*, 157.

54. Christopher Caldwell, "The Southern Captivity of the GOP," *Atlantic*, June 1998, http://www.theatlantic.com/magazine/archive/1998/06/the-southern-captivity-of-the-gop/377123/, accessed 18 July 2015; Berke, "Ford Urges G.O.P."

55. *PPPUS, 1976*: 555; Leonard Benardo and Jennifer Weiss, *Citizen-in-Chief: The Second Lives of the American Presidents* (New York: Morrow, 2009), 20; Evan Wolfson, "Enough Marriage to Share: A Response to Maggie Gallagher," in *Marriage and Same-Sex Unions: A Debate*, ed. Lynne D. Wardle et al. (Westport, Conn.: Praeger, 2003), 28; Bob Roehr, "Gerald Ford Remembered as Gay-Friendly President," PrideSource, http://archive.fo/lFeuR, accessed 18 July 2015; "Ford Believes G.O.P. Should Steer to Center," *New York Times*, 27 July 1998; Tim Weiner, "Ex-President Displays Many Sides in KC Visit," *Kansas City Times*, 17 April 1981; Greene, *Betty Ford*, 113–114.

56. Roy Rowan, "Professor Ford Speaks His Mind," *Fortune*, 16 January 1978, 112; Richard Wennekamp, interviewed by Richard Norton Smith, 13 December 2009, http://geraldrfordfoundation.org/centennial/oralhistory/richard-winnekamp/, accessed 18 July 2015; Tom DeFrank, interviewed by Richard Norton Smith, 24 February 2011, http://geraldrfordfoundation.org/centennial/oralhistory/tom-defrank/, accessed 18 July 2015; Peter Secchia, interviewed by Richard Norton Smith, 5 August 2008, http://geraldrfordfoundation.org/centennial/oralhistory/peter-secchia/, accessed 18 July 2015; Ann Cullen, 17 August 2009, interviewed by Richard Norton Smith, http://geraldrfordfoundation.org/centennial/oralhistory/ann-cullen/, accessed 18 July 2015.

57. "Ford Offers Bush Advice," *New York Times*, 8 June 2000; Gerald R. Ford and Bob Dole, "The Wisdom of Choosing Dick Cheney," *New York Times*, 31 July 2000.

58. Paul Krugman, "Don't Prettify Our History," *New York Times*, 22 August 2005.

59. Katharine Q. Seelye, "Commission Urges Overhaul of Election System," *New York Times*, 31 July 2001; Benardo and Weiss, *Citizen-in-Chief*, 274.

60. Brinkley, *Gerald R. Ford*, 159; Robert D. McFadden, "A Day of Mourning," *New York Times*, 15 September 2001; David W. Dunlap, "Pataki Offers Peek at Ground Zero Progress," *New York Times*, 23 November 2004.

61. Jeffrey Gettleman, "Anger Rises for Troops' Families as Deployment in Iraq Drags On," *New York Times*, 4 July 2003; Susan Page, "Former President Ford Reflects as He Nears 90," *USA Today*, 10 July 2003.

62. Bob Woodward, "Ford Disagreed with Bush about Invading Iraq," *Washington Post*, 28 December 2006, http://www.washingtonpost.com/wp-dyn/content/article/2006/12/27/AR2006122701558.html, accessed 19 July 2015.

63. Sidney Blumenthal, *The Strange Death of Republican America: Chronicles of a Collapsing Party* (New York: Sterling Publishing, 2008), 134–135; Lewis L. Gould, *The Republicans: A History of the Grand Old Party* (New York: Oxford University Press, 2014), 335, 340–342.

64. Warner to Ford, 21 August 1974, Gerald R. Ford Presidential Library, President Records, Box 49, and Gerald Ford, interviewed by Maury de Jonge, 21 August 1975, Gerald R. Ford Presidential Library, President Records, Box 55, BHL.

65. Martin Waldron, "Nixon Hails Johnson Library at Dedication," *New York Times*, 23 May 1971; Terence Smith, "Carter and Kennedy Share Stage at Library Dedication" *New York Times*, 24 October 1979; Kaufman, *Post-Presidency from Washington to Clinton*, 440.

66. Dick Ford, interviewed by Richard Norton Smith, 4 November 2008, http://geraldrfordfoundation.org/centennial/oralhistory/dick-ford/, accessed 11 July 2015; "Ford Lets Committee Run Museum Planning," *Grand Rapids Press*, 2 March 1977; Radock to Ford, 12 April 1978, Gerald R. Ford Library, President Records, Box 69, BHL; John Brosky, "A Monumental Task," *Grand Rapids Magazine*, September 1981, 67, 68–69.

67. Maury DeJonge, "3 Sites in Running for Ford Museum," *Grand Rapids Press*, 15 March 1977; Maury DeJonge, "Ford Gives Approval to West Riverbank Site for Museum," *Grand Rapids Press*, 9 April 1977; Maury DeJonge, "Ford's Plea Wins Grant for Museum," *Grand Rapids Press*, 26 May 1977; Brosky, "Monumental Task," 68.

68. Laura D. Walker, "Dedication Lift-Off," *Grand Rapids Press*, 15 September 1981; "Presidential Picnic's a Treat for Pine Rest," *Grand Rapids Press*, 16 September 1981; Jim Mancarelli, "Thursday at the Airport . . . When the World Came to Town," *Grand Rapids Press*, 18 September 1981; "Tributes to Ford Open Museum," *Grand Rapids Press*, 18 September 1981; Jim Mancarelli and Chris Meshan, "It Was a Night to Remember in the Civic Auditorium, Too," *Grand Rapids Press*, 18 September 1981.

69. Gerald Ford, interviewed by James Cannon, 25 April 1992, Ford, Gerald—

Interview, 4/25/92, JMCRIN, Box 1, GFL; Nancy D. Meyers Benbow and Christopher H. Benbow, *Cabins, Cottages and Mansions: Homes of the Presidents of the United States* (Gettysburg, Pa.: Thomas Publications, 1993), 198.

70. Kaufman, *Post-Presidency from Washington to Clinton*, 436.

71. Ibid., 436–437.

72. Ibid., 437–438; "Executive Changes," *New York Times*, 8 March 1985; Timothy F. Bannon, "The Board Game," *Harper's*, December 1982, 10–11; oral history, Gerald Ford, 13 November 1990, interviewed by James Cannon, Ford, Gerald—Interview, 11/13/90, JMCRIN, Box 1, GFL; "An Ex-President Is Available," *Time*, 18 February 1980, 27; "Jerry Ford, Incorporated," *Newsweek*, 11 May 1981, 28.

73. "An $800,000 Yearly Tab for Nixon, Ford," *Newsweek*, 16 April 1979, 30–31; Kaufman, *Post-Presidency from Washington to Clinton*, 439; Robert Lewis, "Ford's Moneymaking Raises a Key Question," *Grand Rapids Press*, 13 September 1981; "What I Would Have Done," *Parade*, 4 April 1982, April 1982—Clippings, GRFS, Box 34, GFL; "Ex-President Is Available," 27; Koziol, "Ford Becomes a Big Investor"; Marjie Lundstrom, "Jerry Ford Takes a Look at His New Digs in Vail," *Denver Post*, 24 December 1981; Megan Barber, "No One Wants President Ford's Ski Chalet in Beaver Creek," *Ski Curbed,* 25 September 2014, http://ski.curbed.com/2014/9/25/10042932/no-one-wants-presidents-fords-ski-chalet-in-beaver-creek, accessed 19 July 2016.

74. Jerald F. terHorst, "President Ford, Inc." *Washington Post*, 29 May 1977.

75. Hendrickson, "Jerry Ford Likes His Leisurely Life"; "What I Would Have Done."

76. Robert Lindsey, "Busy Gerald Ford Adds Acting to His Repertory," *New York Times*, 19 December 1983; Richard Cohen, "The Carter Distinction," *Washington Post*, 11 May 1989.

77. Brinkley, *Unfinished Presidency*, 287; Ford interview, 25 April 1992.

78. Van Natta, *First Off the Tee*, 100; Ted Roelofs, "Former President Beloved Here, Too," *Grand Rapids Press*, 31 December 2006.

79. Robert Lewis, "Gerald Ford's Tax-Paid Luxuries May Dwindle," *Grand Rapids Press*, 8 November 1979; "Ex-Presidents, Libraries Receive $26 Million a Year," *Los Angeles Times*, 25 April 1983; "Ford Asks Congress to Let Ex-Presidents Keep Funding," *St. Louis Post-Dispatch*, 16 June 1996; Benardo and Weiss, *Citizen-in-Chief*, 60; Gregory Korte, "House Bill Could Give Former Presidents a Pay Cut," *USA Today*, 16 April 2015, http://www.usatoday.com/story/news/politics/2015/04/16/former-presidents-act-how-much-do-former-presidents-make/25837949/, accessed 21 July 2015; Gregory Korte, "Obama Vetoes Cuts to Former Presidents Expense Accounts," *USA Today*, 23 July 2016, http://www.usatoday.com/story/news/politics/2016/07/22/obama-vetoes-cuts-former-presidents-expense-accounts/87462850/, accessed 6 October 2016.

80. Oppenheimer, "Gerald Ford on His Family and Future," 6–7; "Ford Has Knee Replaced," *New York Times*, 5 April 1990; Matthew Purdy, "Ford Is Treated for an Infection at Hospital after Being Honored," *New York Times*, 2 August 2000; B. Drummond Ayers Jr., "Hospitalized after Suffering a Stroke, Former President

Ford Is Expected to Recover Fully," *New York Times*, 3 August 2000; B. Drummond Ayers Jr., "Ford Is Said to Be Better; Bush Allowed in for Visit," *New York Times*, 4 August 2000; Martin Kasindorf, "Ford's Post-Stroke Prognosis Positive," *USA Today*, 4 August 2000.

81. "California: Ford Has Dizzy Spell," *New York Times*, 17 May 2003; "Ford Is Released after Brief Hospital Stay," *New York Times*, 18 May 2003; "Faces in the Four Thousand," *New York Times*, 12 June 2004; Mark Bixler, "Friendship Unites Carter, Ford," *Atlanta Journal-Constitution*, 21 February 2005; "Presidents for Gun Control," *New York Times*, 17 July 2004.

82. "California: Gerald Ford Is Hospitalized" *New York Times*, 14 December 2005; "California: Ford Hospitalized," *New York Times*, 17 January 2006; "California: Ford Leaves Hospital," *New York Times*, 26 January 2006; "Minnesota: Ford Gets Pacemaker," *New York Times*, 22 August 2006; "Minnesota: Ford Undergoes Heart Surgery," *New York Times*, 26 August 2006; "Minnesota: Ford Leaves Hospital," *New York Times*, 29 August 2006; "Ford to Be President Who's Lived Longest," *New York Times*, 12 November 2006; Allison Hoffman, "Family Was Able to Say Goodbye," *Grand Rapids Press*, 29 December 2006.

83. Tom Rademacher, "Boy Scouts Will Offer Final Salute," *Grand Rapids Press*, 28 December 2006; Rachel L. Swarns, "Funeral a Reunion of White House Old Guard," *Grand Rapids Press*, 2 January 2007; Dave Mussary, "Fords Say Quiet Goodbye," *Grand Rapids Press*, 5 January 2007.

84. "'History Will Treat Him Well,'" *Atlanta Journal-Constitution*, 28 December 2006.

85. Ibid.; Dionne, "New Image Is Surfacing for Ford's Presidency"; "Clinton Bestows Medal of Freedom," *New York Times*, 12 August 1999; "Michigan U. to Name School for Gerald Ford," *New York Times*, 18 November 1999.

86. Bixler, "Friendship Unites Carter, Ford"; Anthony Lewis, "For Gerald Ford," *New York Times*, 5 August 2000; Mark J. Rozell, "President Ford's Pardon of Richard M. Nixon: Constitutional and Political Considerations," *Presidential Studies Quarterly* 24 (1994): 134; Richard Reeves, "I'm Sorry, Mr. President," *American Heritage* 47 (1996): 55; Brinkley, *Gerald R. Ford*, 154; Adam Clymer, "Hindsight and the Eye of the Beholder," *New York Times*, 27 May 2001.

87. Jane C. Timm, "Clinton, Bush Team Up to Launch Leadership Program," 29 August 2014, http://www.msnbc.com/morning-joe/clinton-bush-team-launch-leadership-program, accessed 27 July 2015.

88. "What Happened to This Party?," *Time*, 21 March 2016, cover.

Conclusion

1. Richard Norton Smith, eulogy at funeral for Gerald Ford, 3 January 2007, https://www.fordlibrarymuseum.gov/grf/funeral/smith.asp, accessed 18 March 2016.

2. "A Long Goodbye," *Newsweek,* 15 November 1976, 26.

3. Bud Vestal, *Jerry Ford, Up Close: An Investigative Biography* (New York: Coward, McCann, and Geoghegan, 1974), 11.

4. Edward L. Schapsmeier and Frederick Schapsmeier, *Gerald R. Ford's Date*

with Destiny: A Political Biography (New York: Peter Lang, 1989), 52, 100–101.

5. Joseph M. Siracusa, *Encyclopedia of the Kennedys: The People and Events That Shaped America*, vol. 1 (Santa Barbara, Calif.: ABC-Clio, 2012), 240.

6. Elizabeth Drew, *Richard M. Nixon* (New York: Times Books, 2007), 53.

7. Gerald R. Ford, *A Time to Heal: The Autobiography of Gerald R. Ford* (New York: Harper and Row, 1979), 53.

8. John Robert Greene, "'A Nice Person Who Worked at the Job': The Dilemma for the Ford Image," in *Gerald R. Ford and the Politics of Post-Watergate America*, ed. Bernard J. Firestone and Alexej Ugrinsky, vol. 2 (Westport, Conn.: Greenwood, 1993), 645; Farley Yang, "Turning a Runaway into a Race: The Role of Foreign Policy Issues in the 1976 Republican Primaries," *Michigan Journal of Political Science* 7 (1986): 116.

9. Peter Spikoel, "He Led by Listening," *Los Angeles Times*, 28 December 2006.

10. Ron Nessen, *Making the News, Taking the News: From NBC to the Ford White House* (Middletown, Conn.: Wesleyan University Press, 2011), 187; John J. Casserly, *The Ford White House: The Diary of a Speechwriter* (Boulder: Colorado Associated University Press, 1977), 284.

11. "Weakened Presidency . . . ," *New York Times*, 16 February 1975; Shuman to Nessen, 6 August 1975, Nessen, Ron (3), RTHF, Box 38, GFL.

12. Clark R. Mollenhoff, *The Man Who Pardoned Nixon* (New York: St. Martin's, 1976), 297; Yanek Mieczkowski, *Gerald Ford and the Challenges of the 1970s* (Lexington: University Press of Kentucky, 2005), 307; Lou Cannon, *Governor Reagan: His Rise to Power* (New York: PublicAffairs, 2003), 402.

13. See, for instance, J. Edward Lee and H. C. "Toby" Haynsworth, *Nixon, Ford, and the Abandonment of South Vietnam* (Jefferson, N.C.: McFarland, 2002), 74; Michael Schudson, *The Rise of the Right to Know: Politics and the Culture of Transparency, 1945–1975* (Cambridge, Mass.: Harvard University Press, 2015), 9; Stephanie A. Slocum-Schaffer, *America in the Seventies* (Syracuse, N.Y.: Syracuse University Press, 2003), 49; Paul S. Boyer et al., *The Enduring Vision: A History of the American People*, vol. 2, *Since 1865*, concise 7th ed. (Boston: Wadsworth, 2013), 736; John M. Murrin, *Liberty, Equality, and Power: A History of the American People*, 5th ed. (Boston: Thomson, 2008), 938.

14. Paul Charles Light, *The President's Agenda: Domestic Policy Choice from Kennedy to Carter* (Baltimore: Johns Hopkins University Press, 1982), 53, 112; Max J. Skidmore, *Presidential Performance: A Comprehensive Review* (Jefferson, N.C.: McFarland, 2004), 303; Stephen J. Wayne, *The Legislative Presidency* (New York: Harper and Row, 1978), 85; Philip Shabecoff, "Appraising Presidential Power: The Ford Presidency," in *The Presidency Reappraised*, ed. Thomas E. Cronin and Rexford G. Tugwell, 2nd ed. (New York: Praeger, 1977), 35.

15. Ford, *Time to Heal*, 263.

16. Jules Witcover, *Marathon: The Pursuit of the Presidency, 1972–1976* (New York: Viking, 1977), 45; Max Brodnick, ed., *The Jerry Ford Joke Book* (New York: Times Books, 1976), 14.

17. Richard Reeves, *A Ford, Not a Lincoln* (New York: Harcourt Brace Jovanovich, 1975), 204.

18. Roger Porter, "Gerald R. Ford: A Healing Presidency," in *Leadership in the Modern Presidency,* ed. Fred I. Greenstein (Cambridge, Mass.: Harvard University Press, 1988), 227; James Cannon, *Time and Chance: Gerald Ford's Appointment with History* (Ann Arbor: University of Michigan Press, 1994), 415–416; Mieczkowski, *Gerald Ford and the Challenges of the 1970s,* 3, 303, 354–357; Thomas L. Friedman, "The First Energy President," *New York Times,* 5 January 2007, http://www.nytimes.com/2007/01/05/opinion/05friedman.html?_r=0, accessed 19 March 2016; Robert M. Gates, *From the Shadows: The Ultimate Insider's Story of Five Presidents and How They Won the Cold War* (New York: Touchstone, 1996), 87; Andrew J. Bacevich, *The New American Militarism: How Americans Are Seduced by War,* updated ed. (New York: Oxford University Press, 2013), 179.

19. On this score, see Raymond Garthoff, *Détente and Confrontation: American-Soviet Relations from Nixon to Reagan,* rev. ed. (Washington, D.C.: Brookings Institution, 1994); and Daniel C. Thomas, "Human Rights Ideas, the Demise of Communism, and the End of the Cold War," *Journal of Cold War Studies* 7 (Spring 2005): 110–141.

20. *Gerald R. Ford, Late a President of the United States: Memorial Tributes Delivered in Congress* (Washington, D.C.: GPO, 2007), 26.

Bibliographic Essay

For overviews of the primary and secondary literature on Gerald Ford, there are two places to begin. The first is *Gerald R. Ford: A Bibliography*, compiled by John Robert Greene (Westport, Conn.: Greenwood, 1994). Comprehensive in its coverage, it lists and, in many cases, offers commentary both on archival materials related to Ford and on a wide array of books and articles on his life and presidency. The second is *A Companion to Gerald R. Ford and Jimmy Carter*, edited by Scott Kaufman (Malden, Mass.: Wiley Blackwell, 2016), a compendium of thirty historiographical essays written by experts in their fields. Approximately half the contributions are in whole or in part on Ford, with one devoted solely to Betty Ford. Because of the extensive coverage of the literature in Greene and Kaufman, the annotated bibliography that follows offers those who want to learn more about Ford a more selective list of monographs and articles.

The most important repository of materials related to Gerald Ford's life is the Gerald R. Ford Library, located on the University of Michigan campus in Ann Arbor. Aside from the papers of the former president, researchers will find here as well those of his wife, Betty; of key administration aides; and of some members of Congress, including longtime Ford ally Melvin Laird. Unlike a number of other presidential archives, the Ford Library offers travel grants for those who would like to conduct research on the country's thirty-eighth president. Next door to the Ford Library is the Bentley Historical Library, which has a number of collections with documents relevant to Ford's life.

The Ford Library has a small collection of papers on Ford from other presidential libraries, but it is not complete. Hence, researchers will want to spend time at those repositories as well. The Alphabetical Name Files at the Richard Nixon Presidential Library and Museum in Yorba Linda, California, has a number of documents related to Ford. The Jimmy Carter Presidential Library and Museum in Atlanta, Georgia, and the Ronald Reagan Presidential Library in Simi Valley, California, house materials on the 1976 and 1980 presidential elections. Of importance as well is the Library of Congress, which stores numerous collections for individuals who have served both on Capitol Hill and in the White House, as well as oral history interviews conducted by Former Members of Congress, Inc.

In addition to materials posted online by the Ford Library, researchers will find a growing body of documents on the web. The Dirksen Center in Pekin, Illinois, is the home of the papers of Everett Dirksen, who served for a time as senate minority leader when Ford held the same post in the House. Included in those papers are the Joint Senate-House Republican Leadership Minutes. Available on both the web and in hard copy are *Foreign Relations of the United States*, a rich resource collected by the Office of the Historian at the Department of State for those wishing to learn about America's diplomacy; *Public Papers of the Presidents of the United States*, where researchers will find the presidents' public speeches, writings, and press conferences; and *Congressional Quarterly Almanac*, a summary of the history, debate, and outcome of legislation approved or rejected by Capitol Hill. It is important to note that not all the volumes of *Congressional Quarterly Almanac* are online. Finally, researchers will want to look at *Congressional Record*, a collection of the statements made by lawmakers alongside articles, editorials, and other documents they submitted as evidence. The online volumes for *Congressional Record* begin with the year 1995, so researchers will want to visit a library that has it in hard copy or on microfilm.

The title of Ford's reminiscences, *A Time to Heal: The Autobiography of Gerald R. Ford* (New York: Harper and Row, 1979), researched and ghostwritten by Trevor Armbrister, emphasizes what the ex-president considered his most important accomplishments while in the White House. Despite a sometimes disjointed writing style, readers will learn about his upbringing, his relationship with Betty, his desire to climb up the ranks of the House of the Representatives, his accession to the presidency, and his failure to win the presidency in his own right in 1976. Ford spoke extensively with Thomas DeFrank, a *Newsweek* correspondent, with the caveat that their discussions were not to be published until after his death. Hence, it was not until 2007 that DeFrank's *Write It When I'm Gone: Remarkable Off-the-Record Conversations with Gerald R. Ford* (New York: Putnam) appeared in print. In it, Ford opens up about his difficult relationship with Nixon, his dislike for Reagan, and his disappointment with Vice President—and formerly Ford's chief of staff—Dick Cheney.

Several authors have written biographies of Ford, though all have their shortcomings. Two of the earliest are those published in 1974 by journalist Bud Vestal and by Ford's first press secretary, Jerald terHorst. The subtitle of Vestal's *Jerry Ford, Up Close*, is *An Investigative Biography* (New York: Coward, McCann and Geoghegan, 1974), but it offers more anecdotes than analysis. TerHorst, who resigned as press secretary following Ford's decision to pardon Richard Nixon, views his ex-boss in *Gerald Ford and the Future of the Presidency* (New York: Third Press) as honest but at times too loyal to his fellow Republicans. A particularly damning assessment of the thirty-eighth president is that of former reporter Richard Reeves. In *A Ford, Not a Lincoln* (New York: Harcourt Brace Jovanovich, 1975), Reeves portrays Ford as an unintelligent, unwavering Republican who, despite his numerous flaws, was loved by his colleagues in the GOP. Edward L. and Frederick H. Schapsmeier's well-researched *Gerald R. Ford's Date with Destiny: A Political Biography* (New York: Peter Lang, 1989) is marred by a lack of analysis and a disorganized, chronologically jumpy writing style. Doug Brinkley's *Gerald R. Ford* (New York: Times Books, 2007), was the first full biography of Ford. As part of the *New York Times*'s series of short books on the presidents, though, it is selective in its coverage. James Cannon, who served as executive director of the Domestic Council during Ford's tenure, authored *Time and Chance: Gerald Ford's Appointment with History* (Ann Arbor: University of Michigan Press, 1994) and *Gerald R. Ford: An Honorable Life* (Ann Arbor: University of Michigan Press, 2013). The former focuses on Ford's life up to his accession to the presidency. The latter was an attempt to chronicle Ford's life in full, but Cannon passed away before he could complete it. Furthermore, his description of Ford's presidency reads more as a memoir of his time on the Domestic Council and less as an analytical biography.

Ford's home city of Grand Rapids is the subject of several books. Old but still very useful is Z. Z. Lydens, ed., *The Story of Grand Rapids* (Grand Rapids, Mich.: Kregel, 1967). Also of possible interest to readers are G. Christian Carron, *Grand Rapids Furniture: The Story of America's Furniture City* (Grand Rapids, Mich.: Public Museum of Grand Rapids, 1993), and Ellen Arlinsky and Mary Ed Kwapil, *In Celebration of Grand Rapids* (Northridge, Calif.: Windsor, 1987).

Hendrik Booraem V has written two volumes on Ford's early years: *Young Jerry Ford: Athlete and Citizen* (Grand Rapids, Mich.: William B. Eerdmans, 2013) and *The Education of Gerald Ford* (Grand Rapids, Mich.: William B. Eerdmans, 2016). The latter is superior to the former in the depth of its analysis and, unlike *Young Jerry Ford*, includes both footnotes and a bibliography. Yet *The Education of Gerald Ford* is weakened by the author's propensity to make assumptions about what Ford was doing at particular moments in his life.

While serving in the U.S. Navy, Ford nearly died when the ship on which he served was among those hit by a typhoon. This episode is captured in C. Raymond Calhoun, *Typhoon, the Other Enemy: The Third Fleet and the Pacific Storm of December 1944* (Annapolis, Md.: Naval Institute Press, 1981), and Bob Drury and Tom Calvin, *Halsey's Typhoon: The True Story of a Fighting Admiral, an Epic Storm, and an Untold Rescue* (New York: Grove Press, 2007).

Not long after he returned to Grand Rapids from the Pacific theater, Ford met and married Betty Warren. Years later Betty Ford penned her memoir, *The Times of My Life* (New York: Harper and Row, 1978), a frank account of her life as the wife of Congressman and later President Gerald Ford, the loneliness she felt, and her struggle with alcoholism. Since then, a number of biographies about her have appeared. The best is John Robert Greene's *Betty Ford: Candor and Courage in the White House* (Lawrence: University Press of Kansas, 2004). As it is part of a series on America's first ladies, *Betty Ford* focuses primarily on her time in the White House. Even so, readers learn about her upbringing, the psychological toll of raising a family while being married to a man she loved but who was often absent, and the flak she faced because of her outspokenness. Readers may also wish to consult Jeffrey S. Ashley, *Betty Ford: A Symbol of Strength* (New York: Nova History, 2003), and John Pope's chapter on Betty Ford in *American First Ladies: Their Lives and Their Legacy*, 2nd ed. (New York: Routledge, 2001), edited by Lewis L. Gould. There are a number of books where readers can learn about the Fords' children, but a good starting point is Doug Wead's *All the Presidents' Children: Triumph and Tragedy in the Lives of America's First Families* (New York: Atria, 2003).

The Republican Party that Ford sought to represent in Congress in 1948 had undergone significant changes during its history and had not controlled the White House since 1933. Lewis Gould has written an outstanding, readable account of the party from its formation in the nineteenth century. His *Grand Old Party: A History of the Republicans* (New York: Random House, 2003) skillfully demonstrates the rightward shift that gradually took hold of the GOP after World War II. In *The Republicans: A History of the Grand Old Party* (New York: Oxford University Press, 2014), a shortened, revised edition of *Grand Old Party*, Gould carries his narrative and analysis into the second decade of the twenty-first century. The declining influence of moderates in the Republican Party in the postwar period is the sole focus of Geoffrey Kabaservice's *Rule and Ruin: The Downfall of Moderation and the Destruction of the Republican Party, from Eisenhower to the Tea Party* (New York: Oxford University Press, 2012). Sidney Blumenthal, a former aide to Bill and Hillary Clinton, contends in *The Strange Death of Republican America: Chronicles of a Collapsing Party* (New York: Sterling, 2008) that by 2008, the Republican Party was on the verge of falling apart because of the growing influence of its conservative wing. Timothy Thurber chronicles the difficult relationship between African Americans and the GOP in the period from the end of World War II through Nixon's resignation in *Republicans and Race: The GOP's Frayed Relationship with African Americans, 1945–1974* (Lawrence: University Press of Kansas, 2013). There were Republicans who, alongside colleagues in the Democratic Party, civil rights activists, labor unions, public interest groups, the media, and academics, sought to reform Congress, as described by Julian Zelizer in *On Capitol Hill: The Struggle to Reform Congress and Its Consequences, 1948–2000* (New York: Cambridge University Press, 2004).

Not much has been written on Ford's years as a congressman. William A. Syers, in his article "The Political Beginnings of Gerald R. Ford: Anti-Bossism, Internationalism, and the Congressional Campaign of 1948," *Presidential Studies Quarterly* 20, no. 1 (1990): 127–142, concludes that a desire by voters in Michigan's Fifth District to reform a political system run by party bosses and to turn away from isolationism helped Ford defeat Bartel Jonkman in the 1948 Republican primary.

In "Prelude to the Presidency: An Examination of the Gerald Ford–Charles Halleck House Minority Leadership Contest," *Presidential Studies Quarterly* 25, no. 4 (1995): 767–785, Henry Scheele cites a number of reasons for Ford's defeat of Halleck as minority leader, including the outcome of the 1964 presidential election, Halleck's personality, and the impact of television.

There is a large body of literature written by or about members of Congress who served in office during Ford's political career. Joseph Martin, whom the "Young Turks" ousted from his position as minority leader, is the focus of James J. Kenneally's *A Compassionate Conservative: A Political Biography of Joseph W. Martin Jr., Speaker of the U.S. House of Representatives* (Lanham, Md.: Lexington Books, 2003). Halleck, who replaced Martin, held a series of joint press conferences with Dirksen to present the Republican rejoinders to President John F. Kennedy's initiatives; this is the subject of Henry Z. Scheele's "Response to the Kennedy Administration: The Joint Senate-House Republican Leadership Press Conferences," *Presidential Studies Quarterly* 19, no. 4 (1989): 825–846. In 1965, Halleck found himself the target of the Young Turks, who successfully replaced him with Ford. Though the book is weakened by a failure to look at some key archival materials, readers will want to consult Henry Z. Scheele's *Charlie Halleck: A Political Biography* (New York: Exposition Books, 1966). One of those Young Turks who helped oust Halleck was Donald Rumsfeld. Although much of his *Known and Unknown: A Memoir* (New York: Sentinel, 2011) is devoted to a poorly argued defense of President George W. Bush's decision to invade Iraq in 2003, readers will find interesting his rationale for challenging Halleck and, later, his experiences as Ford's chief of staff and secretary of defense. Rumsfeld's political career is the subject of Bradley Graham's *By His Own Rules: The Ambitions, Successes, and Ultimate Failures of Donald Rumsfeld* (New York: PublicAffairs, 2009). As the title suggests, Rumsfeld sought to climb the ladder of power and succeeded in doing so, serving as both White House chief of staff under Ford and defense secretary under Ford and George W. Bush. However, concludes Graham, he will ultimately be remembered for his failures vis-à-vis the war in Iraq.

Upon assuming the position of minority leader, Ford developed a close working relationship with Melvin Laird and attempted but failed to keep John Rhodes from becoming chair of the Republicans' Policy Committee. Dale Van Atta's *With Honor: Melvin Laird in War, Peace, and Politics* (Madison: University of Wisconsin Press, 2008) provides a phenomenal study of a man who, like Ford, served in the U.S. Navy, Congress, and the White House. With the assistance of Dean Smith, Rhodes discusses his relationship with Ford in his memoir, *John Rhodes: "I Was There"* (Salt Lake City: Northwest Publishing, 1995). Minority Leader Ford had an at-times tense relationship with Dirksen. Brothers Edward L. and Frederick H. Schapsmeier offer a well-researched but overly laudatory account of the Illinois lawmaker in *Dirksen of Illinois: Senatorial Statesman* (Urbana: University of Illinois Press, 1985). Among those Democrats who served in Congress while Ford was there—and who continued to represent his state on Capitol Hill when Ford moved into the White

House—was Jim Wright. A Texan who later became speaker of the House, Wright recalls his experiences in *Balance of Power: Presidents and Congress from the Era of McCarthy to the Age of Gingrich* (Atlanta: Turner Publishing, 1996).

Bella Abzug, a Democratic member of Congress who hoped to prevent Ford's confirmation as vice president, is the subject of *The Political Life of Bella Abzug, 1920–1976: Political Passion, Women's Rights, and Congressional Battles* (Lanham, Md.: Lexington Books, 2013), by Alan H. Levy. Senators Frank Church and Henry Jackson caused headaches for President Ford by their positions on the U.S. intelligence community and on American policy toward the Soviet Union, respectively. Biographers LeRoy Ashby and Rod Gramer praise Church in *Fighting the Odds: The Life of Senator Frank Church* (Pullman: Washington State University Press, 1994). A similarly laudatory account of Jackson can be found in Robert Kaufman's *Henry M. Jackson: A Life in Politics* (Seattle: University of Washington Press, 2000).

The roles played by many of these lawmakers in policy making is the focus of Robert David Johnson. In *Congress and the Cold War* (New York: Cambridge University Press, 2006), Johnson relies on dozens of congressional archives to ably demonstrate how blocs of lawmakers and individual legislators pressed for the foreign policies they believed the United States should adopt.

To understand why Barry Goldwater became the Republican nominee for president in 1964, readers will want to consult Rick Perlstein's *Before the Storm: Barry Goldwater and the Unmaking of the American Consensus* (New York: Nation Books, 2009). In this excellent work, Perlstein explains that Goldwater personified the rise of the conservative wing of the Republican Party in the 1960s, which decried New Deal liberalism and opposed efforts to improve relations with the Soviet Union. Of interest as well is *Barry Goldwater and the Remaking of the American Political Landscape* (Tucson: University of Arizona Press, 2013), edited by Elizabeth Tandy Shermer.

As a congressman, Ford endorsed President Harry Truman's foreign policies but was more critical of the Fair Deal. One of the best biographies of Truman is David McCullough's Pulitzer Prize–winning *Truman* (New York: Simon and Schuster, 1992). For more on Truman's initiatives as president, readers will want to consult Donald R. McCoy's *The Presidency of Harry S. Truman* (Lawrence: University Press of Kansas, 1984). Ford supported Truman's decision to have U.S. forces stop the North Korean invasion of South Korea. That war, argues Paul G. Pierpaoli Jr. in *Truman and Korea: The Political Culture of the Early Cold War* (Columbia: University of Missouri Press, 1999), fomented a garrison-state mentality that had enormous consequences for American politics and the economy.

Ford was only partially supportive of Truman's policies, but he did, by his own admission, strongly back the initiatives of Truman's successor, Dwight D. Eisenhower. A solid biography of the former president is *Ike: His Life and Times* (New York: Harper and Row, 1986). The author, Piers Brendon, offers a balanced account of the former general and president, one that views him as an intelligent, insightful, and politically astute man who could also, however, be indecisive and overly cautious. Chester Pach, in his revision of Elmo Richardson's *The Presidency of Dwight*

D. Eisenhower (Lawrence: University Press of Kansas, 1991), provides an excellent overview of the former general's tenure in the Oval Office. Useful but older is Herbert S. Parmet's *Eisenhower and the American Crusades* (New York: Macmillan, 1972). A short, easy-to-read synthesis of the literature on Eisenhower's presidency is provided in *Eisenhower* (New York: Pearson Longman, 2005), by Peter Boyle.

As he had with Truman, Ford tended to favor John F. Kennedy's foreign policies over his domestic initiatives. Kennedy is the subject of numerous biographies, but for a good start, readers will want to consult Richard Reeves's *President Kennedy: Profile of Power* (New York: Simon and Schuster, 1993). In this critical account, Reeves views Kennedy as an intelligent and ambitious politician who, as president, reacted to events rather than preparing for contingency. James Giglio's *Presidency of John F. Kennedy*, 2nd ed., rev. (Lawrence: University Press of Kansas, 2006) is also an excellent study, though readers will find that the author devotes more attention to Kennedy's diplomacy than to his domestic policies. Readers may also want to consult Michael O'Brien, *John F. Kennedy: A Biography* (New York: Thomas Dunne/St. Martin's, 2005). Ford disliked Kennedy's proposal for what became Medicare. In *The Politics of Medicare*, 2nd ed. (Hawthorne, N.Y.: Aldine de Gruyter, 2000), Theodore R. Marmor provides a history of that program.

Though Ford supported President Lyndon Johnson's decisions to escalate the war in Vietnam and to send troops to the Dominican Republic, he believed the president was not doing enough to contain Cuba and was particularly critical of the Great Society. There are several biographies of Johnson. One is Robert Dallek's magisterial two-volume work, *Lone Star Rising: Lyndon Johnson and His Times, 1908–1960* (New York: Oxford University Press, 1991), and *Flawed Giant: Lyndon Johnson and His Times, 1961–1973* (New York: Oxford University Press, 1998); combined, they present a detailed, readable account of one of the most complex personalities to sit in the Oval Office. More recent is *LBJ: Architect of American Ambition* (Cambridge, Mass.: Harvard University Press, 2006), by Randall Woods. Woods depicts Johnson as an ambitious politician who wanted to pursue a liberal agenda but could never please liberals. Over the past three decades, Pulitzer Prize winner Robert A. Caro has published four volumes of a planned five-part biography of Johnson that centers on his drive for power in the U.S. government. The most recent of those volumes, *The Years of Lyndon Johnson: The Passage of Power* (New York: Vintage, 2012), takes Johnson from 1958, when he was Senate majority leader, through his vice presidency and ends about two months after he began his tenure in the Oval Office. Readers will also want to look at Charles Peters's contribution to the *New York Times* series on the presidents, *Lyndon B. Johnson* (New York: Times Books, 2010). Useful essays on Johnson's domestic programs can be found in Robert A. Divine's edited volume, *The Johnson Years*, vol. 2, *Vietnam, the Environment, and Science* (Lawrence: University Press of Kansas, 1987). For more on Johnson's foreign policy, see H. W. Brands's *The Wages of Globalism: Lyndon Johnson and the Limits of American Power* (New York: Oxford University Press, 1995) and Brands's edited volume, *The Foreign Policies of Lyndon Johnson: Beyond Vietnam* (College Station: Texas A&M University Press, 1999). The president's crime-control measures are covered by David B. Wolcott and Tom Head in *Crime and Punishment in America* (New York: Facts on File, 2010).

The Vietnam War not only grew increasingly unpopular but also divided the Republican Party over whether to continue the war or leave it. While there are dozens of books on that conflict, two good overviews are *America's Longest War: The United States and Vietnam, 1950–1975*, 4th ed. (Boston: McGraw-Hill, 2002), by George C. Herring, and *Where the Domino Fell: America and Vietnam, 1945–1995*, 6th ed. (Malden, Mass.: Blackwell, 2014), by James S. Olson and Randy Roberts. An excellent work on the antiwar movement is Charles DeBenedetti's *An American Ordeal: The Antiwar Movement of the Vietnam Era* (Syracuse, N.Y.: Syracuse University Press, 1990). In *Vietnam's Second Front: Domestic Politics, the Republican Party, and the War* (Lexington: University Press of Kentucky, 2010), Andrew Johns skillfully shows not only that the Republican Party was divided over prosecution of the war but also that domestic politics constrained the flexibility of those in the White House in prosecuting that conflict.

It was during the presidency of Richard Nixon that Ford rose from the ranks of minority leader to vice president. The literature on the country's thirty-seventh president is voluminous. Why the liberal consensus that allowed Lyndon Johnson to win the 1964 election broke down and opened the door to the Nixon presidency is the subject of Rick Perlstein's masterful *Nixonland: The Rise of a President and the Fracturing of America* (New York: Scribner, 2008). The election that brought Nixon into the White House is the subject of Lewis L. Gould's *1968: The Election that Changed America* (Chicago: Ivan R. Dee, 1993). For Gould, bitterness with the Democrats' positions on Vietnam and civil rights led a substantial number of individuals who identified with that party to join the Republicans' ranks in 1968. Part of the *New York Times* series on the presidents, Elizabeth Drew's balanced but critical *Richard M. Nixon* (New York: Times Books, 2007) focuses primarily on Nixon's time in the Oval Office, with particular emphasis given to his foreign policies and Watergate. Melvin Small offers a lengthier, evenhanded account in *The Presidency of Richard Nixon* (Lawrence: University Press of Kansas, 1999). Richard Reeves, in *President Nixon: Alone in the White House* (New York: Simon and Schuster, 2001), describes an administration poisoned by the president's paranoia, penchant for secrecy, and determination to concentrate decision making in the Oval Office. Readers may also want to consult Stephen Ambrose's *Nixon*, vol. 2, *The Triumph of a Politician, 1962–1972* (New York: Simon and Schuster, 1989), and *Nixon*, vol. 3, *Ruin and Recovery, 1973–1990* (New York: Simon and Schuster, 1991). However, in light of the author's history of plagiarism and evidence that he falsified data in his biography of Eisenhower, his volumes on Nixon should be used cautiously. Ford endorsed Nixon's opposition to forced busing, a topic addressed by Lawrence J. McAndrews's *The Era of Education: The Presidents and the Schools, 1965–2001* (Champaign-Urbana: University of Illinois Press, 2006).

Once referred to as the "lost decade," the 1970s in recent years have received growing scholarly attention. In *Mad as Hell: The Crisis of the 1970s and the Rise of the Populist Right* (New York: Knopf, 2011), Dominic Sandbrook effectively describes the rise of a right-wing populist movement of predominantly white, middle- and working-class Americans who came to see big government and corporate and political elites as enemies. For how the decade's films depicted the political environment of time, see David Cook's essay, "Movies and Political Trauma," in *American Cinema of the 1970s: Themes and Variation*, edited by Lester D. Friedman (New Brunswick, N.J.: Rutgers University Press, 2007). David Farber, in "The Torch Had Fallen," one of the essays in *America in the Seventies*, which he edited along with Beth Bailey (Lawrence: University Press of Kansas, 2004), explains how Ford failed to restore a sense of hope to a country in despair because of Vietnam and Watergate.

A number of authors have written on Ford's tenure in the Oval Office. The best book on this score is John Robert Greene's *The Presidency of Gerald R. Ford* (Lawrence: University Press of Kansas, 1995), which effectively disproves the thesis that Ford was simply a "caretaker" president. In 1989, Hofstra University gathered a group of scholars and members of the Ford administration—including President Ford—at a conference where they addressed the president's foreign and domestic initiatives, including the Nixon pardon, détente, policy toward the Middle East, Ford's handling of the economy and the New York City financial crisis, and the 1976 presidential campaign. Both the papers and the comments delivered by the participants have been collected in the two-volume *Gerald R. Ford and the Politics of Post-Watergate America* (Westport, Conn.: Greenwood, 1993), edited by Bernard J. Firestone and Alexej Ugrinsky. In a study that focuses predominantly on Ford's domestic initiatives, Yanek Mieczkowski contends in *Gerald Ford and the Challenges of the 1970s* (Lexington: University Press of Kentucky, 2005) that although in the short run Ford failed to revive the economy or help the country reduce its dependence on foreign sources of energy, in the long run he was the right person for a country shaken by Vietnam and Watergate. Although Andrew Downer Crain devotes far more attention to foreign policy than does Mieczkowski, he shares Mieczkowski's positive appraisal of the nation's thirty-eighth president. However, his *The Ford Presidency: A History* (Jefferson, N.C.: McFarland, 2009) offers virtually no background on Ford and is much weaker in its analysis.

The relationship between Ford and his advisers has been addressed by Anthony J. Bennett in *The American President's Cabinet: From Kennedy to Bush* (New York: St. Martin's, 1996) and Michael Medved in *The Shadow Presidents: The Secret History of the Chief Executives and Their Top Aides* (New York: Times Books, 1979). The latter is far better in addressing Dick Cheney's role as chief of staff than Donald Rumsfeld's. For more on staffing during the Ford presidency, see Karen M. Hult and Charles E. Walcott, *Empowering the White House: Governance under Nixon, Ford, and Carter* (Lawrence: University Press of Kansas, 2004).

Many of those in the Ford administration have written memoirs of their experiences. Ford friend and confidant Robert Hartmann detailed his own battles with holdovers from the Nixon administration as well as the conflicts between Vice President Nelson Rockefeller, on the one hand, and Rumsfeld and Cheney, on the other, in *Palace Politics: An Inside Account of the Ford Years* (New York: McGraw-Hill, 1980). Speechwriter Jack Casserly depicts an administration replete with infighting and lays much of the blame for Ford's failure to win reelection at Hartmann's feet. However, in *The Ford White House: The Diary of a Speechwriter* (Boulder: Colorado Associated University Press, 1977), he writes that what happened in 1976 was more than anything else the result of Ford's lack of vision for the country. Former Treasury secretary William Simon openly expresses his conservative leanings in his memoir, *A Time for Truth* (New York: Reader's Digest, 1978). The title of Ron Nessen's *It Sure Looks Different from the Inside* (Chicago: Playboy Press, 1978), expresses what it was like to be at one point a reporter whose job it was to question what the White House was doing and to serve at another as the administration's press secretary and defend the president's initiatives. But his memoir is more than simply a recounting of his relationship with the press, for he offers insight into the personalities and policies of the Ford administration. Shorter but equally absorbing is Nessen's 2011 memoir, *Making the News, Taking the News: From NBC to the Ford White House* (Middletown, Conn.: Wesleyan University Press). In *Shooter* (New York: Newsweek Books, 1979), White House photographer David Kennerly demonstrates his fondness for the Ford family and his dislike for Secretary of State Henry Kissinger. Kissinger recalls his experiences working for Ford in his tome, *Years of Renewal* (New York: Simon and Schuster, 1999). Significantly, the former secretary of state traces his own decline in influence as he came under criticism from both the left and the right. Four years later, Kissinger published *Ending the Vietnam War: A History of America's Involvement in and Extrication from the Vietnam War* (New York: Simon and Schuster, 2003), in which he recounts the difficulties the Ford administration faced as it sought to defend America's credibility in the face of strong resistance to continuing the commitment to South Vietnam. Like Rumsfeld, Dick Cheney (with the assistance of his daughter, Liz Cheney) spends a good portion of his recollections, *In My Time: A Personal and Political Memoir* (New York: Threshold Editions, 2011), defending his actions as President George W. Bush's vice president. But he also gives readers details about his work as Ford's chief of staff.

Biographies have also appeared on a number of these administration officials. Aside from Graham's above-mentioned book on Rumsfeld, readers will want to consult *Kissinger: A Biography* (New York: Simon and Schuster, 1992), an insightful, balanced study of the former secretary of state. The author, former *Time* magazine editor Walter Isaacson, is sympathetic to Kissinger where deserved but also demonstrates that his subject was more than prepared to lie and conspire to achieve his goals. Richard Norton Smith effectively captures Nelson Rockefeller's tenure as New York State governor, his desire to become president of the United States, and his trials and tribulations as Ford's vice president in his captivating *On His Own Terms: A Life of Nelson Rockefeller* (New York: Random House, 2014). Ford's national security adviser, Brent Scowcroft, is the subject of Bartholomew Sparrow's *The Strategist: Brent Scowcroft and the Call of National Security* (New York: Perseus, 2015).

There are numerous books and articles that address in whole or in part President Ford's decision to pardon Nixon. The fullest account of this episode is Barry Werth's *31 Days: The Crisis That Brought Us the Government We Have Today* (New York:

Doubleday, 2006), a daily recounting of the events that occurred between Ford's assumption of the presidency and the pardon. Clark Mollenhoff, who had quit the Nixon administration after becoming disenchanted with his boss, condemned Ford's action in *The Man Who Pardoned Nixon* (New York: St. Martin's, 1976). James Doyle, an assistant to Watergate prosecutors Archibald Cox and Leon Jaworski, seconded Mollenhoff. However, as he writes in *Not above the Law: The Battles of Watergate Prosecutors Cox and Jaworski* (New York: Morrow, 1977), Jaworski favored the pardon on the grounds that Nixon could not get a fair trial. A number of scholars who have since looked at the pardon have judged Ford favorably, among them Mark Rozell in his article "President Ford's Pardon of Richard M. Nixon: Constitutional and Political Considerations," *Presidential Studies Quarterly* 24 (1994): 121–137. Even Richard Reeves, who condemned the pardon in the 1970s, apologized in "I'm Sorry, Mr. President," *American Heritage* 47 (1996): 52–55.

Paul Charles Light, author of *The President's Agenda: Domestic Policy Choice from Kennedy to Carter* (Baltimore: Johns Hopkins University Press, 1982), argues that the ability of a president to get his agenda through Congress is based both on the ability of the president and his aides to determine what issues are most important to them, and on the circumstances of the time. But getting those initiatives passed became more difficult in the post-Watergate period.

As a congressman, Ford had an interest in environmental protection, though he believed that the effort should be left primarily to state and local governments; as president he considered it more important to promote economic growth than to defend the environment. For more on the history of environmentalism in America, readers will want to look at Hal K. Rothman's *Saving the Planet: The American Response to the Environment in the Twentieth Century* (Chicago: Ivan R. Dee, 2000), Benjamin Kline's *First along the River: A Brief History of the U.S. Environmental Movement*, 2nd ed. (Lanham, Md.: Acada Books, 2000), and Thomas R. Wellock's *Preserving the Nation: The Conservation and Environmental Movements, 1870–2000* (Wheeling, Ill.: Harlan Davidson, 2007). For specifics on Ford's environmental policies, see Byron W. Daynes and Glen Sussman, *White House Politics and the Environment: Franklin D. Roosevelt to George W. Bush* (College Station: Texas A&M University Press, 2010).

On Ford's energy policy, see David Howard Davis, "Energy Policy and the Ford Administration: The First Year," in David E. Caputo's edited volume, *The Politics of Policy Making in America: Five Case Studies* (San Francisco: W. H. Freeman, 1977). Ford did not get along well with George Meany, the president of the AFL-CIO, as detailed by Archie Robinson's biography, *George Meany and His Times: A Biography* (New York: Simon and Schuster, 1981).

Both domestic and foreign policy came together in congressional hearings that took place during Ford's tenure on the U.S. intelligence community. Loch K. Johnson, in *A Season of Inquiry: The Senate Intelligence Investigation* (Lexington: University Press of Kentucky, 1985), provides a detailed look at the inquiry led by Senator Church that convinced Congress to call for a larger role in overseeing America's intelligence agencies. In fact, though, writes Kathryn Olmsted in *Challenging the*

Secret Government: The Post-Watergate Investigations of the CIA and FBI (Chapel Hill: University of North Carolina Press, 1996), little real reform ultimately came out of the hearings led by Church, Rockefeller, and Otis Pike.

Graeme Mount has produced the only book that focuses solely on Ford's foreign policy. His inappropriately titled *895 Days that Changed the World: The Presidency of Gerald R. Ford* (Montreal: Black Rose Books, 2006) is a collection of essays written by ten of the author's students that offers little new material and fails to explain adequately just how the Ford administration "changed the world." Although this book does address some unique subjects, such as U.S. policy toward Argentina and what the death of dictator Francisco Franco meant for U.S.-Spanish relations, both laypersons and scholars interested in U.S. diplomacy during Ford's tenure in the Oval Office will want to begin their research elsewhere.

One of the key facets of Ford's foreign policy was to continue the policy of détente with the Soviet Union. However, he found himself on the defensive, to the point that he stopped even using the word "détente" in his speeches. Though over twenty years old, Raymond Garthoff's *Détente and Confrontation: American-Soviet Relations from Nixon to Reagan* (Washington, D.C.: Brookings Institution, 1994) holds its own as one of the best works on superpower relations in the 1970s. Former Soviet ambassador to the United States Anatoly Dobrynin provides an insider's account of the relationship between Washington and Moscow during Ford's presidency in *In Confidence: Moscow's Ambassador to America's Six Cold War Presidents* (New York: Times Books, 1995). One of the reasons why détente ran into trouble was because of superpower differences over Soviet machinations in Angola, as detailed by Daniel Spikes in *Angola and the Politics of Intervention: From Local Bush War to Chronic Crisis in Southern Africa* (Jefferson, N.C.: McFarland, 1993). As suggested by the title of Anne Hessing Cahn's book *Killing Detente: The Right Attacks the CIA* (University Park: Pennsylvania State University Press, 1998), it was political conservatives who ultimately succeeded in wrecking détente by charging that the Central Intelligence Agency had underestimated the military threat posed to the United States by the Soviet Union.

Matching Ford's disappointment with the lack of support for détente was his dissatisfaction with Congress's unwillingness to stand behind South Vietnam. That assessment is shared by J. Edward Lee and H. C. "Toby" Haynsworth in *Nixon, Ford, and the Abandonment of South Vietnam* (Jefferson, N.C.: McFarland, 2002). To Ford, Kissinger, and others in the administration, Cambodia's seizure of the U.S. cargo ship *Mayaguez* offered an opportunity to defend America's prestige, which they believed had been damaged by the fall of South Vietnam to the North. In *A Very Short War: The* Mayaguez *and the Battle of Koh Tang* (College Station: Texas A&M University Press, 1995), John E. Guilmartin agrees with Ford and other administration officials that the administration's handling of that crisis was successful.

The administration's management of the Middle East peace process in the 1970s is covered by Burton Kaufman, *The Arab Middle East and the United States: Inter-Arab Rivalry and Super Power Diplomacy* (New York: Twayne, 1996); William B. Quandt, *Peace Process: American Diplomacy and the Arab-Israeli Conflict since*

1967, rev. ed. (Washington, D.C.: Brookings Institution, 2001); and H. W. Brands, *Into the Labyrinth: The United States and the Middle East, 1945–1993* (New York: McGraw-Hill, 1994). The growing interest in the 1970s of making human rights a component of U.S. foreign policy has been detailed in Lars Schoultz's *Human Rights and United States Policy toward Latin America* (Princeton: Princeton University Press, 1981) and Barbara Keys's *Reclaiming American Virtue: The Human Rights Revolution of the 1970s* (Cambridge, Mass.: Harvard University Press, 2014).

Ford's image as an unintelligent klutz hurt him politically both before and during the 1976 presidential campaign. The television program *Saturday Night Live* was partly responsible for that image, as demonstrated by Doug Hill and Jeff Weingrad in *Saturday Night: A Backstage History of "Saturday Night Live"* (New York: Beech Tree, 1986). The media also played a role, contends Mark Rozell. In *The Press and the Ford Presidency* (Ann Arbor: University of Michigan Press, 1992), Rozell writes that despite the effort of the president and aides to demonstrate that he was anything but a dull-witted oaf, the press crafted an image of Ford more reminiscent of that on *Saturday Night Live.*

The 1976 presidential campaign has received a large amount of scholarly attention. Published only a year after Americans chose Jimmy Carter over Ford as president, Jules Witcover's *Marathon: The Pursuit of the Presidency* (New York: Viking, 1977) remains essential reading. Witcover effectively uses his skills as a journalist to cover in detail the people and events that led to Carter's victory. Those wanting to learn more about Ronald Reagan's rise in the Republican Party and his nearly successful effort to seize the party's nomination in 1976 will be disappointed by his memoir, *An American Life: An Autobiography* (New York: Simon and Schuster, 1990); far better on this score is Lou Cannon's outstanding *Governor Reagan: His Rise to Power* (New York: PublicAffairs, 2003). In their revised edition of *The Presidency of James Earl Carter, Jr.* (Lawrence: University Press of Kansas, 2006), Burton I. Kaufman and Scott Kaufman describe how a Cinderella-like Carter was able to make his successful bid for the presidency. Patrick Anderson, who wrote speeches for Carter during his campaign, became disenchanted with his boss and authored a largely critical account of both Carter and Carter's aides in *Electing Jimmy Carter: The Campaign of 1976* (Baton Rouge: Louisiana State University Press, 1994). In *Packaging the Presidency: A History and Criticism of Presidential Campaign Advertising*, 2nd ed. (New York: Oxford University Press, 1992), Kathleen Hall Jamieson points to the impact of Watergate on the advertising of both the Ford and Carter campaigns. Political ads are also the subject of Darrell M. West's *Air Wars: Television Advertising and Social Media in Election Campaigns, 1952–2012*, 6th ed. (Thousand Oaks, Calif.: CQ Press, 2014) and of L. Patrick Devlin's "Contrasts in Presidential Campaign Commercials of 1976," *Central States Speech Journal* 28 (1977): 17–26. For the relevance of polling to presidential campaigns, see David W. Moore, *The Superpollsters: How They Measure and Manipulate Public Opinion in America* (New York: Four Walls Eight Windows, 1992). On the question of race and the election, see Jeremy D. Mayer, *Running on Race: Racial Politics in Presidential Campaigns, 1960–2000* (New York: Random House, 2002).

American diplomacy became a central factor in the 1976 campaign. One of the topics that Reagan used to try to win the Republican nomination was Ford's support for the negotiations with Panama over the Panama Canal, as explained by ex–*New York Times* reporter Adam Clymer in *Drawing the Line at the Big Ditch: The Panama Canal Treaties and the Rise of the Right* (Lawrence: University Press of Kansas, 2008) and by Farley Yang in "Turning a Runaway into a Race: The Role of Foreign Policy Issues in the 1976 Republican Primaries," *Michigan Journal of Political Science* 7 (1986): 108–128. In fact, though, Ford faced opposition from both the right and the left, in part because his endorsement of the Helsinki Accords was taken as proof of his unwillingness to contest Soviet domination of Eastern Europe. On this score, see Sarah Snyder, "Through the Looking Glass: The Helsinki Final Act and the 1976 Election for President," *Diplomacy and Statecraft* 21 (2010): 87–106. Ford's poorly worded comment regarding Poland in his second debate with Jimmy Carter severely wounded his bid to stay in the White House, as described by Leo P. Ribuffo, "Is Poland a Soviet Satellite? Gerald Ford, the Sonnenfeldt Doctrine, and the Election of 1976," *Diplomatic History* 14 (1990): 385–404, and by Lev E. Dobriansky, "The Unforgettable Ford Gaffe," *Ukrainian Quarterly* 3 (1977): 366–377.

The idea that Ford was a caretaker president has come under increasing criticism. Aside from the above-mentioned works by Greene, Crain, and Mieczkowski, see Roger Porter's essay "Gerald R. Ford: A Healing Presidency," in Fred I. Greenstein's edited work, *Leadership in the Modern Presidency* (Cambridge, Mass.: Harvard University Press, 1988).

For Ford's post-presidency, readers will want to start with Burton I. Kaufman's *The Post-Presidency from Washington to Clinton* (Lawrence: University Press of Kansas, 2012). Kaufman finds that instead of going into quiet retirement, ex-presidents have, from the days of George Washington, involved themselves in national or even international affairs. Ford, argues Kaufman, sought to use his post-presidency to "mass market" himself through continued involvement in politics and took advantage of his title as a former president to make money. In *The Presidents Club: Inside the World's Most Exclusive Fraternity* (New York: Simon and Schuster, 2012), *Time* magazine editors Nancy Gibbs and Michael Duffy describe the relationship that developed among former and sitting presidents. Ford and Carter offer one example of the friendship that developed among ex-presidents. Here, readers will want to consult Douglas Brinkley's sympathetic account of Carter's post-presidency, *The Unfinished Presidency: Jimmy Carter's Journey beyond the White House* (New York: Viking, 1998) and Carter's own *Beyond the White House: Waging Peace, Fighting Disease, Building Hope* (New York: Simon and Schuster, 2007).

Ford loved to play golf as president, and in retirement he continued to spend a lot of time on the links. His friend, Bob Hope, offers an amusing look at Ford's prowess on the golf course in *Confessions of a Hooker: My Lifelong Love Affair with Golf* (Garden City, N.Y.: Doubleday, 1985). Readers will also want to peruse Don Van Natta Jr.'s *First Off the Tee: Presidential Hackers, Duffers, and Cheaters from Taft to Bush* (New York: PublicAffairs, 2003).

Index